Critical Essays on Erskine Caldwell

Critical Essays
on Erskine Caldwell

Scott MacDonald

G.K. Hall & Co.   •   Boston, Massachusetts

Copyright © 1981 by Scott MacDonald

Library of Congress Cataloging in Publication Data
Main entry under title:
Critical essays on Erskine Caldwell.

  (Critical essays on American literature)
  Includes index.
  1. Caldwell, Erskine, 1903–   —Criticism and
interpretation—Collected works. I. MacDonald,
Scott, 1942– . II. Series.
PS3505.A322Z54   813'.52   80-28914
ISBN 0-8161-8299-X

CRITICAL ESSAYS ON AMERICAN LITERATURE

This series seeks to collect the most important previously published criticism on writers and topics in American literature along with, in various volumes, original essays, interviews, bibliographies, letters, manuscript sections, and other materials brought to public attention for the first time. Scott MacDonald's volume on Erskine Caldwell is the first collection of criticism ever published on this popular and neglected writer. Professor MacDonald's introduction is a valuable overview of the development of Caldwell scholarship and an important presentation of Caldwell's fictional creed. In addition to an original essay by Sylvia Cook on Caldwell's nonfiction, the volume offers essays by the foremost scholars in American literature, among them Carl Van Doren, Joseph Warren Beach, Malcolm Cowley, Henry Seidel Canby, Kenneth Burke, and James T. Farrell. Also included are Richard B. Sale's interview with Caldwell and twenty essays by Caldwell himself. We are confident that this collection will make a permanent and significant contribution to American literary scholarship.

James Nagel, GENERAL EDITOR

Northeastern University

For Patricia

CONTENTS

Introduction   xi

REVIEWS

T. K. Whipple and Malcolm Cowley, "Two Judgements of
'American Earth' "   3

Norman Macleod, "A Hardboiled Idealist" [review of
American Earth]   6

Gerald Sykes, "The Poetry of Unfeeling" [review of
American Earth]   7

Vincent Wall, "Poor Whites" [review of *American Earth*]   8

Anonymous, "Erskine Caldwell to Publish Novel, 'The Old
Tobacco Road' "   10

J. Raiford Watkins, "Caldwell's Novel Is of Georgians"   11

James Gray, "New Realist Depicts South's Poor Whites'
Pitiable Existence"   13

Anonymous, "Library Admits Caldwell Novel"   15

Edward Dahlberg, "Raw Leaf"   16

Jack Conroy, "Passion and Pellagra"   17

Kenneth White, "American Humor"   18

Erskine Caldwell, "Ripe for Revolution"   20

Edwin Rolfe, [*God's Little Acre*]   23

James T. Farrell, "The Author of 'Tobacco Road' Takes Us
Again to Georgia"   25

Anonymous, "People *v.* Viking Press, Inc., *et al*"   27

Anonymous, "Caldwell Novels Banned"   31

Erskine Caldwell, "Mr. Caldwell Protests"   32

Arthur Ruhl, "Seventeen Tales by Erskine Caldwell"
[review of *Kneel to the Rising Sun*]   33

Randall Jarrell, ["Ten Books"]   35

Hamilton Basso, "Sunny South"   38

James T. Farrell, "Heavenly Visitation"   39

Albert Halper, "Caldwell Sees America"   41

Arnold Gingrich, [Telegram]   44

Anonymous, [Editorial Commentary in *The New Republic*]   44

Anonymous, "A Long Road"   45

Guy A. Miller, [Letter to the Editor of *The Nation*: "Judicial
Calm"]   47

Anonymous, " 'Tobacco Road' Winds Its Way Into Congress"   48

Erskine Caldwell, "Tobacco Roads in the South"   50

Robert Van Gelder, "A Compelling Album of the Deep South"
[review of *You Have Seen Their Faces*]   53

Malcolm Cowley, "Fall Catalogue"   54

W. T. Couch, "Landlord and Tenant"   56

Donald Davidson, "Erskine Caldwell's Picture Book"   59

Jonathan Daniels, "From Comedy to Pity" [review of
Southways]   67

Dorothy Van Doren, "Out of Georgia"   68

Otis Ferguson, "Caldwell's Stories"   69

Maurice Hindus, "The Land That Is No More" [review of
North of the Danube]   71

Richard Wright, "Lynching Bee" [review of *Trouble in July*]   72

Burton Rascoe, "Caldwell Lynches Two Negroes"   74

Jonathan Daniels, "American Lower Depths"   78

Maurice Edgar Coindreau, Preface to *Poor Fool*   80

Harrison Smith, "Well-Controlled Anger"   82

Anonymous, "Cop Reviews Caldwell Novel, St. Paul
Prosecutor Bans It"   84

Anonymous, "Denver Police Ban Penguin Edition of 'God's
Little Acre' "   85

Anonymous, "Caldwell's Collapse"   86

Lon Tinkle, "Crumbled Georgia Crackers"   87

Harrison Smith, "Comic Citizens of the South"   89

Anonymous, "Attorney General *v.* Book Named 'God's
Little Acre.' "   91

CALDWELL, *the New York Post*, and *the Augusta Chronicle*

Erskine Caldwell, "Georgia Poverty-Swept, Says Caldwell"   97

Erskine Caldwell, "U. S. Aid Forces Out Georgia Share
Croppers"   100

Erskine Caldwell, "Georgia Land Barons Oust Dying Girl
and Her Father"   102

Erskine Caldwell, "Starving Babies Suckled by Dog in
Georgia Cabin"   105

Anonymous, [Editorial from *The Augusta Chronicle*: "What
Will Good People of Jefferson County Say of This?"]   107

Anonymous, "Caldwell Story Called Untrue; Probe Ordered"   109

James Barlow, Jr., [Letter to the Editor of *The New York
Post*: "Share Cropper Conditions Denied"]   111

Anonymous, "Erskine Caldwell's Story Starts Two-Way
Inquiry"   111

John R. Lewis, [Letter to the Editor of *The Augusta
Chronicle*: "Answers Caldwell"]   113

Warren H. Pierce, [Letter to the Editor of *Time*: "Caldwell's
Hog Wallow"]   115

I. S. Caldwell, [Letter to the Editor of *Time*: "Father"]   116

Anonymous, "Investigation Is Made To Determine Basis
Caldwell Had For All His Writings"   117

Anonymous, "Erskine Caldwell"   119

Anonymous, "Erskine Caldwell"   122

Anonymous, "Erskine Caldwell"   125

Anonymous, "Erskine Caldwell"   128

I. S. Caldwell, [Letter to the Editor of *The Augusta
Chronicle*: "Mr. Caldwell Writes"]   131

J. T. Avret, [Letter to the Editor of *The Augusta
Chronicle*: "Mr. Avret Writes"]   133

L. E. Holmes, [Letter to the Editor of *The Augusta
Chronicle*: "From a Social Worker"]   134

Anonymous, [Editorial, from *The Augusta Chronicle*:
"Investigation—Now What?"]   135

Anonymous, [Editorial from *The Augusta Chronicle*: "The
Caldwell Issue and Long Range Rehabilitation"]   136

Anonymous, [Editorial Commentary in *The New Republic*]   139

Erskine Caldwell, "Caldwell Declares AAA Ruins Thousands
in South"   140

Erskine Caldwell, "Landlords Chiseling South's Poor on FERA"   143

Erskine Caldwell, "Negroes Who Ask Pay Beaten in Alabama"   145

Charles Malcolmson, "Share-Crop Life a Bed of Roses,
Senator Holds"   148

Erskine Caldwell, "Georgia Tenants, Ousted by Landlords,
Eat Dirt as Change From Bread and 'Lasses'"   149

Anonymous, [Editorial from *The New York Post*: "Hell on
Earth"]   152

ESSAYS

Carl Van Doren, "Made in America: Erskine Caldwell"   155

Lawrence S. Kubie, " 'God's Little Acre': an Analysis"   159

Kenneth Burke, "Caldwell: Maker of Grotesques"   167

J. H. Marion, Jr., "Star-Dust Above 'Tobacco Road' "   174

Joseph Warren Beach, [*American Fiction: 1920–1940*]   180

Malcolm Cowley, "The Two Erskine Caldwells"   198

W. M. Frohock, "Erskine Caldwell: Sentimental Gentleman from Georgia"   201

Henry Seidel Canby, "Introduction" to *The Pocket Book of Erskine Caldwell Stories*   214

Erskine Caldwell, "Introduction" to *American Earth*   221

Erskine Caldwell, "Introduction" to *Tobacco Road*   223

Erskine Caldwell, "Introduction" to *God's Little Acre*   225

Erskine Caldwell, "Introduction" to *Kneel to the Rising Sun* 227

Erskine Caldwell, "Introduction" to *Journeyman*   229

Erskine Caldwell, "Introduction" to *Tragic Ground*   231

Erskine Caldwell, "Introduction" to *A House in the Uplands*   233

Erskine Caldwell, "Introduction" to *This Very Earth*   235

Thelma M. Smith and Ward L. Miner, [*Transatlantic Migration*]   237

Carl Bode, "Erskine Caldwell: A Note for the Negative"   246

Erskine Caldwell, "My Twenty-five Years of Censorship"   249

Stewart H. Benedict, "Gallic Light on Erskine Caldwell"   255

Mikhail Landor, "Erskine Caldwell in the Soviet Union"   262

James J. Thompson, Jr., "Erskine Caldwell and Southern Religion"   268

Richard B. Sale, "An Interview in Florida with Erskine Caldwell" 279

Calder Willingham, "True Myth-Maker of the Post-Bellum South"   294

R. J. Gray, "Southwestern Humor, Erskine Caldwell, and the Comedy of Frustration"   298

Malcolm Cowley, "Georgia Boy: A Retrospect of Erskine Caldwell"   315

Scott MacDonald, "Repetition as Technique in the Short Stories of Erskine Caldwell"   330

Scott MacDonald, "An Evaluative Check-List of Erskine Caldwell's Short Fiction"   342

Sylvia Jenkins Cook, "Erskine Caldwell and the Literary Left Wing"   361

Robert H. Brinkmeyer, Jr., "Is That You in the Mirror, Jeeter?: The Reader and *Tobacco Road*"   370

Sylvia Jenkins Cook, "Erskine Caldwell's Nonfiction"   375

Index   393

INTRODUCTION

I

Erskine Caldwell's more than 50 volumes of novels, short stories and nonfiction have probably been the subject of less, and of generally less effective, serious critical discussion than the life's work of any American writer of comparable stature. There is no better example in our literature of the degree to which traditional and conventional critical assumptions about the nature of literary art have hampered a recognition of what is most interesting and inventive about a writer's achievement. Because of the bizarre qualities of so many of Caldwell's early stories and novels, fascinated, puzzled critics have tended to label what seem the most recognizable aspects of his work, and then stay consistently within the parameters implied by these labels.

The most pervasive critical label in the early thirties was that of "born humorist."[1] From the beginning critics saw a keen sense of humor or burlesque as Caldwell's strongest quality.[2] In some stories or novels Caldwell's humor might seem "ruthless" or "trivial," but in general it was seen as giving him the power of detachment over his often grotesque materials.[3] Humor seemed so fundamental to Caldwell's reputation, in fact, that by the late thirties, when Caldwell's interest in social causes seemed to be growing increasingly explicit in his fiction, even admiring critics were worried: "There may have been always a will to expose and reform behind the cackling laughter he evoked out of the Southern lower depths, but it was unobtrusive in short native comedy which was excellent for its own sake. . . . But now, though in this book [*Southways*] much comedy remains, fresh as stories told about the gin house door, five of the last six stories in the new collection are perilously close to that deliberate stirring of pity for a purpose which is permissible in preachers, but is scarcely a basis for such a substantial reputation as properly belongs to Caldwell."[4] Despite an occasional doubt, critics seemed, and have continued to seem, convinced that whatever reputation Caldwell's fiction would sustain would rest very largely, if not entirely, on his abilities as a humorist.[5]

While critics assumed that being labeled "humorist" was to Caldwell's credit, the other label consistently applied to Caldwell during the thirties—that of "social reformer"—meant different things to different critics. Caldwell's social concern, particularly about the tenant system and racism, found strong supporters in some quarters. As early as 1931, *New Masses* editor Norman Macleod saw the author of *American Earth* as "an idealist of the finer sort who (as most of our young writers do today) hesitates to admit it. . . . When he goes deeper into the life of the working class of the South, he promises to become one of our most signifi-

cant writers. . . ."⁶ When *Tobacco Road* was published, James Gray
seconded Macleod: "We are blandly unconscious in America of the
squalor that exists in hidden corners. . . . 'Tobacco Road' should be read
aloud to everyone who has ever made a glib, ignorant generalization
about the high standard of life in the United States."⁷ By 1938 J.H.
Marion, Jr. felt he could already detect changes in the South brought
about, at least in part, by *Tobacco Road* (both the novel and Jack
Kirkland's long-running dramatic adaption): "however unwittingly and
indirectly, he is helping . . . to free the South from an unworthy and
socially crippling tradition." Marion did not claim, of course, that
Caldwell was entirely responsible for "the interest and zeal which have
lately been aroused over the plight of the croppers": "Neither *Tobacco
Road* nor *God's Little Acre* is the sort of book that pulls a man out of his
chair to do something about it right away, but they are the kind of books
that do subtly prepare the people's emotions for suggested reforms."⁸

Other critics and reviewers grew increasingly concerned about the
accuracy and fairness of Caldwell's "realism" and about the power, even
brutality, with which he expressed his apparent outrage. The strongest attacks appeared in *The Southern Review*. While admitting Caldwell's considerable gifts, John Donald Wade suggested that his "literary output
would be more impressive if—a good Southerner still—he were not as
anxious as he is to please the kind and class of people he has come to be af-
filiated with—the detached, nervous, thrill goaded Metrocosmopolitans
["New Yorkers and would-be New Yorkers," especially] of his own day."⁹
By the time Caldwell and Margaret Bourke-White published *You Have
Seen Their Faces*, Donald Davidson was fed up with Caldwell's success.
He attacked the accuracy and honesty of the picture-text, which he found
both hypocritical and dangerous: "The South can never even make a decent beginning toward settling its economic problems if while engaged
earnestly in the process of studying them, it is constantly summoned to
court and forced to answer libelous and malicious proceedings against its
character." Why would Caldwell be willing to do so much damage to his
native region? "Are the proceeds of *You Have Seen Their Faces* and other
notable works devoted to charity?"¹⁰

Even some of those who admired Caldwell's willingness to attack the
South were—by the publication of *Kneel to the Rising Sun* in 1935—
growing doubtful about the manner of his attacks. While admitting that
some of Caldwell's stories, like Goya's paintings and etchings, can create
in us "a horrified protest" and a violent wish "that we could do something
about such things," Randall Jarrell was suspicious of other stories in
which "the obscene or gruesome subject matter is used deliberately,
merely to increase the effect. . . ."¹¹ Arthur Ruhl admitted the
undeniable "kick" of the stories in *Kneel to the Rising Sun* ("the kick of a
mule, sometimes") and "the fine economy of their craftsmanship," but had
an uneasy feeling that Caldwell might be exploiting "beastiality" and horror for their own sakes.¹²

While most thirties' reviewers and critics were primarily concerned with defending or attacking Caldwell's identification as "humorist" or "social reformer," implicit within many discussions was what later came to be understood as a fundamental disparity between the two labels. By the mid-forties, in fact, this apparent disparity had become, and has remained, the central issue of what little serious Caldwell criticism we have had. Unfortunately, the nature of the debate about this issue has distracted critics from following up tenuous, but insightful suggestions by two commentators that the disconcerting power of Caldwell's best work has sources and implications apart from either humor or an involvement in social issues.

Carl Van Doren was, perhaps, the first to recognize that Caldwell is, to some degree, "impenetrable." Van Doren saw Caldwell as "a little puzzled" by his popularity with various coteries: "He has not thought of himself as writing in special ways or for the deliberate ends with which he is credited. He wants, as he has always wanted, only to write as truthfully as he can about what he knows, and to be read by as many people as he can interest." Further, "it is as difficult for an outsider as it is for Mr. Caldwell to find in his work any systematic, even any very conscious, doctrine. He has not shaped himself by reasoning. . . ."[13] What differences such assumptions might, or should, make in our evaluations of Caldwell's writing Van Doren did not say. Given the grotesque quality of so many of Caldwell's "decerebrated" characters, Kenneth Burke found it "positively incredible that his extravaganzas, imagined in a world essentially as fantastic as Swift's, should ever have passed for realism." Burke related Caldwell's work to dadaism and surrealism—"the plots are subtly guided by the logic of dreams"—and suggested that "Caldwell's particular aptitude has been in scrambling or garbling proprieties." The source of Caldwell's "fantastic simplification," according to Burke, was a "balked religiousity" which resulted in the permeation of *Tobacco Road* and *God's Little Acre* with "symbolic sins, symbolic punishments, followed by symbolic purification." Whether "one so apt at entertaining us by *muddling* our judgments will be equally fertile in *stabilizing* judgments remains to be seen. . . . My guess is that he won't, since he would have to master a whole new technique of expression. His very abilities work against him."[14]

The longest, most positive, most carefully considered assessment of Caldwell during the forties was a two-chapter section of Joseph Warren Beach's *American Fiction: 1920–1940*. Beach took as a starting point his feeling that Caldwell "is probably the best example we have of the artistic imagination working consistently in matter of concern to the social conscience, and yet not subdued, like the dyer's hand, to what it works in. By this I mean that, dealing consistently with data of the most obvious economic and sociological significance, he does not treat it in the manner of sociological treatise or reformist propaganda, but keeps—in his novels and short stories—within the strict limits of esthetic presentation. And the result is, curiously enough, that he is the cause of bewilderment and scandal to many serious and cultivated readers."[15] Beach saw Caldwell in an aesthetic dilemma: how could the horrible social conditions he was so serious and well-informed about be recreated so as to give aesthetic pleasure? Caldwell's solution, Beach felt, was the development of a brand of Bergsonian humor (humor results when human beings with intelligence and free will exhibit the wooden and automatic movements of puppets) with which to present his chief theme: "the agony of the impoverished land." The comedy of the Lesters' less-than-human activities was not only a result of terrible socio-economic conditions; it was, Beach concluded, a means of making painful realities aesthetically palatable to the reader.[16]

While Beach seemed satisfied with his explanation of the dialectic relationship between Caldwell's social concern and his humor, other critics continued to see a disparity, and to see it as a serious limitation to a substantial talent. According to Cleanth Brooks, Caldwell's "real ability to use folk materials for comic effect, has frequently been pushed into propaganda for various causes with the resulting confusion of his attitude toward his material. . . . Mr. Caldwell frequently misunderstands his own purpose."[17] In "The Two Erskine Caldwells" Malcolm Cowley saw Caldwell as two writers: a social novelist, and a creator of "impossible fancies and wild humor"; "Sometimes in short stories they achieve an almost perfect union between the social doctrines of the first and the exuberance of the second. In novels, however, they always seem to be working at cross purposes." In *Tobacco Road*, for example, Cowley felt that Caldwell's sociological essaying in Chapter VII was out of place with the imaginative creation of Jeeter Lester, "who is not a tragic or typical figure of decay, but rather a sort of earth spirit, dirty, goatish, morally irresponsible, and given to picturesque language."[18] In Caldwell's three subsequent novels, and especially in *God's Little Acre* and *Tragic Ground*, Cowley found the two Caldwells even more at variance. Brooks' and Cowley's conclusions were reiterated by W.M. Frohock: when we read the novels "as comedies, Caldwell carefully and disconcertingly knocks the props from under the comic element; we look then for serious, socially-conscious reporting, and the comic element spoils our view. . . . So we come finally to the conclusion . . . that Caldwell's novels suffer from a multiplicity of meanings which are incompatible with one another. This is another way of saying that Caldwell's own attitude toward his materials is ambiguous."[19]

As Caldwell's forties novels appeared, nearly all reviewers came to feel that whatever abilities Caldwell had demonstrated in the thirties were no longer in evidence. *All Night Long* (1942), *Tragic Ground* (1944), *A House in the Uplands* (1946), *The Sure Hand of God* (1947), *This Very Earth* (1948), and *Place Called Estherville* (1949) seemed to reviewers and critics to have neither humor nor honest social concern. The newer novels seemed so unimpressive, in fact, that some reviewers became increasingly suspicious of the acclaim the earlier books had received. If Caldwell could write books *this* bad, they seemed to feel, those famous earlier novels must be less significant than we've realized. Only one area of Caldwell's work—his short stories—continued to seem worthy of attention; it is ironic that Caldwell ceased publishing short stories altogether during the fourteen years following the appearance of the well-received *Georgia Boy* (1943).[20]

During the fifties and early sixties, Caldwell's critical reputation—at least in the United States—continued to decline, despite the development of what has become a rather astonishing expansion of critical attention to American literature.[21] The only effective, positive discusssion of any extent during the fifties was Robert Cantwell's introduction to *The Humorous Side of Erskine Caldwell*. Cantwell went into considerable detail about Caldwell's background in order to demonstrate that Caldwell was not an untutored country bumpkin but the child of educated, sophisticated parents, and that, as a result, his stories and novels should not be considered the products of a primitive "born humorist," but "the work of a great humorous imagination." Cantwell saw Caldwell as creating "a home-made mythology" populated by characters whose spontaneous eloquence, fantastic beliefs, and unexpected insights "make the backwoods of Caldwell's imagination a ceaselessly interesting place."[22]

Except for Cantwell and one or two others, however, critics were generally ignoring or attacking Caldwell.[23] While admitting the quality of some of the short stories, Carl Bode contended that, largely because of Caldwell's use of sexuality and feverish narrative, "*God's Little Acre* and the rest of Caldwell's hot and shoddy novels make much money for him but add nothing to his literary reputation." According to Bode, "Caldwell's is not the true South. But the important thing for the multitude of customers in the reprint market is that it is true enough for them. And it invites them to feel superior to it."[24] A number of critics complained about Caldwell's characterization: Walter Allen—"Sex apart, the characters of *God's Little Acre* are not even animals: they are mindless automata"; John M. Bradbury—"Caldwell's characters never come across the printed page as people, but only as absurdly amusing or grotesquely fascinating examples of a new subhuman species"; Louise Y. Gossett—"The mirror which Caldwell says he holds up to human nature reflects not a representative selection of mankind but a private chamber of horrors."[25] The sloppy off-hand comments of still other critics are an indication of how unimpressive Caldwell's reputation had become. Ray B. West, determined to interpret "Kneel to the Rising Sun," read the rising sun at the end of that grim story as "the regenerative warmth of social reform"—a reading for which there is no textual support whatever—and simultaneously complained that *Caldwell* was reaching outside the story for a sentimental conclusion.[26] In "What's Happened to Erskine Caldwell?" Sidney Finkelstein concluded that the publication of *A Lamp for Nightfall* in 1954 was powerful evidence of the dissipation of one of the early thirties' brightest talents without even being careful enough to learn that *A Lamp for Nightfall* was itself written in 1933, after *Tobacco Road* and before *God's Little Acre*.[27]

The seventies began with the publication of the first "full-length" work on Caldwell: James Korges's pamphlet *Erskine Caldwell*. Korges usefully enlarged the scope of Caldwell criticism. Previous critics had tended to limit themselves to a single novel—generally a novel of the thirties or early forties—or to a single theme or aspect of method. Korges, on the other hand, not only discusses the novels of Caldwell's "cyclorama," he comments interestingly on Caldwell's pre-*Tobacco Road* novels—*The Bastard* (1929) and *Poor Fool* (1930)—and finds value in two recent books: *Close to Home* (1962) and *Miss Mamma Aimee* (1967), which contains "characters as grotesque as any in recent 'gothic' fiction; yet the whole is again grandly rendered in the comic mode, as though in his full maturity Caldwell had returned to his major themes with renewed vigor."[28] More important—because it was so long overdue—was Korges's attention to Caldwell's nonfiction. Korges discusses *Some American People*, *Call It Experience*, and *In Search of Bisco*, as well as the text-picture collaborations with Margaret Bourke-White: *You Have Seen Their Faces*, *North of the Danube* ("what may be the masterpiece of their collaboration"), and *Say! Is This the U.S.A.* Generally, Korges is more useful for creating increased awareness of the extent of Caldwell's achievement than for his specific insights into particular works. He repeats some of the standard conclusions about Caldwell, though he doesn't take traditional ideas for granted. He doesn't place heavy emphasis, for example, on Caldwell's humor. While the Korges pamphlet was certainly the most significant contribution to Caldwell criticism in 25 years, it is weakened by a general tendency to stretch for interpretations of the novels and to suggest that the books have dimensions which are never convincingly demonstrated. Further, while Korges considers Caldwell "one of the American masters of the short story," the stories are given only a single paragraph.[29] Of course, these weaknesses may be a function of Korges's need to work within a limited space, but I have a suspicion the problem goes a bit deeper: like so many of Caldwell's admirers, Korges *feels* the significance of Caldwell's accomplishments in certain books, but he never developed an approach which could account for this feeling while illuminating the books.

During the past ten years there have been periodic calls for a Caldwell revival, the most interesting of which is Malcolm Cowley's "Georgia Boy: A Retrospect of Erskine Caldwell." What is significant about Cowley's informal overview of Caldwell's career is not so much what is said—there is little new information or critical insight in the piece—but that Caldwell's "magic" is strong enough to have maintained Cowley's high regard.[30] But, despite the seemingly widespread suspicion

that a serious revaluation of Caldwell's career is due (and the likelihood
that the scarcity of good Caldwell criticism must be an attraction for doc-
toral students overwhelmed by the immense bodies of material which
have accumulated around many of Caldwell's contemporaries), the
seventies have produced surprisingly little solid insight. The 1979 issue of
Pembroke Magazine, which contains a 183-page section on "Erskine
Caldwell: America's Great 20th Century Author," is the most recent
disappointment. The dozens of individual essays included in the issue are,
in general, not only remarkably short on ideas, many are not even com-
petently written.

There are exceptions to this trend, of course, though even the most
interesting tend to pursue lines of investigation established during earlier
decades. R. J. Gray returns to the question of Caldwell's comedy, relating
Jeeter Lester to the tradition of Southwestern humor (in particular, to
George Washington Harris's character Sut Lovingood) and suggesting
that Caldwell creates a "comedy of frustration" by having his characters
act in a way which is comic but which is the result not of any intrinsic evil
in themselves but of the deterioration of traditional Southern agriculture:
"it would be putting matters in their right perspective . . . to say that
Caldwell insists on the difference between Jefferson's tillers of the earth
and his own Georgia crackers, and then imposes full responsibility for this
difference upon a corrupt social machine precisely so as to arouse *our*
anger and encourage *our* demands for change." According to Gray,
Jeeter's philosophizing in *Tobacco Road* and the passages in which
Caldwell explains the historical reasons for the Lesters' degeneration are
not structural lapses but a form of Brechtian *Vermfremdung* in which
"the audience, instead of being invited to involve themselves in the action, should be forced to adopt an attitude of clinical detachment toward
it."[31] Robert H. Brinkmeyer, Jr. suggests that a crucial dimension of the
meaning of *Tobacco Road* derives from the relationship between reader
and characters. However, instead of reiterating the standard assumption
that the Lesters are notable because they are so different from "normal"
people, Brinkmeyer suggests similarities between Caldwell's characters
and his readers: "While the Lesters no longer have any hold on the
American scheme of things . . . Caldwell makes it clear that they still
hanker for the same material successes that the typical American does. As
they grovel for food and money, Jeeter and his family become grotesque
parodies of the American drive for wealth and power. And even more
American is their lust for Bessie's new car, the central prestige symbol of
American culture. Distorted as the images are, Jeeter's and his family's actions mirror those of American society." Creating a bond of identification
between the reader and the Lesters was crucial for "the social purpose of
the novel": "By educating the reader both in the injustices of the
economic order and the essential falseness of looking down on people like
the Lesters, Caldwell hopes the reader will better sympathize with the

cause which undoubtedly was a major motivating force behind the work—the destruction of the system of tenant farming."[32] A few other critics—Sylvia Cook, most notably—also provide useful insights.[33]

II

What is one to make of Caldwell criticism? That it is very largely a failed enterprise seems obvious. Although most commentators, even the hostile ones, agree that Caldwell is strongest as a short-story writer, not a single critical article on this sizable body of work (to date Caldwell has published around 150 short stories) was published until 1977 when my own, very limited piece on the uses of repetition in the stories appeared.[34] While those Caldwell critics who have read Caldwell's dozen or so volumes of nonfiction have generally found them quite impressive, not a single serious critical discussion of any of these books (except for Korges's comments in *Erskine Caldwell*) appeared until Sylvia Cook's "Erskine Caldwell's Nonfiction," published for the first time in this volume. That leaves the novels, and what have we learned about them? Not much. Of Caldwell's twenty-six volumes of longer fiction, only five—*Tobacco Road*, *God's Little Acre*, *Journeyman*, *Trouble in July* and *Tragic Ground*—are even mentioned with any frequency, and while *Tobacco Road* has at least generated something like consistent interest, after forty-seven years we have had little more than a series of attempts to account for certain apparent disparities in the kinds of information included in that novel.

Perhaps the answer is very simple: Caldwell is not a good enough writer to sustain serious criticism. And yet, if that were true, why do critics continue to return to his work, at least to the thirties novels and stories? Doubtless, some return because they are under pressure from the academic system to publish, or because they themselves want to be published, and Caldwell's work is obviously still wide open. But others—Malcolm Cowley most recently—seem to write out of a sincere, and somewhat mysterious, unwillingness to let Caldwell disappear. In the past few years I have grown more and more convinced that the failure of Caldwell criticism derives from a fundamental refusal to face the nature of Caldwell's goals and achievements. Faced with a writer they could not account for in conventional ways, critics have avoided talking in detail about his work. When the sheer volume of Caldwell's writing—and its various forms of notoriety—has made discussion unavoidable, or when enthusiasm for individual Caldwell volumes has created a need to discuss them, critics have generally assumed that if they simply analyze Caldwell in the way they have successfully analyzed Hemingway or Faulkner or Fitzgerald, interesting insights will be generated, at least if Caldwell is any good and if they are adequate critics. But, examining Caldwell for coherent underlying structures or for patterns of meaningful imagery has proved consistently unsatisfying. The result: Caldwell's detractors have judged him second rate; and even his most coherent supporters have been forced to rest their case on essays which begin confidently and degenerate into vagueness or confusion, or simply peter out before any specific line of investigation has been completed.

If we are to understand the real meaning of Caldwell's magical pull, we must first recognize what he *means* to do—what his own goals for his work are and how he attempts to reach them. We may not agree that these goals are worth attaining, or that attaining them makes for "good" literature, but when a writer has been as clear and as consistent about his intentions as Caldwell has, it seems futile to avoid the obvious.

For Caldwell, writing seems less a matter of conscious choice than of emotional necessity: "I consider creative writing to be motivated by a certain state of mind; and believe that only those who are born with the gift or who acquire the indefinable urge to express themselves in print can accomplish it. This state of mind, as I call it, is an almost uncontrollable desire that seeks fulfillment at any cost. It is a craving that will not be denied. It is similar to the emotional need, as some find it, to seek love and companionship; to others it is as the physical necessity for food and drink."[35] Though he comments infrequently about the deeper sources of his desire to write, Caldwell repeatedly has been quite explicit about the sort of writer he needs to be:

> I'm only a story teller; and what I do, or have done, and tried to do, is be able to tell the story of people and the life that they live. . . .
>
> I think if you set out to be a storyteller, that's more important than anything else. And that's what I still try to be, a storyteller in the written word. If you don't have a story, I don't know what else you've got in writing fiction. I don't know what else there is.
>
> The present writer has no delusions concerning his work. I can only say that the pieces on the following pages [of *The Caldwell Caravan*] are readable, honest, and the result of hard work. I do not consider them to be examples of artistry, or of earth-shaking importance; they are not indicative of a trend in fiction; and they were not written to make propaganda. The one and only thing they do is tell stories; if they do anything else, something is wrong somewhere.
>
> I think you must remember that a writer is a simple-minded person to start with and go on that basis. He's not a great mind, he's not a great thinker, he's not a great philosopher, he's a storyteller. I mean that's the field I belong in; there are, of course, writers who have great minds, but I don't pretend to.[36]

"Storyteller," then, not "humorist" or "social critic," is the label Caldwell is most comfortable with. While this term would seem to indicate that Caldwell's primary concern is with fiction, however, these statements do not tell us what Caldwell means by "fiction," what he considers a "story." But again, Caldwell himself seems quite clear about the matter:

> People say, "Well now, is this true to life? Did this really happen?" Well, you see that always bothers me. . . . Did this really happen? Well, if it did, it's non-fiction. Fiction is a creation. So, of course, it never happened. It never happened until it happened in the book that you are writing. That's when it happened, not before or after.
>
> I would not want to, or could not, sit down and relate a story that happened to me many years ago, verbatim. I could not do it; I would not be interested to do it because then I would know how it was going to end. I would have no interest in starting that story if I already knew what the ending was going to be. . . .
> What interests me, as a writer, is having an idea that's based on some solid, factual incident . . . but has no relation to how it's going to end, what it's going to do in the middle. . . .
>
> *Dr. Tharpe:* I'm interested. . . . Is it literally true that when you start a story, you do not know how you are going to end it?
> *Mr. Caldwell:* That's right.
> *Dr. Tharpe:* Do you care to elaborate on that?
> *Mr. Caldwell:* Well, you see, if you—I don't like the word create, but I don't know how else to express it right now. If you're making something, creating something, if it already has an ending, then you're not creating anything. All you're doing is filling in the blank spots, blank words, blank lines, and so forth. To me, that story has . . . to build itself as it goes. One thing has to lead to another. Sometimes it might be improbable; sometimes it might be irrational, but that can't be helped.[37]

Caldwell's aesthetic statements are so down-to-earth that their novelty can easily be overlooked. Caldwell believes that the fiction writer's job is to tell what might happen in life, not to try to provide solutions to life's dilemmas or answers to life's mysteries. On the basis of his experience, Caldwell imagines characters—his versions of people who *might* exist—and then, using his observation of human activity, he describes, step by step, what these particular characters *might* do. The actual writing of a fiction for Caldwell, in other words, is not—as often seems the case with other writers—a process of molding a series of imagined events so that they demonstrate truths about life which the writer feels he or she has discovered; rather, it's a process of discovery during which Caldwell can see where his imagination will lead him.

The particulars of the way Caldwell composes a book reflect his general approach:

> I have to be satisfied page by page as I go, not with the end result but with the page result. One page may be done a dozen times, but I won't go to the next page until I'm satisfied with that page. I just have to go at it that way.
> *Sale:* Has that always been your working procedure?
> *Caldwell:* Yes.
> *Sale:* You don't write a number of pages and then make serious revisions?
> *Caldwell:* No, I like to see the page. I like to see the typewritten page the way it should be in a finished condition. If I have to cross out something or write something in, well, I'll go back and do that page over again to make it look better, to make it look more like print, rather than look like a sprawling mess or something. So I'll do it over maybe a dozen times because I might change one word or ten words or one sentence or take out half a dozen. But if it doesn't look right, if it looks messy, if it looks imperfect, I have to go back and do that page over on the typewriter to make it look clean and finished.
> *Sale:* Have editors ever severely edited your work?
> *Caldwell:* No, no. I learned early in life that that was not necessary. . . . Now if I make a mistake in grammar or something, I'm very happy to have it brought to my attention. . . . But as for changing something, no. I say just forget it. Nothing has ever been changed that I have written.[38]

Caldwell's commitment to his unusual method of storytelling is reflected in the kinds of people he has tended to write about and in his characteristic fictional style and organization. Almost by definition, Caldwell's method precludes his writing about his own life: "I couldn't write autobiographically . . . because I know what my life was at the time. If I were going to write an autobiography, I would write an autobiography, not . . . try to clothe it in fiction."[39] Instead, Caldwell has consistently chosen to write about people who, he is sure, might be found in geographic areas he has had ample opportunity to observe, but whose lifestyles are likely to be unfamiliar to most readers: people whose lives reflect the folkways of specific regions ("I think regional writing is much more important than trying to be universal or . . . trying to write the great American novel") or people whose lives are strongly affected by economic deprivation.[40] The benefits of this choice are at least two-fold: Caldwell has been able to give his imagination free rein in exploring what his fictional characters do, while locating their activities within vivid renditions of real environments; and he has been able to make the reader's experience more fully a process of discovery: he takes us to places we've never been and shows us people we couldn't have imagined.

Caldwell's fundamental commitment to explore the activities of his characters implies his attitude toward style: "to me content is far more important than style. Anyone can probably spend a good part of his life working up a certain style, but then he has to make content conform to the style. Whereas I believe that your style will come out of your content, that your content will dictate the method, the style that you're going to write in. So I'm always a little bit suspicious of people who are stylists. . . . I'd . . . be more content to be a common practitioner of content in writing."[41] The conscious creation of a highly visible style—as in the fiction of Stein or Faulkner, for example—frequently implies an overriding attitude toward character; it functions as an indicator of the meaning of their activities. Since Caldwell is committed to revealing what his characters *might do* (which he feels he is capable of knowing, or guessing) rather than what their activities *mean* (which he is sure he cannot know) conscious stylistic "artistry" is outside the parameters of his work. This is not to say, of course, that Caldwell has no style, but that for him style is effective only insofar as it provides the reader with a clear view of the characters, their activities, and their environment. The desire to write clearly informs Caldwell's language in several ways. For one thing, he has been consistently determined to simplify his language. At the end of *Call It Experience* Caldwell asks himself, "There must be some one thing that you consider the most important element in your writing. What is it?" The answer: "Not using a word of many syllables when a shorter word will do. Not using a word that has to be looked up in a dictionary for definition or for spelling. Once I revised my copy of the dictionary by striking out all the words in it that had more than four syllables."[42] A second result is an almost complete absence of imagery. From time to time one may read a simple comparison—"the crater was hotter than a pail of barbecue hash"—but any search for a consistent pattern of imagery deriving from the implications of Caldwell's language is almost sure to be unrewarding. The goal of Caldwell's "plain style," then, is to get his stories told clearly enough so that whatever energy readers expend as they read will be devoted to considering the activities of the characters, rather than to deciphering the meanings and implications of his language.

Caldwell's method of composition has implications for the way in which his narratives are constructed. For one thing, his page-by-page discovery of what his characters do implies a chronological presentation of events. One thing simply leads to another. Even in those instances when Caldwell develops multiple narrative strands—in *Trouble in July*, for example—no complex interweaving of time or place is developed. Caldwell merely follows one strand of action step by step for a while, and then step by step brings the next strand up to date. Since Caldwell cannot interpret his characters' activities before he discovers them, and since he refuses to revise what they have done later, his organization of events into chapters tends to be arbitrary. The beginnings and endings of chapters may signal changes in time and place, but often they seem to occur in the middle of on-going activities, for no apparent reason except, perhaps, that Caldwell assumes his readers need a breather.

Caldwell's attitude toward the contributions of other writers is also a corollary to his fictional method. While many authors feel they must be aware of what has been written in order to know where they can make a contribution, Caldwell has been consistently unapologetic about the limitations of his literary background: "Many years ago I divided the population into two parts: those who read and those who write. I wished to belong in the latter category."[43] He admits to reading "a few books a year," but rarely more than a single book by a given author: "When I read one book by a writer, I'm satisfied. I don't have to read four of them to form an opinion."[44] Among the books he has read, he includes *As I Lay Dying* ("a superb book"), some of the short stories of Sherwood Anderson and Hemingway ("I can't remember anything of his I've read. I'm sure I read something"), and one book each by Steinbeck, Dreiser, O'Connor, McCullers, and some others. His limitations as a reader, however, are obvious: "Never read anything by Mark Twain"; "As for the Russian writers, I don't read them"; "the so-called New England school. I never read it, but I've heard about it being the seat of American writing."[45] We may feel that Caldwell is missing a good deal; yet since his goal is simply to provide readers with a clear look at what he thinks certain imaginary characters might do, one is hard pressed to see how his lack of reading compromises his own efforts: "When I write something, that's the way it's going to be as far as I'm concerned. Whether somebody else likes it or doesn't like it means nothing to me at all. That's the way it is. Not that I think I'm perfect or anything of this sort, but I did the best I could and I don't think anybody else could tell me how to do it any better."[46]

III

A moment's serious consideration of Caldwell's aesthetic makes obvious the limitations of the persistent critical complaint that Caldwell's fiction is flawed by its lack of overall coherence. The very function—and value—of Caldwell's one-page-at-a-time compositional procedure is to make certain kinds of inconsistency possible, or, to put it another way, to prevent considerations of literary form from constricting the moment-to-moment human truth he is attempting to capture. Instead of revising his characters' activities so that they conform to a preconceived view of what people are like or what readers are likely to accept, Caldwell allows his stories and novels to create for the reader the same sorts of exploratory experience that writing them was for him. Though the "plain style" always provides a clear view of what is going on, we never know what might happen next. We may understand, for example, why middle-aged Ben Hackett gets sexually aroused by finding a pair of woman's silk panties in an abandoned car which is blocking his road, but there is absolutely no way we could predict that when he subsequently runs into Fred's wife he will grab her, throw her to the ground, and, despite her cries for help, proceed to put the panties *on* her. Nor is there any way to predict that Fred's wife will finally realize what Ben is trying to do and will be pleased, or that they will end their encounter with a dignified "Good day." Like "Midsummer Passion," many of Caldwell's most interesting stories—"A Swell-Looking Girl," "The Growing Season," "The Fly in the Coffin," "Country Full of Swedes," "A Woman in the House," "A Short Sleep in Louisiana," "Savannah River Payday," dozens of others—almost defy the reader to guess what will happen from one minute to the next. The scope of the novels is larger, but the effect is much the same. Who could ever predict that an entire family would dedicate itself to digging for gold on land which quite obviously will never yield a nugget, or that Ty Ty would throw his "scientific" approach to digging aside and capture an albino to divine for gold, or that, once he sees Darling Jill, the captured albino will fall desperately in love with her and not want to go back to his family, or that when Ty Ty finds them having sex behind the house he'll be delighted, or that . . . the list could continue until the conclusion of *God's Little Acre*; and of course, *Tobacco Road*, *Journeyman*, *Tragic Ground* and other novels would yield similar results.

When we are not mystified about what the characters in Caldwell's short stories and novels might do next—and, usually, even when we are—we are likely to be puzzled by the apparent disparities between the various things we see them do. How can Lonnie, the protagonist in "Kneel to the Rising Sun," have so little to lose and still be so afraid of Arch Gunnard that he'll betray his closest and most valuable friend? What can Roy hope to do with the sharpest corn-bread knife (in "A Knife to Cut the Corn Bread With") when he cannot move his body? How can Jule Robinson (in "The Negro in the Well") be so greedy as to demand two of Bokus Bradley's hounds as the price for pulling Bokus out of the Robinson well, and further, how can Bokus decide to refuse? How can Tuffy Webb (in "A Day's Wooing") be so confident that with his new straw hat he'll successfully woo Nancy and then be unable to say a word to her; and how can he fail to see how obviously she wants him? How can Jeeter Lester (in *Tobacco Road*) steal Lov's turnips and gorge himself on them, to the frustration of the rest of his starving family, and then suddenly grow concerned about God and the moral implications of his actions? How can he expect to make money by chopping and selling broom sedge that won't burn? How can Semon Dye (in *Journeyman*) call himself a man of god and, at the same time, be a gambler, a thief, an adulterer, a pimp, and a murderer; and how can Clay Horey, after all Semon does to him, conclude, "God help the people at the next place Semon picks out to stop and preach. . . . But I reckon they'll be just as tickled to have him around as I was"? To read Caldwell is to be consistently confronted by such questions. In some instances, in fact, they are so fundamental and so pervasive that readers have ignored them. When *Trouble in July* was published, a number of reviewers—and, subsequently, the majority of Caldwell critics—complained that Caldwell's lynching novel is weakened by the obviousness of Sonny Clark's innocence of the patently false rape charge of sexually frustrated Katy Barlow. Yet, that Sonny's innocence *is* so obvious and so unquestionable is what makes the activities of the residents of Andrewjones so interesting. The individual members of the social structure of the small town perform their ritual parts in a racial revenge, despite their own consciousness of the complete absurdity of their actions. The blistering speed of this Caldwell narrative reflects the speed with which even the most ridiculous social tradition can play itself out.

Taken as a body of work Caldwell's stories and novels provide us with a panorama of human vagary. Whether the inconsistencies and the absurdities of his characters' activities are a product of large sociopolitical realities—economic deprivation, the co-existence of two races in a single place and time—or of each character's individual make-up is hard to say; Caldwell rarely hazards a guess. He is confident only that they exist and that they are the aspects of human nature which he, and his readers, will find most interesting. It is as though Caldwell were saying, "Before you make any judgments about Human Nature, consider *these* people, and how at least one experienced observer of the human drama sincerely believes they might act under certain circumstances." The basic truth about life for Caldwell cannot be determined simply by deciding what is "normal" or what is understandable" to make any sensible judgments— or to decide that no sensible judgments can be made—one must understand what is, in fact, possible, what people are capable of saying and doing. One of the central ironies of his career is that by choosing to capture what characters who might exist might actually do, and by refusing to compromise his findings so as to conform to the assumptions of a literary establishment, Caldwell has been considered a creator of "grotesques." Certainly, compared to most literary characters Caldwell's people do seem impossibly strange. But if we honestly compare them with real people, do they really seem more grotesque than the rest of us? We find each other so frustrating and so fascinating, after all, not so much because we are basically coherent beings who undergo a meaningful and understandable development—like most fictional protagonists—but because we are, within a single, limited period of time, quite likely to drastically change our minds, our moods, our feelings, and our statements with no apparent motive; to tediously repeat ourselves; to offer passionate justifications of the most absurd activities; to worry outrageously about the most insignificant details; to procrastinate action on conditions which require our immediate attention; to labor doggedly for the most impractical ends; to be angry at others for failing to do what we ourselves would not think of doing. As self-contradictory as it may sound, in other words, "normal" human beings—like Jeeter Lester, Sister Bessie, Ty Ty Walden,

Semon Dye, and the rest of Caldwell's characters—are consistently inconsistent, and often outrageously so. Instead of bemoaning Caldwell's failure to make life seem fundamentally orderly and comprehensible, we should be congratulating him for finding a way of presenting interesting narratives without being false to the puzzling realities of human experience.

The tendency of most critics to label Caldwell "humorist" or "social critic" can be seen in this context as indicative of a critical failure to recognize, or accept, what actually goes on in his stories and novels. Since we tend to laugh at what strikes us as unusual, and since Caldwell's characters seem rather unusual to most readers, the conclusion that Caldwell is being funny is not surprising. It is, however, inaccurate. Puzzled critics have sometimes noted that Caldwell himself has resisted the label of humorist, and while his reticence may seem to some a rather perverse attempt to deny the obvious, Caldwell has made the reasons for his attitude clear:

> I can only say that consciously I could not write anything that was comic or humorous if you want to use that word. . . . To me, there is comedy in tragedy and tragedy in comedy; they are inseparable; they're interchangeable. It's like the old saying you hear sometimes, "I couldn't laugh for crying; I couldn't cry for laughing," and so forth. To me, they are such interchangeable things that it's all one; it's life; it's a person's life that you are writing about, and he's going to have tragedy; he's going to have comedy in his existence willy-nilly. It's inescapable.
>
> I would not set out to try to distinguish these two elements. Say I am going to write a comic interlude here, or I am going to write a tragic interlude here and so forth to try to prove something or try to show something in a person's character. No, it would have to be such a natural result of this person's living that I wouldn't know whether it was going to be funny or sad. By the time I got half way through the chapter, I still wouldn't know whether the effect was going to be funny or sad. It all results in the delineation of this person as he is going to reveal himself, not what I am going to do about it, but what he is going to do himself.[47]

Ultimately, according to Caldwell, comedy "depends on what your point of view is"; "the same situation" can be "both; it can be really tragic, or it can be humorous. . . ."[48] As he has said so often, Caldwell merely tells us what might happen. Whether we find it funny or not depends on *our* attitudes and *our* experiences, not on Caldwell's. Instead of talking so extensively about Caldwell's humor, critics should have been talking about their own.

The label of "social critic" is inadequate for much the same reason.

True, Caldwell did knowingly draw attention to specific social evils—the tenant system and racism, most obviously—and in nonfiction works like *Tenant Farmer, Some American People,* and *You Have Seen Their Faces,* he explained his objections to these institutions in no uncertain terms. It is even conceivable that his writing has had some practical effect in changing the South. And yet, Caldwell has always resisted the suggestion that he writes from a specific political orientation, and he has denied that he tries to be a social critic: "I have not consciously and knowingly set out to be a social critic in any sense of the word."[49] Again, the apparent contradiction here is understandable within the context of Caldwell's aesthetic. Caldwell's fictional narratives develop out of his observations of the interesting things that people do, or might do. Living and traveling in the South, especially during the Depression, would have made frequent observations of conditions which we would consider evidence of serious social problems almost inevitable. Regardless of his politics or his feelings about specific social reforms, Caldwell could have been expected to chronicle in his fiction some of the more interesting human aberrations resulting from such conditions. To accurately chronicle what might happen, on the basis of what one has observed, however, is not necessarily to be a "social critic," as that term is usually understood. At most, Caldwell functions as a social observer in his fiction and carefully restricts his opinions about what ought to be done about social problems to his nonfiction. I can remember only one instance where this seems contradicted: the frequently discussed comments Caldwell makes about the background of Jeeter Lester's problems in Chapters 7 and 13 of *Tobacco Road.* It seems likely, however, that Caldwell considered these comments less an analysis than a straightforward presentation of information that would have been common, observable knowledge for anyone living in Northern Georgia in the thirties, but with which readers from other regions might not have been familiar. Incidentally, the objection of several critics that *Tobacco Road* is flawed by Caldwell's inclusion of this expository background material is based on the assumption that a writer is aesthetically justified in presenting only one type of information in a specific work, an assumption which is not only highly questionable in this particular instance— Caldwell's own fictional voice is quite consistent throughout the novel— but is questionable in general.[50] Our observation of history and our observation of our immediate experiences provide us with different kinds of information; yet they are perfectly capable of being mutually illuminating within an individual context.

Once the labels of "humorist" and "social critic" are recognized for what they are—reflections of how some critics have attempted to make sense of Caldwell's puzzling stories and novels—rather than as insights into Caldwell's methods or goals, one can more easily understand that while Caldwell's fiction offers a considerable challenge to readers, it is a challenge of an entirely different order from that which most fiction is thought to provide. Faulkner's fiction, for example, is often difficult to understand because readers may have difficulty, at least during early readings, recognizing precisely what is taking place and because careful study is required before the complex vision implied by Faulkner's style, his complex imagery, and his experiments with point of view, declares itself. Hemingway's fiction can be deceptive because the surface simplicity of his style can seduce the reader away from subtle but immensely rewarding deeper levels. In both instances, the reader is challenged to understand the intricacies of what these writers mean to communicate to us. The difficulty of Caldwell's fiction, on the other hand, is a reflection of the difficulty of life itself. Instead of being faced with deciphering the components of a coherent vision which informs particular novels and stories—something most trained readers can do, given enough time and effort—Caldwell readers are up against the mystifying incoherence of real life. The result is that while Faulkner's and Hemingway's fiction becomes clearer with each successive reading, Caldwell's fiction continues to perplex both trained and untrained readers as long as it is read. The "plain style" turns out to be one of the central ironies of Caldwell's fiction because, as is true in the paintings of Bosch or Dali or Magritte, this style so clearly reveals the most bewildering possibilities.

A word about Caldwell's nonfiction is in order. Since Caldwell's aesthetic is based on a definition of "fiction" as narrative discovered by a writer as a story or novel is written, and of "nonfiction" as a writer's description of something which has already occurred, Caldwell's nonfiction—by definition—cannot be surprising and puzzling in the same sense his fiction is. Nevertheless, in many of his nonfiction books Caldwell found means of developing reading experiences which would create a feeling of exploration. In a number of instances Caldwell combined expository essays and reminiscences with fictional narrative. *You Have Seen Their Faces* includes detailed essays about the agricultural system of the South; passages of first-person narrative which have the feel of fictional portraits, though they are presumably transcriptions of actual statements by particular people ("nonfiction" in Caldwell's definition); and—for the Bourke-White photographs—brief fictional legends, "intended to express the author's own conceptions of the sentiments of the individuals portrayed," rather than the actual statements of these people.[51] Especially in conjunction with the Bourke-White photographs this combination of methods (and *Say! Is This the U.S.A.*, *Some American People*, and *Deep South* use similar strategies) provides the reader with a multi-dimensional exploration of his subject. Even in those nonfiction works where Caldwell does not ostensibly use multiple types of writing—in the opening section of *Some American People*, for example—his recollections are presented in a variety of ways, from direct reminiscences in which Caldwell is the identifiable narrator, to sketches like "The Barber of the Northwest," "After Eighty Years," and "Grandpa in the Bathtub" which would fall within the parameters of most standard definitions of "fiction." In still other nonfiction works Caldwell effectively employs many of the traditional narrative devices that his own method of writing tends to eliminate. Most notably in *North of the Danube*, Caldwell uses a rather highly descriptive language full of imagery to present a series of sketches during which we simultaneously see Caldwell travel spatially from eastern to western Czechoslovakia and feel the relentless movement of history which is bringing heavier and heavier Nazi influence. Anyone under the illusion that the unconventional form and effect of Caldwell's fiction results from his inability to handle the demands of more recognizable fictional forms would be well advised to pay careful attention to this beautifully constructed nonfiction novel.

IV

When all is said and done, how significant a writer is Caldwell? The critical consensus, as of 1979, was that he is an interesting, but unquestionably minor figure, whose work never fulfilled his early promise. And yet, as we have seen, this consensus is largely a result of a consistent failure on the part of Caldwell commentators to deal with Caldwell on his own terms. Of course, even the most careful attention to the ways in which Caldwell's aesthetic functions in his work does not negate the fact that this work has limitations, some of which are a direct result of the aesthetic itself. For one thing, there are certain kinds of reading pleasure Caldwell does not provide, even at his best. The enjoyment of re-reading a story or novel, carefully exploring its subtleties until its full implications are apparent—an enjoyment Faulkner, Hemingway, Bellow, and so many of the most respected contemporary writers give us again and again—is almost entirely absent from the experience of reading Caldwell. By and large, re-reading a Caldwell story or novel not only fails to uncover subtleties missed the first time through, it eliminates the suspense originally generated by our curiosity about what the characters might do next. To put it another way, once we've finished a Caldwell story, it ceases to be "fiction"—at least according to Caldwell's definition—and becomes memory. Secondly, since Caldwell's fiction is centered entirely on his characters' statements and actions, we do not experience the exploration of fictional forms which makes Stein or Faulkner enjoyable volume after volume. Third, no matter how many of Caldwell's books we read, we do not grow aware—as we do, say, in Elliot or Hardy or Steinbeck—of a World View, a model against which we can measure our interpretations of our own experience.

These would seem to be significant limitations, and yet to judge Caldwell as a minor writer simply because he is "limited" is to ignore the obvious fact that *all* writers are limited and that, as is true in Caldwell's case, their limitations are generally a function of fundamental aesthetic choices. For example, all the reading pleasures described in the previous paragraph are available *only* to those people who can devote substantial periods of time to reading. A single careful reading of *The Ambassadors* or *The Sound and the Fury* or *Ulysses* requires many hours; anything like a comprehensive understanding involves many days of re-reading and study. Such books demand more than just hours and patience, however. Most of us could never have become comfortable with any of the major works of Joyce, James, Faulkner, or even Hemingway had we not first experienced years of intensive academic training, much of it devoted in particular to classic literature. Of course, to develop what is normally considered an expertise about such writers, a serious on-going commitment over a period of years is a necessity. In practice, then, whatever riches these authors offer are available to a relatively few, highly privileged readers. For most people—even most intelligent people who love to read—novels like *Wings of the Dove* or *Finnegans Wake* are rather like white elephants.

It is one thing to have deep respect and admiration for the writer who can create a large, dense novel capable of fascinating the most astute student of literature for a substantial portion of a lifetime. It is quite another to presume that the production of such masterworks is the only accomplishment in fiction which is worthy of our deep respect. Such a presumption, after all, implies that the greatest literature is that which is comprehensible to the smallest number of highly trained specialists; and while few of us would feel completely comfortable with such an attitude, it is nevertheless very widespread: a great many scholars and teachers of literature assume that the most significant writers are those who are demanding enough to have stimulated the most research and discussion. Part of Caldwell's particular difficulty with critics stems from his awareness of, and implicit contempt for, this attitude. In a number of instances, in fact, he has suggested that the real reasons for such restrictive thinking just may be somewhat less estimable than an abiding love of literature:

> I would much rather have the appreciation of a reader than the appreciation of a critic, because a critic is usually paid, or he makes money out of his judgements, whereas a reader goes out and pays to buy the book. Therefore, if he likes what he has bought, then I think I am more pleased that I would be if someone wrote a praise-worthy review.
>
> You see, for one thing I have not been writing for the edification or the education of the university community. That's the last thing that would come to my mind, to write a book, write a story for the purpose . . . of edifying or amusing or educating a college student. My aim is different. . . .
>
> My aim is . . . for the casual reader . . . the man in the street. . . . I can appreciate his comment about what I write

much more than I can that of a critique . . . written or
delivered by a professor to students, because that's forcing me
upon someone else . . . being forced to appreciate me in some
way or read me in some way. Whereas, the other person comes
along and sees the story, and likes and dislikes it, but he has not
been forced . . . to read this work of mine."[52]

Is it too much to suggest that literary critics and literature teachers
prefer fiction which requires intensive study because difficult literature
makes their particular expertise necessary? Obviously our students *need*
us to understand Faulkner and James. And the most illuminating critical
discussions can be written about the most complex authors. While
Caldwell himself has never betrayed the slightest annoyance at not being
taken seriously by the academic literary establishment, I am growing
increasingly convinced that his failure to develop a critical reputation
comparable to that devoted to such contemporaries as Fitzgerald, Hemingway, Steinbeck, and Wolfe says nothing at all about the intrinsic
merits of his accomplishment and a very great deal about the potential effects of the increasingly widespread pressure to publish and to justify the
need for specialists in literature in institutions of higher education. Since
Caldwell's work does not need to be deciphered, since analysis of it rarely
uncovers surprising new dimensions which can be revealed to students
and colleagues, the academic establishment would just as soon forget
Caldwell and devote its attention to more "valuable" writers. This constitutes what amounts to the irony of ironies, at least for those thousands
of professionals who teach both literary analysis and expository writing.
We have grown more and more to accept a professional disparity worthy
of Jeeter Lester himself: we beg our students to be clear, concise, direct,
honest, and well-informed, to write prose which communicates its
message in a single reading, while reserving our highest accolades for only
those whose work mystifies almost everyone.

For Caldwell to attain his rightful place in our culture we need only
recognize that in any area of the arts there are different kinds of excellence, and that they need not compete with one another. We don't
need to stop loving James or Faulkner in order to love Caldwell, any more
than we need stop loving Old English ballads to love *Paradise Lost*. The
opposite is more nearly the truth: to appreciate what Caldwell has given
us can create a more sensible perspective about writers with radically different talents and goals. True, Caldwell has written some uninteresting
books; and his later work is generally much less impressive than the books
he published during the thirties and early forties. But the same can be said
of Hemingway, Faulkner, Fitzgerald, Anderson, and many other writers
accepted today by the literary establishment.

In the final analysis, Caldwell has as much to offer us—despite his
perfectly obvious "limitations"—as any other first-rate modern writer.
Working within an unusual but cogent definition of fiction, he has

created dozens of interesting stories characterized by a courageous will-ingness to be honest about the mysterious complexities of human lives and by a determination to communicate the fruits of his intensive observation in a form which is clear enough, direct enough, and powerful enough to be read, understood and vividly remembered for years by both trained literary critics and lay readers. His dogged determination to see what he can and to stand by what he sees has resulted in works of immense integrity and individuality. And despite all he has accomplished, he has consistently refused to pretend he is a seer or a prophet; if he deserves more attention than he has received, he doesn't even know it: "You see, from my point of view, I have no reason to suppose . . . that I have been neglected because I don't know that what I have done is important enough to entitle me to any kind of different judgment than I've already had, because I am just a simple storyteller."[53] Yes, I believe the author of *Tobacco Road, God's Little Acre, American Earth, We Are the Living, Southways, Kneel to the Rising Sun, North of the Danube, Trouble In July, Journeyman, Some American People, You Have Seen Their Faces, All-Out on the Road to Smolensk, The Sacrilege of Alan Kent, Say! Is This the U.S.A., Call It Experience, Tragic Ground*, and *Georgia Boy* is a great writer, and he may be the most refreshingly unpretentious great writer we've ever had.

V

The present volume is divided into three sections. "Reviews" presents responses to individual Caldwell books at the time of their publication. Specific reviews are included either because they illuminate some aspect of Caldwell's work or because they reveal trends in its public and critical reception. Also included in this section are materials which reveal crucial aspects of Caldwell's literary career not evident in discussions of individual books. The decisions of City Magistrate Greenspan and Justice Spalding in the two most important court cases involving Caldwell's work are included, as are a number of responses by Caldwell himself and others to Jack Kirkland's dramatic adaptation of *Tobacco Road* and the public furor it raised.

The second section, "Caldwell, *The New York Post*, and *The Augusta Chronicle*," documents one of the most interesting interludes in Caldwell's career as a public witness of social injustice. Like Hemingway, Caldwell was a significant public figure, especially during the thirties and early forties. His career can be seen as a dialectic between his private imaginative explorations as a storyteller and his public attempts to have some positive effect on larger developments—the Depression and World War II, in particular—which so profoundly affected the period during which he did his most interesting writing. In February, 1935, and again in April of that year, Caldwell attacked the Southern agricultural system in *The New York Post*, drawing national attention to grotesque conditions he claimed to have witnessed near Augusta, Georgia. His eight *Post* articles are reprinted here, along with the reactions of Georgia citizens and a series of investigations and editorials from *The Augusta Chronicle* which were prompted by the first group of *Post* exposés.

"Criticism," the final section, presents critical overviews of Caldwell's career. As suggested earlier, so little solid critical work has been done on Caldwell that, as of 1979, I am able to include nearly all of the most interesting, the most useful, and the most influential discussions of his work to date. New insights into Caldwell's nonfiction are provided by Sylvia Cook in an essay published here for the first time. Since Caldwell's own explanations of his goals and methods have been so consistently neglected in critical assessments, I have also included Richard B. Sale's illuminating interview, Caldwell's own "My Twenty-Five Years of Censorship," and the eight introductions, reprinted here for the first time, which Caldwell wrote for new Duell, Sloan & Pearce editions of his books during the period 1948–1951.

I would like to thank all those whose support and expertise contributed to this volume. I might never have become interested in Caldwell had it not been for my former teacher Peter Lisca, whose admiration for Caldwell's early novels was a catalyst for mine. The Utica College research librarians—Pat Dugan, Jim Williamson, Gisele Skinner, and Barbara Grimes—and Walter W. Wright, Chief of Special Collections at the Dartmouth College Library (where an excellent collection of Caldwell materials is housed), helped with my research. My friends Diane Matza and Verne Snyder read the introduction and provided useful suggestions for revision.

I am especially grateful to Erskine and Virginia Caldwell for their consistent support and generosity. In particular, Erskine Caldwell's willingness to allow me to reprint twenty separate essays has added immensely to the collection.

I don't know how to thank Patricia Reichgott Burg, whose attentiveness during every part of this project has been a constant help, and whose love and courage and sensitivity and good humor are a constant inspiration. The book is dedicated to her.

Notes

1. The phrase is Randall Jarrell's, in "Ten Books," *Southern Review*, 1 (1935–36), 402.

2. James T. Farrell, "One of Our Minor Young Writers Sheds Some Literary Tears," *The Sun* (N.Y.), 25 Sept. 1933, p. 22, col. 6.

3. See Carl Van Doren, "Made in America: Erskine Caldwell," *Nation*, 137 (Oct. 18, 1933), 443–44.

4. Jonathan Daniels, "From Comedy to Pity," *Saturday Review of Literature*, 18 (June 18, 1938), 7.

5. Harold Strauss considered Caldwell's humor "debatable," on the grounds that the mood evoked by an incident depends on where the reader stands: "in the case of a man slipping on a banana peel, your interpretation depends on what you are. If you are close to the man who hurts himself or to the Negro who wastes his slim substance on "Nine Dollars' Worth of Mumble" to conjure the love of a pretty high-yaller gal, you will perceive the tragic implications. But if you are a casual passer-by, you are unlikely to keep from laughing." "New Stories by Erskine Caldwell," *N.Y. Times*, 19 June 1938, Sec. 6, p. 7, cols. 2–4. Strauss's comments are very close to Caldwell's own; see Sec. III of the present discussion.

6. "A Hardboiled Idealist," *New Masses*, 7 (July, 1931), 18.

7. "New Realist Depicts South's Poor Whites' Pitiable Existence," *St. Paul Dispatch*, 16 Feb. 1932, p. 8, col. 8.

8. "Star-Dust Above 'Tobacco Road,'" *Christian Century*, 55 (Feb. 16, 1938), 204, 206.

9. "Sweet Are the Uses of Degeneracy," *Southern Review*, 1 (1935–36), 466, 453.

10. "Erskine Caldwell's Picture Book," *Southern Review*, 4, No. 1 (1938–39), 25.

11. Jarrell, p. 402.

12. "Seventeen Tales by Erskine Caldwell," *Saturday Review of Literature*, 12 (June 8, 1935), 5.

13. Van Doren, pp. 443–44.

14. See "Caldwell: Maker of Grotesques," *New Republic*, 82 (April 10, 1935), 232–35.

15. (New York: Macmillan, 1941), p. 219.

16. See Beach, pp. 219–31. In the second half of his essay ("Substitutes and Compensations," pp. 235–49), Beach reviews examples of ways in which Caldwell's poverty-stricken characters compensate for their boring, often empty lives: in *Journeyman* the characters turn to orgiastic religion; in *Trouble in July* to racism and racial murder; in *God's Little Acre* to the search for gold (Ty Ty) and ritual sex (Will). Beach sees Caldwell as a master of "the *naive* style": "There is an almost unfailing irony in the representation of character and action. But it is in the conception, in the arrangement of the elements, not in the phrasing or the moral tone" (p. 247).

17. "What Deep South Literature Needs," *Saturday Review of Literature*, 25 (Sept. 19, 1942), 9.

18. *New Republic*, 111 (Nov. 6, 1944), 599.

19. "Erskine Caldwell: Sentimental Gentleman from Georgia," *Southwest Review*, 31 (Autumn 1946), 358.

20. During the mid and late forties, six collections of previously published Caldwell stories appeared. The best of these, *The Pocket Book of Erskine Caldwell Stories* (New York: Pocket Books, 1947), was selected and introduced by Henry Seidel Canby.

21. In other countries—particularly France and the Soviet Union—Caldwell was faring better. In *Transatlantic Migration* (Durham: Duke Univ. Press, 1955), pp. 146–60, Thelma M. Smith and Ward L. Miner describe the generally favorable critical and popular reception of Caldwell in France, from the publication of the French edition of *God's Little Acre* in 1936 until the early 1950's. In "Gallic Light on Erskine Caldwell," *Southern Atlantic Quarterly*, 60 (August 1961), 390–97, Stewart Benedict reviewed the discrepancy between the French and American critical response to Caldwell and suggested possible reasons for it. Americans, suggests Benedict, don't like Caldwell because they are generally amelioristic and chauvenistic, because they are humorless about sex and sexless about humor, and because Caldwell writes patriarchical novels and the United States is a matriarchical society. The French do like him because they admire style, organization, and dispassion: "Clearly . . . the reader of Caldwell must establish his own emotional rapport with the characters," rather than expect that the author will supply the emotion; "The French, convinced by the technical excellence that it is worth the effort, are willing to do so; the Americans are not" (pp. 396–97). Finally, Benedict

contends that "American critics like their emotions one at a time" (p. 397) and therefore cannot appreciate Caldwell's humor. Mikhail Landor reviews the highly favorable critical and popular reception in the Soviet Union, in "Erskine Caldwell in the Soviet Union," *Soviet Literature*, No. 3 (1969), 183–86.

22. (New York: Duell, Sloan & Pearce, 1951), pp. xvi, xxviii, xviii. Cantwell discusses a number of ways in which the incongruities in Caldwell's stories and novels—"the sober recitals of odd happenings"; "the odd recital or ordinary ones" (p. xxi) create humor. In another essay, "Caldwell's Characters: Why Don't They Leave?" *Georgia Review*, 11 (1957), 252–64, Cantwell suggests that the relationship of people to the land is the essential catalyst in all Caldwell's novels, and that even when the land has ceased to be productive, Caldwell's characters can't leave: "The threefold destiny of Caldwell's characters hinges on their certain doom if they remain where they are, the numbed sense of helplessness that prevents their getting away, and a third element, a real or imaginary semi-organized force . . . which harries them through the third rails and live wires of an industrialized society if they do attempt flight" (p. 259).

23. C. Hugh Holman, "The View from the Regency-Hyatt," in George Core, ed., *Southern Fiction Today* (Athens: Univ. of Georgia Press, 1969), pp. 16–32; and George Snell, *The Shapers of American Fiction 1798–1947* (New York: Cooper Sq., 1961), pp. 263–88, are exceptions. Both commend Caldwell's work, especially as a short story writer. Holman suggests that "Kneel to the Rising Sun" has "a controlled fury that lingers in the mind and heart," which is presented with "an apparently artless simplicity which the artist can achieve only after many hours of seeking for clarity and grace" (p. 27). Snell feels that in general the stories from *American Earth* to *Southways* are of high quality, and that, "Two or three . . . are undoubtedly the most powerful examples of the literature of social protest written in America" (p. 266). Snell singles out "Candy-Man Beechum" and "Kneel to the Rising Sun."

24. "Erskine Caldwell: A Note for the Negative," *College English*, 17 (Oct. 1955), 358.

25. Allen, *The Modern Novel* (New York: Dutton, 1964), p. 119; Bradbury, *Renaissance in the South* (Chapel Hill: Univ. of North Carolina Press, 1963), p. 101; Gossett, *Violence in Recent Southern Fiction* (Durham: Duke Univ. Press, 1965), p. 25.

26. *The Short Story in America 1900–1950* (Freeport, N.Y.: Books for Libraries Press, 1952), p. 55.

27. See *Masses and Mainstream*, 5 (Aug. 1952), 59–64. Caldwell describes the experience of writing the book that was later entitled *A Lamp for Nightfall* and Maxwell Perkins's decision not to publish it in Chapter 9 of *Call It Experience* (New York: Duell, Sloan & Pearce, 1951).

28. No. 78 of the Univ. of Minnesota series of pamphlets on American writers (Minneapolis: Univ. of Minnesota Press, 1971), p. 44.

29. Pp. 45–46.

30. Cowley's "Retrospect" was published in Matthew J. Bruccoli and C.E. Frazer Clark, Jr., *Pages* (Detroit: Gale, 1976), pp. 62–78.

31. "Southwestern Humor, Erskine Caldwell, and the Comedy of Frustration," *Southern Literary Journal*, 8 (Fall 1975), 4, 17, 22–23, 20.

32. "Is That You in the Mirror, Jeeter?: The Reader and *Tobacco Road*," *Pembroke*, No. 11 (1979), 49, 50.

33. Cook provides an informative review of Caldwell's involvement with the Left during the thirties in "Erskine Caldwell and the Literary Left Wing," *Pembroke*, No. 11 (1979), 132–39; in the Caldwell chapter of her *From Tobacco Road to Route 66* (Chapel Hill: Univ. of North Carolina Press, 1976), she makes an interesting distinction between the female power of the land and the male power of the factories in *God's Little Acre* and provides a valuable comparison and contrast of Caldwell and Faulkner; and in her new essay, "Erskine Caldwell's Nonfiction"—published for the first time in this volume—she provides the most illuminating survey to date of Caldwell's nonfiction. James J. Thompson, Jr. discusses three

themes—sexuality, degenerated ethical standards, and fatalism—which he sees as characteristic of Caldwell's presentation of religion. See "Erskine Caldwell and Southern Religion," *Southern Humanities Review*, 5 (1971), 33–44. Harvey Klevar, in "Some Things Holy in a God-Forsaken Land," *Pembroke*, No. 11 (1979). 65–76, details his contention that Caldwell's characters project "instinctive life-forces and longings for transcendence" into the void created by the absence of an efficacious God, as a means for adding hope and meaning to their lives.

34. See "Repetition as Technique in the Short Stories of Erskine Caldwell," S.A.F., 5 (1977), 213–25. Further discussion of Caldwell's stories is included in my "An Evaluative Check-List of Erskine Caldwell's Short Fiction," SSF., 15 (1978), 81–97, along with a detailed, annotated listing of the first publication of each of Caldwell's stories. Both Henry Seidel Canby and Carvel Collins comment on the short stories in introductions to collections of Caldwell's short fiction. Canby, who regards Caldwell "as primarily and essentially a short-story writer," suggests that Caldwell is the first great American short-story artist "who has consciously viewed the rich materials of his native experience as sociology, and then turned them into successful art." See "Introduction," *The Pocket Book of Erskine Caldwell Stories* (New York: Pocket Books, 1947), p. ix. As is evident in his selection of stories, Canby is well aware of the range of Caldwell's accomplishment in short fiction: "He is not a naturalist, like Dreiser or Zola, in spite of his sociological basis; he is not a realist, if being a realist means to let life speak for itself without focus upon some inner significance; he is certainly not a romanticist, except about the land. . . . No one of these critical terms seems of much use in describing Mr. Caldwell's work, unless negatively. He will not be pigeon-holed easily by literary historians" (p. xv). In his brief "Introduction" to *Erskine Caldwell's Men and Women* (Boston: Little, Brown, 1961), Collins discusses possible reasons for Caldwell's popularity.

35. *Call It Experience*, pp. 180–81.

36. Jac Lyndon Tharpe, *Interview with Mr. Erskine Caldwell Eminent American Author*, Vol. 13 of The Mississippi Oral History Program (Hattiesburg: Univ. of Southern Mississippi, 1973), p. 5; Richard B. Sale, "An Interview in Florida with Erskine Caldwell," *Studies in the Novel*, 3 (Fall 1971), 329; Caldwell, "Introduction" to *The Caldwell Caravan* (Cleveland & New York: World, 1946), p. 7; Carvel Collins, "Erskine Caldwell at Work," *Atlantic*, 202 (July 1958), 27. Tharpe's interview is particularly valuable, though his failure to carefully edit the transcription of his conversation with Caldwell results in Caldwell's sounding less coherent than seems fair.

37. Tharpe, pp. 21, 32, 36.

38. Sale, pp. 320–21.

39. Tharpe, p. 37.

40. Sale, p. 331. Caldwell's interest in American regional life was demonstrated by his editing the 25-volume American Folkways Series. See also Caldwell's comments in *Writing in America* (New York: Phaedra, 1967), pp. 118–20.

41. Sale, pp. 328–29.

42. P. 188.

43. *Call It Experience*, p. 189.

44. Sale, p. 327.

45. Alan Lelchuk and Robin White, "An Interview with Erskine Caldwell," *Per/Se*, 2 (Spring 1967), 15, 16; Tharpe, p. 58.

46. Sale, p. 321.

47. Tharpe, p. 98.

48. Tharpe, pp. 99–100.

49. Tharpe, p. 5.

50. The most recent critic to raise this objection is Sylvia Cook. See *From Tobacco Road to Route 66*, pp. 66–69.

51. Caldwell and Margaret Bourke-White, (New York: Viking, 1937).

52. Tharpe, pp. 85, 86.

53. Tharpe, p. 85.

REVIEWS

"Two Judgments of *American Earth*"

T.K. Whipple and Malcolm Cowley*

Anyone who has ever spent much time where the untutored sons of these States forgather—as, for instance, in the army—must have heard, for hours on end, reminiscences poured forth in floods of anecdote—incidents pointed and pointless, significant and insignificant. In such storytelling is to be found the true popular or vulgar oral literature of America, the germ, the unformed beginning of narrative. The complaint is often made that this country has no folk tales; and while the complaint is mistaken, inasmuch as America is rich in folk tales, it is true they are local and generally have a look of quaint relics of a vanished age. But the endless stories which men tell each other of their own lives—into these taken in the mass, though each is individual in origin, the whole characteristic life of America is digested and distilled.

With such stories our politer letters have never condescended to have much traffic, perhaps for the excellent reason that most of our literary men, being somewhat orchidlike of nature, have seldom been where these recitals take place. Picaresque, proletarian, peasant America, though the most interesting as well as the largest part of the nation, has appeared in literature but little, and then as if viewed *de haut en bas*—almost never has it appeared in the terms of its own chosen mode of expression, the reminiscent anecdote.

Mr. Erskine Caldwell's collection of stories, "American Earth," is closer to this kind of narrative than any other book I know. To be sure, his field is limited—his first dozen sketches and incidents are entitled "Far South," his second twelve "Farthest East"—and he is so good a writer that the flavor of locality is strong in his work; but there is nothing necessarily local about the genre which he has chosen. It could be used equally well for all other parts of the Union.

While presumably one must not suppose that Mr. Caldwell's stories are autobiographical, it is as if he were telling offhand of things that had happened to him or that he had run into—insignificant in themselves perhaps, but somehow, though one could not say why, memorable.

*Reprinted from *New Republic*, 67 (June 17, 1931), 130–32, with permission.

Always he is, or pretends to be, the unsophisticated raconteur. Character, emotion, significance, are secondary, at most implied; plot is nonexistent; he deals in sheer incident, the primal germ plasm of narrative. Of the many contemporary efforts to get back, in revolt against the overelaborate and artificial productions of recent art, to some unexhausted original rootstock, Mr. Caldwell's is one of the most successful.

Mr. Caldwell goes back even farther than the folk for his fresh start; he reverts to boyhood. Much of his best work shows that bright, wide-eyed innocent fascination with everything dirty, nasty, horrible or gruesome which is one of the strangest and most unfailing traits of small boys. Even Mr. Caldwell's treatment of sex seems somehow preadolescent. His writing has a fresh, direct immediacy of juvenility which is extremely rare—and since his folk, even his adults, are the sort who stay juvenile all their lives, there is no incongruity.

One reason undoubtedly for his success is that, as the jacket of his book tells us, he has had a varied and extensive career among the people of whom—and like whom—he speaks. Not only, however, has Mr. Caldwell picked cotton in Tennessee, served as night cook in the Union Station at Wilkes-Barre, and reported for The Atlanta Journal; he has lately published his stories in Pagany, This Quarter, Transition and other such periodicals. And as his biography indicates the source of his strength, so do these names suggest his weakness, or at least the dangers which beset him. These occult magazines, priding themselves on making no compromise with common humanity, these purveyors of caviar, are insidious poison for Mr. Caldwell.

Since this is his first book—with the exception of "The Bastard," which was privately printed—one expects the unevenness and uncertainty which one finds; the serious peril is not his occasional fumbling, but his too frequent affectation. His naïveté too often is plainly a self-conscious pose. He is not free from preciosity—and of all kinds of stories, preciosity is most fatal to his kind. In part, this quality springs from a too devoted imitation of Sherwood Anderson; in part from a deference, perhaps, to the journals which have printed Mr. Caldwell's stories but with which, one suspects and hopes, Mr. Caldwell has little really in common. Especially are these effects evident in the third part of "American Earth," which contains only one long piece consisting of numerous tiny disconnected bits of fact and phantasy—a type of thing which seems, now at least, not to be the writer's forte.

Mr. Caldwell's unmistakable ability, his out-of-the-ordinary and interesting talent, and his very remarkable achievement justify us in having great hopes of him. Let us pray, however, that he may be delivered from the highbrows.   T. K. WHIPPLE.

In a year of generally dispiriting fiction, Erskine Caldwell's book of stories is important enough to justify the publication of a dissenting opinion. Not that I disagree with most of Mr. Whipple's admirably phrased review: what he says about the anecdotes that compose more than two-thirds of the volume is acute and unexceptionable; but he adopts a more questionable position in his last three paragraphs, when he takes "American Earth" as an excuse for attacking the influence of the little magazines.

During the last twelve years, almost every new writer destined to have any influence on the history of American literature has begun by appearing in the little magazines. The statement is more than justified by the facts. Leaving aside The Little Review and Others, which would carry us far into the past; leaving aside Transition and Pagany for an opposite reason: namely, that most of the writers they introduced are still too young to be widely known, one can quickly gather an impressive list of publications and writers. There is The Dial, which brought forward E. E. Cummings, Glenway Wescott, Kenneth Burke, Hart Crane, Elizabeth Madox Roberts—Broom, which published Matthew Josephson and Kay Boyle—The Fugitive, which produced Allen Tate and Robert Penn Warren among others—The Transatlantic Review, with Ernest Hemingway and Nathan Asch—"The American Caravan" (belonging at least in spirit among the little magazines), which first published the work of Erskine Caldwell himself, as well as printing Joseph Herbst, Katherine Anne Porter and others whose names are certain to be widely known. The list could easily be continued: it is enough to say that the primary function of the little magazines is discovering talent, and that they have performed this function successfully, having revealed such new talents as there were to be unearthed.

But the little magazines have a secondary function: that of encouraging experimental writing, which is another term for original writing. Originality is not a virtue mysteriously born into writers: it can be developed in talented people by force of reflection and reworking; it can also be destroyed in them if they write only for publications which demand that everything be done according to formula. The little magazines as a class have encouraged originality in the writers they printed. In so doing they have also encouraged affectation, mannerism and unintelligibility, but this, I think, was also desirable—not because I admire these literary vices for themselves, but because they often lead to admirable qualities. The young writer adopts them as a means toward developing a personal style; in the end he sloughs them off. If he doesn't, he isn't worth lamenting.

Mr. Caldwell is a literary child of the "occult" magazines, a child with eight foster-parents: "The American Caravan," Blues, Front, The Hound and Horn, Nativity, Pagany, This Quarter and Transition. By publishing his work, the best and the worst of it, they have encouraged him to develop something original. What I dissent from in Mr. Whipple's review is that he attacks precisely the portion of "American Earth" in which the author's original qualities are most evident.

I refer, of course, to the "disconnected bits of fact and phantasy" which compose the third section of the book. Here Mr. Caldwell achieves a sort of violent poetry, simple, romantic, arbitrary and effective; it is a mood unique in American prose (though suggested by the poems of Phelps Putnam). His figures of speech are expressed in terms of hyperbolic action. "Once," says Mr. Caldwell, "the sun was so hot a bird came down and walked beside me in my shadow. . . . In the chill frost of winter," he says elsewhere, "I left Memphis and rode on the outside of freight cars all the way to the Atlantic. The nights were so cold that my fingers froze around the iron bars and at daybreak each morning I had to bite them away with my teeth." The effect of hunger on the imagination is conveyed by one statement of fact: "A man walked into a restaurant through the front door and ate all he wanted to eat." Approaching death is a picture of buzzards in a field:

> There was an old Negro who was almost a hundred years old. When he worked in his cotton patch, the buzzards walked behind him all day and clawed the red earth with their feet and pecked at it with their beaks, and at night they roosted on top of his house and flapped their wings till the sun rose.

I don't mean to imply that the whole third section of the book is on the same high level. There are trite and sentimental passages which move one to personal fury against the author; there is also, as Mr. Whipple says, a good deal of preciousness and affectation. But for figures of speech like those quoted, and for the episodes which surround them, one could forgive any amount of faulty writing. Erskine Caldwell brings a new quality into American fiction: may due credit be given to the little magazines which recognized his talent.   MALCOLM COWLEY

"A Hardboiled Idealist"

Norman Macleod*

For the most part, Erskine Caldwell deals with the un-class-conscious proletarians in the sticks of America: down south and up east. As a cotton picker, lumber worker, hack driver, professional football player, night cook and waiter, he has penetrated the lower crust of the south without having come into contact with the organized worker. These proletarians of which he writes are always on the verge of starvation but with no perception of the class struggle or the economic forces operative in the United States which produce the conditions responsible for their poverty.

*Reprinted from *New Masses*, 7 (July, 1931), 18.

Not having workers en masse to deal with where the individual is insignificant in comparison with the group, Caldwell has turned to the "primitive" in his prototypes. Caldwell is, first of all, interested in sex. His workers are as unaware of Russia as any South Sea Islander and are as isolated from the world as god. And for that matter so is Caldwell. His style is staccato and sometimes "hardboiled" but beneath the surface one often perceives a fine strain of sensitivity to human emotions. He is in reality an idealist of the finer sort who (as most of our young writers do today) hesitates to admit it. As far as his characters have led him, he has done an excellent piece of interpretive writing. What he lacks is the ability to place them in the social scheme of things. When he goes deeper into the life of the working class of the South, he promises to become one of our most significant writers in America. Stories such as *Saturday Afternoon* prove him capable of good proletarian work.

We need writers like Caldwell.

He should go left.

"The Poetry of Unfeeling"

Gerald Sykes*

Erskine Caldwell is formally introduced in this volume to his country. One of his qualifications, apparently, is his knowledge of that country, for his publishers take pains to tell us that he has lived in several Southern States, in the East, in New England, and in the Far West. Another qualification is his combination of youth and experience; his years are twenty-seven, and his jobs have been almost as many. A third qualification—his publishers do not mention this, but it is implicit throughout the book—is his lack of feeling. For Mr. Caldwell is one of that group of young writers who have surpassed even the hard-boiled generation in callousness; in fact he has been called one of our "new barbarians." Rape and lynching, these are typical incidents in his stories; and he writes about them in the uncomprehending manner approved in our day.

Most of the volume is devoted to rather short short stories having the flavor of homely local anecdotes. The style is influenced by Ernest Hemingway, yet possesses a quality of its own. The truth is that Mr. Caldwell writes quite capably, and knows both what a story consists of and how to drive its point home. It is his capability, in fact, that subjects his stories to criticism. For many of them, perhaps all, are deliberately aimed at the reader, with the purpose of getting a definite response from him. The

*Reprinted from *Nation*, 133 (Oct. 21, 1931), 436–37. Copyright © 1931 The Nation Associates.

response usually desired is a coarse laugh or a shudder. There is little attempt to record a thing seen in pure terms of the author's vision. Effect is the prime consideration. As a result, there is little artistic difference between these stories and those which appear in some of our large-circulation magazines, except that these, being more "advanced," are aimed at a smaller audience. They tell us nothing new about our country, as the stories of Sherwood Anderson did, for example; because there is no new seeing here. The naivete is not genuine; it is simply the standard hard-boiled device. Despite their title, which may also have been aimed at us, we cannot go to these stories for new knowledge of the soil of America.

But the volume ends with three fantasies in the first person. It is here, in my opinion, that Mr. Caldwell has contributed the most attractive side of himself. His lack of feeling, which is not feigned but real, has a charm in the fantasy that it has not in the short story. A short story is built with the bricks of feeling; otherwise it comes to nothing. But in the fantasy anything is possible, and youthful violence does no harm. "When the woman who told fortunes went crazy, we had to carry her into another tent and cut her throat there." This is a diminutive "chapter" of one of the three fantasies. The reader is willing to accept it, as he is not willing to accept the same unfeeling when it is engaged supposedly in the portrayal of real people in real life. For unfeeling has a poetry of its own, even if it is chiefly a matter of verbal abandon. Tracing Life with a Finger—that is the title of the first fantasy, and, though it has nothing to do with "life," it shows Mr. Caldwell at his best. "Ever since then I have been tired. Oh, my God, how tired I am! The days are long—long. The sun rises quick like a bat out of hell and roosts forever in the sky biting my eyeballs with its black gums, and the blood of me drips all over the world." There is no creation here; but there is a certain freshness and novelty.

"Poor Whites"

Vincent Wall*

This book is titled rather appropriately. Its characters are the poor whites of the South and the damyankees of the North. Such men and women existing in the lazy backwash of American life have been done often enough in folk story and in popular fiction. It is seldom, however, that they have been done with greater honesty and less sentiment.

The author's style is that of the early Hemingway. He uses clipped sentences, literal, factual, sometimes crude, and sometimes flat, as well as the technical tricks that such a treatment permits: the deliberate

*Reprinted from *Saturday Review of Literature*, 8 (March 19, 1932), 604.

understatement, and the repeated phrase or epithet which suggests a lyric note. We are told, for instance, in "The Mating of Marjorie," that the heroine's "arms and legs are cool and firm, like the young pines in winter," and like a theme in music this phrase is repeated at intervals. Mr. Caldwell's attitude, not unnaturally, is that of the objectivist, and more often than not he is convincingly real. He writes of many things—of young love, a village quarrel, and the death of an old woman—yet it is always an impersonal, detached, and restrained account. When he writes of a lynching, it becomes an incident which he reports vividly and with clarity. His interest is purely literary, he makes no pretence of presenting a social document. He has taken a stand on no moral issues. His interest is in revealing character, and this he does—sometimes with humor, sometimes with pathos, and often with apathy.

The most distinguished contribution of the book is the story, "The Sacrilege of Allan Kent," which is the whole of the last section. It is the brusque, disconnected autobiography of a youth who eventually achieves a rather bitter maturity. The story is told by means of a bewildering variety of incidents and mental states briefly announced by the author in some one hundred and fifty numbered statements. The events described are often discolored and ugly; the statements are often chaotic and puzzling; occasionally they seem unimportant, and are like childhood memories which have unaccountably escaped oblivion.

There is almost no plot. Incidents are recorded incoherently and are apparently without significance. It might be a section from an author's notebook in which material for a novel had been collected. Childhood and boyhood are briefly suggested. Thereafter, the youth gives many years to aimless wandering about the South and the Middle West. He roustabouts with a carnival and works with niggers and poor whites on farm, levee, and plantation. Time and place mean nothing, and the account is always blurred and chaotic.

There are almost no characters save himself and those who pass briefly in and out of his life. His father and mother are dimly seen in the first section, Tracing Life with a Finger. Many women and some few men appear later for an instant, but they have life only in their relation with the ego of Allan Kent. This type of fiction is the stream of consciousness technique developed almost to the limit of its possibilities.

It is evident that the book has some value. Mr. Caldwell has something to say, although he is not always quite articulate. There is also a certain immaturity that makes certain of the stories seem trivial. The work on the whole, however, has strength and vigor, and the characters are full-blooded and convincing. Those who keep an ear to the ground for the new voices in literature will be interested in reading his next volume.

"Erskine Caldwell to Publish Novel, 'The Old Tobacco Road' "

Anonymous*

Erskine Caldwell, well known Georgian who has won literary fame within a few years, has just had notification of the acceptance of another novel of Georgia life, it was learned yesterday by his father, I.S. Caldwell, Chronicle columnist who resides at Wrens, Ga. Erskine Caldwell, who formerly resided in Wrens with his father and mother, now resides in Maine, although he spends much time in Wrens with his parents.

His new novel, which is to be published by Scribner's, is entitled "The Old Tobacco Road," which name was taken from the road by that name in this country. It is a novel with Richmond county as a setting, Mr. Caldwell says.

A number of his short stories have been published in periodicals of high literary standard, and the publishers of his last book, "American Earth," advertised its author as a "young genius." Before that time, he published "The Bastard," a novel with a small textile mill town as the setting.

"American Earth" is a collection of short stories, and its title describes the book. The stories are of a type, which, while not rapidly becoming a fad among average readers are praised by the best literary critics of the country as outstanding contributions to American literature. The author writes in the modern style; his sentences are brief, reduced to their simplest elements, and critics have described his writings as sincere in every word.

The title of the book is aptly chosen. The stories are "earthy;" the characters are slow moving, tied to the earth. Their humor springs from it, and a fundamental primitive brutality which no attempt is made to veil, frequently shows itself.

One of the stories in "American Earth" explains this characteristic. Take the story "Dorothy"; on the streets of Atlanta he finds a girl, jobless and penniless. She is too proud to ask for money; a lone quarter rests in his pocket and he is too proud to offer it. Instead, he directs her down Forsythe Street, across the viaduct to a cheap hotel. The memory of it torments his conscience afterward.

In another, "John the Indian and George Hopkins," George dies and his two daughters quarrel and separate over whether the iron fence about his grave should be painted. The dispute leads to the theft of the body by one of the daughters, with the aid of John, the Indian. Because of the

*Reprinted from *Augusta Chronicle*, 1 July 1931, p. 7, cols. 2–3.

underlying rock, they cannot bury it again. So they keep it in John's house. John rids himself of it by piling it into a canoe, hooking a bull-headed salmon and tying the line to the boat, and the corpse, towed by the salmon, sails blithely out of the story.

Between the extremes of reality in the stories are a host of pictures in which vice and virtue mingle, stories of stubbornness, love, age and death. They are worth reading, and the idea is inescapable that Mr. Caldwell is bound for a greater success.

Mr. Caldwell, who is now residing in Mount Vernon, Maine, is now devoting his time entirely to writing, and it is said that he has made a success of every one of his works.

"Caldwell's Novel Is of Georgians"

J. Raiford Watkins*

On two or three blocks of Broad Street, at both ends of the busiest center of the town, are dwellings situated over stores, and on the front of these dwellings are little iron balconies on which sit daily and nightly from two to six young women of varying degrees of attractiveness. To all men they smile, and to some who look interested they beckon. In cold weather they perch in the windows, so that at least one side of them is warmed by the fire within the front room while they scan the passing lines of pedestrians and automobiles.

In the warm afternoons, they descend to the sidewalk dressed in brilliant red, blue or green, shining frocks, and stand around for a while discoursing among themselves or with rough looking men until other men stop in automobiles and beckon to them, whereupon they lean against the windows of the cars, one foot in the street and one foot on the running board, and talk. Sometimes they get into the automobiles and ride away.

Chaste ladies and gentlemen glare at them and make remarks about what the authorities ought to do, and say that Augusta is the only place in the world where that could happen. And then they consider the girls themselves, and feel sorry for them, and say they are to be pitied rather than condemned.

If the aforesaid gentry will read Erskine Caldwell's new novel, "Tobacco Road," they will cease to wonder whence come the demimonde of Broad Street, and will know that they are happier than they were in the homes of their birth, and they will cease to grieve for them. The author

*Reprinted from *Augusta Chronicle*, 14 Feb. 1932, Sec. 1, p. 3, cols. 2–5.

never mentions any of these people; the reader himself must put them in his own conclusions.

That is, this will happen if the pride of the reader as a Georgian is not stung to deny vigorously the truth of the book and to castigate the author. For this will be the result with many readers whose loyalty is stronger than their eyes. Mr. Caldwell illustrates his points with extreme cases, and no good citizen will admit anything worse than average.

Mr. Caldwell is the only son of Mr. and Mrs. I.S. Caldwell of Wrens, Ga., both of whom are teachers in the Wrens high school, and the former of whom is also pastor of a church there and a daily editorial columnist in The Chronicle. He knows Georgia and her people. His latest work is a valuable addition to folklore and literature.

"Tobacco Road" is the second of his novels to deal with the lowest element of the white race in this state. It will be called a great story by half its readers, blatant and commercial perfidy by the others. I belong to the first half. Of those who like it, most will realize that it is the story of the pitiable small percentage of backwoods people reduced to miserable semi-savagery by malaria, pellagra and ignorance.

The author introduces a new technique in this book by having a principal character who never appears on the scene, and who is never even directly quoted. Little Pearl—the golden haired illegitimate daughter of the wife of "Jeeter," a man who would be a farmer if he could ever get around to the plowing—becomes the outstanding personage in the first chapter when her husband goes to the house of Jeeter to describe to him Pearl's strange actions. But—and this may sound strange—the story never becomes wholly the story of Pearl until next to the last chapter when her husband tells Jeeter that she has run away. This can only be understood by reading the novel itself, for such is the treatment that only Mr. Caldwell could handle it in this manner.

The utterly loathesome if humorous people whose life and characters are described throughout the novel are, as has been said, extreme cases, and Mr. Caldwell builds the entire story about them. When he announces that little Pearl has fled, badly frightened, to Augusta, all the reasons why she should—nay, must—take flight have become so obvious that the reader cheers her on. Her family thinks that she will go to work in a mill, and Mr. Caldwell doesn't say that she does not, but he knows that the reader knows better. She will follow the course of her half-sister, Lizzie Belle, who when last seen was strolling, brightly dressed and perfumed, up Broad street. Her folks thought she made all that money working in a cotton mill.

Reviewers have said that Mr. Caldwell "is like Bret Harte, Mark Twain and Fielding" and others call him Rabelaisian. But this is better praise than simile. He is distinctly an individual. He is not "of a school." He is unique in that although his language is as simple as the characters he draws, his ideas are subtle and the situations often obscure. In order to show the true character of the people with whom he deals, he describes their lowest emotions in great detail for emphasis, in words that will shock many. But therein lies the force of the book. There are several angles to it, including the futility of the life of the farmer in Jeeter's circumstances, and the helplessness of his brood, but it is the story of Pearl that makes it great.

Mr Caldwell has a delightful sense of humor, and it shows itself throughout the "Tobacco Road." While he deplores the condiiton of his characters, he finds much about them at which to laugh and thereby lighten the thought.

Augustans will be doubly interested because the novel took its title from the road in Richmond county known as "The Old Tobacco Road," and because the people in it often discuss Augusta and her "rich folks." It is in the book stores today. Scribner's are the publishers.

"New Realist Depicts South's Poor Whites' Pitiable Existence"

James Gray*

Erskine Caldwell is a new American realist to whom we are going to listen very attentively during the next few years. His first book called "American Earth" appeared a year or so ago. It was a volume of short stories in which he demonstrated clearly that he possessed the shrewdness and the detachment for telling harsh and horrible little truths about certain aspects of the American scene.

His first novel, just published by Charles Scribner's Sons, is in the same mood. But it has as much more power as a novel should have. "Tobacco Road" is a grimly fascinating study of the degraded conditions under which the poor whites of Georgia live out their meaningless, pitiable and altogether distressing existence.

Jeeter Lester is one of those utterly forlorn creatures who may perhaps be aptly described as disinherited by nature. He lives on the ungracious land from which all the men and women, in whom ambition and protest have not quite died out, have long since fled. He has lost any desire to compete and even the will to survive is sluggish in him.

He lives with his wife, mother, son and daughter on the ruins of his farm, slowly starving to death. Every virtue that we claim for human nature has sickened and died within him and he has sunk far, far below the animal level. For he has lost even the impulse to find food for himself and his family. His torpor is complete and consciousness survives in him

*Reprinted from *St. Paul Dispatch*, 16 Feb. 1932, p. 8, col. 8.

only as a warped, perverted and absurd burlesque of human intelligence. His vague mental retrogression is somehow more distressing than madness.

At first it is difficult to believe in the picture. From its explicit portraiture the imagination of the well-fed and comparatively secure reader retreats into incredulity. But gradually one becomes aware that no one could have made up such horrors. Not even a man of letters could be so morbid as to plague us with despair like this unless he had the justification of telling the awful truth.

In the first scene the Lesters are revealed in all their hopelessness. Jeeter's son-in-law, Lov Bensey, has come to complain about his wife. Pearl will not behave as a wife should. She will not talk. Even when Lov tries such disciplinary measures as throwing rocks at her she only runs away. He cannot think what is wrong. He wants advice and help.

But Jeeter and his family are not thinking very concentratedly of Pearl. They have seen that Lov has a bag of winter turnips on his back. On that they fix their attention. When Ellie May Lester, whose one flaw as an example of feminine loveliness is that fact that she has cleft lip, distracts Lov into a flirtation, Jeeter catches up the bag of turnips and runs into the woods. There he gorges happily, until his son Dude descends upon him to claim a share in the booty.

But much worse is to follow. A woman preacher, Bessie, visits the Lester home to pray their sins away. She casts her eyes upon Dude, the sixteen-year-old boy and straightway decides that God means him to become a preacher, too. So she marries him. The boy is lethargic and unconcerned until Bessie promises to buy him an automobile. This distressing little romance has its complete fulfillment for Dude when he drives the car down the Tobacco Road releasing all his inner soul by honking the horn incessantly.

The appalling episodes pile up. Dude runs into a truck. The negro driver is thrown into the street and his skull crushed. The Lesters decide that probably he is dead and drive unconcernedly on. In a terrific family battle over whether Jeeter is to be allowed to ride in the car, a break comes between Dude and his parents. He backs the car out of the yard running over the grandmother as he goes. No one pays the slightest attention. Several hours later Jeeter examines the body and decides that though she isn't yet dead she soon will be and goes to dig a grave.

Later still in the same eventful day, Jeeter has one of his rare impulses to assert himself. He will farm his land once more. The first step is to burn the sedge. He sets fire to it and retires to bed. The fire envelopes everything in the neighborhood including the hut in which Jeeter and his wife lie asleep.

The next day Dude and Bessie come to survey the ruins. And presently as they drive away Dude is saying:

"I reckon I'll get me a mule somewhere and some seed cotton and guano, and grow me a crop of cotton this year. It feels to me like it's going to be a good year for cotton. Maybe I'll grow me a bale to the acre, like pa was always talking about doing."

The hideous story of Jeeter is to be told all over again.

All this is told by Erskine Caldwell with complete objective detachment. It is as though Mr. Caldwell took the reader by the hand, led him to the scene of these dreadful happenings, commanded: "Look! Listen!" and then retired to let the onlooker draw all of his conclusions for himself. From beginning to end, he makes no comment, no interpretation. He resists every temptation to point a sociological moral.

He does not consider them inevitable, of course. It is his literary slyness to force a sense of responsibility upon the reader by seeming to take none himself. It is a triumphantly successful method. I think I have never been so depressed by a book nor so filled with a desire to do something about all this.

We are blandly unconscious in America of the squalor that exists in hidden corners. We talk with reproachful horror of the conditions of life in Soviet Russia, unaware that far worse things exist at home. "Tobacco Road" should be read aloud to everyone who has even made a glib, ignorant generalization about the high standard of life in the United States.

"Library Admits Caldwell Novel"

Anonymous*

A "marked disagreement" between the chairman of the book committee and the board of directors of the Young Men's Library association was settled yesterday afternoon at a meeting of the board and it was voted to admit to the library shelves the recent novel "Tobacco Road" by Erskine Caldwell, of Wrens, Ga. S.D. Copeland, the committee chairman, who told The Chronicle last night that he had previously decided not to admit the book, which concerns Georgia people in the territory of Augusta, said that the board of directors had convinced him that the volume should be on the library shelves.

Mr. Copeland said he had NOT read "Tobacco Road," but had talked to several people who had read it. He said it probably was all right for mature people, but that he did not believe it would be advisable to permit indiscriminate reading of it by young people. He ordered it yesterday afternoon, however, and said it will be on the library shelves as soon as it arrives.

Joseph B. Cumming, president of the association and chairman of

*From *Augusta Chronicle*, 9 March 1932, p. 2, col. 5.

the board, led the dispute yesterday afternoon in favor of "Tobacco Road." He declared that the library has "always been proud of its liberal spirit and open-mindedness" and mentioned several classics which he said could not be admitted into the library if strict morality and purity of thought were to be demanded of literature. Mr. Cumming informed the board that "The Boston Transcript" had called Mr. Caldwell one of the leaders of modern American authors, and that his publishers, Scribner's, had classed him as one of three American geniuses.

Mr. Cumming added that he did not think the library should set itself up as a guardian of the public morals.

"Raw Leaf"

Edward Dahlberg*

"Tobacco Road" is the story of a family of Georgia crackers, their serfdom, slow starvation and economic and social stupefaction. Erskine Caldwell has caught with phonographic accuracy the illiterate and repetitive gibberish which reveals the seedy background, the scant hopes and the ineluctable vassalage of these poor whites. He is a much easier writer than William Faulkner or Elizabeth Madox Roberts. Without tortuous effort, he can chronicle simple statements of fact.

The Lesters live in a leaky, broken-down shack on a sandy, recalcitrant and neglected farm. Most of the day Jeeter Lester, the father, sits around meditatively mumbling over his hunger, his worthless black-jack wood and his prospects, hoping that when he dies he won't be buried in his overalls. His old woman, Ada, is always pining for a silk dress and some boxes of snuff. She wants the snuff to keep her mind off food, and the silk dress for her burial.

There have been seventeen Lester kids, at least one of whom is illegitimate, besides some other farm urchins in the vicinity which Jeeter claims must be his. Most of them have casually left home at different times, without ever bothering to tell Jeeter or Ada of their intentions or their destination. Besides the parents, Dude, who is sixteen and has never gone to school, and Ella May, who has a harelip, still live there. The grandmother, Jeeter's mother, is also about the place, and they wish she were dead so that there would be more crackers and fat-back for themselves. The land, like all the property around there, has passed into the hands of absentee landlords. However, still clinging to the soil, rooted to the barren farms by a superstitious fear of the industrial cities and mill towns, these American muzhiks wait and pray for succor and a year of pentecost which never comes.

*Reprinted from *New Republic*, 70 (March 23, 1932), 159–60.

The novel opens on a warm February day. Lov Bensey, the son-in-law of Jeeter, is coming up Tobacco Road carrying a gunnysack of turnips. Almost a year ago Jeeter had traded in his twelve-year-old daughter, Pearl, to Lov for a week's wages, seven dollars, and some odds and ends. Lov complains that he hasn't been getting the benefits of a wife, for Pearl has slept on the pallet on the floor ever since their marriage. Jeeter, whose eyes have completely passed over into the gunnysack, promises to talk to Pearl if Lov will give him those bright gargantuan turnips. Failing to make him agree to this, Jeeter hits him over the head with a stick, and while the others hold Lov down, runs off to the woods with the bulging gunnysack.

There are incidents and passages in the book which evoke the grim cupidity and astringent humor of the peasants in "La Terre." The marriage of Sister Bessie, a female preacher and Holy Roller, to sixteen-year-old Dude, has this same Zolaesque texture. And the episode in which Sister Bessie and Dude kneel down in prayer in a motorcar showroom before the automobile she has just purchased is Middletown in fantastic bas-relief.

In one of the Scandinavian countries or in Russia, I believe, "Tobacco Road" would be hailed as something of a literary event. Here the chances are that it will be quietly buried like "The Enormous Room" and other unclean documents. Not until Mr. Caldwell has learned to make poverty, hunger and sex something that can be nostalgically mistaken for art rather than truth will his writings be widely praised—at least that is one reader's guess.

"Passion and Pellagra"

Jack Conroy*

Erskine Caldwell has told with a great deal of skill the story of the decay and dissolution of the Lester family. Yet somehow his characters fail to emerge full-blown. They are all dying of pellagra and starvation, yet other organs beside their stomachs seem to plague them the most. Lov's twelve year old bride for example, refuses to sleep with him, so he stops to ask the advice of Jeeter Lester, her father. He has a sack of turnips which he watches warily, lest the ravenous Lesters steal it. Ellie May, the harelipped daughter, begins "horsing," and slides her bare bottom along in the sand toward Lov, just as a hound does to allay its itch, according to Dude, the son. Dude also fears that Ellie May will thus get herself full of sand. Finally she springs on the frustrated bridegroom, and Dude cries excitedly: "Lov's going to big her. He's getting ready to do it right now, too.

*Reprinted from *New Masses*, 7 (April, 1932), 24–25.

Look at him crawl around—he acts like an old stud-horse." Then Lov doesn't give a damn who gets the turnips and consequently old Jeeter runs off to the woods with them and eats most of them.

There's a great deal more about a passionate "woman preacher" who lusts after sixteen year old Dude, and marries him. Old Jeeter knows he shouldn't yearn after the "woman preacher" as he does, and considers "cutting himself off" in order to forestall further temptation. Dude is a little uncertain as to what the forty year old widow wants, but she soon teaches him.

The ancient grandma gets run over by a new car which the bride had bought with her former husband's insurance money. Grandma lies in the yard with her head caved in and everybody seems to be glad to be shut of her. Without being certain she is dead, they unceremoniously dump her in a shallow grave. This and other macabre touches suggest William Faulkner and the new school of Southern realists.

When the author ventures to explain the reason for the Lesters' degradation, he adduces that it is because a benevolent landlord has moved out of the vicinity, leaving his hapless serfs to fend for themselves. If the landlord had stayed and taught them "cooperative and corporate farming" he would have "saved them all." Bad sociology does not improve fiction.

Nevertheless, the story is gripping and Caldwell possesses a simple yet forceful style. The successive efforts of old Jeeter to pump up the worn out tires so he can take a load of wood to town, his annual nostalgia for the cotton fields and the fresh turned earth, Dude's contempt for his parent, and many other situations are vividly and convincingly portrayed. The author has also etched the effect of Jeeter's alternate hope and his steadily cumulative despair in a masterly fashion.

Caldwell is palpably capable of much better work, and it is a little disappointing to see him fall just short of his mark. He lacks social understanding which is the life of revolutionary prose. He is like a "bored and bilious God," unmoved by his subjects' agonies. Yet out of the welter of detective thrillers, the amorous adventures of society dames, and the vicissitudes of poor but honest virgins, this book emerges as a social document of no small importance.

"American Humor"

Kenneth White*

All the events in "Tobacco Road," Erskine Caldwell's first novel since "The Bastard," pass in a monotone through Georgia seasons, through

*Reprinted from *Nation*, 135 (July 6, 1932), 16–17. Copyright © 1932 The Nation Associates.

hunger and shiftlessness, through death and marriage. No one event receives more emphasis than another: Bessie, the woman preacher, is "ganged" in a cheap hotel, the grandmother is run over, the Ford is bashed in, a Negro is killed, but the sentences have no bumps to show that the story has been jolted out of its slow pace. Caldwell's method is completely identified with the casual happenings to his characters, who seem thereby to acquire some of the comic properties intrinsic in chickens. The notion has gone about that the deliquescent characters, their squalor, their utter placidity, make Caldwell's writing "primitive"; his sentence structure has made possible the belief that his work is naive; and because the setting is rural and the humors supposedly exaggerated, he is said to resemble Mark Twain and Bret Harte. These false notions have completely obscured what is an original, mature approach to the incongruities existing in a people who ignore the civilization that contains them as completely as the civilization ignores them.

By the simple construction of his sentences, by the fact that he deals usually with isolated rural people who come into contact with other ways of American life only at its more amusing points, and by giving only an external account of events, Caldwell is able to build a series of comic meanings about events—hunger, death, property—which have a totally different significance for the reader. The comic meanings are never explicit in his work; the author leaves it to the reader to call them up for himself; and his stories and novels take on an immediate kind of humor and, occasionally, a kind of pathos which is far from sentimentality. On the surface the method is like Hemingway's; but Hemingway makes it known that one thing matters more than another, if nowhere else than in the dialogues which indicate that there is more than can be said in words. Caldwell makes no such concession; everything is told baldly; the event is all. The reader gets the effect he pleases, but he will be pleased to get a bracing kind of humor. It is probable that Caldwell could not obtain any high emotional response to his characters by this method, which, fortunately, and unlike Hemingway, he does not force on to every and any kind of material he is interested in. When, however, in the last paragraph of the book he tries to be ironic, to suggest just how the reader should take the last stretch, he falls into cheap sentimentality notably absent from his characters' pronouncements anywhere else in the novel. There is nothing sentimental, for example, about Jeeter's lyrical speeches of complaint, for everything is complained about. The error of the last words of the book is the error of dropping the comic method to point a moral.

"Ripe for Revolution"

Erskine Caldwell*

Ministers plenipotentiary pecking out a column of book chat daily and weekly for advertisers and reading clubs found themselves recently in an uncomfortable position. Edward Dahlberg's new novel of American life had appeared. However, they rose to the occasion and, with two or three notable exceptions, threw dust in their readers' eyes. It did not matter what the excuse was just as long as it was an excuse.

The trouble, it seems, was that here had been written a book about people undeniably similar to the majority of readers of their columns. Dahlberg's story of their lives was far from flattering. Hence the throwing of dust in everyone's eyes. Dahlberg doesn't know how to write; Dahlberg doesn't know what people want to read about; Dahlberg isn't nice company; Dahlberg makes things appear worse than they actually are. If these men who make a business of filling a column or two reading matter next to advertisements had fulfilled the functions of a critic, they would have hastened to report that Dahlberg's people chew gum and rent books at the lending library like fifty million other Americans.

From Flushing to Calvary is the story of Lorry Lewis. He had once been in a Cleveland orphanage, but when the story opens he is living with his mother, Lizzie, in Bensonhurst. Bensonhurst, Dahlberg tells us, is low, flat, rheumatic marshland studded with ashen stucco houses shaped like Camel cigarette boxes. It is one of those real estate developments in every suburb that are created without plan and inhabited without reason. It is in this section of New York, on Long Island, that we find Lorry working as a shipping clerk. His mother is trying to make some money. At the moment, she is getting a few dollars by trimming corns and digging bunions. But that is only a side-line, or rather one of many side-lines. The answering of matrimonial ads is, perhaps, the most important to her of several interests.

One evening Lizzie meets a fellow named Jerry Calefonia. Jerry, who runs a bicycle repair shop, picks her up. He doesn't like Lizzie so well after he gets to the house, but he stays a while just the same. Jerry had said over and over to himself: "Cheap people live here." He was speaking of America in general and of Bensonhurst in particular, as well as of Lizzie's mean street. He wished to go back home, to his own country, but in the meantime he picked up Lorry's mother. The story has broken into a run by this time.

Lizzie isn't getting on so well with her side-lines as she had hoped. She takes in a boarder at four dollars a week. That helps, but not enough, and she begins borrowing money from him. Lizzie has remembered that

*Reprinted from *New Masses*, 8 (Dec., 1932), 26–27.

back in Kansas City, where she had been a lady barber, she used to make money on the side with an Indian remedy. She secures a customer, and guarantees to bring about an abortion. One or two others come to her for help after that, and the money begins coming in. She goes out and tries to drum up trade. After a while the income from this source begins to peter out, and Lorry loses his job.

By this time a matrimonial ad has brought in Hervey to her. Hervey isn't sure if he wishes to marry her. He stalls. Lizzie wishes first to find out how much money he has, and whether he will sign over half of his property to her. They fight over her demands. Lorry sits on his bed in the next room and listens to them argue. He wishes to help his mother, but he doesn't know what to do.

The story has gathered a powerful momentum by this time. Dahlberg is writing calmly but we are dry-mouthed with excitement. We know nothing is going to happen, not much out of the ordinary, anyway; but we wish to go on with Lorry and Lizzie at an increased tempo, trying in a way to push them out of the mess. But Dahlberg holds us back and forces us to examine the evidence more closely. There's nothing to get excited about, he says; these people can't do a thing with themselves, not because they are incapable of direct action but because they do not know what can be done with their lives. They are the products of a native environment that most of us have struggled against, and lost. Everybody, in the story will lose in the end, just as we have done so far. Lorry and Lizzie have no contact with growth, either social or economic; they are in the backwash of America. He does not tell us that we all could get out of the slums and into clean rooms; out of the life-sapping routine of weary job-hunting and into a factory with decent pay—Dahlberg doesn't tell us that, but he knew and we know that we'll continue looking for jobs where there are no jobs and pinching pennies until there is no penny left until the gut-rotting disorganization of unplanned society is thrown bag-and-baggage overboard.

All this stench of Bensonhurst will continue to sweep into the nostrils of men until our system of life is changed. Only a complete reorganization can erase the mean streets, the packing-box flats, the hamburger-and-coffee meals, the body-crushing existence of four-fifths of America. Lorry didn't know what to do about it; he did not even realize that anything could be done about it. He was caught in the backwash. Lorry and Lizzie had grown up in pre-1930 America, and they did not know the world was changing. One cause lies there.

It is at this point in the narrative that we as readers become fully convinced that Lorry and Lizzie will continue their degraded existence until some means are devised to furnish them with direction and leadership out of the slough of capitalism that had defeated them. If a man be ignorant, then teach him; do not damn him for his ignorance. There is not a person in this tale who would not be capable of becoming revolutionary if only he knew how to go about it, or had someone to direct him. The incentive to rise needs only a single spark to set a man free, but the spark has yet to come into contact with millions.

This is not a proletarian novel. Before such a book can be written there must first be a revolutionary change of life in America. We cannot expect to write or to read genuinely proletarian novels until we live in a proletarian world. At our present stage, we find that we can only begin where our previous existence dumped us. We were dumped by a capitalist system on hard ground, and here we lie. Our first step is now being taken; we are scattered, broken, and bewildered; we are lifting our heads and looking ahead into the future. *From Flushing To Calvary* is the hard ground, the working-model from which we hope to get away. There is use, then, in such a book. Without such books we would not know our materials.

This is the kind of story of which revolutionary literature is made. This is the beginning, the initial step. Here are the people; this is the environment. With this we know we cannot continue to live. This is the clay for the mold. The next step is that of contact and teaching. Dahlberg's people are ripe for revolution.

Men who throw dust in readers' eyes are not the only enemies of Communism. Some few reviewers carefully forgot to read this book, or, having read it, forgot to write about it; but the greatest menace has almost come unnoticed. There are those who have elbowed their way into what they consider the inner circle of revolutionary activity. They write glowingly of "Communism" for their magazines and papers, gush about it over speakeasy glasses, and await the time when they think they will take "Communism" away from the worker and make it respectable for themselves. There is a menace in this, and Dahlberg's book was eagerly grabbed to work upon. The sooner these bogus "Communists" are kicked back to where they breed, the better will revolutionary activity proceed. Men who edit magazines and papers read largely by bondholders and stockowners can easily reach out the back door and shake hands with a worker, but it is not so easy to go out the front door and walk down the street arm in arm with the same man. Workers are not interested in whether an investor's bonds are defaulted; a worker must have a job and food and shelter. He will gain none of these by holding on to the coat tails of some literary racketeer who is out to make "Communism" fashionable.

Dahlberg's people lift their voices and sing, "America, you've made us what we are today." There is no quarter given, no feeble excuse offered; the fact that Lorry and Lizzie and Jerry and Hervey are what they are, is sufficient reason to indict the environment in which they were forced to exist. It is an unhealthy, squalid, painful environment imposed upon America by the barons of coal and steel, wheat and cotton.

Although *From Flushing To Calvary* attempts to cover too much territory, and the over-ambitious plan of the novel does jerk us from coast to coast with too much speed, the successful study of Lorrie and Lizzie is so overwhelmingly accurate that such criticism seems insignificant in retrospect.

"God's Little Acre"

Edwin Rolfe*

All of Caldwell's previously revealed aptitudes and limitations are crystallized in his new novel. His story of the Walden family discloses a disastrous unfamiliarity on his part with his characters. Ty Ty Walden, who with his sons, Buck and Shaw, has been digging holes on his Georgia farm for more than fifteen years, in a vain effort to strike gold; his daughters Darling Jill and Rosamond; his son-in-law and daughter-in-law, Will and Griselda—not to mention a half-dozen others, never really come to life. As in *Tobacco Road*, where the only impressive character was Jeeter's daughter Pearl, whose part throughout the book was created in the conversation of other characters, the only real persons in *God's Little Acre* are the prostitutes, the cops, the mill workers who crowd around the factory on the eve of Will's murder by the mill thugs. And all of these people appear in single, isolated scenes, so that it is merely an impression of life that we receive, not an actual developed creation. Aside from these fragmentary figures, the best integrated character of *God's Little Acre* is Pluto, Darling Jill's fat suitor. But here too it is significant to observe that Pluto is a complete caricature, developed through a series of witty exaggerations of description and action, and not through any synthesis of his character with the unfolding situation. Pluto, after his first presentation, remains static. Our first glimpse of him has revealed everything that Caldwell can tell us about him. Further scenes merely verify our first reaction; Pluto acts as we expected him to act; the sense of growth or change is conspicuously lacking.

As for the story itself, it consists of a series of skillfully connected incidents which are never integrated into a cental all-important theme. Some of these incidents, such as the capture of the albino Dave, the early-morning pleasantries of Will and Darling Jill, Ty Ty's expedition to town to borrow money from his wealthy son, are as amusing as anything that has been published in America for a long time. Other scenes, notably the one during which Will turns on the power at the cotton mill and is killed for his part, are as weird and fantastic as the author meant them to be straightforward and genuine.

It can truthfully be said that *God's Little Acre* marks a definite advance on Caldwell's part. But it is an advance that is fraught with danger.

*Reprinted from *New Masses*, 8 (Feb., 1933), 26.

Caldwell's facility in handling the short story has within itself the power to trip him, to arrest his further growth, unless he consciously attempts to overcome it. While the inclusion of the mill scene in *God's Little Acre* marks a definite increase in Caldwell's social awareness, his treatment of it—fantastic, disconnected, unbound to any semblance of reality, artificially grafted to the rest of the book—neutralizes the very growth that its presence in the book indicates. Had Caldwell attempted a more thorough investigation into the causes of southern industrial struggle, I am sure that he would not have made of the unemployed textile worker, Will, the grotesquely-heroic and unconvincing legend that he becomes. The man would have been more firmly built of flesh and blood.

The technical proficiency of Caldwell's writing cannot conceal the obvious fact that he has not mastered the novel-form, and that he is not likely to grow as a novelist until he discovers the importance of a highly-integrated, central theme. He must learn to write more than a series of skilfully-connected short stories before he can assume the stature of a full-fledged novelist.

Another drawback which may assume more serious form soon is Caldwell's pre-occupation with sex as a theme. While his approach to sex is thoroughly healthy, he ought, in the future, to avoid this over-emphasis. The scene in which Will strips Griselda of her clothes, while Darling Jill, Rosamond and Pluto look on, smacks too much of D. H. Lawrence. The humor of his treatment of this and similar scenes should not blind us to the decadent possibilities latent in such writing.

Finally, and most important of all, it is time for Erskine Caldwell to begin to think consciously of the material which exists for writing in America today. It is a comparatively simple thing to write of characters isolated from the main trends and struggles of decaying capitalism, insulated against the conflicts and influences that inevitably make deep impressions on all of our lives. It is more difficult, and therefore more honest and important, to choose themes that actually cry out for expression. Caldwell possesses that very important item in the equipment of any writer—the ability to select his material. But so far he has consciously dealt with minor themes, and with characters removed from the larger struggles of modern life. As a result, his work is definitely of a minor character.

His talent deserves a higher plane on which to function, a broader perception of the struggles of men than he has seen fit to reveal. He is surely aware of the class conflicts raging throughout the country and of the crisis in which not only American, but world capitalism finds itself; his support of the Communist candidates in the last presidential election would indicate this. His logical development as a writer must begin to parallel his development as a social being; if it does not, the artificial cleavage will become increasingly apparent in his further work, as it is apparent in his achievement thus far, and destroy the vitality which mere technical proficiency in writing can never sustain by itself.

In order to achieve this greater importance and value, Caldwell's future work must go beyond the skilful but static presentation evident in his work until now. His understanding must, with further practise and maturity, acquire the dynamic qualities of developmental continuity and change, (coupled with the choice of more vital subject matter) which his present works lack and which is essential to all truly great art in writing. In short, he must go beyond mere sympathetic depiction into the higher sphere of dialectical development of characters placed in situations that clamor for treatment today.

"The Author of 'Tobacco Road' Takes Us Again to Georgia"

James T. Farrell*

I have read, in succession, "American Earth," "Tobacco Road" and "God's Little Acre," by Erskine Caldwell (Viking. $2.50). In these volumes there is no question of the author's talents and artistic integrity; the cumulative effects reveals these qualities readily. However, Erskine Caldwell still seems to exist in a state of potential promise.

A phrase like psychological immaturity might be applied to his work to suggest its weakness. He possesses a sharp and exact reportorial eye, and he has fresh material upon which to draw. He can tell what people say and do, often with a keen sense of humor, and he can make his readers feel their environments; but he has, as yet, not matched these abilities by a clear perception of what they feel, and of how their feelings and attitudes change in a time of stress. He seems to be so gifted that he writes like a "natural" writer, but he does not give the impression of having completely mastered his technic. Thus he is at his best in developing a single impression, or a relatively limited situation. When he attempts something broader his powers are thinned out by melodrama and sentimentality, or by the introduction of more violence than his themes can absorb.

While Mr. Caldwell has advanced beyond his "American Earth," I believe that that book is an excellent illustration of the analysis I have made. As a whole, the volume impresses one as a striking prediction of future work that will be important. Its most successful pieces are the humorous stories, such as the "Corduroy Pants," "Midsummer Passion," and "Rumor." Using violence as a theme but limiting himself to a small canvas he has produced a truly excellent story in "Saturday Afternoon." But when he strove to write stories that would reveal how people feel and are motivated, when his theme was more psychological, he came off less well, as in the story, "The Lonely Day." It seemed to be mere sentimentality. In brief, he was most successful in short reportorial pieces. The last

*Reprinted from *The Sun* (New York), 7 Feb. 1933, p. 22, cols. 7–8.

section, "The Sacrilege of Alan Kent" revealed, though, that he was genuinely an artist and not a mere reporter. It was a flashlight or impressionistic sort of biography, set down in a series of separate and disconnected paragraphs, many of them single sentences. On the one hand, these demonstrated a fine and delicate lyrical quality, and a warm responsiveness to life. On the other hand, many passages were pervaded with an extravagant romanticism, with meaningless paradoxes such as "I could have been a giant but thoughts made me weak," or with bald statements of little significance: "A millionaire lived across the street but I never saw him." Violent incidents were piled on top of each other, until the effect was overdrawn, just as in a totally different book, "The Boy" by James Hanley, horror was reiterated until it lost all its effect as a theme. This section symbolized the whole book as a groping and uneven work done by one who seems certain to develop.

In "God's Little Acre," Mr. Caldwell has split his novel in two, and while it contains many well described incidents it does not hang together, and its main virtues are some good reporting and some finely done slapstick humor. The locale of the book is a section of Georgia near the Carolina border and not far from "Tobacco Road." Ty Ty Walden has been digging holes on his farm for fifteen years in an unrelenting search for gold. In his effort, he has absorbed the energies of two sons, Buck and Shaw, and neglected to farm his land properly. He is convinced that he will find gold and that he is proceeding in a scientific fashion. The nature of his science is revealed when he takes his two sons and goes into the swamps to capture an albino, because he has heard that albinos are good gold diviners. Many years previously he had set aside one acre of his ground to God, giving its produce to the work of the Deity. The exigencies of digging have continually forced him to shift "God's Little Acre" about, because God shouldn't expect him to give away all the gold if it were to be found on His acre.

Ty Ty's son-in-law, Will Thompson, is a millworker in a company town across the Carolina border. For eighteen months the mill in which he works has been shut down, and Will is determined that the workers shall seize the mill and turn on the power. During this layoff Ty Ty brings Will and his wife to the farm to help in the digging, because with his albino divining for him, and the discovery of gold imminent, he needs all the help he can get. Will refuses to dig, and is unhappy away from the mill. He is also anxious to "get" Buck's wife, Griselda, and the two brothers-in-law quarrel threateningly, so that Ty Ty, anxious to avoid having blood spilled on his land, consents to let Will return. When they return in the automobile of a friend, Pluto Swint, Griselda and Ty Ty's unmarried but promiscuous daughter, Darling Jill, go along for the ride. Back in the mill town Will sees his fellow workers, and they determine to turn on the power the next morning. This prospect exalts him. His exaltation is intensified by Griselda and there is an extravagant scene in which

Will tears her clothes off, and the others, Will's wife, Darling Jill, and Pluto Swint, are awed in watchful respect. Here Mr. Caldwell's attempt is to portray a deep and reverent adoration of a man for a woman, but he is extravagant and melodramatic so that the passage sounds like a twisted fairy tale. In the morning Will goes with the workers.

They seize the mill. Will turns on the power, but is shot by company guards. This scene is also described in extravagant fashion and reads as much like a fairy tale as the taking of Griselda. When Griselda, Will's wife, and Pluto return to the farm Buck senses what has happened and becomes mean and surly. A gratuitous anti-climax occurs. Ty Ty's other son, James Leslie, a rich cotton broker, comes to steal Griselda, and Buck shoots him.

The split in the novel occurs with the return of the group to the company town. Previous to this occurrence we have had excellent slapstick humor. Then there is a sudden and unsuccessfully motivated change in the characters, and they seem like different people. As a result the book is unconvincing, and when Mr. Caldwell changes from reporting to a description of deeply rooted feelings he kills his novel. He is a much better writer than "God's Little Acre" would indicate.

"People
v.
Viking Press, Inc., *et al.* *   Anonymous

City Magistrate's Court of New York City, Fourth District, Borough of Manhattan. May 23, 1933.

> *Harold Frankel*, Deputy Asst. Dist. Atty., of New York City, for plaintiff.
> *Hays, Hershfield, Kaufman & Schwabacher*, of New York City (Wolfgang S. Schwabacher and James M. Grossman, both of New York City, of counsel,) for defendants.

Greenspan, City Magistrate.

This prosecution is instituted by the New York Society for the suppression of vice, through Mr. John S. Sumner, its secretary and attorney, against the Viking Press, Inc., the publishers of a certain book by one Erskine Caldwell entitled God's Little Acre, and against Helen Schiller, clerk in the employ of the publishers, who sold the book to an agent of the society.

*264 N.Y.S. 534 (1933)

[1, 2] It is claimed that the sale of the book is a violation of section 1141 of the Penal Law and that the book is, within the meaning of that statute, "obscene, lewd, lascivious, filthy, indecent or disgusting." In order to sustain the prosecution, the court must find that the tendency of the book as a whole, and indeed its main purpose, is to excite lustful desire and what has been rather fancifully called "impure imaginations." *People v. Muller*, 96 N.Y. 408, 48 Am. Rep. 635. The statute is aimed at pornography, and a pornographic book must be taken to be one where all other incidents and qualities are mere accessories to the primary purpose of stimulating immoral thoughts.

The courts have strictly limited the applicability of the statute to works of pornography and they have consistently declined to apply it to books of genuine literary value. If the statute were construed more broadly than in the manner just indicated, its effect would be to prevent altogether the realistic portrayal in literature of a large and important field of life. The Court of Appeals has consistently frowned upon such an interpretation of the statute. *People* v. *Wendling*, 258 N.Y. 451, 180 N.E. 169, 81 A.L.R. 799; *Halsey* v. *New York Society for Suppression of Vice*, 234 N.Y. 1, 136, N.E. 219. See, also, the opinion of The Appellate Division, First Department, in *People* v. *Brainard*,192, App. Div. 816, 183 N.Y.S. 452, regarding the book called Madeleine, an anonymous autobiography of a prostitute.

It is claimed, on behalf of the defendants, that the book in the instant case, Caldwell's God's Little Acre, has high literary merit. In support of this claim, counsel for the defendants have collected and presented to this court a large number of testimonials from people eminent in the literary life of this city and country, as well as from others distinguished in social work, education, and other fields. Some of these testimonials were written especially for presentation to this court. Others are culled from literary reviews and newspapers. Among the latter, which are necessarily to be given more weight than those written especially for the purpose of defeating this prosecution, the court finds praise of the merits of the book by the following: Franklin P. Adams in the New York Herald Tribune of January 28, 1933; William Soskin in the New York Evening Post of April 29, 1933; Horace Gregory in the New York Herald Tribune Book Review of February 5, 1933; an unnamed reviewer in the London Times Literary Supplement of March 23, 1933; James T. Farrell in the New York Sun of February 7, 1933; Louis Kronenberger in the New York Times of February 5, 1933; a reviewer in the New York Evening Post of February 7, 1933, who refers to the book as a "passionately honest book"; Gilbert Seldes in the New York Journal of February 11, 1933, who describes the book as "engaging and impressive at once"; Jonathan Daniels in the Saturday Review of Literature, as quoted in the Raleigh, N.C., News Observer of March 5, 1933; and Joseph Henry Jackson in the San Francisco Chronicle of February 17, 1933. The court regards this as a fair

cross-section of American literary opinion, by a group of men competent
to judge with reasonable accuracy the value of contemporary American
books.

The brief presented to this court by Mr. Sumner makes the following
references to these reviews: "We have seen this attempted before and the
question arises as to whether a criminal prosecution is to be determined by
interested parties having access to the newspapers and no interest in
public welfare or by the Courts existing for that purpose and representing
the whole people and not only the literati." Mr. Sumner also refers to the
following quotation from *People* v. *Pesky*, 230 App. Div. 200, 203, 243
N.Y.S. 193, 197: "These matters must be judged by normal people and
not by the abnormal. Conditions would be deplorable if abnormal people
were permitted to regulate such matters." Mr. Sumner then says: "Substitute the word 'literati' for 'abnormal people' and we have an exact explanation of the letters, reviews, and other favorable comments presented
in behalf of this book and its author."

Letters have been presented to this court praising the value of the
book in question, from Mark Eisner, president of the board of higher
education of the city of New York; Lewis Gannett of the New York Herald
Tribune; John Mason Brown, dramatic critic of the New York Evening
Post; Sidonie M. Gruenberg of the Child Study Association of America;
Solomon Lowenstein, executive and director of the Federation for the
Support of Jewish Philanthropic Societies; Marc Connelly; Horace M.
Kallen, honorary vice president of the American Jewish Congress; Carl
Van Doren, a distinguished literary critic; Herbert Bayard Swope, former
editor of the New York World; J. Donald Adams, editor of the New York
Times Book Review; Prof. Raymond Weaver, of the English Department
of Columbia University; Malcolm Cowley, one of the editors of the New
Republic; Henry S. Canby, the veteran editor of the Saturday Review of
Literature; Nathan Ottinger; Elmer Rice, playwright; John Cowper
Powys; and finally Sinclair Lewis.

This court cannot subscribe to Mr. Sumner's opinion of the capacity
for fair judgment of these leaders of American literary and educational
thought. The court declines to believe that so large and representative a
group of people would rally to the support of a book which they did not
genuinely believe to be of importance and literary merit. The court is of
the opinion, moreover, that this group of people, collectively, has a better
capacity to judge of the value of a literary production than one who is
more apt to search for obscene passages in a book than to regard the book
as a whole.

This court has carefully read the book in question. It is an attempt at
the portrayal, in a realistic fashion, of life as lived by an illiterate
Southern white farm family. A daughter of this family is married to a
worker in a Southern mill town. There is interaction between the run-
down farm life and the mill town life. Both on the farm and in the mill

town the people are primitive and impoverished. They are deprived of the opportunity for development, and their activities are largely sexual. They are of a simple nature, and savage passion is found close to the surface.

[3] This court is not sufficiently familiar with conditions in the portion of the county described to say, at first hand, that the description is accurate. Nothing in this opinion is to be construed as an expression by the court as to whether or not the book is an accurate piece of reporting. As fiction, however, it contains internal evidence that it was written with a sincere attempt to present with truth and honesty a segment of life in the Southern United States. The author has set out to paint a realistic picture. Such pictures necessarily contain certain details. Because these details relate to what is popularly called the sex side of life, portrayed with brutal frankness, the court may not say that the picture should not have been created at all. The language, too, is undoubtedly coarse and vulgar. The court may not require the author to put refined language into mouths of primitive people.

[4, 5] The book as a whole is very clearly not a work of pornography. It is not necessary for the court to decide whether it is an important work of literature. Its subject-matter constitutes a legitimate field for literary effort and the treatment is also legitimate. The court must consider the book as a whole even though some paragraphs standing by themselves might be objectionable. "No work may be judged from a selection of such paragraphs alone. Printed by themselves they might, as a matter of law, come within the prohibition of the statute. So might a similar selection from Aristophanes or Chaucer or Boccaccio or even from the Bible. The book, however, must be considered broadly as a whole." *Halsey* v. *New York Society for Suppression of Vice*, 234 N.Y. 1, at page 4, 136 N.E. 219, 220. The test is whether "not in certain passages, but in its main purpose and construction" (*Halsey* v. *New York Society for Suppression of Vice*, 234 N.Y. 1, at page 10, 136 N.E. 219, 222), the book is obscene and lewd, and, therefore, violative of the statute.

[6, 7] The court holds that it is not. This is not a book where vice and lewdness are treated as virtues or which would tend to incite lustful desires in the normal mind. There is no way of anticipating its effect upon a disordered or diseased mind, and if the courts were to exclude books from sale merely because they might incite lust in disordered minds, our entire literature would very likely be reduced to a relatively small number of uninteresting and barren books. The greater part of the classics would certainly be excluded. In conclusion, God's Little Acre has no tendency to inspire its readers to behave like its characters, therefore, it has no tendency to excite "lustful desire." Those who see the ugliness and not the beauty in a piece of work are unable to see the forest for the trees. I personally feel that the very suppression of books arouses curiosity and leads readers to endeavor to find licentiousness where none was intended. In this book, I believe the author has chosen to write what he believes to be

the truth about a certain group in American life. To my way of thinking, truth should always be accepted as a justification for literature.

No complaint will be entertained against the defendants and the summons herein will be dismissed.

"Caldwell Novels Banned"

Anonymous*

Erskine Caldwell's "God's Little Acre" and "Tobacco Road" were banned by the Library of Teachers College of Columbia University last week. The books were withdrawn after several faculty members had complained that they were "indecent and tending to corrupt." Both novels, however, are included in the required reading lists of several English courses at the University.

Other censorship activities in the news recently were a drive on a certain type of magazine by License Commissioner Paul Moss of New York City, who published a list of 63 proscribed magazines and pamphlets and ordered police to check up on whether any of them were being offered for sale at newsstands, and a crusade for "Christian decency" in regard to reading by the Catholic women of New York. At a meeting of the Catholic women to inaugurate their campaign, Mgr. Lavelle characterized "Anthony Adverse" as the rottenest book he had ever handled, saying "I don't think there is a form of bodily vice and obscenity that is not treated in the book." Mgr. Lavelle said that in response to a request from the Vatican, Cardinal Hayes had appointed him head of a local committee to fight the spread of indecent books.

Newsdealers answered Commissioner Moss's edict by threatening to use "Ulysses" and "God's Little Acre" as reasons why such magazines as "Pep Stories" and "Gay Parisienne" should not be banned.

Reports indicate that John S. Sumner, secretary of the New York Society for the Suppression of Vice, is considering an attack against "Ulysses." Mr. Sumner sent a copy of the book to District Attorney William C. Dodge and asked him to read it to see if there should be a prosecution on an obscenity charge. Mr. Dodge is now reading the book.

*Reprinted from *Publishers' Weekly*, 125 (March 10, 1934), 1045, published by R. R. Bowker Company. Used by permission.

"Mr. Caldwell Protests"

Erskine Caldwell*

Sir:

Teachers' College of Columbia University has banned two of my novels, "Tobacco Road" and "God's Little Acre." Well, what of it?

Well, a lot of it! It means, for one thing, that my struggle for honesty in writing was not completely won in May of last year when "God's Little Acre" was vindicated by the courts of New York City of charges of obscenity. It means that another book of mine, "Tobacco Road," has been misunderstood. And it means that for a writer honesty is his most difficult problem.

I have been told by those who should know that "you can get away with anything if you will be smart and write in double meaning." I suppose that advice is good enough for those who have vulgarity for sale. In the first place, I have nothing for sale; and in the second place, vulgarity is a poor substitute for obscenity. And in the third place, if the time has come when a writer is forced to clothe honesty with tricks in order to be published, then I would much rather remain unpublished.

At this point I pause to ask myself a question. Are the Columbia censors following the lead of William Lyon Phelps, who, in a published interview, after declining to say that he had read "Tobacco Road" or seen the play made from it by Jack Kirkland, announced that all of it was merely "a small boy's scribbling on a fence"?

But to continue:

Probably the thing I abhor above all else is moral and intellectual dishonesty. I am prompted to make the statement in this connection because the action of the Columbia University unit recalls an experience I had when I was attempting to get an education in a small college in South Carolina.

I was taking a course in American history. We had reached the Civil War period in our books and lectures. The professor at this point began deleting sections and pages from the text. He explained that the author of the book was a Northerner, and that he did not present the South's history in a favorable light. That was, I think, my turning point. I read every word of the deleted sections and chapters, I read all histories of the Civil War I could find in the library. My grade, was, as I recall, 12 for the year's study.

"Tobacco Road," the play now running on Broadway, and "Tobacco Road," the novel, is, in a way, my reaction to the dishonesty of the South Carolina college which taught, by suppression and censorship, that the Southern point of view was the true version of the history of the Civil War. And, too, it is my reaction to the present-day attitude in the South

*Reprinted from *New Republic*, 79 (June 27, 1934), 184–85.

of covering up any phase of life that might cast reflection upon Southern institutions and people.

It seems to me that Teachers' College of Columbia University has placed itself in an intolerable position: it has by its own act relegated a major educational institution to the level of Southern demagoguery. By presuming to suppress the story of a phase of American life, it violates one of the governing principles of education. The students of this college have enrolled to train themselves for the important role of instructing the youth of a nation. When this unit of Columbia University by example encourages future teachers to ignore an important section of the population, it follows that to ignore is to be ignorant, and likewise our own children, who will be influenced by them, will be taught to ignore and to be ignorant. These future teachers go to all parts of the nation; they will now go with prejudiced minds to your community and to mine, to teach our children that the people of Tobacco Road in Georgia are not worthy of thought or notice. This, then, is condemning thousands of people in America without trial. It is safe to say there is not a court in America that would sentence a man to extinction without first giving him a hearing. But this is exactly what Teachers' College of Columbia University has done: it has beheaded the teeming thousands of Tobacco Road by the simple method of refusing to admit their existence.

Mount Vernon, Me.

"Seventeen Tales by Erskine Caldwell"

Arthur Ruhl*

There's no denying the "kick" of these stories—the kick of a mule, sometimes—nor the fine economy of their craftsmanship. Nobody at all interested in the technique of the short story can be indifferent to them. The way the thing itself—character, scene, the ultimate thrust, generally that of horror—comes through, in a minimum of words, with nothing of the writer, seemingly, hanging to it, unburdened by the least touch of literariness, is superb in its way.

If these tales were the first of their kind, not read in the light of other examples of Caldwell's work, one might leave it at that. But so read, it is a bit hard to escape now and then a certain sense of being tricked, of being the victim of a pose which is no less a pose because the stuff in hand happens to be more or less sub-normal humanity instead of the fancier varieties with which pose and snobbishness are usually associated,

*Reprinted from *Saturday Review of Literature,* 12 (June 8, 1935), 5.

In other words, isn't Mr. Caldwell, with his unbroken procession of animalistic negroes, decadent share-croppers, and sadistic white bosses, leading us on a bit? Aren't his chosen material and "stark" realism, instead of being something which springs instinctively from his inner consciousness, now and then merely a new-fangled device for "shocking the bourgeois"?

An uneasy feeling of something of the sort does come over one in reading one or two of these stories—"Masses of Men," for instance. A man worked for a street-railway company for thirty-five years and then was killed by an automobile while jacking up a rail to replace a rotten tie. The company never gave the widow anything and when she called at the office nobody seemed to know anything about the matter. They didn't know which "Hugh Miller" she was inquiring about. The woman and her three children get colder and hungrier until finally the mother brings in a man to rape her ten-year-old daughter while she takes the quarter he gives her and goes out to buy a loaf of bread and a little meat.

About "Kneel to the Rising Sun," hideous as it is, we feel differently. An abject negro share-cropper stands helplessly by while his fiend of a white boss chops off the tail of the negro's hound-dog with his jack-knife—just to torture the dog and plague the negro. The latter's old father, on short rations like everybody else on the place, wandering off in the dark in search of something to eat, falls into the hog pen and is half eaten up by vicious hogs. The son and his pal, the one black on the farm who will stand up to the owner, drag out the body in the middle of the night and wake up their boss.

The negro with some gumption tells the latter that the boss knows good and well how the old man happened to be eaten up by the fattening hogs. The boss flies into a fury, whangs the negro with a single-tree, and the negro finally runs away. The white posse which soon gathers forces the abject cropper to tell them where his friend has gone. The white men shoot the latter down like a coon. In a kind of delirium, the negro who has helped to kill his best friend staggers homeward across the ploughed field, falling every now and again, then struggling to his knees to face the rising red sun.

There is bestiality and horror enough here, goodness knows, but given the neighborhood, the custom of share-cropping, and the humans concerned, the story has, nevertheless, a certain logic. It not only "could have happened," but it has a certain heroic quality in the sense that the poor helpless Lonnie and the vicious Arch Gunnard are by way of being symbols of masses of men—exploiters and exploited—of something bigger than themselves. And in the telling, in the rhythm and sense of life, there is a certain macabre beauty.

Caldwell once said of himself that "all I am, I attribute to my dislike of reading books. I'll read anything in print I can put my hand on if the medium is a magazine, but I dislike books as I do a steel trap."

All very well for a young writer of stories like Mr. Caldwell's at the moment of his being "discovered," piquant and in character, and possibly his idiosyncrasy may actually have helped to preserve his earthy style from contamination. But Mr. Caldwell is now regarded as a serious artist; whether or not he reads books, he writes them, and in the nature of things he addresses an intellectual .elite. For he isn't a primitive bard twanging the lyre for his own people. If the sub-normal types which preoccupy him as subject-matter ever read at all, they would be the last to be interested in such tales as these. Those capable of appreciating his work will accept bestiality and horror if they seem to have some significance. It's another matter when one gets the notion that they are being exploited for their own sakes.

["Ten Books"]

Randall Jarrell*

Mr. Caldwell's effects range from particularly brutal to quite unusually sensitive ones; who else would have named three poor girls on a Georgia farm, Rosemunda [sic], Griselda, and Darling Jill? He is certainly a born humorist—if one ever doesn't laugh when Mr. Caldwell wants one to, it is only because one is too horrified. He is equally at home with the typical and the odd, a deputy sheriff and an albino. He generally depends on understatement and repetition, rather than exaggeration, for comic effect. The best thing one can do with Mr. Caldwell's peculiar variety of humor is to accept it with gratitude.

However, there is another element in his serious work—a preoccupation with brutal, violent, and obscene subject matter—that is not in the least peculiar to Mr. Caldwell. It is more evident than it has ever been in his latest book of short stories. There is no mixture of elements in them; they class themselves automatically as serious or humorous. Not a single story in Kneel to the Rising Sun is without a murder, a rape, or some scene of the utmost violence and brutality. Most of them, if merely related baldly as anecdotes, would have a considerable physiological effect on the reader; told by Mr. Caldwell, who lavishes all of his very considerable powers on them, and whose attitude and methods are those of the humorist, they are horrible to an extraordinary extent: the reader can actually feel his stomach contracting. If Mr. Caldwell is subjecting one to this nausea gratuitously, it is difficult not to feel for him a violent dislike; one is forced to look for circumstances which will explain or justify his methods.

*Reprinted from Southern Review, 1 (1935–36), 401–04. Copyright © 1935 by Randall Jarrell. Reprinted with the permission of Farrar, Straus and Giroux, Inc.

About most of these stories one can say, as Goya did, "I have seen it." or, as Ambrose Bierce said in a different connection "Can Such Things Be?" That is, they are social documents, instruments of protest against society; we accept the discomfort that attends reading such a story because we feel that it is true, that we ought to know it. After reading the *Agamemnon* or *Lear* we feel no desire to *do* anything at all; but after reading a successful story of this other kind, we are full of a horrified protest, we wish very violently that we could do something about such things.

Some of the stories, however, are not of this sort. In them the obscene or gruesome subject matter is used deliberately, merely to increase the effect of the story. This is, in the last analysis, an insult to the reader, an implicit assumption of his aesthetic stupidity; the writer believes that the reader will not be able to differentiate the effect of the shocking subject matter from the effect of the story as a work of art proper, and since the total effect is so large, will assume that the story must have been extraordinarily fine. I do not mean this condemnation to be so sweeping as it sounds (nor do I mean to say that this assumption about the reader is necessarily conscious on the part of the writer), but certainly the indiscriminate or evident use of the principle can only result in failure. After all, the entire point of a trick is that you don't see how it is done. In such scenes as the death of Emma Bovary, Kiriloff's suicide, the blinding of Oedipus, the subject matter has its effect; but, in the first place, the scenes are so carefully done that we notice the form more than the matter; and, in the second place, the blinding of Oedipus means something, it has an obvious relevance. Mr. Caldwell would have told you of the act for its own sake, and besides have told you so vividly, and in so much detail, that you would virtually feel your own finger nail against your own eyes. The writer had better remember that even the most gruesome and tragic art must give the reader pleasure. If the aesthetic pleasure we get from these stories outweighs the unpleasant effect of the subjects, then they are successful; but if this is not the case, there is no reason why we would show the slightest mercy to Mr. Caldwell.

It is much easier to understand than to pardon such conduct on the writer's part. In the first place, if you habitually write about murders and rapes, under peculiarly trying circumstances, in a peculiarly brutal manner, who will have the courage to call you sentimental?—and we live in an age that eschews sentimentality as if it were a good deal more than the devil. (Actually, of course, a writer may be just as sentimental in laying undue emphasis on sexual crimes as on dying mothers: *sentimental*, like *scientific*, is an adjective that relates to method, and not to matter.)

There is another more important cause. Valery says about the poet that he is like a man who carries ten-pound weights up to the roof, and finally drops them all at once on the head of a passer-by. That is, the writer does not get from his work as he writes and reads it the same aesthetic shock that the reader does; and since the writer is accustomed to reading other stories, and having them produce a decided effect on him, he is disquieted at not being equally affected by his own. But the bare facts of murder and rape have as much effect on the writer as on the reader: and the writer, confusing this shock with aesthetic shock, may take always to writing stories of the kind that have so much effect on him as he writes them. (Just so, an author frequently chooses solemn or over-whelming subjects to write about; he is so impressed at writing about Life and Death that he does not notice that he is saying nothing of the slightest importance about either. Miss Millay's "Renascence" is one of the best ex-amples of this fault.) The writer's subject matter will of course become more violent and more shocking all the time; the appetite grows with feeding, and the writer after a time will be unmoved by things that would have once made him shake like an aspen.

Mr. Caldwell's technical ability is quite unusual. He writes his stories almost as if he were writing music. He has set themes or motifs, which he repeats time and time again—there are few writers who use repetition to the same extent. He brings you with extraordinary delicacy and care up to a climax or anti-climax; he loves that sort of suspense you get in the movies when someone is about to be killed by gangsters. He has a peculiar style, bare, precise, about halfway between the conversational-common-place and the naive-literary—the latter element is almost chemically pure in such first-person stories as "The Cold Winter."

About half the stories in his present volume are sketches rather than stories; but certainly no one could think of saying that about such a story as "Kneel to the Rising Sun." Mr. Caldwell's people are frequently not people at all, but merely very much simplified response-systems. The easiest way of seeing what he lacks is to read Chekhov's stories about peasants. Nevertheless, such stories as "Kneel to the Rising Sun," "The Growing Season," and "A Day's Wooing," are stories well worth reading. "The Growing Season" is, in fact, one of the most extraordinarily in-genious stories I have ever seen. It is about the extremely bloody murder of something called "Fiddler." Fiddler is chained to a tree in Jesse English's yard; whether Fiddler is an imbecile, a dog, God himself couldn't say for certain, since never once is he called anything but Fid-dler. Fiddler, "with his undeveloped legs," "rattling his chain," "crawling around the tree," getting up "as if to stand," Fiddler "making more noise than he had ever made before," is something the reader will hardly forget.

"Sunny South"

Hamilton Basso*

I have some slight knowledge of the Tobacco Road country in Georgia and, because of that, I have often been asked if there are people really "like" those who appear in the novels and short stories of Mr. Erskine Caldwell. The only answer I can give is that while I have never come across a Jeeter Lester or Ty Ty Waldon[*sic*], I have sometimes encountered their approximations. If Mr. Caldwell's characters do not actually exist, in all their various shapes and meanings, the circumstances of life and economics in that part of the world would all seem to conspire to create them. There will be many persons who, reading this book, will ask the same question and question Mr. Caldwell's "realism," and I would like to make the point that he is not a realist at all, not a person drawing exact cartoons, but a very fine and sensitive artist whose characters are idealistic creations; from which comes both the strength (as in *Tobacco Road*) and the weakness (as in *Journeyman*) of his writings.

The story *Blue Boy* in the present collection will further illustrate what I mean. Realistically, in the everyday prosaic sense of "could this have happened?" one might argue about it all night long. It is my feeling that it could not have happened—that no middle-class farmer (as the farmer in this story is), regardless of moral decay and degeneracy, would entertain his guests after a holiday dinner by having an idiot Negro indulge in self-abuse. And yet, beyond the shock of horror (strengthened, perhaps, by the fact that I come from the South and do not want such a thing to be true) I also feel that, idealistically, as a creative and artistic truth, it not only could happen but did.

The title story in this collection, *Kneel to the Rising Sun*, by any critical standard whatsoever, is one of the finest short stories any American has written. It is not a pretty story, when you read it there is a sick, dead feeling in the middle of your stomach, but it is a story you are not likely to forget. It is bitter and merciless in its indictments, but it also has that quality of tenderness that so few critics who have tried to assay Caldwell have remarked upon; and a strength, a rightness, derived from its idealness which, if taken away, would make it no more memorable than the report of a lynching in a newspaper. It is one of those rare pieces in which everything is right; element fusing into element to make a hard, complete, compact whole and not any striving for effect or a single doubtful note.

I do not intend to hand down a ruling on each of the sixteen stories in the present collection. My own tabulation reads: one fine story, three good ones, five that are fair and seven that, for one reason or other, fail to come off. All of them, however, with one or two exceptions, are worth

*Reprinted from *New Masses*, 15 (June 11, 1935), 25.

reading at least once and many of them may be read with profit several times. In the latter category I would include as well as the stories already mentioned, "Honeymoon," 'A Day's Wooing," "The Growing Season," "Slow Death" and "Travel [sic] Island." Mr. Caldwell has completed another section in the picture he is painting of one kind of life in the backwoods of Georgia and he has done it with his own gifts of economy, poetry and skill.

If, to get back to the question of "fact," one seeks an extra-artistic substantiation for Mr. Caldwell's writings I suggest a reading of *Tenant Farmer*—the result of the tour Mr. Caldwell made through the South for The New York Post. In this pamphlet, Mr. Caldwell becomes a reporter and puts down, as a reporter, what he has heard and seen. (It is worth remembering, if any further authentication of his accuracy is required, that an investigation conducted by The Augusta Chronicle verified Mr. Caldwell's more important findings.) This is a pamphlet I would like to see read by every Southerner who professed to be interested in the welfare of his section. If any further condemnation of the tenant-farmer system is needed and the whole plantation economy as it is now practised, here it is. And here also, is a graphic picture of the thing that Southerners, among them men of pride and decency, want to defend—a system based upon exploitation and greed and a total disregard of human beings.

There have been times when reading Mr. Caldwell, I have felt he has almost exhausted the soil from which all his writings have sprung. I felt it most strongly in *Journeyman* and I felt it in some of the stories in this book. I remember some things Mr. Caldwell has written that do not derive from the Tobacco Road country and I am sure that Mr. Caldwell does not depend, as so many southern writes depend, upon their region. But each man to his own plowing. Only Mr. Caldwell could have written *Kneel to the Rising Sun*, it could only have come out of that part of the world he has made his own and it is a contribution of first importance to the literature of our time.

"Heavenly Visitation"

James T. Farrell*

Erskine Caldwell can best be described as a natural-born story teller. Looking over the period of his last five books, it seems quite apparent that he writes neither as a self-conscious craftsman nor as one driving towards the increase of an understanding of human relationships and social processes. Rather, he seems to catch his material on the wing and to pour it out in a hit-or-miss manner, with the result that he seems to miss more

*Reprinted from *New Masses*, 15 (April 2, 1935), 32–33.

often than he hits, and his work, taken as a body, includes a great deal of repetition and an unmistakable unevenness in accomplishment.

To date, he has indicated that he can rise to his best within the space of a limited canvas, more readily in the short story than in the novel. His most impressive work is of two types: stories of adolescent love and of the first vague stirrings of amorous and sexual emotions in the lives of his blushing Hamlets and Evangelines of the backward rural areas; and tales in which there is a surface of burlesque that covers grim and grotesque tragedy, and reveals people who are implacably bent on their own self-destruction because of ignorance, and because of social conditions and pressures which they cannot understand. In the most satisfying of these stories, it is noticeable that he deals with a single impression, or with a small number of closely knit impressions.

When he seeks to deal with a narrative which requires lengthier development on the one hand, or the delineation of characters either in a process of growth or of genuine emotional crisis on the other, he seems unequipped to handle his material. The result is often bathos, sentimentality, even banality. A study of his work reveals that he is more at home in his treatment of a rural environment than when he seeks either to write of characters with an urban background or in a modern industrial setting. Thus, his stories of poverty in the city, such as *Masses of Men*, and *Rachel* are among his poorest, and thus his failure in the strike scene of *God's Little Acre*.

With his rural characters and environment he shows a precision in observation of details of speech and habits, in almost glaring contrast to the generalized treatment he affords in his strike scene of *God's Little Acre*, or the dependence on stereotyped detail in his tales of urban poverty and degradation. In such sections of his writings there is melodrama—improperly motivated and developed emotions—rather than the genuine aliveness, gusto, passion and ecstasy which we can feel in the most effective of his Georgia tales.

His recently published novel, *Journeyman*, is a miss rather than a hit. When one thinks of *Tobacco Road*, or even of *God's Little Acre*, *Journeyman* reads like a parody written on Caldwell himself. It is the story of an itinerant preacher, Semon Dye, who travels through Georgia spouting the word of God on his own authority. Lusty, hypocritical and crooked, he happens into a backward Georgia community and immediately begins to feather his own nest. He seduces one of the Negro girls working for his host and shoots her man for protesting; drinks liquor wholesale, wins his host's automobile, watch, and even his wife, in a suspicious crap game, and sells back part of his winnings for a hundred dollars of borrowed money; seduces the wife, blackmails his host for sexual relationship with a former wife, and concludes with a revival meeting in which he leads the whole community into an insane orgy of jerks and twists and rollings until he himself froths at the mouth. When he leaves, the community regrets his departure.

If this story be taken simply as a fantastic burlesque, it is passably humorous and diverting. However, if it is to be considered as a serious novel, purporting to reveal an understanding of a section of the American scene and intending to give us an awareness and a sense of the people in this milieu, an estimation of the novel becomes a different question. It is difficult to note any underlying theme. Rather, *Journeyman* seems to be just another story hastily rolled off Caldwell's typewriter. The characters are repetitions of the Tye Tyes[*sic*], the Jeeters, and the Darling Jills already created. Here they are given with less understanding, and there is almost nothing in the book to suggest that Caldwell has gone back into this material either to perfect his previous statements of it, or to expand and deepen his awareness of it. We find the same facility of dialogue, the same tricks and mannerisms, the same ease and fluency in writing, the same presentation of those amusing and unintelligible quirks of habit and character which lead to such tragic and grim consequences. He has simply reproduced the same article, but with a lessened impact.

One chapter alone stands out as a contrast and an exception to this thin repetitiveness. Here, three of the male characters, including Semon Dye, sit in a barn drinking liquor and gazing through a crack in the wall at a field which they could vision more fully merely by stepping outside the barn. This act becomes for them an emotional release, a kind of poetic experience, acquiring a meaning in their personal experience totally disproportionate to its apparent value and usefulness. And Caldwell here manages to convey this impression through their dialogue in a manner which is genuinely poetic. It is the one passage in the book which carries a weight of feeling.

The social implications of *Journeyman* are familiar, or else negligible. It is again merely a picture of the life of primitive and undeveloped American folk. Since it does not end in tragedy, it does not contain the same agitation, the same sense of life, that we find in *Tobacco Road*. Since it is so much of a repetition, it does not increase our consciousness of this life and these people as a few of his stories and the first half of *God's Little Acre* did. It is Erskine Caldwell—not at his best.

"Caldwell Sees America"

Albert Halper*

In some respects this collection of travel sketches and jottings can be called the best book Erskine Caldwell has yet done. The whole work continues more or less on one high level and the finish (the Southern tenant-farmer section) gathers weight to close the volume with a mighty wallop aimed flush at the jaw of industrial and agrarian exploitation.

*Reprinted from *New Masses*, 17 (Dec. 10, 1935), 22–23.

Now let us examine the book more closely.

Mr. Caldwell opens his volume with a blast against the average American traveler's method of traveling, giving out an indictment to the effect that the average traveler (who has the means) either speeds like the whirlwind across his fatherland, or merely views the physical sights such as the Grand Canyon or Niagara Falls, then goes on to the next sight. There is some truth to this statement, but on the whole the indictment is far-fetched. The American, in the main, is a good sound traveler, when he is not rushing across the continent on business. He takes his time (the only time he does), stops off at tourist camps, is friendly and loquacious, prepares food with the assistance of new-found acquaintances, talks politics and business and, in short, gets to know his fellow American. Sometimes people who have met in Ohio or Pennsylvania will pass and re-pass each other on the road all the way to California, renewing their friendships and comparing notes as they go along. This is no bad way of traveling by any means.

Mr. Caldwell started out from the West Coast and covered the drought area. He tells us tales picked up at gasoline and hot-dog stands, in itself a makeshift way of getting information. We get the feeling of a population being affected by the drought and yet we do not get the feeling of the drought. There is hardly any description of the land at all, save for a few phrases of its bareness. This reviewer recalls an article he once read about the drought in The Saturday Evening Post two years ago which described the topography of the land, the look of the trees with the blown soil hanging in the branches like lichen, the glare in the sky, the effect of the heat, how much top soil was blown away, how far it blew, how the cattle stood it, the reaction of the farmers' families, etc. In short, the drought was depicted as the drought and became a dramatic thing, charged with life and death. In Caldwell's book there is none of this. It is true Caldwell admits in his foreword that his volume lays no claim of being an exhaustive study, but nevertheless he is criticized by this reviewer for falling down on the job. Caldwell had only to throw a stick to hit a state farm-school graduate along the road who, in an hour's time, could have given him all kinds of information and data.

This is not to minimize Caldwell's swell job of reporting. When he comes to Detroit he is on firmer ground. He reports the speedup in the automobile industry, the spy terror and the accidents with harrowing detail; and it is evident to the reader that Caldwell had had some entree to the facts behind the scenes.

And when he comes to his native South, Caldwell is on home soil in-deed. Here we get facts and figures and the blazing rage of a man who not only feels for the people but *knows*. Caldwell piles up such a case against the program of exploitation of the sharecropper and wage laborer that this reviewer confesses he has never read anything to beat it. *Tobacco*

Road's author's unrelenting honesty and fierce clean prose cut through the layer of lies and false reports like a surgeon's knife. The book closes with a charge against the federal government which has, and is, bungling Southern agrarian relief in such a fashion that whole families and communities have been driven to subsist on the roots of the field and, in some cases, on clay.

The grimness of the volume is relieved at times by several deft sketches in the well-known Caldwell manner, namely, "Grandpa in the Bathtub," "A Country That Moves," "A Badland Tale" and other little stories, any one of which is worth more than a bushel's weight of the type of "introspective" tales turned out by Alvah Bessie, William Saroyan, Whit Burnett and other stooges of The Story Magazine-Arch-deaconess Edward J. O'Brien clique.

Erskine Caldwell, to this reviewer, is one of the few young American writers who seems to be definitely advancing and not just standing still or slipping backward. The fact that he is not an inhabitant of New York stands vastly in his favor. In Manhattan most of the writers for years have never set foot beyond a ten-mile radius, except to pay a visit to a writers' colony or to spend a week-end with a friend on a Connecticut "farm." Many of these writers originally come from the South, the Middle West or the Far West, but they have not gone home for years to see how the home folks have been hit. Their writing, consequently, has flattened out and staled and anything they have to say about their birthplaces is gleaned from the files of newspapers or occasional letters from home. A writer, if he is to amount to anything at all, must return to his people again and again for nourishment, even if he hates or despises them. Failing to do this, he is doomed to rootlessness and creative poverty. Literary history is strewn with the corpses of exiles and expatriates whose works, before they expired (from a creative point of view) thinned down to repetitious water or stopped completely. The letters of Turgenev are recommended to the interested reader, Turgenev, that big lonely hulk of a bachelor who couldn't stand Russia but felt castrated every time he left her soil. His talent and his honesty literally forced him to return to Russia every year or two, and it is noteworthy to recall that after almost every trip his output received a spurt and another great book was added to the rollcall of the times.

In fine, Erskine Caldwell, by writing *Some American People*, not only has done a good job of reportage but has also set an example to his fellow writers to come out of their Manhattan shells and Connecticut "farms" and to rub shoulders with the people if they are to find out really what it's all about. This goes for the young fledgling poets as well, who have been recently receiving a mild sort of ballyhoo. Poets are writers as well as novelists and to vegetate forever in Manhattan in order to send forth a small annual crop of verses in the hard-guy lingo directed against

Wall Street, the cops or the noise of the "L" above Third Avenue, is insufficient. The times are such that in order to write one must have *contact*. Erskine Caldwell, in his new book, demonstrates that he has it.

[Telegram]

Arnold Gingrich

OV CHICAGO ILL OCT 22 1935
ALBERT HALPER MAXIM LIEBER
545 FIFTH AVE NYC
COMMITTEE CHICAGO WRITERS ASKING ALL AUTHORS WHO WORKED IN OR EMANATE FROM CHICAGO TO JOIN IN PUBLIC PROTEST AGAINST ARBITRARY THEATRE CENSORSHIP EVIDENCED BY SUPPRESSION OF THE PLAY TOBACCO ROAD BY CHICAGOS PROVINCIAL MINDED MAYOR KELLY STOP PLEASE JOIN US BY WIRING YOUR EXPRESSION COLLECT TO MEYER LEVIN NINE NINETEEN NORTH MICHIGAN AVENUE
ARNOLD GINGRICH

[Editorial Commentary in *The New Republic*]

Anonymous*

The exclusion of "Tobacco Road" from Chicago by virtue of the action of Mayor Kelly in withdrawing the license of the Selwyn Theatre is one of the most outrageous cases of current censorship of the arts. The intervention of Judge W.H. Holley, an enlightened member of the federal bench, in granting a stay was met by a counter action on the part of the city, and unless public protest is successful, the play is banned from Chicago and necessarily from smaller cities in the Middle West. Once more Chicago, in which both Coquelin and Mansfield were forbidden to play "Cyrano de Bergerac" on the ground that the drama plagiarized the work of one of its leading real-estate men, is the victim of the provincialism of its officials. Mayor Kelly finds a play that has interested and informed audiences in New York for two years "a mass of filth." That Mr. Caldwell's play is a true picture of conditions as they actually exist cannot be denied. When Mr. Caldwell was challenged by Georgia newspapers as to the reality of such conditions, he offered to take a group of reporters and show them. He did. The policy of concealment, of covering up, in the

*Reprinted from *New Republic*, 84 (Nov. 6, 1935), 348

interest of American complacency is especially short-sighted in view of the avowed policy of the national administration to rescue the forgotten man. The characters in "Tobacco Road" are forgotten people. Mr. Caldwell deserves the gratitude of all who honestly care for decency in American life by bringing them so powerfully to mind.

It is difficult to believe that Mayor Kelly is acting in good faith. The Mayor rose to prominence and wealth in Chicago as engineer of the Board of the Sanitary District. In this position he was a spectator of the orgies of this gang, carried out in junketing trips to various cities. He must have known that the funds of the district were drawn upon to pay for the pleasures of members of the Board, which, with unusual effrontery, were specified in the vouchers in words which it is not permissible to quote. This mess of filth, generally known to the public, sat easily upon Mayor Kelly's conscience. Again, during the two seasons of the Century of Progress Exposition, Mr. Kelly was not only mayor of the city but also president of the South Park Board, on whose grounds the fair was held. Every visitor knows the extent to which shows were constantly permitted whose only attraction was their obscenity. These exhibitions were offered in the most salacious terms by barkers to a multitude of people, including children. If there is such a thing as lust of the eye, that lust was appealed to by every known device; and the good name of the city was stained. The Cardinal Archbishop of the Diocese, whose spiritual lamb Mayor Kelly is, was appealed to, apparently without avail. If the Mayor is now ambitious to obtain the reputation of Cato the Censor, he has something to live down.

"A Long Road"

Anonymous*

In a few more weeks "Tobacco Road" will be able to claim a longer run on the New York stage than has ever been enjoyed by any other play except "Abie's Irish Rose" and "Lightnin' "—neither of which it greatly resembles. Like Miss Anne Nichol's masterpiece, the drama received a less than dubious reception from most of the critics—though *The Nation* was enthusiastic—and no one guessed that it would achieve any outstanding success. Indeed, it was very near to closing during its early weeks, but attendance gradually grew and it has now become possible for the press department to compile horrifying statistics. The actor who plays "Dude" is said, for example, to have consumed more than fifteen hundred raw turnips at the rate of two a performance, and several Ford fenders have

*Reprinted from *Nation*, 141 (Nov. 20, 1935), 582. Copyright© 1935 The Nation Associates.

been worn out in the scene which requires that one be dragged on the stage as part of a rapidly disintegrating car.

Unfortunately, it is not possible to compile statistics to show whether or not New Yorkers are any the worse for their long association with Jeeter Lester and his tribe, but the play seems destined to a career outside the metropolis almost as stormy as that of "Waiting for Lefty," since two mayors have already declared in no uncertain terms that there will be no "horsing around" on the stages of their fair cities. In Detroit a circuit judge has just refused to prevent the police from closing the play after a four weeks' run; in Chicago injunctions, restraints, orders to show cause, and the like have been flying back and forth for some time in a yet undecided battle.

The case has a certain peculiar interest because of the fact that it is difficult to see how objections to the play can be rationalized in either of the two most usual ways. Though Erskine Caldwell, from whose novel it was dramatized, has since thrown in his lot with the radicals, the passing reference in the play to absentee landlordism can hardly be called sufficiently subversive to endanger the state. On the other hand, it certainly cannot be charged that vice is rendered attractive. Surely no one who observes the goings-on between the turnip-eating youth and the hare-lipped imbecile is likely to be impelled to go and do likewise. If the mayors object, their objections must be based upon a purely mystical recognition of the force of the taboo. Certain things must not be said or done simply because they must not be said or done, or because—as the immortal Jeremy Collier replied to those who defended swearing on the stage when it was in character—"the sin sticks to the syllables."

Summoned into consultation and asked for an opinion, *The Nation's* dramatic critic declared, perhaps a bit paradoxically, that the play is not only highly moral but beautiful and heartening. "The real point of this drama," he said, "lies in the fact that its chief characters, despite the wretchedness of their lives, are admirably salty fellows in whom the lust of life—in the more general as well as the more specific meaning of the words—has never died. They represent the indomitable persistence of two of the best of human characteristics—wit and desire—through lives which seem calculated to extinguish both. Fortitude—gay loving and gay mocking in the face of bludgeoning fate—is one of the most exhilarating as well as one of the most beautiful things in the world, and the inhabitants of Tobacco Road have fortitude."

Circuit Judge Guy A. Miller characterized the play as "devoid of merit, stupid, profane, obscene, and degrading." He added, "It is difficult to imagine any play so completely devoid of literary or artistic merit." To *The Nation's* critic, however, these were mere weasel words by comparison with those used on another occasion by a very famous American dramatic critic, who wrote as follows about a certain dramatist:

———'s sociological plays neither impart nor enforce helpful significance as to the social themes they present: they suggest no improvement. Their author was not only dreary and dejected himself; he was the cause that dreariness and dejection are in the minds of all clear-brained thinkers who study his writings. . . . A reformer who asks you to crawl with him in a sewer, merely to see and breathe its feculence, is a pest. . . . The movement of the world is onward and upward, but that movement has never been helped, and it never will be helped, by any such gospel of disordered mentality, distrust, despondency, bitterness, and gloom as that which proceeded from the diseased mind of ———. And if the reader is half as sick of the whole subject of his plays as I am, he must be indeed rejoiced to come to the end of this chapter!

The critic was William Winter; the dramatist under discussion was Hendrick Ibsen. No wonder that when this famous critic finally ceased his labors, a commentator quoted Shakespeare: "Fear no more the heat of the *Sun*, nor furious Winter's rages."

[Letter to the Editor of *The Nation*: "Judicial Calm"]

Guy A. Miller
Judge of the Circuit Court for Detroit*

To The Editors of *The Nation*:

I suppose that I should be flattered by the notice which you have taken of a very brief opinion of mine upon the subject of a very poor piece of stage literature. I refer, of course, to your editorial entitled A Long Road, in the issue of November 20. On two points I am not quite able to agree with your editorial writer. I do not pretend to be able to qualify as a dramatic critic with William Winter, nor do I think that Mr. Caldwell quite ranks with Henrik Ibsen.

It takes a great deal of fortitude for a farmhand to clean out a pigsty or privy vault. His language during the process is apt to be quite lurid. Would you consider portraying on the stage this process, including a reproduction of the stench? I would think that such a portrayal might be used for purposes of instruction at least as well as the spineless shiftlessness

*Reprinted from *Nation*, 141 (Dec. 25, 1935), 741–42. Copyright © 1935 The Nation Associates.

of Jeeter Lester. At least, manure is used as fertilizer to produce food, and nothing in "Tobacco Road" suggests any such useful purpose.

It probably takes a more competent mentality than mine to discover anything in the Lester family except inexcusable degradation and decadence. I imagine that if I lived in New York City perhaps the superior atmosphere of that world center might sharpen my intellect. But then, of course, New York City is the front doorstep of America. Only, sometimes, I am tempted to think that it would be more accurate to say that it is the front doormat.

Oh, and by the way, legal literature does not aim at more than adequately to express a subject. That is the reason why my words were merely "weasel words."

I hope, however, that you will not get the idea from anything that I say that I am insensible of the benefits of being panned by *The Nation* and Theodore Dreiser. I cannot conceive of any two sources from which I would more thankfully accept criticism and disagreement.

Detroit, November 29

" 'Tobacco Road' Winds Its Way Into Congress"

Anonymous*

WASHINGTON, April 6—"Tobacco Road's" scarcely idyllic portrayal of life in rural Georgia was loudly resented in the House today by Representative Braswell Deen, Democrat, who is proud to hale from the "Tobacco Road" belt himself.

The curious play from Erskine Caldwell's novel of love and starvation among the sharecroppers has just started a run here which promises to fill the cavernous spaces of the National Theater for a full week. Rumors about the play reached the ears of Representative Deen early. Fearful that he might not be able to maintain his indignation, he did not visit the playhouse himself.

Instead, he sent two spies, who brought back reports that made the Representative's hair stand straight up with horror. He did not know whether he was more outraged by the general gaudiness of the play's biology or by "the infamous wicked untruth" of its portrait of life in his district.

"We never lived thataway down in our part," cried he. "Never at all.

---

*Reprinted from *New York Herald Tribune*, 7 April 1936, p. 14, col. 2, by permission of the I.H.T. Corporation.

Why, we got churches and schools for everybody. Even the Negroes have churches and schools."

Early in the day there was some hope that the District Attorney's office in the District of Columbia might step in on Mr. Deen's side. Miss Rhoda Milliken, leader of the city's feminine police, was upset by the Caldwell-Jack Kirkland opus, and advised that so much of it be excised that there would have been about twenty minutes of drama left. A posse of six assistant district attorneys was dispatched to the National Theater to see for themselves, however, and they returned a verdict favorable to the play.

Undiscouraged, Representative Deen, a tall, lanky rural Georgian with a fine gift for public passion, rose in the House to demand instant action by the entire Congress to put an end to the libel on the pastoral South. His eyes flashed, his arms waved like flails when he warmed to his task, and his voice roared out over the rows of Representatives, listening unexcitedly enough.

"I have asked this time," shouted the Representative, "to request my colleagues of the House to either see this most infamous, wicked and damnable play, or to talk with some one who has seen it and to join with me in requesting the District Attorney of the District of Columbia and the commissioners of the District to have the presentation of the play stopped in this city today. The Mayor of Chicago even a few weeks ago declined to permit this infamous and wicked play to be presented in the city of Chicago.

"It is predicated on conditions which are as far from the truth and the facts as the East from the West. It is based on a condition that never existed, based on conditions supposed to exist in my Congressional district. There are millions of tenant farmers in this country, there are thousands of them in my district, and they are today working the tobacco on their farms and, as their humble Representative, for the first time in this session I open my mouth and resent with all the power of my soul this untruthful, undignified, undiplomatic and unfair sketch of Southern life, which, it is said, is worse than savagery 200 years ago. There is not a word of truth in it. I denounce it and resent it."

Representative Deen admitted that the "dreadful" play was "well acted," and pointed with quivering horror to the fact that the play was sold out. This, he felt, indicated the depths of depravity of taste which could be reached by the citizenry of Washington. He mentioned with warm approval the unsuccessful demarche of Miss Milliken, intimating that she was a credit to Washington womanhood and the Washington police force. And he was emphatic that, at such a time as this, when thousands of visitors have come to Washington with the refined intention of inspecting cherry blossoms, they should not be allowed to come in contact with so soul-shaking an exhibit as "Tobacco Road."

"Of all times and places that this play should not be shown," he said, "it is at the present time in this nation's capital, when thousands of visitors from every part of the country come here to attend the cherry blossom festival. Thousands of them attending this show will cary back with them to their homes the impression that Georgia sharecroppers live in a barren land where there is no God, where there is no romantic love, no religious training, no schooling, no standards of right or wrong. They will carry back with them to their homes the impression that sharecroppers in Georgia are living in environments inferior to savages of 200 years ago.

"For thousands of sharecroppers and their families who are not in the nation's capital to defend themselves against this infamous, vile and wicked web into which they have been woven by those who would commercialize upon them, I am calling upon the bar of public opinion and public justice to render its decision against the appearance of 'Tobacco Road' in the nation's capital."

Representative Deen explained that he was convinced that "Tobacco Road's" action was laid in his district, because the old Tobacco Road runs down from Augusta, right into his counties. He said that his district was a great tobacco-growing district, and he also thought that the large numbers of offspring produced by "Tobacco Road's" characters were suggested by his district's citizens. He said he knew families of twenty-two children, but, he declared, they were all refined, God-fearing citizens. His own brother, he said, is a sharecropper, with four virtuous youngsters.

"Tobacco Roads in the South"

Erskine Caldwell*

One of the most realistic and vivid plays revealing a revolting phase of American working class life is "Tobacco Road" by Erskine Caldwell, who was reared in the South. It portrays the poor whites, the real forgotten men for at least two-hundred years in this country. The play has stirred the resentment of politicians and the aristocracy of the South, who want to conceal this economic and social ulcer. Congressman Braswell Deen of Georgia recently denounced "Tobacco Road" and its author on the floor of Congress, and the author in the drama section of the New York Times answered these critics. Herewith follow some leading sections of the reply, an excellent portrayal of the life of a large section of the underlying population in the South today.—EDITOR

*Reprinted with permission from *New Leader*, 19 (June 13, 1936), p. 4, cols. 5–6. Copyright © 1936 The American Labor Conference on International Affairs, Inc.

The obiter dicta of a Mayor Kelly, a Governor Talmadge, a Congressman Deen have by no degree changed the basic social and economic condition of Tobacco Road people. Inversely, however, their remarks have drawn the attention of many interested persons who have made it possible to conduct experimental investigation of the life and death of the genus Jeeter.

As time goes on, I hope that this study can be enlarged to include the whole basic background of the so-called poor-white. And so, as one Cracker to another, it can be said, in reply to the remarks of Congressman Deen on the floor of Congress, that the bellies of some of his constituents are just as hungry now as they were before his Cherry Blossom Week speech.

The concurrent political criticism of "Tobacco Road" reveals that the static ignorance of many men holding public office is a thing to marvel at. Year after year Congressmen, Governors and Mayors stand up and denounce "Tobacco Road" as an untruth. Some even circumvent the basic facts of the drama by declaring it is (1) immoral, (2) sacreligious, (3) calumnious.

Behind this screen of vote-teasing verbiage lies the awful truth of the Tobacco Road country. Stretching from South Carolina to Arkansas, its stench is a complacent nation's shame. White and colored, its thousands upon thousands of men, women and children exist in an inhuman state of landlord and politician imposed slavery. For fifty years, while churches were sending missionaries to save the heathen in China, Africa and Mexico, its own people were being subjected to the economic blood-sucking of the landlord-elders and the politician-deacons. Many of the ministers who pointed out the inconsistencies of the church were branded heretics and exiled. Today there remain the carcass, the rags and the depleted, sterile soil.

* * * *

I do not hesitate to say that I believe I hold just as much love for the South and for my native State of Georgia as does Congressman Deen. It is because I have this love that I insist upon such a story as "Tobacco Road" as a means of exposing the shame of its civilization. It has never been a pleasing sight in my eyes to see men, women and children born, live and die in poverty, ignorance and degradation. I have picked cotton with them, eaten bread with them and dug graves for their dead with them. If ever a man was one of them, I am he.

But I did not like to stand and see one of them tied to a tree and beaten into insensibility by a landlord. I did not like to stand and see one of them cheated out of his year's labor by a small-time politician passing as a part-time lawyer. I did not like to stand and see one of them killed in cold blood by an overseer for protesting against the rape of his daughter before his very eyes. It is because I did not like those things, among others, that I attempted to show in "Tobacco Road" that the South has not only produced a coolie serfdom but, more than that, has turned around and deliberately kicked it in the face.

* * * *

One of the reasons why even those Georgians who protest the most loudly against "Tobacco Road" do not know what they are talking about is that they are ignorant of this life either because they are uninformed or because they do not wish to be informed. Of the latter, little else need be said. But for the benefit of the former, I wish to repeat here what I have said many times before. The Tobacco Road people are to be found throughout Georgia, and other cotton-growing states as well, wherever the soil has been eroded or depleted. Many are share-croppers, but by no means all of them. Perhaps the majority of them, just as Jeeter Lester, have been forced out of the sharecropper class. They cannot secure farms to till. The reasons for this are many, but perhaps the most common one is that many landowners prefer Negroes, because they have learned they can get the best of Negroes by means of threats, whereas white tenants are more inclined to demand what is rightfully theirs.

* * * *

That well-known figure, the professional Southerner, has ever denied any such condition, even the mere whisper of it. Today he is as pugnacious in attitude as he ever was. "Tobacco Road," novel and play, sends him into spasms of apoplectic rage. The display of anger is the first stage. The second stage is his statement that there are no such people. And the third stage is his offer to take you in his car and show you people who are just as educated, thrifty, intelligent, industrious and presentable as any North, East or West. Perhaps the great error of my life was in not appending a preface to "Tobacco Road" stating that the story did not pretend to typify the entire South, but that it was my purpose merely to sketch a representative family among five million persons who are actual residents on Tobacco Road, who are likely future residents there. As it is, we have the spectacle of a man entering a room full of people, crying "Thief," and seeing nearly every person present in the act of running away.

* * * *

Regardless of whether "Tobacco Road" is performed in American theatres one time or a thousand times more, Tobacco Road itself will continue to extend with increasing mileage through every county in the

South. It can be halted in its progress with the help of science, economics, sociology, and common humanity; eventually it could be wiped completely off the map.

"A Compelling Album of the Deep South"

Robert Van Gelder*

Erskine Caldwell—author of "Tobacco Road," "God's Little Acre" and a number of other novels and stories—went back to his home South and got the people talking hard times while Margaret Bourke-White—star photographer for Life and Fortune Magazines—took their pictures. I don't know that I've ever seen better photography, but Mr. Caldwell, a powerful single-tracker, pretty much makes the book his own by main force and conviction.

Miss Bourke-White's pictures allow for the confusion of reality. They capture beauty and reveal the existence of ease, sometimes of contentment, of courage, even happiness, in settings where Mr. Caldwell's mind refuses to admit that these qualities exist. Her pictures show some cheerful people who are ragged and possibly hungry and almost surely ignorant, but are proud of themselves, anyway, and hold themselves superior to the great mass of other people.

There are views of a dressy Negro preacher who obviously believes in the value of what he is saying and doing, who knows that it is enough to bring the sinners in. A group of men who probably never have had a telephone to answer are lazy in the sun watching the river; an old man grins that he is doing all right because he is paid a dollar a day when he works; a woman stops plowing to reassure the visitors that she and her family are getting along.

The pictures show the people as they are. Not all the people. None of the young bucks who kill a jug of corn and drive eighty miles to hire an orchestra are here, none of the pretty girls at the soda fountains. But most of the people who are shown prove in the way that they are shown that in spite of dirt and lack of a radio they are living, and living about as completely as most of us in the richer North.

But in effect Mr. Caldwell claims that though this is in the pictures it isn't so, that the people and the land are dead. Unlike the camera he looks beyond the people and sees the malign diseases of the Southern social system behind them, the worn-out soil, the insufficient diets, the hopeless desperation that he—healthy-minded, educated and sensitive—knows

*Reprinted from *New York Times*, 28 Nov. 1937, Sec. 7, p. 11, cols. 1–2. Copyright © 1937 by The New York Times Company. Reprinted by permission.

must come to all men with the knowledge that little improvement of conditions is possible.

The South has always been shoved around like a country cousin. It buys mill-ends and wears hand-me-downs. It sits at second table and is fed short-rations. It is the place where the ordinary will do, where the makeshift is good enough. It is that dogtown on the other side of the railroad tracks that smells so badly every time the wind changes.

The plantation system wrung "the blood and marrow" from the South through two centuries; sharecropping is extracting "the last juice of life from its prostrate body." And the system of sharecropping is not self-perpetuating; "it can survive only by feeding upon itself, like an animal in a trap eating its own flesh and bone."

These two systems have ruined the people and ruined the land. The South is an agricultural empire that is all worn out. The soil was never any too rich except in a couple of sections that seemingly nothing could damage, and now except in those sections all the richness is gone and the "rains and the winds are eroding the land, washing away and blowing away the earth, until it takes on the appearance of a country cut and scarred by deep valleys and gorges."

The people work harder there in the South, Mr. Caldwell says, than do the people anywhere else in this country and they get less for their work. The people he is talking about have been taking their beating since long before "the Surrender" and now the pain and indignity are "Beginning to tell." He speaks of unrest, not warningly. The one hope of the sharecropper, in his view, lies in organization, in throwing out the bosses, taking over the spoiled fields for themselves. And for the whites, particularly, this is necessary, for on many of the more productive plantations the whites are being pushed out to make room for Negroes, because the Negroes are easier to control, less likely to show their bitterness, to break under frustration.

Mr. Caldwell has done some of his finest writing for this book, but he has turned the book into a sledgehammer to pound home an idea that the pictures somehow go beyond.

"Fall Catalogue"

Malcolm Cowley*

From the reader's point of view, this has been a dispiriting autumn, even though the books published have been good enough, when judged in bulk. There has been the usual number of sound scholarly studies, of

*Reprinted from *New Republic*, 93 (Nov. 24, 1937), 78–79. Copyright © 1937 by Editorial Publications, Inc. Reprinted by permission of the author.

entertaining travelogues, of workmanlike novels that prove a mild thesis; there has been more than the usual quantity of fairly distinguished verse. But there has been an almost total absence of memorable books, of books that open or close horizons, of books, in short, that have in them enough fire and excitement to cast a glow on their more ordinary companions, and thereby make the whole process of writing and publishing and reviewing seem richer in rewards.

It is always dangerous to draw close parallels between the books published in a given season and the mood prevailing in the intellectual public—dangerous, that is, unless you are eager to endow all writers with the gift of prophecy. Political critics often forget that books take a long time merely to be published, and a much longer time in the writing, so that a novel like "To Have and Have Not"—to give one example—might represent the author's state of mind in 1934 or 1935, with some last-minute revisions. Yet after these concessions it remains true that there is, this year, a curious analogy between the dullness of the new books and the dull mood that afflicts the literary world. Writers, like everybody else, are carrying on mechanically while waiting for something to turn up, some new hope to avert catastrophe.

At the National Book Fair in Rockefeller City, all the newest books of 110 publishers are displayed side by side. The jackets make a brave show, but having sampled the text they advertise, I feel more dubious about it. Still, I did see one book that impressed me to the point of breaking all the rules of the exposition and reading it on the spot. It was the volume of photographs by Margaret Bourke-White with text by Erskine Caldwell: "You Have Seen Their Faces."

The two authors made a trip through the cotton states from South Carolina west to Arkansas and Louisiana. They kept away from the cities, the textile mills and the big plantation houses; their sole interest was in the ten million sharecroppers, white and black, who form the most depressed and hopeless class in American society. Writer and photographer worked in close collaboration, Mr. Caldwell contributing his knowledge of the people and his ability to talk to them in their own language; Miss Bourke-White waiting until they had forgotten to be suspicious of strangers, then snapping them in their characteristic attitudes—plowing, chopping cotton, kneeling by the fireplace to mix corn-cakes, shouting and dancing in church, working on the chain gang, and finally sitting in the sun waiting for death—"There comes a time when there's nothing to do except just sit."

In one photograph, a scared little Negro boy, barefooted, in patched overalls with nothing beneath them, stands at the door of his father's cabin beside a long-legged mongrel hound. The board wall is papered with pages torn from Collier's and The Saturday Evening Post—pages that illustrate beauty, romance, affluence, all the good things of civilization. Here one reads the slogans of a hundred corporations: "The most talked of gift on the Christmas horizon!"—"Five kinds of insulation give you a new 'hushed ride.' "—"Out to win—you can't afford to coast!"—"Hey kids, come see my new play rug!"—The cabin, with its floor of cracked boards, has no rug of any sort. The dresser is heaped with dirty clothes. "Blackie ain't good for nothing," the little Negro boy is saying, "he's just an old hound dog."

In another photograph, a Negro woman with big sad eyes is looking through the bars of the St. Tammany Parish jail: "I've only been misbehaving." In still another, a white woman with a child in her lap sits on the top step of a Louisiana mansion, against a background of high stucco pillars with their surfaces pitted as if by smallpox. She says, "I don't know what ever happened to the family that built this house after the War. A lot of families live here now. My husband and me moved in and got two rooms for five dollars a month." These quotations printed beneath the photographs are exactly right; the photographs themselves are almost beyond praise.

They belong to a new art, one that has to be judged by different standards from those applying to painting or sculpture. The composition may be good or bad—usually it is good, but that doesn't really matter. Here the important qualities are those which used to be conveyed in words rather than pictures—drama, for example, and class conflicts, and stories to the extent that they are written in the gullied soil, the sagging rooftree of a house or the wrinkles of a tired face. The roles of text and illustration are completely reversed, as Ralph Thompson said a few days ago in The New York Times. The pictures state the theme of the book, whereas the prose serves as illustrative material.

"Landlord And Tenant"

W. T. Couch*

The latest production of Erskine Caldwell, "You Have Seen Their Faces," cannot be judged without reference to his other writings. His intention in this book seems to be that of arousing sympathy for Southern tenant farmers, black and white. I believe this intention is good and that nothing effective will be done to correct the bad conditions now prevailing generally throughout the South until the sympathy of the nation is aroused. At the same time, I am convinced that sympathy is not enough. There must be some real understanding, and the ideas in people's minds must have some correspondence with actual conditions as they exist. If the pictures of tenant farmers and of poor people in the South generally, as rendered in "God's Little Acre" and "Tobacco Road," are authentic, then

*Reprinted from *Virginia Quarterly Review*, 14 (Spring, 1938), 309–12.

there is little which can be done by landlord or tenant, by government or God, unless, of course, Mr. Caldwell's writings should so arouse the interest of the Deity that He would then proceed to make tenant, landlord, and land over again.

The short text of "You Have Seen Their Faces" contains much that is true, much that has been written many times before and that needs to be repeated over and over again until something effective is done. But if Mr. Caldwell in this work paints a more accurate picture of the tenant and the system in which he lives than we have been led to expect from him, this is not to say that he reproduces faithfully the colors, the true proportions, or the significant forms of those aspects of Southern life which he has chosen for his subject. It is not possible here to refer to more than a few of the aberrations in this book.

When Mr. Caldwell condemns the South for its "refusal to assimilate the blood of an alien race of another color, or to tolerate its presence," I cannot go along with him. It is not clear that the best future for Southern people could be achieved by intermingling of blood. A good case might be made out for the opposite view. The intermingling of blood in South American countries has not resulted in a high level of culture, and it is not beyond dispute that any high state of civilization has ever resulted from such intermingling. Furthermore, there is a substantial array of facts to support the argument that better relations exist between black and white in the Southern United States than between peoples of such widely different colors and heritages anywhere else in the civilized world. One has to know only a very little about the Negro in South Africa or in French West Africa to know that the nine million Negroes in the South have a far better chance to enjoy civilized life. I doubt whether anything can be done to improve living conditions for the Negro in the Southern United States unless the advantages which he already enjoys are recognized. Nothing is to be gained by a large indefinite sympathy which wishes to improve conditions, but which does not have knowledge of conditions elsewhere as a basis for comparison, and which therefore is of necessity lacking in any definite idea of what improvement is.

The South, says Mr. Caldwell, is a worn-out agricultural empire. Nevertheless, it produced last year eighteen million bales of cotton, the largest crop in the history of the region. "Cotton," says Mr. Caldwell, "was king, but it is not king any longer." But in spite of this pronouncement, the price of cotton remains the dominant factor in Southern life.

Mr. Caldwell is not optimistic about the plans which have been presented for the alleviation of the South's poverty. "What the South has most to fear," he writes, "are well meant, but irresponsible, plans for its regeneration." If those who have been studying Southern problems during the last ten or twenty years had formulated no better proposals than those Mr. Caldwell mentions, then I can understand how he could regard them as dangerous. "Sociologists of one school," he writes, "stake their reputations on a plan for the sterilization of the mentally and physically unfit among the tenant farmers." I should like to know who these sociologists are. "Another school," he continues, "hold to the belief that educational advantages and health instruction will suffice." He does not mention the regional planners or the Agrarians or other important schools of thought. He pooh-poohs the attribution of the South's poverty to such causes as slavery, climate, hookworm, insect pests, and high tariffs, and puts the whole burden on the greed of Southern landlords. He asserts that no plan thus far advocated for the relief of the South will be sufficient. He follows this with these two statements: "There is no reason to believe that any plan will succeed unless it were accompanied by reeducation and supervision," and "there are two means of bringing about a change, collective action by the tenant farmers themselves, or government control of cotton farming."

I fail to find anything new or enlightening in Mr. Caldwell's proposals. He is either woefully ignorant or he is simply indulging in the old political method of misrepresenting or inadequately representing the platforms of others, and then proposing measures which have long been familiar and are already partly in operation. But if Southern tenant farmers are at all like the Jeeter Lesters and Ty Ty Waldens with whom Mr. Caldwell has peopled his South, I cannot help wondering what good could come out of their collective action. Nor can much good be expected from government control if the persons controlled are the type that Mr. Caldwell has led us to believe now populate the South.

Margaret Bourke-White's photographs in "You Have Seen Their Faces" are as nearly perfect as any I have ever seen and they are excellently printed. However, the pictures do not confirm "the South's despair." On the contrary, many of them show people who seem to be healthy and happy in spite of poverty. The most extreme poverty is revealed by some, but those showing even the worst conditions may be matched many thousand times in New York City or in other metropolitan centers. A few weeks ago on a Saturday afternoon I walked by Manhattan Bridge and saw a crowd of several hundred men gathered together in a small space on the sidewalk near the bridge. I doubt whether as much misery could be found in several Southern counties as was huddled in this small space of a few hundred square feet. I do not offer this as an excuse for Southern complacency. On the contrary, I believe the South must recognize that evils of the kind Mr. Caldwell describes actually exist in this region, and must do what it can to correct them. But I do not believe anything good can be accomplished unless those who work on the problem have a balanced view of it.

Harry Harrison Kroll's "I Was a Share-Cropper" presents an entirely different picture of the tenant farmer, and I believe a much more authentic one than Mr. Caldwell has ever imagined. Mr. Kroll's work is autobiographical, and his recollections, I fear, have taken on a glow that is perhaps too warm and romantic. However, when you read his book, you know that events like those in his book have lived. He is a little too inclined, I think, to place the blame for the tenant's poverty on the tenant himself, whereas Mr. Caldwell places it all on the landlord. "I Was a Share-Cropper" is a book which will grow in favor, and which will rank with such classics as "The Time of Man." If we ever pass out of the present era of sentimental slush, of undiscriminating sympathy on the one hand and of merriment over psychopaths on the other, Mr. Caldwell's works will be forgotten.

"Erskine Caldwell's Picture Book"

Donald Davidson*

As might have been predicted, *You Have Seen Their Faces*, by Erskine Caldwell and Margaret Bourke-White, was prominently discussed in the metropolitan press, and here and there, as might also have been predicted, accusing fingers were leveled at a South "so sick from its old infections of prejudice and poverty that it is a menace to the nation." (The quoted remark is from a review in the New York *Nation*.) Less predictable, perhaps, was a tone of disappointment that ran through many of the reviews and that made the usual expressions of moral indignation over Southern conditions seem more perfunctory and forced than on many previous occasions, easily remembered. *You Have Seen Their Faces* was doubtless expected to be a Caldwellian *Uncle Tom's Cabin*, which through matter-of-fact pictures and text would substantiate Mr. Caldwell's previous matter-of-fiction accounts of Southern life. A public already accustomed to the visual treats of *Life*, *Look*, and *Pic* could hope for something supremely juicy from Mr. Caldwell and Miss Bourke-White.

To all who may have expected such as this, *You Have Seen Their Faces* must have seemed as tame as the magazine section of the New York *Times*. There are no *erotica curiosa* in the book. There are no candid camera shots of the harelipped girl tumbling lasciviously in the weeds, or of the mill-hand of *God's Little Acre* and his enamorata ceremonially unclothed, like Jurgen and Anaitis, before the staring rustics. Nor are there any *gesta turpia et diabolica* - no share croppers devoured by the boss's hogs, no old grandmothers bumped and flattened by ruthless automobilists; and (though there are chain gangs in authentic stripes) no Negroes are being hanged in chains or tortured in sweatboxes.

Instead, we have a group of sixty-four excellent photographic

*Reprinted from *Southern Review*, 4 (1938–39), 15–25.

studies, on the whole far more romantic than realistic in selection of subject and treatment. To accompany the pictures we have appropriate "legends," or dramatic speeches put into the mouths of the characters depicted. These, Mr. Caldwell states (in suitably small type, inconspicuously placed!), are in no case the actual words of the subjects. Mr. Caldwell has made them up to fit. "The legends under the pictures," he writes, "are intended to express the author's own conceptions of the sentiments of the individuals portrayed; they do not pretend to reproduce the actual sentiments of these persons." And here, as in the pictures, the average Southern reader, if not the Northern one, is compelled to admit that Mr. Caldwell has behaved a little more handsomely than might have been expected from his previous record. The legends too are more romantic than realistic. Often they are quite near to the genuine country idiom, and are surprisingly nonrebellious and uncomplaining. "It never felt much like Sunday to me till I picked the guitar some," is the sentiment attributed to a merry-looking fellow who picks a guitar while Grandpap listens. A nursing mother is made to say, "The littlest one gets taken care of." A pipe-smoking shanty-dweller says: "I spent ten months catching planks drifting down the river to build this house, and then the flood came along and washed the side of it off. Doggone if I don't like it better the way it is now." This easy-going philosophy is offset to some extent by a sharper pointing up of other "legends," and even more specifically by certain longer dramatic interludes in which share cropper, overseer, and landlord are made to speak either bitterly or overbearingly, in the roles one would expect a Marxian critic of the system to ascribe to them. But the general effect, while at times partial, is by no means offensively unfair, as documents fictional or non-fictional, when dealing with the complex problem of tenancy, sometimes have had a way of being.

Since the pictures are the most prominent objects in the book, they call for some special analysis to justify the observation I have made above, as to their romantic and realistic quality. Of the sixty-four pages of illustration, twenty-four would fall, by my classification at least, into the romantic category; twenty-three would be "realistic"; and seventeen are neutral, or may be put under either head according to one's personal tastes and predilections. I call romantic those pictures that give us faces smiling, happy, cheerful, vigorous, that tell or imply a sentimental or humorous story, or that suggest the fallen grandeurs and lush natural abundance traditionally associated with the "Deep South" and the "Cotton Kingdom." Of this order, for example, would be the following (since Mr. Caldwell has supplied no titles or page numbers I must make up titles): "Boy Ploughing" (it is "child labor," of course, but he is a ruddy strong fellow and seems to take it well!); "Negro Loafers Watching Ol' Man River"; "Crumbling Mansion, Mother, and Child" (used for a cover piece; it makes a looker think of Tara and *Gone with the Wind*); "Negro Granny, Laughing"; "Ploughed Hillside with Cloud Effects"; "Child

Eating Watermelon"; "Share Cropper Picking Guitar"; "Negro Sermon"; "Old Women on Porch." Of the realistic order are those pictures that show some notable excess of rags, dirt, disease, bad housing, or depressing environment; or that are meant, possibly, to suggest some brutality. For example, "Poor Folks Near Ringgold, Georgia, Pulling Wagon"; "Black Boy in the Jailhouse"; "Chain Gang with Armed White Guard"; "Paralyzed Negro Boy"; "Poor Whites Eating a Crust"; "Malnourished Whites"; "Old Woman with a Goiter"; "Shacks Covered with Bill Posters"; "Ragged Woman and Infant"; "Eroded Field"; "Snuffdipper and Infant"; "Overcrowded Negro School." Of the neutral type are those faces which have been photographed apparently because they make interesting subjects rather than because they convey any very explicit social message, and such items as the pictures of the political candidate, the white school room (which unlike the Negro one, at least has desks), the signboards put up by evangelists, and so on—all of which, though they may be intended to carry overtones of meaning, are not particularly exciting one way or the other.

Two general features of the photographs are worth some special note. First, they probably magnify the art of photography a good deal more than they magnify the social ills of the share-cropping system. They are camera studies done with a fine eye for composition and for the possibilities of the subject; they are not candid camera shots. They show that the faces of country people in the South have individual character, flavor, life. These faces are not flabby, they have not been smoothed and rounded out into undistinguished uniformity, as a similar collection of city faces might seem to be, but they are strong, irregular, often beautiful, with a wild and touching nobility. Even when ugly and coarse, they conceal no guile, they betray not overmuch frustration.

Second, the photographs, with their legends, may be taken, within limits, as representative, anyway, of conditions in regions where tenancy is heaviest. It would be absurd for a Southerner to set up any claim of unfairness here. Though he may easily think of photographic representations that might be more flattering in the social sense, he will have to concede that the photographer might have shown worse scenes, worse-looking folks. I have seen a share cropper's place in the Black Tobacco Patch where the cropper lived in a splendid house, owned hogs and cattle, and had upstanding sons who belonged to the Four-H Club. Also I have seen other share croppers' places in the Deep South that were more like the dens of wild animals than human habitation. The photographs hit between these two extremes.

But of course the photographic job is punily, sickeningly incomplete in quite another respect. Croppers and farmers are not the only tenant problem of the South. Nearly all Southerners are tenants, in effect or actuality. We have tenant-bankers, tenant-merchants, tenant-manufacturers, tenant-teachers, tenant-clergy, yes, and even so-called farm owners who are little better than hired hands. And the absentee landlord over these tenants and hired hands is the North. Rarely before in human history has a population of such numbers, in a land so rich, exerted so little responsible control over its own economic fate. We are all held in a bondage that is the more subtle because the chains and indentures are not actually visible. To be complete, therefore, Mr. Caldwell's photographic journalism would have to find a way of picturing these things, placing in juxtaposition, after the manner of *Life*, the eroded land and people of the South and the certainly noneroded land and people of the North. And there ought also to be pictures of matters that do not photograph well, but that may be charted or written about, such as economic imbalances and historic causes. Then there might be, too, some city squalors to show off against country squalors. But such completeness is not to be hoped for in photographic journalism. Mr. Caldwell's picture book, considered simply as picture book, is certainly fair-to-middling, by the strictest possible estimate. He shows fewer horrors, more variety, more poetry and strength than the same kind of photographs, made under nonpartisan auspices, that appear in the report of the President's Committee of Farm Tenancy.

But it is quite another thing when we come to Mr. Caldwell's text, which is a discussion of the tenancy problem itself. When we discover what interpretation we are supposed to make of the faces we have seen and what social action we are supposed to enter into, we are back in the dumps again. As a student of farm tenancy in the South Mr. Caldwell would make a splendid Curator of a Soviet Park of Recreation and Culture. The admirable photographs turn into fearsome cartoons and horrible effigies. The imagination of Mr. Caldwell may be a fine thing when it is behaving as an imagination should, though it does have a lamentable partiality for the grotesque. When it operates directly upon the data of Southern life and opines forthrightly on that subject, the Caldwellian imagination becomes irrepressible and sinister. It brings us to the dim lake of Auber, the dank tarn of Usher, the ghoul-haunted woodland of Weir.

There is a factual basis for Mr. Caldwell's argument about the evils of share cropping. Beneath his highly colored account of the situation it is possible to discern some dim outline of social and economic truth. One can tell that he has done a little reading; he has learned about erosion; he has a smattering of Southern history—a little less than a Georgia high school student, a little more than the average contributor to *The New Masses*. The share cropper biographies that he uses as *exempla* may be accepted as factually correct, as far as they go. Here and there he shows a half-hearted disposition to weigh in the balance the regional disadvantages of the South. It "has always been shoved around like a country cousin," he says. "It sits at second table and is fed short rations . . . It has been taking a beating for a long time . . . [It] will never be understood by the rest of America." And so on. But immediately such concessions are colored and changed by another kind of talk. "Mark against the South its failure to preserve its own culture and its refusal to accept the culture of the East and West. Mark against it the refusal to assimilate the blood of an alien race of another color or to tolerate its presence." Or, "the South perpetrated a feud, which was excusable in the beginning, and now it is guilty of perpetuating the quarrel, for which there is no excuse."

The South is "guilty," and, secondarily, Southern landlords of any and every sort are "guilty." That is the leading motif in Mr. Caldwell's interpretation. The factual basis, the occasional concessions, the scattered historical references—all mean nothing. Mr. Caldwell's argument puts the case of United States vs. the South back where it was a hundred years ago. It is the same old story of prosecution and judgment combined in one act:

> Fury said to a mouse
> Whom he met in the house,
> "Come, let's both go to law.
> I will prosecute you . . .
>
> "I'll be judge, I'll be jury,"
> Said the cunning old Fury.
> "I'll try the whole case
> And condemn you to DEATH!"

The only difference is that a Southerner with Marxian affiliations, who takes a Marxian line, assumes the rôle of Fury. All the rest is unchanged: we have the same errors and distortions of fact, the same innocent simplifications, the same nonchalant exclusion of testimony that might acquit the defendant, the same willingness to hand down a verdict beneficial to the prosecutor-judge. It is Olmstead, Garrison, John Brown, Thad Stevens, Charles Sumner, with modern trimmings.

The following is a summary of Mr. Caldwell's diagnostic description: i.e., what we are supposed to think that the pictures and legends demonstrate about the South.

Ten million [sic] people now live under the "yoke" of the sharecropping system. This system is a direct outgrowth of the plantation system, which is an "anti-social" device for raising cotton. The plantation system which depended on slave labor was ruined by the War; the South then discovered it could not catch up economically with the East and West. So it retreated into isolation. It thought up share cropping (1) as a means of keeping the Negro, and with him the poor white, in a kind of slavery and (2) "as a means of getting even with the North." The general villain is the South, which insists on being "a worn out agricultural empire." The particular villain is the Southern landlord. If he has a hundred tenants, each of whom makes six bales of cotton, he gets three hundred bales and each tenant gets only three. The landlord makes the profit; he is wealthy and generally cruel. He has the power of law and wealth behind him. He is the pernicious agent of an agricultural system "that acquires share croppers and mules for their economic usefulness and disposes of them when no more profit can be extracted from their bodies."

Such is the economic diagnosis, but we should not neglect to point out that Mr. Caldwell has added a little sociological-journalistic coloring to it. Upon this economic picture we must superimpose the picture of the South which has great currency in the North—being first disseminated in the 1920's by Mencken and Company and by Gerald Johnson and other Southern "liberals." That is, it is a South which makes women work in the fields; which knows not the blessings of the birth control movement; which releases its "pent-up emotions by lynching the black man in order to witness the mental and physical suffering of another human being"; which makes every white face the Negro sees "a reminder of his brother's mutilation, burning, and death at the stake"; which has rabble-rousers as leaders; which has, for religion, an opium of the people contrived to keep them servile—it excites "the ignorant who live primitive lives to give vent to their feelings by rolling on the floor, shouting, and dancing in the aisles"; which takes a contrary delight in race prejudice, backwardness, poverty, illiteracy, and social snobbery. Furthermore, this is the only South that exists at all! It is the only South presented in Mr. Caldwell's discussion, and he has taken pains to add some photographs that echo this long-established caricature.

Now for the remedy, which is as simple as the diagnosis. Mr. Caldwell would welcome a government investigation into the share-cropping evil. He would also welcome government control of cotton farming. But in any case, over and above all else, the remedy is collectivism. What Mr. Caldwell wants is a labor union for the share croppers—not farm ownership (for many of them would prefer not to have the responsibility of ownership) but "adequate pay" . . . "the same protection from unscrupulous employers that workers in steel mills and department stores receive." If we do not seize upon this remedy, we are warned to expect a genuine social uprising. The tenant farmer will, Mr. Caldwell assures us, takes matters into his own hands; and he will find that his long experience of hardship will "stand him in good stead when the time comes for him to begin thinking *about taking over the job of raising cotton* [*Italics mine*]."

It is easy enough to check off Mr. Caldwell's grosser errors of fact. The 1935 Census reports only 716,356 share croppers for the entire South, including the border states. There cannot be *ten million persons* living under the "yoke" of the share-cropping system. Share cropping was not a devilish invention got up by the South to reënslave the Negro and spite the North. It was the only resource of the postbellum South, which still had land to work, but no money. It was, and still is, one practical means of raising staple crops in a section that gets relatively little return on its produce, and that does not know how else to guarantee its annual labor supply, which is likely at any time to move to the nearest city. Or if one wants to be broadly historical, it is no more an outgrowth of the plantation system in particular than of America's historic fondness for the old fee simple system of land tenure, which, however abused by later generations, seemed to our forefathers the very "palladium" of liberty. Furthermore, there is share cropping everywhere in the United States, not only in the South. It sometimes works badly in the big-plantation regions, but it has not always worked badly elsewhere. It is entirely possible that the relatively serious condition of the tenant farmers in the South and the recent large increases in tenancy are not a specific indictment of the plantation system, but are symptomatic of the critical condition of agriculture, bad everywhere, but naturally worst in the cotton regions, which were economically sick long before the day of photographic journalism.

These facts are well known to all serious students of farm tenancy and share cropping. They are available in all kinds of documents—magazine articles, pamphlets, books, and government reports. They were available to Erskine Caldwell, but I doubt whether, even if such material had been put into his hands, he would have used it. The facts indicate a highly complex situation; and Mr. Caldwell could do nothing with a complex situation. He wanted it simple and stark. He made it simple and stark. He does not want a solution. He wants a fight. His book, published first in a deluxe edition at $7.50 for the penthouses and later in a seventy-five cent edition for the newsstands, has the beautiful simplicity of all engines of propaganda. The North is supposed to read it, as it once read abolitionist pamphlets; and next comes, I suppose, the 1938 equivalent of Beecher Bibles; and then in Arkansas and Mississippi the modern parallel to Bleeding Kansas. If we could be certain that *You Have Seen Their Faces* would have the effect apparently intended, it would be easy enough to predict the course of events and Mr. Caldwell's share in them.

One can hardly deem his intentions innocent, for he is a Southerner, and he himself knows what he has left out of his account. He was left out, for example, the entire tale told by Webb in *Divided We Stand*: the whole tragic story of the great agricultural region dominated and exploited by the careless sway of the still greater industrial region. He left out of account the well-known fact that the average Southern landlord is almost as much a victim as the share cropper. But for the recent intervention of the Triple-A there might not have been any Southern landlords for Mr. Caldwell to rail against; most Southern plantations would now be among the frozen assets of banks, mortgage companies, or insurance companies (chiefly Northern-owned), as many of them are, indeed, at this moment. Faulty as the Southern landlord may be in some respects (and I certainly do not propose to whitewash him) he does not deserve to be the villain of Mr. Caldwell's piece—except, perhaps, in certain limited areas where highly commercialized plantations are administered with studied irresponsibility by absentee landlords. If the cropper has a case against the landlord, the landlord also has a case against the cropper. No farmer in Vermont, New York, Ohio, or Kansas would put up with, in his farm labor, what the Southern landlord inescapably *must* put up with. But in any case the ultimate villain is the industrial system which makes machinery, fertilizer, and clothing high and cotton low in price; and the industrial system is not controlled by the South, least of all by the Southern cotton-grower.

As for investigation by a government commission, that has already been done, and little has come of it.

As for share croppers' unions, they are reasonable enough in theory, I suppose, if the great plantations are going to become simply units of an industrialized agriculture—which is probably what Mr. Caldwell wants. But even with an industrialized agriculture and share croppers' unions, the relative economic disadvantage of the Southern producer would remain untouched. If the plantation gave the share cropper "adequate pay," according to some scale devised by Mr. Caldwell, he probably would be not only without profit but without a plantation. If that is to happen, the cotton land of the South had as well as signed over to Northern capital at once, without the agony of a further decay. But Mr. Caldwell does not really want that either. He wants an uprising. He is a Marxian, who has learned nothing from Stalinized Russia.

But it is probably useless to make such points. It is useless to subject Mr. Caldwell to critical analysis. He will never mend his ways. There is no easy way, either, of reaching, with the coolest possible critical analysis, the people whose opinions he hopes to influence. They do not read *The Southern Review*. Most of them do not know that it exists. But they will read *You Have Seen Their Faces*, and, because their minds are already "conditioned" in a certain direction, will accept Mr. Caldwell's interpretation of his pictures. There is no effective means open to the South for combating that interpretation. The best that the South can hope for is that the thousands of readers of *You Have Seen Their Faces* will, like some of the reviewers, be bored and inactive, since after all it is a very old story.

Is there any particular admonition that a Southerner could give to those readers, provided he should by some miracle be able to reach them? I can think of one admonition of special importance. Let the Northern reader, before he grows indignant over Southern conditions, be sure, be *very* sure, that in no way he himself is profiting at the expense of the Southern share cropper—and landlord. If any part of his income is derived from the sale of high-priced manufactured articles, if he clips any coupons from industrial paper, insurance stocks, *et cetera*, he is in all likelihood *particeps criminis*—he is sustained by the lifeblood of the victim he would pity as the victim of "an outworn agricultural empire."

And one more admonition. The South can never even make a decent beginning toward settling its economic problems if while engaged earnestly in the process of studying them, it is constantly summoned to court and forced to answer libelous and malicious proceedings against its character. That has been said before. It cannot be said too often.

From all this it should appear that a great deal is the matter with Mr. Caldwell. Just what, I do not think I need to say in the most precise terms. What is the matter with any Southerner who turns state's evidence under circumstances like these? Are the proceeds of *You Have Seen Their Faces* and other notable works devoted to charity?

"From Comedy to Pity"

Jonathan Daniels*

The time has come to worry about Erskine Caldwell. He was safe as long as the so-called forces of righteousness were trying to save the American reader from the contamination of his American writing. But queerly and increasingly, in the midst of tales which the conventional American moralist would never approve, he seems to be becoming, in more and more conventional and sentimental form, an American moralist himself. There may have been always a will to expose and reform behind the cackling laughter he evoked out of the Southern lower depths, but it was unobstrusive in stout native comedy which was excellent for its own sake. If Caldwell began as one of the later day Abolitionists (which I doubt), he was a rare exception to their screaming solemnity. But now, though in this book much comedy remains, fresh as stories told about the gin house door, five of the last six stories in the new collection are perilously close to that deliberate stirring of pity for a purpose which is permissible in preachers but is scarcely a basis for such a substantial reputation as properly belongs to Caldwell.

Of course, comedy remains among these stories. From old Governor Gil who decided to marry his tenant's young hellcat of a daughter to Gus Richards who came home once a year or so to fuss with his wife and tear up her chairs, Mr. Caldwell has made in his excellent and apparently effortless characterization a whole gallery of folk who stir a laughter which not only amuses but disturbs. But when Mr. Caldwell writes of young people, boy and girl, man and woman caught in love and hunger at the same time, it seems to me that his implicit demand for economic improvement takes the art form and the art attitude used by backwoods evangelists in shaping anecdotes aimed at eliminating sin. Mr. Caldwell makes sound laughter, but when he turns deliberately heart-rending, in my case at least he makes no tears at all.

*Reprinted from *Saturday Review of Literature*, 18 (June 18, 1938), 7.

But if a new solemnity is slipping into his writing, there is in it no loss of veracity in the people about whom he writes. They rise in Georgia as indigenous as a Georgia hill. That they are Southern folk, clearly, honestly, and vividly drawn, is certain; but that their doings are "Southways," as a Southern patriot I presume to doubt. The pitiful and the peculiar, the greedy and the hungry and the lustful and the ridiculous had shaped stories in a wide, sometimes weird world long before Mr. Caldwell opened his on the too many insanities and injustices of the South. This South is a strange land, but so are all lands strange and readers and writers are sometimes as queer as the far folk they put in or take out of books. Southways in general are the ways of the world.

"Out of Georgia"

Dorothy Van Doren*

By comparison with the number of novels published in a year, volumes of short stories are few and far between. Volumes of good short stories are fewer and farther. The great bulk of short stories appear in magazines; they are ephemeral, inconsiderable, written, one sometimes suspects, without conscience; obviously written without art. Once in a while a Ring Lardner comes along, a writer who appeals to a wide public and at the same time gains the highest sort of critical approval. Lardner's baseball stories appeared in the *Saturday Evening Post* and commanded an extremely high price. Mr. Caldwell has not yet reached these heights. But if Lardner wrote "Alibi Ike" and "You Know Me, Al," he also wrote "The Champ" and "Some Like Them Cold," too grimly satirical, perhaps, for the popular taste. And Mr. Caldwell's compact and cruel stories of the South deserve to be compared with them.

It would be interesting and instructive to analyze one of the stories in "Southways" to see exactly how a good short-story writer achieves his effects. The first story is less than twelve pages long. It is about a Southern landowner who wants to marry the daughter of one of his tenants; but the girl will not have him. That is all there is to it, yet Mr. Caldwell in a few pages manages to say so much more than merely that. He says, for one thing, that the South is poor, not poor with a genteel, pretty poverty, but poor in every sense: the land is poor, the only crop is cotton, the houses— even of the gentry—are without paint, weeds crowd up to the front doors; the tenants have one garment to their backs and without surprise or complaint make a meal of bread and molasses; the landowners, if they have enough to eat and to wear, are poor in spirit and in character. There is a kind of dour democracy between master and tenant which arises out of a

*Reprinted from *Nation*, 146 (June 25, 1938), 730. Copyright © 1938 The Nation Associates.

mutual desperation, and expresses itself sometimes in wry humor. Daisy, when Governor Gil—he was governor of his state for a term many years before—commands her to come up to the big house to go to bed, has only one comment to make. She says: "You damned old fool." When her father hears from the Negro houseboy that she has bitten and scratched her elderly suitor, he laughs until he falls off his chair. Mr. Caldwell does not describe the eyes or hair or height of his characters. He merely says that Governor Gil habitually strikes off the heads of weeds with his stick—except the weeds around his own front door. He makes Daisy known to his readers by having her father say: "Just about all she's got to her name is that little slimsy gingham jumper she's wearing." He illuminates the gulf between Negro and white by having the Negro houseboy say to the poor tenant: "Mr. Walter, Governor said to tell you if you ever raise another hellcat like Miss Daisy, he'll chop your head off. Now, Mr. Walter, I didn't say it! Please, sir, don't think I said it! . . . You know I wouldn't say that myself, don't you, Mr. Walter?"

In the space of eleven and a half pages, in short, a culture is revealed, a land is described by indirection, a situation is created, suspense follows, and the resolution is at last snapped off. A good deal to have done in a short space, and only the greatly skilled can do it. The other stories in the volume are almost all equally skilful. They are laid in Mr. Caldwell's Georgia, which, if no other Georgian would acknowledge it, has as much reality as Gulliver's Lilliput. It exists in Mr. Caldwell's mind, and he projects it into the mind of the reader. It has length and breadth, heat and cold, squalor, cold jest, and contention. There is no crepe myrtle blooming around the dooryards in this book, but its men and women are real. A great many readers will be grateful for them.

"Caldwell's Stories"

Otis Ferguson*

If you have any interest in the way the quick turn of a short story can give you glimpses of people living their lives, you couldn't do much better today than Erskine Caldwell's new collection.

Caldwell is getting closer than ever to bringing two ways of seeing and feeling into a single way of writing. In most of the early stuff you could (many did) trace a social meaning if it pleased you, but it hadn't been consciously put there: it was a mere necessary adjunct to a writer's delight in his material and his craft. But ideas were afoot and Caldwell knew a writer just couldn't sit around and be delighted. So he began to impose social point from outside, and one of the classic examples of the

*Reprinted from *New Republic*, 85 (July 6, 1938), 258.

dividing line between what is inside and what is spread on is still "God's Little Acre," where the unspoiled real-fantasy of the first half (almost as if the writer had read a copy of The Daily Worker overnight) turns into the last half, where the symbols of fun-in-bed and strike-in-the plant are brought together, to their mutual confusion and embarrassment. The writing is of course swell all the way through: you can't unlearn to be a writer just by reading the exhortations of those who aren't.

"Southways" has two types of story: the picture of men being stunted or wrecked by powers as immanent, inscrutable and everlasting as the old gods; the picture of men caught in their own foibles or catching them by the tail, bawdy and unashamed on the lower levels of sophistication, drinking, handseling, swapping hound dogs or beating the old woman a little, all with more natural shrewdness and pure gusto than it takes to get into the Senate or the magazines. Still, I cannot remember one of the sixteen pieces in which the idea is not conceived and worked out in the vein appropriate to it. The wretched ways of social injustice crop up in more places than that of the primary boss-worker conception. Three stories are concerned with the tragedy of white over Negro, one of them comical on the surface. Three have to do with some warping personal devil. But while there are in addition only two direct class indictments ("Wild Flowers" and "A Knife to Cut the Cornbread With"), there is felt throughout, just as you might sense it in the ordinary world, the many strong teeth just under and behind the easy grin.

For a touch of humor in humanity, a touch of sweetness, I'd pick "Uncle Henry's Love Nest"; for deepness of human trouble, "Return to Lavinia" and the two purely social ones mentioned. "The Night My Old Man Came Home" is nearest to the Caldwell of "The Grass Fire" and the way they preserved God's little acre—but the old crazy zest seems to have sobered a little. The wild marchgrass of the imagination is thinning, and at the same time a more utilitarian crop, with deeper roots, is being matured.

Without prediction or devices of exhortation (the Lord knows a man of Caldwell's prose could tell any critic writing today to go read his own work for a change), I should say this book was an interim report. Caldwell has been most successful as he has brought his life-as-observed material into the fantasy of story-telling and legend, by such tricks of private vision and such an ear for the lift of speech, by such imperceptible planning and joining, that he couldn't help being book-reviewed as a "realist" from the first. But from this book you can see that he is handicapped in handling straight tragedy by the very simplification, and heightening to the unreal, which served him so well in the earlier vein. He seems to plot and stage and stack the cards a little. But if at the same time he can bring what he has in him out in something of novel length and flight, he will *have* something there.

"The Land That Is No More"

Maurice Hindus*

This is a travel book. The text is by Erskine Caldwell and the photographs by Margaret Bourke-White. The subject is Czecho-Slovakia as it was in the pre-Munich days, with catastrophe shadowing land and people. It is a thin book with comparatively little text—eight short sketches (there should have been twice as many)—and with not too many photographs.

Yet it is one of the most extraordinary travel books I have ever read. Author and photographer wander at will in city and village, in Bohemia, Moravia, Slovakia, Ruthenia, and they record only those scenes and experiences which have inner meaning. Caldwell writes entirely in terms of symbols. Consider the titles of some of the chapters: "The *Roads* of Uzhorod," "*Bread* in Uzok," "*Dogs* in Ceske Budejvice." By means of these symbols the author unfolds, with a striking economy of words, now a drama, now an epoch, now a mood and now, as in the opening chapter, a sweeping panorama of things and people. The purely Slavic flavor of his conversations with peasants, especially the Ruthenians (who are as magnificent in their eloquence as are Russian peasants) eludes Caldwell. But he never fails to perceive the inner meaning of their words or their lives.

The chapter on "Peace in Brno," in the light of Hitler's recent seizure of Bohemia and Moravia, is especially significant. Brno is the capital of Moravia. Caldwell found it an attractive and humane city, with Czechs, Germans, Jews, living in peace with one another and giving generously toward the support of the refugees that had come from Austria and Germany. Left to itself Brno, as well as all Czecho-Slovakia, would have been an example to the rest of the world of racial amity and religious tolerance. Now, with the swastika flying over it, the place has already become a citadel of savagery. The group of brilliant writers who published the Brno Lidovy Noviny, one of the most famous newspapers in Europe and often spoken of as Czecho-Slovakia's Manchester Guardian, has been broken up and several of them have already been sent to concentration camps. The photographs are even more impressive than the text. They reveal more of the lyric of Czecho-Slovakia as it was and more of the tragedy of the country as it is now. Consider the photographs bearings the inscriptions, "The Hungarian Boss and Slovak Peasants," "Hungarian Landlord at Ease" and "Field Workers' Dormitory." Here you have the medievalism of Hungarian civilization boldly and unforgettably depicted. This of course is not the civilization of Budapest, with its brilliant cafés, its gay night clubs, its social swank. This is the Hungary that Budapest seldom sees but

*Reprinted from *New Republic*, 98 (April 12, 1938), 284.

which supplies the nutriment that goes into its glitter and swank. Here side-by-side with the swagger, the self-confidence, the charm and the brutality of the work-hating Hungarian nobleman, are the misery and degradation of the toiling Slav peasantry. The Czecho-Slovak republic had effectively undermined the powers and prerogatives of the Hungarian landlord. It had brought to Slovakia and Ruthenia schools, medical services, a new system of agriculture and a respect for the human individuality which the peasantry there had never known. Munich has smashed it all, and now the Hungarian nobleman is once more enthroning serfdom over all Ruthenia and a part of Slovakia. In the above-mentioned photographs Miss Bourke-White has caught all the drama and pathos of an aspect of the Munich agreement and its aftermath which no journalist has as yet bothered to record.

"Lynching Bee"

Richard Wright*

This time Erskine Caldwell's theme is lynching, that haunting symbol of America's desire to right "wrongs" with adolescent violence. In language as simple, melodious and disarming as the drawl of his outlandish characters, Caldwell depicts the bucolic tenderness and almost genial brutality that overtakes a Southern community when a white woman has been "raped." Hovering grimly in the background of the lynching is King Cotton, an inanimate character whose influence is as fatal as that of any living being, and whose rise and fall on the commodity market sets the narrow channel through which the political, social and even personal destinies of the other characters flow.

The character in the foreground, Sheriff McCurtain, turns out to be a damp rag in the face of a whirlwind. Caldwell accounts for his sheriff and the subsequent lynch panic in wider terms of social and political reference than he has heretofore used in his fiction, and the result is a picture of an unheroic man who is pitiably human. With a political boss to order him about; with two hundred pounds of fat to tote around at ninety in the shade; with a desire to "keep this lynching politically clean"; with a political opponent seeking to send all Negroes back to Africa; a bitter hatred of swamp mosquitoes; and a sentimental love for "niggers" who commit petty wrongs—with all this against him, the sheriff tries to follow his wife's advice to go fishing until the lynching "blows over." In his blundering generosities and naïve sense of fitness, Sheriff Jeff makes us understand why lynchings are possible.

Katy Barlow, Aryan and oversexed, is surprised by Narcissa

*Reprinted from *New Republic*, 102 (March 11, 1940), 351–52.

Calhoun, an aspiring political spinster, as she solicits a Negro boy on a Georgia road. The boy, Sonny Clark, runs away because he is not only mortally afraid of her, but is a virgin. Narcissa persuades Katy to give the traditional alarm of "rape"; a mob forms under the leadership of Katy's father and terrorizes the Negro quarters. Just as small boys pour salt on snails to watch their agonized convulsions, so the mobsters casually pour turpentine on the bodies of Negro women to see them writhe and tear their flesh with their nails.

Fear is the pivot of the story: plantation owners are afraid that their fields will be ruined by the mob; Katy is afraid that her claim of rape will be revealed as a falsehood; her father is afraid of what neighbors will think if he does not avenge his daughter; the sheriff is afraid that if Sonny Clark is *not* lynched his political enemies will drum up enough racial panic to make him lose the impending election; the political boss, Judge Allen, is afraid that something will happen *one* way or the *other*; Sonny Clark is really more afraid of leaving home than of facing the mob, since he has never been away from his grandmother before. The most poignant fear of all is that of Glenn, the cotton farmer, who, discovering Sonny Clark hiding out in the woods, is afraid to help him escape for fear of being called a "nigger-lover." Some of the most laughable, human and terrifying pages Caldwell has ever written deal with Sonny trotting with doglike obedience at the heels of Glenn, who is trying to decide what to do with him. When the perplexed boy learns that he is to be given over to the mob, he pleads for Glenn to shoot him, and Glenn, choking with pity because "the niggers has always to put up with it," answers, "I ain't got a gun to do it with."

Katy basks in the glory of her martyrdom until the taunts of her fiancé prod her to hysteria. Then, shamed and fearful, she screams out the Negro boy's innocence when she sees him swinging from a tree. "It ought to put an end to lynching the colored for all time," the disconsolate sheriff mutters as he stumbles away from Katy's body. She had been stoned to death by the mob when it learned that she had lied.

P.S. Do not accept as good Caldwellian fun Narcissa Calhoun's idea of shipping the Negroes back to Africa. Caldwell was serious, no matter how fantastic it sounds, for such notions are being aired in the halls of Congress today.

"Caldwell Lynches Two Negroes"

Burton Rascoe*

Bogey in reading time for the new Erskine Caldwell novel is two hours flat. Like Steinbeck's *Of Mice and Men*, it is a tour de force; but, unlike the Steinbeck, it is neither original in theme nor novel in treatment. For fluidity, concision, clarity, proper balance of narrative and dialogue, deft use of suspense in the building of climax, and precise employment of vocabulary it might serve, to students of composition, as a classical example of how to write an exciting novel—and as a classical example of what not to write about.

It begins to look a little as though the Arvin Hickses and Freeman Cantwells of the League of American Writers had creased Caldwell with their Marxian dumdum bullets, roped and dragged him into their corral, branded this literary Meddlesome Jack with the hammer and sickle, rechristened him Social Significance, and even got him into believing that he is something quite different from what he is. Critics who get a reputation for profundity by writing great gobs of stuff that is almost impossible to read and quite impossible to understand—except for some unconnected sentences here and there—have been known to do this, after they have adopted some simple genius at story-telling as a pet exemplar of their theories and as a special recipient of their encomia. Waldo Frank and Paul Rosenfield nearly ruined Sherwood Anderson by writing 3000-word articles for highbrow periodicals, declaring somewhere therein something to the effect that Sherwood was a great naïf *intuitif*, undoubtedly an autochthonous *philosophe*. Sherwood couldn't find out what he was from his pocket-dictionary and had to go ask Lewis Galantière what the words meant. When he learned that he was supposed to be a natural-born wise man who thought great thoughts instinctively, Sherwood got to thinking he *was* one and got to writing out so much of the stuff he imagined was deep thought that it was hard for his friends to get him back to writing his short stories again.

Caldwell is a marvellously clever literary technician, especially expert in depicting with finesse both the comic and pathetic aspects of lubricity. As Carl Van Doren says in *The American Novel*, Caldwell with his sure art, never feverish or foggy like Faulkner, can invent a story and so write it that the reader instinctively accepts it as an old folk-tale. And he can make his most outrageous invention sound as though it were an exact, naturalist record of something that happened.

This quite precious art of Caldwell's is what has misled the Marxian muttonheads. Incapable of accepting creative imagination as creative im-

*Reprinted from *American Mercury*, 49 (April, 1940), 493–99.

agination, they have taken *We Are the Living, God's Little Acre*, and *Tobacco Road* to be authentic transcriptions of life among the Georgia crackers, social documents designed to expose the horrors of capitalist exploitation. If *Tobacco Road*, either as a play or novel, is a naturalistic transcription from life, so is Wycherley's *The Country Wife*. People have wondered why *Tobacco Road* has the longest continuous run of any play in the history of the American theatre. Such people must never have been to a burlesque show. The scene from *Tobacco Road* in which the girl squirms on her belly and writhes her legs is shrewdly designed to produce more caloric suspense in the audience than a strip-tease by the best bump and grind *artiste* in burleycue show business. And the to-do on the stage about the nuptial peepshow, faithfully transcribed from the novel, is another conspicuous example of Caldwell's genius so to invent and treat an incident that it seems as though it weren't something Caldwell had thought up but a marvellous example of bawdy old barnyard folk-tale.

Caldwell displays some of his fine talent for grim but robust humor in *Trouble in July*, but the central theme is so trite and has been exploited so often that one can explain his using it only on the assumption that he is beginning to take seriously his rôle as a crusader for social and economic reform. The idea was used by Waldo Frank in *Chalk Face*, by Roy Flannagan in *Amber Satyr*, twice by T. S. Stribling, once in *Birthright* and again in *Teeftallow*, and it appears in an English variation in E. M. Forster's *A Passage to India*. In the earliest version, of course, it is the story of Joseph and Potiphar's wife. It is about the white girl who wants a Negro to lie with her and who, when frustrated in her desire, accuses the innocent boy of raping her; and a lynching of the boy follows.

Caldwell gets hold of an incidental theme of profounder aesthetic and social importance but he muffs it and makes little out of it, chiefly, I believe, because his comic sense causes him first to conceive the sheriff (protagonist of the incidental theme) as a ridiculous character, callous, insensitive, henpecked, given to jailing Negro wenches for carnal reasons or suspected of it by his wife, and constantly falling into comical difficulties through stupidity and incompetence. A caricature can't be made to carry a deeply serious argument *and realize it*; and not all of Caldwell's talent can make it credible that this buffoon of a sheriff is brought to an acute critical realization of all the flaws in the democratic process of government, through the means Caldwell supplies. The idea is, simply, that the sheriff is an old man, really holding a sinecure; he depends upon the people's vote to keep him in that sinecure; if the people want to hang a Negro, he will lose their vote and his livelihood if he tries to prevent them.

Caldwell attempts to make the ethical implication of the sheriff's cogitation on that personal aspect of his problem dawn upon him, not through the hanging of the Negro boy or through the girl's confession that she lied, but through the hanging of an old idiot Negro he had given to the blood-thirsty mob as a hostage against his promise to deliver the Negro boy to them. Caldwell ends on a bathetic note as incongruous as when the burlesque queen, wearing a G-string, a black lace brassière and a purple scarf draped over arms and shoulders, shakes a couple of small American flags and sings, "Land . . . of . . . thuh . . . Pil . . . groms' pride." He has the sheriff recall an officer's oath to do his duty as he sees it, without fear or favor, and then say aloud, "That's a mighty pretty oath for a man in public office to swear to. . . . I guess I had sort of forgotten it," and walk blindly down the road, alone.

II

Incidentally, according to Monroe W. Work, department of records and research, Tuskegee Institute, and editor of *The Negro Year Book* (the authority quoted in the 1940 *World Almanac*), there were six lynchings in the United States during 1938, all of Negroes; none of the persons lynched was in the hands of the law when seized; there were forty-two instances in which officers of the law prevented lynchings. Also, since 1882 there have been in Arizona twenty-nine lynchings of whites, no Negroes; in Colorado, sixty-six whites, two Negroes; New Mexico, thirty-three whites, three Negroes; California, forty-one whites, two Negroes; Oregon, twenty whites, one Negro; South Dakota, twenty-seven whites, no Negroes; Washington, twenty-five whites, one Negro; North Dakota, thirteen whites, three Negroes; Nebraska, fifty-two whites, five Negroes; Idaho, twenty whites, no Negroes; Oklahoma, eighty-two whites, forty-one Negroes. There have been seventeen Negro lynchings in Illinois, fourteen in Indiana, twenty-seven in Maryland, sixteen in Ohio, seventy in Missouri, six in Pennsylvania. Caldwell's native Georgia, in fifty-six years, is second. Mississippi leads with a total of 568 lynchings, forty-one being of whites. Georgia's total is 507, of which thirty-seven were of whites.

Caldwell's book and these statistics, taken in conjunction with Percival Jackson's *Look at the Law* and Ralph H. Gabriel's *The Course of American Democratic Thought*, and correlated with such earlier publications as Oberholtzer's *A History of the United States Since the Civil War* and the Chapel Hill publication, *Culture in the South*, edited by W. T. Couch, bring to my mind the fact that the literary exploitation of Negro lynchings in the South, particularly the invariable use of the dramatic device of making the Negro innocent, has made it important, if not actually imperative, that quite a number of contingencies should be clarified and that a lot of smug, pharisaical Northern heads should be shaken around and cuffed with a little knowledge in the interests of common fairness, if not of intersectional amity.

Northern writers and Southern writers (who have to depend in large measure upon New York publishers, New York critics, and New York outlets to Northern bookstores for their acceptance, critical notice and appreciation, advertising, promotion and royalty checks), by appealing directly or indirectly, consciously or unconsciously, to Northern preconceptions, Northern ignorance, Northern taste, Northern temperaments and Northern complacency, have not only over-emphasized flaws in the South but have falsified the South by this very over-emphasis and have done it with full appreciation of the fact that the South cannot effectively hit back, dissipate the fallacies, or even plead very cogent factors in extenuation. Except for its subsidized university publications, the South has no media but its newspapers, which are often owned by Northern capital and even when not are restrained from correcting Northern misconceptions simply by the knowledge that whatever they might say would be discounted in the North as mere ebullitions of professional Southern pride.

I herewith set down, as concisely as possible, some salient facts:

The North, after the Civil War, imposed upon the South the most humiliating and crippling peace ever imposed by a victor upon a conquered people, short of complete annihilation. The North enfranchised the Negroes and, under the "iron clad" test oath of 1862, disfranchised the Southern whites! Under the act of March 2, 1867, "to provide for the more efficient government of the rebel states," this test was invoked to make it impossible for any Southern white who had served the Confederacy or had in any way given aid and comfort to the rebel forces, to become a registrar at the polls, and, in the cases of hundreds of thousands of literate whites of voting age, even to vote. The North freed the Negroes but left them where they were and did nothing about them except provide the means for scoundrelly Northern carpetbaggers to exploit them for the theft and expropriation of Southern property. (*Vide*, Oberholtzer, Vol. II, *The Klan*, pp. 1–391.)

We have heard a vast deal about the Ku Klux Klan, old and more recent, most of it justifiably abhorrent. Well, the first Klan was organization in defense, and in retaliation, against the hugest, most horrible, most sinister secret society the country has ever known—the Loyal League, a federated society of Negroes and Northern white skunks, with branches in every county of every state in the South. These Northern swindlers, selling the ignorant Negroes four wooden pegs for four dollars, told them a Negro could stick them down anywhere at four corners of a piece of land and the government would deed it to him even if it embraced his late master's choicest lands. They played on the Negroes' voodoo superstitions and put them up to killing off all the cattle of the whites, stealing their horses and mules, and plundering their fields and storehouses at night. They sold the Negroes whiskey in exchange for stolen cotton, tobacco, horses, mules and other chattels.

Northerners, swarming down and controlling the electorate, the constabulary and the judiciary throughout the South, made such a mockery of the law, the courts, and of justice that they implanted in the minds of decent Southerners such contempt for judicial procedure and such loathing for shyster trickery that not until very recent years have they been able to get over the effects. In serious matters such as rape and murder, the Southerners had come to have such a low opinion of the judicial process that they would not entrust the issue of such matters to corruptible, incompetent judges, tricky lawyers and the delays and loopholes of the law. They sometimes took the law into their own hands, and not merely for the sadistic pleasure of it, as they have so often been pictured as doing by the litterateurs, but out of a feeling of grim necessity. One almost entertains a half-wish that an honorable group of decent men would arise in New York and go expeditiously about such a prophylaxis in cleaning out the corruption of our New York courts so hideously revealed in *Gang Rule in New York* by Craig Thompson and Allen Raymond.

In spite of the sentimentalists, there are Negroes capable of committing rape, just as there are whites who are capable of it. There were 8,302 rape cases tried in the courts in the United States during one year, 1938! Of the 8,302 defendants quite a few, who were found guilty and punished, were Negroes. In New York City, whites outnumber the blacks in the committing of rape and murder; but, as the records show in the Thompson and Raymond book, if you are a successful mobster you can commit rape and murder with relative impunity: a rape charge seems especially hard to make stick. Finally, as Percival Jackson quite conclusively shows, it *is* very hard for an ordinary, decent American citizen, with little money and no political resources, to get a square deal in the courts of the USA, particularly in large Northern cities. But the answer is: the law is just what the layman makes it, no more. It is high time for some Northern laymen, particularly litterateurs, to wipe their noses and shut up about the South.

"American Lower Depths"

Jonathan Daniels*

It seems to me that it is time for some decision as to whether Erskine Caldwell is a writer concerned with the socially significant in the lower depths of American life or whether he has found modern pay dirt in comedy at the expense of the half-wit and the deformed, which so delighted audiences long ago.

This new "Tragic Ground" is certainly ground that could be tragic but it comes out in straight Caldwellian fashion as a farce about hunger, about homesickness, about nakedness, and juvenile delinquency. Indeed, if anything distinguishes this book from "Tobacco Road," it is that the town lights are brighter even when seen from the trash dump and the

*Reprinted from *Saturday Review of Literature*, 27 (Oct. 14, 1944), 46.

little girls, who thoroughly enjoy juvenile delinquency, are prettier. There is not a harelip among them and somehow the deformed social situation which makes them prostitutes at twelve and fourteen seems more amusing than heartbreaking.

In this book Mr. Caldwell makes a part of his comedy from the obvious ludicrousness of some social workers facing tragedy either with big, misunderstood words out of the books or the flat-footed distaste of a cop. While there are passages which should be deeply moving about some of Spence Douthit's neighbors in the shanty settlement of stranded war workers, the relationship of Spence with his next-door neighbor, the marihuana salesman, seems to derive from the literary tradition of Happy Hooligan and the Katzenjammer Kids.

Altogether, "Tragic Ground" is a very strange book. Essentially Mr. Caldwell is writing about a depressing home possibility, glossed over in much of our talk about a decent peace, in his description of peoples left behind by the closing of the war plant. The Beasley County from which they were lured by labor recruiters with promises of liquor to the men and cheap frilly underwear to the women may still hold some hope for Spence. Basically, however, he is not so much homesick as caught in his poverty and secretly well pleased with town opportunities for adult delinquency in the settlement of the stranded.

There could be a significant warning here about people no longer needed in a possibly productive America. There is fearful tragedy in American families only serving to breed pretty little girls for cheap mass service whore houses. Maybe it is this warning in tragedy that Mr. Caldwell wants to make to intelligent and literate America. Maybe we, as a people, can be made to guffaw our way out of complacency. It seems doubtful, however, that the audiences which year after year filled the seats at the dramatization of "Tobacco Road" were so much moved as amused. It is doubtful whether "Tragic Ground" will stir thoughtful readers as much as it pleases those who love a loud and bawdy tale.

As entertainment there can be no question of the merit of "Tragic Ground" for those who like strong humor, or raw sex. Mr. Caldwell has written his tragic farce with much of his great skill. There is credible realism in his little snickering prostitutes. Old Spence, drunk or sober, seems an entirely possible and rather appealing American gutter-dweller. His wife, who spends her life in sick nakedness between debauches on patent medicines, seems a little less real but often even more noisy. The social workers, the family that moved in to contest with the Douthits for their ramshackle house, the young pimp who gets murdered and the father who murdered him, all seem very real figures suffering for our amusement. The American lower depths are very funny, indeed. In "Tobacco Road" they amused more people than even "Abie's Irish Rose" did. "Tragic Ground" emphasizes the faith that there are still customers who like to laugh at the deformed.

"Preface to
Poor Fool"

Maurice Edgar Coindreau*

If the French reader were not already familiar with Caldwell's best work, I would be careful not to present *Poor Fool* to him as an introduction to this writer's art. I have, in fact, no illusions about the imperfections of this small early work, and I know that it could alert the public against the man who dared to conceive its strange subject. But I know also how much we can derive from it regarding the mind of an author who is known, and rightly so, as the most original of his generation.

In the history of American literature, the years following the First World War will remain years of violence. It was the period when the young brutally rejected those of their elders whom they regarded as too timid. Under the aegis of Theodore Dreiser, of Sinclair Lewis, and of Sherwood Anderson, they practiced full-fledged naturalism or undertook explorations of the unconscious, toppling idols and disregarding taboos. They thought of nothing but violent action. Gangsters, boxers, and whores replaced the genteel characters of Edith Wharton and Willa Cather. Hemingway wrote his first and best stories. Joseph Moncure March published *The Set Up* and *The Wild Party*. Erskine Caldwell got his hand in with *The Bastard* (1929) and *Poor Fool* (1930).

The first of these two narratives is distinctly inferior in quality. After a series of adventures as bestial as they are monotonous, Gene Morgan, son of a prostitute and an unknown father, finally goes to live with Myra Morgan (the same name—a half-sister perhaps?). A baby is born of this union, a hideous little monster with a hairy face. One evening Gene, pretending to take the baby out for some air, throws him into the river and then leaves, after a last glance at the window where the silhouette of Myra is visible as she anxiously awaits the return of the man and her son. There is nothing fanciful to brighten this grim story, which at times makes one apprehensive of discovering that the whole thing is a kind of provocation inspired by the desire to find out, through the accumulation of gratuitous horrors, how far an author can go before a reader revolts. Erskine Caldwell is not yet himself in *The Bastard*.

He is, on the other hand, completely himself in *Poor Fool*. When I asked him what had impelled him to write such a disconcertingly macabre story, he replied:

*Reprinted from *Un Pauvre Type*, by Erskine Caldwell (Paris: Gallimard, 1945), © Editions Gallimard 1948. Translation by George McMillan Reeves, in Maurice Edgar Coindreau, *The Time of William Faulkner: A French View of Modern American Fiction* (Columbia: University of South Carolina Press, 1971), pp. 119–21. Copyright © 1971 by the University of South Carolina Press. Reprinted by permission of the University of South Carolina Press.

I wanted to use the methods of realistic writing on a purely imaginary subject. When I was working on *The Bastard*, I was careful never to get away from the real, or at least the possible. More than anything else I wanted realism with verisimilitude. *Poor Fool*, on the other hand, belongs to the literature of dreams. It is something like those diabolical dreams that come out of opium, except for the fact that I have never used opium. I simply let my imagination run free, without barriers or restraints. Nevertheless, I tried all along the way to make my story ring true, and I believe that if it has any interest, the reason is the contrast between the madness of the subject and a style that is cold, concise, and perfectly reasonable in its strict objectivity.[1]

It is certainly true that this little nightmare derives part of its value from that contrast. But only part. *Poor Fool* is more than a bad dream. It is the seed from which the true Caldwell will soon be born and, consequently, the thread of Ariadne which will eliminate the errors that are always possible in the interpretation of *God's Little Acre*, of *Tobacco Road*, and of the stories in *Nous les vivants*.[2] *Poor Fool* contains everything that makes up the fundamental originality of Mr. Caldwell: his taste for horror and cruelty, his very special way of regarding sexual matters, and that deadpan impassibility to which he owes his finest successes. Already we find the tragicomic marionettes which reveal him as a master of caricature: Mrs. Boxx and Jackie, whose naughty games prefigure the frolics of Dude and Sister Bessie (*Tobacco Road*), and the more cruel doings of Pluto and Darling Jill (*God's Little Acre*); and the alarming Mr. Boxx, a familiar of the kingdom of the dead, thanks to whom we understand why, in *Tobacco Road*, Ada Lester insists on being buried in a pretty, stylish dress. But it is especially the "poor fool," Blondy Niles, who should be set beside all the "poor fools," all the abulics that populate Caldwell's novels. In a very interesting study of *God's Little Acre* Lawrence S. Kubie insists that Caldwell is the painter of impotence and sterility. His male characters, even those who boast of their virility, never succeed in escaping entirely from their childhood. Against them are their mothers, who never appear in a normal light. "As the figures of women become clearer," writes Mr. Kubie, "the maternal role is distorted more and more towards perversion and prostitution." In Caldwell's works "there are good mothers who are dead, good mothers who suffer, bad mothers who hoard their sustenance and will not share, mothers who breed and transmit disease, erotic mothers whose bodies exist to nurse men, and women who exist only to destroy."[3] This comment sheds light on the ignoble Mrs. Boxx, the monstrous mother, the source of destruction who turns all the "poor fools" into her slave-sons. *Poor Fool* is a chromo illustration of the Oedipus complex and of the castration complex. "I want to, but I can't get away," Blondy groans, in the grip of the terrible

Genetrix. And the liberation which Dorothy brings him comes only as a prelude to death. Because *Poor Fool* is, by the author's own avowal, a novelized dream, one could not study it completely except by using Freudian methods. Psychiatrists will be grateful to Erskine Caldwell for having offered them a naturally savory dish that, for good measure, he has seasoned with a pinch of sadism and necrophilia.

There is, then, much more than one might believe in this narrative which is at once violent, horrible and grotesque, awkwardly executed, and slowed by the repetition and the monotony of a style whose rough staccato I have willingly respected. It was because of the profound resonances in this work that I developed an interest in presenting it to the French public.

I present it also for bibliographical reasons. *Poor Fool*, like *The Bastard*, has been published only in a limited edition.[4] Today it is an extremely rare work. Hence the present version has the interest of a first edition not only in Europe but for most American readers as well.

Notes

1. Since there is no record of this conversation, the phrasing in English is not Caldwell's but mine[Reeves'], translated directly from Coindreau's version in French.

2. For details about this collection of stories from *We Are the Living* and *Kneel to the Rising Sun*, see "Preface to *Nous les vivants*" in this volume.

3. "*God's Little Acre*: An Analysis," *Sat. Rev. of Lit.*, 11 (Nov. 24, 1934), 306.

4. *The Bastard* (New York: Heron Press, 1929), illustrated by Ty Mahon, was published in an edition of eleven hundred copies. *Poor Fool* (New York: Rariora Press, 1930), illustrated by Alexander Couard, was limited to one thousand copies. M.E.C.

"Well-Controlled Anger"

Harrison Smith*

In Erskine Caldwell's latest novel he abandons the poor white trash, who have furnished him with characters and plots for his satirical and possibly libelous novels of Southern life, for the equally desperate poor-white aristocracy. Since "Tobacco Road," written in 1932, was turned into a brave and bitter drama intended for the intellectuals, to wind up as a bawdy and timeless successor to "Uncle Tom's Cabin," Mr. Caldwell has written seven novels, creating stereotyped human beings who have become the familiar subjects for cartoonists and the advertisers of Cream of Wheat. All of us know them and the miserable shacks on the edge of an arid field that are supposed to shelter them; we know the randy old

*Reprinted from *Saturday Review of Literature*, 29 (May 18, 1946), 8–9.

grandma, with two teeth in her head clinging to a corncob pipe; pappy, all ribs, ramshackly legs, and a pair of torn pants; we know voluptuous little Judy, a juvenile delinquent at fourteen, a hag at twenty-two, and we know what is going to happen to all of them in almost any of Mr. Caldwell's novels, from that masterpiece of uncensored melodrama, "God's Little Acre" to "Tragic Ground," his last year's saga of white poverty in the South.

What we don't know, and will doubtless never know, is whether these incredible products of the hookworm and the hired cotton field that he has invented have ever existed in human form. Let us say that they were the creation of a talented writer who was so filled with compassion for poor whites and with hatred for the conditions that produced them that he deliberately made them objects of ridicule. It is easier to laugh at a blind man falling safely on his face at the curb than it is to weep, though both are the products of outraged pity. But at some time or other Mr. Caldwell had to call a halt to his hookworm novels; he had set them on the edge of the industrial South, in the barren lowlands, and in the freer air of the famished hills, and always with grandma, pappy, and the sexually starved youths surrounding little Judy, who always provided them with the drama of her surrenders.

From the theme of "A House in the Uplands" it is obvious that Mr. Caldwell had come to the end of his rope. But, what is the result of his moving from his poor white trash to the thin end of Southern aristocracy? It is a bitter, dramatic novel, written in crisp language and easily divisible into three acts, as if he hoped that at last Broadway and Hollywood might be interested. It is an "Uncle Tom's Cabin" rewritten for today. In 1946, the elegant and wealthy St. Claire of Mrs. Stowe's novel has become a debauched, sadistic, plantation owner whose fields and house are mortgaged to the hilt. Uncle Tom has become the pitiful grandson of a slave who cannot escape from the white master for whose family he has worked without pay all his life. The black or mulatto women who are the servants and field workers are frightened to death of this bankrupt aristocrat and yield to his fantasies as they have to his father's. Little Eva has become in an easy transition the neglected child-wife, and Simon Legree has been changed almost out of recognition to a frightened plantation manager, born on the wrong side of the fence, whose son is in love with the master's wife. But Harriet Beecher Stowe, bless her innocent 1852 heart, could never have invented the Northern crook, whose successful bawdy-house and gambling den corrupted town justice, and who brought down the scion of generations of plantation owners with a bullet in his black insides.

It is sad to have to say that Erskine Caldwell has changed his tune with no profit to his art. Nor can he continue on this new road for very long. Surely the number of sadistic, broken ex-aristocrats whose goings-on are tolerated by the neighbors must be as severely limited as the white hookworm victims are numberless. Let us grant Mr. Caldwell one more novel on this new theme and after that he will have to return to his original victims, grandma, pappy, little Judy, and the delinquent boys. Or if that is no longer commercially possible, he might look around him at the struggling, mighty colored people of the South.

There is no single laugh, covert or otherwise, in "A House in the Uplands." When Mr. Caldwell settles finally down to the great theme which he must eventually undertake, he will find no laughter there, either. We can imagine that he might be now through with the clever device of humorous satire and sex on a broken bed, which has covered what his publisher rightly calls "a controlled and deadly anger at a world which allows such poverty to exist." The anger is still there, strong enough, and the gift for terse characterization and intense drama. This new theme to which we might commend Mr. Caldwell is limitless; he can never come to the end of it. And let us hope that the symbols of Southern poverty and negligence he has created (not William Faulkner or any other Southern writer) will finally disappear from the newspapers and comic sheets of this country.

A joke is a joke, to be sure, Mr. Caldwell, but the hunger and lack of education of the underprivileged white population of the South are slowly, let us hope, being remedied. They are no longer subjects for the satirical novelist, or the comic draftsman, but for the investigator and the social worker. Racial prejudice remains. Twelve million colored people of the South remain subject to dangerous economic hazards in the next decade. Give up grandpappy and Julie, Mr. Caldwell, and go to work on something worthwhile. You have been a powerful propagandist, disguised as a novelist and satirist. Get to work!

"Cop Reviews Caldwell Novel, St. Paul Prosecutor Bans It"

Anonymous*

A St. Paul patrolman's review of "God's Little Acre" by Erskine Caldwell led to the banning of the book by the City Prosecutor on April 7, according to a United Press report. Whatever the ban did to sales in St. Paul, it was evidently a windfall to booksellers in neighboring Minneapolis, for a later press report quoted Minneapolis dealers as saying "their sales of the book jumped by leaps and bounds." Duell, Sloan & Pearce, publisher of the book, has no comment to make as yet. Another

*Reprinted from *Publishers' Weekly*, 149 (June 1, 1946), 2907, published by R. R. Bowker Company. Used by permission.

novel by Mr. Caldwell, "Tragic Ground," is at present the subject of censorship litigation in Ontario (*PW*, February 16).

The St. Paul case started when a customer of Harry Fredkove, book dealer, returned the book, complaining it was obscene. The chief of the police morals squad promptly obtained a copy and gave it to Patrolman Don Wallace to read and review. Wallace read the book, pencilled passages he thought objectionable, and wrote a review calling the novel "immoral, obscene and lewd." The City Prosecutor banned the book after reading this review and holding a hearing.

"Denver Police Ban Penguin Edition Of 'God's Little Acre' "

Anonymous*

The Penguin Books 25-cent edition of Erskine Caldwell's "*God's Little Acre*" has been banned by police in Denver, Colorado, and up to the present no local newsdealer or other seller of the Penguin line has come forward to contest the ban. The book was suppressed, according to the *Rocky Mountain News*, Scripps-Howard daily in Denver, without any charge being issued, a procedure which Lee Casey, associate editor of the *Rocky Mountain News*, calls illegal. The action instructing newsdealers to cease to sell the 25-cent edition was issued by the Morals Bureau of the Denver Police, and the local dealers have complied.

No action was taken against the trade edition of the book, according to Morals Bureau Captain John F. O'Donnell, because the main idea of the ban was to "keep the book out of the hands of teen-age children." Children, he said, would be unlikely to buy the more expensive trade edition at bookstores. He did not, however, make any charge that the book was indecent.

The *Rocky Mountain News* has given considerable attention to the case. Mr. Casey, in an article headed "Denver Police Have No Right to Tell Us What Not to Read," says "the Police Department has put itself in the absurd and illegal position of passing not upon matter but upon prices." Erskine Caldwell and more than a dozen Denver authors and university professors are quoted at length in denunciation of censorship in general. The American Civil Liberties Union has offered its services to any dealer who wishes to challenge the police decision.

*Reprinted from *Publishers' Weekly*, 151 (Feb. 15, 1947), 1135, published by R. R. Bowker Company. Used by permission.

"Caldwell's Collapse"

Anonymous*

Erskine Caldwell, chronicler of the seamy side of the Southern woes, is the leading bestseller-novelist in the world.[1] Quarter reprints of his *God's Little Acre*, *Tobacco Road*, *Trouble in July* and others have pushed the sales of his books above 9,000,000 copies. Perhaps some of his appeal is to hunters of the salacious: it is possible to read his novels as if they were extended dirty jokes. But the Caldwell of these early novels and stories had real talent besides.

He wrote in a mode of grotesque comedy rarely found in recent American fiction. With the irresponsible zest of a primitive jokester, he reveled in the high jinks of such moronic sub-humans as Jeeter Lester and Darling Jill, whom he twisted into creatures of ribald fantasy far removed from everyday human character.

Caldwell was especially good at mimicking Southern folk rhetoric, its mixture of lecherous filth and vivid images drawn from rural life, its passages of whining literalness relieved by sudden bright patches of corrupt folk poetry. His ability at recording poor white and Negro speech was, in fact, greater than his ability to make creative use of it in the framework of a novel, which is why his best pieces read more advantageously as off-center anecdotes than as realistic narratives.

Scrawny Turkey. Once he gained fame, Author Caldwell abandoned his narrow, though unusual gift. Prompted perhaps by the party-line critics and earnest sociologists who misread his sordid stories as profound exposures of Southern society,[2] Caldwell undertook to write "seriously." The result was lamentable: each of his recent novels is more inept than its predecessor, and the latest one is as scrawny a literary turkey as has been hatched in 1948.

This Very Earth reads as if it were written by a man under a deep spell, as if Caldwell himself were aware that something was the matter, and simply did not know what to do about it. Its prose has the glassy, elaborately monotonous décor of the language of hypnosis, beneath which the reader can sense the hysteria of someone trying to re-establish communication with the world. In what is obviously a rigorous act of will rather than the product of a freely flowing imagination, Caldwell puts his characters through his standard novelistic paces without once indicating what motivating idea or feeling can possibly be behind them. The reader, no matter how patient, can never find out.

Slobbering Sadist. *This Very Earth* runs its weary preordained course of rape, murder and stupidity without once arousing the slightest emotional response. The dialogue bears no living relationship to the

*Reprinted from *Time*, 52 (Aug. 30, 1948), 82–84. Reprinted by permission from TIME, The Weekly Newsmagazine; Copyright © Time Inc. 1948.

character speaking it, and the characters are all pressed from the same worn Caldwell dies: the lazy, immoral man; the cheap woman who sells herself cheaply; the slobbering sadist who beats his wife. The reader soon gets the uncomfortable feeling that he is watching the uncoordinated performance of a once-talented dancer who still remembers all the steps and postures but has forgotten how to dance.

Notes

1. Except for thriller-writers like Erle Stanley Gardner, Agatha Christie and Ellery Queen.

2. Caldwell is one of the Soviet Union's favorite U.S. authors. One hundred thousand copies of his short stories were printed by a Russian state publishing house last year. However, Moscow's *Literary Gazette* recently complained that Caldwell "in his latest works has fallen victim to the baneful influence of anti-popular, decadent ideas."

"Crumbled Georgia Crackers"

Lon Tinkle*

Erskine Caldwell's latest novel sharply arrests the distressing nose dive taken by his talent in the two preceding novels, "A House in the Uplands" and "The Sure Hand of God." Chism Crockett and his family, whose fortunes are the concern of "This Very Earth," are authentic and powerful Caldwell creations. The mingled violence, comedy, and tragedy of their lives yield nothing in inventiveness to the best of Caldwell's work.

But if the novelist's virtuosity again finds assertion in "This Very Earth," it cannot be said that he has regained the classic level of "God's Little Acre." The reason might be that the destinies of the stubborn, weak (though, for once, not degenerate) characters of the new novel leave the author actually indifferent. His attitude toward Chism Crockett and the others is not the artistic detachment which characterizes such a master as Flaubert; it's just indifference.

In this day when fiction has been captured by the critical mind that longs to be creative, it is easy to sell Erskine Caldwell short. No one, of course, would ever say of Caldwell what used to be said of Jules Romains: "It's not that Romains is too intellectual, but too *exclusively* intellectual." And of late Caldwell has even shown a belligerent tendency to pretend to a mindlessness as extreme as that of his own Georgia rustics.

This pose should fool no one. Caldwell's writing is astringent and his mood acescent. He can write out of lucid hatred, as he occasionally does in this novel, notably in a blistering attack on a Congressman. But what forestalls the reader's complete capitulation to his skill is the fundamental

*Reprinted from *Saturday Review of Literature*, 31 (Aug. 28, 1948), 12–13.

ambiguity mentioned above: Caldwell seems indifferent—and one suspects that is because he no longer feels sure where to assign the blame for human cussedness.

Take Chism Crockett, for instance. As this book opens, Chism is savoring the pure pleasure of possum hunting, now that autumn has come with its frosty and luminous nights. This indeed is the only pure pleasure Chism has known since leaving the farm and moving his motherless brood of three girls and two boys to town. But he won't return to the farm. Farming is what he hates most. He hates it enough to reject it even though he sees the town is wrecking his family.

Grandpa, one of Caldwell's occasional tender portraits, is forever reminding Chism of doom. Daughter Vickie works the night shift in a downtown café, conveniently near a hospitable hotel. Vickie is as promiscuous as her sister Dorisse is fatally faithful—faithful to a psychopath who ultimately kills her with a flatiron. Jane, still in high school, is seduced by the football coach, more than twice her age and married. Chism himself teaches eleven-year-old Jarvis to drink corn whiskey, and takes the boy along on what is surely as shocking a rape episode as you'll ever find, even in Caldwell's work.

There is no need to catalogue the evil into which Chism falls. The question is whether the reader is legitimately entitled to ask why he falls into it. We think so, but Caldwell himself has recently commented that the only function of the novelist is to show the reader what people actually do.

Well, people do think now and then; they even modify their impulses by reason. It is this realm of "doing" which is so markedly absent from "This Very Earth." It would be absurd, however, to defend this lack on the grounds that Caldwell is picturing simpletons. Far from it; Chism himself is as wily as any possum and has all the brainpower needed for craftily selling his daughters to the highest bidder or for practising blackmail on their lovers.

So, as a novel, "This Very Earth" is basically unsatisfying. It will prompt instinctive admiration from any but the intellectual snobs, who ought to admit that as a craftsman Caldwell perfectly frames the exact pictures he wants to paint. But what he paints is not "this very earth"; it is the world of Erskine Caldwell. And that world is becoming increasingly artificial instead of deeply felt. It can hardly be more important to the reader than it is to the author. Can it be that Caldwell's experience on an international scale has made him impatient of provincialism?

"Comic Citizens of the South"

Harrison Smith*

In a review of Erskine Caldwell's "Tragic Ground," Jonathan Daniels wrote that the American lower depths were very funny, indeed, and that "Tobacco Road" had amused more people than "Abie's Irish Rose." Almost any critic who attempts to be fair about any of Mr. Caldwell's latest books has to curb his wrath at his obvious attempt to get a laugh out of the sick souls, the moral delinquents, rapists, idiots, and sadists whom he has turned into cartoon strips of citizens of the South. Obviously, there are customers by the tens of thousands for anything he writes, for the million or so Americans who have read him know by this time that they are going to get a strong dose of eroticism and bawdy humor along with whatever brutal lesson in race relations and poverty he chooses to teach.

Now that prosperity has flooded or crept into the South Mr. Caldwell has moved away from the drooling grandpappies and the rest of the creatures he found among the sharecroppers, and has concentrated on the plight of the hapless Negroes living amongst lecherous and murderous whites in the slums of Southern cities and towns. These are in turn becoming caricatures, and it is to be hoped that in time either his audiences will be sick of them, or that he will run out of new material to exploit for gruesome laughs.

He has called his latest book "Place Called Estherville," and it is fortunate for the author's continued health and the future of the town itself that there is no such place on the map. Estherville is an outwardly peaceful little town, sleeping under the hot sun. The tourist might drive through it and think how pleasantly monotonous life would be in this calm retreat. According to Mr. Caldwell, it is a sink of iniquity, a nest of drowsing copperheads and rattlesnakes.

In the afternoon the pale and slack manager of the bank is meditating the seduction that evening of the high-color gal slaving for his wife who pays her in old clothes instead of cash. The cop on the corner is licking his lips while he muses on the Negro he hopes to beat up later and throw into the jail house. The boys loafing along the street are planning to gang up on a colored girl after sundown, strip her, and rape her in a shed around the corner from the drugstore. Two or three abandoned or neglected wives and the lovely and degenerate daughter of the town's rich man are trying to get their hands on the handsome and terrified colored youth who delivers the groceries, or cooks and waits on the family table. One of the town's physicians is plotting with the owner of the hardware store to get a colored boy to buy a bicycle at twice its value and then take it away from him when he can no longer pay the doctor five dollars a

*Reprinted from *Saturday Review of Literature*, 32 (Sept. 10, 1949), 14–15.

week. Estherville is a merry town, all right, and there is a laugh on every other page.

Oddly enough he succeeds in making fun of the miserable colored boy and his almost white sister who came to Estherville from the country to live in a hovel with penniless and sick Aunt Mattie. Both of them are so amusingly naive. The eighteen-year-old boy falls squirming and protesting into every trap; the girl permits herself to be outraged repeatedly with wonderfully philosophic calm. The boy is, of course, doomed from the start. He has had a year or two of rural education, an unforgivable affront to Estherville, and he is obviously old enough to relieve the boredom of spinsters, neurotic girls, and lecherous wives, and also to afford any gang of white lads a pleasant evening of torture. One day he is murdered by a farmer who is a notorious "nigger-hater" because the half-insane girl he is living with accuses the poor wretch of attacking her.

For the reader it is like living in an insane asylum specializing in sex maniacs and sadists; you become used to the inhabitants and are not at all surprised that they are all alike. It is a surprise at the end, however, to find one decent white human being, an elderly doctor, who had spent his life sacrificing himself to the maladies of Negroes and their natural enemies. And it is odd to discover that this familiar character out of so many romantic melodramas is the most unlikely and unbelievable white man in the cast. Pretty Kathyanne, who has nobly endured seduction and rape so many times, had to be saved somehow to balance the story. Something good must somehow come out of Gomorrah! The deus ex machina in this case is a fine young colored man who has loved her all along and has endured patiently her continual defeats. When she has a beautiful girl baby by her first seducer, he agrees to marry her. As the doctor leaves the girl, he delivers as corny a valedictory as we have read in a long time. ". . . It's my guess, she's a quadroon . . . the baby's going to outdo her mother for looks, and that's going a far piece, I can tell you . . . It's just what nature always strives for—to produce a beautiful woman—and there's no arguing with nature in this life." Thus consoled for her misadventures with white human nature Kathyanne blesses the doctor, who is so overcome with astonishment that he opens the door and falls dead. At least, he must be dead, for here is the last sentence of the novel, "And then, suddenly, and without a murmur of protest, the gray overcoated body fell to the freezing ground of Gwinnett Alley."

So here is Erskine Caldwell's latest success. Perhaps it will finally answer Jonathan Daniel's comment five years ago: "It is time for some decision as to whether Erskine Caldwell is a writer concerned with the socially significant in the lower depths of American life or whether he has found modern pay dirt in comedy at the expense of the half-wit and the deformed." This writer made his decision some time ago. "Place Called Estherville" merely serves to confirm it.

"Attorney General
v.
Book Named
'God's Little Acre.' "

SUPREME JUDICIAL COURT OF MASSACHUSETTS. SUFFOLK.
ARGUED DEC. 8, 1949. DECIDED JULY 26, 1950.*

J. J. *Kelleher*, Boston, J. J. *Bresnahan*, Asst. Atty. Gen.,
and L. E. *Ryan*, Dorchester, for plaintiff.
R. W. *Meserve*, Boston, *Joseph B. Ullman*, New York
City, for defendants.
Before QUA, C.J., and LUMMUS, RONAN, WILKINS,
SPALDING, WILLIAMS and COUNIHAN, JJ.

SPALDING, Justice.

The Attorney General, under the provisions of G.L. (Ter. Ed.) c.
272, §§ 28C–28G, as inserted by St. 1945, c. 278, § 1, seeks by this petition to have the novel "God's Little Acre" by Erskine Caldwell ad-
judicated obscene, indecent, or impure. In an answer filed by persons interested in the book it was admitted that it was being sold and distributed
in this Commonwealth. From a final decree in favor of the book the Attorney General appealed. The case comes here on a report of the
evidence, including a copy of the book itself, and findings of fact by the
trial judge.

While conceding "that if one were seeking so called racy, off-color or
suggestive paragraphs, they can be found in the book," the judge was of
opinion that the "book as a whole would not stimulate sexual passions or
desires in a person with average sex instincts," and concluded that he did
not believe that it would have "a substantial tendency to deprave or corrupt its readers by inciting lascivious thoughts or arousing lustful desires."

[1] The tests to be applied in determining whether a book is obscene,
indecent, or impure are fully set forth in the recent case of *Commonwealth* v. *Isenstadt*, 318 Mass. 543, 62 N.E. 2d 840. They were quoted
with approval and applied in *Attorney General* v. *Book Named "Forever
Amber,"* 323 Mass. 302, 81 N.E. 2d 663. They need not be restated. Comprehensive and complete as are these tests, their application in a given
case is by no means easy. Indeed it is not indulging in hyperbole to say
that no more difficult or delicate task confronts a court than that arising
out of the interpretation and application of statutes of this sort. On the
one hand, an interpretation ought not to be given to the statute in question which would trim down the fundamental right of the public to read

*93 N.E. 2d 819 (1950)

"to the point where a few prurient persons can find nothing upon which their hypersensitive imaginations may dwell." *Commonwealth* v. *Isenstadt*, 318 Mass. 543, 551–552, 62 N.E. 2d 840, 845: On the other hand, care must be taken that it be not construed in such a way as to render it incapable of accomplishing the objects intended by the Legislature.

We turn to the story itself. It has to do with life of a poor white farmer and his family on a run down farm in Georgia. The father, Ty Ty Walden, is a pathetic figure with the mentality of a moron. Believing that there is gold on his land, he and two of his sons dig for it incessantly, leaving the raising of cotton to two colored share croppers. Ty Ty, who is pious, dedicates one acre of his land to God and intends to turn over the proceeds of that acre to the church. But he is so busy digging for gold that he never gets around to raising anything on it, and he relocates it from time to time to meet the exigencies of his digging. Ty Ty's sons, daughters, and daughter-in-law become involved in numerous sexual affairs. These lead to quarrels among the brothers, and as the story closes one brother kills another and departs with his shotgun, presumably to kill himself. Ty Ty, who had always tried to keep peace in the family, in despair resumes his digging for gold.

[2] Viewing the book as a whole we find ourselves unable to agree with the conclusion of the trial judge that the book was not obscene, indecent, or impure as those words have been defined in our decisions. The book abounds in sexual episodes and some are portrayed with an abundance of realistic detail. In some instances the author's treatment of sexual relations descends to outright pornography. Nothing would be gained by spreading these portions of the book on the pages of this opinion.

[3] Evidence was introduced at the hearing below by literary critics, professors of English literature, and a professor of sociology touching the "literary, cultural or educational character" of the book. See § 28F. In general the literary experts regarded the book as a sincere and serious work possessing literary merit. The sociologist was of opinion that the book was of value as a sociological document in its portrayal of life of the so-called "poor whites" in the south. The judge, who had the advantage of hearing these witnesses, has indicated in his findings that he accorded considerable weight to their testimony. We accept his findings on this aspect of the case. But the fact that under § 28F evidence may be received as to the "literary, cultural or educational character" of the book does not change the substantive law as to what is obscene, indecent, or impure. Those provisions were undoubtedly inserted to clarify doubts as to the sort of expert evidence that may be received in cases of this type. See *Commonwealth* v. *Isenstadt*, 318 Mass. 543, at pages 558–559, 62 N.E. 2d 840. In reaching the conclusion that the book offends against the statute we have taken into consideration the expert testimony described above. In the Isenstadt case we recognized that sincerity of purpose and literary

merit were not to be entirely ignored and could "be considered in so far as they bear upon the question whether the book, considered as a whole, is or is not obscene, indecent, or impure." 318 Mass. at page 554, 62 N.E. 2d at page 846. But as we said in that case, "In dealing with such a practical matter as the enforcement of the statute here involved there is no room for the pleasing fancy that sincerity and art necessarily dispel obscenity. * * * Sincerity and art can flourish without pornography, and seldom, if ever, will obscenity be needed to carry the lesson." 318 Mass. at page 553, 62 N.E. 2d 846.

Our attention has been directed to two decisions in other jurisdictions in which the book in question has been held not to be obscene under statutes somewhat similar to ours. One of them, *People* v. *Viking Press, Inc.*, 147 Misc. 813, 264 N.Y.S. 534, is an opinion by a city magistrate. The other case, *Commonwealth* v. *Gordon*, 66 Pa. Dist. & Co. R. 101, was decided by a court of first instance in Pennsylvania and was affirmed by the Superior Court on appeal in a per curiam decision, 166 Pa. Super. 120, 70 A. 2d 389. A discussion of these decisions would not be profitable. It is enough for present purposes to say that the interpretations placed on the statutes there involved differ materially from that which this court has placed on our statute.

[4] The contention that a decree adjudicating the book as obscene, indecent, or impure would be an abridgment of the rights of freedom of the press guaranteed by the Fourteenth Amendment to the Constitution of the United States requires no discussion. A similar contention was made without success in *Commonwealth* v. *Isenstadt*, 318 Mass. 543, 557–558, 62 N.E. 2d 840. What was said there is applicable here.

It follows that the decree below is reversed and a new decree is to be entered adjudicating that the book in question is obscene, indecent, and impure.

So ordered.

CALDWELL, the *NEW YORK POST,* and the *AUGUSTA CHRONICLE*

"Georgia Poverty-Swept, Says Caldwell"

Erskine Caldwell*

Erskine Caldwell was born in 1903 at White Oak, Ga., where he attended grammar school one year, high school one year and preparatory school for two years. He attended the University of Virginia for three years.

Caldwell has written a series of four articles on the share croppers of the South for the New York Post.

He worked as a cotton seed shoveller in an oil mill, hod carrier on construction, plowed and picked cotton, harvesting strawberries and beets, as a bottle washer in a dairy, cook and counterman in a restaurant, newspaper reporter on the Atlanta (Georgia) Journal.

His novel, TOBACCO ROAD, was dramatized and is now in its second year on Broadway.

For four years economic conditions in the South have been as acute as any in the United States, but in this fifth year of the depression conditions have never been as bad. In parts of Georgia human existence has reached its lowest depths. Children are seen deformed by nature and malnutrition, women in rags beg for pennies, and men are so hungry that they eat snakes and cow dung.

The State of Georgia provides no direct relief. Governor Eugene Talmadge, the self-styled "wildman," the dictator of three million people, who exercises more power than Huey Long, passes along to the Federal Government the responsibility the citizens placed upon him—and without co-operation, Talmadge, when prodded, shouts that the State is not a relief agency. While he is shouting himself red in the face he holds one hand behind his back to receive money sent down from Washington to keep alive the men who voted him into power.

Talmadge is riding to greater power on his program of clearing the State of debt. By refusing to furnish food, clothing, and work to one-third of the population he intends to close his present term of office with a surplus in the treasury.

In some sections of the State, particularly in South Georgia and East

*Reprinted from *New York Post*, 18 Feb. 1935, Sec. 1, p. 1, cols. 4–7; p. 7, cols. 6–8.

Georgia, men who are unable to qualify for the meager relief provided by the FERA offer their labor—eight, ten, twelve, fourteen hours a day of it—for what they can get. What they can get, one or two days a week, if they are lucky enough to find employment, is sometimes twenty-five cents a day. Thirty-five cents is the average, in this agricultural empire. Exceptional pay is fifty cents a day.

The day laborer, white or black at this season of the year when farming is almost at a standstill, may work one day a week, he may even work ten days a month; or he may, as hundreds do, search fruitlessly day after day, week after week, for half a day's employment. On the other hand, if he happens to be one out of five, he may qualify for relief work and earn five or six dollars a week. These relief workers are the aristocrats of Georgia labor. They earn enough to provide food for their families.

The real sufferer in agricultural Georgia is the former share cropper. Share cropping, once the backbone of the South's cotton empire, is rapidly giving way to an even more vicious system of labor extraction. The new style is driving men away from the fertile land, away from schools for their children, away from civilization. The share cropper of yesterday is the day laborer of today, the man who peddles his muscle and brawn for 25 and 35 cents a day and who is lucky if he works one day a week during the winter months. The share cropper's place has been taken by the tenant farmer, who pays for the rent of the land, whether there is anything left over for himself or not.

This once-flourishing farming country in the month of February, 1935, is a desolate land. Crop control has reduced the quantity of products without raising the quality. Fewer workers can find employment. White men are being replaced by cheaper, more tractable Negroes. Land is concentrated in the hands of corporations, banks and individual land owners, thereby forcing whole sections of the State into domains of absentee landlordism.

Starting in the north near the Savannah River with Columbia County and continuing in a southerly direction through McDuffie, Glascock, Jefferson, Richmond and Burke Counties for a hundred and fifty miles to the Atlantic Ocean, East Georgia is experiencing the decay that spreads westward through Alabama, Mississippi and Arkansas. Railroads that contributed to the once healthy growth of the cotton empire are being scrapped and in their places weeds are growing. Tenant houses, rotted and roofless, are the homes of families hoping that 1935 will provide food, clothing and shelter. When the house falls in, the family starts out with their belongings strapped to their backs in search of another home where hope may be continued.

These American people of the cotton country, robbed of their means of livelihood by the downfall of systems of farming, are being forced into the swamps, the stony acres, the waste land. The ground they are forced upon will not yield crops. It is a soil that will not even grow a good crop of broom sedge.

There are hundreds of these communities in East Georgia, and they exist throughout Georgia, Alabama, Mississippi and Arkansas. Usually there are no roads, and travel is done across creeks without bridges, fields without even so much as a cowpath.

These are the unknown people of 1935, the men, women, and children who hide their nakedness behind trees when a stranger wanders off the main-traveled roads. Here are the deformed, starved, and diseased children born since 1929. Here are the men who strip leaves off trees, dig roots out of the earth, and snare whatever wild animal they can. These are the people who were forced off the tillable land, these are the women and children, the urban residents deny that exist, these are the men who tramp to the county seat week after week in an effort to secure the relief they have heard about but which somehow is always exhausted when they apply.

There is hunger in their eyes as well as in their bellies. They grasp for a word of hope. They plead for a word of advice.

The FERA in Georgia is inadequate to help them. Neither has heard of the other.

None of them wishes to kill and steal. He wishes to work, to secure food for his children, medicine for his wife, clothes for warmth in a winter temperature of 12 degrees below the freezing point. He has covered the country in search of even a rumor of a job as far away as the county seat, and there is no means to travel any further. The mule has died of old age, or overwork, or starvation; or the mule was sold by the sheriff of the county to satisfy a judgment. There is no mule with which to work or on which to ride. There is nothing left except the roofless shack and a few pots and pans and a corn-shuck mattress.

The Federal Government says that nobody starves, but the Federal Government does not know what its left hand does. The FERA in Georgia, as everywhere, is administered by local citizens. A local citizen is an urban resident who knows the city streets but who would be lost ten miles from home where there are no highway signs. Without co-operation from the State, the Federal Government is helpless in trying to feed and clothe a million persons. Even with an increased appropriation for Georgia the relief sent from Washington would be inadequate for the State's dire needs.

Talmadge takes off his coat, snaps his suspenders and shouts from every cross-road that the wild man of Georgia is everybody's friend. If the people who are made to suffer because of their Governor's refusal to allow State relief appropriations could have their way, it is not unlikely that they would petition the Federal Government to nationalize the State of Georgia.

Under present conditions, that is the wisest step that could be taken. Laying aside the possibilities of a local upheaval, it would at least give some of them the opportunity to vary their fare of snakes and cow dung.

"U.S. Aid Forces Out Georgia Share Croppers"

Erskine Caldwell*

This is the second of a series of four articles by Erskine Caldwell, famous novelist and playwright, on the share croppers of Georgia and other Southern States. In this series Caldwell deals with the economic conditions in the South which have brought upon the day laborers of that part of the country an almost unbelievable plight. Caldwell is a Georgian and has himself been a laborer in the country about which he writes so vividly.

In an agricultural country such as East Georgia there is rarely an opportunity for the worker to find employment in a mill or factory. All he makes is squeezed from the soil. There are days when it rains and he is forced into idleness, there are days when the soil is dry and he is forced to become idle until moisture makes the earth tillable. And there is always fall and winter, a long stretch of months between harvest and planting when there is little that can be done.

The agricultural worker without land, implements or stock of his own may enter into an agreement with a landowner to farm a portion of land. The landowner may agree to supply the worker's needs, including food and clothing, against repayment at harvest time. The worker becomes a share cropper.

The agreement varies. In some cases, the landowner receives half the crop produced by the worker and his family; in some cases, the worker agrees to give the landowner a certain number of bales of cotton. In any event the landowner stands to come out ahead at the end of the year, but there is no assurance the worker will. More often he comes out even after a year's work. But frequently, if he does not question the landowner's system of keeping books, the worker finds himself deeply in debt at the end of a year.

In that case he has no alternative but to remain and try to work off his debt during the next year. There are workers in Georgia white and Negro, who have been trying for the past twenty years to work themselves out of debt, and most of them find themselves going deeper into debt each

*Reprinted from *New York Post*, 19 Feb. 1935, Sec. 2, p. 24, cols. 1–2.

year. It is easy for a landowner to juggle accounts when the worker can't read or write.

But times have changed. Landowners were forced to sign crop control agreements. That meant that the number of acres of cotton they were allowed to plant were reduced. In reducing the acreage the number of bales was cut. The landowner woke up to find that his share cropper was gaining on him. One share cropper was making as much as the landowner and in some cases more.

It did not take the landowner long to find a way to force farming back into the profitable paths. He told the share cropper there would be no more food on credit, no more clothing for his family and no more advances of money for medicine, school books and tobacco. He told the share cropper to go shift for himself. It was then left to the worker to decide whether he was going to remain and work under the new system—to become a tenant farmer or a day laborer. The landowner gave him the chance to choose for himself.

What there is today of the share-cropping system is mostly confined to workers with large families, generally Negro. A man with six, eight, ten or more children in his family old enough to work in the fields is given preference over the worker with only three or four grown children. A share-cropper with ten field hands in his family can raise more cotton than a man with only his wife to help him. The landowner appreciates that. He will have twelve bales of cotton in the fall instead of two. Legalized birth control would soon wipe out the last remaining share cropping agreements.

The Federal Government, since the breakdown of the individual system, has gone into the game of share cropping in the form of sustenance homesteads. An agreement is made with a worker who wishes to farm but who has no mules, implements or grown children to help him raise cotton. Land is provided, mules and implements are furnished and seed and fertilizer are supplied. During the waiting and preparatory seasons several dollars a week are supplied for food, clothing and stock feed. The worker then has what he has asked for. He is once more a share-cropper, nationalized from the crown of his head to the tip of his big toe, but he has plow handles to walk between and a mule to talk to. He has no worry on his mind. He is working for the Government.

This would be a pretty picture but for the fact that for every worker who signs such an agreement there are five workers who have no such opportunity. They make trips to the county seat week after week, trying to find out what is holding up their papers. They receive many evasions, traceable either to local politics or to lack of Government appropriation. The man goes back home, waits another week and returns to hear the same story. In Georgia it is called "getting the Talmadge razzberry."

In the meantime the applicant asks for relief from the local FERA office. If it is learned that he has applied for a Government homestead he is told to stop trying to get two hand-outs at the same time. Back he goes home, hungry. His family meet him at the door, hungry. They go to bed hungry.

Twenty miles away at another county seat, the food warehouse of the relief agency is overflowing. There is more food than can be given away. People are called up on the phone and invited to come and get five pounds of cheese. The car is backed out of the garage, and the warehouse is crowded with people who would like to have five pounds of cheese for the asking. Inside the relief office the phone rings. Somebody working in a store can't get off from work until 6 o'clock, and asks if the warehouse will stay open until he can get away from his job. The warehouse stays open.

Twenty miles away hundreds of families go to bed hungry. Families of five, ten, fifteen, twenty, crowd into quilt-covered corners and try to get a little sleep on empty stomachs. These are the would-be share-croppers for the Government, for the absentee landlords, for anybody who would give them a start on this year's crop. In the morning they get up and look at the sky wondering which way to turn. These are the people who once were share croppers in debt maybe, but share croppers with food nevertheless, and who want to share-crop again if they can find anybody to share-crop for. They say the Government plowed them under last year. They laughed at that. It is something to take the mind off an empty stomach. But the laughter is short lived. They are serious now.

There are cotton mills and fertilizer plants in Augusta, there are fertilizer plants and sugar refineries in Savannah, but there are no jobs there for the share-cropper forced from a farm.

The small lumber mills on the Savannah River and along the creeks of East Georgia already have more labor at hand than can be used. Road building and repair are done by machine. There is nothing else.

Rabbits that once furnished food for the hungry have been almost completely killed off. There is nothing in sight after that.

"Georgia Land Barons Oust Dying Girl and Her Father"

Erskine Caldwell*

This is the third of a series of four articles by Erskine Caldwell. . . .

A tenant farmer in East Georgia pays rent for tillable land either in money or in bales of cotton. If he fails to do either, the contract with the landowner is broken, and the tenant is likely to be evicted.

Tenant farmers last year were unable to purchase the necessary

*Reprinted from *New York Post*, 20 Feb. 1935, Sec. 1, p. 7, cols. 1–2.

amount of fertilizer, and consequently their cotton crop was far below average. Those with short crops failed to produce enough cotton to pay their rent.

Their hope today is to secure Government-rented farm land which will enable them to become share-croppers. That failing, they will be forced into the day-laborer class, the most insecure group of agricultural workers in the entire South.

In 1934 a tenant farmer in Jefferson County was unable, because of old age and illness, to work out his crop. A physician prescribed for his ailment, but the man could not buy the medicine, and no relief agency would supply it. A four-year-old girl in the family died at the end of the year of anemia. The tenant moved several miles away to another farm, but after several weeks the landowner decided that he was too old and ill to work a crop on a tenant-farmer basis, or on any other basis, and he was evicted.

The household goods were carried to the land-limits and deposited by the side of the road. Another tenant took the goods under shelter, and the landowner gave notice that if they were not removed from his land, he would come to the house and burn them.

In the meantime the old man had gone off into the swamp, without ax, hammer, or saw, with the intention of felling trees and building a log house for his family. He had not been heard from since he left.

This tenant farmer had lost his health, and nobody would allow him to work, either on shares, on the promise of rent, or for wages. There was no house to shelter his family, there was no food to feed even one of them. The girl died in January 1935, from the effects of malnutrition, her body twisted and knotted by rickets and anemia.

This section in East Georgia is the scene of cases of human want that no relief agency, Government or private, has touched. More than that, it has been publicly denied that the section exists. And yet it is only five miles from U.S. Highway No. 1, twenty miles from the county seat. Hundreds of families in the tenant and day-laborer class live in this strip of America twenty miles wide and a hundred miles long. In other parts of Georgia, in Alabama, Mississippi, and Arkansas, there are hundreds of other similar communities. There is starvation, deformity, even death for want of a loaf of bread.

Like the slums of a city, it contains the backwash of America. But unlike the slums of a city, it is unknown and unseen. Officially, on the rolls of the FERA and on the mind of the Governor of the State it does not exist.

Here is another tenant farmer. He begs to know how he can get a small acreage to farm. He is a young man, not over thirty-five. He has a wife and three children. He has been to the county seat, but each time he has visited the official in charge of Government homesteads, he has been told nothing can be done for him for a while. He has worn out his shoes walking there and back.

His children have not enough clothing to wear to school. He will not talk about what they have to eat. Several miles away is an FERA adult school, which provides a job for one teacher. The grown men and women who attend the school, learning to read and write, have to leave their children at home because they have no clothes to wear to the district school. The young tenant farmer cannot understand why an adult school is provided when his three children are unable to attend the district school. He thinks it must be the Governor's fault. Governor Talmage will not cooperate with the Federal Government in supplying the necessities of life, because the Governor has some political ambition up his sleeve. He would like to become President of the United States. He may have to share the White House with Huey Long, but since they are on friendly terms he is willing to do that if he can only get there.

Across the field is another tenant farmer. He had moved into a cabin recently occupied by a Negro share-cropper who was forced out by the landowner, and the white man had to have shelter for his family. It was the only available dwelling within ten miles, and the landowner had promised full co-operation because the new tenant owned a pair of strong mules. No one knew what had become of the Negro family, but it was supposed they had moved into an abandoned barn several miles away. The roof had fallen in, but otherwise the building was habitable.

Only a half a mile in the other direction is a tenant farmer who has set his family up in an abandoned school house. None of the six persons in the family can read or write. The man sits on the schoolhouse steps wondering where he can find a plow to break the ground for his 1935 cotton crop. He has got to pay rent whether or no, and plowing time will soon be at hand.

Up the creek is another tenant farmer. In January and February there is little that can be done in the way of farming. So the man is splitting "splinters," small slabs of fat-pine used for the kindling of fire. There are eleven children helping him, their ages running from one year to seventeen. His wife was in bed, white-faced with pelagra.

Somebody had heard of an organization of some sort that tried to help share-croppers, tenants and day laborers, but nobody could find out where it was or what could be done about it. The rumor was that share-croppers, tenants and day laborers could join it and force the landowners into paying living wages. The organization was like a rainbow after a storm, but nobody knew where or how to look for it.

The man splitting the pine continued to tie the splinters into small bundles, each one weighing two or three pounds each. Sometimes he was able to get a cent a bundle for a load in Augusta—sometimes he could not even give them away. He had sold a load for four dollars before Christmas, but out of that he had spent two dollars for gasoline and oil to run the broken-down truck. He had earned two dollars in two months, and it had kept his family alive. There were six or seven months ahead of him before he could harvest a crop. He did not know how he would be able to keep his family alive until then. He was a tenant farmer with the benefits of a landlord to supply the necessities of life on credit.

The tenant wore an old sweater pinned across his chest, a pair of overalls and shoes. His wife had not been out of bed in eight months. One of his children, a girl of sixteen, had a growth closing over one eye that could be removed by a surgeon. The growth had been there eight or nine years, and it is becoming larger each year. Soon the girl will lose the sight of one eye when the growth closes over it.

The owner of the land on which the tenant lives is the justice of a State court. The owner comes to the farm occasionally, always once to see that the crop is planted on time, and always once to see that it is harvested on time. Rent is collected as the gin when the cotton is baled. The rest of the time the owner is too busy to consider advances for food and clothing.

"Starving Babies Suckled by Dog In Georgia Cabin"

Erskine Caldwell*

This is the fourth and last of a series of articles by Erskine Caldwell. . . .

Working for a few cents a day, the farm laborer in East Georgia cannot afford to rent a house for the exclusive occupancy of his family. When the rate of pay is twenty-five cents a day, and when half a day's work a week is common, there is nothing to be done except double up with another family.

Near Keysville a two-room house is occupied by three families, each consisting of man and wife and from one to four children each.

While two eighteen-year-old girls from the house were chopping wood from a stump across the road with a plowshare tied to a hickory pole, one of the men came home in the middle of the day. He had finished half a day's work at noon, the first in two weeks' time, and with the pay he had bought a pound of salted hog-side, and two pounds of corn meal.

The third family refused to share in it, because the wife insisted that her husband would be home with something to eat before night.

In one of the two rooms a six-year-old boy licked the paper bag the meat had been brought in. His legs were scarcely any larger than a medium sized dog's leg and his belly was as large as that of a 130-pound woman's. Suffering from rickets and anemia, his legs were unable to carry

*Reprinted from *New York Post*, 21 Feb. 1935, Sec. 1, p. 20, cols. 5–6.

him for more than a dozen steps at a time; suffering from malnutrition, his belly was swollen several times its normal size. His face was bony and white. He was starving to death.

In the other room of the house, without chairs, beds, or tables, a woman lay rolled up in some quilts trying to sleep. On the floor before an open fire lay two babies, neither a year old, sucking the dry teats of a mongrel bitch. A young girl, somewhere between fifteen and twenty, squatted on the corner of the hearth trying to keep warm.

The dog got up and crawled to the hearth. She sat on her haunches before the blazing pine-knots, shivering and whining. After a while the girl spoke to the dog and the animal slunk away from the warmth of the fire and lay down again beside the two babies. The infants cuddled against the warmth of the dog's flanks, searching tearfully for the dry teats.

The two girls who had been hacking at the pine stump across the road with a rusty plowshare dragged two sacks of wood across the yard and into the house. Pieces of fat-pine were thrown into the fire, and the quick blaze warmed the whole room. The woman in the quilts stopped shivering and began to snore lightly. The girl squatting on the hearth moved back from the intense heat. The dog got up and shook herself and lay down several feet away. The babies crawled crying after her.

In the other room the meat and meal were being baked in a skillet over the open-hearth fire. Five persons crowded around the blaze watching the hoe-cake brown. The boy with rickets ducked under his father's arms and tried to snatch the hoe-cake from the pan. He burned his fingers and his mother rubbed some of the grease from the salted hog-side on them. He stopped crying while he was eating his portion, but as soon as that was gone, he began crying again, and he did not stop after that. He said his head hurt him, too.

There was a laborer across the fields who earned twenty-five cents a day. He received from the landowner eight dollars a month. The only trouble was that the landowner usually brought him meat and meal and took it out of his pay.

Formerly, this eight-dollar-a-month laborer had had a job on relief, and he received seven to eight dollars a week. But the FERA told him one day he was fired, because he had only one arm and could not do a man's full share of work. Cut off from relief, he was forced into the day laborer class, and everyone of his neighbors said he was lucky to get a full-time job, at 25 cents a day. He did not know how he was going to send his seven children to school.

In the room with the two babies there was no food. The husband should have been back the day before, but it was doubtful if he would return before another two or three days.

The two girls who were the wood-gatherers sat down on the floor, one on each side of the dog and babies, warmed themselves before the fire. It kept them busy most of the time getting wood, because the fat-pine stumps burned as if kerosene had been poured over them. They wiped the babies' faces, and scolded the dog for moving so often.

There was nothing in that side of the house to eat, and there had been nothing for three days. The dog began to whine again, and tried to get up to go outside and hunt for something she could eat, but the girls would not let her leave the babies. She had to keep them until the mother had finished her nap.

The girl on the hearth, raising her corn-sack skirt to let the warmth of the fire fall upon her body, said it ought to be easy to get something to eat if you only knew where to find it. Her sisters looked at everybody, but said nothing. The girl then asked herself a question. What wouldn't I do for a heaping dish of hog sausage?

Editorial from the *Augusta Chronicle*: "What Will Good People of Jefferson County Say of This?"

Anonymous*

Erskine Caldwell, author of "Tobacco Road" and "God's Little Acre" is conducting a column for the sensational New York Evening Post, which has gone from one extreme to another, from the ultra conservative paper owned by the late Cyrus H. K. Curtis, of Saturday Evening Post fame, to a sensational sheet which is out Heroding Herod and beginning to make the yellow tabloids feel ashamed of their conservatism. At any rate Caldwell is making such an indictment against his old home county of Jefferson, that the Chronicle is printing excerpts today and asking the question, "What will the good people of Jefferson county say of this?"

In his "Tobacco Road" Caldwell portrayed the ignorance, poverty, depravity and degeneracy of a white family that lived not far from Augusta. That the picture was grossly overdrawn we have always believed, although Dr. I.S. Caldwell, of Wrens, father of the author and a man of the finest integrity and a Christian minister asserts that the picture in "Tobacco Road" by his son is not exaggerated. Frankly, we believe it is, and if it were strictly true the fact that Erskine Caldwell used a single family, afflicted with low mentality and vice, as a type, is certainly grossly unfair. No one seems to have taken the trouble to call for an investigation as to the statements in "Tobacco Road" and the book was dramatized and has been running on Broadway in New York as the outstanding success of the past decade.

*Reprinted from *Augusta Chronicle*, 4 March 1935, p. 4, cols. 1–2.

The Chronicle feels that without further ado we should quote from the last writings of Erskine Caldwell reprinted in "Time" magazine from the New York Evening Post of a recent issue:

"In 1934 a tenant farmer in Jefferson County was unable, because of old age and illness, to work out his crop. A physician prescribed for his ailments, but the man could not buy the medicine, and no relief agency would supply it. A four-year-old girl in the family died at the end of the year of anemia. The tenant moved several miles away to another farm, but after several weeks the landowner decided that he was too old and ill to work a crop on a tenant-farmer basis, or on any other basis, and he was evicted.

"The household goods were carried to the land-limits and deposited by the side of the road. Another tenant took the goods under shelter, and the landowner gave notice that if they were not removed from his land, he would come in to the house and burn them.

"In the meantime the old man had gone off into the swamp, without ax, hammer, or saw, with the intention of felling trees and building a log house for his family. He has not been heard from since he left. . . .

"Near Keysville a two-room house is occupied by three families, each consisting of man and wife and from one to four children each. . . .

In one of the two rooms a six-year-old boy licked the paper bag that meat had been brought in. His legs were scarcely any larger than a medium-sized dog's leg, and his belly was as large as that of a 130-pound woman's. Suffering from rickets and anemia, his legs were unable to carry him for more than a dozen steps at a time; suffering from malnutrition, his belly was swollen several times its normal size. His face was bony and white. He was starving to death.

"In the other room of the house, without chairs, beds, or tables, a woman lay rolled up in some quilts trying to sleep. On the floor before an open fire lay two babies, neither a year old, sucking the dry teats of a mongrel bitch. A young girl somewhere between fifteen and twenty, squatted on the corner of the hearth trying to keep warm.

"The dog got up and crawled to the hearth. She sat on her haunches before the blazing pine-knots, shivering and whining. After a while the girl spoke to the dog and the animal slunk away from the warmth of the fire and lay down again beside the two babies. The infants cuddled against the warmth of the dog's flanks, searching tearfully for the dry teats."

Could such horrible conditions as Caldwell describes exist in any civilized community? What of the churches, of the Christian men and women of Jefferson county? Are they are so indifferent to conditions around them that they would allow them to continue, if such they are? What does the relief administrator of Jefferson county say? What does Judge Hardeman of the superior court say? We know many outstanding citizens of Jefferson county and we do not believe that they would allow such human wretchedness, poverty and depravity to exist. We have in mind Judge B.F. Walker, of Wrens, Judge John R. Phillips, Mr. Robert Bethea, Dr. John R. Lewis, Mrs. Virginia Polhill Price and other outstanding citizens of Jefferson county.

We have an idea that the good people of Jefferson county will go to the bottom of the most recent charges of Erskine Caldwell and do it quickly. If such conditions are true, let's know the truth and if they are not true then let Jefferson county place the world on notice that she is being grossly and outrageously maligned. We are frank to say that we do not believe such condition exists as described by Erskine Caldwell, for some of the good people of the county would have heard about and corrected them.

Is it not time for judges of the superior court in Richmond, Jefferson and other counties where conditions such as depicted in "Tobacco Road" and in the recent article by Caldwell to have grand juries to probe to the bottom? Certainly we know that there is poverty, ignorance and consequently the accompanying vices of filth and depravity, among some of the wretched poor whites of our section and we should bestir ourselves to improve the situation, but we cannot believe that a condition exists anywhere in this section of the South such as Erskine Caldwell depicts in his sensational article. And once proven not to be true let's tell the world about it, so that millions of people in this country may not believe that we are heartless heathens. If by any chance Caldwell is right, let's know the truth, admit it with shame and humiliation and go about correcting it.

"Caldwell Story Called Untrue; Probe Ordered"

Anonymous*

Citizens of Jefferson and Burke counties, incensed over writings of Erskine Caldwell purporting to describe conditions existing in poverty-stricken homes of the Keysville section, yesterday rose to the defense of their counties and branded Caldwell's statements as unfounded.

An editorial in The Augusta Chronicle yesterday morning called attention to Time's reproduction of a column by Erskine Caldwell printed in the New York Evening Post, in which the writer told a sordid tale of

*Reprinted from *Augusta Chronicle*, 5 March 1935, p. 1, cols. 1–2.

squalor and depravity and of the mistreatment by a landlord of one of his land tenants.

Investigations will be launched immediately in both counties to determine whether there is any truth to Caldwell's assertions.

A cotton control conference at Waynesboro yesterday morning developed into an indignation meeting in protest of the Caldwell articles and the gathering voted to call upon the county board of commissioners to conduct an exhaustive investigation.

Dr. John R. Lewis, chairman of the Jefferson county board of commissioners at Louisville, told The Chronicle over the telephone he would start an investigation in his county immediately.

A delegation of four, one man and three women, from Burke county called on Thomas J. Hamilton, editor of The Chronicle, yesterday afternoon and reported proceedings at the cotton conference. They asked Mr. Hamilton's and The Chronicle's help in publicizing their protest. They were Sidney C. Jones, Mrs. Louisa W. Cox, Waynesboro, and Mrs. Grady Adkins and Mrs. G.E. Chandler, Keysville.

Mrs. Cox, an FERA case worker in the Keysville district of Burke county, declared that she had personally investigated every needy family in her district and found none answering the description given by Caldwell.

"I can speak only for Burke county," said Mrs. Cox, "and I know of no such conditions existing in the Keysville section in our county.

"We have some destitute and unfortunate people, of course, but none in the circumstances described in that article. It just seems that Mr. Caldwell is making money at the expense of his own home people."

Mrs. Cox called attention to the fact that while Keysville itself is in Burke, it is located in a corner between Richmond and Jefferson and very near the lines of both of these counties.

Mr. Jones, Mrs. Adkins and Mrs. Chandler substantiated Mrs. Cox's statements.

In his statement to The Chronicle, Dr. Lewis said:

"The statements of Erskine Caldwell, I believe, are entirely unfounded."

"I will start an investigation through the county commission and make a detailed report of true conditions as they are in Jefferson county."

Dr. Lewis said also he has started a survey of relief work in the county and will furnish The Chronicle with a detailed report of money expended, the number of case workers and the number and character of cases, in order to give the truth of the comprehensive coverage of all sections of the county and assistance to all destitute cases.

Letter to the Editor of the *New York Post:* "Share Cropper Conditions Denied"

James Barlow, Jr.*

To the Editor of New York Post:

Sir—Erskine Caldwell has not been to Georgia recently or he writes on hearsay or he treats veracity too lightly. Never have I seen any one in Georgia eating cow dung, but perhaps Mr. Caldwell is referring to his own experience. Such silly stuff as he writes about will make excellent copy for Russian newspapers. Please inform Caldwell that Georgians would prefer that he cease referring to Georgia as his birthplace. Poverty exists everywhere, but such poverty as he writes of is not evident in Georgia.

Being here on the scene of discussion, I am in a position to present the true picture. We are complaining of a second "carpet baggers' " rule. Too many Yankees have been imported to administer relief. They take it as an excellent opportunity to equalize the races by giving much to the Negroes and little to the whites. It is not unusual for a Negro to cash a relief order for $20 or $30 on silk underwear. Georgia's complaint is that residents of the state and not outsiders should administer the relief.

Caldwell's claim that Governor Talmadge is a dictator may be discounted along with everything else he says. These almost pure-blooded people of Anglo-Saxon strain believe as much as ever in rights.

JAMES BARLOW, JR.

*Reprinted from *New York Post*, 6 March 1935, Sec. 1, p. 10, cols. 5–6.

"Erskine Caldwell's Story Starts Two-Way Inquiry"

Anonymous*

Declaring his "county's good name had been maligned" by the writings of Erskine Caldwell, John R. Phillips, Sr., prominent citizen of Jefferson county and former member of the state highway board, last night told The Augusta Chronicle he would make a personal investigation today of conditions in poverty-stricken homes of the Keysville section.

"This is an outrage on the county," Mr. Phillips said. That there is considerable poverty is not to be denied, he explained. "But Caldwell's

*Reprinted from *Augusta Chronicle*, 6 March 1935, p. 1, cols. 2–3; p. 5, col. 3.

story leaves an entirely wrong impression. I want to help clear the good name of my county and its good people," he added.

Mr. Phillips said he expects in his investigation today to study the cases referred to by Mr. Caldwell as far as they can be identified and isolated. He affirmed his confidence that he would find they had been inaccurately pictured.

Dr. J.R. Lewis, chairman of the Jefferson county board of commissioners, after a comprehensive inspection tour of his county yesterday, reported he had been unable to discover any such conditions as described by Caldwell.

He told The Augusta Chronicle over the telephone that while "there was a good deal of poverty" in Jefferson county, he was positive after his investigation that conditions had been greatly exaggerated.

Dr. Lewis said he had talked with relief workers on his tour and had found no one who could confirm the allegations imputed to Mr. Caldwell.

Definite efforts toward overcoming unfavorable publicity given Jefferson and Burke counties through Mr. Caldwell's writings in the New York Evening Post and his novels went forward yesterday when Thomas J. Hamilton, editor of The Augusta Chronicle, made formal request for publication of the answers to Mr. Caldwell's charges.

Mr. Hamilton addressed his request to the magazine Time, in which Caldwell's article in the Evening Post was reprinted, and enclosed clippings of an editorial and a news story printed in The Augusta Chronicle, asking that Time publish a statement on the basis of the clippings "in justice to this section of the South."

Meanwhile, Joel Chappell, county agent in Burke county, told The Augusta Chronicle over long distance telephone last night that Mr. Caldwell "is all wet" when he says anyone has been evicted from a Burke farm under the circumstances cited in the article reprinted in Time and again quoted in The Augusta Chronicle's editorial Monday morning.

"That is plain boloney," said Mr. Chappell. "I have never heard a single complaint from tenants in Burke county occasioned from eviction. I know there certainly has been no such case as that described by Caldwell. We have had and are now having fine cooperation between landlords and tenants and tenants are glad to live on Burke county farms. Right now we are short of tenants, but are placing some every day.

"Caldwell is all wet when he says any Burke landlord ever treated a man as he has described."

In his letter to Time, Mr. Hamilton characterized Mr. Caldwell's statements as "outrageously false" and enclosed the editorial from The Augusta Chronicle and an account of the indignant repudiation of Caldwell by prominent Burke and Jefferson county citizens.

He declared the people of this part of the South "would not tolerate" such conditions as Mr. Caldwell described.

The letter in part was as follows:

"I am enclosing editorial from the Augusta Chronicle of Monday, March 4 and a front page story from today's paper in which Erskine Caldwell's contributions to your paper are discussed. You can readily see from the enclosed clippings that Caldwell's charges have not the slightest vestige of truth and, although we are not proud of the condition of some of our poor whites, none of them have reached the point of utter degradation Caldwell describes in his recent article, or, as for that matter, conditions he depicts in 'Tobacco Road.'

"In justice to this section of the South, I sincerely hope you will print a statement based on the enclosed clippings setting your readers right on this question."

Letter to the Editor of the *Augusta Chronicle:* "Answers Caldwell"

John R. Lewis*

Editor, The Augusta Chronicle:

I note your editorial and the quoting of Mr. Erskine Caldwell, as to the pitiable condition that he pictures in Jefferson county. His father, for whom I have respect as a preacher and teacher, several years ago criticized the county officials in regard to a blind couple in the upper part of the county. He was in error as to the county not assisting this couple. We were providing funds for their maintenance at the time. We had offered them a place in the county home. He was simply mistaken. I corrected his error in the paper. I believe the Rev. Mr. Caldwell was sincere and is sincere in seeking to do deeds of charity. It has always been a pleasure to cooperate with him in his work.

In justice to the splendid communities of Wrens, Matthews and the entire county, I feel it my duty to reply to Mr. Erskine Caldwell's article. After a painstaking investigation, I can not locate the family where the babies were nursing the teats of a mongrel dog. I have been unable to locate the starving man. I believe I have located the anemic little girl mentioned. She received every care at the hands of a very competent physician, Dr. J.J. Pilcher, of Wrens, Ga., who states, "she did not die from neglect but from pneumonia." She was buried in a white casket, furnished the family by Jefferson county.

The relief organization in Jefferson county denies Mr. Erskine Caldwell's assertion. Mr. Roach, in charge of the relief work is my authority. Miss Hall, county aide at Wrens, Ga., further denies it. They admit there is some poverty and want in Jefferson county which is not an

*Reprinted from *Augusta Chronicle*, 10 March 1935, p. 4, cols. 4–5.

exception to any other county—or section. That in some instances you find families with a low mentality that do not appreciate, comprehend, or take advantage of the opportunities offered them for improvement. To a great extent are satisfied with their lot. I am frank to state that I believe Mr. Caldwell has over-exaggerated. That possibly he has a very imaginary mind that creates such vivid imagination that he actually believes to be true things that are not true. That he does not stop to think or realize that he reflects on the intelligence and high type of citizenship that Jefferson county possesses. That he is endeavoring to commercialize on a possible instance of poverty in a community at the expense of humiliating a majority of good citizens. Publicity and commercial remuneration at the expense of a poor, unfortunate person or family is regrettable. His desires should be to assist, aid and endeavor to uplift humanity to a higher type of living and citizenship. One that does not do so is a party to the wants and needs of others. Therefore, I respectfully request that he furnish the name of the family in question, giving the location, address, etc. If he can not furnish these facts, he must admit his statements were an exaggeration of facts, misleading and unwarranted.

New York city and other cities have gangsters but this does not mean every inhabitant is one. Quite the reverse is true.

The idea presented is that he should not overstate conditions, to the detriment of the majority of citizens or to the injustice of those in the minority though poor.

Jefferson county is full of culture and refinement. As intelligent people live within its bounds as are to be found anywhere. Certainly, we have poor people in the county—among them I number myself. Being poor is no disgrace—nothing to be ashamed of in the sight of God or man. People here are prompt to visit others and assist any in distress or want, day or night. I can name instances if need be the case.

Jefferson county levies the maximum amount of tax rate that is allowed to care for those in need or distress. We have a well-kept county home. Admits both white and black people that need the services it renders. We have a health officer, a county health nurse. We have a county agent to assist the farmers. A large part of home supplies are raised on the farms of this fertile agricultural county. Milk in many instances has been furnished undernourished children. We have splendid schools, various industries that speak for progress, intelligence and culture. We are proud of our county, its citizenship.

Jesus Christ was poor; born in a manger. The only perfect man that ever walked this earth. We have poor people but an honorable people. A people that make their living according to the scriptures, by the sweat of their faces. Were the entire country in as good shape as Jefferson county the relief rolls would soon banish.

Mr. Caldwell does an injustice to his native county and state. He does an injustice to himself and does not deserve any credit for his criticisms if he does not assist in correcting them. I wish to call his attention to the two characters in the Bible. The only perfect man—he was poor. And one of the perfect man's disciples that went wrong for the love of silver. A splendid lesson to study. It is to be hoped that Mr. Caldwell's pen, mind and endeavors will direct him to a higher plane of usefulness. That he will be found in person trying to improve as best he can any human being's lot. It is regrettable that he should try to commercialize and advertise the poverty of some individual case at the expense of the good citizens of this splendid county. To seek to commercialize on the poverty of some unfortunate human being, one that may be handicapped by being intellectually off, or may be poor, honest, upright and intelligent and have some illness wreck him physically and financially. Many good people in Jefferson county resent his articles. Some consider the cause that prompts it, believing he is desirous of advertising himself and commercializing for the advancement of himself in a financial way.

I wish to thank The Chronicle for calling the attention to these articles he has written, and feel certain that there will be other protests to his writings.

Respectfully,
JOHN R. LEWIS

Louisville, Ga.

Letter to the Editor of *Time:*
"Caldwell's Hog Wallow"

Warren H. Pierce*

. . . Erskine Caldwell is seizing upon an isolated instance or two of injustice to tenant farmers by Jefferson County landowners to paint the county as a sink of iniquity. As a damyankee of many generation's standing, I cannot be accused of rushing to the defense of my native State. But by profession trained to accurate observation and impartial reporting, and speaking from six years' intimate familiarity with Jefferson County, I can say that a more contemptible libel has never been uttered about any community.

What Caldwell would term the bourgeoisie of that county are cultured, kindly and humane people. Their attitude toward, and relationship with, the tenant classes, white and colored, is friendly and sympathetic in the highest degree. To be sure there are cases of social injustice in Jefferson County, as there are in every county in every State in the

*Reprinted from *Time*, 25 (March 25, 1935), 8. Reprinted by persmission from TIME, The Weekly Newsmagazine; Copyright © Time Inc. 1935.

Union. But I have yet to see the community with as low a percentage of social injustice as that one which Caldwell would hold up to the world as a horrible example.

Erskine Caldwell is one of those neurasthenic egomaniacs in the infliction of which upon mankind the Creator seems to have been guilty of unnecessary harshness to an erring world. . . .

One superb talent Caldwell has. Give him a single stink and he can create a magnificent hog wallow, a singularly appropriate gift for those of his ilk.

WARREN H. PIERCE

The Daily Clintonian
Clinton, Ind.

Letter to the Editor of *Time:* "Father"

I.S. Caldwell*

Sirs:

ERSKINE CALDWELL'S STORY ESSENTIALLY TRUE. NO INVESTIGATION MADE, EFFORTS BEING TO COVER UP FACTS. NEWSPAPER PROPAGANDA IS BEING SENT IN EFFORT TO HIDE FACTS IN CASE. PEOPLE NOT ON GROUND DENOUNCE THE STORY AS FALSE.

I.S. Caldwell
(Father of Erskine Caldwell)
Pastor

Presbyterian Church
Wrens, Ga.

Since sending the foregoing telegram, Father Caldwell was given the opportunity to assist in an investigation.

Editor

*Reprinted from *Time*, 25 (March 25, 1935), 8. Reprinted by permission from TIME, The Weekly Newsmagazine; Copyright © Time Inc. 1935.

"Investigation Is Made To Determine Basis Caldwell Had For All His Writings"

Anonymous*

EDITOR'S NOTE

The Augusta Chronicle today begins a series of articles dealing with conditions existing in certain very small sections of Jefferson and Burke counties. The Chronicle wishes it understood at the outset that these articles are not being printed with a view of indicting any county or section or individuals. This newspaper was prompted to make an investigation because of national unfavorable publicity given this section by articles written by Erskine Caldwell. The controversy over the Caldwell articles had reached such an intense stage that The Chronicle felt that an investigation was demanded, and therefore has gone to considerable expense and time to present what it believes is an accurate and unbiased picture to its readers in Jefferson, Burke and Richmond counties. The Chronicle holds no brief for Erskine Caldwell, and does not defend either his writings or the manner in which he purportedly presented conditions as they existed in the section in which he was reared. The two members of The Chronicle staff who visited the families described in The Chronicle articles found the conditions recorded existing in such an exceedingly small and isolated section of these two counties that it can not help but believe that the true picture of conditions will clear once and for all the name of our good neighbors in Burke and Jefferson counties.

Seeking to probe beneath the surface of Erskine Caldwell's descriptive writings which have aroused the resentment of Jefferson and Burke county residents, we have visited the section from which Caldwell drew his material and have observed the most poverty-stricken people of the Wrens-Keysville region.

What we have seen, coupled with the information we have obtained from official and other sources, leads to the conclusion that there exist families in utter need of rehabilitation, not typical of Jefferson county alone, but such as are to be found in all parts of the country.

The number of these families in the so-called Sand Hill section of the county, an elongated area extending along a creek dividing Richmond and Jefferson counties, and continuing a short distance into Burke county, is variously estimated from 10 or 12 to 35.

*Reprinted from *Augusta Chronicle*, 10 March 1935, p. 1, cols. 4–5, p. 19, cols. 4–5.

Regardless of the figure, maximum or minimum, it is still true, and it is a direct assertion as a result of our survey, that the persons referred to by Erskine Caldwell in all of his writings form a minute portion of the population of Jefferson county. We have been told, and we believe, that investigation in any area would produce a similar proportion of human derelicts. Some live in backwoods section of rural areas, others inhabit filthy quarters in city slums.

Most of these people are not only poor but wretched, living in want and squalor, victims of their own shiftlessness and ignorance. Their like, authorities point out, are everywhere, the unfortunate substratum of any region's population.

There are some instances of dire degeneration, our survey discloses. Many of these families have been for years what they are now. Efforts to better their condition often meet with no response. They are ignorant and content with little. They are a prey to disease, often subject to moral laxity and almost entirely divested of civilized ideals.

The problem presented to relief workers is a difficult one to cope with. Ignorance and stubborn reserve frequently cause the most needy families to refuse medical aid or food to satisfy their want. Cases have been reported in which blankets and like articles, sorely needed by the sufferers, have been sold as soon as they were received from relief agencies.

Nevertheless, our study shows, relief work continues. Eligible families are provided with their pro rata share of food and clothing when their cases are reported or discovered. But, relief workers say, their aid is often futile, for even though it may be accepted it is likely to bring no permanent improvement.

Among citizens of Jefferson county, it appears there is a feeling that Erskine Caldwell by using such families as types has created a false impression in his writings, an impression that in the area about Keysville there are pitiable conditions of human degradation peculiar to the region alone. There is further feeling that Mr. Caldwell has exaggerated his descriptions with lurid details not drawn from fact.

The Rev. I.S. Caldwell, father of the writer and principal of the Wrens high school, believes implicitly, we found, in the fairness of his son's descriptive sketches and other works treating of the locality. He sees in them in humanitarian purpose, a desire on his son's part to focus attention upon unfortunate conditions in the hope they will be amended.

The writer's father himself guided The Chronicle's representatives to a number of the worst afflicted dwellings. We saw, in some instances, large families living amidst extreme poverty in dilapidated one and two-room houses, unfit for human habitation. We observed unmistakable evidence of malnutrition, disease and moral degeneration.

We were met by dull, stolid, stupid people, seemingly unaware of all their ills save hunger. Their clothes were rags, in many cases. They seemed to possess no jot of pride of appearance. From babies to adults, nearly all were unkempt and dirty.

These people, we found, may be divided into three general classes. There are tenant farmers and sharecroppers, whose condition is usually above that of the others. There are wage hands, who manage to do some labor and earn a small and irregular income, but who suffer serious want. And there are what may be called derelicts, wretched people either unwilling or unfit to work, who beg what they eat and live where they can, possessing practically nothing.

It is these last who are in the most miserable plight, our investigation disclosed. The tenants and wage hands, squalid as their circumstances may be and however acute their want, still have something. But the derelicts, suffering from disease and near starvation, shorn of all initiative, are to all intents and purposes irresponsible. They are, in the full meaning of the phrase, a burden on society.

Recognizing these conditions as existing to a limited extent, several prominent citizens of Jefferson county see a need for corrective measures wherever such degradation is found throughout the county. The consensus seems to be that, in many instances, scientific sterilization would play a great role in removing from society its worst enemy, the dregs of itself.

"Erskine Caldwell"

Anonymous*

Following is the second of a series of articles . . .

Visiting scenes purportedly described in the writings of Erskine Caldwell, we found in the "sand hill" section of Burke and Jefferson counties striking examples of poverty and human degeneracy.

These examples, we learned, are not so numerous as to be typical of the county. They are, on the contrary, only a number of individual cases, variously estimated at from 10 to 35, of a universal class of poverty-stricken, shiftless, helpless people distributed everywhere throughout the county.

Guided by the Rev. I.S. Caldwell, father of the writer and principal of the Wrens high school, we made a tour of the area considered most thickly populated by families of the most unfortunate type. This narrow region extends roughly from Wrens to Keysville, centering about Noah and dipping into Burke county.

When we started our trip, accompanied also by W.J. Wren, Jr., son

*Reprinted from *Augusta Chronicle*, 11 March 1935, p. 1, col. 1; p. 4, col. 5.

of the founder of the town Wrens, it was understood we were to see chiefly those families suffering most acutely from poverty, ignorance and disease, which are but a minute part of the whole population.

The condition of these families differs. As a general rule, those who are tenant farmers and sharecroppers are in the least pitiable circumstances, while the wage hands, poor as they are, still have something to rely upon. It is the derelicts, doing no work and having no property, who usually are faring worst.

Of the families we observed perhaps the most prosperous is one living about three miles from Matthews. The head of this family of 16 is a tenant working a two-horse farm, for which he pays 800 pounds of cotton rent a year. Last year his crop amounted to four bales. After paying two bales for rent and the other two for fertilizer and funds previously advanced to work his farm, this tenant was left with a profit of 62 cents. For cutting his crop he was to receive $55 from the government, but his check never came, he said. In his ignorance he has no idea why.

There are eight children in the family, only one of whom, a 17-year-old boy, can so much as write his name. The father has an old car, practically a wreck, which the boys use in gathering pine sticks. These they carry to Augusta and sell as kindling wood at one cent a small bundle. They make about five trips a month, when there is a demand, and realize approximately four dollars a load, from which they must deduct their expense for gas and oil.

The head of this family has no other source of income and must provide for 16 persons besides himself. His dwelling is a ramshackle two-room house. His children and the other members of his family are dirty and poorly clad. But they seem in their ignorance fairly satisfied with their lot. Food is their only real concern, but they are not starving.

In the same vicinity we observed a squalid one-room shack occupied by a family of four. The father earns 50 cents a day as a wage hand when he can find work. He has no other means of support and is not eligible for relief. He was described to us as a hardworking, unmoral man. Like many of his counterparts he lacks almost completely a moral sense. But he is not vicious, merely unthinking, stolid and dumb.

His one-room house is in a state of dilapidation. The furnishings, worthless and scanty, consist of two beds covered with rags for bedding, two cheap broken chairs and a few boxes for seats. Otherwise the room is empty except for plunder and trash.

About four miles northwest of Wrens we visited a two-horse farm occupied by the tenant, his wife, five children and two grandchildren. The mother of the two smallest children has shown evidences of social disease for years. Her health and appearance are pitiful. Her child, when we saw it, wore only one garment, a soiled dress.

The head of this household is not eligible for relief since he is a tenant farmer. Last year he decreased his acreage but received nothing from the government due to his failure to sign a crop control contract. He suffers from high blood pressure and is unfit to work much. His house is small and run-down.

No effort is shown to keep the premises tidy. The children wear filthy rags. A little boy, who should be in school, cannot attend for lack of shoes.

A short distance within the limits of Burke county we inspected a wretched two-room shack that feebly houses four half-starved people. The father is unable to work because of heart trouble. The wife, a 60-year-old woman is so weak from malnutrition she sometimes can hardly walk. Yet she has plodded at times 10 weary miles to Wrens that she might be able to beg a little food.

Her son, 21-year-old boy suffering from inadequate nourishment, does relief work as often as there is an opportunity. Since Christmas he has had 12 days work, earning $1.20 a day. They have no land for a garden.

When we visited this house there was not a bite of food in it. All they ever have is cornbread, the woman said, uncovering her empty meal barrel.

Despite its impoverished condition the family has made a place in its home for a young woman who had no place else to turn. The shelter she shares is almost futile, for the roof of the house is riddled with holes. The son has attempted patching the roof with odd scraps of wood, so that one small corner is partly waterproof. For furniture these people possess only two rickety rag-covered beds, three wabbily chairs and two rough home-made tables.

Working in a field was a 69-year-old woman with her young daughter. Both had nothing but rags for clothing. The woman's canvas shoes, her only pair, were worse than worn out, holding together only by shreds.

Having no men to support them, the woman and the girl both must work for a living. A few times, whenever there is work, the girl does relief work. She is paid $1.20 for a day's work but must spend fifty cents each time for transportation. During 1935, the old woman said, the only things she received from relief agencies were two and a half pounds of cheese and three cans of beef.

Utterly resigned to her lot, she feels no shame in her penurious circumstances. "I'm ragged and poor," she said. "I was born poor and I'll die poor, but I work for an honest living."

At one house we visited we saw a 13-year-old girl from another family. Having been a victim of a social disease all her life, her appearance was revolting. One eye was totally gone and the other in the last stages. Her face was distorted by the ravages of disease. Since her infancy, we were told by people who knew her, she has had no medical attention. There was no reaction to a statement the child may go blind.

About three miles from Matthews we found a dirty one-room house occupied by a mother, her 20-year-old son and an imbecile daughter who has two children and apparently is expecting another. Stupidly the young woman told that different men were the fathers of her children. She evinced no shame or sense of propriety. One man was her cousin, she told us.

In the house were two filthy beds with tatters, for bedding, a fireplace, a bench and a chair, all needing repair. There was nothing else in the room save junk and trash.

When he can get work, the son earns 40 cents a day. This is their sole income and it is irregular. We found the mother washing a few ragged clothes at a spring a half-mile from the house. When the spring dries up, she said, she must carry water a mile to do her washing.

Perhaps the most pitiful case we encountered was one a few miles north of Matthews. Here a man and his 16-year-old daughter are living together in a squalid one-room shack made available to them by a sympathetic landowner. The furniture consists of two old beds covered with grimy bits of quilting, two makeshift tables and nothing else. His uncle, the man explained, took everything else away from him.

The two of them have nothing to eat but what they can beg from poor people of the neighborhood. The man, who has a wife and other children elsewhere, is physically unfit for labor. Suffering from heart trouble and malnutrition, he is gaunt, weak and emaciated. When we met him he was ascending a slight slope to his house carrying a light piece of tree limb, but he was gasping as if under a heavy burden.

Both he and his daughter are dumb and stolid, their faces vacant of intelligent expression. The girl attended school as far as the first grade only. Now and then, when there is work to do, she earns a little money from relief projects.

One spark of civilized yearnings remains with these two. After we had searched their blank faces in vain for signs of intelligence and had been depressed by the dirty meanness of their household, we were cheered on observing a last single trace of human superiority.

In a small space in front of their wretched hovel, patiently cleared of weeds, were planted a small cedar tree and a few lonely jonquils.

"Erskine Caldwell"

Anonymous*

Following is the third of a series of articles . . .

Fifteen years' practice of medicine among the people of all classes in the territory around Wrens has afforded Dr. J.J. Pilcher an intimate

*Reprinted from *Augusta Chronicle*, 12 March, p. 1, col. 1; p. 4, col. 5.

knowledge of social conditions in those parts of Jefferson and Burke counties dealt with in the writings of Erskine Caldwell.

As part of our investigation into these conditions we interviewed Dr. Pilcher at his office in Wrens. He described to us what he called "gloomy pictures" of the poverty, physical suffering and degeneracy of some families in the region, particularly the "sand hill" area in north Jefferson county.

Dr. Pilcher places the number of these families of his personal experience at only 10 or 12. They exist, he pointed out, in all localities. As a type peculiar to no special region, they are ignorant, shiftless and incapable. They have been for years the same as they are now and will continue to be the same if left to themselves.

During his 15 years in Wrens, Dr. Pilcher told us, he has had ample opportunity to observe these people closely and to mark what few changes come into their lives. As long as he has known them they have remained practically unchanged.

"The plight of these families has been deplorable many years, since long before I began treating them," Dr. Pilcher said. "Even in more prosperous times this degradation was much the same as now."

When we informed him that we had visited some of these families ourselves to study their living conditions first hand, Dr. Pilcher, presuming correctly that our observations were made during the day, explained we had not chosen the proper time if we wanted to view the most impressive scenes.

"You should have gone in the evening," he said. "It is a gloomy picture to see these families huddling in at bedtime."

Dr. Pilcher described to us hurriedly the kind of houses the most unfortunate families occupy, the same sort of dwellings we had seen the day before on our tour into the country not far from Wrens. Most of them were one and two-room shacks, sometimes not sufficiently intact to give shelter against the rain, furnished usually with only one or two beds that had rags and tatters for bedding and little else.

Often Dr. Pilcher has given his services free to these people in their illness. But he finds them difficult patients. Few of them can read. Generally their mentality is extremely low. Consequently it is hard to find anyone among their number capable of administering treatment after the doctor has prescribed.

He recounted several incidents in his medical work around the "sand hill" section illustrative of the ignorance and primitiveness with which a physician must cope.

On one occasion, the doctor said, he answered a call to one of the backward families late at night. He was surprised when his knock was answered to see all members of the family rush to the door fully clothed. Immediately he suspected they were not in the habit of undressing, so he asked how often his patient had a bath and change of clothes. "About once a month," was the reply.

As an example of the stupid stubbornness the people he was discussion so often display, Dr. Pilcher related another story from his medical experience. The case of a member of one of the most poverty-stricken and degenerate families was reported to him. When he went to investigate he found the man suffering from cancer and in a serious condition.

He immediately offered to have his patient carried to Augusta for proper treatment. But the man refused over all the doctor's urging. Later Dr. Pilcher learned that the same person had fallen into the hands of a "quack" who brought him no improvement. In a few years the man was dead.

Dr. Pilcher also investigated the case of a child believed the same one referred to by Erskine Caldwell as dying of anemia. Actually, he said, she had a violent hookworm infestation, influenza and pneumonia.

The authorities sought to remove the child to a hospital for medical care, but the mother refused her consent because another member of the family had died in a hospital. The child did not live long afterward.

Due to the nature of the soil on which they live, to their unhygienic mode of living and to their lack of shoes, hookworm is highly prevalent among these people.

This class usually understand nothing about the general principles of hygiene, according to Dr. Pilcher, but they often show great faith in "pills and medicine." For this reason they are easy dupes to "quacks" and hoodoo doctors.

Perhaps their greatest menace, it was indicated, is the prevalence of social diseases among them. From his close observation Dr. Pilcher has been led to the conclusion that within this particular class certain forms of these diseases are increasing.

In his opinion their chief immediate needs are food and an exhaustive examination for symptoms of social diseases. Their salvation, if it is to come, he believes lies in some scientific improvement program administered by the federal government.

There is no doubt Dr. Pilcher has a deep sympathy for these families. Although he recognizes that they are almost universally ignorant and degenerate, sometimes appallingly debased, at times believed to be guilty of incest, he has found good qualities among them. He acknowledges their honesty and appreciation.

Among the many heart-rending scenes he has witnessed, he remembers vividly being called once to the bedside of a man with heart disease who had long been his patient. The man's case was incurable and the doctor found him writhing in agony while other members of the family sat about solidly in apparent unconcern.

Within two hours of Dr. Pilcher's arrival his patient died, but not before he had thanked the doctor for his long help and sympathy. Dr. Pilcher considered himself amply repaid. The next day the man's family came to him to ask for a coffin.

By way of comment Dr. Pilcher added, "If we could get these people concerned about their manner of living as about their burial, it would be far better. Jim had nothing in life in keeping with a $35 casket."

"Erskine Caldwell"

Anonymous*

Following is the fourth of a series of articles . . .

Having viewed conditions of poverty, disease and want in some eight families, and having been told during our investigation of possible bases for the controverted writings of Erskine Caldwell that there were other families in Jefferson county variously estimated to a total of 35 in similar condition, it was only natural that we should desire to inquire into the administration of relief and charity in the county.

For this purpose, we found a willing helper in Dr. John R. Lewis, chairman of the Jefferson county commission of roads and revenues. First he explained the help that the county itself is giving to the poor.

He placed the income of Jefferson county from real estate taxes and from the county's share of the state gasoline tax at approximately $70,000 a year. Of this, he said, about 10 per cent, or $7,000 a year, is devoted to the care of the poor of the county.

A large part of the fund is expended on the county poor house which at present houses 16 inmates, eight white and eight colored. Salaries of attendants, which include a superintendent, seamstress, cook and two assistants for the institutional farm, form the chief expense since most of the meat, vegetables and milk, for the table of the home are produced on the farm.

Diets according to needs as described by physicians are furnished the inmates, and medical attention is afforded to all persons needing it.

In addition to care of these inmates, the county regularly contributes to the support of other families, contributions being made on a monthly basis according to the need of the family. In December, 1934, when the Federal Emergency Relief administration ordered all persons listed as unemployables taken from its direct relief rolls and returned to the county for care, the Jefferson county commission agreed to contribute to the support of 61 such persons, Dr. Lewis told us.

In summing up his survey of county work, Dr. Lewis said "no one suffers for food, clothes or medical attention in Jefferson county if we know they are in need."

*Reprinted from *Augusta Chronicle*, 13 March 1935, p. 1, col. 1; p. 3, cols. 2–3.

It was through Dr. Lewis that we gained most of our information concerning the activities of the Federal Emergency Relief administration in the county.

We were told that allotments to the county for work relief projects usually varied from $4,000 to $5,000 a month, with cost of supervision to be deducted. In addition, the county administrator receives various supplies from the Surplus Commodity Purchase corporation which are distributed to eligible families numbering about 400. These supplies include butter, cheese, canned beef, cloth, and other commodities purchased on a market stabilization basis by the government. The receipt of supplies varies from month to month according to the purchases effected, we were told.

Farm rehabilitation activity through the FERA has reached a rather mature stage in the county, and some 75 farmers have been returned to workable farms and given their stakes for the first year's operation.

We were told that a majority of the 400 persons on relief roles are negroes.

In our investigation, we visited families which fell into three classes: tenant farmers, wage hands and those who were neither, living purely on what they could beg.

These first two classes, the tenant farmers and wage hands, are not eligible for FERA aid in any form. It is a rule of the administration, and no matter how much relief investigators—all of whom know the families we visited—want to aid them, there is no provision for them in the present set-up.

Of the third class—the drifters—there are few who are eligible for relief at the present time since they are listed in most cases as unemployables. Whether it is disease, malnutrition, laziness, incapacity, mental inability or stubbornness, it is still true that there are some persons who are not able to do the day's work required on FERA work relief projects. Relief records, however, show that others have been given aid from time to time, some starting as far back as November, 1933, others as late as January 1934. Official records were not available on these families.

In the main, these families have been given commodities, especially during that period before the unemployables were ordered off relief roles.

We found instances among the families we visited of young women, some of them girls about 15 years of age, having been given according to their own statement, two or three days of work on a woman's project. They said they were paid at the rate of $1.20 a day, and that they had to pay 40, and in one case, 50 cents, for transportation into Wrens to arrive at the work. These transportation charges are not made by the FERA, but by individuals, so far as we could learn, since the FERA has no way of providing transportation for the people.

In every case, it appeared to us, the relief work afforded these women or girls was "around Christmas" and the project upon which they can be employed apparently does not run regularly, but depends upon a large budget for the months in which it can be conducted.

In reference to the ability of the male members of the family to work, we talked with a prosperous farmer living on the edge of the section we visited. His farm includes some 1,000 acres, and he has several high type tenants helping him to operate it.

He depicted the people as unable to work. His assertion that "I would not let one of the families come on my place" was prompted, he said, by the fact that the men are unable to do a day's work and do not know how to farm if given an opportunity.

This same farmer has seen futile attempts to aid the families. Food can be carried in, and is eaten quickly. Clothes and bedding given are never seen again, and he presumes they are sold. At the present time, his wife is a member of a society preparing clothes to enable some of the young girls to attend an opportunity school operated by the FERA. We were told there were some 12 of these schools in various sections of the county.

We found one boy who had attended. He learned to write his name, and went no more. He was the only member of a family of 16 whose education extended that far.

This prosperous farmer told us that the families—their names are on the tongues of many people of Wrens and Louisville—live the best way they can, begging most of the time, and being very proficient at the art; that they associate apparently only with each other, inter-marry, and bring forth children to be raised by the same standard; that they have been in that particular section for many years, and that all indications are that they will remain there until something is done about it.

It is a conclusion of a doctor with whom we talked, a conclusion of farmers, a conclusion of the relief workers and a conclusion of ours that there are no rules in the FERA manuals applying to these families. There are no methods of ordinary charity, we were told, which will better their lot more than temporarily.

We were told that these families—backed by generations of poverty and ignorance, want and disease, moral laxity and lack of ambition— must be cared for in some particular manner, a manner which yet is to be devised.

Rehabilitation with them, a physician told us, is not a matter of a farm and a stake for a crop. It is a matter of institutional care for the olders ones and many of the younger ones; slow rehabilitation and education of the better of the younger ones not for themselves alone but for their children.

Apparently, and from the best information available, it has taken generations to breed the worst degenerates of the group; it is the opinion of those who know these families best that what has taken so long to do can not be undone in a short time, and then, only with expert sociological direction backed by large funds and compelling authority.

"Erskine Caldwell"

Anonymous*

Following is the last of a series of articles . . .

Our investigation of conditions of living of a small group of families in a particular area of Jefferson and Burke counties having been started as the result of writings of Erskine Caldwell, one of our foremost purposes was to discover what, if any, truth was behind his statements.

In our contacts with several families of the type about which he wrote, and in our conversations with other people of the section, including farmers, relief workers, physicians and leading citizens, we had several questions prodding our minds for answers. Among these questions were:

1. Was there any basis at all for his writings?

2. If such people and conditions as he wrote about existed, was Caldwell the only one who knew of them, or did other people of Wrens and Louisville know them also?

3. If conditions as described by Caldwell existed, what was the objection to the publishing of his articles?

We found answers to all of these questions. In a series of articles concluded with this one, the conditions as we found them existing among eight families have been described. Poverty, disease, ignorance and lack of ambition, coupled with moral laxity in some cases, were typical of what we found. We were told that there were between 10 or 12 and 35 families of the type in Jefferson county.

In answering the first question, we are forced to say that there is some basis for the writings of Erskine Caldwell. We did not observe the details of what he said in his writings, but we did observe the conditions under which depicted events could have happened. We observed a group of people lacking in ambition, lacking in concern for the conventionalities of civilization and lacking in any connection with the world which comprises civilization and thrives within a short distance from their squalid abodes.

Perhaps the most piquing description made by Caldwell in one of his articles was that of two babies attempting to find food from "the dry teats

---

*Reprinted from *Augusta Chronicle*, 14 March 1935, p. 1, col. 1; p. 8, cols. 3–6.

of a mongrel bitch." We did not see this, nor did we find anyone who had seen it. We did find families with scant food, with no income, with nothing but hope that they could beg food on which to keep alive, and in some there were infant babies.

In making the statement that there is some basis for the writings of Erskine Caldwell, we are not endorsing all the details as depicted by him, for we did not view them. We merely are making a statement that there exist a few families in the most destitute circumstances imaginable— destitute not only economically, but morally as well.

The second question does anyone else know of the families, must be answered in the affirmative. We were surprised at the number of people who named the very families we had visited before we told them where we had been. We were told of several events surpassing those which we had seen.

It was quite common for those with whom we talked to relate the story of a man suspected of having raised a family by his oldest daughter after his wife died.

The fact that these conditions exist among a small number of people and the fact that their condition is known by residents of Wrens and Louisville does not mean that no attention is paid to them. In a previous article, the extension of relief to them was described, eligible persons under the rules of the FERA receiving their pro rata share of all commodities distributed in the county.

There are several answers to the third question, what is the objection to the writings of Caldwell?

We found those who said there was not a word of truth in what Caldwell wrote, that he had exaggerated small details to make large ones.

We found, too, a prosperous farmer on the edge of the section where the most destitute persons live who said he believed there was a basis for every statement made by Caldwell, but that Caldwell had written his articles in "a sensational manner to make them sell."

Among those who admitted conditions of degradation among a small number of families, we found several who held to the opinion that Caldwell should not have had his articles published in northern newspapers and magazines, but should have spent his time at home getting aid for the families.

The greatest objection to the Caldwell articles we discovered to be the possible interpretation from them that he was describing a typical family of Jefferson county.

We have tried in this series of articles to convey the impression that the people of whom we were writing comprised a minute portion of the population of the county, less than one per cent, and we have found that Caldwell drew his material from these same people.

There was no statement in the Caldwell articles to give an impression that he was writing about all the people of Jefferson county; nor was there any statement to give the impression that he was writing about a small group.

His greatest error, it appears, was in not prefacing his remarks with an explanation that the people of whom he was writing, purportedly in a true manner, were limited in number and were to be found only on side roads, on poor land which no one else wanted to use or had abandoned after getting the best from it.

There were residents of Louisville and Wrens who denounced Caldwell in unprintable terms; there were others who defended him.

He was accused of commercializing the wretched condition of a poverty stricken group of people, of using his imagination with a touch of sensationalism.

Some recalled that he had written of conditions equally as bad that he claimed to have found on travels through the west; others said he was going to the north with slanderous writings against the south.

Naturally, we attempted to find some reason behind his articles, some motive for his writings.

It is a true statement that Caldwell's father, the Rev. I.S. Caldwell, has spent a large part of his lifetime in investigating people of that class which we visited. The Rev. Mr. Caldwell says they are not to be found alone in Jefferson county. His work has carried him to many counties of the state, and he proclaims a small group of degraded people live in every section, along the back roads on poor land; it is his belief that similar conditions exist all over the nation. Nor are these conditions limited to rural sections. Slum of large cities furnish scattered tales of degradation, and cities of all sizes have such families living in their border sections.

Erskine Caldwell, since the time he was 11 years old, lived in Jefferson county, went with his father on visits to the poverty stricken class, observed them under all conditions; he made many trips alone, or with friends.

The Rev. Mr. Caldwell preaches on necessary assistance to the class of people we visited. He maintains not ordinary charity is needed, but specialized sociological work. He says their condition is the result of poverty and ignorance bred through generations, and that their presence is not an indictment against anyone. Prevention of the development of such people in the future is his chief desire.

Both the Rev. Mr. Caldwell and Mrs. Caldwell say Erskine's interest in the class of people is with a motive of having something done to correct their condition and their future development. They say that through his writings he hopes to center attention on their deplorable lot and have a movement started to eradicate such conditions, and preclude the possibility of conditions of the like in the future. They explain, too, that Erskine knows the conditions exist all over the nation but that he writes of Jefferson county because he knows Jefferson county.

The Rev. Mr. Caldwell said Erskine sends money home to be used to ease the conditions of existence among the people.

It is not to be denied that Erskine reaps a rich harvest from his writings. His "Tobacco Road" alone yields him a good income, especially since it was dramatized on the New York stage. Those who charge him with commercializing the conditions of the people say his success with that book prompted his subsequent articles.

Generally speaking, we found feeling over Erskine Caldwell and his work sharply divided with everyone willing to express an opinion on one side or the other.

Nevertheless, we discovered a peculiar race of people, limited in number, suffering a number of diseases, living in squalor, displaying ignorance.

One of the most remarkable facts connected with the entire investigation was the repeated assertion that the people of that class never came in conflict with the law, never resorted to stealing to relieve acute want and suffering, but plodded along in the best manner possible, getting food where it was given or where it could be earned with some simple work.

Letter to the Editor of
The Augusta Chronicle:
"Mr. Caldwell Writes"

I. S. Caldwell*

Editor, The Chronicle:

Many years ago when I was in the teen age a good neighbor of ours died of malignant cancer. For a long time she was able to conceal the thing from her husband and children. When it could not be longer concealed a physician was called but he was helpless because of the advanced stage of the disease. There was nothing the family could do except to watch her life ebb away.

For many years our rather boastful and for a time cocksure civilization has been developing the cancer of social injustice that has been weakening the fabric of our civilization. We have been kidding ourselves and going on our hilarious way in the foolish faith that the government at Washington would stand until the end of time. All the while the deadly cancer of social injustice was spreading in all levels of our social order. We have tried to keep the thing hidden from sight. When gaunt poverty dared show itself in public we told ourselves that these people were only few in number and that they were the authors of their own undoing.

When Christmas time came the public conscience was salved by the bestowing of gifts upon the needy by individuals, churches and civic organizations. These gifts were nothing more than a temporary anodyne.

*Reprinted from *Augusta Chronicle*, 17 March 1935, p. 4, cols. 5–6.

The disease continued its ravages unabated. We continued to put up a front and to talk foolishly about developing rugged individuality.

At last we have come to that stage where the disease of crushing poverty can no longer be concealed. Thoughtful people are thankful for the fact that the Augusta Chronicle violated general custom in newspaper circles by giving to the public a glimpse of conditions in Jefferson and adjoining counties. The conditions are worse and poverty has a wider spread than The Chronicle stories indicated but a good beginning has been made.

Of course unthinking people will dismiss the subject by saying that these unfortunate people are the authors of their own misfortunes, but thoughtful people are beginning to realize that every individual is to a large extent the product of his environment, of the institutions that men have set up, of the social forces that society lets loose. No man is self-made and no man is self-unmade. The families depicted by the staff men of The Chronicle are the products of our social institutions. An investigation reveals the fact that at least ninety per cent of the poverty crushed people of this part of Georgia are members of the Christian church and these same people as well as other observant people realize that often time helpless men are exploited without any semblance of mercy by members of their own church.

Unfortunately The Chronicle writers counted the unfortunate by tens when they ought to have been counted by hundreds or thousands. It is to be hoped that the revelations made will suffice to end once and for all time the foolish cover-up policy that has kept society from sensing the imminent danger in which our social order stands.

Owing to the pull of the business office it is hard for the average managing editor to use his paper as an instrument for social welfare. But as a matter of fact the public is more than ready to support a newspaper that will stand like a stone wall for social justice to all people. Practically every city in the United States offers a fine field to the newspaper that has the courage to make a determined fight for social justice. During the past twenty-five years the newspapers of this country have lost much of their leadership. Whether this leadership is regained depends on the attitude of the editorial page towards the social injustice that is sweeping the vitals of our social order.

Wrens, Ga.,
March 16, 1935.

Letter to the Editor of
The Augusta Chronicle:
Mr. Avret Writes

J. T. Avret*

Editor, The Chronicle:

I have been reading with a good deal of interest several articles in your papers of recent date relative to social moral mental and other conditions in Burke, and Jefferson counties as related by Mr. Erskine Caldwell.

To anyone who has not been accustomed to seeing or of hearing of such conditions as are outlined by Mr. Caldwell, it would seem almost impossible for them to exist in a so-called civilized country. Now I am not agreeing that these conditions as portrayed are not somewhat exaggerated. But I am very glad indeed that the matter has been brought to the attention of the public. For to my own personal knowledge there are conditions existing, not only in the above named counties that are a shame to a civilization. Right here in my own adopted county (of Screven), there are conditions that are pitiful.

Now I am not placing the blame for these conditions on any one class of society, neither on any one class of industry. But I do believe that by the proper administrations of the means at hand by good sympathetic Christian people, these conditions could be materially changed until those of us who had taken a part in the change would be very grateful to an all wise maker for having had the opportunity of doing something worth while.

For my own part, I am ready to go, and have already been going some, and have gotten everlasting good from the little that I have been able to do. So let us thank Erskine Caldwell for an effort to open our eyes, and now instead of criticisms, let's do something about it. I admit that we will probably meet with opposition, even from those whom we are trying to help at first, but I believe that if the matter is gone into in a diplomatic way, results can be obtained.

Yours for the good of all mankind.

Sylvania, Ga., R.F.D. No. 1
March 12, 1935.

---

*Reprinted from *Augusta Chronicle*, 17 March 1935, p. 4, col. 5.

Letter to the Editor of
The Augusta Chronicle:
"From a Social Worker"

L. E. Holmes*

Editor, The Chronicle:

Having been a social worker for many years, and dealing with the class of people about whom Mr. Caldwell writes, I submit a suggestion.

These people can not be lifted to any standard of normal life as long as they are permitted to control themselves. There should be a place, not a prison, but some kind of institution where they may be placed under the law, and forced to stay. There should be industries of all kinds suitable to the various members, so that every one one would have some occupation.

All children should be removed from such parents, not permanently but far enough to not be affected by their influence. This is not an impossible idea and until something is done to correct and stop it, the South will be infested with this sore spot. These people are not necessarily natives of Georgia, but because of the mild climate here they drift to the South from every other section, and they can find miserable huts all over the state, which they can crawl into, and find wood to burn, so they do not freeze to death as they would do in other parts of the country.

I also suggest a campaign to burn or tear down all the wretched old huts and shacks that are such an eyesore on every farm in the state. If these people could not find these hovels to crawl into, they would not tarry long. Any man who permits these people to live on his place is contributing to the menace. There is no use to be sentimental about the matter. If a patient has a cancer it is cut out. These people are a cancer on society, a menace to themselves and the state; and to perpetuate the condition only increases their number. There should be a law to control the situation and a remedy to back up the law.

Augusta, Ga.,
March 12, 1935.

*Reprinted from *Augusta Chronicle*, 17 March 1935, p. 4, col. 6.

Editorial from
The Augusta Chronicle:
"Investigation—Now What?"

Anonymous*

When The Augusta Chronicle recently dispatched two of its reporters to make an exhaustive study of social conditions in that section of Jefferson county of which Erskine Caldwell has written so vividly, this newspaper's sole purpose was to conduct an unbiased investigation for the sake of a true representation of facts.

In a series of articles, with which our readers are acquainted, the reporters recounted their findings, harboring no desire either to embarrass Mr. Caldwell or to support him. They merely sought the truth and they found it.

Their inquiry has done this, if nothing else. It has shown that what we may call the mercilessness of Mr. Caldwell's writings is a matter of slight importance when contrasted with an issue of far larger proportions, the salvation of a small but almost hopelessly degenerate part of the race.

It is indisputable that in every quarter of the globe there exists an element of population which would seem to give the lie to the dignity of civilization, unfortunates who live amidst a more or less cultivated world without being a part of it.

Their brand is not poverty, for the poor are always with us. Weakness is their stigma. They are people incapable of caring for themselves. What their origin was and why they have failed to develop forward, perhaps the social sciences can tell us. That is not our problem.

We know we have these lost people among us in the United States. They are a small portion of the population but still an alarming number. And we may rest assured they will remain with us through time interminable if left to themselves. They want the pride, the strength and the will to raise themselves above their present state.

Living in squalor and primitive ignorance, they are breeders of disease and imbecility. They have no share in those higher aspirations which have glorified history three thousand years. They are shorn of almost every trace of moral responsibility. In truth, they are humanity's dregs.

Their only hope, as we see it, lies in the sympathy extended them by society as a whole, not mere charitable sympathy but a studied scientific understanding of their pitiable condition and the remedies it calls for. A nation-wide program of rehabilitation for those not too far lost in degeneracy, together with sterilization of the unfit and institutional care

*Reprinted from *Augusta Chronicle*, 17 March 1935, p. 4, col. 2.

of the totally irresponsible, would do much to remove from our civilization one of its ugliest blots.

At some time not far in the future, we hope, the seriousness of this problem will weigh itself upon the minds of legislators and whoever else has a hand in the fashioning of our social life. It is time one lesson was learned—that a pro rata share of food and clothing will not make a new man.

Editorial from *The Augusta Chronicle*: "The Caldwell Issue and Long Range Rehabilitation"

Anonymous*

There is not an author's note that we have seen anywhere in any of Erskine Caldwell's excoriations of this section of the Southeast to indicate that the conditions he describes are not typical, but relate to considerably less than one per cent of the population. The impression created by "Tobacco Road" and his other writings is that here is a true picture of the condition of illiterate, degenerate, hopeless Southern whites, and through the printed page he drags all of the slime and filth that appeals to an unthinking, gullible public, and particularly the morbidly curious, those who delight abnormally in the grotesque, in sensationalism, and all those who still would keep alive sectional prejudice and animosity.

Mrs. Harriet Beecher Stowe, in "Uncle Tom's Cabin" used as a type of Southern treatment of slaves Simon Legree, mythical overseer of a plantation, and after magnifying the brutality of Legree, after multiplying the heinousness of the worst type of Southern slave driver many times, presented a book to the nation which so incensed the North that the War Between the States was made almost inevitable. Therefore, the injustice to a section by presenting isolated cases as typical is very apparent.

Erskine Caldwell's "Tobacco Road" is playing night after night in New York city, after a run in a Broadway theater of more than year. What do the tens of thousands of people who have seen it or who have read the book think of us of this section? That they consider us as heartless and without any regard for human suffering and degradation is inevitable. And Erskine Caldwell pursues his sensational way, painting in a series of articles in a New York newspaper an even worse picture of conditions, with the bizarre statement in one of his articles that two miserable, starving white babies of one year of age in the filth and squalor of a cabin

*Reprinted from *Augusta Chronicle*, 24 March 1935, Sec. 2, p. 16, cols. 6–7.

near Keysville suck the dry teats of a female dog in vain quest for nourishment. Perhaps Caldwell had read the mythical story of Romulus and Remus suckling a she wolf and went the absolute limit in his tale of conditions in order to give something that would make even his metropolitan New York audience gasp.

Summing up Caldwell, we would say that he has drawn a horrible picture of conditions, but without a constructive remedy, that he has taken the cases of a few degenerate white families (and a few of the same species can be found in almost every American community) and makes the world believe that they are numerous in this section of the South; he has laundered our dirty linen and rattled the skeletons in our closet before hundreds of thousands of people. His motives? We hesitate to ascribe motives to any person. Caldwell's father says that his motives are the finest, that he expends money of his own in alleviation of conditions in the Wrens and Keysville sections. Whatever his motives he has been grossly unfair in not isolating his cases and not making it clear that they are a relatively small number.

The Chronicle has every desire to be fair to Erskine Caldwell. He has stated that he presented conditions as he found them to arouse the people of America to a sense of their responsibility to the illiterate, wretched, poverty stricken whites of this section, that his own father, a sincere, consecrated minister of the gospel and teacher, had worked for many years to arouse public opinion in Jefferson county to the necessity for remedying conditions, and had not been able to awake the people from their lethargy and indifference.

Whatever may have been Erskine Caldwell's motives and however unjust we ourselves and a large share of the public feel that he has treated this section, the result is certain to be constructive, for our people are aroused following The Chronicle's publication of conditions as our staff men found them, and we hope that Caldwell himself will make amends by telling patrons of "Tobacco Road" that this is not a typical picture, but that he used poetic license to adorn his tale. Perhaps he would express it that way, while the great majority of us call it plain exaggeration. At any rate Caldwell is not the important thing right now, so let's forget him in the quest for a remedy.

The Chronicle admits, without cheerfulness, that there is a wretched situation among a few of the poor whites of our section. We did not denounce Erskine Caldwell for his sensational article in the New York Evening Post, but our managing editor, Mr. R.L.M. Parks, designated City Editor Josh Skinner and Dudley E. Brewer, one of our very capable reporters, to go into Jefferson and Burke counties and investigate. Then we printed conditions as we found them truthfully, fearlessly and graphically. We found that from ten to thirty-five families only were involved in a large area; that the families in question had been habitual, professional mendicants and recipients of charity for a long time, some of them for generations. They toil not, neither do they spin, and when food and clothing are presented to them, with habitual improvidence, they consume, squander and sell the surplus as of the moment, and the next week are in want again. They are of a class that may be found in the slums of the cities and in the nooks and corners of almost all rural communities, people whom the neighbors have helped until they have wearied of well doing, people who will not send their children to school even after books and clothing to wear are provided, and the children, morons themselves even as their parents, grow up in filth and ignorance.

The Chronicle has suggested long range rehabilitation for these human derelicts, these people whom civilization itself cannot adopt or assimilate. Frankly, we see little hope of the present generation, but there is hope in segregation and sterilization of the children who have been born to lives of degredations and degeneracy with "eyes that do not see, ears that do not hear and neither do they understand."

The only possible hope for the adults of this hopeless class is for them to become wards of the state and federal governments, with institutional care, or closest of supervision outside, with insistence upon cleanliness in better homes than the shacks and shanties that they now occupy. For the states by themselves to take up such a burden would be rather large when we consider the total number of such people in the aggregate, and with our federal government planning toward social security, with a deeper consciousness than ever before of our responsibility to the individual citizen and to the unfortunates of our land, then we may be approaching a time when these people, the flotsam and jetsam in the sea of human misery, may be taken care of until they themselves pass out, with the knowledge that their progeny will be sterilized and that their race will be extinguished with the next generation. We may be contemplating the impossible for this generation, we may be idealizing toward the land of Utopia, but our idea of long range rehabilitation would be some such plan as this. And if we cannot attain all of this soon, and if the adults must be allowed to drift, so to speak, squandering the aid the relief agencies afford, then let us hope that a selective sterilization law will take care of the offspring. The poor we shall always have with us, we know, but there is poverty with pride and poverty with degradation. The latter class is the one which is so hopeless and which presents such a problem to the individual cities, counties, states and the nation.

After many years of campaigning this newspaper, in alliance with forward looking, patriotic Georgians, has worked ceaselessly for a sterilization law which has finally passed both houses of the legislature and is up for the governor's signature. Let us hope that he will promptly sign it and we shall have taken the first step forward in our great social problem.

Editorial Commentary in
The New Republic

Anonymous*

Although Mr. Erskine Caldwell is the most distinguished modern novelist to come out of Georgia, his native state has never hailed his writings with any great enthusiasm. Going to the poor whites of the backwoods and pine barrens for material, rejecting the moonlight and magnolias of the plantation tradition, his books have aroused the anger and resentment of many Georgians. He was charged with an excessively lurid imagination and with creating a race of subhumans the like of which was never seen in Tobacco Road or elsewhere. Recently Mr. Caldwell, reexamining Governor Talmadge's domain in a series of articles for The New York Post, reported conditions equal to anything described in his books. Thereupon The Chronicle, a morning newspaper published in Augusta, Georgia, decided to conduct an investigation of its own. It sent two members of its staff into the immediate rural districts to discover the true nature of affairs. The reporters returned, not with a clean bill of health, but with evidence substantiating many of Caldwell's charges— and, what is perhaps the most surprising feature of the entire incident, The Chronicle published their findings.

> What we have seen, coupled with the information we have obtained from other sources, leads to the conclusion that there exist families in utter need of rehabilitation. . . . The number of these families in the so-called Sand Hill section of the county is variously estimated from 10 to 12 to 35. . . . Regardless of the figure, maximum or minimum, it is still true that the persons referred to by Erskine Caldwell form a portion of the population of Jefferson County. Most of these people are not only poor but wretched. . . . There are some instances of dire degeneration. . . . On one occasion, a doctor who was questioned said, he answered a call to one of these families late at night. He was surprised to see all members of the family rush to the door fully clothed. Immediately he suspected they were not in the habit of undressing and he asked how often his patient had a bath and a change of clothes. "About once a month," was the reply.

The Chronicle points out, with entire truthfulness, that the people described, like Jeeter Lester, are not "typical" of the average Georgia tenant farmer. But Mr. Caldwell, if we have read his books correctly, does not intend his shiftless patriarch to be considered "typical" in that sense of the word, but rather "representative" of a certain section of Southern society. Charges of undue exaggeration against him may now be dropped. The investigation of the The Chronicle has definitely estab-

*Reprinted from *New Republic*, 82 (March 27, 1935), 172–73.

lished that there are Jeeter Lesters in the world and that something should be done to remedy the conditions under which they are forced to live. We congratulate The Chronicle, not only for conducting its investigation, but for its courage in publishing its conclusions.

"Caldwell Declares AAA Ruins Thousands in South"

Erskine Caldwell*

This the first of four articles on the South's share-croppers by Erskine Caldwell, famous novelist, whose present outstanding success is "Tobacco Road." It is the second series on this subject by Mr. Caldwell, his first revelations in the Post having met with wide hostility throughout the South. Following this criticism, Mr. Caldwell went back, this time accompanied by his father, The Rev. I. Caldwell, of Wrens, Ga., to make a more complete investigation, not only in Georgia but also in Alabama and Mississippi. The photographs which accompany the series were taken personally by Mr. Caldwell and are the subjects and scenes of his story.

Having passed through one of the hardest winters in American history, the Southern tenant farmer today realizes that somebody, somewhere, is trying to squeeze him through the little end of the horn. What he does not yet realize is that his end of the horn is to be a great deal smaller than he had anticipated.

The winter of 1934–35 was a hardtimes period in the cotton States of the South, but the winters to come will bring to the majority of tenant farmers an even greater depression.

The share-cropper, the renter and the wage-hand of the cotton country are earmarked for economic slavery. Present methods of Federal crop control, the pressure of the landowning class, and the machinery of error can bring only one thing, and that one thing is slavery.

Whatever benefits a few receive under the present system of cotton production are completely wiped out by the hunger, poverty and human disintegration of thousands.

The crop control plan as it is practiced in the cotton States of Mississippi, Alabama and Georgia penalizes the tenant farmer and enriches the landowner. The tenant has even less than he ever had before; the landowner has much more than before.

Whatever may be said for the plan for limiting production and equalizing income, there is much more to be said concerning the plan in

*Reprinted from New York Post, 17 April 1935, p. 1, cols. 4–5; p. 26, cols. 1–7.

actual everyday practice. The tenant farmer who receives without delay and without discount his parity check from Washington, who receives without deductions his Government rental check, and who receives various other forms of relief—this tenant farmer is matched against a hundred others who receive nothing.

On paper and on record the crop control program is no doubt marked up in Washington as a great success. In Mississippi, Alabama and Georgia there are thousands of tenant farmers who have not received one red penny of the money due them.

In certain counties of these three cotton States, the parity and rent checks have been placed in the hands of the tenants to whose order they were drawn in Washington. In certain other counties the money has been collected and deposited to the credit of landowners who have neither legal nor moral right to it. It would seem that the fault in such cases lies in the local administration of the crop control act. However, it is difficult to understand how such widespread thieving continues month after month, in county after county, without detection in Washington.

If there were only a few isolated instances of this practice, the condition could be laid to oversight by the supervisors; but throughout these three States one comes upon case after case where tenants have signed or made their marks on mysterious papers as long ago as September, 1934, without since receiving anything.

The buying power that appears to be the thought uppermost in the mind of the Administration is merely a feeble gesture today in cotton States because of this misappropriation of money. The individual landowner who collects not only his half of the rental checks, but who also collects the tenant's half as well, deposits the money in his bank.

The next step has been to take over and deposit his tenant's parity check. A hundred such checks in one man's hand makes the buying power of ninety-nine other men equal zero. There can be no lasting buying power when such widespread areas as Mississippi, Alabama and Georgia are honeycombed with sections where this practice is common.

The pressure of the landowning class is becoming increasingly acute. This class has almost entirely dissolved the system of farming known as share-cropping. Share-cropping, once the backbone of cotton production, is a rarity in the South today. What has taken its place is a system of renting which produces more for the landowner without any of the risks connected with share-cropping.

The renter is obligated to pay a stipulated sum, either in cash or in numbers of bales of cotton. The landowner is certain to receive his income, and if there is anything left over, the tenant is entitled to receive it. Under the share-cropping system, the landowner and tenant divided half-and-half the product of the worker's toil. Today under the renting system if a tenant agrees to pay $75 rent for a certain acreage, he pays that $75 whether or not he makes anything more than that amount.

The owner of a plantation who rents his land to a hundred tenants usually goes even further. He sets up his own store, forbids tenants to buy goods elsewhere, forces them to sell their cotton to him, and in the end no actual cash is paid to the tenant. If the worker buys goods at the plantation store, he is charged 10 to 12 per cent interest.

At the end of the year, he is notified that he is $40, or $50, or $100 in debt, in spite of the fact that he turned two or three bales of cotton over to the plantation owner to sell for him. Such cases, especially, among Negro tenants, are common rather than exceptional on large plantations.

The white tenant farmer fares even worse than the Negro. Because he usually questions the landowner's bookkeeping methods, and because he openly rebels against the system of economic slavery, the landowner in many cases has systematically excluded the white tenant from his plantation.

Consequently, the white tenant farmer has been forced away from the rich productive soil of the plantations to the stony acres and steep barren hillsides of the uplands. Here he can make practically nothing.

Without means of buying fertilizer, his land cannot be cultivated profitably. Without credit he is unable to buy farm implements or stock. Here he becomes a liability to himself and to the State and nation. After a few years he has become what is sometimes known as "a poor white." His children grow up uneducated and diseased; finally, broken in health and in spirit, he becomes a member of a vast army of hangers-on.

The plan of the Government to give employment and a bare living through the FERA, PWA, and other agencies, reveals in the States of Mississippi, Alabama and Georgia that the efforts are only 50 per cent successful. Half of the needy are either classed as unemployables, and consequently receive nothing, or else they do not receive enough to live on.

Unintelligent direction of Government relief work is a machine of error. One of the most misguided phases of this machine of error is the ditching operations, which go under the head of drainage projects. In the face of a rapidly sinking water-level, the arid country is being drained bone-dry. The additional land thus made available for cultivation is a liability since already there is a surplus of land.

What actually happens is that this new bone-dry land drains off the surface water which if left to itself would supply the underground streams with drinking water. As a result, wells are rapidly going dry. On the surface, the earth dries up and is blown away in dust and sand storms. Unless this squander of water is stopped, the Great American Desert will cross the Mississippi River.

"Landlords Chiseling South's Poor on FERA"

Erskine Caldwell*

This is the second of four articles on the South's share-croppers by Erskine Caldwell. . . .

The State of Mississippi never has been widely known for its prosperous citizenry. If any one were to take a trip by automobile through the central part of the State he would find out the reason for its impoverished condition. Here, starting at Forest and traveling northward, lies the answer.

Past Forest, through Carthage, Kosciusko, Ackerman, and beyond, there are hundreds of families of tenant farmers trying desperately, but without hope of success, to make a living from these stony acres and steep hillsides. They have been trying for many years, a long time before 1930, to woo, entreat, beg, curse, and flail a living from this unproductive land. They are white persons, forced away from the rich river-country lands by plantation owners who breed Negroes for their labor.

These white tenant farmers of Central Mississippi average from one to three bales of cotton a year, one of which goes for rent. Their mules have become weakened and broken because of lack of food, and consequently the tenant is able merely to scrape the top of the ground with his plow. When enough earth has been scraped together to make a row, the seed is planted.

Fertilizer is almost a necessity in this country, but the tenant farmer who can buy any is forced to drill it so thinly that its effect is barely worth more than the effort of hauling it from the nearest town.

The income from one of these tenant farms, together with the Government rent and parity checks, usually amounts to less than $200 a year.

On some of these farms are tenants who are well satisfied with their income. If they make three bales of cotton, and receive their Government checks, they see no reason for wishing more. On other farms are tenants who are unable to make enough to supply their needs, and, even with allotments of food and clothing from the FERA, they still have less than enough.

Men with families of eight to ten children, whose income is $10 a month in wages, cannot begin to live without want. Years of malnutrition and disease have made small children bedridden. Tuberculosis can be treated by the county health officer, but there can be no cure without change of climate or living conditions.

*Reprinted from *New York Post*, 18 April 1935, p. 1, cols. 2–3; p. 30, cols. 1–8.

The landowning class does not suffer from want. Its income is assured. It has all the Negro labor it needs.

The Negro, who far outnumbers the white man in Mississippi, has fallen into two kinds of circumstances. He in both cases is an exploited slave of 1935, the man who was promised many years ago a mule and forty acres of land. As far as he is concerned, the war is not over yet.

The Negro is a slave of the large landowner, the plantation holder who has perhaps 2,500 acres of rich river-country land. He has fallen from the relatively high standards of the share-cropper. Now gradually falling from the renter class, he has become a worker promised $10 a month, when he works.

He may work three or four months a year from half an hour before sunup until half an hour after sundown. If he can collect his $10 a month from his plantation boss, he has a lot more than the Negro wage worker who cannot collect a penny of the money promised him.

By renting land from the owner under the crop control plan the Government has unwittingly given the landowner an opportunity to double his income.

If the landowner takes the opportunity offered—and the gradual removal of the tenant from the share-cropper and the renter classes to the wage worker class is proof that many of them do take it—he receives all the money that ordinarily would have gone to the individual tenant.

Merely by changing terms, the plantation owner is enriched to the extent of $1,000 to $5,000 a year. The Negro tenant, doing the same work he has always done, finds that his condition is even worse than it was ten, twenty, fifty years ago.

The Negro is ruled by the white man and, notwithstanding the relief agencies set up to aid him, he is still the victim of his white overlord. On FERA projects he works long hours for small pay while the white man on relief is given the job of bossing him.

It is not uncommon to find a gang of workers on such a project composed of fifteen or twenty Negroes, who work with pick and shovel while five or ten white men stand above them bossing and receiving a higher scale of wages. Even for the same labor a white man will receive more and do less than a Negro.

In the matter of distribution of food and clothing the Negro again is at the mercy of the white. Food is sorted into classes, the good and the bad, and the Negro receives the worse.

If the Negro lives on a plantation he may find himself among those others of his race who have been forced to pay the landowner store prices for clothing that had been sent by a relief agency for free distribution. If he is unable to pay in cash for a pair of overalls he is charged 10 to 12 per cent interest.

Mississippi is not alone in such things. Throughout the cotton States the various practices of discrimination and theft against the Negro can be found with startling regularity.

In traveling through these areas one comes upon sections where there is no complaint against the landowners, in other sections one will hear of county-wide cases affecting hundreds of Negro families.

As a whole, these conditions have the appearance of a checker-board design. One county will be black with discrimination and theft, the next will be white with relatively few.

Instead of buying thousands of acres of timberland, the Government should buy this vast territory of stony acres and steep hillsides in Central Mississippi. By taking over this section and supplying suitable farms elsewhere, the Government would be performing a greater public service.

These tenants would be moved to other sections of the State, sold land on low terms, or, in exchange for the former farms, supplied with stock and implements on terms that could be met, and given a start in life they never had to begin with.

Only such planning will ever bring any real help to such sections.

Supplies of food and clothing can never be more than a temporary makeshift for a situation that demands foresight into the future.

If some such plan is not put into effect, the result can mean but one thing to Mississippi, the forcing to a still lower level of living of these thousands of American citizens.

"Negroes Who Ask Pay Beaten in Alabama"

Erskine Caldwell*

This is the third of four articles on the South's share-croppers by Erskine Caldwell. . . .

Alabama has natural resources that make it one of the richest States in the Union. In the north it has more potential water power than any one State could use, in the north-central portion it is underlaid with millions of tons of coal and ore, and in the southern part its land is so fertile that few areas of it require fertilizer. In spite of all this, Alabama's human beings are among the most exploited of any in America.

The fertile areas have been cornered by landowners whose cotton plantations cover from two to five thousand acres each. To work these acres Alabama excels in its breeding of Negroes. The white tenants have gradually been forced to the hills to till the best they can the unproductive slopes. Where these slopes abound there is a section of poverty and injustice unknown to the rest of the country. Even large numbers of the State's own citizens are unaware of these conditions.

In a large section of the State lying east of Birmingham and Mont-

*Reprinted from *New York Post*, 19 April 1935, p. 19, cols. 2–4.

gomery, hundreds of white and Negro tenant farmers are trying to exist under circumstances only a few degrees removed from slavery.

The landowners, having in their hands farms that should be turned back into forests, employ every known method of exploiting labor. Tenants are threatened, cheated and whipped in efforts to extract the last penny of profit.

Any effort on the part of the tenant to protest against his treatment is met with warnings to keep his mouth shut. The landowners' riders, covering the farms on horseback, keep constant watch over the tenants.

Where this method of control is not practiced openly, it is done in other ways. Any stranger passing through the country is likely to be watched closely, if not actually questioned and threatened by the landowners' overseers. A stranger who would stop and sympathize with one of the tenants, runs the risk of being escorted to the county line and left there with the silent but unmistakable warning not to come back again.

In a State where such methods are employed by the landowning class, it is not surprising to come face to face with cases of human want and suffering brought about by a tenant's failure to take warning where warning was given.

Within a few miles of the University of Alabama are areas inhabited by tenant families living on the ragged edge of life. Here are families without land trying to live in shacks that are little more than abandoned lumber piles. Some of them do not receive any relief at present and never have received any.

Some are heads of families with six, eight and ten children, and are at present employed by the FERA for $3.60 a week. Some are forced to sell their few remaining possessions in order to keep a roof over their heads.

In one way or another these tenant farmers are the victims of the landowners. Either they once rebelled at being cheated out of their year's labor, or else they had rebelled at the stealing of their Government rental and parity checks.

It would be difficult to estimate how many children up to ten years of age, both white and colored, have never attended for a day any kind of educational institution. It is enough to say that in one county (Tuscaloosa) eleven children of this class were found in an hour's time, and what was even more surprising all of them were white children. Only a State-wide census would reveal the true extent of Alabama's negligence.

The State can be crossed and recrossed, but no matter what portion is visited, instances of the landowners' slave-hold on the tenant class come to light. One plantation in the central part of the State (Dallas County) is farmed by nearly a hundred tenants of the renter classification. Several cases on this plantation appear to be representative of the landowner-tenant problem.

One Negro tenant had not received his share of the Government rent check, nor had he received his parity check. He stated that none of the other tenants had received their checks, even though all of them had been called to the plantation office and forced to sign away their rights on papers they were not allowed to read.

One of the tenants said that whenever he asked about his Government check, the landowner threatened to whip him if he ever asked about it again. This particular tenant had made nine bales of cotton over a three-year period, but had not received a penny from his work.

The plantation owner had deducted $75 a year rental, the tenant had bought $22.50 in goods at the plantation store over the same period, but in the spring of 1935 when the tenant asked for his cotton money, the landowner told him he was $40 in debt and would have to remain there until he worked himself out of debt. The tenant declared this had been a yearly happening for the fifteen years he had worked on the plantation.

By any fair means of accounting for the year 1934, this Negro tenant should have received not less than $150 in cash. He was entitled to receive this amount or more, even after paying $75 rent and the $22.50 store account. On top of that amount should be added his half share of the Government rent check and the entire amount of his parity check. For the year (1934) this would amount to about $48, which added to the return from two bales of cotton due him would be $198.

The tenant received nothing, according to his statement, and neither did the other hundred tenants on the plantation. To arrive at the landowners profit, aside from the rent collected from each tenant, which averaged $75 per tenant, multiply $198 by 100 and the estimate would be nearer true than wrong.

Other sections of the State present conditions equally as bad. Within the eastern area of the State (Macon County) the tenant farmer who has to some extent escaped from the confines of a plantation system, finds himself hounded as well as cheated. Here are instances of tenants working worn-out land who complain to the landowner that they cannot make anymore than enough to pay their rent.

The landowner's interest in his tenant's welfare stops short when sufficient cotton has been made to pay the rent. When the tenant persists in asking for better land, or credit for stock and fertilizer, the landowner issues his warning. This warning has taken the form of verbal threats, whippings and killings in Eastern Alabama.

The tenant is warned not to discuss with other tenants or with outside persons any matter connected with the landowner's interests. Strangers who might stop and discuss any such matter with the tenant are sometimes followed and trailed by the landowner's riders. If they do stop and talk, the riders point out the nearest exit from the county.

A continuation of the tenant system of cotton production means serious trouble for the future. The share-cropping plan was almost universally abandoned when the Government stepped into the agricultural States of the South not because the Government put a stop to it, but because the landowners saw more money in the renting system.

The renting system will not remain long, however. The next step is to be the wage system, which has already worked its way throughout the cotton States because it offers the landowner a sure means of making money.

The wage system, which means payment of thirty to forty cents a day, usually paid in the round sum of $10 a month enables the landowner to obtain labor at its cheapest price, and, furthermore, it enables the landowner to gather all of the Government rental checks without going through the form of stealing required under the share-cropping and rental systems.

And, with this technicality removed, the landowner is still under no obligation to pay or to allow the tenant to receive anything, because he can warn the tenant against asking for his wages of $10 a month, just as he has warned him in the past against asking for his share of the Government rental and parity checks and for a yearly settlement of accounts.

Until the agricultural worker commands his own farm, either as an individual or as a member of a Government allotted farm group, the Southern tenant farmer will continue to be bound hand and foot in economic slavery.

"Share-Crop Life
A Bed of Roses,
Senator Holds"

Charles Malcolmson*

WASHINGTON. April 19. The share-cropper's life, according to Senator Ellison D. Smith, South Carolina Democrat, and plantation owner, is just one long day of sunshine, security and song.

Compared to the plight of the Southern landlord, it is "Heads I win, tails you lose."

Challenging the statements of Erskine Caldwell in the New York Post, Mr. Smith has told the Senate that Mr. Caldwell's description of the plight of the share-croppers are "vicious propaganda and gross exaggeration."

According to the Senator, it is the Southern landlord who is getting it in the neck in this depression.

"A share-cropper," said Mr. Smith, "is furnished a home, a house, a

*Reprinted from New York Post, 19 April 1935, p. 19, col. 1.

garden plot. He is furnished all the fuel he needs. He is furnished the animals with which to cultivate the land, he is fed and clothed during the year, and then given one-half the crop.

"If there is a failure of the crop and practically nothing is made, the share-cropper has had a living for a year at the expense of the landlord. If any profit is made, he gets one-half of all the profit on every article.

"He pays no taxes except some slight personal tax. He has no expense of up-keep. It is heads I win and tails the landlord loses."

Bubbling with indignation, Mr. Smith assailed as "grossly exaggerated" the conclusions of "individuals and newspapers who submit special reports" of conditions among share-croppers and laborers. The laborers he characterized as "just as happy and contented as the share-croppers."

He insisted that only Southerners can be trusted to report such conditions as they truly exist.

He said he does not want to see the still-unpublished Myers report of the AAA on the plight of plantation workers and share-croppers.

"If it is like a good many other reports," he said, "I do not care to be familiar with it and I do not want to know anything about it. I have other ways of getting the facts. Some of us in whom Senators have confidence can make statements, and if they are contrary to the conclusions of individuals who submit special reports, our statements should be accepted.

"The making of these reports is in many instances disturbing the morale of our people."

"Georgia Tenants, Ousted by Landlords, Eat Dirt as Change From Bread and 'Lasses"

Erskine Caldwell*

Georgia, like most States, has been so busy telling the world about its natural assets and tricky golf courses that it has neglected to look into the mirror occasionally. Many of its up-and-coming citizens wish the world to know that Georgia is the Empire State of the South, quite a few of its common herd would far rather that the State pay some attention to its home folks. Georgia's common herd is its thousands of tenant farmers.

Central Georgia is a fertile land whose center is Macon. Extending in all directions lies land that produces abundantly and yields a handsome profit. If one were able to buy a farm in that section, even a few acres, he should be comfortable for life.

*Reprinted from *New York Post*, 20 April 1935, p. 4, cols. 3–5.

But this is not all of Georgia. This is only half of the State. There is a circular rim beginning in the west, passing through the north and terminating in the east that holds thousands of tenant farmers, who cannot find much to brag about. The land is poor and hilly.

Just why white tenants should be pushed back from the fertile lowlands and be forced to struggle on the clay hills for a living is a matter no one has given much attention to yet. As conditions are now, Negroes are welcome wherever the land is fertile, but white workers are not welcome.

The landowner can make Negroes work more for less pay. A white tenant cannot be so easily defrauded of the fruit of his labor, and consequently he has been pushed back into the gully-washed hills to get along the best he can.

Back on the hillsides the white tenant farmer found that he could barely make a living. Food was scarce, clothing was limited, medicine was reduced to a few pills and chills-and-fever tonic. There was little more to be had. Too poor to ride out of the hills, the tenant farmer was forgotten. The outside world did not know he existed and he knew nothing beyond what he could see from his hillside.

Among themselves the tenant families fell prey to various forms of religious excitement, which served to take the place of normal entertainment. Physically, they became abject specimens of humanity.

They ate what they could get, usually cornmeal and molasses. As a change, many of them began eating the earth, and today communities of clay eaters exist almost wholly on meal, molasses and clay. Clay eaters may be identified by the color and texture of their skin which looks and feels like putty.

In many such Georgia communities syphilis is as common as dandruff. Incest is as prevalent as marriage in these tenant regions, where normal access to the outside world is shut off because of the inability to travel. They are unable to travel except on foot, because there is a scarcity of live stock and automobiles, and, since there are few of either, there is no incentive for building roads into the regions.

This is not a description of a past age; it is a description of certain Georgia tenant regions in 1935.

The machine of error whirs throughout Georgia, just as it does in the other cotton States. The plantation system is still a barbaric method of making money. Some of the Government relief agencies are in incapable, or, rather, ineffectual hands. Nearly all the organs of public opinion are in reactionary hands.

And the victim of it all is the tenant farmer. He is too poor, generally, to pay a poll tax and hence cannot vote. He cannot read or write and the newspapers never receive his political and economic protests. His charges against the local administration of relief are thrown out the window. He is a pretty helpless person, this Georgia tenant farmer of 1935.

The desire of the landowning class is to keep the tenant in his place. The dominating voice in the matter is that of the local county official who holds office by means of a political machine. He may be the county health officer who refuses to furnish medical aid; he may be the county school superintendent who refuses to establish a school in a tenant community.

Their reasons for not providing what elsewhere amount to public necessities are dictated solely by the landowning class. There is nothing that can be done about it until the stranglehold of the landowner on the tenant farmer has been broken.

It is astonishing to find in this Jim Crow State that the economic condition of this class of white tenant is lower than that of the Negro. His standard of living is lower, his education is more limited and his health is worse. The Negro can be threatened into submission; the white tenant still thinks he should have what he earns and as a result he is discriminated against.

The local administrators of the FERA and PWA have in many cases been reluctant to recognize these tenant families. Where their eligibility for relief has been forcibly proved to the administrators, the result has been a disgraceful, misguided rule.

In many cases, rather than lend or give money for the rental of land or the purchase of seed or a work animal, the relief has taken the form of mattresses, which can neither be eaten nor made to pull a plow. In other cases a ditch will be dug at an expense of several hundred dollars, draining the earth dry of any chance moisture in this semi-arid country, and which eventually lowers the water level until wells go dry.

Now tenant homes that are without wells or other water supply can be counted by the hundred in many Georgia counties. In spite of this devastation of the land, the program for 1935 is deeper and longer drain ditches.

The landowner-tenant system will have to go. No act of its own is motivated by any desire save that of profit at the expense of the physical and moral and economic welfare of the worker. No other system has yet come to take its place, and, until it does, the demoralizing spectacle of seeing thousands of men, women and children, both black and white, being cheated and squeezed and crucified by a profit system that should have no place in modern civilization—until it does come, the present system should make the American people hang their heads in shame.

The sytem of agricultural labor that will take its place in the cotton States is still problematical. And yet it is difficult to visualize any system that will embody the present-day landowner.

A unionized wage-scale system would be ideal in theory for a capitalistic nation, but in practice it is difficult to imagine any such relationship succeeding between the present-day landowner and the worker. A far greater step would be the discarding of the landowner and the cultivation of the large farm on a collective basis, or else the breaking up of large fertile units of land into small parcels for intensive cultivation by one or two persons.

In any event, the tenant-farming system must be abolished.

Editorial from
The New York Post:
"Hell on Earth"

Anonymous*

The Post has just concluded a series of four articles by Erskine Caldwell on conditions in Georgia, Mississippi and Alabama.

The South that Mr. Caldwell presents is not brisk and bustling Atlanta, nor rapidly growing Birmingham, nor quiet, leisurely Montgomery.

His is the South of the tenant farmer, which can, without the slightest exaggeration, be termed a hell on earth.

The Agricultural Adjustment Administration has paid subsidies to the landowners. But these subsidies have not been passed on to the tenants. A plantation owner who is paid for not growing cotton, in many instances does not pay his tenants for not working in the cotton fields.

Thus the tenant farmers, who previously were in a state bordering on serfdom, have now descended even lower in the economic scale. Owners of slaves have, at least, an interest in keeping them alive. The Southern plantation owners in many sections seem to have lost even that incentive to responsibility for their tenants.

A diet of cornmeal, molasses and clay in the worst districts is producing the expected results upon the health of the inhabitants.

The South has special problems which may be beyond the power of any one Administration to solve.

But, at the very least, officials of the AAA should see to it that their policies do not aggravate an already frightful condition.

An official report of the status of the Southern tenant farmer was suppressed by the AAA last month.

We challenge Secretary Wallace to make it public.

*Reprinted from *New York Post*, 22 April 1935, p. 10, col. 2.

ESSAYS

"Made in America: Erskine Caldwell"

Carl Van Doren*

Life for Erskine Caldwell has lately been a kind of chronic tap day. One coterie after another has expected him to join it, and he has even been claimed as a member already of this or that society. Though he is pleased he is also a little puzzled. He has not thought of himself as writing in the special ways or for the deliberate ends with which he is credited. He wants, as he has always wanted, only to write as truthfully as he can about what he knows, and to be read by as many persons as he can interest.

Mr. Caldwell has interested different readers for different reasons. He, or his reputation, interested the screen, and he was called to Hollywood, which at once found it did not need him. He kindled the busybodies who look for vice in books, and they found they could not suppress him. He excites Communists and collectors. He has satisfied any number of aspiring, precarious magazines and has won a prize from the solid *Yale Review*. He is praised for his animal humor and for his spiritual elevation, for his bluff realism and for his tender insight, for his faithful use of folkspeech and for his creative reworking of his themes.

A writer who attracts a variety of readers with a variety of qualities does it not because he is himself a miscellany but because he is something single and impenetrable, and so rouses curiosity. Typical, glib writers are easy to analyze. They analyze themselves. Mr. Caldwell does not. Asked what a story of his means, he would probably give the best of all answers to the silly question: that the story means what it says. If he had known how to make it say more he would have done it. He does not talk well about what he has written, and seems not to like to talk about it at all. He prefers to talk about the aspects of life he has knows at first hand, particularly in Georgia and Maine.

Mr. Caldwell himself is no more a Cracker than he is a Yankee. The son of a clergyman, he spent three years at the University of Virginia and another at Pennsylvania. But during his Georgia youth he lived so close to

*Reprinted from *Nation*, 137 (Oct. 18, 1933), 443–44. Copyright © 1933 The Nation Associates.

the people that he absorbed their folk-ways and learned to speak their language. When he tells stories about them he does not condemn or apologize, as he does not condescend. He never puts in explanatory asides, as if to remind his readers that he too, of course, knows how strangely his characters behave. He believes that the men and women he writes about would in these circumstances do precisely what he shows them doing. The frenzies of religion and of sex which he recounts are not, he holds, exaggerated. Ty Ty, Griselda, and Will Thompson in "God's Little Acre" are exceptional persons. Mr. Caldwell is telling their story, not the story of ordinary beings. His heroic figures, however, come from the people, and in their characteristics and actions follow the people's customs.

Although Mr. Caldwell accepts the usages which rule the lives of his poor whites, he is not sunk in them. Always he keeps the detachment of a powerful humor. When in "Tobacco Road" Sister Bessie and Dude buy the new automobile they go about it with the single-mindedness and irresponsibility of children. Dude is willing to marry a woman who is almost three times as old as he and whom he does not love, for the sake of being allowed to drive a new car and of blowing the horn as much as he likes. Bessie spends all the money she has and then takes no care of what she has bought. Like children she and Dude are incapable of looking farther ahead than the present moment and the present desire. They witlessly follow their impulses and completely fail to understand why there are consequences. They are callous to everything outside themselves because they have no imagination. Dude does not even stop long enough to find out if the accident he has caused has been fatal to its victim. "He looked like he was dead," he tells his father. And his father observed: "Niggers will get killed. Looks like there ain't no way to stop it."

This is appalling, but it is humor of a ruthless kind. At other times Mr. Caldwell can be humorous more lightly. In his latest volume of short stories "We Are the Living" there is a bawdy masterpiece. Meddlesome Jack, based on the popular superstition that a jackass has a disturbing effect on women, is as truly a folk-story as if the writer were unknown. Its materials and its assumptions are all taken from the poor whites. Mr. Caldwell can be humorous in a trivial way, as in The Medicine Man in the same volume. Here he has missed the substantial laughter of the true folk-story and has told what belongs to the shoddy stage of a burlesque theater. After all, it is hardly more than a strip act in print. Yet whatever the uncertainty of his taste, Mr. Caldwell sees human life with the eye of humor. He sees more than his poor whites. "We Are the Living" contains four Maine stories. Folk-stories of another folk, they are as convincing and as funny as any of the Georgia tales. His humor has power over cautious Yankees no less than over Crackers running wild in the sun.

If humor gives Mr. Caldwell power over his materials, so does his faith in instinct. With no ascetic code to govern his approvals and disapprovals, he prefers life always to death. "The trouble with people," Ty Ty says, "is that they try to fool themselves into believing that they're different from the way God made them. You go to church and a preacher tells you things that deep down in your heart you know ain't so. But most people are so dead inside that they believe it and try to make everybody else live that way. People ought to live like God made us to live. When you sit down by yourself and feel what's in you, that's the real way to live. It's feeling. Some people talk about your head being the thing to go by, but it ain't so. . . . People have got to feel for themselves. . . . It's folks who let their head run them who make all the mess of living."

"Tobacco Road" is a novel without heroes. Its characters slouch about their affairs unreflectingly, like animals, and brutally, like peasants. "God's Little Acre" is heroic. Ty Ty, setting aside an acre of his land for God and digging feverishly for gold, year after year, his the nobility of character that comes from passion and assurance. "When you get God in your heart, you have a feeling that living is worth striving for night and day." As he believes in God, he believes in love. He better than any of the others understands the fierce attraction between Griselda and Will. Old and wise, he has never come to think of love as young folly. "If there's anything in the world He's crazy about, it's seeing a man and a woman fools about each other. He knows then that the world is running along as slick as grease."

It is with Ty Ty as a kind of chorus that Mr. Caldwell lifts the story of Will Thompson into tragedy. Seen in another light, he might have been regarded as a milltown stallion, a brawling striker killed in a senseless enterprise. But for Mr. Caldwell Will is a hero of the people, who acts out what Ty Ty feels. Nor is he a mere poor white, land-bound and custom-ridden. He belongs to the mills, and he feels about them a passion like Ty Ty's for God and gold. He is a proletarian hero if American literature has ever had one.

Yet it is as difficult for an outsider as it is for Mr. Caldwell to find in his work any systematic, even any very conscious, doctrine. He has not shaped himself by reasoning and he does not make up stories to prove abstract points. He is seldom better than he is in such tales as Meddlesome Jack and Over the Green Mountains, which have in them a kind of traditional note. They somehow sound as if they had been invented a long time ago and cherished in the popular memory, waiting for the hand of art if it should chance upon them. Mr. Caldwell, handling these matters, partly goes back to a manner at least a hundred years old. Again and again he brings to mind the native humorists before Mark Twain, when American humor had not yet been sweetened but was still dry, blunt, and broad. Not that Mr. Caldwell must be supposed to have read their books. He now reads little and seems never to have read much. But in telling his folk-stories he has naturally taken over a manner which was ready for him. It suited the kind of stories the earlier humorists told, and he tells more or less the same kind. He has no critical doctrine which forces him to devise a new method when a good one is at hand. He would rather give his whole attention to his materials.

Nor is he doctrinaire in his general attitude toward life, which is so simple that it may be summed up as a love of human nature and a hatred of social artifice. Will Thompson is not a mouthpiece for revolutionary principles but a man exalted by love and rebellion. "I'm Will Thompson. I'm as strong as God Almighty, and I can show you how strong I am." He is heroic for his ecstasy, not for his valiant death in a specific cause. Old Ty Ty is fanatical and foolish, but he is heroic to Mr. Caldwell because he so incessantly loves life and so accurately sees what is alive and what is dead. It is in Mr. Caldwell's choice of heroes and in his boldness with which he speaks of their love and religion that he goes beyond any of the older humorists. Yet here too a way has been cut for him during twenty years of warfare between writers and censors in the United States. He does not parade his frankness. He takes it for granted that he and his characters may speak out. With a candor as truly made in America as his humor, he is free to write as well as he can about as much as he knows and feels. In the use he has made of his heritage and his opportunity he is a model for all young American novelists.

" 'God's Little Acre': an Analysis"

Lawrence S. Kubie, M. D.*

[Some readers may not have seen the editor's Introduction to Dr. Kubie's series of articles applying the principles of psycho-analysis to the modern literature of neuroticism. For them it may be well to repeat that these essays are not literary criticisms but scientific analyses of the perplexing phantasies which have caused so much discussion of widely read books in this characteristically modern variety of fiction. These essays will supply a basis for a later literary estimate—Editor.]

Men have always known that the romantic picture of love and marriage is false. They have known that the eager yearnings of adolescence meet with strangely bitter disappointments in the effort to translate themselves into the realities of adult experience. Only recently, however, has any understanding come of why this is true, through the realization that, from childhood on, each step in Everyman's psychosexual evolution is taken in the face of opposing forces which threaten to drive him from the path of normal development. If then the impulse to write and to read bears any relation to human needs, it would seem to be inevitable that a struggle which begins in earliest years and continues throughout life must find insistent expression in literature. It is not strange, therefore, that novelists and readers have always been concerned with sex.

To meet the needs of different temperaments, however, literature assumes varied forms. The simplest and most childlike response to disappointment is to retreat into phantasies in which the frustrated yearnings are gratified. In this way simple people can console themselves with the adolescent and sentimental prevarications of the movies and the cheap magazines. Even the better forms of the romantic novel serve essentially the same simple need. Such writings might therefore be called the romantic and consolatory literature of sex.

More complicated temperaments cannot make use of this elementary device of phantasy and romance; but instead react to disappointment with bitterness and irony, which expresses itself in an effort to belittle that

*Reprinted from *Saturday Review of Literature*, 11 (Nov. 24, 1934), 305–06, 312.

which is unobtainable. Much of the so-called "classical" erotic literature satisfied the needs of such readers; Rabelais and Casanova, Boccaccio and Cellini. But whether it be naive or sophisticated, romantic or ironical and bitter, all of this literature constitutes merely varying forms of literary escape. In neither group is sex recognized as a serious, perplexing, and vital human problem.

Out of the modern temper, however, there has arisen a third group of books: one in which sex is treated frankly and seriously, and yet with a confused pattern of tension and distortion. These books form the great bulk of the so-called morbid modern literature, a literature which attempts not merely a safe and literary escapade in sex, but rather a mirror of the moving realities of sexual problems in all their intricacy.

Certainly a compelling drive to portray and solve the problems of sexual unrest and dissatisfaction is not an obscene or morbid purpose. Yet just as the problem play will be violently attacked while the naked revue passes unmolested, so, too, the cheap and "sexy" magazine, or the subtler waggery of classical erotica, will be accepted unprotestingly by the very people who raise the cry that these modern books are deliberately capitalizing the morbid and perverse in human nature. In other words, an honest and vivid literature, which is struggling to express the confused problems of sex, arouses such hostile, uncomfortable, and suspicious feelings, that it is attacked as dirty, obscene, sick, useless, ugly, etc. This is a strange and paradoxical social phenomenon, the explanation of which may lead to a deeper understanding of the psychological and artistic significance of these books.

The most obvious point is that the protesting reader has been made uncomfortable in a special and peculiar way. Furthermore, not only is he uncomfortable, but he is resentfully aroused as well; and it is out of this constellation of feelings that he throws up the epithet "obscene."

To define what is meant by obscenity is impossible, because the word does not carry quite the same implications to any two people. Nor is there any one type of scene or phrase which will make all people squirm. Yet the experience is almost universal, a feeling which everyone has encountered and can recognize, even if its effective stimulus varies from one human being to another. And since it is universal, it must have some common underlying quality.

This experience might well be called the "sense of the obscene," and with regard to it we will take as our premise: (1) that a reader's phantasies, be they conscious or unconscious, arise from his personal needs; (2) that this angry, resentful sense of the obscene arises when confused and troubling unconscious phantasies are stirred into activity; (3) that his happens when such phantasies have been awakened in the reader by the vigor of the author's art.

From what has been said already it should be clear that our search leads directly into the problem of psychosexual illness. The difficult

lifelong struggle towards adult normality is pursued through a maze of infantile and childish impulses, which, though normal enough at their own
levels, become disturbing if they persist with dominating force into adult
life. It is inevitable, therefore, that in a literature which deals with a
blind groping towards normal sexuality one should find much of the
psychopathology of sex dramatized in literary expression. This will appear chiefly in descriptions of adult distortions of infantile impulses; and
it is just here that the reader, either for lack of technical knowledge, or
because of inner problems, is most likely to mistake the portrayal of
distorted sexual development for the manifestations of a supernormal
lustiness and release. Often enough the picture of sickness is taken for an
example of a greater freedom. It becomes therefore a most difficult problem to estimate the esthetic significance of this confused borderland between sickness and health.

Since no problem in science or in art can be solved by generalizations
alone, our first step must be to subject a typical example of this literature
to a frankly psychoanalytic scrutiny. To do this one must use the tale and
the people and their words as dreamlike products of imagination, dissect-
ing the story for the conscious and unconscious content of the characters'
minds or acts to see how much of sickness or of health lies within its pages.

For this purpose we have chosen the novel, "God's Little Acre," by
Erskine Caldwell, first published in the spring of 1933 by the Viking
Press. It is an earthy and vivid story of Southern whites, who struggle in
the land, and in town, and in their bodies to reach some kind of peace.
And because here and there this struggle is infused with activity which is
technically known as "perverted," the book drew upon itself the curiosity
of all and the wrath of many.

In the tale, as in a dream, there are confused and kaleidoscopic shifts
forwards and backwards between desolate farm land and a turbulent
strike-weary mill town; from deep pit holes in the red and yellow clay to
hilly eminences, from swamp land to solid earth. Unlike an actual dream,
however, the movement from scene to scene is carried along on a thread
of story; whereas in a dream which has not been artificially elaborated
the episodes would follow one another without even this pretence of conscious reason. To the analyst, therefore, the story serves as a rationaliza-
tion, an effect to give an appearance of logical order to the sequence of
free phantasies. This conscious elaboration of spontaneous phantasy succeeds in making the tale appear simple and realistic; but it also interjects
elements which are extraneous to the fundamental dreamlike structure. It
is necessary, therefore, to confine the analytic interpretation to the main
outlines of the story, considering only the characters and their outstanding acts.

As in many dreams, one may recognize two groups of characters,
those that are clear and those that are vague. There are some shrouded
and ominous figures who hover dimly in the background, like those un-

seen persons in a dream whose presence one senses but never sees. There are others who stand out with all the hallucinatory vividness of the lions and tigers of a child's nightmare. Their clarity is a tribute to the author's skill, particularly because, despite their sharp outlines, they retain their fantastic and unreal quality; and when closely examined these figures fuse until they seem to become different aspects of a single human spirit, split up by a legitimate and effective literary artifice into the semblances of separate beings.

Among all the characters one finds no living mother in the book. Yet everywhere throughout the tale brood the spirits of unhappy, frustrated, and forgotten mothers, dimly seen, yet constituting the essential but unrecognized object of all the conflict which the story contains. The figures of women can be arrayed in order from the most dim to the clearest; and then one sees that the shadowy figures are the frank mother-images, and that as the figures of women become clearer the maternal role is distorted more and more towards perversion and prostitution. It is as if the book were saying that the only good woman is a dead and legendary mother—and that even there danger and sin may lurk.

First there is old Mrs. Walden, who, before the tale is begun, has died of heartbreak because her oldest son was ashamed of her. She is a dim phantasy of a good mother, dead and therefore forever unattainable. Then there is the witch-like figure of Gussie, supposedly diseased and hoarding gold, whom this oldest son had married and with whom he hid himself away. This is the "bad woman," the "sterile mother," no mother at all and yet more mother than wife, who is heard wandering eerily off-stage and who never appears directly in the action of the book.

The first woman to emerge even dimly from these shadows is Rosamond, Ty Ty Walden's oldest daughter, and the wife of Will Thompson. She remains vague in outline, but at least she is alive. She weeps in the background of the story, taking humbly and gratefully what Will has left over to give her, mothering him, feeding him, spanking him with her hair-brush when she catches him *flagrante delicto* with her younger sister, Darling Jill. Then she tries in a sudden rage to shoot him; but in the end she mourns his death in a paroxysm of grief.

And finally come the only two clear and vivid women in the tale, standing as the direct objects and instruments of primitive lusts. One is Griselda, the wife of Buck Walden, the daughter-in-law in the Walden family, no mother in spirit or in fact, but whose body stands to all the men as a perverse symbol for nursing. The other is Darling Jill, the youngest Walden daughter, who devotes her life to conquering men with her body, insatiable and destructive, tantalizing men, using them, throwing them aside, demanding pain as her only physical joy, and turning for peace at the last to the fat, infantile, and eunuchoid figure of "Pluto."

This much, then, can be safely concluded: that in this tale are found only certain limited conceptions of women. There are good mothers who are dead, good mothers who suffer, bad mothers who hoard their sustenance and will not share, mothers who breed and transmit disease, erotic mothers whose bodies exist to nurse men, and women who exist only to destroy. There is no image of a woman whose body is to be loved as an adult,—genitally, confidently, happily, tenderly, reproductively. By some undefined magic of the moon, as Ty Ty Walden says, no act of intercourse in the book results in the conception of a child. In the confused and childlike phantasy, babies would seem to be conceived and born in some other manner; and, as we shall see, sex itself comes to mean either nursing or destruction.

It is the result of a deep inner logic then that the book is a story in symbolic language of the struggle of a group of men to win some fantastic kind of sustenance out of the body of the earth, the "body" of factories, and the bodies of women; and that the living women struggle through the mazes of a queer, disjointed, erotic travail to give sustenance or death to the bodies of men. Throughout the book the recurring themes are those of food (watermelons, hams, grits, and ice cream); or of biting, grabbing, sucking, and licking; and of haunted efforts to rend or tear or suck or bite out of the bowels of the earth a golden magical food. Furthermore, since in the tale nursing and intercourse have become confused and interchangeable yearnings, it is logical that the chief protagonists should chant obsessively the beauty of a woman's breasts, that the woman's body should always be described in unreal terms more applicable to a man's and finally that the woman's body itself should be transformed into a fantastic well at which a man may slake his thirst, and ease with his mouth a torment of neurotic and perverse cravings.

But who are the men in this confused and fantastic tale, who play out their needs against these figures of women? First, there is Ty Ty Walden, an old man and a widower, seeking endlessly for gold by digging into the bowels of his farm, rendering his land sterile with mounds of earth from fruitless excavations. Despite his years he digs as a child might, because his "Daddy" told him there was gold in the ground, and because of the echoing rumor that negroes have found nuggets. His gold fever is an obsession, which in his life has taken the place of women and drink. He is sensitive, visionary, a mute artist with an eye for beauty in painting and an ear for beauty in words; but he lives out his lusts and fears at a childlike level. With his words he arouses other men's fever equally to hunt for gold or to assault his daughter-in-law, Griselda. But for himself, he is afraid of women, afraid that they "wear a man to a frazzle." He is willing to look at them but not to go too near them; and even when he looks upon Darling Jill in the very arms of Dave, he does not take in what he sees, but stands uncomprehending as a child. With his eyes he feasts on the body of his daughter-in-law, Griselda, yet he thinks of her and of his yearning for her as though she "were inside" him, as though his erotic impulses were "the rising up of something deep within" his own body. And he carries this feminine identification further by likening himself and Griselda "to a hen with a lone chick."

As an expression of these strange phantasies we find that his objective energy is directed solely towards tearing things out of the earth as if it were a human body; and that when the ground won't yield it up, he flails it like a reluctant living thing. Nor is it strange that he talks of science, yet resorts to a negro "conjur," until finally he effects a confused compromise between the white man's science and the negro's magic by capturing in a swamp the albino, Dave, to use him as his divining instrument, an all-white figure fashioned out of the black mud with which to combine white magic and black.

Furthermore, to Ty Ty the things of the spirit also lie within the body. His formulation of religion is that "God resides inside one," that "there are secret things hidden in every man," that "one hunts for the things that are inside and brings them to the outside." Thus it is clear that his gold hunt, his erotic obsession, and his religion are all part of one confused and largely unconscious system of obsessive phantasies. *He is fascinated and yet terrified by that which lies within the body.* Therefore he cannot approach the body; and though he is an old man, he is still a child, interested in the outside that he can see with his eyes, an aged Peeping Tom. Finally, and like a baby, he is concerned with the earthy products of the body, prizing that which other men discard, heaping mud-pies while he hopes to find in the mud the seed of a supreme and golden treasure.

Will Thompson is Ty Ty's son-in-law, the husband of Rosamond. He is the effective instrument of Ty Ty's frustrated desires; for it is through Will that Ty Ty mates with both of his daughters and his daughter-in-law.

By trade Will is a weaver of cloth who lives and works in the town; yet it is his obsessive ritual to tear cloth into tiny pieces when he turns on the power in the mill; and similarly he must tear to pieces the garments of Griselda when he is about to attack her. For Will, then, intercourse, "to turn on the power," must be preceded by a rending or tearing or deflorating; whereas weaving is like repair and restitution. Will is thus portrayed as a violent man, a "male man" to the negroes, the man whom all women seek and whom all other men hate and envy. With his own words, he likens himself to an almighty and omnipotent phallus. When aroused, his whole body plays this role. He compares his strength to that of "God Almighty." Yet all of this megalomanic phantasy of power can be punctured by a bullet; and in the end he is punished by death for his presumption, that is for his assault upon Griselda and his assault upon the mills.

Thus the bravado and pretended invulnerability of Will cover simple human weakness; and like all weak mortals he must restore himself with food, the most primitive of all restoratives. So Will is pictured as a hungry man who eats as the women wait upon him, and who is brought home by the lure of food; and in his final frenzy it is the mouth which becomes the focus of all his erotic desires. To Will, as to an infant, the most fundamental contact between bodies is through eating; and because his expressed phantasy of himself is of his whole body as a phallus his mouth becomes the instrument of the phantasy.

The other five male figures are less clear and less important fragments. Each of them is dominated by anxiety. None is in any true sense living. These figures of men nurse and dig and beat and threaten, or they peep and yearn and blush. They never love. They never procreate. Their woman are either dim shadows of mothers out of the past, or destroying women of the vivid present. It is out of the stuff of phantasies such as these that sickness itself arises.

It is necessary to stress the elimination of the author from our study, because the book has frequently been spoken of as "sick," a characterization which might be taken as meaning that the author was sick as well. Such a deduction is not at all warranted on the basis of what is evident from the book. The relationship of an author to his work is always complex; and to judge of an entire man from an isolated fragment of his stream of conscious or unconscious thought would be both unscientific and unsound. We can speak with some measure of confidence only of that which we have in hand, namely the book itself, and draw no conclusions about the author.

Readers of the book can be observed directly, however, and one finds them to be variously affected. Some are carried away by the compelling picture of unchecked passion, finding in this a vicarious freedom from their own habitual restraints. Others react with violent and unhesitating aversion. More often, however, they are likely to be fascinated, repelled, and puzzled, all at the same time, hardly knowing whether to envy the characters for their unchecked and hypothetical lustiness, or to look down upon them as sick and bad. Thus we find the reader either caught by the lure of illness which masquerades as primitive power, or stirred by deeply buried impulses within himself which respond to the picture which is painted, or yet revolted at times and resentful of a note of arrogance which he may feel in the protagonists of the tale.

It is inevitable that a book which stirs deep and confused phantasies or feelings must exert a fascination upon the sensitive reader. Whether in any individual in whom such confused misconceptions are active, the inner turmoil will ever break out in active sickness is a matter which depends upon too many variable factors to allow of any generalizations. One can say with confidence, however, that among healthy readers it is unlikely that such a picture of illness could cause a serious disturbance, and that it is highly probable that anyone whose precarious balance could be upset by the book would have been shaken in any case by the pressure of his own sick inner needs. One need not feel too anxious, therefore, about the influence of the book upon the health of the reader; although one may deplore the confusion which the book may churn up within him.

And still, perhaps, the question remains, why such books are, or should be. To that the only answer possible is that they are because they have to be. As long as there is a group of people who cannot be fooled or consoled by romance, whether it be cheap and tawdry or delicate and sophisticated; as long as there are those who refuse to content themselves with the cold comfort of an ironical sneer; and as long as those who reject either of these escapes have courage and honesty, there will be a literature which seeks to write its way out of confusion and restraint into some pathway of passionate relief and happiness. It would seem to be inevitable that in all such literature the portrayal of illness must play a role.

For some readers one may be sure that there is achieved at times a therapeutic relief of feeling through the translation of inner problems into literary forms. For society at large, the question of the value of this literature is more difficult. On the one hand, such books to some extent inevitably break up bigoted and inhibited attitudes towards the body; but on the other hand, when, as in "God's Little Acre," the values are confused, the book may seem to attempt to set up as standards of high normality forms of behavior which are in reality the expression of potential sickness. In all probability, with the passing years and with the deepening and clarifying growth of psychoanalytic knowledge, and the subjection of this new material to the needs of art, much of this confusion will gradually be eliminated. In the meantime it must be borne in mind that the search for beauty leads through strange fields; and that to touch deep chords in human nature, even those instinct with illness, may have subtler values than it is possible as yet to characterize.

"Caldwell:
Maker of Grotesques"

Kenneth Burke*

Erskine Caldwell's most revealing work is a "sport." I refer to the last story in "American Earth," "The Sacrilege of Alan Kent." It is divided into three sections, with wholly non-Caldwellian titles, "Tracing Life with a Finger," "Inspiration for Greatness," and "Hours Before Eternity." In these words we catch a tonality of brooding which though as much a part of America as to have been pronounced by Poe, is more generally associated with the pious satanists who developed the ways of Poe in Europe: Baudelaire, Rimbaud, Lautréamont, and the early Gide. This work is as unique to Caldwell in manner as it is in mood. Whereas his other stories, long or short, are written with the continuity of the undulations along a moving caterpillar's back, "The Sacrilege" is a chain of brief numbered paragraphs, each bluntly set off from the rest. Done with the solemnity of a farewell or a testament, they contain a kind of aphoristic rhetoric, except that the aphorisms are less ideas than tiny plots. We note here a formal resonance, a stentorian quality, obtained by a swift recital of plagues, monstrosities, horrors, obsessions, disasters and gigantesque imaginings, set against a tender counter-theme: "I never heard a girl whose face and body and eyes were lovely say anything but lovely words." Here we have the symbol of the wanderer, driven by unnamed sins and called by vague visions of a homecoming in female sweetness. The swift segments shunt us back and forth between brutality and wistfulness. Perhaps the grandiose, the violent, and the gentle qualities of the piece are all fused in this bit of purest poetry: "Once the sun was so hot a bird came down and walked beside me in my shadow." A section in "Pagany" containing this item was the first thing by Caldwell I ever saw. For days I was noisy in my enthusiasm—but I could not understand how it went with some of his other work.

Now that we have five books to examine, the connections are more easily discernible. It seems to me that Caldwell has elsewhere retained the same balked religiosity as distinguishes "The Sacrilege," but has merely poured it into less formidable molds. We may detect it, transformed, as

*Reprinted from *New Republic*, 82 (April 10, 1935), 232–35; subsequently included in Burke, *The Philosophy of Literary Form*, now published by the U. of California Press.

167

the incentive leading him to blaspheme and profane for our enjoyment. We may glimpse this balked religiosity in the symbolic transgressions and death penalties that give shape to the plots of "Tobacco Road" and "God's Little Acre." It is the explicit subject matter of much conversation in all his novels. It is revealed by an almost primitive concern with sexual taboos, and with fertility rites rising in opposition to the theme of castration. In its temperate, more social aspects, it shows as a tendency to deny humans their humaneness, as though the author, secretly abased, wanted to "drag others down" with him. Entertainingly, it appears in still more attenuated form as caricature and humor, the mental state of "refusal" here inducing extravagant incongruities that sometimes can be received with laughter, but are frequently so closely connected with degradation and acute suffering that the effect is wholly grim. Towards the end of his longer works, the goad of balked religiosity provokes grandiloquent moralistic passages wherein his sub-normal mannikins, strangely elated by the story's symbolism, transcend themselves and speak of vital purpose with almost evangelical fervor (plus a slight suggestion that they had read D.H. Lawrence). And in an unexpected episode of "Journeyman," his latest book, Caldwell has even gone so far as to introduce a quality of other-worldliness into the very midst of his human rabbit hutch—for in no other way can I interpret the section (which Horace Gregory has selected for approval) where three men take turns at peering out through a crack in the wall of the barn, while one sermonizes: "It's sitting there and looking through the crack at the trees all day long that sorts of gets me. I don't know what it is, and it might not be nothing at all when you figure it out. But it's not the knowing about it, anyway—it's just sitting there and looking through it that sort of makes me feel like heaven can't be so doggone far away."

In taking balked religiosity as the underlying theme upon which his successive works are the variations, I do not want to imply that Caldwell, like Hemingway, is preparing himself for a return to Rome. His recent powerful story in Scribner's, "Kneel to the Rising Sun," indicates that he can make the change from negativism to affirmation by choices usually called secular. In so far as he is moved by the need of salvation, he seems minded to find it in the alignments of political exhortation, by striving mainly to see that we and he take the right side on matters of social justice. But as partial vindication of my proposal that his cult of incongruity seems to stem from the same source as his social propaganda, I should note that, precisely in this story of a lynching, his emphasis upon the playful scrambling of the old proprieties abates: instead of the humorist's refusal, as shown in his earlier zest to garble the conventions, we get a sober assertion of positive values. He does not merely act to outrage an old perspective by throwing its orders of right and wrong into disarray: he subscribes to an alternative perspective, with positive rights and wrongs of its own, and with definite indications as to what form he

wants our sympathies and antagonisms to take. Incidentally, this development suggests the ways in which a motivation essentially non-political or
non-economic can be harnessed in the service of political or economic
criticism.

Whether one so apt at entertaining us by *muddling* our judgments
will be equally fertile in *stabilizing* judgments remains to be seen. My
guess would be that he won't, since he would have to master a whole new
technique of expression. His very abilities tend to work against him.
Recently I heard one man complain that Caldwell "has yet to learn that
the revolution begins above the belt." And I incline to suspect that, in the
learning, he may begin to find himself psychologically unemployed. A
literary method is tyrannical—it is a writer's leopard-spots—it molds
what a writer can say by determining what he can see; hence I should
imagine that Caldwell would have to develop by satirizing more complex
people rather than by pleading unmistakably for simple ones. But that is a
guess about tomorrow's weather.

When I say that Caldwell's particular aptitude has been in scrambling or garbling proprieties, I refer to his deft way of putting the wrong
things together. An unendowed writer, for instance, might strain to
engross us by lurid description of the sexual act—and the result would be
negligible. But such an uninventive writer would probably be quite
"proper" in the sense that he accepted the usual conventions as to the
privacy of this act. Caldwell can be much more stimulating by merely so
altering the customary situation that people are looking on and comment-
ing in the blandest fashion, as in the comically inappropriate episode of
this nature in "God's Little Acre." Or he may have Ty Ty say, without
confusion, such things to his daughters and daughter-in-law as would
"properly" be said only under the greatest of morbid intensity. By an as-
tounding trick of oversimplification, Caldwell puts people into complex
social situations while making them act with the scant, crude tropisms of
an insect—and the result is cunning, where Lawrence, by a variant of the
same pattern, is as unwieldy as an elephant in his use of vulgar words for
romantic love-making. Probably only in the orgy at the end of
"Journeyman" does Caldwell become so undiplomatic in his treatment.
Here, with almost the literalness of an inventory, he has us observe in
each member of the congregation that phenomenon which so mortified
Saint John of the Cross, the fact that, since the body has less channels of
expression than the mind, acute religious ecstasy may be paralleled
neurologically by sexual orgasm.

In the psychology textbooks, we read accounts of experiments whereby the higher centers of an animal's brain are removed, with the result
that the animal's reponses to stimuli are greatly simplified. A frog, so
decerebrated, may jump when prodded, eat when fed, and croak when
caressed—but it is evident that with the operation the poor fellow's personality has vanished. He has become less like a living organism, and

more like a doorbell, which rings when you press the button. He has lost the part of himself that is sometimes called free will and which Bergson names the "center of indetermination." And his ways, as compared with the ways of a whole frog, are distinctly grotesque. Caldwell often seems to have performed such an operation upon the minds of his characters. As Ty Ty Walden complains in "God's Little Acre," "There was a mean trick played on us somewhere. God put us in the body of animals and tried to make us act like people." It is a just complaint of Ty Ty's, as the creature of his own private creator. What the decerebrated frog is to the whole frog, Caldwell's characters are to real people. In view of which, it is positively incredible that his extravaganzas, imagined in a world essentially as fantastic as Swift's, should ever have passed for realism.

Pearl, the image of better things in "Tobacco Road," does not even *speak.* Anderson's gropers stuttered, but in this book the golden-haired child-wife who is charged with the novelistic duty of upholding a little corner of glory in the midst of degradation, is totally inarticulate. For her there is no such verbal key as that with which the great sonneteer unlocked his heart. Though married, she sleeps alone; she will not look at her uncouth husband; she refuses to discuss his appetites with him (she cries when he beats her, but "Lov did not consider that as conversation"); and in the end, still wordless, she vanishes, doubtless to become a prostitute in Augusta. Silk stockings in the city, we feel, is her noblest conceivable utopian negation of the physical and spiritual impoverishment all about her; but to her understanding of this little, she will bring a deep, innate delicacy, invisible to all but the novelist and his readers.

In this discussion of Pearl, I may seem to have involved myself in a contradiction. For I speak of Caldwell's subhuman characters, yet I credit them with great delicacy. Here we come to the subtlest feature of Caldwell's method. Where the author leaves out so much, the reader begins making up the difference for himself. Precisely by omitting humaneness where humaneness is most called for, he may stimulate the reader to supply it. When the starved grandmother in "Tobacco Road" lies dying, with her face ground into the soil, and no one shows even an onlooker's interest in her wretchedness, we are prodded to anguish. When these automata show some bare inkling of sociality, is may seem like a flash of ultimate wisdom. I suspect that, in putting the responsibility upon his readers, he is taking more out of the community pile than he puts in. Perhaps he is using up what we already had, rather than adding to our store. He has evoked in us a quality, but he has not materialized it with sufficient quantity. In any event, the silence of Pearl in "Tobacco Road" and the sober burlesque of the men peering through the crack in "Journeyman" are of a piece with the strange albino of "God's Little Acre," the "conjur" who makes the simple, lyrical declaration to Darling Jill (herself graced with one of the loveliest names in all fiction):

"I wish I had married you," he said, his hands trembling beside her. "I didn't know there was a girl so beautiful anywhere in the country. You're the prettiest girl I've ever seen. You're so soft, and you talk like bird-song, and you smell so good. . . ."

I have denied that Caldwell is a realist. In his tomfoolery he comes closer to the Dadaists; when his grotesqueness is serious, he is a Superrealist. We might compromise by calling him over all a Symbolist (if by a Symbolist we mean a writer whose work serves most readily as case history for the psychologist and whose plots are more intelligible when interpreted as dreams). In The Saturday Review of Literature a few months back, Dr. Lawrence S. Kubie took as particularly significant the absence of the motherly woman in Caldwell's fictions, with attendant cult of sterility. And his article gave many relevant clues as to the *nonrational* linkages involved in the imagery of "God's Little Acre."

In books of complex realistic texture, such as the great social novels of the nineteenth century, we may feel justified in considering the psychologist's comments as an intrusion when he would have us find there merely a sublimation of a few rudimentary impulses. The important thing is not the base, but the superstructure. With fantastic simplifications of the Caldwell sort, however, the symbolic approach has more relevance. Thus, the selection of extreme starvation as a theme of "Tobacco Road" is found to take on a significance besides that of realistic justification when we link it with passages in "God's Little Acre" where Ty Ty, admiring Griselda, declares that the sight of her "rising beauties" makes him feel inspired to "get down and lick something." How possibly explain as mere reporting the episode in "God's Little Acre" about the girls who have replaced the men in the factory, and of whom we read the dreamlike statement, "When they reached the street, they ran back to the ivy-colored wall and pressed their bodies against it and touched it with their lips. The men who had been standing idly before it all day long came and dragged them home and beat them unmercifully for their infidelity"? A factory that could induce such surprising antics must have peculiar connotations not realistically there. And perhaps we come closer to them when recalling how, in this same factory, where the rebellion of the workers takes very unreal forms, Will finally fulfills his determination to "turn on the power," but only after his perverted rape of Griselda. When the old grandmother dies, the sight of her face in the dirt simply reminds her son Jeeter that the soil is right for planting. Immediately after, he is destroyed by fire.

The symbolic relations submerged here begin to suggest themselves when we recall the following facts: In both "Tobacco Road" and "God's Little Acre" we are told that there are two types of people, those who stay on the farm and those who go to the factory. Both Jeeter of "Tobacco Road" and Ty Ty of "God's Little Acre" are the kind that stay on the farm, the first hoping to plant again (a frustrated hope) and the second digging in the bowels of the earth for gold (an exceptional obsession to motivate an entire book about contemporary Georgia, though we may legitimately remember here the golden-haired Pearl of "Tobacco Road"). In one of the short stories, "Crown Fire," we learn from the course of the plot that the fire symbol is linked with partial female acquiescence; and in "The Sacrilege," where the "offense" is unnamed, we are told, "My mother saw from her bed the reflection in the sky of red wind-fanned flames. She carried me out into the street and we sat in the red mud shivering and crying"—sitting in this same soil with which Jeeter is so impotently preoccupied (since he cannot buy the seed for planting) and which Ty Ty turns into sterility by digging there for gold. After Will carries out in actuality the perverse inclination Ty Ty speaks of, Will can "turn on the power" in the factory. But though Will here seems to deputize for Ty Ty, Ty Ty's son commits a murder and must run away. Ty Ty moans that blood has been spilled upon his land, whereupon he is freed of his obsession to dig gold; and as the son is leaving, Ty Ty wills that God's little acre be always under him. Both books are thus permeated with symbolic sins, symbolic punishments, followed by symbolic purification. At the end of each, and following the orgy in "Journeyman," there is the feeling that a cleansing had taken place, that the character who, at the last transformation, is the bearer of the author's identity, is free to "start anew." All this is magic, not reason; and I think that we are entitled to inspect it for the processes of magic. The balked religiosity of which we spoke is evidently linked with the devious manifestations of "incest-awe"; the plots are subtly guided by the logic of dreams.

I am not by any means satisfied by the psycho-analytic readings of such processes to date, though I do believe that in moralistic fantasies of the Caldwell type, where the dull characters become so strangely inspired at crucial moments, we are present at a poetic law court where judgments are passed upon kinds of transgression inaccessible to jurists, with such odd penalties as no Code Napoleon could ever schematize.

The short stories (republished in "American Earth" and "We Are the Living") as a whole seem too frail. They are hardly more than jottings in a diary, mere *situations* that Caldwell, with his exceptional turn for narrative and his liquid style, manages to palm off as plots. I call them diary jottings because they often give the impression of having suggested themselves to him in this wise: If you were sitting alone in a strange room, you might think, "What if someone knocked at the door?" If Caldwell were similarly placed, such a thought might occur to him, and there he would have his story.

He has a sharper sense of beginnings than most writers, as witness in the long story, "Journeyman," Semon Dye's formal entrance in the lavishly balky and noisy car. Here is a mock announcement of the hero's approach, done with such a blare and fanfare of brasses as Wagner summons to herald the approach of Siegfried. Thus, the author tends to begin with some oddity of situation, which as likely as not suggested itself without a resolution, so that the story merely fades away rather than closes. He shows a surprisingly naive delight in all the possible ramifications of the thought that girls may be without panties, and he seems to have searched the length and breadth of the country for new situations whereby some significant part or parts can be exposed for us. The basic formula seems to be the use of two unrelated orders of events until they are felt to be related. He gets very appealing pictures of adolescent love—but his most successful venture in the shorter form is probably "Country Full of Swedes," where a family returns to their house across the road after a couple of years' absence, and their sudden prevalence in the locality is amusingly magnified until, for all their obvious peacefulness, they take on the qualities of a vast invasion.

Caldwell's greatest vice is unquestionably repetitiousness. He seems as contented as a savage to say the same thing again and again. Repetition in his prose is so extreme as almost to perform the function of rhyme in verse. In analyzing the first four chapters of "Tobacco Road," I found that it was simply a continual rearrangement of the same subjects in different sequences: Jeeter wants Lov's turnips, Lov wants Jeeter to make Pearl sleep with him, Jeeter's own turnips all have "damn-blasted green-gutted turnip-worms," hair-lipped Ellie May is sidling up to Lov, Dude won't stop "chunking" a ball against the loose clapboards, Jeeter hopes to sell a load of wood in Augusta—about ten more such details, regiven in changing order, make the content of forty pages. Sometimes when reading Caldwell I feel as though I were playing with my toes.

"Star-Dust Above 'Tobacco Road' "

J. H. Marion, Jr.*

Pious people of an older day used to speak of the way God could make even the "wrath of man" to praise him. But I suspect that many such moderns who have read Erskine Caldwell's *Tobacco Road*, or have seen the play based on the book, have sadly concluded that not even the Almighty could make *that* to praise him!

What about it? Are they right?

Undeniably, when so enlightened a place as Teachers College of Columbia University bars *Tobacco Road* from its library, and when numbers of other liberal souls have concurred in that verdict, one who finds in *Tobacco Road* anything wholesome or uplifting may appear perverse and foolhardy indeed. Yet no one who walks carefully around the whole matter, I venture, will end by damning that production as completely and hopelessly "of the earth, earthy." For while the story may not wear a halo exactly, there is star-dust above it.

Helping to Free the South

History may never call Erskine Caldwell a great writer, yet to some of us he does have unusual significance because, however unwittingly and indirectly, he is helping by his best known works to free the south from an unworthy and socially crippling tradition.

Until recently southerners have been much too sentimental, on the whole, in their views of literature. If one must read books, we have said, let them be scented with fragrance of honeysuckle! Let stories be written with the perfume of magnolias flooding the author's nostrils! Let the odors of injustice and vice be carefully sealed in the bottle of social indifference. Such has been the prevailing mood, and, so brought up, many southerners respond to Caldwell's work as a man with a weak stomach might react to the sight of garbage while eating his dinner. To this group, as one critic suggests, Caldwell's writing is not authentic literature of the soil—it is merely soiled literature.

*Reprinted from *Christian Century*, 55 (Feb. 16, 1938), 204–06.

Others, however, are beginning to think differently. Cried Gilbert Maxwell impatiently:

> I am sick in my soul of the poets who sing
> Of the star in the sky and the bird on the wing,
> While Life lies down in a filthy shroud,
> And cannot be spoken about out loud.

That is the view to which, more and more, many southerners are at last coming. If life anywhere is lying down in a "filthy shroud," then in God's name let us throw light upon it! Maybe the shroud ought not be there. Maybe the light will keep the shroud from becoming the winding-sheet of living men who are now in danger of social maladjustment and decay. At any rate, no good purpose will be served by playing the ostrich. So a growing group in the south is now thinking, and *Tobacco Road* is a definite factor in producing the change.

Over appalling social evils people do not become aroused, usually, until somebody has written about them dramatically. All peaceful reforms, if history is any guide, must have their scribbling prophets or their literary groundbreakers. Charles Dickens was such a man in 19th century England. Victor Hugo and Emile Zola were such men in France. If there is one thing reformers have learned, it is that not even the most hateful conditions will stir mass action as long as they remain intellectual abstractions. They need to be emotionalized, made vivid through the medium of colorful words, transferred, as it were, from the brain to the blood of the people.

No one who saw the motion picture version of "The Life of Emile Zola" could easily forget the scene where Zola, fired from the publishing firm of Monsieur Larue, turns upon his erstwhile employer and says: "While you, Monsieur Larue, continue to grow fatter and richer publishing your nauseating confectionery, I shall become a mole, digging here, rooting there, stirring up the whole rotten mess where life is hard, raw and ugly. You will not like the smell of my books, Monsieur Larue. Neither will the public prosecutor. But when the stench is strong enough, maybe something will be done about it." More than once, when a writer with that determination has come along, some far-reaching social reform has been set afoot.

The South That Read Scott

There are plenty of signs, to take a negative example, that the absence of the right books in the slave-holding south was a considerable factor in bringing on the Civil War. Up to around 1830 slavery could be opposed in the south as vigorously as a man pleased. During the next generation, however, this was far from true. Intellectually and morally, the Dixie of that period lay under a mist of romantic moonshine. There was not a single influential writer who ably and fearlessly portrayed the inhumanity of slavery. Reality was about the last thing a writer was supposed to face. Penetrating social criticism was practically nonexistent. What voices there were, including the preachers, spoke softly of soothing and agreeable generalities. The novels of Sir Walter Scott, with their glorification of an older feudalism, were, significantly, widely read; those of Charles Dickens were not. Nothing must disturb the genteel tranquility of the southern scene. Thus by 1850 the south was so immured in self-righteousness, so sensitive to criticism, that the few who did dare lift a voice against slavery were quickly silenced or driven into exile. A new feudalism, no less immoral for being superficially humane in spots, had taken root.

An awakening book, *Uncle Tom's Cabin*, finally came, but it came too late and from the wrong section. Had several such books been written earlier by southern writers, and accepted by a south with any capacity for self-criticism, history might have been different. Coming as it did from the north as late as 1852, and calculated to inflame northern abolitionists at the same time it angered and stiffened the defense of the southern pro-slavery element, *Uncle Tom's Cabin* was bound to spur the sections on toward further enmity, cleavage and conflict. Lincoln called Mrs. Stowe the author of the war.

Growing Capacity for Criticism

One hopeful thing about the present south is her growing capacity for honest self-examination. The ante-bellum priggishness and provincialism are dying—in many minds, indeed, they are quite dead. Frankness is no longer the sin against gentility it once was. Erskine Caldwell digs around in southern muck, flings the muck into the literary sky (smack among the magnolias!) and the south—part of it, anyway—watches. Nor does it miss the meaning of the show. With no pretense of being a prophet or reformer (he would laugh if you called him either!) Caldwell throws a beam of uncolored light upon one segment of a demoralizing social system; and now the average southerner, thanks partly to these stark and vivid stories, is much more willing to face and talk about conditions than ever before.

Here and there, to be sure, a shocked voice cries that Caldwell's pictures of poor-white life are caricatures, his characters grotesque. One could only wish they were! But while the poverty and depravity of old Jeeter Lester and his family are not universally typical, they are at least accurately symbolic. For, by and large, life is like that among the dispossessed of this region. If the cropper-tenant civilization were a human body, one would have to regard it as not merely diseased but, in some quarters, in the last stages of putrefaction. The characters in *Tobacco Road* are an integral part of what someone has called that "miserable panorama of unpainted shacks, rain-gullied fields, straggling fences, rattle-trap Fords, dirt, poverty, disease, drudgery and monotony that stretches for a thousand miles across the cotton belt."

Nor can the wretchedness of the scene be explained away by talking eugenics. Lazy, licentious and low as they often are, what damns these people is not something inside them but something outside. Bad blood may flow in many a cropper's veins, but it isn't bad blood at bottom that blights these tragic lives. It is chiefly the present system of cotton tenancy—that system plus upper class indifference and blindness: the bland confusion, for example, that makes many a well-fixed southerner hope for a mild winter lest there be great suffering among the poor, but which makes him, in the same breath, cry loudly against any change in the setup that is the root cause of that suffering! What Caldwell unconsciously indicts, therefore, is not so much the immorality and misery of a single family, but the corrupt and degrading influence of this entire social order itself.

Seeing Only the Surface

Just how badly we needed Caldwell's beam of light to "stab us broad awake" may be pointedly illustrated by my own life. Born and brought up in a middle class family, I was automatically shielded from the harsher aspects of rural reality. As the son of a prominent small town lawyer, I was vaguely aware of poverty and vice, but I looked on them as immutable features of a divinely ordered society. Some people were just "that way," and that was all there was to it! Agriculture was as foreign to me as French or Sanskrit. Tenant farmers were rough, queer folk who once a week trickled out of their rustic haunts to make Saturday the liveliest day of the week downtown. The "cabin in the cotton" was a pleasant phantom which I encountered mainly in sentimental songs or from the vantage point of a peacefully shaded swimming hole.

What scabrous horrors might lie beneath the surface of cropper life most of us never suspected. That we favored townsmen might be living off the misery and depravity of surrounding sharecroppers—fed like vultures, as it were, from the flesh of a rotted carcass—was a thought which might not have concerned many of us had it occurred to us, but a thought too which never had a chance to make its appeal because the facts that might have provoked it were never impressively brought to light. Together with thousands of others, I went through high school and college with scarcely a glimmer of the actualities of poor farm life. Up to the dawn of Caldwell's realism I was sure that people like William Gilmore Simms, "Uncle Remus" and Thomas Nelson Page had said the last word. Romanticism had swept all corners. But—not any more! Now I know better, and others do too.

Moreover, some of us are convinced that these ugly revelations will help to call forth adequate remedies. Like bugs under a dead log, the cropper system has thrived on darkness; but now under the piercing light of these rough but realistic stories it will, beyond question, begin to crack. Or it might better be said that the cracking process which already has begun will be thrown into higher gear. For whatever may be Caldwell's faults—and I am not trying to whitewash him—he is not letting southerners live in a world that is only a painted lie. The smug or squeamish may dismiss him as a crude purveyor of raw sex or bawdy burlesque, but his stories are really far more. Dramatizing social decay, and touching men's minds with fire as books like *The Collapse of Cotton Tenancy* and Arther Raper's *Preface to Peasantry* fill men's minds with facts, they point with flaming and accusing finger at the open sore of the south.

Books Opening the Way

One cannot claim, of course, that Caldwell is entirely responsible for the interest and zeal which have lately been aroused over the plight of the croppers, though I do think that his work has made a real contribution by baring conditions that never would have been properly dramatized by the depression alone. While it may be too early to estimate his influence on current sociological thought and activity, it is not too soon to predict his influence on the south's tomorrow. Amused or enraged as southerners may be at first, his telltale pictures are sure to prick the southern conscience. Neither *Tobacco Road* nor *God's Little Acre* is the sort of book that pulls a man out of his chair to do something about it right away, but they are the kind of books that do subtly prepare the people's emotions for suggested reforms, making men more amenable to change and less opposed to governmental measures like the "triple-A" and other rehabilitation programs. People generally may not trace their new thoughts to the new literature or the new drama, but they will unconsciously catch from it the conviction that a section which puts up with such cancerous farm conditions thereby forfeits the right to call itself civilized, much less Christian.

There is a mounting body of evidence to show that southern critics, journals and teachers are not only seeing all this but saying it. Recently the editor of a South Carolina daily, quoting from a letter which Erskine Caldwell had written to the *New York Times* in defense of his realism, went on to make this quotation the text for an approving editorial. The editorial was then reprinted by at least one other paper and allowed to speak for itself, without comment. Thus from occasional newspapers, scattered classrooms and from library shelves the essence of Caldwell and other kindred spirits is seeping slowly into the public mind, disturbing old complacencies, opening shuttered eyes, and giving promise of increasing dissatisfaction with the south's common and corrupting system of farm tenancy.

To call *Tobacco Road*, the book, another *Uncle Tom's Cabin* would be far-fetched. To compare the play with *Main Street*, as Carl Van Doren does, is, from the standpoint of popularity, more accurate. My own feeling is that the book and the play are even more akin to Jacob Riis' *How the Other Half Lives*. For what that book did for city slums a generation ago, Caldwell's *Tobacco Road*—at once an exposé and a challenge—may help to do in time for the country "slums" of an exploited south.

We may not like the smell of Caldwell's book, but Zola's words are worth pondering: "When the stench is strong enough maybe something will be done about it."

[American Fiction: 1920–1940]

Joseph Warren Beach*

X. Erskine Caldwell: *The Comic Catharsis*

Erskine Caldwell is probably the best example we have of the artistic imagination working consistently in matter of concern to the social conscience, and yet not subdued, like the dyer's hand, to what it works in. By this I mean that, dealing consistently with data of the most obvious economic and sociological significance, he does not treat it in the manner of sociological treatise or reformist propaganda, but keeps—in his novels and short stories—within the strict limits of esthetic presentation. And the result is, curiously enough, that he is the cause of bewilderment and scandal to many serious and cultivated readers. For intellectual cultivation and moral seriousness do not necessarily mean a capacity to enjoy works of the imagination on the esthetic level. The enjoyment of art is natural enough to men in general, cultivated or uncultivated; but a certain measure of cultivation is only too likely to confuse a reader with other than esthetic concerns, and moral seriousness may lead a man to attribute frivolity and corruptness to a work in which matter of conscience is treated artistically.

The human spirit, on its moral and practical side, is given to self-distrust, anxiety and dread. It dreads unsettlement, distraction from its strenuous aims, and division of its forces. This sort of fear is natural enough, and grounded in experience of our own limitations. We know that our energies are limited, and we fear that anything short of a total devotion of them to our practical aims may lead to weakness and ineffectualness in action. And in our concern that right should prevail or that we should be successful in our endeavors, we are likely to forget that the narrowest view of any subject is not the most correct view or that most likely to promote success. We forget that our very concept of rightness is based in the notion of value, and that in the notion of value there is an appreciable tinge of the esthetic. Value is attributed to that which yields

*Reprinted from Joseph Warren Beach, *American Fiction: 1920–1940* (New York: Macmillan, 1941), pp. 219–49. (Copyright © 1941, 1969 by Joseph Warren Beach and Northrup and Warren Beach. New York: Russell & Russell, 1960)

180

satisfactions to human beings; and satisfaction is as clearly an esthetic concept as it is a moral one.

We have no reason to conclude that puritanism is the code most likely to promote the general well-being of the race or even to insure its survival. In any case, it would be a dreary world in which men's imagination was confined within the strait-jacket of puritanism. There is some reason to think that the spirit is better for an occasional holiday. If nothing else, this brings a certain relaxation to the strained nerves. Our psyche is a mechanism of great complexity and varied needs. It craves exercise of various kinds. Even in matters of conscience, the esthetic and the scientific approaches may be purgative and salutary to the spirit—calming it, stabilizing it, raising it above the anxiety and nervousness of the puritan attitude. More than that, they may be broadening—the esthetic and the scientific attitudes; they may lead to discriminations and refinements, to wise attenuations and humane indulgences. Given a spirit of some gravity and depth, every gain in breadth and imagination is in the end an ethical gain, an enlargement of moral wisdom.

The inexperienced or unimaginative reader may at first blush question the social seriousness of Erskine Caldwell in such novels as *Tobacco Road*, such tales as those included in the volume, *Kneel to the Rising Sun*. He may take him to be a cynical soul, one that delights in the miseries and degradations of human nature. And that, because the life of poverty and humiliation is presented in the manner of fiction, without expository comment, in speech and action, pointed up with the resources of humor and irony and imaginative high lighting. For such a reader it is important to explain that Caldwell is the author of several volumes of sociological studies of the utmost earnestness based on careful personal observation, notable for their plain matter-of-factness in reporting conditions, for the obvious concern with which the writer views the unfortunate conditions reported, and his modest but serious effort to suggest means of ameliorating these conditions. In 1935 he published *Some American People*, based on leisurely travel through the Pacific Northwest, the Middle West, including Detroit, and through certain counties in Georgia, and on numerous interviews with persons in distress mainly as a result of unemployment. In 1937 he published *You Have Seen Their Faces*, with some sixty or seventy odd photographs by Margaret Bourke-White, now Caldwell's wife. The pictures represent typical men, women and children from the poorer agricultural regions of the South, whites and negroes, seen in their homes, in the fields, in church, in school, in the chain-gang. Each picture is accompanied by some characteristic sentiment or statement about himself from the person represented. There are, also, serious essays on the history and present state of tenant farming and share-cropping, and the economic and social condition of the people involved.

The ordinary comfortable reader, unacquainted with government reports and other statistical studies, will be amazed and shocked at the desperate conditions reported by Caldwell even in those deepest years of the long depression, and above all with the almost universal state of hopeless misery prevailing thoughout large regions in Georgia, Alabama, Mississippi, Louisiana, Arkansas and Tennessee. If the reader's patriotism requires him to assume that extreme injustice and bestial living are not possible under our system of government, he may be inclined to discount some of the plain facts reported by Caldwell, and still more to question the connection he draws between the facts and certain of our economic and industrial arrangements. Caldwell does not make any such comparisons; but one is led to wonder whether, under the system of tenant farming in the South either whites or negroes are much better off economically, politically, or morally than peasants in Poland, Russia, Yugoslavia or even China, at least in time of peace. One wonders whether the condition of the unemployed workman and the homeless girl turned prostitute in Detroit (with a municipal permit) is so much better than that of similar groups in London, Marseilles, Birmingham or Budapest. Such thoughts are highly distressing to a patriotic American, and the easiest way to deal with them is to deny the facts, to assume that they are grossly exaggerated, or to attribute them not to any defect in our social and industrial arrangements but to the natural shiftlessness and depravity of shiftless and depraved people.

There will be ways for the reader to break the force of the facts presented by Caldwell. But even so, the average open-minded person cannot fail to be impressed either by the facts or by the serious intentions of an author who has taken the pains to inform himself so widely and to set down what he has observed in so straightforward and matter-of-fact a manner. He will realize that he is dealing here not with an irresponsible sensation-monger and spinner of shocking tales. And then if he will look into the studies of federal officials and the staid publications of Southern University presses, he will realize that what Caldwell is dealing with is a set of conditions having their roots in a long and tragic industrial history. He will come back to Caldwell's pamphlets and ponder his general assertions—that the plantation system was one which resulted in the rapid impoverishment of the soil over a region larger than Europe; that the sharecropping system was one in which a small class of owners enriched themselves at the expense of millions of men who could never make enough from their toil in the cotton fields to free themselves from debt; that in vast sections the owners regularly forced the white share-croppers to give up the land and replaced them with negroes who could be more easily cheated and exploited and maintained in a state of virtual serfdom; that the system of tenant farming represents a still more hopeless outlook than that of share-cropping, a still lower level of subsistence and decent living.

The chief theme of Caldwell's writing is the agony of the impoverished land, which has now so nearly reached a state of complete exhaustion in large sections of the old South that it is only a matter of time (he thinks) when the dust storms will cross the Mississippi and extend the desert to the east. That is the material basis for the social conditions which he sets forth in his stories. But, of course, it is the people who interest him as a student of human nature; and with the people, it is not so much their material sufferings as the moral degradation which follows steadily on the decline of their material well-being. It is the illiteracy passed on from generation to generation of those who cannot find time to go to school or have not clothes to wear to school. It is the benighted ignorance of people without books or newspapers, often without even a church, with little more than the superstitions and traditional error of bygone ages to guide them in the conduct of life. It is a state of poverty which leads parents to marry off their twelve-year-old daughters in order to have one less mouth to feed; the isolation which makes incest as common as marriage. It is the diseases caused by malnutrition and excessive childbirth which turn women into sickly slatterns. It is the dull indifference to others' sufferings, the want of imagination and sympathy, engendered by a life obsessed by the constant craving for food. It is the shiftlessness and improvidence and irresponsibility wrought by habitual want of hope.

This is not the exclusive subject matter of Caldwell's stories. But it is the central and dominant theme. The pitiful state of the white agricultural laborer in Georgia is what possesses his imagination above all other subjects. And it is clear enough that it has taken deep hold on the moral feelings of this son of a Presbyterian minister. He might have dealt with this matter as an economist, as a sociologist, as a social reformer—as the John the Baptist of some gospel of social reorganization. He has, I think, the seriousness for any of these ways of dealings with his subject. But it so happened, by some chance of birth or circumstance, that this man is by bent an artist rather than a scientist or propagandist. As a student at the University of Virginia, as a mill hand, a farm laborer, a cook, it was not for sociology that he was preparing himself; it was for a still more serious endeavor, as it must have seemed to one of his temperament—that of molding the stuff of life as he knew it in the shapely and significant forms that gratify the esthetic sense. He was one destined to follow in the steps of Chaucer and Dickens, of Balzac and Gorky.

We say, in a general way, that the artist is one interested in beauty and skillful in the representation of beautiful things. But that—as beauty is frequently understood—is a very limited definition and leaves out of account a large part of the action of the esthetic faculty. The artist is one interested in shape and color and quality and in the representation in some medium of whatever is characteristic in shape and color and quality. He appeals to our own interest in the *characteristic* and the pleasure we take in its representation. And so it comes about that anything in human nature may be the subject of artistic representation provided it can be shown as characteristic; and that the reader esthetically disposed can take a positive pleasure in the skillful representation of anything characteristic in human nature, provided only that his pleasure is not inhibited by some more powerful emotion. The human spirit is many-sided, and we are fortunately capable of taking esthetic pleasure in subjects which, on some other view of them, are painful or disgusting. This is a happy provision of nature, since it makes it possible to reap a benefit from circumstances which otherwise might be a total loss to us as human beings. Thus it comes about that a spirit as serious and feeling as Erskine Caldwell's may take a positive pleasure, on the esthetic side, in the representation of characters and situations which are abhorrent to him as a moralist or a man of feeling.

Caldwell's subject in *Tobacco Road* (1932) is a Georgia farmer whose dominant instinct and passion is to grow cotton. He is, that is, a potentially useful and productive member of the community. He is living on land once owned by his grandfather, in a tumble-down shack whose present owner has retired to Atlanta and left it with all other buildings on the land to be occupied without rent by the families established there as long as it will stand up. The land was once fertile, but was long since worked out. Lester Jeeter's[*sic*] father planted exclusively cotton and completed the exhaustion of the soil; the land he and his father lost parcel by parcel as it was sold to meet their debts. The present Jeeter owns nothing whatever but a change of clothing, a bed, and a few utensils. He has long since been unable to secure credit at the store or the bank; and for several years he has not planted even a small patch of cotton, not being able to get either seed or fertilizer. He and his family are slowly starving to death; but, being deeply religious, he cherishes the hope that God will somehow come to his relief before it is too late.

Jeeter's wife has borne him many children, but only three are left. Some have died, and most of them, at an early age, have abandoned the farm to marry or seek employment in the mills. The Jeeters cannot read or write; they have no means of locomotion but a broken-down car whose tires will not hold up the distance to the nearest town. They have no communication with the children who have left them, and have only the remotest notion how many grandchildren they may have scattered about the country. Jeeter's wife has long suffered from pellagra; she is a languid drudge; her sole preoccupations are a little food, snuff (which cannot be had), and a proper dress to be laid out in when she dies—of this she has small hope or prospect. They have one daughter, a young girl whom they cannot marry because her hare-lip makes her so repellent. Her father has long meant to take her to town and have the hare-lip sewed up; but with no money and less enterprise, he has always postponed it for something more urgent. The still younger Pearl has already been married; her husband earns a living shoveling coal for the railway. But Pearl is not old enough to be fit for matrimony; she is a frightened little animal, who cannot be persuaded to sleep with her husband or to speak a word to him. In the Jeeter household there is also a grandmother, so old and decrepit that no one ever has anything to say to her except to scold her. Everyone resents her existence, and they give her nothing to eat out of their scanty store. She lives on odds and ends; and she is so hungry that she regularly gathers wood and lights the fire three times a day in hopes there may be something to cook. Then finally there is the son Dude, who spends his time bouncing a ball against the side of the house to the evident damage of that rickety structure.

The moral status of these people is hardly recognizable as human. They do possess language; they wear clothes; they handle implements; they can do the manual work of men; and they believe in "God." That is about all there is to distinguish them from other mammals. Their most distinctive traits, as human beings, are their extreme ignorance and incompetence and their shocking moral callousness. And yet there is nothing to suggest that they are naturally depraved—if such a thing is conceivable—or even that they are naturally shiftless and improvident. Everything distinctively human in sentiment has been withered away by the unremitting pains of hunger. And their shiftlessness is too natural a growth of conditions so utterly hopeless. It is true that Jeeter might have moved to town and become a mill hand. He might have secured for himself and family that measure of humanity which is possible under such conditions. But his not doing so is the result of his one virtue—his deep attachment to the land, his instinctive craving to be productive.

Now, the Jeeters are representative of conditions widely prevailing in the agricultural backwaters of Georgia and elsewhere in the South. Here is matter of the highest sociological and moral interest. And the esthetic problem is this: what angle of approach to take, what tone to assume, and how dispose the subject matter so as to distill from this painful stuff the esthetic pleasure derived from the skillful representation of the characteristic in human nature. There will be several possible solutions of this problem according to the gifts and temper of the author. Caldwell's solution is something like this. He will choose a succession of incidents, characteristic and familiar, but such as to bring out in high relief the childish naïveté of these people. By any civilized standard their behavior is outrageous in the extreme. At every turn they violate our notions of decency and good sense. They are like animals of some inferior species, or like little children not yet trained in the ways of adults. But they are dressed and labeled men; they have the stature and responsibilities of adults. If we judged them strictly as men, we should have no choice but to be severe. But what prevents us from judging them so is their utter helplessness and ignorance, their incredible innocence, their total lack of awareness that their behavior is shocking.

There is an element of paradox and incongruity here, and there is an element of surprise, which—as the psychologist will tell us—is of the essence of comedy. Indeed, these characters fit in rather well with the special theory of the comic developed by Henri Bergson in his famous treatise on Laughter. Bergson holds that the comic effect results where human beings, who are supposed to act like human beings, with intelligence and the flexibility of free agents, exhibit instead the wooden and automatic movements of puppets. We take them for human; we look for the human reaction; we are caught with sudden surprise by movements not proper to human beings; the shock of this recognition, this absurdity, releases some nervous spring within us, and we laugh.

There are many kinds and degrees of comic effect, and the reaction varies with the other emotional elements present in the experience. There are absurdities of action which we do not need to take seriously since the moral sense is not deeply involved; and we can laugh at these with a heartiness not dampened by any feeling of the gravity of the subject. Where subjects of grave importance are concerned, our laughter may be checked or minimized. Not many readers will laugh very heartily over the absurdities of the Jeeters. The play taken from *Tobacco Road* introduces many circumstances which we do not feel to have a moral bearing, like Jeeter's childish shrinking from the touch of cold water, his disinclination to washing. So that one laughs more over the play than over the novel. The Jeeters are not funny in quite the same way as Mr. Micawber or Sairy Gamp or Tom Sawyer or Tartarin. The moral seriousness of the situation is too near the surface for us to laugh. But the essence of the comic is there, and it is what saves the day. It is our defense against the intolerable degradation of human nature. It furnishes a sorely needed psychological relief. And it is what keeps this sociological matter within the limits of imaginative art.

It is very hard to draw the line between the tolerable and the intolerable in the esthetic representation of degraded types. It is doubtless in the last analysis a subjective matter, depending on the point in the reader's make-up where reactions of disgust come in to inhibit all pleasurable response. There are two early novels of Caldwell, *The Bastard* and *Poor Fool* (both 1930), in which, I must acknowledge, the accumulation of horrors is so great, and the elements of relief so slight, or non-existent, that the net result for me as a reader is much more displeasing than pleasing. I have the impression, here, of a beginning writer exploiting his knowledge of the underworld and rather straining his imagination to produce a sensational effect. Prizing Caldwell as I do, and wishing to put him in the best light with the intelligent reading public, I find myself inclined to soft-pedal these early efforts, hoping that only specialists will come upon them, or only persons already favorably disposed toward the author from the riper products of his genius. Brutal criminality so holds the center of the stage in these books, and even perversion, that the comic effect is hardly to be discerned. And while many of the characters may be regarded as mentally subnormal, as well as illiterate, there is not the same suggestion about them of childish innocence, let alone sweetness of disposition, which lends a wistful charm to the mellower creations of the author's maturity. And there is not the same provision of lighter incident to reduce the strain of the cruel and shocking.

In *Tobacco Road* a large part of the story is made up of misadventures with an automobile. What particularly impresses the reader is the criminal waste of money where money is so tragically needed; and that becomes a symbol of the childish incompetence of this whole outfit. But along with this the automobile episodes are so contrived as to bring in every other aspect of their topsy-turvy life, and mainly in forms that are consistent with the comic spirit. Sister Bessie, the preacher woman, has cast her eyes on Dude, and the Lord directs her to make him the successor to her late husband as her partner in the gospel business. Sister Bessie is not pleasant to look on; she is not of a suitable age for Dude; Dude has no present inclination to matrimony or to the gospel business. The whole idea is essentially immoral. But neither Sister Bessie nor Lester Jeeter has the slightest notion that there is anything wrong about it. Their type of religion and their social code are not such as to admit these niceties of sentiment. Sister Bessie lives in a shack as ruinous as the Jeeters'; but she has a banking account of eight hundred dollars, left her by her late husband. And that is a great attraction to the Jeeters. This eight hundred dollars wisely disposed would go a long way toward lifting these people out of the bog in which they are sinking. But the sole idea of Sister Bessie is to buy herself a fine new car in which she and Dude can tour the country and spread the gospel abroad. This, under all the circumstances, is an idea as criminal as it is cockeyed.

None of these innocents has the remotest idea of the values of anything more than a jar of snuff, nor of the precautions one takes in bargaining not to be cheated by the other party. It does not occur to Sister Bessie that she might spend part of her fortune on a car and keep the rest for incidentals, like sewing up Ellie May's hare-lip or stocking the Jeeters' larder or providing Lester with cotton-seed and guano for the summer's crop. (This doesn't occur to Lester either.) She marches straight into the dealers'; they ask her what priced car she wants, and she says an eight hundred dollar car. Within five minutes they have sold her a car which, for aught we know, cost them no more than three hundred dollars, and with insufficient oil to run any distance. Such a thing as oil is beyond their range of vision. Neither she nor Dude knows anything about driving, or that there is anything that should be known. Dude's sole concern is for the noise he can make blowing the horn. Within two days they have broken the back spring, smashed the right front fender, torn off the left front headlight, burned out the bearings, ruined the upholstery carrying firewood to town, and killed two persons—a negro driving his cart, and grandmother run over in a heedless maneuver. They are less disturbed by the deaths of the negro and grandmother than by the damage to the upholstery.

The moral obliquities of these people are on all fours with their mental defectiveness. And their mental defectiveness is that of a race of people who have never been able to sign their own names or read a newspaper, whose cultural heritage is that appropriate to men without land, without money, and without experience of any of the simplest amenities of life.

XI. Erskine Caldwell: *Substitutes and Compensations*

In *Tobacco Road* the mentality of the characters is not merely defective. It is confused and topsy-turvy. They do not associate ideas in the manner of civilized beings. And that is one reason why we are both amused and scandalized by the peculiar tie-up in them between piety and shameless conduct.

In *Journeyman* (1938) Caldwell has given us a glimpse of the type of religion that flourishes among the more ignorant of the poor whites. The central character is one Semon Dye, an itinerant preacher, who is making a few days' stay with Clay Horey, a slightly more prosperous Jeeter. Semon Dye is a big lanky ruffian with a gift for words and a dynamic personality, who first charms people by his wit and wisdom and then rules them with a tyrannous will. His being a forceful and sincere preacher does not exempt him from the natural proclivities of a man. He can drink corn liquor with the best. With women he has had a wide and uniformly successful career. He is well along in years, but his day is not yet done. "My day is a long way from being over. But when my day is done, it's going to have been a long one." His will brooks no opposition; and when he cannot have it peacefully he imposes it at the point of a gun. He shoots the negro man who comes to protest against his seducing his yaller girl. He wins Horey's car with loaded dice, and then wins Horey's young wife Dene. And all this while he maintains his intention of preaching to the people of this district on Sunday.

Sunday afternoon they gather in great numbers at the schoolhouse; and he holds forth all the afternoon and evening. He takes the greatest pride in his gifts as a preacher. His aim is to make every man and woman "come through," and also to take up a generous collection. "Coming through" is the final stage in a series of convulsive seizures in which one thrashes round on the floor, tears one's clothes, loses consciousness, and generally comports oneself like an epileptic. It appears to be a means of throwing out the devil, cleansing oneself of sin, and attaining a state of holiness. It offers intense and gratifying excitements to people on the lower and more brutal cultural levels, and serves to compensate them for the normal boredoms and deprivations of their starved lives.

Semon Dye on this occasion has a very large measure of success. All but one of the company come through, including the preacher himself. But one person holds out, and that, the one he is most concerned to bring to God—the prostitute Lorene. She is, he considers, the worst sinner in the schoolhouse and most in need of his ministrations. And when he comes to after his own paroxysm and finds that he has not been successful in this supreme instance, he regards the whole thing as a failure. He has met a will that is stronger than his. He is so deeply moved by his unsuccess that he even forgets to take up the collection. He spends the night at Horey's and the next day drives off in Horey's car with Lorene. He has an understanding with her by which he will go fifty-fifty with her on her earnings "putting out."

The reader accustomed to some reasonable logic in religion, some association between religious faith and moral conduct, will be shocked and perhaps incredulous, and may be inclined to think that Caldwell has made this all up out of whole cloth. But the phenomena he is here presenting are too well and widely known to admit of that conclusion. That he has selected and arranged things dramatically so as to point up his idea, that he has rounded them out and developed their inherent logic, is no doubt true. But the fact remains that, on certain cultural levels, there is a curious discontinuity between religion and morals, in spite of the religious emphasis on the concept of sin. Caldwell does not suggest that Semon Dye is a fakir or a hypocrite—that he takes no stock himself in sin and hell fire. The point is that he trades upon them like any commercial exploiter. They are his stock in trade; and his success in putting them across is the chief source of his personal pride. But it does not follow that he is a good man himself, or that he has a genuine abhorrence for sin. On the contrary. He is going to preach to the people of Rocky Comfort. He is confident that they are sinful, and the sinfuller they are, the better he likes it. He is superior to the settled preachers with parishes. "I'm a traveling, ranging, journeyman preacher, and I know just about every sin there is in Georgia. And then some!" Sin is the means by which he works these people up into a lather of fear and delight. They are afraid of hell fire, but they get a great kick out of his allusions to sin, above all the sins of the flesh, and his suggestive anecdotes in illustration of the theme. It is all a part of the orgiastic excitement which culminates in the "coming through." They will feel purified and assuaged on the following day, but it is not so certain that their morals will be improved.

As for himself, it never occurs to him to carry over his religion into his personal conduct. He seems to enjoy special exemptions as a man of God. "I'm Semon Dye. The Lord don't have to bother about me. He sort of gives me a free rein." And other people take him largely at his own valuation. There is something demonic about him that lifts him above the ranks of common men. His personal charm is so great, he offers so much relief from the monotony of life, that even those who suffer most at his hands are sorry to see him go. He is to Rocky Comfort what a poet is to New York or Paris. "Somehow I sort of hate to see Semon go away now and leave us," thinks Horey. "Semon was a sort of lowdown scoundrel, taking all in all, but he had a way with him just the same. I couldn't put up with a rascal like him very long, because I'd sooner or later go get my shotgun and blast away at him. But it does sort of leave a hollow feeling inside of me to know he ain't here no longer."

Such a tribute from Horey has something pathetic as well as something funny about it. It makes one feel not merely how benighted these people are, but how terribly boresome a life it is that craves to be relieved in ways like this. Religion is but one of the means by which these people seek diversion, make up for the meagerness of their lives, and violently discharge their pent-up nervous energies.

Another classic indulgence of the poor white is the lynching of negroes. This is Caldwell's subject in the most recent of his novels, *Trouble in July* (1940). When Sheriff Jeff McCurtain hears of the search for Sonny Clark, charged with rape of a white girl, he is of two minds whether to try to prevent a lynching or to go fishing for several days till the trouble is over—so he may "keep this lynching politically clean." But he is ordered by Judge Ben Allen, the political boss, to check the mob—Judge Allen has been telephoning round and has decided it is politically expedient at this time to have no lawbreaking. Meantime, Jeff gets concerned over possible harm to another negro whom he had in the jail on some minor charge and whom the mob has taken as a hostage; if they cannot catch Sonny Clark they will string up Sam Brinson. Sam Brinson is a man whom Jeff regards as a special friend of his, even if he is a nigger, and he starts out on an earnest search for him. In the meantime it has been made perfectly plain to the reader that Sonny Clark is entirely innocent of the charge against him; he is a well-meaning kid; the white girl Katy had taken a fancy to him, and Mrs. Narcissa Calhoun, fanatical nigger-hater, had come up at a critical moment and drawn the wrong conclusion. The case is so clear that even Katy's steady will not believe a word of the charge; he tells her she is nothing but a cotton-field slut, and she ought to be ashamed to let people lynch a little nigger boy that's as innocent as the day is long.

But even if Katy were willing, it is too late to stem the tide of passions that have been roused in the mob. Katy's father is a man who has killed more than one nigger, and white man too; and the whole mob are driven on by sadistic instincts that fiercely crave expression. There are many obscure impulses which mark the negro as the natural victim of their savagery. The white men's fear of the negro raper is in part an oblique reflection of their own craving for negro women. Their own offenses against the negro can be given a kind of vicarious atonement through the crucifixion of the black man. There is doubtless a kind of perverse religiosity involved. The negro becomes a physical symbol for men's consciousness of sin. The puritan fanatic, Narcissa Calhoun, is circulating a monster petition to send all negroes to Africa where they came from. This involvement of nigger-hating with religious fanaticism is a theme of other Southern writers; it is prominently featured in Faulkner's *Light in August*.

Above all, with the white man who is nearest to the negro in economic and cultural status, there is the powerful urge to establish and maintain a superiority which there is little to confirm but the difference of color. The negro is an economic competitor with the impoverished white; he is capable of enduring poverty with more good nature; and sometimes it is the humiliating experience of a white man in the country store to see a nigger with more money to spend than himself. This had happened to one of the men in Caldwell's story, and it made him feel "it was getting about time to clamp down on a nigger again. . . . Hell, this is a white man's country! Ain't no nigger going to flash a bigger roll of money than I can, and me not do nothing about it. It ain't right." But more than all these psychic inducements to victimize a negro is the simple need for animal excitement strong enough to make up to these poor creatures for boredom and deprivation, for their almost total want of civilized pleasures and diversions, for empty bellies and the threadbare poverty of their emotional life.

These men have no grudge against Sonny Clark; many of them, like Jeff, are fond of individual negroes. They have themselves no disposition to spare the purity of white women; no reason to think of Katy Barlow as anything but a perverse little chippy. But all that is beside the point. The emotional drive is beyond reason. They must have blood; and when once they have strung up Sonny and riddled his body with bullets, when now Katy has a change of heart and confesses that her charges were baseless, they cannot stay the force of their passion till they have stoned to death the white woman whose honor they had set out to avenge.

I will not stop to note the strain of comedy that runs through the gruesome incidents of this story, or discuss the esthetics of the case; but instead pursue a little further the law of psychic compensation which operates so regularly in Caldwell's fables. In *God's Little Acre* (1934) there are two main examples of this psychic phenomenon, objectified in the two leading persons of the story. The one is Ty Ty, a Georgia farmer, and the other is Will Thompson, his son-in-law, a weaver in a South Carolina factory town. Ty Ty is possessed by the fantastic notion that there is gold on his land, where he lives with his family and his negro dependents; and he and his sons have spent all their time for years in a frenzied digging in the sand. They live in a shack in extreme indigence, though the land is good enough if they would work it, and all their toil is labor lost. As his son-in-law tells him, "You can raise more cotton on this land in a year than you can find gold in a lifetime." But the search for gold is more exciting; it is a perpetual fever in the blood. It sheds a transcendental glamour over lives otherwise so dull and drab.

In Will Thompson is dramatized the most common and powerful of all psychological mechanisms for supplying excitement and value to a life deprived of normal gratifications. Sexual indulgence is normal enough, to be sure, and calls for no fancy explanation; but when it takes the uncontrolled and extravagant course that it does with Will Thompson, with such an accompaniment of imaginative fireworks, so much of ritual and ostentation, we cannot but feel that it stands for more than itself, expresses more than itself—that all the frustrated urges of flesh are being poured through this one narrow bottleneck, all hungers of flesh and spirit finding their satisfaction here, finding in the lurid intoxication of sex their one supreme, their one available and adequate symbol.

And this impression is borne out by the way in which the other characters respond to the reckless anarchism of Will's behavior. They all of them share, at least vicariously, in the ritual of his loves. Ty Ty is an old and widowed man; but still for him the sexual act is a matter of passionate and sympathetic interest. It is a matter of pride to him that his daughters and daughter-in-law are women of such great beauty. He is forever celebrating in most open fashion their bodily attractions, and without offending the women themselves. But it is the younger man who becomes the effective instrument of his senile lusts. It is not enough for Will to have married his daughter Rosamund; in the course of this brief story he must also mate with his unmarried daughter, Darling Jill, and with his daughter-in-law, Griselda. However grieved Will's wife may be at his infidelities, she cannot hold them against either him or the other women. Griselda and Darling Jill find that he is the one man, besides their father, who treats them as they like to be treated, with a kind of sacred and religious rage. And the father reflects that Will Thompson comes as near understanding the secrets of mind and body as he himself.

The sexual life of Will Thompson is obscurely bound up with his vocation. He is a weaver out of work, because the strikers have not the courage to go into the mill, turn on the power, and run it for themselves. He is filled with a burning desire to turn on the power at the mill, and in the end he loses his life when in carrying out this aim he is shot by the guards. His life follows a ritual of tearing and building. His turning on the power is prefaced by tearing his shirt to shreds; the weaving perhaps, in his unconscious mind, takes the form of repair and restitution. Before going to bed with Griselda he makes a speech, declaring that he will tear her clothes to pieces and look at her as God intended. His whole body becomes an almighty and omnipotent phallus, his mouth the instrument of the phantasy he is enacting. He becomes a god. The men have decided to arbitrate the strike, but he says they can turn the power on and run the damn mill themselves—he is as strong as God Almighty now.[1]

Under any circumstances there is something formidable and demonic in the spectacle of sexual impulse on the rampage. And when, as here, it overrides serenely all social bars and limits, it becomes positively alarming. Even Ty Ty acknowledges that the death of Will was a fortunate thing, since after all there were wives and husbands to be considered, and Griselda and Jill "would have made a mess that the law doesn't allow." Given the jealous nature of men and women, such a course of action threatens the peaceful living which is Ty Ty's great concern. But for all that, there was something about Will that all the characters admired; there was something dazzling about his lunatic exaltation. He was the carrier and symbol of a Power to which they all did homage, as he was the means by which they all gave vent to the stifled cravings of their being.

Even the reader's imagination may be impressed. And that is no doubt the reason why this book became the object of prosecution on the part of those gentlemen who run societies for the suppression of vice. They are in general simple-minded gentry, incapable of distinguishing between incitements to vice in the young and childish and the kind of literature that makes its unprovocative appeal to the mind of maturity and to that alone. The representatives of literature came promptly to the defense of Caldwell, and by good fortune the ruling of the court was made by a man of judgment and intellectual cultivation. He justly pointed out that what we have here is an instance of serious realistic writing, and defended the autonomy of art against the assaults of anxious and unimaginative moralism.

He wisely refrained from going into the finer points of the question. It would take a psychological expert to trace the obscure ways in which the theme of sexuality is associated in this book with that of poverty and deprivation. Throughout, the theme of food-getting constantly recurs in the form of eating, biting, grabbing, sucking, licking. Nursing and normal intercourse become confused. The confusion of woman's function transforms men psychologically into fierce children. The women all become types of the mother, but no actual mothers are portrayed. The maternal rôle is twisted toward perversion and prostitution.

How much of this is conscious on the part of the author we can only guess. We should, I think, do wrong to underestimate the subtlety of Caldwell and his awareness of modern psychological trends. In the case of religious fanaticism, he certainly is deliberate in showing how hunger of the spirit battens on the same conditions as belly-hunger.[2] Of the sexual element in orgiastic religion he is certainly well aware. It is only reasonable to assume that, in *God's Little Acre*, he means to exhibit among other things the sexual instinct as it manifests itself in cultural conditions rooted in poverty. Sexual indulgence is there a substitute for the pleasures of feeding; and sexual hunger is, more than that, a form of spiritual hunger. It is shown running amok and fertile in social effects that frighten and dismay. But it has, for all that, its splendor and exaltation. For it is in part the manifestation of normal instinct, an evidence of vitality; and beyond that, it testifies to the presence of that spiritual hunger which it is easy to divert and drive into devious ways but which it is very difficult indeed to quite suppress and eradicate.

Hardest of all for the hunters of vice to bear is, perhaps, the spirit of comedy that presides over the conduct of this display. For persons of their mentality do not appreciate comedy. They have no inkling of its value as intellectual criticism; nor yet of the aid and comfort it gives to thoughtful men in supporting the else intolerable absurdities and paradoxes of human nature. The most constant of comic paradoxes in Caldwell is the utter innocence of his characters in the perpetration of outrageous acts. They know not what they do. For the most part moral depravity in his stories is the exact counterpart of mental obliquity. We might call it the obliquity of the folk mind; for it seems to represent the natural complexion of mind of the whole community on a given cultural level. Ty Ty mentions in company intimate details of his women's beauty with the completest absence of any sense that he is violating the proprieties.

There is often in Caldwell's characters a callousness in the treatment of other people which suggests a virtual unawareness of the others as human beings. Someone suggests to Ty Ty that albinos have a gift for locating gold and that there is somewhere in the county such an albino. He sets out at once and captures the albino with the help of a lasso. He takes the young fellow away from his wife, brings him home by force and keeps him prisoner in the barn. He shows him off to his friends in the kitchen as if he were some strange animal, discussing his merits as a gold-finder as if he could not hear or care what was said about him. When the albino boy begins gazing with wonder at the beauty of Darling Jill, Ty Ty for the first time realizes that he is a person like another.

This same callousness toward others is shown by the characters in *Tobacco Road*, where it is obviously associated with a state of chronic hunger. All the people in this story are so constantly concerned with the craving of their own stomachs that they have no imagination left for others' sufferings. If they do not worry about grandma or the nigger killed by the car, it is because they have never properly taken in the existence of other beings as real as themselves. In Caldwell's short stories the most cold-blooded cruelty is exercised against niggers or women by men who have never learned that women or niggers have serious claims on white men. The man who is most forward in shouting prayers in the church will not give his negro tenants enough fat-bacon to flavor their corn-bread or pay them compensation for the accident that cripples them for life. The Ex-Governor takes for granted that the young daughter of his white tenant is his for the asking, with or without her parents' consent, and that he need not even wait for the license to "handsel" her. He is mighty surprised and hurt when she lights into him like a hellcat, and "pretty near bites the daylights out of him." The girl's father was relieved, for he was not sure that her mother would approve of the Governor's project, but his reaction was not one of moral indignation. He was carried away by the joke of Daisy's getting the best of the Governor. He sat down in his chair on the porch. "He leaned back and started to laugh. He could not wait for his wife any longer. He leaned back and laughed until he slid out of his chair."[3]

The absurdity often lies in the contrast between a man's shrewdness and his stupidity. The most benighted general state of mind may coexist with the utmost cunning in the calculation of one's own interest. We call it animal cunning, and in a human being it is shocking and ridiculous. Or it may be the contrast of an office that calls for courage and responsibility with a cowardly or irresponsible character in the incumbent. Caldwell is fond of sheriffs who run away from danger or have more regard for community prejudice than for their oath of office. His young men may combine a complete want of sexual morals with the shyness of the chaste. They will spend an afternoon on a girl's porch vainly trying to get up courage to propose to her, and then ride over to the neighboring town to pick up a chippy. When one of them marries, he spends the day of the honeymoon playing pool, and he wakes up in the morning scared to death to find himself in bed with his wife. "What in hell am I doing sleeping in bed with a white girl?"

Strange flowers of humanity push up through this dunghill soil of cultural degradation. The negro Jesse, struggling against the wiregrass in his cotton, amidst the intolerable heat of the dry season, cannot bear to witness the suffering of his donkey; he shoots the animal and goes on sharpening the blade of his hoe. Another negro gives himself up to the law for shooting his daughter; he could not stand hearing her say she was hungry after his landlord on some pretext had taken away his share of the crop. The moral sense of the town asserts itself, and the sheriff goes home so as not to keep the men from freeing the negro.

There is no more self-consciousness about their humanity than about their inhumanity and meanness. The tale is told in the same dry manner. Behavior has the same air of being automatic and inevitable, the outcome of economic pressures and conforming to a primitive code. The characters have the same innocence, the same naïveté. Naïveté is the best single word for describing these people, and the best way to characterize Caldwell as a storyteller is to say that he is an accomplished master of the *naïve* style. His manner is plain and straightforward and without a touch of facetiousness or of verbal irony. There is an almost unfailing irony in the representation of character and action. But it is in the conception, in the arrangement of the elements, not in the phrasing or the moral tone. The story is told simply, and for the most part in terms suitable to the characters concerned. There is no elaborate attempt at dialect, but a modified colloquialism that gives the bloom and accent of the local idiom. There is no far-fetched rendering of the idiosyncracy of thought; but within measure the author follows the rhetoric of the characters' minds, their manner of associating ideas, their way of regarding things. It is all done with deftness and precision, without heavy emphasis, but with a soft-fingered sureness in the disposition of "values." And so, without interference, the characters expose themselves in all their simplicity, perverseness and absurdity.

Caldwell is fond of having his story told from the point of view of young boys, incapable of judging or of quite fully understanding the import of what they recount, thus adding another irony, and a kind of innocence too, to the chronicle of adult folly. He has a tender regard for the sensibility and the opening minds of children, who represent a healthier state of mind than most of the adults he pictures, and a happier view of human nature. Some of the most charming of all his tales are those which open the early volume, *American Earth*, involving a young Southern boy of good family whose sentiments have not been hardened by adult suggestion. There is the story of the aunt who had come South to visit with the boy's family, and who wishes to train him in the tradition of the Southern gentleman. Under her direction he is trying to learn to shoot rabbits, though it goes against the grain to kill an animal of which he is so fond. Fortunately he misses his rabbit with his gun but frightens it so that he can take it with his hands. He brings it home alive and feeds it lettuce, leaving it free to come and go, much to his aunt's disgust. But his father is on his side in the matter, and his mother looks at him as if he had done the right thing after all.

But the author is fond (as an author) of whatever will lend itself to his special gifts for storytelling, will shape itself up significantly for the imagination. For Caldwell nothing is more fascinating than a certain simplicity of mind, whether it goes with a good or a mean disposition; and perhaps it makes more diverting patterns where the disposition is mean. That is something which the moralist in us is reluctant to acknowledge, that in human nature it takes an admixture of the ugly to make the most interesting patterns for the artistic imagination. The moralist shrinks from the mention of evil save in terms of abhorrence, and the puritan of today is inclined to deprecate any disposition to play it up as a subject of art. But the artist insists on the free play of his imagination. Prudence may support the puritan; but in the long run wisdom is on the side of the artist. Wisdom knows that evil will not be done away by ignoring it; that our passion for truth demands the recognition of evil, the examination of it. And wisdom knows that the most innocent of ways to deal with evil is the way of art, and one of the subtlest and most illuminating. Puritan prudence would have confined Caldwell to the way of the sociologist and reformer. But he is obviously more of an artist than he is of a sociologist; and his art is the means by which he gives life and body to what he knows of human nature. Without it, the world would be the poorer by so much of valuable knowledge and insight. Not to speak of the loss of many capital stories!

Notes

1. For much of my interpretation here and in the third paragraph below I am indebted to a highly suggestive article by Dr. Lawrence S. Kubie, the distinguished psychiatrist and psychoanalyst, in the *Saturday Review of Literature*, No. 19 (Nov. 24, 1934), pp. 305–6, 312. I must note, however, that Dr. Kubie confines himself to a study of the action of this story as

an example of adult distortion of infantile impulses, indicative of pathological states in all the persons concerned. He does not, I think, suggest the specific cause or occasion for the development of these psychological disorders, and makes no direct connection between them and poverty or deprivation, though many of the points he makes might suggest this connection to one familiar with the whole of Caldwell's work.

2. See *Some American People* (New York: McBride, 1935), p. 263; *You Have Seen Their Faces* (New York: Viking, 1937), p. 142.

3. References in this paragraph are to "A Knife to Cut the Corn Bread With" and "A Small Day," both in *Southways*. In the two following paragraphs reference is made to the following tales in *Kneel to the Rising Sun*: "The Shooting, " "Candy-Man Beechum," "A Day's Wooing," "Honeymoon," "The Growing Season," and "Daughter."

"The Two Erskine Caldwells"

Malcolm Cowley*

Erskine Caldwell is two writers, both good of their kind, and one a sort of genius in his own narrow field. They collaborate on most of his books, but with conflicting aims; and the result is that reading some of his novels—including the latest, "Tragic Ground"—is like a week-end visit to a bickering household. "I am a social novelist," says the first Caldwell. "I study the Southern tenant farmers, white and black, I describe their hopeless plight, and I suggest means by which it might be remedied—if not in this generation, which is lost already, then at least in twenty or thirty years. If I had my life to live over, I should prefer to be a working sociologist." The second Caldwell doesn't talk about his aims, and in fact he isn't completely conscious of them; but sometimes, pushing his twin brother away from the typewriter, he begins pounding out impossible fancies and wild humor.

These two Caldwells bear a family resemblance as writers; both of them deal with the same background and both are moved by anger and pity. Sometimes in short stories they achieve an almost perfect union between the social doctrines of the first and the exuberance of the second. In novels, however, they always seem to be working at cross purposes. One of them is bent on achieving effects which the other tries to weaken or destroy.

In "Tobacco Road," for example (I mean the novel and not the play, which Caldwell didn't write), the sociologist was trying to present the utterly hopeless life of tenant farmers on worn-out soil. In Chapter VII he wrote a little essay to prove that "coöperative and corporate farming would have saved them all." But the imaginative Caldwell was not impressed by this argument. His contribution to the book was Jeeter Lester, who is not a tragic or typical figure of decay, but rather a sort of earth spirit, dirty, goatish, morally irresponsible and given to picturesque language. "I used to be a powerful sinful man in my time," Jeeter says. "I reckon I was at one time the most powerful sinful man in the whole country. Now, you take them Peabody children over across the field. I reckon

*Reprinted from *New Republic*, 111 (Nov. 6, 1944), 599–600. Copyright © 1944 by Editorial Publications, Inc. Reprinted by permission of the author.

clear near about all of them is half mine, one way or another." There have
been hundreds of poems and stories written in the vain attempt to introduce the god Pan into American folklore. Our woods are still unpeopled with fauns, nymphs or satyrs, but we do have Huckleberry Finn,
who is a sort of river spirit; and we also have Jeeter Lester, who might be
Huck in his old age. How can we pity Jeeter, or try to abolish him, when
he represents our half-conscious desire for freedom from moral restraints?

The two Caldwells are even more at variance in "God's Little Acre."
When this fable about Ty Ty Walden's sons and the beautiful Griselda is
suddenly transformed into a social novel; when Will Thompson, after acquiring heroic strength by sleeping with Griselda, makes the symbolic
gesture of turning on the current in the idle cotton mill, and then defies
the company police, dying not like a man but like a demigod—at this moment the book falls apart; reality corrupts the fable, while itself acquiring
a fabulous character that makes it less than reality. "Trouble in July" is a
more consistent novel, the best that Caldwell has written, but here again
the two authors are in conflict. For one thing, they can't agree about
Katie Barlow: the poet admires her for her unrestrained and quite incredible passion; the sociologist detests her for causing the death of a
Negro boy. And they also differ about the amiable sheriff, Jeff McCurtain, who always went fishing when there was trouble in Julie County,
although there was nothing he hated more than fishing trips. Sheriff Jeff
is a mythical but convincing figure, so long as he hasn't any moral
qualms. At the end of the book, however, after Sonny Clark has been
lynched and Katie stoned to death for trying to save him, Jeff has a sort of
conversion to social responsibility. "To perform his duty as he sees it,
without fear or favor," he says. "That's a mighty pretty oath for a man in
public office to swear to. I reckon I had sort of forgotten it." And the
remark seems just as false and sententious as, let us say, a Puritan sermon
would have been in Falstaff's mouth.

In his latest novel, "Tragic Ground," the two Caldwells are apparently less in agreement than ever before. This time Caldwell One, the
sociologist, is writing about the general plight of workers in a war-boom
town when the powder mill closes and they have no money to get home
again. But Caldwell Two is writing about the special plight of Spence
Douthit, who might well be Jeeter Lester's cousin, and who in any case is
so shiftless that he could never be out of trouble. Caldwell One is inclined
to blame Spence's misfortunes on the fact that he and his family had left
Beaseley County, where they belonged. They now live in Poor Boy, a
group of tumbledown shacks on the banks of a ship canal, where there is
no way to earn a living except by prostitution or peddling marijuana. One
of the characters, a returned soldier named Jim Howard Vance, makes a
touching speech about Poor Boy. "Back home," he says, "people like us
are just as good as people anywhere else in the world. If you want to do
the right thing, you ought to put all the blame on Poor Boy, because it's

Poor Boy that causes all the trouble. The finest folks in the world would get mean and bad if they had to live in a place like this." Then, at this solemn moment, Caldwell Two invents a final speech for Spence Douthit. "I've sort of got used to Poor Boy now," he says, "and I'm mighty afraid I'd be homesick way off up there in Beaseley County if I had to stay there any length of time."

Meanwhile Spence has managed to get himself involved in several hilarious adventures: for example, when he finds his oldest daughter, Libbie, in bed with Jim Howard Vance, and starts a long conversation about Beaseley County, while Libbie tries to make him go away; and again when he goes to "a real high-class place" called the White Turkey to rescue his youngest daughter, aged thirteen, from a life of prostitution that she thoroughly enjoys. Mrs. Douthit lies on her cot all day, except when she drinks a big bottle of Dr. Munday's Tonic and goes reeling naked into the yard. When a social worker appears in the Douthit shack with "a sacred duty to perform," as she says, ". . . the task of adjusting your lives to the complex pattern of modern life," Maud Douthit mistakes her for a necktie saleswoman. "Get going, sister," she says, "I don't allow no women coming around here trying to get sported." But while Spence and his wife have no truck with any sort of moral standards, Jim Howard Vance, who finally marries Libbie, is obsessed with serious notions of reform; and there is also a neighbor with moral compunctions; he murders a young half-wit for sleeping with his daughter and then surrenders to the police. The intrusion of moral feeling spoils the comedy, making you hesitate to laugh; the comedy spoils the social message; and you are left with a book that falls apart into separate scenes, some of them vastly better than the story as a whole.

The two Caldwells have never agreed through a whole novel, but they can, as I said, sign a truce for the time it takes to write a short story. Social purpose and imagination are perfectly fused in stories like "Daughter," "The Negro in the Well," "Horse Thief" and "The People vs. Abe Lathan, Colored." The poet alone, with his wild humor, is responsible for "Maud Island," "The Night My Old Man Came Home" and, best of all, "Country Full of Swedes." All these are included in "Stories by Erskine Caldwell,"[1] a selection of twenty-four made by Henry Seidel Canby. In general Dr. Canby's selections are excellent, although he neglects the early stories of pre-adolescent love. His introduction is good, too; and in fact my only real complaint is that the book is too short. "Jackpot," an earlier collection that can sometimes be found on remainder counters, is better simply because it contains twice as many of Caldwell's stories.

---

[1]Stories by Erskine Caldwell, Selected with an Introduction by Henry Seidel Canby. New York: Duel, Sloan and Pearce. 237 pages. $2.50.

"Erskine Caldwell: Sentimental Gentleman from Georgia"

W. M. Frohock*

There is a special sort of humor in America, native to our earth and of the earth earthy, and peculiar to us because it is deep-rooted in our history. Its material is the man who has been left behind in the rush to develop our frontiers, the man who has stayed in one place, out of and away from the main current of our developing civilization, so largely untouched by what we think of as progress that his folkways and mores seem to us, at their best, quaint and a little exotic—and, at their worst, degenerate. The canon of jokes about families who have one son in an asylum and a daughter in the reformatory and the "little feller" at Harvard—"Yeah, he's in a bottle. He's got two heads"—is enormous, frequently lurid, and invariably fascinating. Geographically, it covers the country, although the bulk of contributions seem to have come from the East: the islands off the coast of Maine, the Vermont hills, the Jackson White area along the lower Hudson, the back counties of the Allegheny Ridge states, Georgia, the swamps of Florida and then over across to the Ozarks. On one level of sophistication it is exploited in the notorious mountaineer cartoons of *Esquire*. In serious literature, it has been the main source, as well as the great strength, of Erskine Caldwell's novels.

If this seems a little strange at first, if it is difficult to square the wild and blood-chilling violence of some of Caldwell's work with his sharing in a great American humorous tradition, we have only to pick up a novel like *Georgia Boy*. In this book the elements which have now and then scandalized a good part of the reading public are for once lacking, and it is possible to see how after all the man has an impressive gift for making literary comedy out of the stuff which we most often associate with the irreverently ribald periodical press, not to say the smoking car. *Georgia Boy* is a sort of *Tobacco Road* obviously sweetened down for the carriage trade. The rampant sexuality, the murderous ignorance, the bitterly depressing picture of Georgia life which characterize Caldwell's other books are gone. What we have left is the feckless figure of Pa Stroup. He

*Reprinted from *Southwest Review*, 31 (Autumn, 1946), 351–59.

carelessly lets the family's goats get on the roof of the house; he goes into politics via the office of dog catcher, and fills the local pound by the highly practical method of baiting the dogs with raw meat; he substitutes for the sexton and tolls the bell for a funeral when it should be pealing for a wedding; he steals a heifer by luring it away from its pasture, and carries off his neighbors' property to sell for scrap; he buys a paper-baler and gets so enthusiastic over its money-making possibilities that he throws into it not only the hymnals which have been entrusted to his wife, but even the wallpaper from the family living room. One may detect a note of seriousness in the comedy, of course. The man is presented as a small-town Southerner, ignorant, lazy, too soggy-minded to be either honest or successfully dishonest, moral only because immorality requires effort, and proud at all the wrong times of all the wrong things. ("Be a good Stroup," says Pa Stroup's brother Ben as he is being taken back to the penitentiary from which he has recently escaped.)

If we like, we may see in all this a condemnatin of the region which produces such fundamentally useless people. But there is no question at all about Caldwell's intention in the book, and there is no mistaking the fact that he is consciously exploiting a comic talent of considerable dimensions, and using for material one aspect of the vein which we have just been at pains to describe. *Georgia Boy*, although there is no point in claiming that it is a great or even a significant book, is something like what Mark Twain might have done had he come from Georgia and found himself in a playful mood, and (we should perhaps add) if he had wanted to be sure of not offending his public. It is also an important key to understanding Caldwell.

For at base most of Caldwell's books have comic implications, and the comedy is always akin to the famous mountaineer cartoons. "Niggers will get killed," says dimwit Dude Lester in *Tobacco Road* just after he has killed one with Bessie's Ford; "don't seem to be nothing you can do about it." "I don't mind seeing a dead darky once in a while," says Clay Horey in *Journeyman*, "but I sure do hate to see one of my hands passing away on me at this time. It's planting time and no other. If Hardy was to die, I'd have to get out and do some work myself." This is pathetic stuff, in a way, and—to the delicate conscience—bitter: certainly all the wormwood of the predicament of the underprivileged Southern white is in it, all the callousness and invincible ignorance for which circumstances are to blame. We have to achieve a certain detachment before we can laugh at it, and laughter is easier if one's taste is not too discriminatingly genteel, and if one is not particularly sentimental. The *Esquire* cartoons are easier to take because they picture preposterous situations which we are sure do not really exist. The things that Caldwell pictures—Hardy, for example, has just been shot by the journeyman preacher for interfering with the latter's pursuit of Hardy's wife—are just as preposterous, but we are afraid they really do happen. The family relationship with the cartoon mountaineers, and with all the lore about the people whom our civilization has passed by, is no less clear for all that.

This is still clear in a book which gives us a much better idea of Caldwell's stature as a novelist than does the facile *Georgia Boy*. There is no doubt that fat Sheriff Jeff McCurtain in *Trouble in July* is another version of the Jeeter Lester-Pa Stroup pattern: gone to seed physically, shiftless, morally vague, too inert for any sort of planned action, spineless. We recognize him by his behavior when his habitual technique for handling a crisis—he always disappears on a fishing trip as soon as he scents trouble and stays out of sight (much as he hates fishing) until everything blows over—for once fails to work. When the county judge who owns Jeff, fat body and soul, decides that this time the law must be enforced for reasons of political expediency, the sheriff does everything he can think of to avoid the issue. His frantic wriggling, his terrified efforts to "keep this lynching politically clean" and to keep himself out of danger, his persistence in blinding himself to every sort of moral question involved, identify his comic type. His best expedient, the product of hours of desperate casting-about for an exit from his impasse, is to sneak into a cell-block in his own jail under cover of darkness and, in hopes of making it look as if he had been locked in by the lynchers, to throw his keys out through the bars. But he discovers with the simultaneous arrival of daylight and his suspicious wife that he has shut himself in the same cell block with a comely colored girl whose presence in the jail has already aroused his wife's jealousy!

At this point, of course, the similarity to *Georgia Boy* ends abruptly. The comedy of *Trouble in July* goes hand in hand with a particularly disturbing kind of violence. The impending lynching is an especially horrid affair, from the moment that the black boy is accused of raping the white girl by the preacher and the erratic woman who is devoting her life to getting all Negroes sent back to Africa. That the white girl is a dubious character with the makings of a nymphomaniac, as one member of the lynching party testifies, makes no difference; neither does the strong chance that the boy is in every way blameless, nor the fact that even the unastute McCurtain can see these things. "It's not an easy thing to say about brother whites," he remarks, "but it has always looked to me like them folks up there never was particular enough about the color line. However, a nigger man ought to be more watchful, even if it is one of those white girls up there in the sand hills." The reader is upset by the knowledge that this black boy stands no more chance than the other Negro stood against Dude Lester's Ford. But what is even more upsetting is the gruesome joy of the participants: the way so many of them make the whole episode a social event, the pathological mass-delight when the girl shows the crowd the great hole which the rapist is supposed to have torn in her dress. The mob, wanting no further proof, starts the man hunt in a welter of deviated sexual excitement by stripping and burning with turpentine a Negro girl who has done nothing worse than fail to have the hunted boy in her cabin. The Negro boy is finally handed over to his pursuers by a man who does not believe him guilty, but who can not face the social consequences of letting him get away. The sheriff, who has never lost hope that somehow his pitiful excuses for not taking action will seem valid, arrives on the scene to find that the lynching is over and that the girl, having confessed that she had never been raped at all, has been stoned to death by the mob in a frightening mixture of sex-lust and blood-lust.

I may have more trouble convincing other people than I do convincing myself that this novel, rather than the all too famous *Tobacco Road*, is Caldwell's most successful novel to date. But here comedy and violence blend together and support each other. We accept Jeff McCurtain originally under the comic convention which permits the creator of a comic figure to exaggerate. Then we accept the story of the lynching because we have previously granted the existence of the character whose weakness, which we have seen as comic, is what makes the abomination of the lynching possible. We have known from the beginning that however comic Jeff may be, trouble is inevitable, and when it comes it is the more terrible because we have seen it coming so long. There is no clash between the comic mood and the horrid catastrophe into which it resolves. The effect of the book is thus powerful and unified.

The violent shock of its impact on the reader identifies *Trouble in July* as belonging to the Novel of Violence type which I have mentioned recently here in connection with Steinbeck.[1] Men like Steinbeck and Caldwell and Hemingway and Faulkner in America, and Malraux, Sartre and Céline in France have, in recent years, made violence a necessary ingredient, and perhaps the central ingredient, in their work. They frequently aim at a dramatic form of the novel which is akin to tragedy and which, as good tragedy does, in turn aims at producing shock. How important violence is to these men is apparent when we remember that Steinbeck writes well only of characters who, when the squeeze is on them, have no recourse but to violence; that from the contemplation of violence Hemingway derived the peculiar discipline of vision which is responsible for his greatest prose and also for his inability to make characters who can not appropriately see the world through his eyes; that Malraux has in the past considered, and presumably still considers, violence as the only tolerable way of life.

To this picture of the contemporary novel Caldwell contributes, when he is at his best—as I believe he is in *Trouble in July*—two special characteristics: the strangely powerful admixture of comedy and violence which he contrives, and the particular nature of the violence in which he deals. In relation to this second factor, a comparison with Steinbeck is obligatory. There is violence and to spare in Steinbeck's books, but it is violence into which the characters are forced by circumstances that are clearly, immediately visible. If these people (in *The Grapes of Wrath*, for example, or in *In Dubious Battle*) are not violent, they will perish. If they are successful in their violence it will lead them to a better life. But Caldwell's people are frequently violent only because this is the one available satisfaction of their depraved emotions; they torture and burn and murder for the same reasons that they writhe and howl in church; their compulsive frenzy must be assuaged through a sort of blood-letting before they are able to bear the wretchedness of their lives. There is nothing unhealthy about Steinbeck's characters; but Caldwell's are in process of degeneration, they smell of rot. Part of this is attributable to Caldwell's material; he works with life in rural Georgia, or else with rural Georgians transplanted in the towns, and he counts as one of the important group of writers who, in interpreting the South to the rest of the world, have "taken the magnolias out of the South." His material, as Caldwell interprets it, is especially rich in the comedy which we have examined, and in extraordinarily repulsive violence. The old South of bygone literary tradition was a beautiful, sometimes cloying never-never land. The present South, in the new tradition which Caldwell is helping build—with Faulkner in particular—is a kind of Gothic horror-chamber.

This may make it seem merely that one sort of Romanticism has been supplanted by another; but surely by this time the word Romantic must have ceased to be a term of critical reproach. It is certainly not unfair or uncomplimentary to identify Caldwell with the line of the great exponents of horror. On the basis of his juxtaposing of comedy and horror, he might even be placed in the line of contrivers of antithesis which runs back through Hugo to Shakespeare. Impressive literary reputations have before now reposed on less.

But now we have to ask why it is that Caldwell's literary reputation in America is not more impressive than it is. Why is it, not that the French and Russians—to whom the appearance of a Caldwell translation is a literary event which brings staid reviewers to their feet cheering—like him so much, but that we, as a reading people, like him so much less? Why, in other words, is he a good author who has written only one completely successful book? The answer lies in his handling of violence and comedy in the rest of his output. We may take *Tragic Ground* as an example.

Taste, space requirements, and the postal regulations all inhibit a detailed rehearsal of the episodes of this book, not to say the quotation of certain passages which identify the comedy element with the tradition of American humor habitually exploited by Caldwell. But Spence Douthit and his family come straight out of this American folklore. Hillborn poor whites, now transplanted and stranded in an industrial slum, they are certainly below what we like to think of as the human level. Maud, the slattern wife, arises from her sickbed only when under the influence of "Dr. Munday's" richly alcoholic tonic, on which occasions she is prone to rocket about the neighborhood in the buff, or to threaten the social worker, the family's only source of help, whom she regularly mistakes for a fancy-woman with designs on Spence. Spence catches his elder daughter in his own house *flagrante delicto* with a semi-hospitalized veteran, but fails to do anything about it because of their argument that they are almost married, i.e., they have the license but no time for the ceremony. The younger daughter, Mavis, has just left home after being seduced by the next-door neighbor, against whom Spence does feel a certain resentment since "he might have let nature take its course." It is Mavis' employment in a combination roadhouse-brothel called The White Turkey that brings in the social worker—a type, we should note, appearing rather frequently in the back-country humor from which Caldwell draws his comedy. "You must feel free to talk to me," she counsels Spence, "because I am here to help you. You must not consider me a stranger trying to pry into your private affairs, but a sincere and trustworthy friend who wants to help your family adjust itself to the complex pattern of modern life. During cycles of economic and social readjustment, each member must co-operate as to—well, as to unity. Is that clear, Mr. Douthit?" "I can't say as it is, Miss," replies Spence. The social worker tells him that Mavis has become a prostitute within four days after leaving home. "That makes her my daughter if anything does," Spence avers somewhat proudly; "when I set out to do something, I go whole hog or nothing."

From here in the story revolves around this lady's efforts to get the Douthits out of trouble and out of town, and with Spence's valiant attempts to remain in both. He does agree to try to get Mavis out of The White Turkey ("They tell me it's a real high-class place") but the inevitable happens: he gets drunk on the money he has stolen from Maud, fails to find Mavis, and spends the night with one of the other girls.

All this should suffice to identify Spence with the other Caldwell characters we have scrutinized, but a bit more is necessary. Spence returns home the next day without Mavis, but with a curious individual named Bubber in tow. He has had the thought that Mavis, with all the things she must have learned recently, will make someone a particularly interesting wife. Bubber, whose interest in the talk about a marriageable daughter has led Spence to think of him as a prospective husband, turns out actually to be a sort of talent scout for The White Turkey. Once the pair get to Spence's house, Spence, unable to produce Mavis, strips the drunken Bubber and locks him in for safekeeping until the errant child turns up.

But enough of this. Obviously it will take a *deus ex machina* to close the story. The social worker—who, be it remembered, is our agent and society's agent—is utterly incompetent to cope with such people. Caldwell rings down the curtain by bringing back the now completely married elder daughter, who with her husband will take the family back to the hills. Maud does not want to go: Mavis has been committed to a home where it would be so nice to visit her on Sundays. And Spence is already thinking of ways to persuade his son-in-law to finance a return, one of these days, to the slums. "You just can't," he thinks, "keep digging a man up by the roots and setting him down in different parts of the country and expect him to be satisfied the rest of his life."

Thus most of *Tragic Ground*, in spite of its title, is straight comedy of the type which we have seen Caldwell consciously exploiting elsewhere. Admittedly it is comedy of people who cannot cope with life, a dreary enough picture of adult debauchery and juvenile delinquency, of drunkenness and prostitution and worse; but the whole tradition of humor to which we have attached Caldwell's comic materials is open to the same charge. So is most comedy. One could raise somewhat similar objections to *Candide*; and it would be entirely possible, by identifying ourselves with and sympathizing with Arnolphe, to make a powerful tragedy of *School for Wives*. *Tragic Ground* is the comic reflection of an undesirable social situation. And it would not be too unreasonable to claim that *Tragic Ground* even follows the prescription to instruct while giving pleasure—always provided, of course, that we can take pleasure from the comic type which resorts, when reduced to lowest terms, to wondering whether now that April is here is it not appropriate to get Gran'daddy out of the privy.

I insist on this aspect of *Tragic Ground* because one can easily imagine how a book like this, however distasteful to the sensitive, could pile up a really tremendous force. If it were written entirely as straight comedy, we could probably be trusted to feel all the searing irony which arises from the discrepancy between the ludicrous antics of the characters and the circumstances which make them behave as they do. We would be entirely aware that they are unfortunate, depraved animals, and that we, as members of a free society which resolutely persists in considering itself enlightened, are in some measure responsible for their depravity. Knowing that the central figure of any comedy is in a sense a victim of the audience, we would realize that a society which does no more about the sufferings of a Spence Douthit than simply to laugh at them might do well to examine its own conscience. Caldwell's book, written as straight comedy, could have been one of those which bridge the gap between comedy and tragedy: comedy so long as author and reader manage to remain somewhat Olympian and detached, but full of tragic implications as soon as the Olympian mood should pass.

But it is not in Caldwell to let the wild comedy of *Tragic Ground* run straight on to its own ridiculous conclusion. Spence has a friend named Floyd who runs a scrubby store in their slum and is surrounded by a raft of children. Unlike Spence, he has enough brains to be unhappy. When Bubber escapes from Spence's house without his clothes, he takes refuge in a shack on Floyd's place, and there Spence and Floyd catch him in the act of seducing one of Floyd's adolescent girls. Floyd murders him, briefly and messily, with an axe. The two men then drop the body in a nearby canal, and the story proceeds. Later Floyd takes to brooding over what is bound to happen to every family in the slum, and attempts, undetected, to burn the place down. And at the end of the story, just as Spence and his family are setting off for the hills, we learn that Floyd has given himself up to the police.

At this point the reader's task becomes a hard one. Up to now Caldwell has been enjoying the comic writer's privilege, and we have not asked him to make a literal report on life or to give us "true" people; we have allowed him to exaggerate, to pick and choose his types without reference to their being "representative," and have absolved him in advance of libel against the actual residents of the locality he chooses to write about. This was what permitted him, in *Trouble in July*, to make such effective use of Jeff McCurtain; this is what has carried us through the early part of *Tragic Ground*. But now, after Caldwell has said, "Here are my people and here is how they act, and here are certain implications which, if you can read, tell you that you have a certain responsiblity for their actions," he still feels that this is not enough, and he cries: "Pretty funny, isn't it!—Now look at how horrible it can be." Naturally we recoil.

And we feel somehow that we have been tricked. This game of suddenly bringing a corpse to the party destroys our confidence, to say the least. Here we have been watching a comedy—a comedy with ominous undercurrents, to be sure, but still recognizable as a comedy—and without warning Caldwell produces a violent catastrophe out of the materials which he has been treating as comic. This is true not merely of one book. Jeeter Lester's monumental shiftlessness makes things like the trip to town to sell the blackjack hilariously funny, but subsequently kills him. Will, in *God's Little Acre*, is shot during the strike because of his energy, which has made him a leader—and which previously had made him the hero of a series of sexual adventures that, in spite of noteworthy ominous qualities, were part of a comic situation. They are killed by the thing which we have taken to be comic, just as Bubber has been killed as much by Spence's foolish whim to marry off Mavis as by Floyd's revolt against the doom which is closing down on his slum-rotten family. Sooner or later the reader comes almost to wonder whether he has not been wrong all the time in looking on any of Caldwell's novels as comic, and even suspects himself of a sort of guilty perverseness for having done so.

Now Caldwell is a famous reporter as well as a novelist, and has made a reputation in the field of the prose-plus-photographs documentary. And such is America that we, the public, automatically attribute special authority to the man who gives us a grim view of things as they are, especially if he does it in the weekly newspicture magazines in collaboration with a talented photographer. It makes no difference that the lens can be made a more deceptive, more convincing liar than the typewriter has ever been, and that the photograph and the printed word can be combined in the most despicable instrument of potential falsehood that the world has yet invented. We have the faith to make us forget how difficult it is for any instrument to be more honest than its user. And this faith, this special authority which we attribute to men like Caldwell, tends to undermine our confidence in our original intepretation of his work as comedy.

We have to grant, furthermore, that there are places in Caldwell's work where obviously no comedy is intended. His latest novel of all, *A House in the Uplands*, is clearly an attempt to get at the sad drama of the decline of the once powerful Southern families, the degeneration of the aristocracy. A kind of dark terror (not horror) presides over this story of a girl who discovers that she has married a man whose blood and character have disintegrated. It is closer to Faulkner than it is to any of Caldwell's other novels, and—whatever its quality—there is no question of any comic intention. We must also grant that in *Tobacco Road*, which we have taken as comedy, there is also a vein of sermonizing in the chapters where Caldwell speaks for himself and explains the course of events which has produced such people. Such considerations as these must strengthen our discomfort.

And yet taking all of Caldwell's novels into consideration the case for documentary realism can not stand alone for long. If it could, heaven help the sovereign state of Georgia.

Read as a documentary piece, a book like *Journeyman* becomes intolerable. Here is a traveling preacher who barges in uninvited on poor Clay Horey, looking for lodging first, and next for a woman. Even Clay doesn't like it, and Clay is another Jeeter. The first night on Clay's farm the preacher makes overtures to Clay's present wife, Dene, and before morning takes the wife of Clay's Negro field hand. Later Clay's previous wife, Lorene, turns up to see whether Clay has ever gotten around to taking their child to a doctor to see about the veneral disease with which they have endowed him. When the preacher learns that Lorene is now a practicing prostitute in Jacksonville, he arranges to travel with her as her pimp on the way back south. Meanwhile he has gotten Clay drunk and started a crap game in which Clay loses, in the following order, his wife's gold watch, his car, his farm, and finally his wife herself—whom he buys back, slightly damaged, for a hundred borrowed dollars. Sex relations are as tangled as any writer has contrived to entangle them since Homer: the preacher with Lorene, Dene, and the yellow girl, Sugar; Clay with Sugar, Dene and Lorene; Dene with the Negro, Hardy, in addition to the ties already noted; and Lorene with a neighbor named Tom.

Now the preacher appears most of all as an upcountry Tartuffe, using the cloth (to which he has only a squatter's title) to dupe a country clown out of all his possessions; he is a thoroughly despicable individual in every respect, and, in his readiness to do anything including murder to get what he wants, very reminiscent of figures like Faulkner's Popeye. The book ends with his Sunday services, in which he demonstrates his ability to induce in his hearers a hysterical state of religiosity, with physical manifestations obviously related to sex, which he calls "coming through." We watch with fascination this process which we assume to be as cynical and self-interested as everything else the man has done. And then, amazingly, he "comes through" himself, is so hypnotized by his own incantation that he fails to take a collection and, instead of going off on the projected trip with Lorene, disappears without warning during the night.

One of the quotations which I brought up at the beginning to identify Caldwell's comedy with a familiar folk-humor is from this book, and it would be possible to make a case for the interpretation of the whole thing as comedy of Caldwell's characteristic type. But again the reader would be disconcerted by the sudden revelation about the preacher, and return to doubting the validity of his interpretations. Yet, on the other hand, to take the tale as literal reporting is almost insuperably difficult. There is, of course, the terrible possibility that much of this stuff is literally true; but the fact that the exaggeration is so palpable defeats the purpose of realistic reporting in the documentary manner. Even if we were predisposed to accept the literal-reporting theory in view of the generally leftist tendency of Caldwell's politics, the whole point of such reporting, in the purview of leftist politics, would be that such things are typical of at least a considerable segment of the population of our country. The merest suspicion of comedy, of comic exaggeration, or of anything of the sort would frustrate the political purpose, and leave us exactly where we were before. In other words, to interpret Caldwell's work as reporting of this kind leaves out too much.

This will not do. If there is an element of reporting in Caldwell's novels, it is of another and less satisfactory sort. Caldwell has always been an inveterate collector of grotesques: in *Tobacco Road* the grandmother, consumed by pellagra until she is a dehumanized hag; Bessie, with no nose; the girl with the harelip, so hideous no male can keep his eye on her; Jeeter himself, a sort of he-witch. In *God's Little Acre* Pluto is so fat he can hardly move about; in *Trouble in July* Sheriff Jeff McCurtain has so big a belly his wife has to lace his shoes. Bubber, the repulsive character in *Tragic Ground*, has a grin permanently built into his face. And these are only show cases. Behind them is a procession of women like Maud, and energy-drained, worm-eaten men like Spence. These are presented by Caldwell as people. They are also, in a sense, gargoyles. We are never sure that they are not in the stories simply because they are picturesque. There is really no good reason why Jeff and Pluto have to be incapacitated by fat, so far as the stories go. A missing nose and a harelip are not essential to *Tobacco Road*, except that they serve to make the men who can contrive to put up with them seem extraordinarily desperate for feminine companionship—in fact, picturesquely so.

In connection with this we remember that Caldwell is at present general editor of a series of books on American Folkways. And what, as Professor Howard Mumford Jones asks in a recent review, is a "folkway"? Of course, it has something to do with being native to a rural place, and characteristic of the people there. Yet although you and I are folk—save for the evil chance which occasionally coops us up in cities—our characteristic manners are not folkways in Caldwell's sense, and neither are the characteristic manners, which Professor Jones cites, of his youth on a midwestern farm. To be folkways, they must also be picturesque.

Getting back now to Caldwell's novels, may they not also be interpreted as a sort of preliminary exploration of certain American folkways? Are they not, as much as anything else, an exploitation of the picturesque? I would hesitate to affirm that they are, but the suspicion exists and must be recognized. Not only may these people be gargoyles, inserted for their ornamentative horribleness, but their conduct may be the conduct of gargoyles; we may be watching both grotesque types and grotesque—intentionally grotesque—human activity.

Now nobody objects to looking at gargoyles, so long as we know what we are looking at. But the identification of these characters as such should, it seems to me, pretty well cancel out the possibility of reading Caldwell's novels as straight socially-conscious documentaries, and also cancel out the value of the books as serious comedy.

By itself, then, the theory that Caldwell is doing some sort of reporting is a completely inadequate basis for the interpretation of his work.

There is, to sum it all up, no completely satisfactory attitude for the reader to assume toward these books. When we read them as comedies, Caldwell carefully and disconcertingly knocks the props from under the comic element; we look then for serious, socially-conscious reporting, and the comic element spoils our view; we resort, unwillingly, to taking them as exhibits of the picturesque, only to realize that Caldwell deserves more from his reader. So we come finally to the conclusion—for which we have been searching all along—that Caldwell's novels suffer from a multiplicity of meanings which are incompatible with one another. This is another way of saying that Caldwell's own attitude toward his materials is ambiguous.

Sometimes it is childish to object to ambiguity. Ambiguity, we are persuaded, is life. And we all love *Hamlet*. Yet we hate to renounce unnecessarily that part of the human heritage which is our ingrained reluctance to admit that it is impossible to make the world conform to the logic we have invented. We demand that if we must finally surrender to ambiguity, we be given something in return; we ask that the ambiguity somehow enrich us, that the meanings of a book be somehow complementary to each other, that there be layers of meaning rather than a number of conflicting meanings on the same level. The ambiguity which we are willing to accept is in the finished work, then, but not in the author's own attitude toward his material.

The difficulty might disappear if we could read Caldwell as we read Jean-Paul Sartre. For in Sartre's world, as he lays it before us in *La Nausée*, the fact that people are very much like what Caldwell says they are like need worry no one; for when people are not absurd they are horrible, and the assumption of any sort of social responsibility is therefore itself an absurdity that we had better commit only with our eyes wide open. This is difficult for us to agree with, but sufficiently cogent and consistent within its parts to satisfy the intelligence.

Or if we could read Caldwell as we read Céline, to whom all men are ultimately insane and thus fit only for the strait jacket (politically, the strait jacket of fascist regulation), Caldwell's attitudes would, in their apparent neglect of consistency, make good sense.

The French, those archenemies of the ambiguous, undoubtedly do read Caldwell—whom they consider an exponent of the new *roman noir*—in some such way, for they do not complain of his ambiguity. They have the additional advantage of being more remote from the material than Americans of our generation can be. They can read *God's Little Acre* without feeling that Pluto is always treated as a picturesque, stock character; that old Ty Ty's frequent redesignation of the plot of ground reserved for the Almighty's benefit comes from a familiar comic tradition; that much of the farming scene is straight documentary stuff; that the fiercely animal sexuality of some of the characters, not to mention the bloodshed, has less to do with the rest of the material than with our present novelistic conventions. Nor are they, as we are, in the position of emotional involvement where Caldwell's material is concerned.

The emotional question is one to which I have not dared to give much importance up to this point, because amateur psychology is a treacherous thing. But the key to the whole discussion may be contained in it. Can it not be that Caldwell's own emotions toward his characters are somewhat unsteady? These are his people; it would be odd indeed if he did not feel strongly about them. "I would willingly trade ten thousand of those [readers]," he writes in his Foreword to *God's Little Acre*, "for a hundred readers among the boys and girls with whom I walked barefooted to school and with whom I sweated through the summer nights in the mills of Georgia." This sounds like emotional involvement. And no one, certainly, would blame Caldwell for it. But unless carefully controlled, it could show up in his writing as a sort of sentimentality. Sentimentality toward material like Caldwell's could, in turn, result in the ambiguity which bothers us. I believe—though I propose it as a suggestion only—that this is true in Caldwell's case.

We may not be so fortunate as another generation of Americans, to whom these various considerations are not immediate. They may rank Caldwell much higher than we tend to rank him. After all, the only justification for spending as much time on the question of his ambiguity as we have spent here is that the ambiguity at times endangers a truly remarkable talent. Despite all the difficulties we have noted, Caldwell's novels have their place with those of Hemingway, Faulkner, and Steinbeck; and one of them, *Trouble in July*, is a really superior piece. His mixture of comedy and violence, when it works well, is a significant contribution to the novel of violence. Some of his creations have become part of our folklore: people who have never read a line of Caldwell know all about Jeeter Lester, and apply to the form of degeneracy to which it is appropriate the slur, "tobacco-road."

When we take everything into consideration we are likely to feel that, in spite of Caldwell's ambiguity, he is greater than we know.

Notes

1. "John Steinbeck's Men of Wrath," *Southwest Review*, 31 (Spring 1946), 144–52.

"Introduction" to
The Pocket Book of
Erskine Caldwell Stories

Henry Seidel Canby*

Erskine Caldwell is one of those rare men in human experience who have done both what they wanted and what they have thought that they wanted. He thought that he wanted most of all to "go places," to see people in a living experience of the sociology he picked up at the University of Virginia. However, he began his travelling—more accurately described as vagabondage—long before he ever heard of sociology. In childhood and youth he was a resident of six Southern states, and wandered through all of them as an amateur tramp, with a tramp's experience, but the mind of an artist and observer. Then, when his reputation was made, he travelled in a big way as a correspondent, notably in Russia.

But something in him wanted all this time to write. He says he would have preferred to be a working sociologist, which reminds me of Vachel Lindsay's passionate desire to be known as an art critic. Yet apparently only the desire to write could neutralize the vagabond in Caldwell, who was always finding his immediate environment too small. And, indeed, as his prefatory notes to the collection of his short stories called "Jackpot" show, many of these tales were written en route by bus or train from one place to another. The truth is, of course, that these two dominant wants in Caldwell's life are as closely related as ploughing, planting, and harvesting. His stories came out of the soil on which he has lived and over which he has wandered. The inexplicable urge which forces the born writer to symbolize life in words and create the significance which actual experience hides in a confusion of events, has done the rest. Gross experience accurately recorded and statistically explained is sociology; but if a man is an artist, this experience sets his imagination to work, and he is not content until he has drawn out the inner truth which is so much more revealing than the facts. That Caldwell has this peculiar sensitiveness, which is indispensable for fiction, is sufficiently indicated by the record. In fifteen years of writing he has published twenty volumes of short

*Reprinted from *The Pocket Book of Erskine Caldwell Stories* (New York: Pocket Books, 1947), vii–xvi.

stories, novels, social studies, war correspondence, and travel notes, which have so impressed the contemporary world as to be represented in thirteen nations and twelve languages in addition to his own.

Erskine Caldwell was born in the middle of December, 1903 (the exact date has been lost), in the hill country south of Atlanta, Georgia, eight miles from the nearest post office. His father, a minister in the Associated Reformed Presbyterian Church, and a North Carolinian, was also a wanderer, who moved on from church to church through the South every year or two, on an average salary of $300 a year. At seventeen, the boy left home to go to school in South Carolina, but spent more time riding freights and as blind-baggage than in school, with arrests for vagrancy and rich opportunities to see life in its picaresque aspects. Just how, with this rich but not concentrated education, he got into the University of Virginia, is not clear—there must have been more direction in his wishes than he admits. But he did stay there—more or less—two years, supporting himself by working in a poolroom as helper and bouncer.

He left to become a cub reporter on *The Atlanta Journal*, which had been his ambition, married and began a family. But he discovered, as so many journalists have done, that newspaper work is not creative writing, and that if to write in a creative way is what you want, journalism is the wrong profession. The only way to write creatively is to write creatively, and forego, at whatever risk, daily news writing. So, with admirable audacity, Erskine Caldwell got as far away from his old environment as possible, perhaps subconsciously feeling the need to get it into perspective. For years he "holed in in Maine," raised potatoes and chopped wood to feed his family, "vowing not to come out until I had got myself published." But in three years—as is recorded in one of his books—he had sold a story (over a telephone) for $350, though he would have willingly taken $50 for it if necessary, and his public career had begun.

I myself regard Caldwell as primarily and essentially a short-story writer. His fame among the masses is due of course to the incredible success of the play, *Tobacco Road*, written by another, but based on a long short story or *nouvelle*, as the French call such stories, by Caldwell. But at his most original, most effective, and certainly at his best, Caldwell belongs in the distinguished list of American short-story writers who have made their place in world literature, beginning with Irving, Hawthorne, and Poe. And it is as a short-story writer that I shall discuss him in this estimate of his work introductory to a new collection. In this career, to an extent surpassing any other American story writer except perhaps Sarah Orne Jewett or William Faulkner, the literal, actual facts of his own country, and thus of his own biography, are vitally important. And in the above-mentioned list of great American short-story writers, Erskine Caldwell is, I should say, the first who has consciously viewed the rich materials of his native experience as sociology, and then turned them into successful art.

Of course, the short story is beautifully adapted to this service. The writer of short stories, if he is gifted in that art, keeps his eye on life until it turns for a moment dramatic, then rebuilds the circumstances and retones the atmosphere to give that moment emphasis. For him, mere action is not necessarily, nor even usually, dramatic; rather it is the revealing word or look or deed which makes action burst into significance. Hence, though his choice of descriptive words or of indicative phrases requires the subtlest and most imaginative discrimination, his technique of construction is—once he has learned it—very simple. All it consists in, is to hold the reader's interest in suspense until the climax is ready, which is not a step in the story but really the story itself, for which all the rest is just a build-up. Note in the stories here included, how true this is of such a tale as *Candy-Man Beechum* or *Saturday Afternoon*.

Perhaps this is why Mr. Caldwell gets so irritated with the "Professor Perkins" whom he constantly addresses in the paragraph prefaces to the stories he put in "Jackpot." "Professor Perkins" is always discussing the construction of the story, whereas there are a dozen possible ways of building most of these Caldwell stories, provided the vital moment, with its implications, is thrown in high relief. If I were "Professor Perkins" and had Erskine Caldwell before my class, I would ask him to retell Bret Harte's *Outcasts of Poker Flat* in his own fashion, and so prove the point very readily. Mr. Caldwell would have liked to rewrite that story, which, under his hands, would change from high-colored (and excellent) melodrama to a rich and objective narrative, as in his *Martha Jean*, with the sentiment concentrated into pity and driven down into the roots of the story, where the careless reader might easily miss it. Caldwell and Harte would tell the same story; that is, the mid-nineteenth and the mid-twentieth century writers would each give you a Mary Magdalene revealed, but as the result of very different methods.

Probably Erskine Caldwell's grandfather, whom he constantly quotes, was right. The true story teller is a man who seems to be too lazy to do more than experiment with all kinds of living. Actually the thorough-going livers of life have lazy imaginations. The writer's eager fancy plucks him away from experience as soon as he sees its significance. Then he must choose a symbolic movement and give his energies to turning that into the reality of fiction which is always more real because more complete and self-explanatory than actual happenings. Note Caldwell's famous story called *Country Full of Swedes*, which is nothing but a symbol of the disturbing rush of vitality over the unvital, like a comber over a sterile beach. Or the simple tale of *Big Buck*, which is essentially a description of exuberant life. Or that most terrible of lynching stories, *Saturday Afternoon*, where the horror is not in the lightly stressed lynching, but in the naïvely callous pleasure of the onlookers who have been saved from a dull afternoon.

Naturally, therefore, a short-story writer is most effective when he writes from deep layers of the subconscious, which every poignant memory stirs into a warmth of emotion. Caldwell's Maine stories, such as his *The Midwinter Guest* and his *Grass Fire*, both in this book, are humorous studies of eccentricity—usually of obstinacy or of fear. They are like tall tales or local anecdotes told over the cracker barrel, and they are good.

He can do the same thing with Georgia, as in the *Handsome Brown* and *My Old Man* stories, than which it would be hard to find much more amusing reading. This is the Mark Twain tradition and it is a good one. Indeed in these tales, and others which throb with indignation against a maladjusted world in spite of the horse-play and mock innocence on top, Caldwell is Mark Twain's spiritual heir.

But when Erskine Caldwell comes home to Georgia he soon drops the quip and the crank for something much hotter and sometimes of deadly power. *Tobacco Road*, by no means as deadly as some of his briefer stories, shows how the artist takes his revenge on life as he remembers it. Jeeter Lester and Preacher Bessie have entertained thousands of playgoers—but the play, which Caldwell did not write, leaves out the background of the story and it is this that gives it power. What made the play so successful was probably the humor of primitive sexuality brought out by skillful acting. But in the story itself you see why these lamentable decadents are so much more than comic-strip satire. Shreds and tatters of moral codes still hang about them, and a pathetic confidence that God will make up to them for their misfortunes. But that they are helpless and hopeless victims of their own love of the land which they have ignorantly, obstinately exploited until it will not support a rat, they never guess. This is the dynamic idea behind the story. The boy Caldwell saw them as he walked along Tobacco Road, laughed at them, probably despised them, then began to wonder. The mature Caldwell keeps the memory of their humor, but now can understand what had happened to them, and so he makes their degeneracy human and significant.

The same, of course, is true of his white-and-Negro stories. The classic tale of a lynching is not to be found in Lillian Smith's recent "Strange Fruit," effective as that novel is, but in Caldwell's very brief *Saturday Afternoon*—where the fly-specked butcher that everyone likes is awakened from his nap just in time to go to the lynching; or in the very terrible *Kneel to the Rising Sun*. Here is entire objectivity. Every word in these stories describes the scene as the actors saw it. The fury of rage with which the author wrote is carefully concealed. It is for you to feel, and, unless you are as naïve as the actors, of course you do feel it. Not even Hemingway's *The Killers* is a more terrible story than these.

Richer and more humorous are the stories of Negro types. Of these, *Big Buck* is a classic of irrepressible vitality. And *Candy-Man Beechum* is the best of all, for here Negro exuberance is checked when it reaches the limits set by the governing race, and is cut down like a weed. There is no preaching in these stories, but only the most insensitive reader can miss the passionate revolt against a vicious system which holds the Negro down in order that a decaying white culture can keep some self-respect in its ignorance and poverty. If Caldwell's sympathy seems always with the Negro, it is probably because he feels that the Negro has retained more humanity and vitality than his oppressors. He is evicted, beaten, shot, lynched, but it is the decadent white who really has been most deeply scarred by what has happened.

This sociologist's understanding of ultimate causes explains the tolerance that enables Caldwell to present his scenes so objectively. There is a false idea that his popular reputation depends upon the freedom he allows himself in describing sexual experience. Read these stories carefully and you will see that this is not really true. Sex spices his stories certainly, but never makes them. Sex, like keeping the Negroes down, is the release from the dull and futureless life of the Georgia whites, who love their very lovable sunshine and piney woods, but never seem to be able to get beyond the most elementary efforts to stay fed and clothed. Sex is the one pure joy and adventure left in a starved environment. This sex element in such an excellent story as *Maud Island* is as pagan as in Naomi Micheson's Greek stories. The women (after youth) still keep up the reprobation that makes amorousness and adventure, but in general this sex experience comes from a primitive instinct which seldom rises to love, and is respected even by husbands and fathers whom it injures. It is vulgar in the true sense of that word. Some of Caldwell's most effective stories, such as *Man and Woman*, and *Martha Jean*, are made from blind, unanalyzed lifts of this primitive instinct into something more civilized.

Probably—though you would never guess it from his flippant prefaces—Caldwell's chief stock of emotion is pity. In the perfectly delightful stories in *Georgia Boy*, this pity does not have to be exercised. The Old Man of these stories is just as worthless as the poor whites of the grimmer stories, and could be just as ruthless if his Negro or his neighbor interfered with his peculiar way of life. But in these stories he is in the sun, and does not have to be cruel in order to keep his meal ticket.

Shift from such stories into the shadow and see how the emphasis changes. Read *Kneel to the Rising Sun*, the ruthless story of the starved share-cropper whose father is gnawed to death by the boss's hogs. He has so little of a man in him that his loyalty to the plantation (which is all he has left of his morale) will not let him protest, forces him to help the lynchers catch his Negro friend who has dared to tell the boss what he thinks of his inhumanity. Or the story of the sadist who collected the tails of his tenants' dogs. Or *The End of Christy Tucker*. In all these narratives, the rage of the writer is tempered and suppressed by his pity for the victims—these Negroes and poor white trash who do not know what is wrong or how to escape it.

The white brutes who are the villains in such stories as these are, with a few exceptions, not creatures of pure evil. They are the same easy-living, land-loving individuals as in *My Old Man*, except that the decline of their economic culture has hurt them more psychologically because they have more to lose. Instead of greed, which is the inevitable reaction in a homogeneous community such as one might find in France, their humor and humanity have degenerated into suppressed fear, unacknowledged cowardice, and open and callous cruelty.

Mr. Caldwell has a very good time bantering the critics in his little prefaces in the volume *Jackpot*. He thinks, and rightly, that they know too much about the alleged rules of writing and too little about life and the art that springs freshly from it. He may think I am taking him too seriously in the remarks above, but that I doubt. He is well aware that many of his stories are only clever anecdotes; yet his eagerness to get in a punch at his reviewers before their gloves are on, shows that not only does he take his own art hard, but fears and expects it will be misunderstood. In this (and in other ways) he is like Chekhov, who wrote with such regard for the seeming trivialities of life, that he was often thought to be only a photographic realist. Mr. Caldwell's art is definitely an art of understatement—understatement, I mean, of the deep issues of the story, though overstatement and repetition often of the humors, the absurdities, and the eccentricities of his characters. He is not a naturalist, like Dreiser or Zola, in spite of his sociological basis; he is not a realist, if being a realist means to let life speak for itself without focus upon some inner significance; he is certainly not a romanticist, except about the land, where, indeed, his characters often speak in pure idealistic romance which gives their author great satisfaction. No one of these critical terms seems of much use in describing Mr. Caldwell's work, unless negatively. He will not be pigeon-holed easily by literary historians.

I should prefer to characterize him finally by a comparison with a very great artist indeed. The little corner of Georgia with which his mind is obsessed is, in some respects at least, like the misgoverned, decadent, economically backward Spain where Goya painted. In its minor way, Caldwell's Georgia presents individuals as racy in their decay as Goya's Spaniards, and also a community as regardless and as truly ignorant of what had happened to it as was Spain in its collapse after greatness. I do not wish to push the comparison further, except to suggest that Caldwell, like Goya, paints what he sees, and feels with evident intensity, yet never sentimentalizes or falsifies the scene by letting his artist's consciousness leak into his words. The decadence, the economic degradation, the pathology of racial or class conflict are for you to feel if you can. The poor white starving on his sand hills, or the Spanish peasant caught in factional warfare, sees no controllable causes, but only the devil in action, or the wicked rich oppressing him, or sins of his youth now remembered by an avenging God.

But let us drop comparisons, and say simply, that the best of these short stories are symbols of an American experience of quite frightening significance, of which the actors are entirely unaware. And that, being unaware, they can be and are utterly themselves—which means as trivial or worthless or amusing or callously inhuman, as most of us are when food is scarce and the satisfactions of vanity hard to find. Whether this be realism or not, it is certainly a powerful way in which to present reality. And for many a reader the sand hills, and eroded cotton fields, the tottering houses, the easy acceptance and hearty laughter of the middle South, will be most vividly remembered in Erskine Caldwell's interpretation. He has made that country particularly human, by giving the life there a world-wide human significance.

"Introduction" to
American Earth

Erskine Caldwell*

I am glad *American Earth* is the first book I wrote, and I feel that it is fortunate that it was a book of short stories.

The particular stories in this collection are obviously far from approaching anything like the finest ever written, and yet I feel now, some twenty years later, that if I were to have the opportunity to live my life over again, I would rather write these same stories than any others. The principal reason for my having such a feeling about this book is that I believe I achieved what I set out to do at the time, which was to prove to myself that it was possible to find the materials of fiction in the everyday life around me.

It will be seen that this book contains stories written about people and things in the Far South, and an equal number of those whose scenes are laid in Northern New England.

It was not chance that made this so.

My desire was to discover at first hand how American life was lived, and to me it seemed, having been born and reared a Southerner, that it would be logical, and worthwhile, to experience a contrasting way of life in Northern New England.

Consequently, the short stories in this volume have been placed in two sections, just as I had consciously sought a new environment to contrast with life as I had known it in early youth. This, of course, does not necessarily make the stories, tales, and incidents in *American Earth* better or worse than they might have been if I had written exclusively about the South, or solely about Down East. However, as far as the reader is concerned, this collection does offer, I trust, a scene more truly American than it would otherwise have been.

It can be said that these two dozen stories constitute the result of ten years of writing. I had put myself to the task of becoming a writer—a published writer—within that period of time. During the first seven years of that decade I was unable to find an editor who wished to publish a

*Originally published in the 1950 Duell, Sloan & Pearce edition. Reprinted with the author's permission.

story of mine in a magazine. That is an unpleasant situation, as anyone who has ever attempted to get a story published can appreciate, but when one has tried for that long a time to attain a goal, he has usually acquired a perverse tendency to reject discouragement, at least until his alloted ten years are consumed.

It was at this point that a surprising event took place. A short story of mine was unexpectedly published in a magazine in Paris, *transition*, the title of the story being "Midsummer Passion," and I enthusiastically destroyed all previously written stories and put myself to the task of beginning a writing career all over again. During the following three years, ending in 1931, sixteen short stories were printed in magazines in America. All of these are contained in *American Earth*. The book itself was first published in 1931.

"Introduction" to
Tobacco Road

Erskine Caldwell*

It has come to be generally believed that at an early age authors acquire a philosophy or creed that impels them to write novels rather than to devote their energies to more commonplace things. This must be true, because a fairly normal person who wants badly enough to write can with little effort convince himself that life would be more interesting if he were a novelist. Thus once becoming destiny's child, and carefully maintaining a delicate balance between calcification and glandular activity, he will possibly endeavor to seek fame and fortune—perhaps in passing effect good or evil upon his social and economic province—or else surrender himself to promiscuous indulgence in the deeper psychological mysteries of the ego.

My credo, if it could be called by such an imposing term, is a very simple one. The desire to write about what people do was created when I realized that I was dissatisfied with, and somewhat provoked by, the manner in which the everyday lives of the people I knew were falsified and perverted by novelists who arbitrarily forced human beings to conform, and perform, to artificial plot and contrived circumstance. The people in such novels had slight resemblance to the reality of life, and even life itself was being made repugnant by the crafty dishonesty of fiction. I stopped reading such bogus literature, probably becoming permanently resentful and mistrustful of teachers and critics who were on the verge of convincing me that the artificial was more desirable than the genuine, and began writing about people as I knew them and about life as I saw it.

*Originally published in the 1948 Duell, Sloan & Pearce edition. Reprinted with the author's permission.

This, then, for the most part, was the motivation that brought me to write my first novel, *Tobacco Road*. I wanted to write about people as they actually lived, not as readers had been misled by ingenious novelists to think they existed. You cannot write an honest story of people if you use dishonest methods in the conception of it. And in the end the most effective story is one that mirrors the life of men and women as they themselves recognize it by its faithful resemblance to their own sorrows and happiness. You know you are being faithful to life when a stranger comes up and says he is a little angry, but glad just the same, that you wrote the truth about his wife's brother in the book. Consequently, when I wrote, I wrote about the people I had been born among, had been raised with, and had come to know.

Tobacco Road is the first book in a series of novels about the South I know. No one will find here the Old South or the New South, the Deep South or the Romantic South, but perhaps he will find, as we know it, a broad expanse of peopled land between the Piedmont and the Low Country that has existed for a long time and will continue to be there for some time to come. Its recognizable characteristics are red gullies, sandy fields, piney woods—and people doing what people do.

"Introduction" to
God's Little Acre

Erskine Caldwell*

It can be said that *God's Little Acre* was written because there are so many interesting people in the world who do interesting things in interesting ways that I wanted to see what happened when some of these fortunate people were given an opportunity to tell the story of their lives in their own way. If they had been forced to behave in the traditional manner of characters in novels, and if I had belabored the story to a preconceived conclusion, this might have been a more professional-appearing novel, cunningly concealing all the time-tested artifices of hackneyed fiction, but it certainly would have been too dull and spent to hold my interest, and few readers would have had enough curiosity to read it to the end. As it was, I became so engrossed in the doings of Ty Ty Walden, and his kith and kin, that I wrote the story as fast as I could wind it through a typewriter in order to find out what was going to happen next. When it was finished, and the last page had been reached, I was saddened, because it was heart-rending to leave them and go back into the commonplace world.

Ty Ty's world differs from the world around us only in the fact that his life was more spiritually rewarding than the secularly imposed lives most of us live. The reason his life was interesting is because he made it so, regardless of the ultimate, inevitable consequences that befell him, while we ourselves are generally too uncourageous, in a circumspect civilization, to allow the spiritual needs of life to take precedence, at all times, over the material. It becomes increasingly evident, as the story is told, that we must either accept or reject Ty Ty before going much farther into his life, because here is a man who will surely ennoble us if we are deficient in human goodness, or defile us if we are satisfied with common morality.

The story itself is much more simple than all this. It is merely a story about a man who wanted to find gold on his land, and happiness in the hearts of his children. It is not nearly so important whether he did or did

*Originally published in the 1949 Duell, Sloan & Pearce edition. Reprinted with the author's permission.

not find these elusive things as it is that he had the undeniable desire to seek them at all costs. We may become envious of Ty Ty, but when we realize we cannot trade places with him, we are quick to seize upon the next best thing, which is to become attached to him. It is this attachment, this close personal association with him, that gives us the satisfaction of knowing that we have been permitted to live for a little while in a world we were privileged to enter only because Ty Ty opened the way for us. After we have lived in it for a while we recognize it as being the very same world we have lived in all our lives, but as only seeming different and more desirable because its spiritual and material values have been changed to reveal their real worth. By the time the story comes to a close, we realize that, for a short time, what we have been reading is a story about a man who was not afraid to rearrange values in life so that he could place the true worth on those things men most avidly seek.

"Introduction" to *Kneel to the Rising Sun*

Erskine Caldwell*

The seventeen short stories in this volume probably would never have been written if, many years ago, I had accepted the advice that the novel was the only form of fiction worthy of major effort and that a young and ambitious writer would do well not to handicap himself by following a belief that short-story writing in the age of large-circulation magazines could produce anything of permanent value. The trouble with counsel on the subject of authorship, always to be found offered freely on all sides, is that it is deceptively akin to appreciation and encouragement, and many young writers eagerly accept it without realizing that they are actually getting questionable advice.

In those days, fifteen or twenty years ago, and perhaps today as well, well-meaning but unperceptive persons, many of whom still look upon the short story as being merely a space filler for magazines of large circulation, argued that only a novice or an outright foolish author would ever devote the larger portion of his time and talent to writing anything other than a novel. If all authors believed this and wrote accordingly, it is doubtful if a short story could ever be defined as anything more than an incident or episode that had failed to fit into the structure of a novel.

Perhaps I did have a desire to refute this argument; but whether it was a conscious desire or a cantankerous notion, I did wish to prove to myself that a short story was capable of being just as interesting and enthralling to a reader as a work of fiction of extended length. I set out to prove this for my own benefit, and this collection of seventeen stories, called *Kneel to the Rising Sun*, was the result of eighteen months of writing. I still feel that it was time well spent and, regardless of whether I proved anything or not, I would not trade this particular book for any novel I have written.

As a writer, I have always felt that there were many incidents and episodes in life that could be told more effectively and compellingly in the compact space of a short story than could be related in a chapter or por-

*Originally published in the 1951 Duell, Sloan & Pearce edition. Reprinted with the author's permission.

tion of a longer and often artificially extended work of fiction. After all, there are relatively few dramatic moments in life that require a hundred thousand words for the telling; the most exciting and memorable happenings are usually brief and explosive. The elastic nature of the short story as a form—within which tales are told in as few as several hundred words or as many as several thousand words—is ample reason for its existence and popularity.

Some may argue that none of the stories in *Kneel to the Rising Sun* would qualify as fiction of major effort. However, as long as these stories continue being read—pleasurably or critically—I will feel that they are capable of speaking for themselves and that there is no necessity for raising my voice in their behalf.

"Introduction" to *Journeyman*

Erskine Caldwell*

It is possible that some novels would forever remain unwritten if the author had any way of knowing beforehand into what strange fields and devious bypaths his story might lead him. In the beginning I had no inkling of what turn the story of Semon Dye in *Journeyman* would eventually take, but I had written only a few chapters when I became convinced that, come what would, I was bound to go along with him to the end. I am glad now that I did, even though there were times when I regretted ever having thought of the man, because when the novel was finished, I felt the satisfaction of having put on paper something of the evasive and tantalizing character of a human being often glimpsed but never before seen face to face.

It is doubtful if Semon Dye, even with all his ingratiating personality and glibness of tongue, could ever justify his own existence in human society. However, the fact remains that he did exist, at least in the lives of the people upon whom he forced his presence, and that, to Semon Dye, was ample justification unto himself not only for living but for glorifying his life of knavery as well.

Fortunately, in a country that has such a population, there are relatively few like this man—knaves who employ the garb of religion to gain selfish ends—and yet the influence they wield pervades a large portion of the land. This is not strange, when we stop and think about it, because every vocation and profession has its quota of swindlers and pettifoggers of whom we must constantly beware.

The trouble was that Clay Horey and Tom Rhodes and Dene and Lorene, perhaps being no better or no worse than most of us, recognized Semon Dye as being exactly what he was but were powerless to cast off the spell he had put upon them. They reproved him and they damned him, yet eagerly became the slaves of his will. In the end they knew full well that they had been victimized by a rogue, but none the less they were sorry to see him leave.

Journeyman, then, is a violent novel. It was destined to be a violent

*Originally published in the 1950 Duell, Sloan & Pearce edition. Reprinted with the author's permission.

novel from the beginning, since the inevitable headlong impact of good and evil made violence unavoidable. Now that I look at the novel many years after it was written, I can clearly visualize calmer and more sedate means of relating the story of Semon Dye; but I feel sure that if the story had been compelled to deviate from its headstrong course, I would have been dissatisfied with the outcome and perhaps never have let it be published. And if it had been told differently, it certainly would not be the authentic story of turbulent Semon Dye, but manifestly a distorted version of his life and deviltry. As it is, *Journeyman* can be said to be, if nothing else, a faithful portrait of a man as I knew him.

"Introduction" to
Tragic Ground

Erskine Caldwell*

If the true intent of an introduction such as this is to tell the prospective reader what the book is about and, at the same time, in an unobtrusive manner, but with unashamed calculation, leave him convinced that he will be regrettably unhappy for the remainder of his life if he does not read it—if such design is the unblushing purpose of an introduction, then I think I can be as forthright as my intention.

Tragic Ground is a novel about those of us who, at some time or other, wander from place to place on earth, either plagued by necessity or gravitated by desire, and who strive to feel not uncomfortable in a strange world, but who can never quite outlive a compelling urge to return, no matter how bleak the prospects, to what we call our homeplace. The homeplace, whether it be a mere plot of ground or an entire region, is a state of mind, a geographical location, and the ultimate retreat of those of us who are dissatisfied with our lot in life. And even though some of us never return, there is always at hand the sustaining thought that if worse comes to worst, one can always find comfort in his native land.

Every man, no matter how strong his determination, sooner or later finds himself swept up by strong currents that blow across the world and, often to his surprise, sees himself being deposited in some strange place. Such was the experience of Spence Douthit in *Tragic Ground*. He had been displaced and misplaced in life, and only a person who has suffered a similar fate could adequately sympathize with him. No person in the story really understood his plight, and he himself wavered from time to time, depending upon the temper of the wind, between the betokened attractions of his new environment and the remembered satisfactions of Beaseley County. What can a mortal man do when he is pulled first in one direction and then in the opposite direction by conflicting and uncontrollable desires? If he is like the rest of us, he never completely comes to a decision.

Now that I have said in so many words what *Tragic Ground* is about,

*Originally published in the 1948 Duell, Sloan & Pearce edition. Reprinted with the author's permission.

I find that I am much more interested in the people in the novel than I am in the story it tells. To me as a writer, and as a writer who sometimes reads, the telling of a story is a tedious task to get done and out of the way so that I can have the time to become better acquainted with the people in the story. As a result, since finishing this book about him, I have probably spent more time in thinking of Spence Douthit, wondering what he would or would not do in this and that circumstance—what goodness would balance what badness, than I devoted to the telling of the story in the first place.

"Introduction" to
A *House in the Uplands*

Erskine Caldwell*

For a long time I had been writing novels about the South when one day I became aware of the fact that actually I was writing only about people and things I approved or disapproved of for the purposes of fiction. Of course, I knew all the time that an important phase of life was lacking in the re-creation of this world I had known since birth, but it was sad and tragic and somewhat personal, and I tried to keep from admitting to myself that I did know. The story I had failed to write was *A House In The Uplands*.

A House In The Uplands, like *Trouble In July*, and *This Very Earth*, and other works in the series, is one of the individual panels in a cyclorama of a people's social and economic history. The story about the South of which I write would be incomplete and prejudiced without this particular picture. Although names change, scenes vary, and actions differ with the times, the basic theme remains the same as it was the first time men tried to destroy, for better or for worse, an established and cherished pattern of life. Here in the South, as elsewhere in the world, the age-old theme is the pain that is inflicted upon the human breast when an outmoded way of life ceases to be beneficial to the common good, and makes a final desperate effort to maintain itself against the inevitable inroads of social and economic change.

The story here told has been fashioned by countless balances and counterbalances that weight both conscious and unconscious acts. Many of these elements appear to be trivial and picayunish—small human irritations and desires that might have been dissipated by a word or a glance—but in sum the cumulative effect of these little things is tragic and overpowering.

It is not surprising that the innocent suffer to as great a degree as the guilty, and the suffering of the innocent in *A House In The Uplands*, while not a justifiable atonement for a whole people, at least serves to ease the pain of violent vengeance for the guilty and unguilty alike.

*Originally published in the 1949 Duell, Sloan & Pearce edition. Reprinted with the author's permission.

There are few persons left now like these in *A House In The Uplands*, and those who do remain are probably resigned to their fate.

Life is many things to many people, and this particular portion of the larger story is only one of many ways of life. Few of us would consent to walk back into time and take up the way of life in *A House In The Uplands*, because we know now it holds no hope or promise of happiness.

However, this is an inherent part of a people's heritage, and contemporary roots, disdainful of the source of their sustenance, are nourished in the soil of the past. Consequently it is inevitable, it seems to me, that what people do and say, for long afterward, will be the fruit of the tree.

"Introduction" to
This Very Earth

Erskine Caldwell*

Writing such a novel as *This Very Earth* has been to me a satisfying experience. Principally, I feel that it is a step toward the ultimate completion of the cycloramic depiction of Southern life that I have been writing in many novels for many years, and also, simply because I like to write about such a person as Daniel Boone Blalock and to trace the influence he has on the lives of the people around him.

When the reader finishes this novel, he may well wonder how it can be said that *This Very Earth* is about Dan Blalock, when, seemingly, the story is concerned for the greater part with the lives of the family Crockett. It seems to me that the story of Chism and Vickie and Jane, and all the others, would have been different if it had not been for the baleful influence, almost imperceptible at times, of Daniel Boone Blalock. As a consequence, the story is rightfully his.

It is probable that I like to write about Dan Blalock because I have never known him in real life. I am convinced that he exists, in varying proportions, in other living persons, and some day I fully expect to see him alive and whole. In my mind, rightly or wrongly, the world is peopled with men and women who came into being from the pages of fiction. The fact that Blalock is a composite character in no way makes him less real to me. I do not always approve of his acts, I rarely admire him, and he is undoubtedly a despicable person, but once brought to life he is, for better or for worse, here in existence.

No doubt one of the reasons why characters in novels—at least the characters in the novels I write—are not exact impersonations of real people is because an author, being human himself, could not resist the urge to improve, or depreciate, such a person as Dan Blalock by attributing to him finer qualities than he actually possessed, or by failing to turn to the light some of the brighter facets of his nature. The fictional character being a creation of the author's mind, a man in a novel is, ideally, a whole man faithfully portrayed. If he is lacking in certain noble traits—the

*Originally published in the 1951 Duell, Sloan & Pearce edition. Reprinted with the author's permission.

nobility we are prone to demand in our fellow men—it is merely because he is not someone else who does possess those admirable traits, but is simply what he is.

I set out to say that the people—especially Dan Blalock—in *This Very Earth* are wholly imaginary, that they are fictional characters. I will be greatly surprised if no one questions a word of this.

The trouble is that writers strive so hard to make fictional characters real and lifelike that they often become victims of their own skillful legerdemain. If these creatures of the imagination are made at all convincing, the reader is assured in his own mind that the author is cleverly concealing actual persons now living. Perhaps, after all, that is exactly what a writer unknowingly does.

[*Transatlantic Migration*]

Thelma M. Smith and Ward L. Miner*

Caldwell's reception in France really begins with the publication of *God's Little Acre* by Gallimard in May, 1936. The translator was Coindreau, by then a familiar name to those who read American translations, and André Maurois's prestige made him an appropriate person to write the preface. Caldwell was, at first, clearly an exotic and did not reach the popular level until after the war, but the book sold and favorable criticism appeared. In June, 1937, Gallimard published *Tobacco Road* and in May, 1938, *We Are the Living*.

Before 1936 there had been scattered mention of the American editions of Caldwell's books—the most important was a review of *Tobacco Road* in *NRF* July, 1934, in which the germs of future Caldwell criticism appeared. Coindreau pointed out here that the writers of the twenties had been fundamentally romantic in their reaction against the war and their world, but that the younger writers are resigned to an evil world. Caldwell laughs at human stupidities. He is both an observer and a satirist. His book is really farce in spite of the constant atmosphere of tragedy—it reminds us of the Guignol. His farmers hold immovably to a faith in the ferocious god of the Puritans. Later in the same year Philippe Soupault wrote an article on "La nouvelle littérature américaine" for *Europe*. He felt that writers like Faulkner in *Sanctuary* and *As I Lay Dying* and Caldwell in *Tobacco Road* and *American Earth* are particularly symptomatic of the new state of mind which attaches itself to essential problems. It seeks to find the true American and not a phantom or a superficial caricature pushing his glasses up on his forehead or chewing a cigar like Babbitt, who seems, when one knows the citizens of the United States, a pseudo-American pictured by a badly informed European. Faulkner and Caldwell, the critic continued, seek to portray the American soul considered not as a literary motif or a picturesque subject but as a living and intense reality.

Maurois, in the preface to *God's Little Acre*, began by pointing out that "this strange book, cynical and remarkable, needs no commentary." He briefly described Caldwell's early life and then explained that when

---

*Reprinted from *Transatlantic Migration* (Durham: Duke Univ. Pr., 1955), 146–60.

the book appeared in the United States it was loudly condemned in some quarters for its obscenity. Forty-five prominent American writers protested and the attorney for the state of New York dropped the case. "Wise decision. The book is certainly brutal and harsh as were in a totally different sense Rabelais and Lawrence, but it is impossible to deny that it is a work of art."

Six months after *God's Little Acre* appeared Coindreau wrote an article of some consequence for *NRF*. In it he defended Caldwell's "indecency" as having in it something of the innocence of the profoundly instinctive. This writer, Coindreau said, glorifies man's instincts, especially his animal instincts. In the same month, November, a review of the book came out in *Europe*. The critic believed that *God's Little Acre* is an admirable tonic which should embolden the reader to accept his own vagrant outbursts of passion. And M. Hertz agreed that Maurois was right in protesting the charge of obscenity. "We learn from this book something of childlike folly, of innocent sensuality, of tragedy tempered with humor in a primitive and jovial society which has all the beauties and cynicisms of youth." A review in *Esprit* suggested that the descendants of the Puritans are in the process of taking a revenge against their heritage which puts to shame the French *petites pornographies romancées*. Lawrence, Faulkner, and now Caldwell. "We used to speak of *gauloiserie*; now we must say *américainisme*."

Pierre Brodin in his book *Roman régionaliste américain* (1937) also took up the cudgels for Caldwell. He recalled that in America not only was the novelist accused of pornography but of downright lies; however, *God's Little Acre* and *Tobacco Road* actually show accurately enough the conditions which existed among many poor whites during the depression. Brodin called *Tobacco Road* a work having two great qualities—an undeniable picturesqueness and a profound accent of truth. And *God's Little Acre* seemed to Brodin, from a literary point of view, even better. Thiébaut in the *Revue de Paris* ("Trois romanciers étrangers: Huxley, Morgan, Caldwell") discussed both books. He emphasized Caldwell's poetic sense, which gives to his burlesque an incontestable grandeur. Lelis reviewing *Tobacco Road* in *Europe* wrote first of *God's Little Acre*, the book which a year before had revealed to the French the name of Caldwell. Echoes of the power of this book still resound, he felt, of its force, originality, and sexual exacerbation. The second novel is just as good as the first. In both, Lelis continued, we find bitterness, humor, despair. We are astonished to discover hungry people in the United States, but Caldwell has depicted men and women as he has seen them. So much the worse for us if it seems too much *nature*.

Jeanine Delpech wrote an article for *Nouvelles Littéraires* in January, 1938, entitled "Visite à Erskine Caldwell, le Céline américain." She put Caldwell outside the pattern of the American regional novelists. His characters, she said, are unforgettable for their wild passions and the

force of their *idée fixe*. Their illogical acts seem a reflection of the il-
logicality of nature; if they are cruel, they are no less cruel than the
elements. The scene of Caldwell's novels is a nightmare universe where
time no longer exists, where instincts express themselves with such brutality that they come close to perversions. These are not thesis novels, though
they arouse in the reader either impotent anger or a desire for immediate
action. He is never left indifferent. These novels force us, in spite of our
embarrassment, in spite of the laughter Caldwell uses to lighten our
agony, to be aware of a suffering humanity whose existence is a shame to
the America so proud of her youth, of her civilization. This is Caldwell's
aim, which he attains without descending to propaganda but by means of
a Rabelaisian vigor and purity of style.

For *We Are the Living,* translated by Ed. Michel-Tyl, Coindreau
wrote a six-page preface. In it he emphasized the importance of
Caldwell's "The Sacrilege of Alan Kent," which for him contains the germ
of all Caldwell's work. In the last sentence of the story Alan Kent says,
"And I knew now that I would always be alone in the world." To Coindreau that confession is Caldwell allying himself to the *grands anxieux* of
present day Anglo-American literature—to Lawrence, Sherwood Anderson, Faulkner. Coindreau went on to speak of Caldwell's lyricism, to
compare it with Faulkner's, and then to emphasize Caldwell's comic sense
based on unconscious burlesque and incongruities. It is a humor *pince-
sans-rire* whose American forebearer is Mark Twain. The French reader
will think rather of Maupassant—the same stripped story, dry irony,
latent pessimism. But in Caldwell this pessimism turns toward sadism and
atrocity. In depicting horror and cruelty, the American triumphs easily
over the Frenchman. Finally Coindreau said the short stories in this
volume, taken from *We Are the Living* and *Kneel to the Rising Sun*, illustrate all the aspects of Caldwell: social satire, humor and lewdness,
atrocities now and then unbearable, pantheistic feeling for nature
translated by symbols as old as the world but eternally beautiful, and the
final unifying trait—a profound originality rising out of an intense savor
of terror.

One critic alone in this first burst of enthusiasm strikes a somewhat
sour note. Wessberge, reviewing *Tobacco Road* in *Etudes Anglaises*
January, 1938, wrote that though these primitive characters are amusingly superstitious, that is not enough to give them an interest truly
human. Caldwell's realism, brutal and cynic, is here as arid as *la Route
maudite*. It does not have the comic nor the dramatic power which made
God's Little Acre a bitter epic. If *Tobacco Road* does not disgust
the French reader, it will be only because of Coindreau's remarkable
translation.

Even during the war years Caldwell received some attention. *Fontaine* printed his "Fin d'été" and *L'Arbaléte* "L'homme de dieu"—a

chapter from *Journeyman*. In 1943, Marc Barbezat, in "Caldwell et le mythe," wrote: The society of Caldwell is a jungle, and the writer takes no pains to hide the claws and the fangs of his characters. If Ty Ty were a Negro, how picturesque he would be, the critic continued, but Ty Ty Walden is you—he is me. We cannot escape from him any more than he can escape from his misery, a cosmic misery—as of shipwrecked beings thrown upon a desert isle or of fallen angels on a continent hostile and sterile. Barbezat put Caldwell above Dostoevski, saying that in *Crime and Punishment* Rechetnikov by his monotony loses the attention of the reader but Caldwell in his books holds it by his humor. This humor is the magnificent proof of the health and youth of America. The reader's laughter never mocks but pays homage to the vitality of the characters, to their ruggedness, to their rage to live. They resemble the people of the first books of the Old Testament. Ty Ty, Noah—Lester, Adam. That a twentieth-century novelist has refound the power of the myths of Exodus and Genesis interests us, the critic continued. We ask ourselves if the method of Caldwell is perhaps not indispensable to the modern writer, if it will not give us back force in our novels, help us grow out of our sterile psychological analyses. Caldwell's characters pertain to eternity; however young, they carry within themselves all the experience of humanity; they invite us to live in a mythic universe.

Not too different from Wessberge's adverse criticism written six years before was Charles Lucet's comment in "Les Français et l'Amérique" published in *La Nef* (Algiers) August, 1944. First the critic quoted William Byrd on the life which the early Americans lived on the *frontière géorgienne*—where the utterly lazy men left all the work to their wives and at the end of the year found themselves with nothing to eat. Monsieur Lucet added:

> Such was certainly the life of the first pioneers—a life which today, describing the same regions, the great novelist Erskine Caldwell offers us again in his *Tobacco Road* and *God's Little Acre*. His characters are lewd villagers, dirty and sly, ignorant of the civilization which has detoured around their mountains, examples little to be recommended to touch the heart of a civilized man.

In 1945 appeared Maurois's *Etudes américaines*. One chapter discussed the American edition of *Tragic Ground*, pointing out that Caldwell's characters might better be described as beasts in their tranquil shamelessness rather than as savages, for savages at least have their code and taboos. The family in *Tragic Ground* respects no longer the taboos of Christian civilization. Maurois suggested that when Mavis describes her new job to her family the situation recalls certain scenes by Zola, though the tone is different. Zola gives his characters a sense of sin and the feeling that they are violating the moral law. Caldwell's people walk about nude and candid; they have shame neither for their bodies nor for their habits. And then the critic, as others had, placed Caldwell in the tradition of the revolt against puritanism in Anglo-Saxon literature.

The postwar burst of enthusiasm for the American novel carried Caldwell to popular success though critical reception of *Poor Fool*, which Gallimard got out early in 1945, was mixed. Coindreau had translated the book before the war. In his preface, dated 1940, he again presented to the French the historical background of the modern American novel—the breaking away from the traditional after 1914 by Sherwood Anderson, Dreiser, Sinclair Lewis. He said that *Poor Fool*, published in America in 1930, is the birth of the true Caldwell. We see already his taste for the horrible and cruel, his approach to sex, his tragic-comic puppets. *Poor Fool* illustrates both the Oedipus and castration complexes.

The reviewers were numerous. Vagne wrote:

> We have delighted in the American novel as the source of new adventures for the mind. How impatient we have been to break the silence of the war years. Now Caldwell returns! Horrors! Is this what we have loved so dearly? This tissue of gratuitious violence, of sordidness? This nightmare which is closer to psychoanalysis than to literature?

Astruc concluded that no other writer could get away with offering to the French public right after the war a work so full of horror. He dismissed the book as awkward but agreed with Coindreau that it shows the themes and tendencies later developed by Caldwell. De Laprade decided the novel left him rather indifferent. Others were favorably impressed and went into long discussions of Caldwell's techniques and ideas. "This novel is man crushed by his world, dominated by what is stronger than he, the incarnation of the ancient Greek and the modern American conception of the wretched, the unlucky being vomited out by his world, the victim of obscure gods."

Blanzat took this occasion to consider the vogue of the American novel. He felt there were many reasons for it, but most important was the ability of Faulkner, Steinbeck, and Caldwell to express clearly the brutality of the age. That gives them their universal audience. Although each differs from the other, they have the same philosophy. Man as they see him lives in a kind of middle age without the faith of the Middle Ages. Modern civilization, far from helping him, enriching him, actually enfeebles him. He is alone and more than ever powerless before his destiny. This image of man is not new. We find it from Greek tragedy to the naturalistic novel. American novelists have much of both in them, but they deviate from naturalism because they are not realists though they begin from the real. They seem to copy reality—to give detail after detail, effacing themselves. All this is why their literature is filled with idiots, drunks, perverts—each with a symbolic value. So builds up a literature of myths and allegories which turns into a neoromanticism. But this new romanticism is not talkative, not sentimental, and its lyricism is always masked under a precise, dispassionate tone. If such are the traits of the American novel, then we can say that no one is more American than Erskine Caldwell. The desolate world of Steinbeck and Faulkner appears civilized and flourishing compared with Caldwell's.

Poor Fool sold. By June, 1946, one critic at least, Sans, was suggesting that certain American novelists were better known in France than in their own country. As a proof he said, "Several thousand copies of Caldwell's story *Poor Fool* have been run off in Paris although in New York the printing, solely for devotees, was limited to 300 copies!"

Over the months from May, 1945, to September, 1946, a group of artists in Paris were working to produce a magnificant de luxe edition of *Tobacco Road* "to honor the great American writer Erskine Caldwell." Nine hundred copies were printed. There were eleven copperplate illustrations by Denyse de Bravura. Marcel Chapuis directed the work. The printing was done at the press of Ernest Puyfourcat fils, the copper plates in the workshop of Paul Haasen. The folio pages were folded chez Jossé, the box cover chez Adine, and the paper chez Mertens. All was under the imprint of Editions du Pré aux Clercs. A review of this handsome book said, "This novel appears to us one of the most remarkable of the young American literature. It has a force at the same time realistic and lyric—the power of the great literary fables where the characters were called Misery, Hunger, Pride, Love, Desire."

In 1946 also, *Action*, a leftist weekly, published three short stories: "Beechum le Beau," "Abe Latham, homme de couleur," and "Le Nègre dans le puits." In August Jacques Vallette wrote "Erskine Caldwell: plan de son oeuvre" for *La Nef* summarizing and praising the American novelist's work. And two books appeared: Brodin's had a seventeen-page chapter on Caldwell, straight biography and criticism, and Coindeau's a twenty-eight-page section which gathered together the opinions on Caldwell he had expressed in his articles and prefaces.

When Caldwell paid a visit to Paris in the summer of 1947, half a dozen papers carried articles or interviews. One of the most entertaining was in *Figaro Litéraire*. The interviewer, Arban, asked:

> "Why did you choose such people to write about, such horror?"
> "Because I knew them as a boy. All the people of *Tobacco Road* exist. It is 100 per cent reality. But *Poor Fool* is 100 per cent imagination."
> "Tell me—have you read especially carefully Edgar Poe?"
> "What?"
> "Edgar Poe. There are in your *Poor Fool* passages which evoke him particularly. This tendency to necrophilia. *L'histoire de cette robe de morte.*"

"Poe. No." Caldwell smiled gently in excuse. "I never read. In any case, not Poe!"

Also in 1947 Guérard in his preface to the short story "Dorothy" by Caldwell in *Ecrit aux U.S.A.* attempted to give the French a picture of American criticism of Caldwell. Guérard asserted that Caldwell is much more admired in France than in the United States, where more and more his last books are unanimously judged not to be fulfilling the promises of his youth. He seems to have lost the indignation he once had. In *Tragic Ground* the condition of children uprooted seems humorous rather than terrible. This kind of thing is hard to see in translation. But certain American critics find in Caldwell as in James Cain or Henry Miller a sort of sadistic compliance in the tortures of their victims and a desire to titillate or scandalize the bourgeois reader. In Caldwell this tendency seems more pronounced in his novels than in his short stories where his greatest qualities—mastery of dialogue and choice of detail—appear to best advantage. But it is in his novels that French readers find this *absurde*, this vision of a world in disorder which interests them so much today.

The same year, 1947, brought Caldwell success on the Paris stage. *La Route au Tabac* opened March 15 at the Renaissance Théâtre. Simon recalls that the play was a striking success though only mediocrely produced. There were favorable reviews which emphasized the play's "fantastic lyricism" and its "deep tenderness hidden under surface ferocity." One in *Europe* admitted:

> Unquestionably *Tobacco Road* dominates this theatrical season as did *Of Mice and Men* the year 1946. But the road of tobacco never attains the emotion produced by the mice. We speak of its naturalism—that it is a slice of life, that it allies the grotesque and the sublime. But the play does not reach its goal. The ideas are too denuded and at the same time too violent to allow the onlooker time for breath. We lose the social significance of suffering humanity.

Another critic, in *Paru*, complained, "It is difficult to be moved by such sordid beings who have no vitality except in their sexual debaucheries (rather disagreeable on the stage)."

Seven thousand five hundred copies of the play version were printed in the winter of 1947 by Editions Laffont, we were informed, and all but a few copies sold. This, according to one French literary agent, was a good sale; the French do not ordinarily buy plays. A well-known play by a French writer might sell as few as five hundred copies.

Finally, near the end of this year which had seen Caldwell's name achieve prominence again and again, Gallimard published the French translation of *Trouble in July*. The book got a mixed critical reception, though the weight was on the favorable side. Again the emphasis on "humor held in check by profound human sympathy." "The writer is not a simple painter of certain customs. Here is the eternal struggle between man and society." "This tragedy classic in its unities," "this whirlwind of astonishing poetry." One critic, agreeing with others bored with lynching, called *Trouble in July* the hundredth version of a hackneyed theme and asked, "Is Caldwell commercializing his subject matter?" Several pointed out that Richard Wright had a more profound approach to the Negro problem.

During these early years after the war Gallimard and other presses also, as quickly as they could get paper, put out new impressions of the prewar publications by all five of our novelists. Discussing the reissues in December, 1947, Blanzat wrote in *Figaro Littéraire* that Caldwell's two first novels done in French, *La Route au Tabac* and *Le petit Arpent du Bon Dieu*, "gave the impression of a novelist particularly American: brutal, cruel, obscene, painter without nuances of people simplified to the point of caricature." *Nous les Vivants* shows an inspiration "more flexible, more varied, closer to reality." This book, the best of his eight, "forces us to reconsider the somewhat premature evaluation we have made of Caldwell." And thus we see that "in the detail as in the whole, each creation of Caldwell has a double dimension. Only by an unjustifiable simplification do we speak of Caldwell's 'caricatures and puppets.' "

Two Caldwell translations appeared in 1948—*Tragic Ground* early in the year, translated by Coindreau, and *A House in the Uplands* just at the end of the year, translated by Robert Vidal. Neither received as many reviews as had *Poor Fool*. So much had been written on Caldwell since the war that perhaps the critics found little new to add. Also it is a familiar pattern to see a novelist somewhat ignored by the intellectuals as he becomes more popular. Third, of course, the question arises whether these books actually have the power of Caldwell's earlier writings. And it is clear enough that by the publication of the seventh volume in French the original shock value of Caldwell had lessened. One critic said of *A House in the Uplands*, "A bad, a very bad Caldwell. Written to measure with all the tricks showing." But Gérard d'Houville, although suggesting that the influence of American novelists on French writers was probably not good, continued, "But let us speak of one of the novels that does please us and does transport us to another world—*A House in the Uplands*. Here the heady atmosphere, the feverish climate of the South, the odor of the marshes, the chants of the Negroes on the plantations, the melancholy of ruined fortunes, the old hopes now become shameful—it is all this that gives value and interest to Caldwell's brief and somber story."

The critical scales swung back and forth. Guyot's slender volume gave Caldwell three pages of extremely favorable comment. Magny refers to him, however, only in passing. The anthology *Courtes Histoires américaines* omitted him, as had the one published at the end of 1946 by *Cahiers des Langues Modernes*. Reviewing this in 1948, Duvignaud wrote, "It is indeed strange that Caldwell, without doubt one of the most original American writers, does not figure in this collection."

In 1949 *Georgia Boy* appeared but made little critical stir. Two short stories were printed during this year, "Dans la prairie" in *Arts-Lettres* and "Fichue journée" in *Lettres Françaises*, and there were several interviews when Caldwell visited Paris. *Journeyman* came out in January, 1950, and the French recognized this as one of Caldwell's best novels—classed it with *Tobacco Road* and *God's Little Acre*. Robert Merle, whose prestige was enormous—he had won the Prix Goncourt two months before for his novel *Week-End à Zuydcoote*—wrote the preface for *Journeyman*. He considered it technically the most successful of Caldwell's novels because it has more unity. Humor, he said, dominates it from beginning to end. But Caldwell is a critic of capitalistic society as well as a novelist. He "has eaten with the people he describes, he has gathered cotton with them, he has thrown dice with them, and at night behind the barn he has slept with their daughters." As economist he deplores their kind of life; as a man he delights in it. The reviewers agreed with Merle's vigorous praise of the novel—"a master work," "of high quality," "perhaps his chef-d'oeuvre," "one of the summits."

Simon's book, *Le Roman américain au XX^c Siècle*, published in 1950, devotes a dozen enthusiastic pages to Caldwell. He wrote: "American puritans detest him, the intellectuals pretend disdain. But each has read him. Popular editions have made him known everywhere and it is only just." His work, so simple in appearance, hides a wealth of richness which too many hurried readers fail to see. He is one of the absolute masters and he characterizes his period; heir of the realists, he has considerably enlarged their domain. The time for perfect but impersonal photography is past. Caldwell is an artist and an artist *qui prend parti*.

Later in the same year *The Sure Hand of God* translated by J. L. Bost and Marcel Duhamel under the title *Le Doigt de Dieu* appeared. *This Very Earth* was published in 1951 and occasioned a serious discussion by Raymond Las Vergnas in *Hommes et Mondes*. *Episode à Palmetto* came out in the summer of 1952 and in November appeared *Soleil du Sud*, which contains twelve of the fourteen stories printed in *Southways*. There is no question but that Caldwell continues to be read in France—four translations in two years. Yet the reviews of these books, and there were not many, showed Caldwell's critical decline.

But the critics' lack of enthusiasm does not worry the general public. And Monsieur Queneau at Gallimard told us that *Place Called Estherville* will be published soon and also *Call It Experience*. M. Hoffman, Caldwell's literary agent in Paris, reported that he is looking for a translator for *A Lamp at Nightfall*, which he feels will greatly interest the French although they may have difficulty understanding the pictured degeneracy of Maine whites and their hatred of new, foreign blood coming in. And so the story of Caldwell in France continues.

"Erskine Caldwell:
A Note for the Negative"

Carl Bode*

"The World's Fastest Selling Book"—such is the publisher's boast about Erskine Caldwell's gamy novel, *God's Little Acre*. It hit the paper-backed reprint market in March 1946, not long after the war, and in a little over two years 4,000,000 copies of it were sold. And it is still selling tremendously. A relevant question is, Why?

Since *God's Little Acre* is a fullblown sample of Caldwell's fiction, the reasons behind its popularity ought to hold as well for the rest of his widely republished novels, *Tobacco Road* and *Trouble in July* among them. *God's Little Acre* has two parts to its clumsy plot. The first deals with an old Southern dirt farmer and his ruttish family, the second with a strike in a mill town near where the farmer lives. One of the leaders in the strike is his son-in-law, Will Thompson. The high point of the book comes when Will beds with a sister-in-law, the gorgeous Griselda, and then (ah, symbolism!) goes out and turns on the power in the strike-bound mill so that the strike cannot be broken.

The slabs of social significance in the novel (fashionable in 1933, when it was published) are today merely interruptions to the narrative. They allow the publisher to murmur something about the sociological importance of Caldwell's writing, but it is inconceivable that they helped to sell the book in postwar years. They didn't need to. Sex did the job. Caldwell used it very effectively. With an instinct amounting almost to genius, he matched his characteristic kind of writing with its perfectly appropriate locale. How appropriate the back-country South, with its corn-shuck mattress and its privy, was for his setting can be realized only if we try to substitute another section of the United States. New England, the Midwest, the Far West—none is as good. Nor is the big city, although James Farrell's Chicago probably comes as close as anything else. Certainly, as many people have pointed out, Caldwell's is not the true South. But the important thing for the multitude of customers in the reprint

*Reprinted from *College English*, 17 (Oct., 1955), 357–59. Copyright © 1955 by the National Council of Teachers of English. Reprinted by permission of the publisher and the author.

market is that it is true enough for them. And it invites them to feel superior to it.

Here is the place to note too that Caldwell has been unusually popular in foreign countries. There are doubtless several reasons but again one of them must surely be the sense of superiority a foreigner can have after a literal reading of Caldwell's tales.

Along with sex Caldwell supplied a feverish narrative. Something is always happening in *God's Little Acre* and the other books. One action swiftly succeeds another. As Caldwell said years ago in the preface to one of his short stories, "Finally, the reader is so dizzy that merely the sudden cessation of motion is sufficient to send him on his way physically reeling and emotionally groggy." Death—either murder (Will Thompson, for instance, is finally shot by the mill company's guards) or of the "Lookit, the hawgs et Grampaw" kind—is frequent, and always under sordid circumstances. Fighting is even more frequent. All kinds of other things take place, many with a grotesque exaggeration that smacks of tall tales and Southern folklore. The reader cannot stop for a moment, if Caldwell has his way. His publishers' figures show the remarkable extent of his success.

God's Little Acre and the rest of Caldwell's hot and shoddy novels make much money for him but add nothing to his literary reputation. This is not true for his short stories. *The Complete Stories of Erskine Caldwell* (1953) gives us a chance to see him to better advantage.

Most of these tales are set, as one might expect, in the same South as *God's Little Acre*. A few of the remainder are set in New England, where Caldwell spent several early years trying to sell what he wrote. The rest of the stories are unlocalized. The Southwest—he now lives in Arizona—furnishes him with no material at all. His characters in these narratives are rarely individual. The poor whites act much alike. Although some of his stories of social injustice are as moving as anything he has ever written, it is hard to tell one suffering Negro from another. If we had to fix the time within which these beaten-down white and colored sharecroppers move, it would apparently be the depth of the Great Depression. Caldwell has selected the period, as he has selected the place, which offers him the best chance for grimy melodrama. The pressures of poverty and exploitation weigh on his people. Actually, the New Deal, World War II, and the postwar boom in the South have all come to relieve those pressures, but Caldwell wisely continues to ignore this fact.

When he abandons his picturing of the impoverished South, his writing nearly always suffers. His conclusion to "The Lonely Day," for example, the story of a Maine farm girl, is pure mawkishness. "The first light of day broke through the mists and found her lying in the road, her body made lifeless by an automobile that had shot through the darkness an hour before. She was without motion, but she was naked, and a smile that was the beginning of laughter made her the most beautiful woman that tourists speeding to the Provinces had ever seen." When he tries to philosophize about Life for the women's magazine market, he sounds just as false, though in a different way. In "Here and Today," first printed in *Harper's Bazaar*, he takes up the problem of the eternal triangle. The solution he recommends pontifically is that the woman who wants to keep her husband must make herself more alluring than the other woman. Says the heroine to her wandering husband, "I've been fighting you all this time, trying to take you from her and bring you back to me. I know now that it is up to me to make you think I'm the most attractive." With Olympian wisdom, the husband agrees.

Half a dozen writers in the prizewinning short story annuals, almost any year, write better than Caldwell. Yet he has achieved some reputation and he once won a literary prize himself. The kind words he has received are not always justified. He has the ability to put vivid sense impressions into simple words, the ability—mentioned before—to keep the action moving, and finally—in his short stories at any rate—the ability to stop before the reader has caught up with him. A fair share of his short stories are memorable ones, although that is partly the result of his matter rather than his manner. Even his crudely constructed stories linger in our mind when they are tragic enough, though a visit to the morgue will too. In general, however, the sagging architecture which weakens all his novels does not develop in the short stories. They are the better for being brief.

One other factor in Caldwell's favor should be mentioned. It appears so obvious that it is sometimes taken for granted yet should not be. It is his literary vitality, his ability to keep on writing nowadays at about the same level he reached two decades ago. More than one able writer has drained his imagination and thereafter has either written less or written aridly, but not Caldwell.

Among the collected stories, "Candy-Man Beechum" clearly proves Caldwell's power to portray pathos and dignity; this is a sharper, keener story than the better known "Kneel to the Rising Sun." "The Medicine Man" is a first-rate sample of what some people have called his Rabelaisian humor, although it is really pornography with a horse laugh. And "Evelyn and the Rest of Us" compresses into three pages the whole story of the loss of childhood innocence. Nor are these stories the only excellent ones.   )

There is a place in the world of literature between William Faulkner and Les Scott. Mythologist of the South and holder of the Nobel award for literature, Faulkner is a great novelist. Les Scott, whose works attracted the animated attention of Congress's Gathings committee of several years ago, is well represented by such a labor of commercial love as his novel "She Made It Pay." Between these two men Erskine Caldwell can be set.

"My Twenty-five Years of Censorship"

I wrote *God's Little Acre* all in one stretch in the Summer of 1932. As I have recorded elsewhere, I wrote out of my memories of myself as a boy in Georgia, I wrote without reading what I wrote, twisting the sheets out of the typewriter and letting them fall on the floor. When I was done, I read the first fifty or sixty pages, and knew that it was all right. When they came back from the publisher printed and bound, I read it straight through and found that I liked it a lot.

Mr. John Sumner, secretary of the New York Society for the Suppression of Vice, did not like the book. Mr. Sumner presented himself at the offices of the Viking Press, and bought a copy from a clerk. He forthwith lodged a suit against Viking Press on the ground that the book was "obscene, lewd, lascivious, filthy, indecent and disgusting."

Those were the days when "free love" and "companionate marriage" were still racy topics for the Sunday features, and Defoe's *Moll Flanders* and Balzac's *Droll Stories* were seized by the U.S. Customs. As a novelist, I was then very much a newcomer. But the literary community rallied warmly to the book's defense. A protest in the interests of "preserving freedom for genuine works of literary importance" was signed by Alexander Woollcott, Dorothy Parker, Gilbert Seldes, Henry S. Canby, Max Eastman, Marc Connelly, H. W. Van Loon, Clifton Fadiman, Lewis Mumford, Burton Rascoe, Elmer Rice, Heywood Broun, H. L. Mencken, and Malcolm Cowley, among others. Such persons as Sinclair Lewis and Mark Eisner, President of the Board of Higher Education of New York City, wrote letters which were presented in court. Magistrate Benjamin E. Greenspan, the city magistrate before whom the case was brought, showed himself a literate and sensible man.

Sumner argued, as he had in the past, that the book should be judged by the standards of "subnormal" persons. The opinions of the "literate" should be disregarded. Greenspan reversed this doctrine. "The Court is of the opinion," said Greenspan, "that this group of people, collectively, has a better capacity to judge of the value of a literary production than one

*Reprinted from *Esquire,* 50 (Oct., 1958), 170–78.

who is more apt to search for obscene passages in a book than to regard the book as a whole."

Greenspan went on: "The author has set out to paint a realistic picture. Such pictures necessarily contain certain details. Because these details relate to what is popularly called the sex side of life, portrayed with brutal frankness, the Court may not say that the picture should not have been created at all. The language, too, is undoubtedly coarse and vulgar. The Court may not require the author to put refined language into the mouths of primitive people."

Furthermore, he declared, "the Court must consider the book as a whole, even though some paragraphs standing by themselves might be objectionable. . . . This is not a book where vice and lewdness are treated as virtues or which would tend to incite lustful desires in the normal mind. There is no way of anticipating its effect upon a disordered or diseased mind, and if the courts were to exclude books from sale merely because they might incite lust in disordered minds, our entire literature would very likely be reduced to a relatively small number of uninteresting and barren books. The greater part of the classics would certainly be excluded. In conclusion, *God's Little Acre* has no tendency to inspire its readers to behave like its characters, therefore it has no tendency to excite 'lustful desire.' I believe the author has chosen to write what he believes to be the truth about a certain group in American life. To my way of thinking, truth should always be accepted as a justification for literature."

Thus Greenspan laid down certain principles which marked a great advance in the fight against censorship: that a book must be considered in its entirety, and not condemned for isolated passages; that literate opinion was more relevant than that of censorious muck-sniffers; that the test was the book's effect on the ordinary reader, not one with sex problems of his own; that "coarse" language was not necessarily "obscene"; that the realistic portrayal of primitive persons was neither pornographic nor censorable, if the book's intent was honest and sincere.

A few months later, Greenspan's general conclusions were given wider scope when Random House was haled into Federal Court for importing James Joyce's *Ulysses*. Judge John Woolsey exonerated *Ulysses*, noting "that although it contains . . . many words usually considered dirty, I have not found anything that I consider dirt for dirt's sake. . . . I do not detect anywhere the leer of the sensualist."

Since Joyce used every four-letter word in the English language, that language taboo was shattered once and for all. Woolsey also agreed with Greenspan that a book must be judged by its effect as a whole, not upon the easily inflammable or the disordered, but "on a person of average sex instincts." A few months later, Woolsey was upheld by the Court of Appeals, thus erecting a nation-wide standard to which the liberal could repair.

But the opinions of enlightened federal judges are not governing on local vigilantes. Some faculty members protested the use of *God's Little Acre* in several English courses at Columbia's Teachers College, and got it removed from the library shelves. The do-gooders' attention turned to the play made by Jack Kirkland from my novel *Tobacco Road*.

Tobacco Road was shut down in Chicago and Detroit by arbitrary edict of their respective mayors, though the *New Republic* pointed out that "The characters of *Tobacco Road* are forgotten people. Mr. Caldwell deserves the gratitude of all who honestly care for decency in American life by bringing them so powerfully to mind." When the play opened in Washington in 1936, Representative Braswell Deen of Georgia rose in the U.S. House of Representatives to protest its "infamous wicked untruth." "We never lived thataway down in our part," he cried. "Never at all. Why, we got churches and schools for everybody. Even the Negroes have schools and churches." I offered to show Representative Deen what went on in his own district, but he never took me up on it.

Things quieted down during the war. But in 1944, the Boston Watch and Ward Society unwound on several books, including my novel, *Tragic Ground*. Municipal Court Judge Elijah Adlow did not give the Society much attention. "It's not for me or for you to try to establish the literary tastes of the community," he told them roundly. He found nothing shocking in the scene where a female character is allowed to see a man stripped to the waist. "Do you think anybody would be astounded by that? Have you seen any of the calendars that successful business firms have been giving out lately?"

For some reason, *God's Little Acre* ran into fresh trouble when it appeared after the war in the twenty-five-cent Signet edition. In St. Paul, Minnesota, the Morals Squad chief got a copy of the book and gave it to one Patrolman Don Wallace to read and review. The patrolman duly found it "immoral, obscene and lewd." The prosecutor promptly banned it. Then the Denver police ordered newsdealers to stop selling the twenty-five-cent edition. The Morals Squad took no action against the hard-cover edition. The idea, the police chief explained, was to keep the book out of the hands of teen-age children, who presumably could not afford a hard-cover copy. The *Rocky Mountain News* pointed out that "the police department has put itself in the absurd and illegal position of passing not upon matter but upon prices."

A year later, Jersey City, Portland, Maine, and Sioux City, banned the book. The authorities were unmoved when my publisher pointed out that no book of mine had ever been declared offensive or indecent by a court of law.

Unhappily, this statement is no longer true. In 1949, acting under a 1945 law which put a book on trial, the State of Massachusetts charged that *God's Little Acre* was obscene. I was allowed to testify that I had lived in Georgia, and was a competent reporter of the people I wrote about. Judge Fairhurst of the Superior Court cleared the book, but the State appealed, and the Massachusetts Supreme Court reversed Fairhurst's finding. The Supreme Court Justices agreed that the novel was a "sincere and serious work possessing literary merit" and had "value as a sociological document" but concluded, in defiance of the weight of judicial opinion in other states over the preceding ten years, that "there is no room for the pleasing fancy that sincerity or art necessarily dispel obscenity." As a result, *God's Little Acre* can be bought almost anywhere in the world except Massachusetts.

About this same time, a posse of high-minded Philadelphia citizens had compiled a list of nine books which, in their higher wisdom, they considered unfit for perusal by the common people. The list included Faulkner's *Sanctuary*, Farrell's *Studs Lonigan*, and *God's Little Acre*. The police obligingly haled five hapless booksellers into court for selling these allegedly "obscene" volumes. Judge Curtis Bok wrote an opinion which any author would welcome as the last word—though it probably is not.

Said Bok: "I should prefer that my own three daughters meet the facts of life and the literature of the world in my library than behind the neighbor's barn. If the young ladies are appalled by what they read, they can close the books at the bottom of page one. It is my conclusion that the books before me are obvious efforts to show life as it is. Far from inciting to lewd or lecherous desires, which are sensorily pleasurable, these books leave one with either a sense of horror or of pity for the degradation of mankind. I cannot be convinced that the deep drives and appetites of life are very much different from what they have always been, or that censorship has ever had any effect on them, except as the law's police power to enforce the peace is censorship. I believe that the census of preference today is for disclosure and not stealth, for frankness and not hypocrisy, and for public and not secret distribution. That in itself is a moral code. It is my opinion that frank disclosure cannot be legally censored, even as an exercise of police power, unless it is sexually impure or pornographic." The scope of censorship, he added, "must be defined with regard to the universal right of free speech, as limited only by some universally valid restriction required by a clear and present danger."

Macaulay once said: "We find it difficult to believe that in a world so full of temptation as this, any gentleman, whose life would have been virtuous if he had not read Aristophanes or Juvenal, will be made vicious by reading them." Commented Bok: "Substitute the names of the books before me for Aristophanes and Juvenal, and the analogy is exact." He might have added Mayor Jimmy Walker's famous observation that he had never known a woman who had been ruined by a book.

Bok's conclusion was that it is impossible to say what an average reader's reaction to any book may be. "If he reads an obscene book when his sensuality is low, he will yawn over it. . . . If he reads the Mechanic's Lien Act while his sensuality is high, things will stand between him and the page that have no business there. How can anyone say that he will infallibly be affected one way or another? . . . The professional answer that is suggested is the one general compromise—that the appetite of sex is old, universal, and unpredictable, and that the best we can do to keep it within reasonable bounds is to be our brother's keeper and censor, because we never know when his sensuality may be high. This does not satisfy me, for in a field where even reasonable precision is utterly impossible, I trust people more than I do the law."

In a word, in Bok's view (and mine), the reading public can be trusted to discard trash and cherish value. No censor is wise enough to make the decision for him. If he is wise enough, he would not want the job. If he wants the job, he is obviously not wise enough. As Morris Ernst has noted, even Judge Woolsey's "average man" cannot always be trusted when in a jury box. He is, of course, confident the book under judgment would never corrupt *him*. But in his sudden accession to the role of arbiter, he becomes as strict as Mother Grundy, and sets out to protect that mythical creature: the other fellow.

Since Judge Bok's decision, the war seems largely over. Curiously enough, the Kinsey reports may be a factor, as the New York *Herald Tribune* once remarked in a musing on my censorious critics. "The standard objection to Mr. Caldwell's novels," said the *Tribune*, "has hitherto been that his characters were much looser in their sexual behavior than actual people are. The Kinsey report has seemed to indicate that the Caldwell men and women behave much as actual men and women do, in the stratum of the population which these novels represent. Who can tell but that many thousands of readers find in Caldwell what seems to them the first realism about sex they have ever encountered in print?"

I think the *Tribune* may be right. In my trips around the country, people often come up to say that I have written about their families or about people who reminded them of themselves. The letters I get are from people who milk cows and pick cotton. They don't feel I am laughing at them or that the books are pornographic.

Censorship has always been with mankind. In their book, *The Censor Marches On*, Morris Ernst and Alexander Lindey point out that Plato suggested Homer should be expurgated. St. Bernard called Abelard "an infernal dragon, and the precursor of the anti-Christ." Sir Walter Scott trembled for the morals of adolescents exposed to Richardson's *Pamela*. Anatole France said of Zola: "His work is evil, and he is one of those unhappy beings of whom one can say that it would be better had he never been born." At one time or another, censorship has been inflicted on Defoe's *Robinson Crusoe*, Cervantes' *Don Quixote*, Swift's *Gulliver's Travels*, Twain's *Tom Sawyer*, Hawthorne's *Scarlet Letter*. It all seems to happen with the best good-will. A few do-gooders decide to do good. Nothing much happens except once in a while we get something like Prohibition.

But today, if his intent be honorable, any serious U.S. author can use just about any word he needs, and describe in adequate detail any action of humankind that is necessary to his purpose. Work which is obviously pornographic—that is, whose sole and deliberate intent is to be obscene—is still proscribed.

Censorship bête noire: where to draw the line

Is censorship necessary in any form? It is arguable that it is not. The French have practically none and, as a people, seem practically immune to pornography. What pornography exists is sold almost entirely to tourists. The difficulty with censorship is to determine where to draw the line. But it is pretty safe to assume that no book published by an established publishing firm today would be pornographic in intent. If there must be some testing ground, I would suggest that a panel of educators, lawyers, churchmen, and critics might be set up to examine a book before it is brought into court.

But censorship is inherently dangerous because when you start controlling what people can read, you are starting to control what they can think. Then you no longer have a democracy. Censorship, in cases where obscenity is not clearly evident, can be a basic threat to the freedom of the press. Sooner or later, it can touch everyone. The danger of corruption is pretty remote. A really objectionable book rarely survives, since competition among books is so keen that a book has to be universally acceptable in order to endure.

From a creative point of view, the threat is that when another author hears of a persecution for obscenity, he may crawl into a hole, and cut himself down to mouse size, in a kind of mental flinch from the criticism he might arouse. For myself, I don't think I've done that. I know what I know, and I have tried to go on writing about it as honestly as I can. *God's Little Acre* has been screened, scrutinized, winnowed and flailed like no other book ever has, and it has come through pretty well. It must have something of value if it can survive all that.

As Ty Ty says: "The trouble with people is that they try to fool themselves into believing they're different from the way God made them. You go to church and a preacher tells you things that deep down in your heart you know ain't so. But most people are so dead inside that they believe it, and try to make everybody else live that way. People ought to live like God made us to live. When you sit down by yourself and feel what's in you, that's the real way to live." That's the real way to write, too, I believe. And if it does not always come out as morally uplifting and tidily decorous as some would like, I can't help it. Anyway, I don't intend to change. I do not think any intelligent reader would want me to. As long as the censors let readers be their own judge of what is worth reading, I will take my chances.

"Gallic Light on Erskine Caldwell"

Stewart H. Benedict*

Erskine Caldwell, one of the major figures of American literature,[1] is above all an artist with powerful and original gifts.[2] His artistry recalls that of Flaubert, Rabelais, and Swift,[3] of Mark Twain,[4] of Dreiser and D. H. Lawrence,[5] of Baudelaire,[6] and, many critics assert, of Maupassant.[7] Continuing the tradition of Poe, Hawthorne, Melville, and James,[8] he writes in a manner free from the impulse to pose which mars the work of Hemingway[9] or from the puritanical horror of sin which is to be found in Faulkner.[10] More than an artist, Caldwell is a poet whose lyricism does not destroy the simplicity or the truth of his work.[11]

Further, as a realist, he is admirable because he is able to suggest, through his ability to reduce everything to its essentials.[12] As a sociologist, he never hesitates to put his art to the service of the people.[13] As a humorist, he is delightful because, never trying to be comical, he becomes irresistible,[14] and because he has a genuine gift of sympathy.[15] As a writer, he has the ability to create unforgettable characters.[16] The result of this is that his work has evolved into that circle which symbolizes the mythical universe, that universe which belongs to a plastic and collective reality and which gives us the illusion of eternity. This is the magic circle by which everything returns to its origins, by which we return from Caldwell to the Bible, from Ty Ty to Noah, from Jeeter Lester to Adam.[17]

To consider some of his books individually: *Tobacco Road* represents a synthesis of all Caldwell's rare qualities.[18] *God's Little Acre* has comic and dramatic power which sometimes raises it to the rhythm of an epic;[19] it is a veritable masterpiece of its type,[20] written with a subtle delicacy of touch.[21] *Journeyman* holds us breathless from the first page to the last because of the author's talent as a storyteller.[22] *Trouble in July* shows that, taken in detail and as a whole, every literary creation of Caldwell has a double dimension; further, it presents in the portrait of Sheriff Jeff McCurtain an unforgettable character.[23] *The Sure Hand of God* provides for the reader the same pleasure that the author must have experienced in writing it.[24] Such short story collections as *American Earth, We Are the*

*Reprinted from *South Atlantic Quarterly*, 60 (Aug., 1961), 390–97.

Living, Southways, and *Kneel to the Rising Sun* justify including Caldwell among the best short story writers in the United States:[25] Some of his stories are, in fact, perfect.[26]

To summarize: a novelist above all, he has solved numerous technical problems, including the mastery of a style. His stories are told with a scrupulous probity and a sense of dispassion. He describes what is, objectively; he animates by means of his human sympathy.[27] Heir of the realists, he has considerably enlarged their domain.[28] He is to be praised for that unique quality which puts him beyond classification and which makes reading him profitable.[29]

Considered from another standpoint, however, Erskine Caldwell seems destined for a place in subliterature; indeed, it is difficult to believe that he ever enjoyed critical esteem.[30] "He promises to be perpetually promising," principally because he devotes himself to material "not worth the whole attention of a first-rate artist."[31] He deliberately vulgarizes his themes, "exaggerating in the direction of the merely shocking and creating a special brand of horror-pornography."[32]

In his "shoddy" novels, all of them "weakened by a sagging architecture,"[33] he has become increasingly inept.[34] He no longer has any "sense of locale" and he "no longer hears the cadences or the idiom of southern speech,"[35] but this makes little difference because his ability "to make creative use" of speech never did match his ability to record it.[36] His characters are "seldom nuanced" and "the range of his emotion is narrow"; thus his novels are, so to speak, "spatially landlocked."[37] His "twisted comic sense," which gives evidence of a "sly and stuttering romanticism,"[38] may well indicate that "he has found modern pay dirt in comedy at the expense of the half-wit and the deformed."[39]

To evaluate some of his works: *Tobacco Road* shows Caldwell as "a purveyor of Gothic tidbits for the delectation of urban sophisticates"; its main characters are "comic grotesques," "pellagra Frankensteins."[40] *God's Little Acre* lacks proportion[41] and seems a rewriting of *Tobacco Road* with a "greater emphasis on perversion and a confused symbolism."[42] In *Tragic Ground* "the intrusion of moral feeling spoils the comedy," making one "hesitate to laugh," while "the comedy spoils the social message";[43] in this novel the author "perverts his talents, insults his characters and disgusts his readers."[44] *Place Called Estherville* is "an obvious attempt to get a laugh out of the moral delinquents, rapists, idiots, and sadists" whom Caldwell has "turned into cartoon strips of citizens of the South."[45] It is doubtful that these "comic strip attitudes" in which they are presented have "any correspondence with either reality or fine art."[46]

"Disciplined out of all contact with his material and with his readers" by the "Marxian line,"[47] "his promise largely unfulfilled,"[48] he has become "so repetitious that he seems to be playing with his toes."[49]

To reconcile these somewhat disparate points of view seems a task too challenging for the moment; it might be better merely to explain them. The first consists of excerpts from French criticism of Erskine Caldwell in the years from 1935 to 1960, the second, of comments of American critics during the same period. It must be said immediately, of course, that the quotations are to some degree stacked. Not all French critics have invariably seen Caldwell as an incarnation of the highest talents of Rabelais, Flaubert, and Baudelaire, nor have all American critics felt him to be a combination of Walt Kelly and Krafft-Ebing, subconsciously hoping to produce another *Gone With the Wind*.

At one time, to be sure, he was exceedingly well thought of by American critics. The successive publication of two such important novels as *Tobacco Road* and *God's Little Acre* stimulated reviewers to predictions of a brilliant future for an outstanding American talent. French critics at the same period felt the same way, but, where the American attitude has changed markedly, that of the French has not. Even such admittedly weaker productions as *Love and Money* and *A Lamp for Nightfall* were handled very gently[50] and, while they did not add to his reputation in France, they appear not to have tarnished it either.[51]

And so just now Caldwell's literary reputation is high in France and very low in the United States, among those who write about writing. And, paradoxically, the American author most read in America has not appealed strongly to the French reading public: a listing in *Les Nouvelles littéraires*[52] of the best-selling translations into French from all foreign literatures between 1947 and 1957 comprises two hundred and ten titles, of which not a single one is by Caldwell.

This list actually is more interesting than it is significant, since the French general reader is as eager as his American counterpart to buy his own copy of such milestones in our literature as *A Tree Grows in Brooklyn* and *Forever Amber*. What is significant, though, is the vast difference in the critical evaluation of Caldwell in the two countries.

A valuable contribution to resolving this paradox is made by Félix Ansermoz-Dubois, who enumerates in *L'Interprétation française de la littérature américaine d'entre-deux guerres*[53] and what he calls the "secondary reasons" for the success in France of both Caldwell and Faulkner, that is, reasons having nothing to do with the literary or artistic caliber of their books. These reasons, he thinks, are three: the brutal element in them accords with the picture that the French reader has formed of the United States; their books establish that everything here is not proceeding so well, and yet they are reassuring; and finally they depict a region of the country which has remained near to the Gallic heart, the South.

Following the lead of M. Ansermoz-Dubois, we may be able to draw up a list of "secondary reasons" to help explain some of the critical aversion to Caldwell on this side of the Atlantic.

First of all, most Americans (including the critics) are melioristic and chauvinistic; they are therefore reluctant to believe that the events or the people in these books either were or are true, especially in the light of social advances made under the New Deal and during World War II.

Second, in a strongly matriarchal society Caldwell has, until very recently, produced strongly patriarchal novels. For him, woman realizes herself fully only in fulfilling her natural biological function and beyond that is of little consequence. The popularity of such a view in the home of Mother's Day is bound to be limited, while in France it is accepted as desirable, if not normal.

Third, the majority of Americans (again including the critics), although they would firmly deny it, are quite humorless about sex and thus somewhat uneasy about sexual humor. At its lowest level, American humor is basically sadistic (see any *Saturday Evening Post* or read Al Capp) and at its highest, topically witty (see the *New Yorker*), but it is reasonably free of sexual associations. The behavior of the great clowns of our mass media who are also favorites of the critics seems to bear this out: Chaplin's tramp is chivalrous toward all women who are potential sexual objects and his humor in general is, to use Havelock Ellis' convenient classification, excrementally-based; W. C. Fields is utterly sexless, managing even to convert a cinematic encounter with Mae West into a contest of orotund badinage; Harpo Marx is the irrepressible gamin forever engaged in the fruitless chase after the unattainable blonde. Our leading humorists, too, have been and are asexual: Ade, Benchley, and Perelman, despite the variety in their approaches and in their subject matter, unanimously avoid the erotic. That this American attitude results from the Puritan heritage is probably true, but irrelevant here; what is relevant is that Rabelaisian humor is un-American.

So much for "secondary reasons." What elements of Caldwell's writing itself contribute to the difference of opinion under discussion?

Most important, probably, is his dispassionate approach; closely allied to this is the tight organization of both his short stories and his novels. It must be kept in mind that almost all French critics have been rigorously trained in the Greek and Latin classics, which most of their American counterparts have not. The result of this is a far greater attention to form and organization on the part of the French. Many of them, for instance, are utterly nonplused by praise of Thomas Wolfe, whom they consider a "sloppy" writer.[54] On the other hand, they see Caldwell's organization and style as strictly disciplined, especially the style, and they greatly admire its element of dispassion.

This very element is what is most bothersome to American critics, who feel that it proves Caldwell to be without sympathy for his characters. The difficulty is, of course, that, just as the buyer of a crossword-puzzle book used to expect to get a pencil with his purchase, the critic of a contemporary American novel seems to expect to find at-tached a prefabricated lump in the throat; that is, he anticipates that the author will supply the emotion, the emotional rapport, and the emotional identification along with the story. This accounts in part for the success of Hemingway, whose pose includes the manful striving for a dispassionate tone and the concomitant inability to keep his deep feeling from intruding. Clearly, then, the reader of Caldwell must establish his own emotional rapport with the characters, must do all of the feeling. The French, convinced by the technical excellence that it is worth the effort, are willing to do so; the Americans are not.

The other significant element is the humor, and here again Old World sophistication can inform New World naïvete. American critics like their emotions one at a time. Proof of this is provided by the critical acclaim given to Chaplin, whose theory of movie making involved alternating scenes of pathos and comedy, on the grounds that by this juxtaposition the pathos becomes more moving and the comedy more sparkling. As a consequence of this emotional one-track-mindedness, Americans are jarred by a character like, say, Jeeter Lester, who is pitiable, disgusting, and hilarious all at the same time. That feeling, plus the heavily Rabelaisian emphasis, causes most American critics to find Caldwell very unfunny, and often in bad taste. Yet characterizing a foreign writer's humor as better than Maupassant's and on a par with Rabelais' represents no mean concession on the part of a French critic, and shows how high Gallic esteem runs for Caldwell as a humorist.

Most disappointing of all the facets of American criticism illuminated by French comment on Caldwell is its snowball quality. After a few anti-Caldwell articles, critics began to hurl invective and have continued to write increasingly violent attacks. At the present time the most perceptive Caldwell critic appears to be the one who can coin the wittiest epigram to excoriate him.

Presumably, however, the French are neither blind nor obtuse. Their views make it seem that American critics might find it worthwhile to undertake a reappraisal of the work of Erskine Caldwell.

Notes

1. Dominique Arban, "Erskine Caldwell a quitté la 'Route au tabac' pour l'avenue Montaigne," *Figaro littéraire*, No. 69 (Aug. 16, 1947), p. 3. See also *Paris-Théâtre*, 11, No. 117 (1957), 3. This and all succeeding judgments of French critics have been translated by the author and are sometimes paraphrased, sometimes translated directly.

2. John Brown, *Panorama de la littérature contemporaine aux Etats-Unis* (Paris, 1954), p. 206.

3. Maurice Edgar Coindreau, "Lettres étrangères—*Tobacco Road*," *Nouvelle Revue française*, No. 250 (July 1, 1934), pp. 126–27.

4. Jeanine Delpech, "C'est à Paris que j'ai rencontré Faulkner nous dit Erskine Caldwell," *Nouvelles littéraires*, No. 1236 (May 10, 1951), p. 1.

5. Jean Simon, *Le Roman américain au XXᵉ siècle* (Paris: Boivin, 1950), pp. 147, 158.

6. Brown, p. 209.

7. Among them Coindreau, Brown, Simon, Annie Brierre, and Cyrille Arnavon.

8. Claude-Edmonde Magny, *L'Age du roman américain* (Paris: Editions du Seuil, 1948), p. 249.

9. Maurice Edgar Coindreau, "Lettres étrangères—Erskine Caldwell," *Nouvelle Revue française*, No. 278 (Nov. 1, 1936), p. 911.

10. Maurice Edgar Coindreau, "Panorama de la Literature Norteamericana Actual," *Mensaje de la Biblioteca Nacional* (Quito), No. 10–11 (July–Aug. 1940), p. 171.

11. Pierre Brodin, *Le Roman régionaliste américain* (Paris: Maisonneuve, 1937), p. 112.

12. Simon, p. 156.

13. Louis-Marcel Raymond, "Erskine Caldwell," *La nouvelle Relève*, 5 (Jan. 1947), 499.

14. Maurice Edgar Coindreau, "Erskine Caldwell," *Sur*, 10 (Jan. 1941), 79.

15. Cyrille Arnavon, *Histoire littéraire des Etats-Unis* (Paris: Hachette, 1953), p. 345.

16. Raymond, p. 500.

17. Marc Barbezat, "Caldwell et le mythe," *Problèmes du Roman* (July 1943), pp. 308–310.

18. Coindreau, "Lettres étrangères—*Tobacco Road*," p. 126.

19. E. H. Wessberge, "Erskine Caldwell: *La Route au Tabac*," *Etudes anglaises*, 2 (Jan.–Mar. 1938), 110.

20. Marcel Thiébaut, "Trois Romanciers étrangers," *Revue de Paris*, 44 (Dec. 1, 1937), 699.

21. Thierry Maulnier, "Erotisme américain," *Revue de Paris*, 64 (Jan. 1957), 155.

22. M. Ftillard, "Erskine Caldwell: *Journeyman*," *Etudes anglaises*, 3 (July–Sept. 1939), 317.

23. Jean Blanzat, "*Bararre de juillet* d'Erskine Caldwell," *Figaro littéraire*, No. 85 (Dec. 6, 1947), p. 5.

24. Rene Lalou, "*Le Doigt de Dieu* par Erskine Caldwell," *Nouvelles littéraires*, No. 1193 (July 13, 1950), p. 3.

25. Coindreau, "Lettres étrangères—Erskine Caldwell," p. 909.

26. Maurice Edgar Coindreau, *Aperçus de la littérature américaine* (Paris: Gallimard, 1946), p. 152.

27. Charly Guyot, *Les Romanciers américains d'aujourd'hui* (Paris: Editions Labergerie, 1948), pp. 102–103.

28. Simon, p. 158.

29. André Gide, " 'Interview Imaginaire,' Ecrivains et poètes de Etats-Unis d'Amérique," *Fontaine*, 5 (Aug. 1943), 11.

30. Edward Wagenknecht, *Cavalcade of the American Novel* (New York: Holt, 1952), p. 415.

31. Herbert J. Muller, *Modern Fiction* (New York: McGraw-Hill, 1937), pp. 220–21.

32. Leslie A. Fiedler, *Love and Death in the American Novel* (New York: Criterion, 1952), p. 415.

33. Carl Bode, "Erskine Caldwell: A Note for the Negative," *College English*, 17 (March 1956), 358–59.

34. "Caldwell's Collapse," *Time*, 52 (Aug. 30, 1948), 84.

35. Willard Thorp, *American Writing in the Twentieth Century* (Cambridge: Harvard U. Pr., 1960), p. 262.

36. "Caldwell's Collapse," p. 82.

37. Leo Gurko, *The Angry Decade* (New York: Dodd, Mead, 1947), p. 138.

38. Alfred Kazin, *On Native Grounds* (New York: Reynal & Hitchcock, 1942), pp. 372–80.

39. Jonathan Daniels, quoted in Harrison Smith, "Comic Citizens of the South," *Sat. Rev. Lit.*, 32 (Sept. 10, 1949), 15.

40. Kazin, pp. 372, 382.

41. Granville Hicks, *The Great Tradition* (New York: Macmillan, 1933), p. 300.

42. Harlan Hatcher, *Creating the Modern American Novel* (New York: Farrar & Rinehart, 1935), p. 273.

43. Malcolm Cowley, "The Two Erskine Caldwells," *New Republic*, 111 (Nov. 6, 1944), 600.

44. "Cartoon of a Theme," *Newsweek*, 24 (Oct. 16, 1944), 96.

45. Smith, p. 14.

46. Wagenknecht, p. 416.

47. Leon Howard, *Literature and the American Tradition* (Garden City: Doubleday, 1960), p. 305.

48. George Snell, *The Shapers of American Fiction* (New York: Cooper Sq., 1947), p. 271.

49. Kenneth Burke, quoted by Kazin, p. 382.

50. Reviewing the former in Etudes anglaises (8, Oct.–Dec. 1955), M. P. says that it is just not Caldwell, while René Lalou observes of the latter (*Nouvelles littéraires*, No. 1513, Aug. 30, 1956) that the French translation seems awkward.

51. The November, 1958 issue of *La Table ronde*, for example, is devoted to a series of answers to the question, "Why Do You Write?" Caldwell is the sole American author included and is found in the company of such writers as Cocteau, Romains, Maurois, Duhamel, Heinrich Böll, Moravia, and Pratolini.

52. No. 1574 (Oct. 31, 1957), pp. 1, 6.

53. (Lausanne: Impr. La Concorde, 1944), p. 134.

54. E.g., Bernard Fay, L'Ecole de l'infortune ou la nouvelle generation littéraire aux Etats-Unis," *Revue de Paris*, 44 (Aug. 1, 1937), 651, 653–54.

"Erskine Caldwell in the Soviet Union"

Mikhail Landor*

Erskine Caldwell's entrance to the Soviet literary scene was very swift. After several magazine publications, the collection *American Stories* appeared in 1936, followed by a second edition in 1937. Opening up to Soviet readers an entirely new world of American Negroes, farmers and city slum dwellers, Caldwell presented it not only from different angles but also in different manners, each one of which was organically suited to him. For he at one and the same time showed himself an adept in the chiaroscuro of the psychological novella and in folkloristic abruptness of delineation, in ringing laughter and the sombre tragedy of a cruel narrative about cruel things, in the artless anecdote and the modern inner monologue.

Caldwell's stories of American backwoods, eccentric characters and monsters were profoundly American, which made all the more surprising their affinity to Russian writings in denouncing stagnation, greed and spiritual emptiness. The first to perceive this affinity was Ivan Kashkeen, the most penetrating of our critics and translators of Caldwell, who drew attention to the unexpectedly familiar quality of Caldwell's intonations and the moral makeup of his heroes. Even the original humour of the story "Country Full of Swedes" was conveyed by Kashkeen with such inspiration and naturalness that it did not appear in the least exotic in the translation.

Caldwell's art was undoubtedly Leftist, and it was genuine art. He had had first-hand experience of hopeless poverty leading to extremes, to loss of the self and of the craving for solidarity amidst despair; he was able to offer such durable testimonies of the crisis years because the truth he expressed was not restricted to those years alone. Soon after the acquaintance with Caldwell's stories, Russian readers were able to assess the qualities of his social novels, *Tobacco Road* and *Trouble in July*.

Interest in Caldwell mounted in Soviet literary circles as well, and when, in May 1941, he came to Moscow for the first time he quickly struck up friendships with quite a few authors, notably Evgeni Petrov, a

*Reprinted from *Soviet Literature*, 3 (1969), 183–86.

fellow-humorist who shared his dislike for narrow-minded utilitarianism and the humdrum of the daily commonplace. Characteristically, among the Soviet books read by him Caldwell enthusiastically singled out *Ilf* and Petrov's *Little Golden America*.

June 22, 1941, found Caldwell on a tour of our country. The ensuing grave months revealed the man's fine personal qualities. For many days he reported from blacked-out Moscow to the United States, sending out features for newspapers and contributions to *Life* magazine. He visited the front line at Smolensk and eagerly questioned people freshly back from the front. On the home front Caldwell was impressed by the same kind of stamina he had found on the battlefields.

Caldwell always retained his presence of mind and his sense of humour, so important in that grim time. Ilya Ehrenburg recalled that even in an air-raid shelter Caldwell kept up his joking banter. But then, Caldwell's Soviet acquaintances working for the front never missed a chance for a joke. Lev Slavin recorded one of Evgeni Petrov's last jokes, inspired by his American friend. At the time Caldwell had a huge steel helmet, which Slavin kept staring at. Seeing this, Petrov said with feigned severity, "I say, Lev, what are you staring at that helmet for? Caldwell is a polite man, and it may well end with his presenting it to you. Then you'll be lost. It'll be like winning a cow in a raffle."

On his return to the States Caldwell published several books about Soviet people. His visit to the front and the months of ceaseless air raids he had shared with Muscovites created a tremendous impression on him. In Moscow his sincere, friendly books were warmly acclaimed. They were followed by *Georgia Boy*, which our readers came to like so much. The inexhaustible humour punctuated with sadness, the underlying humanism of the superficially farcical style appealed to those who had held out in a cruel and exhausting war. The novel was published in 1945—on rough newsprint—in a fine translation by Ivan Kashkeen and Natalia Volzhina. In 1947, the "Ogonyok Library" published several of Caldwell's stories in mass printings.

Then came an interval coinciding with the several years when few translations were printed at all, but from the mid-fifties the circle of Caldwell's readers began to expand rapidly and his popularity in this country rose tremendously.

His stories appeared in many popular journals published in Moscow and other places. Alongside with new stories older but previously untranslated ones were printed, among them such controversial ones as "Masses of Men" and "We Are Looking at You, Agnes." The "Ogonyok Library" put out two more books of Caldwell's stories in a total printing of 300,000. *Georgia Boy* appeared in a similar printing, and the Russian translation was followed by translations into Latvian and Lithuanian. A big volume of Caldwell's novels and stories was produced in 1956. Two new works, *Jenny by Nature* and *Close to Home*, were printed in Moscow first in a magazine and then as separate books, again followed by publications in Baltic republics. His novel, *A Lamp for Nightfall*, appeared in Ukrainian, and then in Russian his travel notes *Around About America* and chapters from the books *Call It Experience* and *In Search of Bisco*.

When Erskine Caldwell revisited our country in 1959, he was greeted by many devoted friends: prominent among them were a group of gifted translators with a very clear realization of the difficulties of conveying Caldwell's "plain style" in Russian and inventively seeking and finding suitable equivalents for his gems of folk idiom. (In addition to the two translators named before, one of them was Nina Daruzes, who translated three of Caldwell's novels about the South.) He also met his critics, active propagandists of his work, with some of whom, notably Elena Romanova, Caldwell become acquainted in Moscow as far back as 1941, and his readers of several generations.

Caldwell's wide popularity speaks for itself: his talent is essentially democratic. But this popularity, naturally enough, only enhances the need for criticism. A naive understanding of his stories in which his bizzare situations and "extreme cases" are treated as the common run is not infrequent among readers. The unsuspecting see them as true-to-life facts, which deprives the stories of their depth and leaves the author's skill unperceived.

Our critics have always warned readers of the fallacy of a literal understanding of Caldwell. As far back as 1939, Leonid Borovoy wrote: "These stories are built on quite obvious, improbable exaggerations. But we tend to forget that because no matter how absolutely fantastic the circumstances Caldwell's heroes act and speak with shattering authenticity, and the author retains a posture of ingenuous simplicity, himself being completely carried away by the events described." But for the artist's daring these stories, which emanate life and reality, would never have been written.

Obviously, the unsophisticated reader is more readily carried away by Caldwell's irrepressible wit than by the subtle psychological patterns of some of his stories. Ivan Kashkeen, writing enthusiastically of the richness of Caldwell's language, made special mention of these stories, written so lucidly and laconically. "Caldwell's laughter," he remarked, "which is often farcically coarse, sometimes dominates his other intonations, both tragic and lyrical, and the reader would do well to penetrate between the lines of such stories as 'The New Cabin' and 'The Cold Winter' and catch the sad undertones of *Georgia Boy*." Kashkeen especially admired Caldwell's command of the most diverse artistic means. "In form his stories may represent a domestic anecdote, a lyrical miniature, a musical poem in prose, a stinging satirical grotesque."

Kashkeen decidedly preferred these small-form works to Caldwell's novels, which, he considered, hardly rated the term "novel": rather they are long stories. According to Kashkeen, "with a few exceptions (to which, for example, belong the charming *Georgia Boy* or the very typical *Trouble in July*) they are simply a drawn-out anecdote spiced with the vivid, racy speech of his favourite characters."

On the whole this is, I think, true enough, especially as regards the writer's postwar books. Only too often they represented variations of familiar themes and were quite obviously "secondary" with respect to his small masterpieces. However, the exceptions are not so few as Kashkeen would have us believe, and in his bigger works, which he wrote at the same time as his best novellas, he expressed himself at least as comprehensively, albeit differently.

Leonid Borovoy saw his *Journeyman* as a sharp and pungent satire of sleepy backwoods; the author's merciless style reminded him of Gogol's grotesque play, *The Gamblers. Tobacco Road* sparked off a lively controversy in our country, and to this day it is regarded as one of the most vivid books about the idiocy of village life with its poverty and stagnation. In 1967, in Irkutsk, Siberia, a young lecturer by the name of Vadim Yatsenko published a small monograph on Caldwell in which he speaks of the unusual quality of his first novels, with their recurrent transitions from tragedy to farce. "Caldwell's temperamental, surging humour bursts out of all boundaries, completely depriving his narrative about horrible things of any trace of sentimentality," writes Yatsenko, and goes on to reproach our critics for having paid too little attention to such an original and widely read novel as *God's Little Acre*.

Yatsenko's monograph contains some interesting observations concerning Caldwell's art. He analyses the novellas and invites us to look more attentively at the simple-minded, garrulous narrators with whom the author seems to identify himself. His characters jibe at one another, but the reader clearly senses the author's irony and hears his laughter. With refreshing exactitude Yatsenko writes of Caldwell's comparisons, which are akin to American folklore, of the lyrical implications and rhythm of his psychological novellas.

However, he often fails to reckon with the fact that Caldwell as an artist is simply unthinkable without elements of the bizzare. This is all the more unfortunate as of late our critics have had some heated debates about the bizzare in literature and put out some penetrating theoretical works on the subject. They may be of help in penetrating deeper into the world of Caldwell who, in turn, reminds the theoreticians that modern grotesque has many facets.

For example, Yatsenko fails to appreciate fully such a fine story as "Daughter." He regards as unique and essentially quite implausible the basis of the plot, in which a sharecropper, robbed by his master, murders his starving eight-year-old daughter. Yatsenko finds that the exceptionality of the case prevents one from seeing the general. In fact, however, the reverse is true, and the exceptional helps reveal the general. The grotesqueness of the situation explodes the everyday reality and reveals its unbearability. Hunger destroys everything natural, and the very name of the story—"Daughter"—acquires a bitter and sinister meaning. But this is not all. To the sheriff, the whole affair is an unhappy but none the less common event. To the crowd milling in front of the jail it is an extraordinary event: "It don't seem right that the little girl ought to be shot like that." And the crowd's reaction is extraordinary: resenting the daily injustices of life, it displays human solidarity. The narrative is permeated with inner motion.

Soviet theoreticians examining the best literary works of the Renaissance and the epochs that followed note that the grotesque in them is profoundly critical and not at all static. This can be said of many of Caldwell's works, and I think Vadim Yatsenko is wrong when he detects in the story "Joe Craddock's Old Woman" the idea that that's how things have been and will be. For the author speaks not only of the bleak and brief existence of the prematurely faded farmer's wife. The story is built on a bizzare twist: thanks to the undertaker's efforts the prematurely aged woman becomes a deceased beauty. This transformation brings out the idea of beauty, and life itself, perishing in vain. It throws a stark light on the squalor of the commonplace, on the unrealized possibilities of which many had not even suspected.

The grotesque appears in Caldwell's bitterest stories as well as in the comic ones, and it adds unity to his creative world. The horrible and the comic continually change into one another. The Soviet critic Abel Startsev, who made a special study of American folklore traditions, regarded Caldwell as a worthy heir to them. Under his pen, Startsev writes, the old-time motifs and methods of "wild humour" come to life. The writer's early novels, which depict the lower strata and in which tragic notes can often be discerned, remind one of the Renaissance art, so full are they of a lust for life and unfettered humour, so challengingly do they refuse to be forced into conventional literary forms.

Despite his highly underivative features, Caldwell is akin to other American masters who came to the fore in the period between the wars. In Moscow in 1959, he spoke with enthusiasm of Sherwood Anderson and William Faulkner. Characteristically, these artists, blazers of new trails, also felt a kindred soul in him. Anderson in his *Memoirs* disassociates himself from writers with a university background, saying that he is "by nature a story teller," like Caldwell. One could add that they both skilfully combined the traditions of oral narrative with modern psychological culture. Faulkner retained to the end of his life the keen impression gained from Caldwell's first books, for he, better than anyone else, could truly appreciate their daring transitions and the freshness with which they depicted the South.

While in Moscow in the autumn of 1959, Caldwell wrote a few lines on Chekhov for the magazine *Foreign Literature*. They are filled with love, and there is in them a sense of profound kinship between the Russian and American short story. In fact, in his brief appraisal of Chekhov Caldwell seems to state his own ideal when he says that Chekhov understood all people and that is why he knew how to write of individuals so that the story acquired general significance.

"Erskine Caldwell and Southern Religion"

James J. Thompson, Jr.*

In the quest for the central theme of Southern history, religion—specifically Protestant religion—plays a crucial role. Throughout the South's past it has influenced the region's social life, pervaded its politics, confused its race relations, and helped to shape and mold the mind of the South. Southern literature has not escaped the all-encompassing influence of the church. Minor writers and literary giants alike have felt the tug and pull of Southern religion and have responded to it through the plots and characters in their works. Although Erskine Caldwell's credentials place him somewhere between the minor figures and the ranking authors of Southern letters, in an examination of religion as a theme in Southern literature Caldwell rises to a position of critical importance. Perhaps no other Southern author has dealt with the subject of religion as fully as has Caldwell.

Caldwell grew up in the "shadow of the steeple," as he tells us in his autobiographical *Deep South* (1968). His father, Ira Sylvester Caldwell, preached and pastored his way across the South as a minister of the Associate Reformed Presbyterian church. Erskine Caldwell feels that to have spent his childhood in such an environment "was my good fortune in life."

> The experience of living for six months or a year or sometimes longer in one Southern state after another, in cities and small towns and countrysides [writes Caldwell], and being exposed to numerous varieties of Protestant sects which were Calvinist in doctrine and fundamentalist in practice proved to be of more value to me than the intermittent and frequently-curtailed secular education I received during the first seventeen years of my life.[1]

The Reverend Caldwell exposed Erskine to the religious life of the rural South in many ways, especially by letting his son accompany him on pastoral visits.[2] But Ira Sylvester never forced his son's mind into any single religious pattern. When Erskine reached the age of seventeen his

*Reprinted from *Southern Humanities Review*, 5 (Winter 1971), 33–44.

father allowed him to decide for himself whether or not to embrace Protestant orthodoxy. Erskine rejected the church, but maintained an interest in it as part of the Southern landscape.

> Having been offered this freedom of choice, I wondered if I would ever lose interest in observing the spectacle of religious practices as I grew older. I thought not. I had been so close to evangelical religion for so many years that I had the feeling that even if I remained unchurched I would want to continue watching the effect its emotional appeal had on people as time went on (*Deep South*, pp. 12–13).

This concern for religion shows clearly in Caldwell's writings. In both his fiction and nonfiction he "observes the spectacle of religious practices" in the two main branches of Southern Protestantism, "watching the emotional appeal" of both traditional, "respectable" Protestantism and of the "holiness" sects, the Pentecostals, the Churches of God, the innumerable fundamentalist groups which hover along the periphery of accepted religious practice.

The middle- and upper-class Southerners who populate Caldwell's world have outgrown the heated rhetoric and overwrought emotionalism of frontier Protestantism. They have become passive participants in a formalized ritual that demands nothing more than regular attendance. Caldwell sees the "well-rehearsed ballet" of an Atlanta church service as assuring weekly salvation without the unpleasant soul-searching of an intense religious experience, with the added incentive that the well-ordered Protestant congregation offers social and business contacts that assure one the amenities of life. Traditional Protestant churches also provide a ready outlet for the energies of the civic activist: "Boosterism," says Caldwell, characterizes the mainstream Southern churches of today (*Deep South*, pp. 78, 127–128). Perhaps the feverish scurrying about to raise funds for a new youth building or Sunday school annex has replaced the socially taboo emotionalism of "old-time religion."

Although Caldwell has only recently set down many of his thoughts on "respectable" Protestantism in *Deep South*, the same ideas have directed his writings over the full scope of his career. In the novel *Episode in Palmetto*, published in 1951, he captured the essence of middle-class Protestantism. He wrote that

> going to church was the most important social event of the week in Palmetto, where dates were made by young people and visiting days were arranged among relatives and family friends, and it was almost unheard of for anyone to appear in a new dress or a new hat until it had first been worn to church on Sunday. For as many years as anyone could remember it had been the custom, both before services began and afterward, for the men to talk about business and political matters, and it was not unusual for a tract of timber to be sold or a vacancy in a

county office to be filled as a result of a few minutes conversation on the steps of the Methodist or Baptist church (p. 70).

Palmetto's churches in 1951 did not differ much from those in the Deep
South of 1968. The social side of religion has always been important.

The mainstream Protestantism of Palmetto, Estherville, and other
fictional towns appears from time to time in Caldwell's work. More often,
however, Caldwell deals with Southern whites who look to the fundamentalist sects for spiritual solace. The sociological function of this brand
of religion first attracted Caldwell's attention in the despair-ridden days
of the 1930's. In two books—*You Have Seen Their Faces* (1937) and *Some
American People* (1935)—Caldwell examined the lives of the forgotten
and dispossessed, the poor whites who appear in his novels as the Jeeter
Lesters and Ty Ty Waldens. Starvation faced these people in many guises,
both physical and emotional. Society denied them the dignity, comfort,
and hope they desired. Primitive, emotional religion gave the poor white
what society would not—the dignity of equality before God, the comfort
of promised salvation, and the hope of eventual release from the trials of
life.[8]

On a more practical plane, fundamentalist religion offered the poor
white a source of entertainment, a means of injecting a touch of color into
a drab and somber life. "Back on the hillsides," said Caldwell, "the tenant
families fell prey to various forms of religious excitement which served to
take the place of normal entertainment."[4] In Caldwell's fiction this facet
of Southern religion often takes on a humor that obscures the suffering
and emotional deprivation revivalism served to alleviate. In this vein,
Caldwell writes of the work camp inmates who petition for a revivalist
preacher to replace free movies as the nightly entertainment.[5] In a similar
fashion, *Journeyman's* unprincipled Semon Dye, who seduces wives,
cheats at dice, and drinks corn whiskey, brings an air of excitement to
rural life, and leaves a "hollow feeling" when he departs. But whether in
the 1930's or 1960's, fundamentalism has served an enduring purpose. In
1968 Caldwell still found lower-class whites drawn to the humorous
stories and electric guitar music of the gospel tabernacle (*Deep South*, pp.
42–43).

Three themes—sexuality, degenerated ethical standards and
fatalism—flow side by side throughout Caldwell's treatment of Southern
religion. Caldwell weaves them together, whether consciously or not, to
form the finished fabric of Southern religion. The three themes appear on
both levels of Caldwell's religious world, on both the respectable and fundamentalist planes. In one form or another, they can be found in the most
elaborate Episcopalian cathedral as in the storefront churches and ramshackle chapels of the sectarians.

In Caldwell's fiction, the sexuality inherent in Southern Protestantism pervades the whole range of religious experience, from the sex-

ual imagery of otherwise sedate sermons to the orgiastic emotionalism of
the revival meeting. Robert Cantwell hints at this when he compares the
sexual acts of Caldwell's characters to "some tribal or underworld rite."[6]
But Cantwell fails to stress adequately the connection between sexuality
and religion. The pulpit descriptions of sexual immorality and the moan-
ing and writhing of revival services furnish an escape from the harshness
of reality into a realm of release and heightened sensibility. Semon Dye
understands this, for he preaches about the most lurid sins imaginable. "I
believe in preaching about the things people want to hear about," he says
to an awed listener. "I've found out what the people want to hear, and I
give it to them" (*Journeyman*, p. 116).

Though the sexually-explicit sermon contributes to the peculiar combination of religion and sexuality, it is in the revival meeting, in
Caldwell's novels, that sex and religion come together most fully. Full-
blown revivalism appears only in *Journeyman*, but it would certainly appeal to the other residents of Caldwell's world. The Lesters of *Tobacco
Road*, the Waldens of *God's Little Acre*, and the Douthits of *Tragic
Ground* would deeply appreciate Semon Dye's artistry. Semon has spent
thirty-odd years perfecting his technique, and at the age of fifty has
become the consummate revivalist. He builds his meetings to a fever pitch
with the power and fascination of his voice. When his listeners begin to
scream out in religious agony Semon drives them into an orgasm of suppressed energy. Sexuality saturates the entire process, as men and women
writhe on the floor in physical ecstasy. A teenaged girl leaps up and
down, shakes her body, and rips off her clothing. Men and women shout,
body mingles with body, and emotion rips through the little clapboard
building as Semon casts out the Devil. The climax of the meeting leaves
the people emotionally spent and physically exhausted. They drag
themselves home like men after a hard night of whoring. But their exhaustion transcends the bone-weariness of physical labor; rather, it recalls the
ebb of passion and bodily vigor that follows sexual gratification. Sex and
religion, compressed into the revival meeting, produce an experience of
profound pleasure, a welcome relief from the stifling continuity of rural
life.

Another aspect of sexuality in Caldwell's Southern religion concerns
the way sex buffets, torments, and mocks the ministers of the fictional
South. They struggle to master their lusts, but inevitably they fail. Ty Ty
Walden, the central figure in *God's Little Acre*, expounds a homespun
philosophy of religion that sets the stage for the fall from sanctification experienced by Caldwell's preachers.

> There was a mean trick played on us somewhere [says Ty
> Ty]. God put us in the bodies of animals and tried to make us
> act like people. That was the beginning of trouble. If He had
> made us like we are, and not called us people, the last one of us

would know how to live. A man can't live, feeling himself from the inside, and listening to what the preachers say. He can't do both, but he can do one or the other. He can live like we were made to live, and feel himself on the inside, or he can live like the preachers say, and be dead on the inside. A man has got God in him from the start, and when he is made to live like a preacher says to live, there's going to be trouble. . . . The girls understand, and they are willing to live like God made them to live; but the boys go off and hear fools talk and they come back here and try to run things counter to God. God made pretty girls and he made men, and there was enough to go around. When you try to take a woman or a man and hold him off all for yourself, there ain't going to be nothing but trouble and sorrow the rest of your days (pp. 299–300).

Ty Ty argues for uninhibited sexuality as an integral part of the "natural" life God intended man to live. Robert Hazel calls this viewpoint a "pre-psychological innocence" that relieves Caldwell's characters of the need to check their insatiable quest for "fulfillment."[7] Using Hazel's suggestion in a religious context, one can see that Ty Ty's belief in natural sexuality leads him to formulate a religious rationale. He says that preachers, the professional men of religion, have perverted and confused the relationship between religion and sex. In Ty Ty's terminology the minister who advocates sexual restraint has lost the essence of life placed in him by his Creator.

In his novels Caldwell pays little attention to the type of minister that Ty Ty so firmly dislikes. To be sure, preachers who are "dead on the inside" crop up from time to time. The Reverend Bigbee, the Methodist minister in The Sure Hand of God, tries to divorce himself from sexuality. His wife Christine confesses to a friend that her husband forces her to undress in the dark; wear long-sleeved, floor-length nightgowns; and listen to him read the Bible in bed. The Reverend Bigbee's cold and unresponsive nature compels Christine to run off with another man. In despair, Bigbee slashes his arm with a broken glass and bleeds to death. How fitting, Ty Ty might say, that a man who had long ago killed himself on the inside, should complete the job by destroying the living façade that harbored a dead interior.

Caldwell does not usually take pains to draw a full portrait of such a man as the Reverend Bigbee. More often, he deals with the preacher who tries in vain to stifle the sexual urge. From furtive encounters with adolescent choir members Caldwell's men of the cloth move on to the beckoning allurements of the prostitute. Dismissal and banishment generally follow these forays into sin, but paradoxically, the promise of sexual redemption and salvation leads the minister to an inexorable conclusion—he falls in love with the whore who has toppled him from his pedestal of righteousness. Only through total commitment to a prostitute, the embodiment of sexuality, can the minister attain that natural state defined by Ty Ty Walden. Caldwell seldom allows his preachers to go the full route implied by Ty Ty's philosophy. But he does suggest enough to enable one to infer that Ty Ty may have been right.

In several novels Caldwell portrays the fallen minister. The Reverend Haddbetter, the Free Will preacher in *Claudelle Inglish*, cannot prevent his own seduction by the "country whore" Claudelle. "I might as well have held up my hand when it was storming and tried to stop thunder and lightning," says the disgraced preacher. "That's how hopeless it was. No man could've stopped her from what she set out to do" (p. 150). Haddbetter loses his pulpit, his dignity, and his wife. He pleads with Claudelle to marry him, but she laughs at him. Unable to enjoy the natural sexuality introduced to him by Claudelle, he shoots both himself and her. Haddbetter almost attains the redemption accorded those who live the natural life. But having thrown off his "dead inside" he fails to complete the transition to the life envisioned by Ty Ty. Death remains the only solution.

Preacher Clough of the Rugged Cross Church has a similar encounter with a prostitute. He justifies his excursion into the pleasures of the flesh as a means of learning about the sins one ought not to commit. Preacher Clough, writes Caldwell,

> had convinced himself that it was his duty as a minister to learn all he could about life in general so he would be able to base his sermons on the realities of personal experience and observation. After that it had not been difficult to convince himself that it was necessary for him to spend a night in a motel so that he would have a first-hand understanding of that particular phase of life.[8]

The Reverend Bisbee of the Four-Square Church and Raley Purdy, pastor, founder, and sole member of the Supreme Being Missionary Church, fall in love with women without realizing they are prostitutes. Purdy fights his seduction at the hands of Connie Mangrum, but then falls in love with her.[9] Bisbee wishes to marry Clementine Bradley after their first meeting.[10] Purdy and Bisbee react differently when they discover the occupations of Connie and Clementine. Pastor Purdy, drawn to the animal sensuality of Connie, offers to give up his religion for her. When she rejects him he follows her to Savannah. The Reverend Bisbee becomes enraged, but confesses his love for Clementine. The dignity of his profession prevents him from marrying her. But in a symbolic gesture, Bisbee accepts the gift of a former whorehouse as the new parsonage. Spurning Clementine, but ensconced in a house once dedicated to the sexuality he has rejected, the Reverend Bisbee rests in a state of suspended animation midway between Ty Ty's natural life and the dead life of the ministry.

A second theme running through Caldwell's work centers on the absence of an ethical code in Southern religion. A religiously based standard of ethics, regulating man's involvement with his fellow beings, simply does not exist among Caldwell's Southerners. The great ethical precepts of Christianity have degenerated into hollow shells—hollow because the core has rotted away. Caldwell's father recognized this in the 1920's. "As he saw it," writes Caldwell in *Deep South*, "exultant Protestantism in the South had degenerated into excessive emotionalism—which was the glorification of religion for religion's sake—and all ethical values inherent in the Bible were ignored and replaced by the theatrical antics of evangelism and the mesmerizing promises of spirituality and immortality" (p. 164). Caldwell's portrayal of Southern religion adheres to his father's view, for in the novels and short stories spanning four decades, the Southerner's lack of ethics comes through strongly. Even the lone Universalist minister who appears in Caldwell's pages concentrates on filling his church on Sundays rather than on the ethical lives of his congregation.[11]

The absence of a sexual ethic is the most glaring form of ethical hollowness amid Caldwell's religious folk. The unbridled sexuality promoted by Semon Dye's orgiastic religion and Ty Ty Walden's "natural" life encourages a view of man and woman that ultimately cheapens and degrades the act of sexual union. Semon Dye, a character who would feel at home in most of Caldwell's books, combines religion with a rapacious sex hunger. The two do not here conflict, for adultery and casual fornication seem natural to many of Caldwell's characters. The unethical nature of adultery never presents itself to the fundamentalists whom Caldwell pictures. But on the second plane of Southern religion—the level of middle-class respectability—the issue is more complicated. George Swayne, the church-going Baptist banker, has never contemplated extramarital sexual activity until his wife hires a young mulatto maid. Because the Southern code justifies abuse of the Negro, George feels no qualms about raping Kathyanne Bazemore.[12] George's Baptist faith has failed to implant within him a respect for the sexual sanctity of woman, especially the black woman.

George Swayne's treatment of the mulatto maid illustrates a larger problem facing all Caldwell's Southerners. In the attitude toward the black female two facets of Southern religion's ethical poverty intermingle. Not only does the religion portrayed by Caldwell fail to protect the sanctity of the sex act, but it also accepts the brutalization of the Negro. Caldwell hints at the relationship between religion and racism throughout his fiction, but he does not make the open condemnation until the mid-1960's. *In Search of Bisco*, a nonfictional work published in 1965, shows the unmitigated suffering of Southern blacks. The whites Caldwell writes about attend church, pray and contribute their dollars to foreign missions, but not once does their religion compel them to denounce the mistreatment of the Negro. In *Deep South*, published three years later,

Caldwell makes his indictment more explicit by writing of the South's "infectious racial hatred—a hatred germinated and cultured by perverted principles of Christian religion" (p. 252). *Trouble in July* (1940) fictionalizes this hatred, for Miss Narcissa Calhoun, a seller of religious literature, circulates a petition to send the Negroes back to Africa, while Preacher Felts helps her set up the situation that leads to the lynching of Sonny Clark, an innocent Negro boy.

The race hatred of Caldwell's churchgoers feeds into a broader stream of ethical barrenness. Race aside, Caldwell's intensely Protestant Southerners treat their fellow man in a casual manner, often bordering on contempt. Madgie Pugh, closely related to seven Baptist ministers, cheats her maid out of her salary.[13] Mrs. Effie Verdery demands rent money from a bedridden woman in order to contribute to the Baptist mission program.[14] Mr. Gene, who "prays the loudest, sings the loudest, and makes the most noise when he puts money in the collection box," lets a white share-cropper slowly starve to death.[15] In "Slow Death" Caldwell tells the poignant story of a family dying of cold and hunger who receive from a church nothing but prayer and "a pair of khaki pants with two holes the size of dinner plates in the seat."[16] One might argue that such examples have nothing intrinsically to do with religion. But Caldwell takes pains to show the religious fervor of those who commit these inhumane acts. Caldwell intimates that the religious devotion of these people convinces them that they need not worry about how they treat the poor and oppressed of either race. Uninspired to do good by their religion, Caldwell's characters lapse into the social apathy too often typical of evangelical religion.

Occasionally, one of Caldwell's characters, usually a minister, sees an act so flagrant that he cannot remain silent. The Caldwell residents of Palmyra treat blacks in the traditional Southern manner, but the brutal and senseless murder of a Negro leads the town's minister to "preach about it in public."[17] More often, Caldwell's preachers condemn only such public "sins" as drinking and gambling. Pastoral condemnation of these vices becomes a joke, for no one takes such tirades seriously. The clergymen of Maguffin assail the horrors of Skeeter Wilhite's roadhouse, but their attacks send dozens of church members rushing to Skeeter's place in order to join in the fun.[18] In short, Caldwell's ministers and church members condemn such minor vices as drinking and gambling, while they miss the whole point of religious ethics. They pay lip service and nothing more to the Christian tradition that demands the accordance of decency and respect to one's fellow man. Ty Ty Walden's conception of "God's little acre" illustrates the plight of Southern religion. Ty Ty dedicates an acre of his land to God but he constantly shifts it about to keep it out of the way. The implication is that God's portion can be set apart and shunted to the side. In the same way, the ethical content of Christianity can be acknowledged—witness the denunciations of gambling, drinking and "immorality"—but it can also be set aside when it gets in the way of such important things as racial dominance and sexual gratification.

Fatalism constitutes the final element in the religious life of Caldwell's characters. This involves a perverted version of the theology of John Calvin, for the Calvinism of Caldwell's fictional world has lost the inner vitality it once possessed. No longer does one strive to prove himself a member of the elect; rather, he sits passively while an omnipotent God has His way. The evangelical tradition of Southern religion does little to mitigate this fatalistic belief in man's inability to forge his own destiny. Technically, the fundamentalist emphasis on salvation through the conversion experience enables the believer to work hand-in-hand with God in the quest for eternal life. But in practice, Caldwell's characters live in a world they cannot control. Caldwell expresses the essence of this plight when he writes of Spence Douthit who "could not see any sense in trying to maintain beliefs to live by when he had no control over his existence, for no matter how strongly he struggled against fate, he was never able to master it."[19]

Caldwell develops the idea of a distorted predeterminism most fully in *The Sure Hand of God*. The novel examines the destiny of Molly Bowser, whose fate lies cradled in "the sure hand of God." Although her life involves a gradual, but continual, decline into the depths of degradation and debasement, she accepts her ruin with equanimity. The final blow comes when Molly, out of money and hounded by her pious Methodist neighbors, ends up in a whorehouse. She harbors no bitterness or malice, only a spirit of resignation. "Maybe it's for the best, after all," she says. "I feel more at home down here than I ever did anywhere else, and maybe it's where I belonged all the time" (p. 243). Molly's fate appears predetermined, but she does not question the wisdom of a God who would subject her to such an existence.

Jeeter Lester shares Molly's sense of fatalism, but he represents the other side of the reaction to predeterminism. Molly passively awaits her fate, and as her rendezvous with defeat draws nigh she gives up and accepts her plight. Jeeter also acknowledges the reign of an omnipotent God who controls the lives of men. But he, unlike Molly, does not let it undermine his ability to grapple with the world, and he expounds his views without any sense of defeat or resignation.

> God is a wise old somebody [Jeeter says]. You can't fool him! He takes care of little details us humans never stop to think about. That's why I ain't leaving the land and going to Augusta to live in a durn cotton mill. He put me here, and he ain't never told me to get off and go up there. That's why I'm staying on the land. If I was to haul off and go to the mills, it might be hell to pay, coming and going. God might get mad because I done it and strike me dead. Or on the other hand, He

might let me stay there until my natural death, but hound me all the time with little devilish things. That's the way He makes His punishment sometimes. He just lets us stay on, slow-like, and hounding us every step, until we wish we was a long time dead and in the ground.[20]

A note of cockiness appears in Jeeter's speech that contrasts with the sentiments uttered by Molly Bowser and Spence Douthit. Optimism softens Jeeter's fatalism. He assures his son-in-law that some day God will "bust loose with a heap of bounty and all us poor folk will have all we want to eat and plenty to clothe us with. . . . God is going to treat us right" (pp. 12–13).

This optimistic tone must not be overemphasized. Black despair can be found to offset it, as when a character in *Certain Women* says, "Sometimes I think the good Lord has deserted us all in this terrible world" (p. 171). Perhaps it suffices to say that virtually all of Caldwell's Protestants share a degree of fatalism and resignation. In a world controlled by fate (in the form of God) sexual license and lack of ethical concern make sense. Man's destiny does not rest in his own hands, so why not pursue the pleasures of the moment? Ethics count for nothing, for could anything unintended exist in a world governed by an all-powerful deity? Lust and race hatred must have some purpose if God allows them to exist, reason Caldwell's characters.

Caldwell's portrayal of Southern religion can be summed up, then, in the three themes of fatalism, poverty of ethic, and sexuality, but does Caldwell's account coincide with historical reality? In most of his work Caldwell can plead poetic license, but in *Deep South* he sheds the cloak of the novelist and becomes a combination of reporter, historian, and autobiographer. With surprising consistency, both in *Deep South* and in the fictional works, Caldwell captures the essence of Southern revivalistic religion. The latent sexuality which he brings to the surface has certainly been a feature of the Southern religious scene, especially of the more fervent brands of fundamentalism. Caldwell's emphasis on the ethical barrenness of Southern religion penetrates to the very heart of the South's religious difficulties.[21] Finally, Caldwell ferrets out the curious Southern blend of John Wesley and John Calvin, of evangelicalism tinged with fatalism.

Caldwell's picture is, of course, partial. Southern life and Southern religion are far more complex than they appear in Caldwell's pages. But Caldwell makes no claim to the completeness of the historian. Rather, he fictionalizes important features of the Southern religious scene, and in so doing creates a fictional religious world which, in its approximation to reality, furnishes an invaluable aid to the historian of the South, who, in all of his attempts to describe revivalism, could never create a Semon Dye. Through this one character, Caldwell has captured vividly the taut emotions and physical vigor of orgiastic religion. In other works, he has transmitted the complacency and hollow boosterism of the middle-class church. The novelist's imaginative perception has enabled Caldwell to offer valuable insights into the nature of Southern religion, and for this, those intrigued by the South should pay him tribute.

Notes

1. Erskine Caldwell, *Deep South: Memory and Observation* (New York: Weybright & Talley, 1968), p. 1.

2. Erskine Caldwell, *Call It Experience* (New York: Duell, Sloan & Pearce, 1951), p. 24.

3. Erskine Caldwell and Margaret Bourke-White, *You Have Seen Their Faces* (New York: Viking, 1937), pp. 142–43.

4. Erskine Caldwell, *Some American People* (New York: McBride, 1935), p. 261.

5. Erskine Caldwell, "A Country That Moves," in his *When You Think of Me* (Boston: Little, Brown, 1959), p. 102

6. Robert Cantwell, "Caldwell's Characters: Why Don't They Leave?" *Ga. Rev.*, 11 (Fall 1957), 256.

7. Robert Hazel, "Notes on Erskine Caldwell," in Louis D. Rubin and Robert D. Jacobs, eds., *Southern Renascence* (Baltimore: Johns Hopkins Pr., 1953), p. 320.

8. Erskine Caldwell, *Jenny by Nature* (New York: Farrar, Straus & Cudahy, 1961), p. 56.

9. Erskine Caldwell, *Miss Mamma Aimee* (New York: New Amer. Lib., 1967), pp. 80, 114.

10. Erskine Caldwell, *Certain Women* (Boston: Little, Brown, 1957), p. 73.

11. Erskine Caldwell, *Georgia Boy* (New York: Duell, Sloan & Pearce, 1943), p. 20.

12. Erskine Caldwell, *Place Called Estherville* (New York: Duell, Sloan & Pearce, 1949), pp. 30–42.

13. Caldwell, *Place Called Estherville*, pp. 64, 75–76.

14. Caldwell, *Place Called Estherville*, pp. 194–95.

15. Erskine Caldwell, "A Knife to Cut the Corn Bread With," in his *Southways* (New York: Viking, 1938), p. 181.

16. Erskine Caldwell, "Slow Death," in his *Kneel to the Rising Sun* (New York: Viking, 1935), p. 176.

17. Erskine Caldwell, *Close to Home* (New York: Farrar, Straus & Cudahy, 1962), p. 149.

18. Erskine Caldwell, *A House in the Uplands* (New York: Duell, Sloan & Pearce, 1946), pp. 188–89.

19. Erskine Caldwell, *Tragic Ground* (New York: Duell, Sloan & Pearce, 1944), p. 176.

20. Erskine Caldwell, *Tobacco Road* (New York: Scribners, 1932), p. 30.

21. For an account of this problem from a specialist's viewpoint, see Samuel S. Hill, Jr., *Southern Churches in Crisis* (New York: Holt, Rinehart, Winston, 1967), *passim*.

"An Interview in Florida with Erskine Caldwell"

Richard B. Sale*

SALE: Mr. Caldwell, I have the impression that for a while your work was picked up by the Marxist critics as an illustration of their point. Then they turned you off when they felt it wasn't. Was that true in the late 1930s?

CALDWELL: I wouldn't know the motivation behind that kind of attitude. What I do know is that when I was trying to write short stories and get them published in the little magazines of the day I had nothing to do with the so-called large circulation magazines; they didn't print my stories. But the little magazines did for a number of years. And to me it didn't matter what the motivation of the editorial policy was as long as they printed the story. So I was probably on both sides of the fence, the conservative and the liberal. I don't know if anybody ever gave me a great fanfare for writing along the Communist line. Maybe they did, but I wasn't aware of it. If I did write that way it was because it happened to be the way I was writing, not because I had any active motivation for it. I vote, but I vote for the man and not the party. That's been my policy. I wouldn't say I'm even a Democrat or a Republican at the present time, or have I ever been.

SALE: Does the Southerner represent a large part of your reading public?

CALDWELL: Well, that's difficult for me to say; I don't know anything about the breakdown of the circulation of a book so much. Traditionally, of course, more people read books per capita in the North than they do in the South, so they say. But as for how you break those sales down, I really don't know.

SALE: Do letters from readers give you a general impression of reader reaction?

CALDWELL: I don't know how to answer that because the kind of letters I get are really from students more than anybody else. I guess students these days are a little more sophisticated or open-minded or whatever you want to call it, and there seems to be no particular pattern to where they

*Reprinted from *Studies in the Novel*, 3 (Fall, 1971), 316–31

write from. Fifteen or twenty years ago, I would get what I call pan letters, pan letters which said, "Why do you write about the bad side of life
in the South? Why don't you write about the good side of life in the
South?" But that has died out completely. I guess that generation's died
off or stopped reading or something. I don't remember getting anything
like that recently because in recent years it's been mostly from students,
and from no particular region. So I don't know who the other book
readers are right now. I've never seen a typical book reader anyway. I
don't know a typical Southerner. Maybe everybody's typical.

SALE: A few minutes ago you mentioned that country people used to
be taken up with fundamentalist evangelical religion. It was true of many
people throughout the country. Is anything around to give the people that
temporary excitement that everyone seems to demand in some form or
another? I have the feeling that those particular kinds of religious institutions are fading out. And if they're fading out, what's going to give people
that emotional kick? What's going to give them all that sex and violence
that they got from the church?

CALDWELL: Of course, speaking lightly of that, it's always been my
theory that all these country musicians and folk singers out of Nashville,
the new generation of the old religious revival people in the back hills of
the country, these people are all the younger generation that came out of
the hills and down to Nashville. They're the country singers of the time
and make more money than their fathers ever made back in the hills making moonshine or anything else. And, as you know, there might be a lot of
good things coming out of that environment. We know all the present day
popularity of Kentucky Fried Chicken.

SALE: Do these little churches or itinerant preachers still get the same
number in their congregation or in their audiences or in their revival ses-
sions as they did in the past?

CALDWELL: They're getting bigger all the time. They're becoming
more sophisticated. Billy Graham and Oral Roberts are the most successful ones.

SALE: Well, are they giving the people that same tremendous emotional kick that they had in small, sweaty one-room church with the
temperature rising?

CALDWELL: I think there are two phases to that old time revival back
in the countryside. One was, of course, the emotional uplift during
rhythmical music and singing songs and preaching, but basically that
emotionalism was stimulated by the fact that these people had something
to do and were being entertained in a way. That was before the advent of
television and before most of the picture shows. I think in the old days the
people sought that out, immersed in it because it was entertainment.
Now, of course, in keeping with the tempo of the times, these evangelists
have to have a great stress upon music. In the old days a small organ
would do but—

SALE: Now they have a minister of music.

CALDWELL: Now they have to have a musical leader with a number of performers in the band or the orchestra or the choir or whatever it is, to make a lot of noise. Something else developed, the musical side of it, just as much as the old hell-fire preaching ever did. There's very little that people can preach against any more. When life becomes so sophisticated, it's hard to arouse anybody by preaching about sin. So you really have to sugarcoat the message with a lot of entertainment. I think entertainment probably is just as important as ever, even more so to attract a crowd. And they do attract the crowds. All up and down—I don't know about Texas, now—but all up and down this Atlantic side, revivals by traveling evangelists are still very much in vogue. They might have them in a convention center. I don't think they use any tents like they used to do, but they'll take over an armory or a school where they draw big crowds. But it's always with this musical accompaniment. That has a lot to do with it. The people still go.

SALE: It's just a more sophisticated replacement? The tradition hasn't vanished?

CALDWELL: I don't know how much longer the religious grip is going to hold the old people, I mean to what extent. I guess it's going to stay because I notice that the collections I hear about in churches are still pretty good. As long as that money comes in, why, it's going to keep on. Of course, if the states begin taxing church properties and churches, making them pay a sales tax on collections, it might make a difference.

SALE: Let's talk a little bit about humor in your books. Some of the short stories that I read seemed to be strictly for fun, and most of your work has humor mixed with serious matters. Humor is a means of relief, a contrast to the serious matter of a novel or story. Do you consider humor as a device when you're putting a story together?

CALDWELL: A question like that is a little bit baffling to me, because I don't know the reasons for these things. I only know what happens when you're doing a story. And I think if I had to find some excuse for this way of doing, say, a short story, I would answer that in life, maybe not in fiction but in life, there's always a balance there between tragedy and humor. The most tragic occurrence can also have its humorous aspects and vice versa. When you are telling the story of an occurrence that does have a tragic overtone or tragic burden, if you look beneath it or beyond it or to the side of it, there's always some humorous incident or some humorous aspect to that story or to that event. And I wouldn't know consciously how to go about doing it. All I would know is that it happened that way when the story was told.

The most serious incident could go to a tragic extreme; yet there's bound to be some light side to that whole affair. A man might be swimming for his life. He might be in danger of being drowned, and yet if he survives that tragedy, and does not drown but comes up on the shore, there's bound to be some reaction in which there's a light side to that great event in his life where he almost drowned. He would say something like, "I thought I was gonna die," or "I thought I was gonna drown." But what he was actually thinking about was something trivial which might be irrelevant to the whole idea. In other words what was going through his mind not only was the danger of being drowned but the thought of some humorous incident that had occurred or might occur.

SALE: A crab was pinching his toe.

CALDWELL: Or something. Anything at all that would sort of balance that great tragic moment. So I think that's what life's like. I think that's real.

SALE: Whether you planned it to be that way or not, humor also heightens that crisis.

CALDWELL: I couldn't explain it. It's just that it's the way it occurred to me. I don't know why or what, but it had to be that way. Otherwise it would not be satisfactory to me.

SALE: In the novel, *Close to Home*, there was a jarring juxtaposing of comedy and the most intense violence. What was your purpose there?

CALDWELL: Well, you ask a question there that embarrasses me because I don't know why I do certain things. I have no forethought. It's just something that develops that way.

SALE: Were you happy with doing it that way?

CALDWELL: Well, I had to be; otherwise, I would have thrown it in the wastebasket.

SALE: You wouldn't have sent it to the publisher?

CALDWELL: When I'm not satisfied with something I throw it in the wastebasket immediately.

SALE: You've never been reticent about throwing things away?

CALDWELL: No, I've got the biggest wastebasket in town. So that's the method I use to file an error. I try, and if there's an error, I throw it out. I have to be satisfied. If I'm not satisfied, I don't want anything more to do with that.

SALE: Can you recall any one particular published book that's given you more difficulty than any other?

CALDWELL: Well, no. No. I couldn't. Because by the time I finish a book I'm sort of numb. I feel that if I've gone that far with it and this is what it says here now, it must be right; therefore I'm satisfied. But as for trying to analyze it, I couldn't do it. I'm just too numb with the idea because it's all been used. It's all been expended and there it is. I have to be satisfied page by page as I go, not with the end result but with the page result. One page may be done a dozen times, but I won't go to the next page until I'm satisfied with that page. I just have to go at it that way.

SALE: Has that always been your working procedure?

CALDWELL: Yes.

SALE: You don't write a number of pages and then make serious revisions?

CALDWELL: No, I like to see the page. I like to see the typewritten page the way it should be in a finished condition. If I have to cross out something or write something in, well, I'll go back and do that page over again to make it look better, to make it look more like print, rather than look like a sprawling mess or something. So I'll do it over maybe a dozen times because I might change one word or ten words or one sentence or take out half a dozen. But if it doesn't look right, if it looks messy, if it looks imperfect, I have to go back and do that page over on the typewriter to make it look clean and finished.

SALE: Have editors ever severely edited your work?

CALDWELL: No, no. I learned early in life that that was not necessary. Maxwell Perkins was the first editor I ever knew and he published a number of my short stories in *Scribners* magazine, when *Scribners* was a respectable periodical. He was also book editor of Scribner's, and he also published a collection of my short stories in a book. The first novel I wrote after that was *Tobacco Road*. I remember very clearly that he wrote to me about it and said that he was going to publish the novel and that it wouldn't be necessary to change anything in it. So I took that to mean that revision could be done by the writer and not by the editor.

Ever since then I've gone on the principle that that's the way it is. Now if I make a mistake in grammar or something, I'm very happy to have it brought to my attention. If it escapes me and it escapes my wife, Virginia, who proofreads, copyreads, everything I do before I send it out, if it escapes both of us, I'd be very happy for an editor to say this is the wrong construction or something. But as for changing something, no. I say just forget it. Send it back. Nothing has ever been changed that I have written.

SALE: So there's never been any serious conflict between you and the publisher about revision?

CALDWELL: No. I've moved enough from one publisher to another for various reasons but not for that reason. I've been with a half a dozen publishers in my life, but not because of any editorial difficulties. When I write something, that's the way it's going to be as far as I'm concerned. Whether somebody else likes it or doesn't like it means nothing to me at all. That's the way it is. Not that I think I'm perfect or anything of this sort, but I did the best I could and I don't think anybody else could tell me how to do it any better. If anybody else could think so, why hadn't I thought of it myself? So I wouldn't take that kind of advice. Well, you know a lot of editors around these publishing houses think they have to take a book apart to hold their job or to get a lot of praise from the upstairs office. But you see that's something that doesn't interest me at all, what their troubles are. I'm only interested in what I'm saying.

SALE: Did you find Perkins to be an excellent editor?

CALDWELL: Well, excellent in the sense that he never changed anything. He gave me a lot of advice, nothing to do with the writing: He said stay out of New York. And he would never take me to a restaurant to eat, even for lunch. We'd go to a hamburger stand, hot dog stand, stand up and eat.

SALE: What was the reason for this?

CALDWELL: He said too many young writers come to New York and eat very luxurious restaurant meals and they get the idea, they get the feeling that this is the way it's going to be. Their ideas get warped about being a writer. They think everybody's entitled to luxuries in life, which is not true. Oh, he'd have a long talk about those things.

That was the best advice I ever had from him. I got out of New York, too, and stayed out.

SALE: Yet you did some writing in New York. You stayed in New York for some work, didn't you?

CALDWELL: Yes, I went there to live because I didn't have anywhere else to go. But I had nothing to do with the publishers at that time. I was living unknown to people, publishers. I was just trying to write stories. I did that off and on for a couple of years.

SALE: Have you ever had any problem finding a publisher since you published *Tobacco Road*?

CALDWELL: No. The reason I left Scribner's was because one of the Scribner's people—someone by the name of Scribner, Junior or somebody else, it had nothing to do with Perkins—didn't like a book I had written. They took me in to their oak-paneled conference room and gave me an hour of advice about writing. The duty fell on one of the editors, who was not Perkins. He gave me a lengthy talk about what I had written, how it was not suitable for the book readers who bought Scribner's books, how many of these readers are very proper elderly ladies who would be offended if they published a book of the nature that I had written. And so he advised me to write another book with that in mind. I said, "No, thank you." And I walked across the street to the Viking Press and they published the book. That was the closest I came to not having a book published.

SALE: Back to the matter of humor. Randall Jarrell, in very warm priase of several of your works, said that one of the better things that he had seen in your humorous writings was the technique of understatement and repetition. Frequently, one of your characters will say something and then very quickly repeat it again and maybe a third, or fourth time. Is this to portray that character more clearly?

CALDWELL: That's just the way he would act.

SALE: People just repeat themselves?

CALDWELL: That's just his nature to say it. I couldn't, I wouldn't want to change his nature. I wouldn't want to edit the character, in that sense. I just have to do what these characters demand.

SALE: Do you work for an incantation effect by repeating key words or key statements several times? Is there some kind of magic to it?

CALDWELL: Well, you see it's difficult for me to make a comment even on that. I always have to write this story about this person the way he is. And he's already formed himself or he is forming himself in my mind because I don't know who he is. I never saw him before. He's a new guy to me. So I have to go along with him whatever he may do. I might not approve of what he does. I might not like his language. He might be too vulgar to suit me, but I can't help that. He's already gone that far. You can't go back and start over with him, make him different. If somebody has certain characteristics, well, that's the way they have been growing in my mind, the way they're living, the way they are. So I have no control over these people.

SALE: Your main interest, when writing, is not the effect on the reader?

CALDWELL: I don't do that intentionally. I don't know what my characters are going to do next, and that keeps my interest up in the book I'm writing. If I knew what they were going to do all the way to the end, I'd be too bored to go ahead and write the thing. Because then I would already know. Now these people have to expand or grow or be as they live from one minute to the next, from one day to the next. So I have no policy or method of doing these things about people. It's just what the people want.

SALE: You don't do any such thing as work out the structure of a novel and know what's going to happen in the last section of the book in advance?

CALDWELL: I fear I wouldn't know how to make an outline. I wouldn't know how to make a progress sheet. I wouldn't know how to do anything like that.

SALE: No kind of interim plot outline?

CALDWELL: Nothing. I don't have any notes. Nothing of that kind. I don't want them, because then you're restricted, you're constricted by what you've presupposed may happen. How do you know what's going to happen? How do you know who's going to come along? It might be a man or woman. It might be a giraffe or an elephant. How do you know what you're going to see when you walk out? So you're not going to sit here and write a story and say there's an elephant coming down the street. So you've got to wait and see what appears. Maybe it's going to be a horse. We don't know.

SALE: Do you make it a practice to notice the details of your surroundings, the sort of details of Georgia sharecropping, what farm gear looks like, what the harness for a team of mules looks like?

CALDWELL: Well, let's put it this way. You see, everything, every piece of fiction, is based on experience.

SALE: Yes.

CALDWELL: We're not considering science fiction, of course. The fiction we're talking about is based on experience, and the experience has to be in the mind of the writer. Now this experience is not necessarily something that you went out to find. It's not something you went out seeking. It might be something very casual at the moment but it might become momentous later if you recall it. So when you ask, do you see details when you're out somewhere, traveling around, going to the country, the answer is sure, you see everything. But it might make no impression at all at the time. No impression whatsoever. But in recollecting, you think, oh, I saw that tree that was bent over by a hurricane. It was falling on a house. I remember that now. But at the time, well, you see nothing. You look beyond that. It's just a flash as you go by, but you recall it. So everything is experience. Every writer has to have some kind of experience to write upon. But you don't go out looking for experience. If you go out and do that you're crowding it. It becomes to obvious and then it's [not] authentic. So you don't have to go out and marry ten women in order to learn something about female characteristics. The mind has a recollecting ability to it and so it will recall something that's made some deep impression upon you earlier. It doesn't have to make a deep impression to begin with. The details of what you have experienced stay with you. You recall them, you recall them because one thing leads to another; it sort of snowballs, builds up, and first thing you know you have the whole clear complexion of certain conditions or circumstances or people.

SALE: What you've said over and over is that you are your only reader, that if the writing says what you want to say then you accept it.

CALDWELL: I'm the reader. I don't know that I have any other readers.

SALE: You wrote somewhere that, if you are not your own satisfied critic, you don't deserve an audience.

CALDWELL: Did I say that?

SALE: Not exactly; but you meant, I think, you were writing for yourself.

CALDWELL: Yes.

SALE: And if you represent enough interests of other people, then they'll buy your books. They'll first accept your books and then buy them.

CALDWELL: Well, of course, I never think of books being read by other people. I think of mine as being printed and bound, and that's as far as I go with a book. I don't consider who's reading a book or how many are. But I'm sort of pleased by someone who says he read such and such a book. And what pleases me most are the people who are *not* critics. They're not dilettantes. They're not people who are trying to put you on. It might be a bellboy in a hotel, somebody you meet in a bar, or just anybody who comes along. You know he's not trying to put you on; he wouldn't have said it if he hadn't read it. Of course, there's a lot of forced reading going on.

SALE: Are publishing patterns changing?

CALDWELL: The impersonality of publishing is becoming very apparent and acute. Someone gave me a *New York Times*, yesterday, I guess it was, in which there's a piece about New York publishers running wild, playing musical chairs. That's no joke because what has happened as we know is that the corporate enterprises are taking over publishing, like RCA or Hertz Automobile Rental. They're buying up publishing houses. And the people in the business, the editors, the presidents are constantly moving the past few years. As I say, I've been with many publishers in my time, and I've noticed that the people I thought were in a publishing house are not there today. They were there yesterday, but now I don't know anybody there. The impersonality of publishing I think does worry a writer who's been accustomed to having a sort of feeling of stability with a publishing house. Now the younger generation of writers will probably grow up being accustomed to this musical-chairs situation.

The younger generatioin will probably become accustomed to it and expect nothing else, but the older generation to which I belong will certainly become disconcerted every once in a while when the guy you thought you knew who was in charge of everything suddenly moves out and some guy you never heard of takes his place. That's one of the trends or changes in publishing which is probably going to continue the corporate idea of mixing up candy companies and automobile rental companies and the publishing house—making a conglomerate of it.

SALE: Did you begin your writing career by emulating other writers? Any specific writer?

CALDWELL: Well, all right, that's very easy to answer, if I can explain myself about it. This is how it happened. You see I'd been in journalism, sort of a country-style journalism, weekly papers and what not, and I'd been the country string correspondent, covering sporting news and what not. Every month you paste up a column. You get two dollars for it. And so when I was in high school, I did have maybe five or six string correspondent jobs in Augusta, Atlanta, Savannah, Macon, all around in Georgia. I got out of high school and was fortunate enough to get a scholarship to the University of Virginia. That was my first window to the world.

When I got to Charlottesville, I discovered that there was a library at the university. I hadn't anticipated finding a library. I thought a library was a place where you had a lot of dusty old books, dictionaries, and so forth. But this library had a basement room, a very small room devoted to contemporary or current publications, publications we now call the little magazines. They were experimental magazines and they came from all over the U.S. There were some from England. There seemed to be dozens of these small magazines in existence which I'd never heard of before. I didn't recognize the names of anybody who was writing these stories, and I still don't know who they were. They were just guys writing short stories they couldn't get published anywhere else, all experimental. I would read these things and I was amazed that all these people were writing stories and being published, and I thought I could do it better than they did. I started trying to write the kind of story that I would write or could write, not imitating what they were doing, but with the idea that they could be written. There were no names that I would recognize even now. That's how I got the idea that I should write my way rather than somebody else's way. I had no models to go by other than the fact that here were sort of offbrand names, guys who were writing and had succeeded.

SALE: So there were no big names to emulate?

CALDWELL: Big names were selling their stories to the *Saturday Evening Post*, and I had no interest in the *Saturday Evening Post*. Oh, I read Octavus Roy Cohen, for example, about Negro life in Birmingham. I read one of his stories and it didn't interest me. It all seemed a fallacious kind of thing to do. Cohen was a big name in those days. His stories were all in dialect, and that immediately set me against writing anything in dialect. I've never written anything in dialect in my life. To me that bogus dialect is nothing. Real dialect should be in the rhythm of speech, not in the clipping off of letters, putting apostrophes and what not. I was convinced the way to go was in the rhythm of speech of the person talking.

SALE: I'm glad to hear you say that. You never play games with speech patterns.

CALDWELL: That's something I learned.

SALE: You discovered that by reading people who write badly? Like Cohen?

CALDWELL: Yeah, well, he's dead now, we can't say anything bad about him. But there were a lot of Negro stories written by white people in those days that try to imitate the sound of dialect which to me was completely false because to me that was not English. That was not the way it should be done. It should be done in the rhythm of speech. Well, that's what you asked and that's my answer.

SALE: I didn't know what you were going to say.

CALDWELL: I know it might be fashionable to say I've been influenced by—I don't know—Thomas Hardy or Joseph Conrad or somebody.

SALE: Do you feel that you in any way helped in breaking taboos—barriers toward the acceptance of realistic fiction?

CALDWELL: Not consciously, no.

SALE: I don't mean through planning, but as a matter of fact.

CALDWELL: Well, I didn't even think of that, you see; I was only thinking of myself and not of the other people. Not what effect my writing would have on other people, but only the need to do it my way. And, so I had nothing to go by as an example of what to do or what not to do. I just did it my way. Now, if it's true that there is a universal Puritan tradition, possibly that influenced me a great deal in that I knew certain limits of conduct, training, or whatever there was in my environment. I knew certain concepts of morality, and that influenced me only to the extent that I stay within those limits.

SALE: So nothing was planned as far as breaking any barriers about what was accepted and what wasn't accepted?

CALDWELL: No, because I was writing my own experience. My experience was the way it was, and you don't change those things to fit some concept. I'm pretty sure I would have known that certain things were offensive to other people because I had learned something in life. I didn't read the work of established writers. As I said, I didn't read any of those things at that time. I was only reading the experimental work. Well, that fitted in with my attitude of writing at that time. I was just going along with the trend, maybe, of writing as I felt I had the experience to write about. It was only later after I left college that I began reading books as a book reviewer. Then, of course, I read many books.

SALE: That's bound to have given you a pretty good picture of what was being published, wasn't it?

CALDWELL: In a way, but I was not interested in anything I read, though. Those books did not interest me because I felt I could do better. Those books were always sort of second rate, and I reviewed them as such.

SALE: Of course; you were right about ninety-nine percent of the time, weren't you?

CALDWELL: I had a lot of complaints from the editors of the papers I was writing for. "Didn't I ever like anything? Why was I always panning every book that came along?" I don't think I missed any masterpieces along the way.

SALE: You said in *Call It Experience* that you're primarily a writer of books rather than a reader of them. Have you any particular affinities toward practicing writers, people who are in the trade now? Have you read books in recent years that you thought highly of?

CALDWELL: I do read a few books a year, maybe four or five. What has been my habit, I suppose for many years, is to read one work of a writer whom I have heard of as being worth reading. That's how I get to a book, and when I read one book by a writer, I'm satisfied. I don't have to read four of them to form an opinion. For example, we'll take some of my contemporaries like William Faulkner. I read one book of Faulkner which I liked very much. I thought it was superior and I still think it's a wonderful book and perhaps it's one of the least known that he's ever done. The title of the book was *As I Lay Dying*, which was not a sensational book. It was a solid book. So I formed my opinion of Faulkner just on that one instance, and I think I was right in forming that opinion. The same is true of other writers. One book only, that's all I read. I read one book of Steinbeck, for example. I read one book of Hemingway. I read one book of Dreiser; I read one book of Sherwood Anderson. Now when it comes to anybody since that bracket of time, I'm at a loss to pick out anybody that I consider in the same field with those writers that I've mentioned. Because I don't think contemporary fiction is as good as it was.

SALE: Why do you think so?

CALDWELL: It could be that the novelists I mentioned were writing about a time that I am more familiar with. I don't know whether that's it or not. But they did leave a deep impression on me. On the other hand, the present fiction bothers me; it has taken a license that I think is not worthy of fiction, which I think is detrimental to fiction: that is the use of pornography.

SALE: Oh?

CALDWELL: Because to me pornography is a dead end. And when you reach a dead end, you do not progress as a writer. What can you do next that is more pornographic than you have done? Basically, you see, pornography takes all the romance out of sex. It completely wipes it out as far as being romantic. To me life does have romantic elements. If you try to eliminate the romantic out of life, what have you got left except dullness and pornography? It can get pretty dull.

SALE: Has it been extremely frustrating to you to have been accused at times of producing pornography?

CALDWELL: Well, of course, to me my work was not. It was only being what you might say romantic, not obscene or anything. It only bothered me to the extent that I thought it was unnecessary to accuse me of these things. I did not think my work should have those labels at all. That's the only thing that's bothered me.

SALE: In *Call It Experience* you mentioned that you sometimes find a certain snobbishness among other writers who make a distinction between *artist* and *professional writer*. How would you describe yourself if you had to use one of those two terms?

CALDWELL: Well, I never thought of that in such a connection. Usually you think of a professional writer as being someone who does odd jobs and he's very professional at it. He can write something for a trade journal, or he can write a speech for the president of his company. That's usually what I would think of being a professional writer, but I'm just a writer with no adjectives in front of it. I am not artistic in a sense and I'm not professional in a sense, just because I work at it making a living. My occupation is writer, that's all. That's my occupation. An artist should be a painter or a sculptor or something.

SALE: There is artistry in words, I think.

CALDWELL: Well, there's artistry in words, of course, but then you're getting very close to preciousness. You're writing style rather than content, and to me content is far more important than style. Anyone can probably spend a good part of his life working up a certain style, but then he has to make content conform to the style. Whereas I believe that your style will come out of your content, that the content will dictate the method, the style that you're going to write in. So I'm always a little bit suspicious of people who are stylists and who might be artists of the word and so forth. I'd rather be more content to be a common practitioner of content in writing.

I think if you set out to be a storyteller, that's more important than anything else. And that's what I still try to be, a storyteller in the written word. If you don't have a story, I don't know what else you've got in writing fiction. I don't know what else there is.

SALE: There is an element of heroism, something of a classical quality, in the characters of your early Georgia stories. More recent works, such as *The Last Night of Summer* don't seem to have that quality.

CALDWELL: Well, I won't talk about the idea of their being heroic or classic. I don't know about that. But there were two different ideas involved there. *The Last Night of Summer* describes a situation in modern society. Society, I think, degenerates, and when it does degenerate, you don't have heroics because everything is taken for granted, that's the way it's going to be. Nobody's going to do anything about it, so go ahead and accept it as it is: a very dull existence. Whereas if you do put up a fight for something, why, then you do have an element of the ability to rebel and change something. I don't consider *The Last Night of Summer* to be an example of anything other than what it was. It's one of those dead-end things where nothing is ever going to get any better or worse than it was before. It's going to stay like it is. The people who are involved in that kind of situation are rather pathetic in the sense that they don't help themselves or they don't have the ability or the courage to help themselves. They just go ahead and live it as it is without taking any action about it. It's sort of contemporary in a way, you might say.

SALE: I guess that one of the definitions of hero is a rebel, a man who fights against conditions as they are, no matter how absurdly he does it.

CALDWELL: As I see a hero, he doesn't always have to win; he can lose too, you know. But he can make an effort. With people who don't make an effort, you don't expect anything better than what they are or what they do. They don't have the courage to make an effort. In this particular book, in this particular story, the people had no ambition and no desire to do anything but what they did. They're willing to stay in their rut and live it out.

SALE: Have you finished the Georgia cycle do you think?

CALDWELL: I don't know. I hope not. I don't know what will happen next.

SALE: What is in the works right now?

CALDWELL: Nothing right now. I'm taking my six months off, so on the first of March I'll have to get busy. Now, the two most recent books I did were set in Tennessee, *Summertime Island* and *The Weather Shelter*. They were Tennessee stories. Now, whether I will do any more in that area I don't know. I'll have to wait and see. I can't have another work which I've already decided upon. I've got no formula. I've got no outline. I have nothing. I've just got some blank paper there and I've got to put down the first words, the first paragraph. Then I'm going to see what happens after that.

SALE: Do you work from the assumption that people's sexual relations are sort of a core to everything else? Or am I misreading much of what I've read of you? Your novels suggest that the major moves the characters make are traceable back to their sexual impulses.

CALDWELL: Well, of course, that's the motivating factor in life as well as physical survival. First you've got to survive and then you have this natural proclivity or this natural instinct. I would put it number two. After number two, then you can build up a whole series of motivations like social status and wealth and all. But I think physical survival is your first. Your first instinct is to have something to eat. Then nature takes over after that and you have this impulse, this built-in impulse or sexual proclivity. It has a great influence on what you do. And in order to support both of those two instincts, the survival and the sexual thing, you have to produce some sort of wealth.

SALE: I realize it is difficult to talk about much of the business of writing.

CALDWELL: Well, I will comment on anything that I know anything about. But there are a lot of things that I don't know much about, so I hesitate to make a statement or give an opinion on them. Writing is one thing I know so little about that I get embarrassed by trying to explain it.

SALE: Critics frequently know little about it, but they seem to be perfectly willing to comment about it just the same.

CALDWELL: I think that's an interesting subject. I wish I knew more about it.

SALE: Do you agree that some people talk out their creations and some people write them?

CALDWELL: Yes. That's one thing I didn't like about Hollywood, the idea that every idea had to be told to the producer or director or whoever before you did anything. Well, to me what's said is already gone. Why do it now? I never got along well in Hollywood for that reason. Pre-made, prewrapped doesn't interest me. But there are a lot of writers, I'm sure, who could explain themselves very clearly. A fellow by the name of William Saroyan likes to talk, and he writes too. He could be an actor, too. He could be all kinds of things.

SALE: Damon Runyon could talk.

CALDWELL: I don't know how he ever got anything written. I only knew him briefly. During that time all he would do was talk.

SALE: How do you react to the term "regional writer"?

CALDWELL: I'm very much impressed by what I call regional writing because I think regional writing is much more important than trying to be universal or whatever the word would be for that, than trying to write the great American novel. I think the regionalist, if he knows what he's doing and can do it well, is a much more important writer than the big overall kind of thing where you write about something that might be applicable to all American life. There are still a lot of regions in this country that I think real fertile for writers. Even now I think they're real fertile. I keep on thinking of that Evangeline country in Louisiana between New Orleans and Lake Charles. To me it has always been very interesting, but I don't know enough French to get along with the people who live there. You have to know the dialect they use there to understand what they're saying. And the Indian reservations always interest me as a good fertile ground, too. There are a lot of things still around up in North Dakota, South Dakota, Utah, Colorado, which are very rarely done, very rarely written about. Apaches in Arizona.

SALE: There seems to be no particular home base, like the Georgia country, that lures you back.

CALDWELL: No, because I like wherever I have traveled. At the time I'm living there; that's why I like it. I have no unpleasant feelings about any place, after having lived there. But I don't necessarily want to go back and live in the same place again.

SALE: Do you feel like that any of these places represented a sort of geographical ballast for your fiction writing?

CALDWELL: Well, you see, I don't know how it affects other writers, but I like to see life in perspective, not so much in retrospect but in perspective. So I like to be away from what I'm doing, what I'm writing about. I like to be at a distance. But I like to go at all angles for that distance. In other words, go around the whole compass. Not, say, live in New Hampshire and look at it for a lifetime through a telescope. I would rather go from New Hampshire to North Dakota or into Oklahoma or Arizona. I like to go around the whole compass and keep that spot in mind as I move around so it gives me a perspective. I work on the theory that it does. And I like the process. I'm not exactly a Southerner or I'm not a Floridian; I'm not a Georgian; I'm not anything you can name or pin down because I have lived everywhere and I like everywhere I've lived. I started out when I was probably three or four years old moving around with my parents like that and I've never stopped. And I still like it.

"True Myth-Maker of the Post-Bellum South"

Calder Willingham*

Much of southern literature until recent times can profitably be seen as a spiritual, emotional, and philosophical reaction to the Civil War; indeed, perhaps all of that literature able to be identified specifically as "Southern" can be so regarded.

The storytelling, joke-swapping, legend-loving, and language-enamored tradition of Southern culture, energized and driven by post-bellum shock, and by the great social changes that have occurred in the nation as a whole, have produced, I believe, the large number of extraordinary American fiction writers who have come from the South.

One of the most remarkable of these writers is Erskine Caldwell, a man who today, rather sadly, is somewhat neglected and ignored in literary circles. Surely that will not always be so. A good case can be made that the inventor of *Tobacco Road*—far more than William Faulkner, Thomas Wolfe, Carson McCullers, Flannery O'Connor, Eudora Welty, Robert Penn Warren, or any other Southern writer one can think of—is the true myth-maker of post-bellum Southern literature.

Comparisons are odious but sometimes illuminating. In 1944 the literary reputation of William Faulkner was at such low-ebb practically all of his books were out of print. I myself paid premium prices (in today's values, almost $50 each) for rare and hard-to-find copies of *The Sound and the Fury* and *As I Lay Dying*. The gifts of Faulkner were denied on all sides; James Thurber wrote savage and amusing parodies of the Faulkner style in *The New Yorker*, Phil Rahv dismissed him in *Partisan Review* as a writer of "horror stories."

Then the tide suddenly changed from low to high, from sluggish neap to roaring rip, as it often does on the shores of literary fashion. An essay in *Kenyon Review* spoke of Faulkner as a creator of Southern legends, as the genius overlord of the small universe of Yoknapatawpah County. Malcolm Cowley soon followed with a more widely read essay saying much the same thing in *Partisan Review*; Cowley said "myth" in-

*Reprinted from *Georgia Historical Quarterly*, 59 (Summer 1975), 243–46. Originally published as a review of a new edition of *Tobacco Road* (Savannah: Beehive Pr., 1974).

stead of "legend," and expanded the idea. French literary intellectuals then awed the American literary establishment by declaring that Faulkner "wrote like an angel." The Nobel Prize followed.

However, although his great gifts for storytelling and language cannot be denied, William Faulkner must be considered a self-conscious and deliberate literary artist rather than a true myth-maker or creator of legend. If myth and legend have any meaning, it is in a context of folk literature; stories or poems or songs that come from an unrefined and uncultivated public and are understood by that public without the help of exegetical notes in *Partisan Review* or other literary or academic journals.

The works of William Faulkner have been enjoyed and appreciated for the most part by a very small and highly cultivated reading audience. None of his books can be said to have been truly popular. To call him a "myth-maker" is a brilliant stroke of reverse snobbery and it simply is not true. A legend that appeals to and is comprehended by a tiny audience of cultivated readers is no legend at all. Perhaps the murky but often dazzling works of William Faulkner can be called great literature—that is debatable—but let us not call William Faulkner a maker of legends because he was no such thing.

On the other hand, Erskine Caldwell *was* a creator of legends and a maker of myths. Such novels as *Tobacco Road* and *God's Little Acre* reached a huge audience and did it naturally. The characters in these strange, unique, and incredible stories are truly "mythic" and legendary. Jeeter Lester in *Tobacco Road*, and Ellie Mae, Lov Bensey, Dude, Sister Bessie are mythical characters larger-than-life-sized; they are figments of creative inspiration that have become permanent fixtures of the American consciousness, and the wild adventures that befell them are truly legendary.

Millions of people know Jeeter Lester and his love of fresh-plowed land and his hatred of the "durn mills." Millions, indeed. Who does not remember Ellie Mae and her harelip, the fantastic Ellie Mae who drags her bare bottom along sandy ground on her way toward Lov Bensey and his sack of turnips, while Dude throws his ball against the collapsing house and Ada stands faint with pellagra on the porch and old Grandma staggers off to gather twigs to light a kitchen stove for which there is no food?

And then Sister Bessie with "no bone in her nose" and her phenomenal experiences in an Augusta hotel, wherein the hotel clerk keeps putting her in the room of one man after another and collecting money for it, too. They just can't figure out what room she's in, says Sister Bessie. All of this, on a mad excursion during which the moronic Dude enjoys his new car filled with blackjack oak firewood, unburnable iron-like wood that is meant for sale to the gentry in white-columned mansions.

Erskine Caldwell was not only the true Southern myth-maker, he was also a master of what has come to be known as "modern black comedy." Although there was, certainly, a core of grim truth and reality to the unspeakable poverty and human degradation of his characters—as witnessed so eloquently by the unforgettable photographs of Margaret Bourke-White in this superbly printed, bound, and made Beehive Press edition—it is a great error to regard Caldwell humorlessly as so many have done in their outrage at the truth in his work.

A great error beyond any question, because Caldwell was primarily, in my belief, a comic genius. One laughs even as one is horrified. It might be (and has been, for many) hard to conceive of the humor of a father in effect selling his harelipped daughter for a bag of turnips, but as Caldwell writes it the scene is hilarious. Terrible, awful, shattering, and very, very funny.

To read *Tobacco Road* again after so many years is a curious and fascinating experience. The book springs to life as if it were written yesterday. The style is simple, unadorned, dry, and immensely supple and powerful; the narration is wholly unpredictable and at the same time unerring; characters are boldly and quickly drawn with broad slashing brushstrokes. How easy it is to understand the great audience reached by such writing. Add to these writing gifts comic genius and a withering moral indignation and one arrives at a very remarkable writer, who deserves far more of honor and comprehension than he has received.

Certainly, for all its popular appeal, Caldwell's writing was highly personal and idiosyncratic. There is much he did not do as a novelist nor even attempt. Paradoxically, therefore, to the cultivated reader, who has prejudices and expectations to shed or forget, he is apt to be an acquired taste, even as early Louis Armstrong is an acquired taste. It seems clear Caldwell was not a realistic novelist at all, but a narrative poet, a wild comic genius and a true myth-maker of a South still reeling in shock and dislocation from a terrible war.

However, Erskine Caldwell's achievement was tremendous by any standard and his direct and indirect influence on American fiction was profound. Many writers of our time owe him a great debt, whether they are conscious of it or not. The ironic vein of much modern writing was discovered on that dirt Georgia path down which Lov Bensey walked with his sack of turnips; there, and on *God's Little Acre*, lies the mother lode—an unacknowledged mine of inspiration that has heard the ring of many hammers in our own day.

Time, I think, will correct this injustice. It is my belief Erskine Caldwell will emerge as the true myth-maker of Southern literature and the real progenitor of "modern black comedy" as well. Comparisons are odious even if illuminating and one would not want to deny William Faulkner or any other wonderfully gifted writer his or her due. But it would seem possible, irony of ironies, that a Nobel Prize was given to the wrong man for the right reason.

This Beehive Press edition of *Tobacco Road* is beautifully made and the photographs of Margaret Bourke-White form a moving adjunctive to it. The volume belongs in the library of any person who appreciates handsome books and has a serious interest in Southern literature, and an interest also in germinal American writing.

"Southwestern Humor, Erskine Caldwell, and the Comedy of Frustration"

R. J. Gray*

Erskine Caldwell enjoys what is, perhaps, one of the most dubious distinctions possible for a writer: he is popular—one of the most, if not *the* most, popular of all modern Southern writers. This has brought him money, security, even fame (who, after all, hasn't heard of him?), but also a great deal of obloquy. It is usual, for example, to claim that Caldwell is a sensationalist posing as a journalist: a historian, of a kind, who tends to forget facts and concentrate instead upon bizarre, intriguing details. The assumption, somehow, is that Caldwell is really after verisimilitude, and that only another, more important ambition—namely, his wish to be successful in the accepted meaning of that term—has prevented him from ever properly fulfilling his desire.

Few things could, I think, be further from the truth. Certainly, there is a journalistic aim implicit in most of Caldwell's work, in a sense that he was in a way trying to tell us what it is like to live in the South now. But with him this aim assumes new dimensions because (as he himself has more than once suggested) he is not so much interested in verisimilitude as in special pleading: the kind of report that tends to emphasize certain chosen aspects of its subject. He has a number of observations, *important* observations as he sees it, to make about the South and he makes them to the exclusion of almost everything else. The result is something which is perhaps closer to the art of the caricaturist than to the comparatively objective account of the reporter: particular aspects of the described situation are continually being exaggerated in the interests of theme.

What is Caldwell's theme? Stated simply, it is one of degeneracy—the reduction of the human being to the lowest possible levels of his experience. In appearance, at least, his rural characters bear no resemblance at all to Jefferson's idea of the noble tillers of the earth. Grotesques responding only to a basic physical urge, they represent an abstraction not merely from the human to the animal but from the complete animal to a single instinct: "Ellie May got down from the pine stump

*Reprinted from *Southern Literary Journal*, 8 (Fall, 1975), 3–26.

and sat on the ground. She moved closer and closer to Lov, sliding herself over the hard white sand . . . 'Ellie May's acting like your old hound used to when she got the itch,' Dude said to Jeeter. 'Look at her scrape her bottom on the sand. That old hound used to make the same kind of sound Ellie May's making too. It sounds just like a little pig squealing, don't it?' "[1] The difference of perspective, when we compare this description of Ellie May in *Tobacco Road*, with, say, most of William Faulkner's portraits of poor whites, is a radical one. Faulkner tends, usually, to take us inside the consciousness of his "peasants," to share the wealth of their inner life as well as the poverty of their condition. Caldwell, however, nearly always insists—as he does here—on keeping his readers at a distance; in other words, on presenting his characters entirely in terms of externals and, in the process, dehumanizing them.

This distancing, dehumanizing approach is responsible among other things, I think, for the nature of Caldwell's comedy. Nearly all of his country folk operate between the poles of greed and sexual desire, they are the slaves of appetite, and such humor as his novels possess is generally the result of the violence which these appetites provoke. In fact, the comic note is at its wildest in his fiction when the two appetites actually clash, throwing the victim of the subsequent crossfire into confusion. The description of Ellie May quoted above, for instance, is part of a much longer sequence in which Ellie's father, Jeeter Lester, uses Ellie to distract his son-in-law Lov while he steals a bag of turnips from him. To summarize the complicated interplay of hunger and lust which follows is hardly to do justice to the Grand Guignol effects of the situation. As soon as Jeeter does grab the bag of turnips Lov turns to recover it, but he is immediately pulled to the ground by his would-be seducer. Jeeter makes off into the woods with his capture and meanwhile his son, his wife Ada, and his grandmother all keep beating Lov down, whenever he tries to rise up in pursuit, until Ellie May can crawl on top of him. With a mixture of excitement and desperation, Lov then resigns himself to his fate; while Dude, the son, goes off to find his father before all the turnips are eaten, and Ada and her mother-in-law sit whimpering over their inability to participate in either the eating session or the rutting. The scene is, as I have said, a long one and throughout it is presented as a *spectacle*, something to be watched with detached amazement. That perhaps is why Caldwell places three Negro passers-by at the gate to the Lester farm, to witness the occasion and register appropriate reactions to it: we share with them, as it were, the role of a self-conscious audience. And that also is why he permits even the participants in the action an occasional note of commentary, as if they too were able to stand back from what they were doing and so become their own spectators. Jeeter, for instance, pauses mid-way in his flight to expatiate on the possible quality of the turnips, and on the relationship between this and his own social condition: " 'Has these turnips got them damn-blasted green-gutted worms in them, Lov?'

Jeeter said. 'By God and by Jesus, if they're wormy, I don't know what I'm going to do about it. I been so sick of eating wormy turnips, I declare I almost lost my religion. It's a shame for God to let them damn-blasted green-gutted worms bore into turnips. Us poor people always gets the worse end of all deals, it looks like to me.' "[2] Here, as when Dude supplies us with a system of deliberate comparisons for Ellie May's behavior, the character seems to be emphasizing the illustrative quality of his own actions—their representative status as part of a series of Georgia Scenes.

The phrase, "Georgia Scenes," is not chosen at random. For it points to one aspect of his Southern inheritance on which Caldwell leans heavily; an aspect that is symptomatic of the radical differences obtaining between him and such other celebrants of the Southern farmer as Ellen Glasgow and Elizabeth Madox Roberts. More than a hundred years ago, in 1835 to be precise, a lawyer and academic named Augustus Baldwin Longstreet published a book with the imposing title of *Georgia Scenes: Characters, Incidents, etc., in the First Half-Century of the Republic*. To the extent that it *was* imposing, though, the title was a misleading one since a major purpose of the book was comedy. In a series of sketches which varied in approach from the purely descriptive to the dramatic, Longstreet presented his readers with illustrations of life in the remoter parts of the state. The sketches were linked by the appearance in nearly all of them of a narrator bearing a suspicious resemblance to the author himself: a kindly, generous but rather pompous and patronising man who tended to treat his subjects as if they were specimens of some alien form of life, with a mixture of curiosity and amusement. A healthy distance was maintained from characters who were presented not so much as individuals as in terms of their common behavioral patterns; and the combined effect of the detachment, the condescension, and the generalising tendency was to create an effect of caricature. Here is a typical passage, where the narrator is describing the aftermath of a fight:

> I looked and saw that Bob had entirely lost his left ear, and a large piece from his left cheek. His right eye was a little discolored, and the blood flowed profusely from his wounds.
> Bill presented a hideous spectacle. About a third of his nose, at the lower extremity, was bit off, and his face so swelled and bruised that it was difficult to discover in it anything of the human visage. . . .
> . . . Durham and Stallings [the fighters] kept their beds for several weeks, and did not meet again for two months. When they met, Billy stepped up to Bob and offered his hand, saying, "Bobby you've *licked* me a fair fight; but you wouldn't have done it if I hadn't been in the wrong—I oughtn't have treated your wife as I did; and I felt so through the whole fight; and it sort o' cowed me." "Well Billy," said Bob, "let's be friends. Once in the fight, when you had my finger in your mouth . . . I was going to halloo; but I thought of Betsy, and knew the

house would be too hot for me if I got whipped when fighting for her, after always whipping when I fought for myself . . ."

. . . Thanks to the Christian religion, to schools, colleges, and benevolent associations, such scenes of barbarism and cruelty as that which I have been just describing are now of rare occurrence, though they may still be occasionally met with in some of the new counties.[3]

In the preface to his book, Longstreet claimed proudly that he was filling in "a chasm in history which has always been overlooked"; and this passage illustrates well, I think, how he reconciled such a claim with the exigencies of comedy. The tone of the description is humorous but the writer clearly hopes that, by means of this humor, he will demonstrate something significant about the backwoods character as well—its simplicity and its capacity for violence. That is to say, the simplification and exaggeration which create the comic note are there because they enable Longstreet to locate what is *different* about the boy and emphasize it at the expense of any qualities he may share, in a Wordsworthian sense, with the rest of humanity.

This is not the place to go into Longstreet's further motives for emphasizing the specific qualities of the Georgia folk that he did. The virtual impossibility of resolving the problem, anyway, is indicated by the fact that the critical field is about equally divided between those who argue that Longstreet admired his subjects for their "free and active simplicity," and those who say that, as a gentleman and a Whig, he loathed and feared them for the threat they offered to his own life-style![4] What *does* matter, though, and needs to be mentioned here is that, whatever his ulterior motives, Longstreet offered his readers a portrait of the poor farmer which was characterized by three things: detachment, a claim to historical accuracy and a tendency towards comic exaggeration. These were the strategies that gave *Georgia Scenes* much of its drive and contemporary appeal; and these were the ones also that were variously adopted by the writers following Longstreet, who are now referred to generally as the "Southwestern humorists"—"Southwestern" because nearly all of them were interested in the younger states of the interior (such as Alabama, Mississippi, Tennessee). Of course, their approach was never uniform. Apart from anything else there was a tendency in later years to reduce the status of the dramatized narrator altogether: the story was then told impersonally or given to the rural character himself to tell. But the qualities I have mentioned continued to supply a point of departure, a common basis as it were upon which the individual writer could improvise. And one result of this is that in the work which certainly represents the culmination of Southwestern humor, the *Adventures of Huckleberry Finn*, we can find the same combination of historical and comic intention recurring. The portrait that Mark Twain develops in his book, of old times on the Mississippi, is presented via a technique of violent exaggeration which makes it simultaneously elegiac and critical, a humorous masterpiece and a piece of social history; and that exaggeration is itself symptomatic of a detachment which enables us to *place* every character—*including* Huckleberry Finn himself—even while we may sympathize with them.[5]

Time (and the sheer complexity of the subject) may prevent us from examining Southwestern humor in any great detail. But as a way of indicating some of its further implications, and in particular its relevance for Erskine Caldwell, I would like to look briefly at a writer who stands somewhere in between Longstreet and Twain in terms of achievement and chronology; and that is George Washington Harris. The choice is not meant to be an obscurantist one, since, apart from the fact that Harris did exercise enormous personal influence on Caldwell (and William Faulkner as well), there can be no doubt that he represents an important moment in the history of American humor; a time when, in opposition to the dominant climate of prissiness and gentility, it could still be pungent, incisive, and above all broad. Just how broad it could be is indicated by the controlling belief Harris attributes to his major character, Sut Lovingood—that "Man was made a-pupus jus' to eat, drink, an' for stayin' awake in the yearly part of the nites."[6] A native of rural Tennessee, Sut is in effect another example of the creature who tended to become an obsession with the humorists: the primitive or natural man, who stands on the periphery of conventional society and yet can still offer significant comments on it. His life, circumscribed by the animal functions, is a continual drag on our own pretensions, about the nature of our personalities and the efficacy or security of the social system we have organized for ourselves. At one point in his narrative, Sut Lovingood admits that he has "nara a soul, nuffin but a whiskey proof gizzard" and Harris's habitual strategy of making us share Sut's life and experience the connection between what he is and how he lives leads us to suspect that in similar conditions we might be forced to say exactly the same.

It will be clear already that Harris's intentions and techniques are rather different from Longstreet's. For while both share the claim to historical accuracy, and the device of comic exaggeration, they differ in the sense that the placing of their subject (the way they invite us to look on rural folk as a demonstration) is based upon almost contrary premises. Longstreet, as I have suggested, offers us the portrait of a world quite different from our own, which may provoke amusement, perhaps even the occasional tremor of apprehension, but nothing more than that. Harris, by contrast, presents us with a kind of test case which paradoxically derives its impact, the sense of its relevance to our own lives, from the distance it establishes between the literate reader and the illiterate protagonist. Suppose, Harris seems to be saying, we had been brought up in surroundings similar to those of Sut Lovingood: would we be that different from him? Would we not, perhaps, speak the same language and

live upon the same level of comic but grotesque animalism? And if this is
the case, does it not tend to undermine our pretensions; the belief in our
dignity as Godgiven, rather than acquired as a matter of special privilege?
Sut Lovingood is detached from us, certainly—the use of an almost impenetrable dialect sees to that: but he is detached from us only in the way
that a mirror image of ourselves is. We watch him and, in doing so,
witness a curious aping and a criticism of our own behavior.[7]

The criticism is made all the more effective because of Harris's
capacity for reminding us, in the middle of Sut's various scrapes, that his
protagonist does possess traces of what we are pleased to call virtue,
waiting for the appropriate conditions to bring them into life. There is his
extraordinary pride and independence of judgment, for instance, which
prompts him to consider himself "the very best society" and to punish
those who he feels have insulted him in any way. More telling still is the
ability which Harris endows him with for sensing who his enemies are,
regardless of whether they have slighted him personally or not. They are,
he realizes, the preachers and the pedagogues, the politic and educated
leaders of society who are there not simply to supply a butt for Sut's fool-
ing, although they certainly do that, but to remind us of the kind of
people—*people like ourselves*—who are indirectly responsible for his condition. For their privileges, we must realize, have been bought at his
expense; they, and we, are the beneficiaries of a system from which he is
excluded and by which he is deprived. The mirror is being held up to the
readers *as a group*, in other words, as well as to the reader as an individual. We see in Sut Lovingood a reflection of possibilities existing in
ourselves—*and* we are forced to acknowledge our complicity in the creation of circumstances which, in Sut's case, have translated possibility into
fact. And just in case we should continue to miss the point, denying Sut a
germ of sensitivity even after all this, there are occasions in the narrative
when more energetic hints of his potential are allowed to appear. Instead
of a cursory reference to some dormant virtue, we may then be confronted
with a passage of extraordinary lyrical beauty—not denying the comic
framework but actually growing out of it—which serves as the most incisive reminder possible of those aspects of Sut Lovingood's character that
remain mostly unexercised. Here, by way of illustration, is what is
deservedly the most famous moment in all of Sut Lovingood's yarns, set
characteristically enough at a meal-time:

> Wirt's wife got yearly supper, a rale suckit-rider's supper,
> whar the 'oman ove the ouse' wer a rich b'lever. Thar wer
> chickens cut up, an' fried in butter, brown, white, flakey,
> light, hot biskit, made wif cream, scrambil'd aigs, yaller but-
> ter, fried ham, in slices es big es yure han, pickil'd beets, an'
> cowcumbers, roas'in ears, shaved down and fried, sweet
> taters, baked, a stack ove buckwheat cakes . . . I gets doing
> hongry every time I see Wirt's wife, ur evan her side-saddil, ur

her frocks a-hangin on the closeline. Es we sot down, the las'
glimmers ove the sun crep thru the histed winder, an' flutter'd
on the white tabil-cloth and play'd a silver shine on her smoof
black har, es she sot at the head ove the tabil, a-pourin out the
coffee, wif her sleeves push'd tight back on her white roun'
arm, her full throbbin neck wer bar to the swell ove her
shoulders, an' the steam ove the coffee made a movin vail afore
her face, es she slowly brush'd hit away wif her lef han',
a-smilin an' a flashin her talkin eyes lovingly at her hansum
husbun.[8]

The occasion being described here is mundane enough, admittedly, but
what matters about it is not so much the occasion itself as all that Harris
allows his protagonist to make out of it. Sut, we are forced to recognize,
has a sensitivity—a capacity for recognizing the beauty and value of a
particular experience—which will emerge at the least available opportunity; although all too often it is left to waste uncultivated. The waste is
articulated in the rest of the narrative, in the scenes of comic violence and
degeneracy that illustrate the actual conditions of his existence; and placed in this context it becomes unarguable, I think, that Harris even more
than Longstreet has *used* his humor to reinforce a serious social and
historical point. If we are willing to simplify for a moment, we can say
that the comedy in *Sut Lovingood* defines the given situation, the occasional moments of lyricism and commentary imply the possibilities which
have been more or less frustrated, and the activity taking place between
these two poles helps to locate the core meaning of the sketches.

Nearly half a century separates the creator of Sut Lovingood from
the creator of Jeeter Lester: but perhaps this gap in time may serve only to
emphasize the relevant connections between the two writers. The difference of historical situation may, after all, help to isolate what is similar
in their purposes and techniques and so concentrate our attention upon it.
Be that as it may, it is patently clear, I think, once we look at him in this
light, that Caldwell owes a profound debt to the Southwestern humorists,
and to George Washington Harris in particular; a debt which is betrayed
among other things by their common dependence on a broad and grotesque type of comedy. The specific borrowings from Harris are at their
most obvious in *Georgia Boy*, published in 1943, in which the boy of the
title recounts the antics of his "old man," and in the process draws us the
portrait of a delightful and impoverished scapegrace not unlike Sut Lovingood himself.[9] But these are less interesting, I believe, than the kind of
understanding of Harris and his methods which can be inferred from
Caldwell's more important fiction: by which I mean from *Tobacco Road*,
God's Little Acre, and perhaps *Tragic Ground* as well.[10] In such cases it is
not merely the surface structure of Southwestern humor which is
recovered but the relationship obtaining between that structure and the
ulterior purposes of the writer. Comic these books may be, but the com-

edy is all the sharper, the wit all the more pungent and the characters that much more striking, because (just as in *Sut Lovingood*) everything is unambiguously attached to an underlying and genuinely serious series of intentions.

Exactly how these intentions manifest themselves is (again as in *Sut Lovingood*) as much a matter of context as anything else, the total situation in which the humorous moments are played out. The comedy is still a comedy of waste, of human potential denied and frustrated, and that fact is communicated to the reader in part by Caldwell's barren landscapes—whether it be the decayed rural landscape where his farmers are described living in reluctant exile or the urban scene, to which they may retreat occasionally in pursuit of an illusory alternative. The description in *God's Little Acre*, of mill-towns populated by farmers looking for some way of making a living, is typical of what I mean:

> Up and down the valley lay the company towns and the ivy-walled cotton mills . . . the men stood on the hot streets looking at each other while they spat their lungs into the deep yellow dust . . . In the rear of the houses . . . tight-lipped women sitting at kitchen windows with their backs to the cold cooking-stoves. In the streets in front of the houses . . . the bloody-lipped men spitting their lungs into the yellow dust . . . The grass and weeds melted in the sun, and the dust that blew down from the . . . uplands settled on the ground and on the buildings like powdered paint.[11]

Even from this comparatively brief passage it is clear, I think, that Caldwell sees the hopelessness of the rural landscape penetrating the town, to make it unavailable as a resource for impoverished farmers. A common dust (similar, perhaps, to the dust which floats in the wake of the Great Gatsby) settles over city and adjacent countryside alike, so creating a pervasive sense of fruitlessness. And this is the stage on which the Lesters, the Waldens in *God's Little Acre* and all their kind must act out their comedies of frustration; or, to be more accurate, this is the environment which prescribes their frustrated lives.

That it *is* a comedy of frustration we are concerned with here, a series of appropriate responses to a thwarting environment, is witnessed by the habitual activity of Caldwell's characters. For the gestures that make them comic have nothing at all to do with intrinsic evil, however violent and grotesque they may appear to be. On the contrary, Jeeter Lester and Ty Ty Walden (in *God's Little Acre*) are exactly like Sut Lovingood in that they are presented as the *victims* of evil, whose strange behavior demonstrates the response of the innocent to circumstances he cannot control.[12] The whole trouble with Caldwell's characters, as with Harris's, is that they have no relevant connection with the emergent social structure; and so are at best anomalies in that structure and at worst encumbrances to it. And Caldwell, *unlike* Harris, makes sure that the reader is aware of this by explaining, very early on in most of his novels, how people like the Lester family and the Waldens have become the way they are. Both the Lesters and the Waldens were, we learn, once well-to-do landowners. But they fell upon hard times—partly as a result of natural fluctuations in the cotton and tobacco markets, and partly thanks to the machinations of the financiers, the bankers, and the Wall Street brokers. In the event, they—like so many of their class, Caldwell reminds us—lost their land and had to resort to cropping on shares; a ruinous system whereby they placed themselves heavily in debt to the landowner, and the landowner in turn remained solvent by borrowing at a high rate of interest from the merchant banks. This was bad enough, perhaps, but (Caldwell goes on) matters have since become worse because the sharecropping system has itself collapsed; and land has now to be cultivated in very large units or—as in most cases—not at all. In effect, big business has assumed *direct* control of farming, rather than working through the power of its credit, and in doing so has created a new, large-scale agricultural system in which the Jeeter Lesters and Ty Ty Waldens of this world have no place. Jeeter, Ty Ty, and their kind have been turned into anachronisms, an irrelevant nuisance to the present owners of the land; and the most they can hope for, really, is that they will be left alone on the farms they occupy, to eke a meagre existence out of them.[13]

This, more or less, is the starting-point for nearly all of Caldwell's fiction, and certainly the basis of his finest novels. The farmer, he argues, has been "robbed of his livelihood by the downfall of the old systems of agriculture"[14]—and this in turn has led to the physical deterioration which we now see and to his moral collapse. Treated like an animal he has become an animal: excluded from the human community in an economic sense he has degenerated into a kind of moral leper as well, whose humanity is more a matter of biology than of character. The argument is an utterly deterministic one, of course. But, then, so also is the argument implicit in most stories of the old Southwest. More to the point, the determinism is not I think objectionable because it can be seen as part of a total strategy of caricature. Life is simplified and character is distorted in Caldwell's fiction, it may be true: but this is done in a conscious and valuable way—so as to isolate certain specific aspects of the author's given experience and, in isolating them, to explain them.

Given this self-conscious determinism of approach, and the tendencies towards caricature and generalization which accompany it, it becomes less surprising, I think, that Caldwell *should* impose the status of a demonstration on every aspect of his character's behavior: the reader is, after all, being summoned to witness what is likely to happen when a certain type of social and historical situation exists. There is a profoundly illustrative quality, for instance, not just about particular scenes in *Tobacco Road* but about its major source of comedy. This is Jeeter

Lester's belief that one year, next year perhaps, he will be able to plant a tobacco crop. Under the influence of this belief he is forever burning the ground in preparation for the planting until eventually at the end of the novel he sets fire to his own house, killing himself and his wife in the process. The belief is an idiosyncratic one, certainly, leading to situations that range from the ludicrous to the macabre: but not so idiosyncratic that it cannot act as a gauge of Jeeter's innocence, and the desperate nature of a situation which imposes such desperate remedies on its victims. Similarly, Ty Ty Walden's habitual activity of digging up his land in search of gold, absurd though it may appear to be, is founded on the supremely illogical and revealing logic of the helpless naif. He cannot live on what he gets *out* of the land, Ty Ty reasons, so why not try to live on what he finds *in* it? There is perhaps a hint of blasphemy in his behavior too, of the kind familiar to readers of *Go Down, Moses*: the idea that rooting about in the land for gold, oil, or whatever represents a despoliation, an act of rape which is the very opposite of the enrichment offered to the soil by the agricultural activity.[15] But whether this is part of Caldwell's intention or not, there can be little doubt I think that he *does* intend Ty Ty's behavior, like Jeeter's, to achieve the apparently paradoxical feat of being representative by virtue of its idiosyncrasy. Its illustrative quality, that is—as an indication of rural decline and the despair to which this decline leads—is made to depend for its impact on the comic absurdity of the illustration.

The humor is not left in isolation, though, to carry the entire freight of meaning of the book unaided. As in *Sut Lovingood*, the dominant strain of comedy is punctuated by an occasional lyric note which reminds us of what *might* have been in more favorable circumstances—of how people like Jeeter Lester and Ty Ty Walden *could* have developed, given the proper opportunity. The few times that Jeeter is allowed to express his "inherited love of the land" offer us some beautiful instances of this:

> "I think more of the land than I do of staying in a durn cotton-mill. You can't smell no sedge fire up there, and when it comes time for planting, you feel sick inside but you don't know what's ailing you . . . But when a man stays on the land, he don't get to feeling like that this time of the year, because he's right there to smell the smoke of burning broom-sedge and to feel the wind fresh off the ploughed fields going down inside of his body . . . out here on the land a man feels better than ever he did. The Spring-time ain't going to let you fool it by hiding away inside a durn cotton-mill. It knows you got to stay on the land to feel good.[16]

This passage deserves comparison with Sut Lovingood's hymn to the good life, which I quoted earlier, and not just because it helps us to recognize and to accept the latent dignity of the speaker. It does this, of course, but what it does as well is contribute a new dimension of feeling to the narrative; a sense of pathos which depends upon our seeing that, within the limits established by the comedy, the desires expressed here are destined to remain unconsummated. Jeeter Lester will never really live up to the ideal of the farming experience he is describing, nor will Sut Lovingood ever be able to develop his sensibilities and sensitivity to the full; and that, as their creators see it, is a cause for our honest sympathy as much as our amusement—or, rather, something to give depth and direction to our laughter.

It is only a step beyond this strategy of contrast between the comic episode and the lyric moment to that of placing active commentary in the mouths of the characters; commentary, that is, which does not simply *imply* a criticism of the given situation but insists upon it. Needless to say, Caldwell frequently takes this step. His characters suddenly pause, as Jeeter does when he is stealing the bag of turnips, and turn upon their own grotesque attitudes in order to explain them. And not only the attitudes but the context of victimization in which they occur as well; for Caldwell differs from Harris in the sense that he makes his characters articulate their own sufferings, so that we are never left in any doubt as to where to place the blame. Thus, when Ty Ty Walden describes the iniquities of the speculative system to his daughter-in-law, and in particular the depredations of the cotton broker, he seems as much as anything else to be offering an explanation of himself to the reader—supplying the kind of direct analysis of the dramatic situation, and its origins, which is normally assigned to a chorus rather than the protagonist: "You know what a cotton broker is, don't you? Do you know why they're called cotton brokers? . . . Because they keep the farmers broke all the time. They lend a little money, and then they take the whole damn crop. Or else they suck the blood out of a man by running the price up and down, forcing him to sell. That's why they call them cotton brokers!"[17] Statements like this may offer a special problem to some readers. After all, it might be argued, can they be reconciled with the deterministic premises of the rest of the narrative which require the characters to behave like automatons? Ty Ty betrays a clear understanding of his situation here, as much understanding, in fact, as would be necessary for him to exercise some measure of control over it; and how does this jibe with an action which elsewhere tends to reduce him to the status of a Pavlovian dog?

The problem is only an apparent one, though (at least, in the case of Caldwell's major fiction it is), because it is based on the assumption that the writer is aiming at verisimilitude. And the plain fact, as we have seen, is that he is *not*. Like Harris, Longstreet, and all the other humorists, Caldwell has complicated the function of reporter by adding to it that of the caricaturist, a creator of the grotesque. On top of that, he has forced on the reader an attitude of radical detachment. Statements such as the one Ty Ty makes about cotton brokers, or Jeeter's comment on the turnips, are part of the pattern of demonstration I mentioned earlier, in which the characters as well as the audience seem to be made aware of the illustrative quality of the action. As a resource this attitude of detachment is, of course, just as much of an inheritance from Southwestern humor as the strategy of caricature is. But Caldwell develops it much further than any previous humorist ever did; so much further, in fact, that perhaps to explain and justify it we need to draw a comparison from a very different field of literature. I mean by this the programme for an "epic" theatre formulated more than forty years ago by the German dramatist Bertolt Brecht. For the distance placed between reader and character in Caldwell's best fiction is, I think, significantly related—both in its purposes and its effects—to Brecht's core idea of "Vermfremdung" or audience alienation.[18] The idea, stated simply, is this: that in an "epic" play the audience, instead of being invited to involve themselves in the action, should be forced to adopt an attitude of clinical detachment towards it. Consequently, what happens on stage will be witnessed as an explicable social phenomenon with its own definite causes and room for subsequent maneouvre. The sense of an experience participated in is forfeited, according to this theory, but what (hopefully) is gained in its place is a new certainty—the knowledge which comes from having located the dramatic action firmly in its historical time and social place. The events the writer describes become part of an explicable series: their origins understood, the problems they pose carefully defined, and solutions to these problems offered, ready and waiting, for the audience to act upon. This is very much the notion of playwright—or novelist, or poet—as scientific historian, and committed scientific historian at that. And regardless of whether or not Brecht entirely adhered to his theories when it came to the actual writing of plays there can be little doubt, I think, that they encouraged him to develop certain specific literary devices. Among these was the device of permitting someone to comment on events of which he was elsewhere shown to be the victim. Time and again in Brechtian theatre, a character will slip into the role of surrogate spectator, to emphasize moments in the drama (or links in the series) which other spectators may have missed. No one worries about this when it occurs in *Mother Courage* or *The Caucasian Chalk Circle* because it is part of the denial of surface realism which is integral to the action—as well as something which helps to place that action within a context of possible remedies. No one should worry about it when it occurs in *Tobacco Road* or *God's Little Acre* either, and for precisely the same reasons.[19]

The sense of problem-solving—the feeling that we are being asked to look at the action in very much the same spirit as a scientist looks at an experiment—is in fact as pronounced in books like *Tobacco Road* as it could be in any "epic" play; more pronounced, even, since Caldwell likes to add his own comments to those he puts in the mouths of his characters. Asides from the author occasionally supplement asides from his creations, so as to make the didactic intention of the story perfectly clear. This, admittedly, has some use simply because it helps to settle any doubts that may be left in the reader's mind—both about what Caldwell is trying to do, and what he is trying to say. But, on the whole, I think it is a mistake. At such moments, it is very difficult for him not to sound like a schoolmaster talking to an exceptionally dull pupil:

> Jeeter could never think of the loss of his land and goods as anything but a man-made calamity . . . he believed steadfastly that his position had been brought about by other people. He did not blame Captain John [his landlord] to the same extent that he blamed others . . . Captain John had always treated him fairly . . . But the end soon came. There was no longer any profit in raising coton under the Captain's antiquated system, and he abandoned the farm and moved to Augusta. . . . An intelligent use of his land, stocks, and implements would have enabled Jeeter, and scores of others who had become dependent on Captain John, to raise crops to be sold at a profit.[20]

Caldwell never tires of offering direct advice like this; and as any reader of *Tobacco Road* or *God's Little Acre* will testify, the specific proposals he makes are pretty various—ranging as they do from pleas for more government aid to the occasional invocation of the principle of self-help, and taking in agricultural schools, crop rotation, and land recovery along the way. The variety of his proposls, however, should not prevent us from seeing that everything he says stems ultimately from one core belief, a single premise. This is how Caldwell states that premise in one of his books: "Until the agricultural worker commands his own farm, either as an individual or as a member of a state-allotted farm group, the Southern tenant-farmer will continue to be bound hand and foot in economic slavery."[21] Caldwell, as I think this brief passage indicates, is finally a traditional writer. His characters are traditional; his humor is traditional (although, certainly, it is broader and wilder than the Southwestern humorists' ever was); above all, the social and political program implicit in his work is traditional. For what that program boils down to is a belief in the pieties of the small farm. The dream of a chosen people tilling their own fields in perfect freedom: *that* is the dream Caldwell expresses here—and that also is the dream which dictates nearly all of his problem-solving. No matter how little we may realize it while we are enjoying some of the surface details of his comedy, Caldwell—in every one of his finest stories—is trying to draw us back steadily into the world of Jeffersonian myth.

Once we realize this—that the ideal of the good farmer hovers as an admonitory image at the back of Caldwell's best novels and tales—then, I think, the principal reason for the almost apocalyptic violence of his work becomes clear. All the events that occur in books like *Tobacco Road* and

God's Little Acre are wild and grotesque, ultimately, because they represent for their creator such a radical departure from the Jeffersonian norm. Jeeter Lester and Ty Ty Walden are not the noble farmers of regional legend and the fact that they are not, the fact that they stand for *a dream or an ideal betrayed*, is I believe meant to be the real measure of their absurdity. No blame attaches to Jeeter or Ty Ty for their plight, far from it, but that only makes it the more difficult to bear: the more difficult for them to bear, that is, for their author to bear—and, most important of all, for us to bear as well. For it would be putting matters in their right perspective, I think, to say that Caldwell insists on the difference between Jefferson's tillers of the earth and his own Georgia crackers, and then imposes full responsibility for this difference upon a corrupt social machine, precisely so as to arouse *our* anger and encourage *our* demands for change. He is not the only humorist to do this, of course: George Washington Harris, as we have seen, tried to do something similar. But he *is*, as far as I know, the only one to supplement this by talking about the brave new world which may emerge when the machine is reprogrammed; to make tentative moves, in other words, towards turning from the dream betrayed to the dream fulfilled.

This, anyway, is what I take Caldwell to be doing when (as in the passage I quoted just now) he refers to the mistakes made by Captain John and his class: he is beginning to talk about an alternative environment. And elsewhere, in some of the stories that he wrote after *Tobacco Road* and *God's Little Acre*, these beginnings are carried through to a detailed portrait of that alternative. Caldwell then shows us the reorganization of farm management and the re-structuring of rural society actually taking place, and being succeeded in turn by a revival of spirit among his characters. Obviously, the intended effect of these stories is one of uplift; the author wants us to experience a sense of release because the oppressive circumstances, and with them the claustrophobic atmosphere, of the earlier narratives have been dissolved. Their actual effect is a lot less exhilirating than that, however, and the reasons for this take us right back to the virtues of that earlier work: we can define why Caldwell succeeded in *Tobacco Road* and *God's Little Acre* by understanding why he is failing now. For what Caldwell does as a preliminary to drawing his portrait of a better life is to take his rural folk out of the grotesque, comic world of the Lesters and the Waldens; which is a necessary step, certainly, but one which deprives him of his previous excuses for the simplifications and determinism of his argument. The one-sided portrait can no longer be defended as part of a satirical strategy. And having done this he does not really know what to do with his people, because he does not have any other satisfactory approach available to him—one which would make them meaningful and at the same time vivid and believable, too. His characters have lost the power of a Jeeter Lester—the power, that is, deriving from the deliberately isolating and exaggerating tendencies of the comic method—without acquiring any of the more complicated interest, or more sophisticated contact with their time and place, which the participants in a more strictly "realistic" fiction should possess. To adopt E. M. Forster's useful terms for a moment, they have no imaginative life of their own either as "flat" characters or as "round" ones. They are merely mouthpieces for utopian attitudes; as two-dimensional and as unprepossessing as some of the less successful heroes of Elizabeth Madox Roberts or Ellen Glasgow are. In *A House in the Uplands* for instance, a novel published in 1946, the protagonist—who is, of course, a simple farmer—talks to his aristocratic fiancée in this way. It tells us a lot, I think, about the strained, self-consciously heroic posture of much of Caldwell's later work: "I'm just as good as you or anybody who lives up . . . in the big house, and you know it. If I lived in one of those rotting old houses and loafed all the time and borrowed money to live on you'd marry me . . . quick . . . I'm going to amount to something in life and I can give you a lot more than any other man will ever give you, and money won't be the only thing either."[22] This is pure melodrama, horribly appropriate to a story which is only a slightly regionalized version of the Horatio Alger dream, and it represents a sad decline from the comic inventiveness of *Tobacco Road*. Admittedly, it *is* based on the same values as *Tobacco Road* is. The difference, however, and it is a crucial difference, is that what constitutes a background to comedy in the earlier narrative has now been carried into the foreground. The values, previously *implied*, have been allowed to occupy centre stage; and—unfortunately for Caldwell—they have not benefited in the process either from an involvement in credible experience, or from contact with the sort of vivifying literary medium that the comic tradition of the old Southwest represents.

What has occurred in the later fiction is really very simple; and one useful way of summarizing it, within the context of Caldwell's total achievement, might go something like this. In stories like *Tobacco Road* or *God's Little Acre*, Caldwell's success depends largely upon two factors. These are his acquaintanceship with, and his use of, the methods of comic journalism which had been perfected by the humorists of the old Southwest; and his commitment to a dream of the rural landscape which he had also learnt from his region. The factors are not just coincidental, of course. On the contrary, they complement and enhance each other here just as they do in the stories of George Washington Harris: with the dream giving power and coherence to the journalism, and the journalism in turn appropriating some sense of urgency and possibility for the dream. Idea and event are made to interact so as to produce a thoroughly traditional reading of the environment; a reading, that is to say, which depends on the earlier history of that environment without being circumscribed by it. But in later novels like *A House in the Uplands* this interaction more or less ceases. The idea remains unenlivened by any contact with experience:

or, on those occasions when Caldwell does return to journalism—a comic account of things as they are—that journalism does not seem to have an ulterior motive any more. It no longer radiates the kind of significance that would come from its being placed within the framework of a controlling idea. Idea *or* event, dream *or* journalistic report: the two things exist separately, even if they both occur within the covers of one book. And what we are left with, consequently, is either heroic posturing of the sort I have just illustrated—or a descent into episodes of comic violence and degeneracy which have no purpose beyond themselves, which are in a word sensationalistic. We are not being asked to register the gap between fact and potential any longer: only to indulge in day-dreaming about what might happen in the best of all possible worlds, or to enjoy the cheaper thrills offered by a random and meaningless enumeration of some of the sordid facts of life. The strategy of detachment is, in sum, replaced by one of vicarious excitement. This is a sad end for somebody, like Caldwell, who started off so well. But even if it does nothing else it helps us, I think, by suggesting what happens when the functions of journalist (that is, a reporter of things *as they are*) and caricaturist or mythologizer (that is, a reporter of things *as they might be*) are separated for a writer; and history is then translated by him into a refuge for some dormant principle or, alternatively, into a series of disconnected happenings.

Notes

1. Erskine Caldwell, *Tobacco Road* (New York: Grosset & Dunlap, 1932), p. 23.

2. Caldwell, p. 39.

3. "The Fight," in Augustus Baldwin Longstreet, *Georgia Scenes* (New York: Harper Bros., 1835), pp. 50, 52–53. Caldwell's debt to the Southwestern humorists is mentioned in passing by Carl Van Doren, "Made in America: Erskine Caldwell," *Nation*, 137 (October 18, 1933), 444.

4. For different opinions of Longstreet's aims and achievement see: Constance Rourke, *American Humor: A Study of the National Character* (New York: Harcourt, Brace, 1931); Walter Blair, *Horse Sense in American Humor: From Benjamin Franklin to Ogden Nash* (Chicago: U. of Chi. Pr., 1942); Kenneth Lynn, *Mark Twain and Southwestern Humor* (Boston: Little, Brown, 1960).

5. The complexity of Mark Twain's purposes in the book, and the various levels of interest on which it consequently operates, are brought out well in Walter Blair, *Mark Twain and Huck Finn* (Berkeley: U. of Cal. Pr., 1960).

6. "Sut Lovingood's Sermon," in *Sut Lovingood: Yarns Spun by a "Natural Born Durn'd Fool"* (New York: Dick and Fitzgerald, 1867), p. 88; also p. 172.

7. I am aware that this is an unorthodox interpretation of Harris, but I think it can be reconciled at least with the expressed opinions of Lynn and Tony Tanner, *The Reign of Wonder* (Cambridge: University Pr., 1956), pp. 100–03. They argue that Harris is in sympathy with Sut Lovingood, and that this is one reason why he adopts Sut as narrator. I am essentially in agreement with this; but I feel that the sympathy is as much for Sut's potential as for what he actually is. The kinds of values expressed by this potential, it need hardly be added, have nothing at all to do with the genteel culture which Sut criticizes.

8. "Trapping a Sheriff," in *Sut Lovingood's Yarns*, pp. 196–7.

9. See, for example, the stories entitled "The Day We Rang the Bell for Preacher Hawshaw," "My Old Man and the Gypsy Queen," and "Handsome Brown's Day Off."

10. *God's Little Acre* (New York: Grosset & Dunlap, 1933); *Tragic Ground* (Boston: Litle, Brown, 1944).

11. *God's Little Acre*, pp. 99–102. Compare *Tragic Ground*, pp. 17, 236.

12. "Ty Ty is irascible and indestructible, but above all innocent." R. Hazel, "Notes on Erskine Caldwell," in Louis D. Rubin, Jr. and Robert D. Jacobs, eds., *South: Modern Southern Literature in its Cultural Setting* (Garden City: Doubleday, 1961), p. 325.

13. For the clearest and most succinct description of this entire process see *You Have Seen Their Faces* (New York: Modern Age Books, 1937), pp. 32–33.

14. "Tenant Farmers," in *Some American People* (New York: McBride, 1935), p. 212.

15. See "The Fire and the Hearth," in *Go Down, Moses* (New York: Random House, 1942).

16. *Tobacco Road*, p. 28.

17. *God's Little Acre*, p. 108.

"Georgia Boy: A Retrospect of Erskine Caldwell"

Malcolm Cowley*

During the early Depression years I was book editor of *The New Republic* and hence was a minor source of income to young writers who were trying to keep alive in New York. Many of them had found that other sources were limited in those bleak days before the Federal Writers' Project. I felt involved in their problems, which were even worse than my own problems had been a dozen years before, when I had sat on the other side of that big, battered desk and tried to explain why I should be given a book for review. Now younger men and women were making the same worried explanations, and usually I did find a book for them if they showed intimations of having talent or if they merely looked hungry; at least they could sell the book on Fourth Avenue and buy a meal. For Erskine Caldwell, however, I didn't find a book, even though he impressed me as having more promise than almost any of the others.

I had read some of his stories in little magazines and later when they were collected in a first book, *American Earth*, published in the spring of 1931. Clearly he had a natural gift for story telling and he had a subject, too, in the small cotton farmers of East Georgia. Sometimes he wrote as if he were one of them; as if he had dropped the plowlines that very morning, stabled the mule, and rushed to the typewriter. There were other stories about Maine country people, in which his tone was that of a quizzical observer, and the book also contained a long prose poem in numbered paragraphs, "The Sacrilege of Alan Kent." This impressed me even more than the stories, for it revealed what seemed to be a new sensibility, with hints of remembered pain, cruelty, hunger, and savage longing. Some of the paragraphs were single sentences as tough and springy as an axe handle: "A man walked into a restaurant through the front door and ate all he wanted to eat."—"Once the sun was so hot a bird came down and walked beside me in my shadow." That sentence about the bird I kept repeating to myself, each time admiring its utter simplicity and rightness.

*Reprinted from *Pages*, ed. Matthew J. Bruccoli (Detroit: Gale, 1976), pp. 62–68. Copyright © 1976 by Gale Research Company. Reprinted by permission of the author.

So I was curious about the author and pleased when he appeared at *The New Republic* with other candidates for books to review. Caldwell, as I afterward learned, had lately finished *Tobacco Road*, which had been accepted by Scribners for spring publication; now he planned to spend the winter in New York while writing a second novel. He was a big young man with a square-cut head, broad shoulders, and enormous hands, but with little flesh on his bones. His orange hair was cut short and lay forward close to his scalp, so that he looked like a totem pole topped with a blob of orange paint. When we talked about his stories he complained that people thought he was a humorist. "I have never tried to be funny," he said, making a wooden gesture. His features were as solemnly inexpressive as those of an Indian chief or a backwoods farmer.

"He's not as innocent as he seems," I said to myself, but what did I say to Caldwell? Though I can't set down the words, I remember feeling experienced and almost patriarchal. I must have told him that he had a truly exceptional gift for story telling, but that he didn't impress me as having a critical mind. When he volunteered that he had written a lot of reviews for the *Charlotte Observer*, I brushed aside the information. "Keep away from book reviews," I must have said. "They wouldn't earn you a living and they would interfere with your real business, which is writing stories." He clumped down the stairs without a book, while I sat in the editor's chair feeling ashamed of myself for having pontificated. I didn't know until much later that he had been living mostly on rye bread and rat-trap cheese, with a ten-cent bowl of soup in the evening.

Still, I had given Caldwell sound advice, even if books for review would have been more appreciated. That winter was to be his last really hard one. *Tobacco Road* came out in February 1932 and was not a commercial success, but it had more than a few enthusiastic readers. One of them was Jack Kirkland, who later asked for permission to dramatize the book. In March Caldwell went back to Maine, where he lived with his wife and three children in a big drafty house belonging to the wife's family. He had finished his second novel, but, after some hesitation, Scribners turned it down (that book wasn't published for twenty years). Then spring came to Kennebec County and everything seemed brighter. Caldwell started a new novel for which he already had a title: *God's Little Acre*. He had acquired a literary agent, Maxim Lieber, who was selling a few of his stories to magazines that paid for them. The new novel had gone well in the writing; it was finished in August and was promptly accepted by the Viking Press. With the advance against royalties, Caldwell bought a new typewriter, having battered away at the old one until it was beyond repair. He also bought three identical dictionaries, to have a copy always at hand, and the first roast of beef his family had eaten in a year. He was still poor, but he would never again go hungry for want of money.

"A man walked into a restaurant through the front door and ate all he wanted to eat." Caldwell could now be the man.

The next time I remember seeing him—though there were other times now forgotten—was in the winter of 1936–37, at a meeting held in a midtown hotel to advance some worthy left-wing cause. Caldwell appeared late and in the company of a spirited young woman, the photographer Margaret Bourke-White. They had lately traveled together through the Deep South, she taking pictures and he recording conversations for a book that was to become a classic record of the Depression years: *You Have Seen Their Faces*. Now, the wife in Maine forgotten, they were radiantly in love, so that their presence transformed the crowded room. Suddenly I thought of Wallace Stevens and his "Anecdote of the Jar":

> I placed a jar in Tennessee,
> And round it was, upon a hill.
> It made a slovenly wilderness
> Surround that hill.

Those two, absorbed in each other, gave focus and form to the slovenly meeting, while we others had become the wilderness in which they gleamed.

Bourke-White was bright, gallant, ambitious, and hard-working, with a habit—not displayed that afternoon—of surveying a room to pick out celebrities, then marching straight up to them. In Caldwell she had found her dearest celebrity. By that time *Tobacco Road*, in Jack Kirkland's Broadway version, had been running for three years—with four more years to come—and it was yielding as much as $2000 a week in royalties to each of the collaborators. One of Caldwell's stories, "Kneel to the Rising Sun," had made him a hero of the left-wing press, which extolled him as a spokesman for the dispossessed. He was published and praised in Russia. *God's Little Acre* had just appeared in a French version by Faulkner's translator, Maurice Coindreau, and with a preface by André Maurois. In this country a respected critic, Joseph Warren Beach, had written of Caldwell (or was soon to write), "He was destined to follow in the footsteps of Chaucer and Dickens, of Balzac and Gorky." That was heady praise, but, in those days, it did not seem implausible.

II

Erskine Caldwell was a preacher's boy raised in genteel poverty. His father, Ira S. Caldwell, had once been secretary of the Home Missions Board of the Associated Reformed Presbyterian Church, an imposing title with little or no income attached to it. The A.R.P., as the boy learned to call his father's church, is one of the smaller and stricter Presbyterian sects, with few rich men among its members, and for some years his

father's occupation was to travel through the rural South, from one struggling congregation to another, and minister to each of them for a few
months, perhaps for a year or more, until its rifts were healed and it could
afford a minister of its own. Sometimes, however, he caused a new rift by
taking the liberal side on racial questions. His salary wasn't always paid.
Even after 1919, when he accepted a permanent post with the A.R.P.
church in Wrens, Georgia, his income was less than $2000 a year.

By that time his only son was a gangling boy of sixteen. Born in
Coweta County, Georgia, in December 1903 (or perhaps in 1902; there is
some argument about the year), Erskine had attended school intermit-
tently—a few months in Staunton, Virginia, four years in Atoka, Tennessee—but he had also been tutored at home by his mother, who had
once taught Latin and French at a fashionable school for girls. After one
year at the Wrens high school, the boy was given a diploma. He wanted to
attend the University of Georgia, and instead he went rebelliously to Erskine, a small denominational college named like himself for the Scottish
founder of A.R.P. He was there for three years and played football on the
freshman and varsity squads, but he had a miserable academic record and
was often away from campus. Once he went to New Orleans and tried to
get a job on a freighter bound for South America, but he was jeered off
the ship. Later in the same month—it was February 1922—he was arrested for vagrancy in Bogalusa, Louisiana, then a sawmill town, and
spent nine days in jail. He might have spent three months there, but he
smuggled out a letter to his father,who wired money enough to pay his
fine and buy a ticket back to Georgia.

In 1923 he got away from Erskine College by applying to the United
Daughters of the Confederacy for a scholarship to the University of
Virginia. He spent four semesters at Virginia, in all, but they were scattered over four academic years. He did well in English, as one might expect, and sociology, but indifferently in his other studies, and he took to
writing stories. In March 1925 he secretly married Helen Lannigan, the
daughter of an athletic coach. Forgiven by the bride's parents, the
Caldwells spent another semester at the University; then Erskine talked
himself into a job as cub reporter on the *Atlanta Journal*. He gave up the
job in the late spring, determined as he was by then to earn a living by
writing fiction. With his wife he went to Maine, where the Lannigans
owned a house and a hundred acres in the town of Mount Vernon, near
Augusta. Erskine fell into the routine of hoeing potatoes or chopping
wood all day, in preparation for winter, then writing through much of
the night. His stories went out to magazines and came back with rejection
slips. In 1929 he received his first letter of acceptance; it was from Alfred
Kreymborg, who was then helping to edit a distinguished yearbook, *The
New American Caravan*.

That is a bare record of Caldwell's early years, based on information
kindly supplied by Dr. William A. Sutton, the author of *Erskine*, an un-

published biography. His account differs at various points from those offered by Caldwell himself, which in turn differ with each other (except in their common quality of being romanticized). I quote from a letter that Caldwell wrote to the compiler of *Twentieth Century Authors* (1942):

When I was eighteen, I enrolled at Erskine College, Due West, S.C., but remained only a short time. I went to sea on a boat that was running guns for a revolt in a Central American republic, and ended up several months later in Mexico. My next attempt to complete my education was when I entered the University of Virginia after having won a scholarship offered by the United Daughters of the Confederacy. I remained there almost a year, working nights in a poolroom for room and board. I had begun to write short stories, though, before I left, and continued writing while working in a variety store in Pennsylvania, playing professional football, managing a lecture tour for a British soldier of fortune, and selling building lots in Alabama under three feet of water. I attended the University of Pennsylvania for a short time, making my expenses, and more, as a bodyguard for a Chinaman. . . .

The article in *Twentieth Century Authors* goes on to summarize information offered by Caldwell on other occasions. It says, "Anyone who doubts Mr. Caldwell's close personal knowledge of the underdogs of whom he writes should note that in addition to the jobs he mentions he has also been a cotton-picker, a lumber-mill hand, a hack-driver, a stagehand in a burlesque theater, a soda-jerker, and a cook and waiter." Some of those jobs he really held, if briefly, while others are as improbable as his running away to Central America. Dr. Sutton said in the course of a long letter, "Perhaps I have left you with the impression that no Caldwell statement about himself can be taken as necessarily true. Exactly right. As one of his old friends told me, 'He is a put-on artist.' "

It would be more accurate to say that he is simply an artist, one who assigns some of his own adventures to a fictional character named Caldwell. That sort of yarning is not at all unusual among poets and novelists. Whitman, Sherwood Anderson, Hemingway, Faulkner, and Nathanael West—to mention only a few names—all created imaginary selves and thereby made trouble for their biographers. In Caldwell's case the process can be broken down into three stages (though I suspect that these developed almost simultaneously). *First stage*: He wrote a great number of stories (often late at night or when he was tired and hungry). Some of the stories surprised him by the feelings they revealed, which were different from those of the daytime Caldwell. *Second stage*: He therefore adopted a persona, that of the man who might logically be supposed to have written the stories. *Third stage*: Even a persona must have a past, so Caldwell constructed it, yarned it out, using a mixture of episodes from his early life with impulses he had never acted upon.

In "The Sacrilege of Alan Kent," the early prose poem that corresponds on a lesser scale to Whitman's "Song of Myself," one notes the beginning process of self-dramatization. Here is what happens to the nine days in the Bogalusa jail:

> I went to a town where lumber was planed, and lay in jail two or three years or more. There was nothing to do at any time other than listen to a Mexican file his pointed yellow teeth and to feel my growing beard.

And here is the episode of his asking for a job on a freighter docked at New Orleans:

> One night I crawled aboard a coaling tramp and begged a man for a job. He heaved a cask-bung at my head and shouted, "Get the hell off here, you God-damn rat!" Before the tramp and the man got half way across the Atlantic, they went down and no one knows where.

Perhaps Caldwell was taking a fictional revenge on the bo's'n who jeered him off the ship. By 1942, however, the episode was to grow into that mythical voyage to Central America on a gun runner. Here is another paragraph, wholly imagined and not pretending to be anything else, that foreshadows a deep feeling expressed in his later work:

> The night when he heated the iron pokers and began burning the Negro girl with them, one of the Negro men and I took two shotguns and killed him. After we had broken the chain around the girl's waist, we walked all night until we reached the town.

The feeling is that blacks and whites of the oppressed classes should join forces against the oppressors. It is a feeling mingled with dreams of miscegenation—as note the presence of a Negro girl—and the dreams become clearer in still another paragraph:

> For a week on the top floor of a seven-story warehouse, a brown-limbed girl fed me every day and warmed me at night. She even helped me lick my wounds. When I threw my cigarette butts out of the window, they fell into the ocean; and I could see all the way across it. Then I went away for two years and came back to get her, but she was not there; and I can't find her now.

That "brown-limbed girl who fed me every day" was to reappear often in Caldwell's novels. Of course "The Sacrilege of Alan Kent" is a fantasy, not a novel, much less a factual memoir. There is, however, a similar dramatization or pure invention of episodes in Caldwell's purportedly true story of his life, *Call It Experience* (1951). I thoroughly enjoy the book, which is full of lively incidents, and have never felt an impulse to separate the fact in it from the fiction. Whether Caldwell really worked on the night shift of a cottonseed-oil mill in Wrens, Georgia, during the spring of 1920 is a question that I gladly leave to Dr. Sutton. A much more interesting subject is the persona he created for himself: its function, its nature, and its effects on his writing, which were good at first, but ultimately disastrous.

III

I should guess that the primary function of the persona was simply to make the author an interesting figure. At one time he must have told himself a continued story in which he was the hero; that is a boyhood practice of many or most authors. Now—again like many authors—he was embroidering the story for others. But the persona also had a secondary function that became always more important, and this was to validate his fiction. Caldwell was presenting himself as, in his publisher's words, "the spokesman for simple people, good or evil, vicious or oppressed," but there might be those who doubted his "close personal knowledge of the underdogs of whom he writes." The obvious answer was that he had been one of the underdogs; that he had worked or looked for work or starved among them as a field hand, a sawmill hand, a carnival roustabout, and a vagrant—not to mention other occupations—and that he had shared their brief pleasures of drinking, gambling, and whoring. One remembers how "Song of Myself" presented its author to the public; he was

> Walt Whitman, an American, one of the roughs,
>   a kosmos,
> Disorderly fleshy and sensual . . . . eating drink-
>   ing and breeding.

In constructing a public image, Caldwell had less to conceal than Whitman and stayed closer to his true self. He was truly a wanderer, truly a listener, truly used to working with those big hands. He withstood hunger and cold like an Indian brave. He truly raged against injustices to Negroes and sufferings endured by the poor whites. On the other hand, he was less of a Deep Southern primitive than he pretended to be, had more schooling than he acknowledged, and had read more contemporary fiction, at least in the days when he was reviewing books for the *Charlotte Observer*. His pose of gullible innocence was combined with a good deal of shrewdness in dealing with editors and in calculating how long his money would last.

One has doubts about a famous telephone call that he received from Maxwell Perkins, who was the Scribners editor in chief. For months—according to Caldwell's account in *Call It Experience*—he had been bombarding Max with stories, usually a new one every week. When he came to New York in the spring of 1930, Max phoned him at his cheap hotel to say that he needn't send any more, at least for the time being. Two of the stories were being accepted, and what about the price: "Would two-fifty be all right? For both of them."

> CALDWELL: Two fifty? I don't know. I thought maybe I'd receive a little more than that.
> PERKINS: You did? Well, what would you say to three-fifty then? That's about as much as we can pay. . . .
> CALDWELL: I guess that'll be all right. I'd thought I'd get a little more than three dollars and a half, though, for both of them.
> PERKINS: Three dollars and fifty cents? Oh, no! I must have given you the wrong impression, Caldwell. Not three dollars and a half. No. I meant three hundred and fifty dollars.

It is a good story, for all one's doubts about Caldwell's perfect financial innocence. Another good story is how, shortly after his return to Maine, he gathered together all his rejected manuscripts, including novels, novelettes, short stories, essays, poems, and jokes; he says that they nearly filled three suitcases. He spent the night paging through them in a lakefront cabin; then in the morning he carried them to the beach and burned them all, adding for good measure a seven years' accumulation of rejection slips. It was a ceremonial bonfire that marked the end of his apprenticeship, and it serves as evidence of his wild fecundity. Dr. Sutton rather spoils the story by noting that the manuscripts of two unpublished novels survive from the same period. They weren't part of the image that Caldwell was trying to project.

The image was that of a man driven to write fiction by "an almost uncontrollable desire," he says, "that seeks fulfillment at any cost . . . as overpowering as the physical need for food and drink." Or warmth or sleep, he might have added. "Upstairs in an unheated room," he says in speaking of his first Maine winter,

> I wore a sweater, a leather jerkin, and an overcoat while I sat at the typewriter. I kept a blanket wrapped around my feet and stopped once in a while to blow on my numbed fingers. . . . For ten and twelve hours a day, and often through the night, I wrote story after story, revising, correcting, and rewriting . . . trying over and over again to make a story sound to the inner ear the way I wanted to make it sound.

Caldwell went south in January when he had burned the last of his firewood and eaten almost the last of his potatoes. He tells us:

> For several weeks I lived in a one-room cabin in the piney woods near Morgana, Edgefield County, South Carolina, eating a can of pork-and-beans three times a day and writing

for sixteen or eighteen hours at a time. After a while I went to Baltimore and lived on lentils and wrote short stories in a room on Charles Street. When money gave out, it was spring. I returned to Maine.

This time . . . I would cut wood during the day and hoe potatoes in the long purple twilight, and, when night came, I would sit down and work on a short story. At that time of year, in that latitude, it was broad daylight at three o'clock in the morning when I went to sleep for a few hours. Time seemed to go so swiftly and there was so much to do that some nights I would stop the clock or turn the hour hand backward while I was at the typewriter.

And what was the purpose of all this labor, beyond the gratification of his physical need for writing? On that point Caldwell has less to say, but still he makes one specific statement:

I wanted to tell the story of the people I knew in the manner in which they actually lived their lives from day to day and year to year, and to tell it without regard for fashions in writing and traditional plots. It seemed to me that the most authentic and enduring materials of fiction were the people themselves, not crafty plots and counterplots designed to manipulate the speech and actions of human beings.

In those early days his writing was never impeded by the want of subjects to write about. He had known hundreds of persons in the Deep South, and later in Maine, whose moments were clamoring to be recorded. If memories failed him, he could always continue his travels around the country making new observations. "Often I would find myself wondering," he says, "what people might be doing at that moment elsewhere in America, in hundreds of villages and small towns." He was so busy at all times observing, experiencing, and recording that he had no leisure for reading books. "Many years ago," he was to say on various occasions, "I divided the population into two parts, those who read and those who write. I wished to belong in the latter category." The one book he carried with him on his travels—besides his typewriter and a cigarette-making machine—was a collegiate dictionary. "I not only consulted it frequently," he says, "but in my free time I read the dictionary instead of reading novels and magazines." Once he went through it striking out every word of more than four syllables.

Such is the image of *homo scribens*, the writing man, that Caldwell presents to the world, and to himself as an ideal. It is a radically simplified picture that omits the problems encountered by others who follow the trade. Caldwell's idealized writer has no problems except material ones; no doubts of himself, no hesitations, no fears of losing contact with his subliminal wealth. He is impelled to write by a physical need that makes him forget the need for sleep; turning back the clock, he goes on working. His only aim is to set down, in the simplest words, a true unplotted record of people without yesterdays. Past literature does not exist for him, and he is scarcely aware of having rivals in the present. As with Adam in the garden, every statement he makes is new. His only mentor is *Webster's Collegiate Dictionary*; his only acknowledged judge and critic is the inner ear.

So far as the author himself accepted that simplified image, he was limiting his possibilities of development. Writers learn from life, if they are lucky, but they also learn from other writers, and Caldwell was learning less than his contemporaries. In the beginning, of course, he had learned somewhat more than he confessed to himself. I suspect that most of his early stories could not have been written without the encouragement offered by *Winesburg, Ohio*, which served as a beacon light to many new talents of that age, including Hemingway and Faulkner. I also suspect that Caldwell owed a debt to Hemingway's Michigan stories, though he never wrote Hemingway prose; and he must have been affected by the experimental spirit of the little magazines that published his early work. But once he stopped reading—except for "half a dozen novels a year," as he tells us—he deprived himself of models to shape his critical sense (that "inner ear") and also lost what Henry James called "the stimulus of suggestion, comparison, emulation." There was no one he cared to emulate—not James, most certainly; not Proust or Joyce or Conrad; he never mentions them. Although he lived in an age of experiments, including his own, he refused to profit from the experiments of others, which he dismissed, in fact, as "crafty plots and counterplots designed to manipulate the speech and actions of human beings." He wanted to depend on his own technical resources. In the proud way of many American writers at the time, conscious as they were of speaking for a new age, in a new country, he wanted to be completely his own man, owing no debt to anyone else's work. All he asked was that his own work be recognized—and recognized it was, after he had served an arduous but relatively brief apprenticeship.

Early recognition—perhaps at a cost to be paid later—is not unlikely to be the fortune of those who cling to a simple image of themselves. So it was with Caldwell, and the bands were already playing in his honor during the winter of 1936–37, when I saw him at that meeting in a midtown hotel. But I wondered even then what his next literary step was to be.

IV

In those days his name was very often coupled with that of William Faulkner, and we have forgotten that the two authors had many things in common. Especially in subject matter: both of them dealt with a society that appeared to be in a violent stage of decay. They came from different, but not strikingly different, sectors of that society. Caldwell's forebears were less prominent than Faulkner's, and he took less pride in them, but they were educated persons, some of whom had fought for the Confederacy. The real difference here was one of election. Faulkner elected, we might say, to speak as an heir of the cotton planters, even while deploring the crime of slavery. Caldwell chose the side of the cotton tenants, especially the blacks, and he painted such an angry picture of their lives that he was often abused as a traitor to his section. Both men, however, were intensely conscious of having roots in the Deep South.

Where Caldwell was outraged, Faulkner was saddened by injustices to Negroes. Both men were fascinated by the theme of miscegenation, with the difference here that Caldwell admired his quadroons and octoroons, while Faulkner portrayed his with sympathy, but still with the feeling that most of them were damned souls. Both wrote about Southern gangsters and prostitutes. One might say that Caldwell's early novelettes *The Bastard* (1929) and *Poor Fool* (1930) are his versions of the material that Faulkner uses in *Sanctuary* (1931). There is no possibility of literary influence, since *The Bastard* and the first draft of *Sanctuary* were being written at the same time, one in Maine, the other in Mississippi, but still there are curious similarities. Other parallels might be noted among short stories, again without any likelihood of literary derivation. "Saturday Afternoon" is Caldwell's "Dry September," "Candy-Man Beechum" is his "Pantaloon in Black," and "Meddlesome Jack" is his "Spotted Horses." Again, in reading novels by both men, one might think of Caldwell's Darling Jill, in *God's Little Acre*, as the sister of Faulkner's Eula Varner and might regard the people on Tobacco Road as the still more ignorant and destitute cousins of those in Frenchman's Bend.

Just as in their work, it is easy to find resemblances in the early careers of the two authors. Both were proud of having taken odd jobs, of which they both exaggerated the number. Both had early moving-picture assignments, and in the spring of 1933 they worked successively on the same picture, never released, which had *Bride of the Bayou* for its studio title. Director Tod Browning was shooting it on the Gulf coast south of New Orleans. Faulkner was fired by MGM, and Caldwell took his place with so little lapse of time that both must have been bitten by the same mosquitoes. Later, during World War II, both men worked in Hollywood without becoming part of the movie colony (and apparently without meeting each other).

Even in the beginning, when they were regarded by the studios and by the public as almost interchangeable values, there were tremendous differences between them. "Faulkner's genius," one says immediately, but genius is hard to define and one has to look for its manifestations in an author's life and works. There is a clue, perhaps, in the image that Faulkner had formed of himself, which was different from Caldwell's self-image and provided more incentives to growth. Very early in his career, Faulkner showed that he wanted to be not only a writer but among the greatest writers. Shakespeare, the Bible, Dostoevsky, Conrad, Joyce: we know that he read all these intensively. A spirit of emulation kept driving him ahead to study and surpass his own contemporaries, then to surpass himself. Some of his good stories became great stories only on revision, as note "That Evening Sun" and *Sanctuary* and "The Bear." Caldwell, with an immense natural gift for story telling, made fewer demands on it. He depended less on imagination and invention than Faulkner did, though both qualities were richly present in his early work. More and more he came to rely on simple observation of what people said and did.

That self-image of Caldwell's was not the best of auguries for his future as a novelist, but still he was to have an amazing career.

For nine years after the publication of his third novel, *Journeyman* (1935), he wrote comparatively little fiction. Instead he traveled to collect material, first by himself and later with Margaret Bourke-White (they were married in 1939 and divorced in 1942). They were in Moscow preparing to do a book of photographs and text on the Soviet Union when Hitler's armies crossed the border in June 1941. For the next few months Caldwell was fantastically busy as one of the first American correspondents on the scene, then later, in Connecticut, as an author rushing books into print to record his impressions. He was summoned to Hollywood as an adviser on the film *Mission to Moscow*, with other assignments to follow. It was not until 1944 that he terminated a studio contract (at four times the salary then being paid to Faulkner) and went back to writing fiction.

His project was to finish a series of roughly a dozen novels dealing with various aspects of the Deep South; "a Southern cyclorama" was his name for it. Perhaps he had looked up "cyclorama" in his favorite *Webster's Collegiate*, where, in the edition he must have owned, he would have found the word defined as "a pictorial view extended circulary, so that the spectator is surrounded as if by things in nature." That came close enough to Caldwell's purpose, which was to encircle the reader with a series of accurate representations. The publisher promised that each of the novels would present a facet of Southern life "seen though the eyes of a sociologist who is also an artist and a humorist. . . . The sum total will give a picture of a society as detailed and complete as Tolstoy's panorama of Czarist Russia."

Grandiose as the project sounds when translated into publisher's talk, it was a mere extension of Caldwell's self-image as a writer. He was simply planning to tell more stories about more and more of the people he knew, "in the manner in which they actually lived their lives from day to day." He was making the most of his travels and his skill as a reporter while neglecting his subconscious resources, including his imaginative power and his talent for transforming the ordinary into the grotesque and apocryphal. He was substituting extensity for intensity, at the risk of exhausting his material and of re-using the same plots as he moved from one Southern background to another. He pushed ahead with the series, however, and a new novel appeared each year without adding to his literary reputation. As late as 1946, Faulkner spoke of him as one of five contemporaries who were interesting to read (the others being Wolfe, Hemingway, Dos Passos, and Steinbeck). A year later Faulkner was quoted as saying to a group of students "that he had once had great hopes for Erskine Caldwell, but now he didn't know."

Great hopes were being realized at the time, but they were of a different and unexpected nature. Caldwell was becoming a central figure in a new branch of American publishing.

Early in 1946, *God's Little Acre* had been the first of his novels to appear as a 25-cent mass-market paperback. His reprint publishers, Kurt Enoch and Victor Weybright, informed him six months later that its sales had passed a million copies, then an unprecedented figure, and were expected to reach two million by the end of the year. Enoch and Weybright had started as American representatives of Penguin Books, but now they had founded their own company, Signet Books (later the New American Library). Of course they were eager to reprint Caldwell's other novels and to promote them vigorously. The rest of the story can be told in phrases and figures that appeared on the back covers of those other books as they were published in Signet editions year after year.

1949. "It is only recently, with the publication of his work in 25-cent editions, that Caldwell has emerged as one of the most influential and bestselling authors of all time. Eleven million copies of six novels have been sold in Signet editions alone (over four and a half million of *God's Little Acre*)."

1949. (There was a second book that year.) "Fifteen million copies of seven books."

1950. "Over 23,000,000 copies."

1952. "Erskine Caldwell is America's favorite author. His books have sold over 25,000,000 copies in Signet editions alone, with *God's Little Acre* topping the list with sales over 6,000,000."

1952. (Again there was a second book for the year.) America's bestselling novelist. Almost 30,000,000 copies of his books have now been sold."

1956. "The world's most popular novelist . . . has written a brilliant succession of novels and volumes of short stories which have sold over 37,000,000 copies in their paperbound Signet editions alone and have been published in twenty-six countries and languages."

1957. ". . . the world's bestselling novelist . . . has achieved international fame as one of the greatest writers of the twentieth century. . . . His books have topped 40,000,000."

1963. "His books have been translated into 27 languages, with over 61,000,000 copies of all editions in print."

As late as 1967, Caldwell was still being advertised as "the world's bestselling novelist," but his publishers had stopped giving figures of "copies in print"; perhaps these weren't growing fast enough. The figures, incidentally, are not the same as for the number of copies actually sold, since they do not allow for unsold books returned to the warehouse. Might one guess that forty million copies would be closer to the actual sales? That is still an impressive figure, though later it was to be surpassed by the total sales of a few younger novelists. Even the unprecedented record of *God's Little Acre* was to be left behind. Caldwell's "unsparing realism" seemed less unsparing in a later age of total sexual candor, and his "earthy, robust" country humor was replaced by kinky urban humor. Still, during a period of fifteen years or more, the demand for his novels had increased the sales of paperback books in general and had helped to establish mass-market publishing as the most flourishing branch of the industry. After being a literary force in a somewhat limited field, Caldwell thus became a commercial property that, for a time, had its national importance.

It should be added that those sales to a vast public were unexpected in the beginning and were never a reflection of his self-image. Unlike many of his successors in the mass market, Caldwell never became a manipulator of plots and characters. He did offer concessions, sometimes in a rather awkward fashion, to what he thought the public expected of him, but even in the weaker novels of his Southern cyclorama, he still was telling honest stories about people he had known from youth or had observed in his travels.

During the 1960s he made some efforts to write more serious books without much thought of whether they would reach a wide audience. *In Search of Bisco* (1965) is an account of how he traveled through the Deep South looking for a black playmate remembered from his childhood. The search, however, is only a framework for his reflections on racial bigotry and for dramatic monologues by others. Caldwell, always an ear-minded writer, is good at catching their voices. Another nonfiction book, *Deep South* (1968), is a report on fundamentalism as he observed it in various white and black congregations. A few of the white ones, always in small towns, had the Reverend Ira S. Caldwell as their pastor. The best passages in the book are tributes by a wayward son to his father's tolerant and courageous Christianity. Some of Caldwell's later novels also treat his material more seriously and even, in one or two cases, with a hint of affection. The best of them is *Weather Shelter* (1969), which is based on two themes that appeared in his earliest writing: miscegenation and the search for a lost son of mixed blood. This time they lead to a happy ending. The son is found; he is rescued from an attempted lynching; and he will inherit his white father's estate.

I read these three of his later books with sympathy and respect for the author, but, it must be confessed, with none of the troubled surprise I had felt on reading his early work. It is the early books—say the first three novels and the stories up to *Georgia Boy* (1943)—on which Caldwell's reputation will stand or fall. Today there is an unfortunate tendency to let it fall; to dismiss the books as having been too popular. We should not forget that they made a contribution to American letters, not to mention their having added a chapter to American folklore.

In a way they continued the tradition of what used to be called Southwestern humor, though more of it was Georgian or Alabamian. What they added was a new vision, combined with new characters and a new sensibility. Caldwell was taking chances and was giving rein to his subconscious feelings. The result in his work was that homely objects or events—a crushed strawberry, a sack of turnips, a crown fire in the piney woods—became charged with emotion and made themselves remembered as symbols. There was a vein of poetry beneath the surface of his early writing; it was laid bare in "The Sacrilege of Alan Kent," but he made no effort to exploit it, and later it disappeared. There was also a hint that many of his "unplotted" stories fall into ritual patterns corresponding to racial memories. In *God's Little Acre*, for instance, why does Will Thompson tear the clothes from Griselda and reveal her "rising beauties" before he turns on the power in the closed-down cotton mill? There is nothing logical in the sequence of events, but still we sense that it is right. In *Tobacco Road*, when the grandmother is dying of hunger with her face in the dirt, why does Jeeter Lester feel that the soil is right for planting, and set a fire to clear his overgrown fields, and die in the flames? "All this is magic," Kenneth Burke said long ago in the best essay that anyone has written on Caldwell's early work. ". . . the plots are subtly guided by the logic of dreams." It is no wonder that Jeeter and Sister Bessie and Will Thompson have become figures in American folklore. The magic is there, and it must have cast a spell on the millions who bought the novels in paperback long after the critics had forgotten them.

"Repetition as Technique in the Short Stories of Erskine Caldwell"

Scott MacDonald*

James Dickey has said that Thomas Wolfe's work is "so rhetorical that it is almost a shameful act. But there should be such rhetorical writing, as the indication of a kind of limit."[1] The converse might be said about Erskine Caldwell's short fiction. In many of his stories Caldwell's style is so spare and so completely unadorned that the reader learns just how few of the traditional literary devices a writer can use and still create stories which are meaningful and effective. While the hallmark of Caldwell's prose style is simplicity, however, a careful investigation of the stories in such collections as *American Earth*, *We Are the Living*, *Kneel to the Rising Sun*, *Southways*, *Jackpot*, *The Complete Stories*, and *Georgia Boy* shows that Caldwell has worked successfully with a variety of technical devices. Particularly impressive is his extensive experimentation with repetition.[2]

With the exception of Gertrude Stein, there has probably never been a writer more fascinated with the possibilities of repetition than Erskine Caldwell. While the amount and the kind of repetition used in Caldwell's stories varies considerably, repetition itself is both the most obvious and the most important literary device in much of his best work. Some of the repetition in his stories is a reflection of the Steinesque idea that people continually repeat themselves in conversation, that, in fact, repetition is one of the most fundamental qualities of speech. Nearly every character in Caldwell's fiction habitually repeats seemingly offhand phrases and sentences which often serve as indices to aspects of the character's personality. Further, instead of purposely avoiding repetitive detail in descriptive passages, Caldwell normally presents the reader with a few well-chosen aspects of a scene and then repeats them whenever the setting needs comment. The result is simple but vivid description often made memorable by the degree to which the simplicity reflects the unsophisticated lives of the characters.

In much of Caldwell's short fiction repetition also functions in more

*Reprinted from *Studies in American Fiction*, 5 (1977), 213–25.

330

complex and unusual ways. In many stories a limited number of repeated phrases and sentences are used to emphasize various types of structure. In "The Automobile That Wouldn't Run" and "Saturday Afternoon," for example, action begins at a certain place, moves to a second location, and then returns to the starting point. In both stories the style reflects this movement. Certain words and phrases are repeated during the first paragraphs of each story. When action moves away, these repetitions cease but are apparent again at the end of the story when the characters are back at the original place. By using repetition in this manner Caldwell gains two results. First, he brings the stories to a decisive conclusion, and second, he creates a strong final emphasis on the basic immovability of the central characters. In "A Swell-Looking Girl," a story in which Lem Johnson tries to prove to his country neighbors that his new wife wears fancy "little pink things" under her dress, a different kind of structure is emphasized by a fairly simple pattern of repetition on the part of Tom, the first-person narrator. As the events of "A Swell-Looking Girl" are presented, the phrase "a swell-looking girl" is repeated periodically, and with each repetition the phrase becomes more emphatic.[3] The regular recurrence of this line not only stresses the growing excitement of the narrator as he watches Lem raise his wife's skirt higher and higher, it also creates an overall pattern which adds coherence to the story.

While repetition is the most important stylistic device in the stories which have been discussed so far, the amount of repetition in these stories is not particularly heavy, at least not for Caldwell. In some of Caldwell's best stories repetitious style is used far more emphatically and results in three different general effects. First, in such stories as "The Medicine Man," "Where the Girls Were Different," and "August Afternoon" heavy repetition emphasizes erotic excitement. In other stories a consistent barrage of repeated lines creates a feeling of almost insane frenzy. Finally, in some stories heavy repetition causes conversations to take on symbolic implications.

The most important aspect of the repetition in the humorously erotic story "The Medicine Man" is the fact that as Professor Eaton and Effie Henderson become increasingly involved in their mutual seduction, repeated words and phrases become more and more emphatic. As Effie takes her clothes off so that the Professor can make what he calls a thorough medical examination, Professor Eaton continually asks if "perhaps" Effie will remove her blouse, if "perhaps" she'd like to hear more about the miraculous powers of Indian Root Tonic, and, when she hesitates to take everything off, if "perhaps" he should go. To reassure Effie, the Professor explains again and again how important it is for her "to place yourself entirely in my hands," or a slight variation, and nine times in about three pages he assures her that everything will be "absolutely" all right. The Professor's repetitive cajolings and assurances are punctuated by Effie's continual questions: "Do you want me to take—"; "And this, too, Professor Eaton? This, too?"; "Professor Eaton, do you want me to take off all of this—like this?" The tension created in the story by the repetition builds until Effie exclaims, "You make me feel so funny, Professor Eaton. And are you sure—." The Professor assures her, "Absolutely" . . . Absolutely," and urges her one last time to "place yourself completely in my hands" before her brother arrives with his town-marshall's pearl-handled revolver. The frustration of the Professor (and the reader) at the brother's arrival is reflected perfectly in the style for the repetition stops as completely as the sexual excitement does.[4]

Still heavier repetition creates the rising excitement in "Where the Girls Were Different," a humorous story about a young boy's adventures when he goes across the county to meet some girls who are supposedly "different" from the girls around home. The general concentration of repeated phrases which is evident all through the story is given direction by Caldwell's use of what might be called verbal counterpoint. The most frequently repeated phrase in the story is "were different," which in some form is used about sixteen times in the five pages of the narrative and creates one rhythmic pattern. A second pattern is developed as Fred drives to Rosemark and gets a date. Only one word is involved at first ("gee") but because it is an emphatic word, Fred's repetition of it is noticeable. "Gee" is used first when Fred explains that he hated to lie to his parents about where he was going, "but—gee—I had to go down to see those girls in Rosemark." As the story continues, and Fred's excitement grows, the author's use of the word becomes increasingly noticeable. Fred explains how the girl he asks for a date says "Sure" and he goes on to comment, "Gee, this was the way to see girls." Later, when Betty sits very close to Fred, he exclaims, "Gee, she was different!"

The rhythms created by the two patterns of repetition are made particularly emphatic by the fact that Caldwell uses the patterns in closer and closer proximity. This is clear, for instance, in the third repetition of "gee" mentioned above and it is clear in subsequent instances as well. After Fred has begun to gain confidence with Betty, for example, he decides to try and kiss her:

> Gee whiz! I reached down and kissed her and she wouldn't let me stop. The old car rocked from one side of the road to the other as dizzy as a bat. I couldn't see to steer it because Betty wouldn't let me stop kissing her, and I had to wait until we ran into a ditch almost before I knew which way to turn the wheel. Gee whiz! The girls in Rosemark were certainly different, all right (p. 413)

Caldwell brings the two patterns together one final time when Betty asks Fred why he has stopped kissing her. When Fred kisses her again, she puts her arms around his neck and her legs across his lap, and Fred exclaims, "*Gee, whiz!* I didn't know girls did like that! Ben said the girls down in

Rosemark were different, but I didn't expect anything like this to happen to me. Holy Cats!" It is just after this especially emphatic use of "gee" in connection with "were different" that Fred pulls into Betty's driveway and is rudely chased away by her father who has been following in the family car. As is true in "The Medicine Man," in "Where the Girls Were Different" the stylistic heartbeat created by the repetition ceases just when the erotic involvement does. The resulting frustration of the protagonist is thus reflected by a calmer style.

A final instance of Caldwell's use of heavy repetition to create erotic excitement occurs in "August Afternoon," a story in which Caldwell's ability to work effectively with different types of repetition is especially apparent. In "August Afternoon" Vic Glover's young attractive wife Willie is courted and won by a man with an eleven-inch hairy-handled knife while Vic and Hubert, a black friend of Vic's, look on. Most of the types of repetition mentioned so far in this study are used in "August Afternoon." There is a generally heavy concentration of repeated descriptive detail and conversational statement, and a specific line is repeated throughout the story in the manner of "were different" in "Where the Girls Were Different": the five-fold repetition of Hubert's question, "We ain't aiming to have no trouble today, is we?" creates a rhythmic refrain which helps to organize the story. In addition to the previously discussed kinds of repetition, however, "August Afternoon" uses two which have not been mentioned. One involves the fact that as Caldwell's characters grow more tense, their manner of addressing each other changes. For example, when Hubert gets worried about the possibility of violence, he begins to address "Mr. Vic" in an unusually repetitive way:

> "Mr. Vic, I'm trying to tell you about Miss Willie. Miss Willie's been sitting there on that high step showing her pretty and he's been looking at her a right long time, Mr. Vic. If you won't object to me saying so, Mr. Vic, I reckon I'd tell Miss Willie to go sit somewhere else, if I was you. Miss Willie ain't got much on today, Mr. Vic. Just only that skimpy outside dress, Mr. Vic. That's what I've been trying to tell you. I walked out there in the yard this while ago to see what he was looking at so much, and when I say Miss Willie ain't got much on today, I mean she's got on just only that skimpy outside dress, Mr. Vic. You can go look yourself and see if I'm lying to you, Mr. Vic"
> (p. 441).

The seven-fold repetition of "Mr. Vic" creates a pounding rhythm which is emphasized by the five-fold repetition of "Miss Willie" and by Hubert's frequent emphasis on how little Willie is wearing. Several times during "August Afternoon" the tension Hubert feels is revealed in similar passages.

A very different type of repetition is used in the two conversations Willie has with the stranger, one of which begins this way:

"How old are you? Floyd asked Willie.
"Fifteen."
Floyd jerked the knife out of the wood and thrust it deeper into the same place.
"How old are you?" she asked him.
"About twenty-seven."
"Are you married?"
"Not now," he said. "How long have you been?"
"About three months," Willie said.
"How do you like it?"
"Pretty good so far."
"How about another kiss?"
"You just had one."
"I'd like another one now."
"I ought not to let you kiss me again."
"Why not?"
"Men don't like girls who kiss too much."
"I'm not that kind."
"What kind are you?"
"I'd like to kiss you a lot" (pp. 443–44).

The erotic excitement this conversation creates during the story is emphasized by the repetitive format of the characters' brief questions and responses and by the combination of this rhythmically suggestive format with the characters' repetition of specific words. The two conversations between Willie and the stranger are particularly noticeable since the many exchanges between Vic and Hubert are composed of generally much longer statements. Both conversations occur at crucial moments in the story and raise the level of tension substantially. All in all, the various kinds of repetition work together in "August Afternoon" to intensify events and to create excitement. Little meaning in a philosophic sense is developed during the story, but for sheer joy in the possibilities of repetition, "August Afternoon" is a *tour de force*.

A second effect Caldwell develops by using heavy repetition is evident in "Country Full of Swedes," Caldwell's famous story about the arrival of a family of exuberant Swedes in a normally quiet valley in rural Maine. "Country Full of Swedes" uses repetition differently from previously discussed stories. No complete sentences or long phrases are repeated consistently throughout the story in the way "We ain't aiming to have no trouble today, is we" is repeated in "August Afternoon." In "Country Full of Swedes" Caldwell repeats single words and short phrases literally dozens of times to create an overwhelming feeling of frenzy.

The most frequently repeated word in "Country Full of Swedes" is "Swedes." Hardly a paragraph goes by without a character referring to the Swedes in one way or another. The intensity of this repetition varies somewhat but is probably heaviest when Stan takes his first careful look at the new arrivals:

There were Swedes everywhere a man could see, and the ones that couldn't be seen could be heard yelling their heads off inside the yellow clapboarded house across the road. There wasn't any mistake about there being Swedes there, either; because I've never yet seen a man who mistakes a Swede or a Finn for an American. Once you see a Finn or a Swede you know, God-helping, that he is a Swede or a Finn, and not a Portugee or an American.

There was a Swede everywhere a man could look. Some of them were little Swedes, and women Swedes, to be sure; but little Swedes, in the end, and women Swedes too, near about, grow up as big as any of them. When you come right down to it, there's no sense in counting out the little Swedes and the women Swedes.

Out in the road in front of their house were seven-eight autos and trucks loaded down with furniture and household goods. All around, everything was Swedes. The Swedes were yelling and shouting at one another, the little Swedes and the women Swedes just as loud as the big Swedes. . . (p. 7).

The seventeen repetitions of "Swedes" in these few lines give the passage an especially frantic effect, an effect not only apropos for the frenzied action which is going on, but also quite expressive of the specific event involved at this point in the story—Jim's discovery of how many Swedes there are. The story is as full of 'Swedes" as the country seems.

Other phrases are repeated over and over and give other sections of "Country Full of Swedes" an equally frenetic feeling. One of these phrases is "Good God"; others include the adjectival combination of "God" with other words, as in "God-awful," "God-helping," and "God-damn." While these phrases are not repeated quite as often as "Swedes" is, they appear again and again, sometimes in combination with "Swedes." Early in the story, for example, Stan hears gunfire:

"Who fired that God-awful shot, Jim?" I yelled at him, leaping down the stairs quicker than a man of my years ought to let himself do.

"Good God!" Jim said, his voice hoarse, and falling all to pieces like a stump of punkwood. "The Swedes! The Swedes are shooting, Stan!"

"What Swedes, Jim—those Swedes who own the farm and building across the road over there?" I said, trying to find the buttonholes in my shirt. "Have they come back here to live on that farm?"

"Good God, yes!" he said, his voice croaking deep down in his throat, like he had swallowed too much water. "The Swedes are all over the place. They're everywhere you can see, there's that many of them."

"What's their name, Jim?" I asked him. "You and Mrs. Frost never told me what their name is."

"Good God, I don't know. I never heard them called anything but Swedes, and that's what it is, I guess" (p. 5).

The heavily repeated phrases mentioned so far, when combined with the less frequent, but still relatively heavy repetition of such phrases as "one-two," "of a forenoon," "yellow-headed," "yelling and shouting," and the repetition of longer phrases and sentences during specific paragraphs, make "Country Full of Swedes" a story of humorous but nerve-wracking frenzy.[5] The style of the story perfectly reflects the hysteria of the narrator, who is unable to understand or adjust to his exuberant new neighbors. The only comparable effect this critic is able to think of is created by the cinematic device called "pixilation," that method of shooting single frames of an activity and running them at normal speed so that characters seem to dance around on the screen like puppets.

In "We Are Looking at You, Agnes" heavy repetition is used to create a different kind of frenzy. Agnes, the protagonist and narrator of the story, is obsessed with the idea that she is being judged by her family for having become a prostitute. Her obsession is clearly reflected by the mad persistence of a series of paranoid thoughts which are presented and emphasized by the very heavy repetition of such lines as "don't sit there all day long and look at me without saying something about it" and "Ask me, Papa; I'll tell you the truth. . . ."

A final effect created by Caldwell's use of heavy repetition is apparent in "Daughter," a story in which the extreme intensity of repeated phrases and sentences results in the creation of symbolic narrative. "Daughter" is about Jim, a black man who has been jailed because he murdered his young daughter when he could no longer stand her being hungry. In presenting "Daughter" Caldwell uses repetition of several types. Certain statements by Jim and other characters are repeated consistently through much of the story. The most important of these repeated statements is Jim's "Daughter's been hungry, though—awful hungry," which with slight variations is repeated eight times. Often, the statement is followed by Jim's averring, "I just couldn't stand it no longer" or by a slight variation of this sentence. The sheriff also repeats himself fairly consistently throughout the story. Because he is afraid that Jim will get excited and dangerous, the sheriff says again and again, "Now, just take it easy, Jim boy" or "Now, don't you get careless, Jim boy," or a similar statement. Other phrases and sentences are repeated during specific sections of the story to emphasize certain points. Early in the story, as the townspeople try to determine exactly what happened, their question, "It must have been an accident, wasn't it, Jim?" is repeated three times in about a page. Later, when Jim indicates that he had no money to buy food, the townspeople say four times "it don't seem right" that Jim should have killed his child when he might have asked for food, and Jim defends himself by responding several times, "I made enough for all of us to eat," emphasizing the fact that he didn't want to ask for handouts since he had worked and made money he never received. Finally, in addition to the many repetitions in conversation, Caldwell uses frequent repetition in his descriptions of events.

The most important and most noticeable aspect of the repetition in "Daughter" is the fact that the repeated statements and descriptive details occur in a very limited space. The story is five pages long, and most of the repetition occurs in the first three pages. As a result, there are passages during which nearly every line is a repeated line. In addition to creating tension, this extremely heavy repetition causes "Daughter" to seem at times less like a straight narrative than a kind of chant, something akin to the responsive reading during a church service or to the dialogue between character and chorus in some Greek tragedies. Through the process of repetition lines like "Daughter was hungry" and "it don't seem right" take on symbolic power as capsulations of regional realities, and the almost ritualistic repetition of these statements by the crowd, the sheriff, and Jim causes their whole dialogue to have significance as a general statement about racial injustice and exploitation. All in all, the heavy repetition in "Daughter" helps to expand a single confrontation between a black man, a sheriff, and a group of townspeople into universal—or at least na-tional—significance.[6]

Another general aspect of Caldwell's experimentation with repeti-tion is his blending of repeated statements with colloquial diction, rhyme and rhythm to create stories which might be called prose folk ballads. The most successful of these stories are "Candy-Man Beechum" and "The Fly in the Coffin," both of which are attempts to portray aspects of black life in the South.

Caldwell uses colloquial diction in "Candy-Man Beechum" and "The Fly in the Coffin" in an unusual way. Most stories about blacks written by both whites and blacks are presented by narrators who use standard white American English. In "Candy-Man Beechum" and "The Fly in the Coffin," however, Caldwell uses third-person narrators who present events in a convincing rendition of black English. The opening paragraphs of the two stories illustrate Caldwell's method:

"Candy-Man Beechum":

It was ten miles out of the Ogeechee swamps, from the sawmill to the top of the ridge, but it was just one big step to Candy-Man. The way he stepped over those Middle Georgia gullies was a sight to see (p. 23).

"The Fly in the Coffin":

There was poor old Dose Muffin, stretched out on the corn-crib floor, dead as a frostbitten watermelon vine in November, and a pesky housefly was walking all over his nose (p. 576).

While the coloquial diction in these paragraphs is not obtrusive, the phrases "it was all just one big step," "was a sight to see," "poor old," and the down-home simile, "dead as a frostbitten watermelon vine in November," create a feeling that the reader is not simply observing events involving black people but that he is listening to tales which are products of black folk culture.[7]

Caldwell uses repetition to develop a prose chorus in each story, and he carefully controls its appearance to emphasize aspects of the action. The chorus in "Candy-Man Beechum" is the periodic repetition of someone asking "Where you goin', Candy-Man," "What's your big hurry, Candy-Man," or a variation of these sentences, and of Candy-Man's response: "Make way for these flappin feet, boys. . . . Here I come!" or a variation. Each repetition of this chorus brings Candy-Man closer to town and to the danger his confidence obviously creates for him in a locale where, as one character puts it, "the white-folks is first-come." By the end of the third repetition of the chorus, the reader has become accustomed to the exuberant rhythm created by the repeated lines. The result is that when the fourth chorus begins with the white policeman's question "What's your hurry, Candy-Man?" and is not followed by Candy-Man's customary response, the stylistic rhythm is as abruptly interrupted as Candy-Man's journey is. For a moment the reader wonders if Candy-Man's confidence has been shaken, if the black man will give in and be taken to jail. But Candy-Man has the triumphant last word. When the policeman warns that if Candy-Man keeps arguing, he'll be forced to "hurry him on" to death, Candy-Man replies, "If that's the way it's to be, then make way for Candy-Man Beechum because here I come." The triumph of Candy-Man's refusal to compromise the vitality of his life is beautifully emphasized stylistically by the completion of the formerly interrupted chorus.

In "The Fly in the Coffin," a yarn in which a dead man interrupts the joyous celebration of his funeral to demand a fly-swatter so he can kill a fly which has gotten trapped in his coffin, the chorus is a three-statement conversation between Aunt Marty and Woodrow. Three times Aunt Marty says, "You, Woodrow, you! Go look in that corncrib and take a look if any old flies worrying Dose" or a slight variation; three times Woodrow hesitates to obey her; and three times Aunt Marty assures Woodrow that he must protect Dose from the flies. The repetition of this conversation creates an expectation in the reader which is frustrated during the last third of the story. After Aunt Marty gets a swatter and Dose lies back down in the coffin, the story ends with a series of rhythmic paragraphs but without a return to the chorus. Caldwell's decision to conclude the story in this manner is perfectly appropriate; the story trails off stylistically just as the party and the dancing continue on into the night.

The ballad-like feeling created in the two stories by Caldwell's combination of colloquial diction and repetition is enhanced by his unusual use of rhyme and rhythm in specific sentences. When Candy-Man is unjustly stopped by the "white boss," for example, he says, "I never bothered whitefolks, and they sure oughtn't bother me. But there ain't much use in living if that's the way it's going to be." The rhyme of "me" and "be" is made particularly emphatic by the rhythmic similarity of the two sentences. In some passages rhythm alone is used effectively. Near the middle of the story, for instance, the narrator explains "Eight miles to town, and two more to go, and he'd be rapping on that yellow gal's door." In "The Fly in the Coffin" Aunt Marty's explanations of why Woodrow must keep flies away from Dose are always rhythmic and in two instances they rhyme: "Dead or alive, Dose cares about flies" is one of these; "Dose sees flies, he dead or alive" is the other. Rhythm alone is used effectively in such sentences as "Poor old Dose, dead a day and a night, couldn't say a word," and "The jumper was dry, the coffin was thrown together, and the grave was six feet deep."

The development of the rhythmically musical folk ballad form for "Candy-Man Beechum" and "The Fly in the Coffin" is particularly apropos. Both stories not only portray aspects of black life in the South as black people might tell of them, but also dramatize positive responses of black people to their situation. "Candy-Man Beechum" portrays a man who heroically ignores social limitations and lives a life which, while tragically short, is vigorous and full of good humor. In "The Fly in the Coffin" even the reality of death fails to kill either the vitality of Dose, whose hatred of flies is so strong that it enables him to come back to life, or the energy of Dose's neighbors, who are able to wring joy out of tragedy and limited surroundings. The syncopated musical style of the two prose ballads emphasizes this theme of people rising above apparent limitations by reminding the reader of that tradition of the spiritual and jazz which itself represents the triumph of black vitality over societal oppression. The style of these two stories, in other words, is a reflection of the idea the stories present.[8]

While the fundamental quality of Caldwell's prose style is simplicity, a careful investigation of his short fiction shows that he has experimented with various kinds of simplicity. The most important stylistic experiments in the stories discussed, as well as in a substantial number which have not been mentioned, involve repetition.[9] Caldwell controls both the number of repeated words, phrases, and sentences and their distribution to create a wide range of effects, many of which are exciting and unusual. He also experiments with colloquial diction and with rhythm and blends these aspects of style with repetition to create vibrantly musical folk ballads, prose pieces which may be unique in English. All in all, Caldwell's ability to work with the possibilities of style is noteworthy even in a period of American literature which includes such brilliant stylists as Gertrude Stein, Ernest Hemingway, and William Faulkner.

Notes

1. James Dickey, *Sorties* (New York, 1971), p. 117.

2. Although most critics who mention Caldwell's short stories seem impressed with their quality, almost nothing has been written about them except for a few reviews and introductions. Even James Korges, who calls Caldwell "one of the American masters of the short story," spends only one paragraph on the short fiction in his pamphlet on Caldwell. See *Erskine Caldwell* (Minneapolis, 1969), pp. 45–46. A few critics have mentioned aspects of Caldwell's style. Joseph Warren Beach describes what he calls the *"naive style,"* and Henry Seidel Canby discusses Caldwell's use of understatement and the strong emotion it often disguises. See Beach, *American Fiction: 1920–1940* (New York, 1941), p. 247; and Canby, "Erskine Caldwell," an introduction to *A Day's Wooing and Other Stories* (New York, 1944), pp. vii–viii. Randall Jarrell mentions Caldwell's heavy use of repetition, a quality which Kenneth Burke feels is Caldwell's greatest vice: "He seems as contented as a savage to say the same thing again and again," but Burke also suggests that repetition in Caldwell's prose "is so extreme as almost to perform the function of rhyme in verse." See Jarrell, "Ten Books," *Southern Review* (1936), 404; and Burke, *The Philosophy of Literary Form* (Baton Rouge, 1941), p. 360. More recently, C. Hugh Holman has called Caldwell's style, "simple, direct, with underlying folk rhythms, resulting in part from repetition and in part from a folk vocabulary." See "The View from the Regency-Hyatt: Southern Social Issues and the Outer World," in George Core, *Southern Fiction Today: Renascence and Beyond* (Athens, Georgia, 1969), pp. 29–30. Finally, in his interesting and painstaking review of French criticism on Caldwell, Stewart Benedict suggests that Caldwell's stylistic discipline is what makes him an important figure in the eyes of the French. See "Gallic light on Erskine Caldwell," SAQ, 60 (1961), 390–97.

3. All quotations are from Erskine Caldwell, *The Complete Stories of Erskine Caldwell* (Boston, 1953). Because of the brevity of most of Caldwell's stories and because of the nature of much of the quotation in this essay, specific page references would often be distracting. As a result, only long quotations include page references. These are included in the text.

4. The ending of "The Medicine Man" involves a final punch line. Having agreed at gunpoint to marry Effie and having been made something of a fool in the process, the Professor is so much the optimistic salesman that when Effie exclaims, "Just to think that I'm going to marry a traveling herb doctor. . . .Why! all the girls in town will be so envious of me they won't speak for a month!" he immediately returns to his former glory: " 'Absolutely' Professor Eaton said, pulling tight the loosened knot in his tie and adjusting it in the opening of his celluloid collar. 'Absolutely. Indian Root Tonic has unlimited powers.' " The Professor's final repetition of "absolutely" is the funniest line in the story, and it is funny because it is a repeated line, because it emphasizes the impossibility of interrupting for long the Professor's irrepressible blarney.

5. "One-two" is an adjectival combination expressing the idea "approximately one or two." Caldwell also uses "three-four," "four-five," etc. Such combinations were presumably common in rural Maine when Caldwell wrote "Country Full of Swedes."

6. "Masses of Men," a story which originally appeared with "Daughter" in *Kneel to the Rising Sun*, is similar to "Daughter" in the way it uses repetition. "Masses of Men" is not a totally satisfactory story, but it contains a brilliant, brutal scene in which a poverty-stricken mother sells her nine-year-old dauthter as a prostitute to a man who pays her twenty-five cents. The scene uses the extremely heavy repetition of several lines in much the way "Daughter" does to build breath-taking tension and to elevate the sordid events into a kind of ritualized general statement about the dehumanizing effects of poverty, cold, and starvation. *God's Little Acre* also uses repetition in this manner in those chapters during which Will goes to the factory to "Turn on the power." See *God's Little Acre* (New York, 1933), pp. 227–54.

7. Similar use of colloquial diction can be found in such stories as "Big Buck" and "Nine

Dollars' Worth of Mumble," though it is not used as consistently or as effectively as in "Candy-Man Beechum" and "The Fly in the Coffin."

8. Like "The Fly in the Coffin" and "Candy-Man Beechum," "The First Autumn" is made memorable in part by Caldwell's development of a chorus which helps to create a ballad-like feeling. The chorus is a series of three-fold repetitions: of "Woof! Woof! Woof!" when the children and father are playing bear; of "Neigh! Neigh! Neigh!" when they're playing horse; and of "Boo! . . . Boo! . . . Boo!" when the children and their mother sneak up on the father when they think he is asleep. The strange mood created by the chorus is enhanced by Caldwell's unusual juxtaposition of the third-person narrator's use of diction one normally expects of a child—the narrator, for example, refers to the father as "Daddy"—and of the use by the children of diction which sounds very adult. Fittingly, the juxtaposition reflects the reversal of roles the story is involved with. The father dies while playing games with children who are playing at being adult, and the reader assumes that as a result of the father's death at a comparatively young age, the children will soon be forced in reality to become more adult.

9. Some stories which have not been mentioned in which repetition is an important device are "Blue Boy," "Dorothy," "An Evening in Nuevo Leon," "The Growing Season," "Horse Thief," "Indian Summer," "Kneel to the Rising Sun," "The Mating of Marjorie," "Mamma's Little Girl," "Meddlesome Jack," "Memorandum," "The Negro in the Well," "Over the Green Mountains," "Picking Cotton," "Slow Death," "Yellow Girl," and "A Woman in the House."

"An Evaluative Check-List of Erskine Caldwell's Short Fiction"

Scott MacDonald*

During the Thirties and early Forties Erskine Caldwell was one of the most prolific and successful American short story writers. Three dozen of Caldwell's stories appeared on Edward J. O'Brien's "Roll of Honor" in his annual *Yearbook of the American Short Story* between 1930 and 1941.[1] Six of Caldwell's stories were chosen by O'Brien to appear in *The Best Short Stories* of various years, and *Kneel to the Rising Sun* was rated the best collection of 1936, ahead of both Fitzgerald's *Taps at Reveille* and Porter's *Flowering Judas*. The best evidence of O'Brien's high opinion of Caldwell came in 1939, when he ranked Caldwell's *Southways* above Faulkner's *The Unvanquished*, Hemingway's *The Fifth Column and the First Forty-Nine Stories*, Steinbeck's *The Long Valley*, and Wright's *Uncle Tom's Children* in his listing of the best collections of the year. Of course, one may disagree with O'Brien about the significance of Caldwell's stories, but O'Brien's overall judgment of Caldwell's importance seems worthy of consideration, especially since it was reaffirmed by nearly all critics who reviewed Caldwell's collections of short fiction as they appeared. Some serious critics complained that Caldwell was repeating himself by the latter Thirties and that the brutality of the events in some of the stories was not sincere or justifiable, but most agreed with Otis Ferguson: "There ought to be some Caldwell in your library . . . if you have a proper appreciation of the short story in American literature and the things from life it brings us. Caldwell is one of the good men writing, and bound someday to have a place in the courses of the professors who irk him so. They may not know a good thing when they see it because it is a new thing; but their literary history has always been a growth of new things which lay familiar on the tongue into the standard things people would not forget because of their being also true and beautiful and craftsmanwise and nice to have around."[2]

Ferguson's prediction that Caldwell's work would last has, unfortunately, not been fulfilled, at least not so far. In fact, judging from

*Reprinted from *Studies in Short Fiction*, 11 (1978), 81–97.

the general critical neglect of Caldwell's stories during the past three decades and the infrequency with which Caldwell's short fiction is included in recent college anthologies, it seems clear that for all practical purposes Caldwell's stories have been forgotten by serious students of American literature.[3] The question, then, is why a body of work which seemed so significant a generation ago is now almost unknown. There are, it seems to me, at least two major reasons. One involves that fact that Caldwell himself appears to have lost interest in short fiction after the early Forties. While he published over a hundred stories during the fifteen years between 1929 and 1943, his output since 1943, a far longer period, has been fewer than thirty-five stories, most of which are a good deal less impressive than the stories of earlier years. Caldwell himself explains, "After I had written about 150 short stories (both published and wastebasketed) I felt I had done enough and wanted to spend my efforts on novels and non-fiction."[4] With few new stories to rekindle enthusiasm, it is not surprising that interest in Caldwell's short fiction did not remain at the level of the Thirties.

A more important reason for the failure of Caldwell's short fiction to sustain the reputation it deserves involves certain aspects of the stories themselves. Caldwell's stories have many impressive qualities. They are powerful, clear, direct, honest, and unpretentious. Technically, they are ingeniously, though not obtrusively, experimental in such stylistic areas as repetition and dialect and they work inventively with the reader's expectations. Quite by design, however, the stories have little appeal for the reader whose primary interest in reading is intellectual exploration. While they are often psychologically insightful and politically committed, they do not offer complex philosophical discoveries or the fascinating webs of imagery which give many great stories their interest. Since philosophical complexity is the quality which for many teachers makes a story "teachable," Caldwell's stories are far less frequently taught in college courses than stories by artists of comparable stature.

The absence of Caldwell's stories from the bookshelves of many serious students of American fiction and from most college courses in American literature is particularly unfortunate. Not only are the stories interesting and valuable reading in themselves, their rigorous simplicity—they may be the simplest effective stories in American literature—can help to illuminate important qualities of more complicated writers. Because Caldwell has been so consistently ignored in recent years, however, a reader who wants to become more aware of Caldwell's accomplishment must deal with some very basic difficulties. For one thing, Caldwell has published a considerable body of short fiction: to date, around 150 short stories, as well as dozens of sketches which have fictional qualities. While a good many of these are of extremely high quality, the very size of Caldwell's output makes inevitable a certain amount of less successful work. At present, it is difficult for a reader not already familiar with Caldwell's career to know which stories to read or how many good stories to expect.[5] There are difficulties, too, in putting what is read into chronological perspective. Many of the stories have been published and republished in a number of different volumes. In some instances, titles have been changed, and in others, material has appeared in different form in different places.

The check-list which follows is an attempt to facilitate a reexamination of Caldwell's short fiction. Starting with 1929 and moving year by year to the present, the check-list describes the contents of every collection of stories published to date, and it lists the first publication of each of Caldwell's stories.[6] Annotations are used to supply information about changes in title or form and to indicate which stories have been singled out for distinction. In addition, under "Other" the listing includes information about nonfiction books which are relevant to the study of Caldwell's short fiction. In such collections as *Some American People* and *Say, Is This the U.S.A.*, for example, Caldwell includes expository essays, short stories, and hybrids of both. The check-list indicates the best of those pieces from nonfiction books which can be approached fruitfully as fiction. Finally, the check-list attempts to evaluate Caldwell's stories by using asterisks to designate those which seem to this critic most worth reading and studying. The asterisks appear only once with a specific story, at the listing of the first publication. No evaluation of this kind is made of full-length collections of stories.

Check-List

1929

Stories:
  *Joe Craddock's Old Woman. *blues,* No. 7 (Fall), pp. 33–34.
  *Midsummer Passion. In Alfred Kreymborg, Lewis Mumford, Paul Rosenfeld, ed., *The New American Caravan* (New York: Macaulay), pp. 96–99.
    Without Caldwell's knowledge this story was published in slightly different form with the title "July" in *Transition*, No. 16–17 (June, 1929), pp. 170–173. See Caldwell's *Call It Experience* (New York: Duell, Sloan and Pearce, 1951), pp. 70–71.
  *Tracing Life with a Finger. In Kreymborg, Mumford, and Rosenfeld, ed., *The New American Caravan*, pp. 100–106.
    "Tracing Life with a Finger" was later published as the first part of *The Sacrilege of Alan Kent*. See listing for *American Earth* (1931) and for *The Sacrilege of Alan Kent* (1936).

1930

Stories:
  *The Automobile That Wouldn't Run. *Hound and Horn*, Vol. 4 (Oct.–Dec.), pp. 75–81.
    On O'Brien's Roll of Honor for 1931.

*Inspiration for Greatness. *Pagany*, Vol. 1 (Winter), pp. 53–60.

"Inspiration for Greatness" was later published as the second part of *The Sacrilege of Alan Kent*. See listing for *American Earth* (1931) and for *The Sacrilege of Alan Kent* (1936).

*John the Indian and George Hopkins. *Pagany*, Vol. 1 (Summer), pp. 43–46.

*The Mating of Marjorie. *Scribner's*, Vol. 87 (June), pp. 639–642.

This story appeared with "A Very Late Spring" with the headnote, "Presenting for the first time in a general magazine the work of one of the most talented of the new American writers. His milieu is the New England of today." Caldwell's description of his finding out what Max Perkins would pay for using "The Mating of Marjorie" and "A Very Late Spring" in *Scribner's* is one of Caldwell's most amusing anecdotes. See *Call It Experience*, pp. 81–86.

On O'Brien's Roll of Honor for 1931.

*Saturday Afternoon. *Nativity*, No. 1 (Winter), pp. 12–16.

In a recent essay Morris Renek tells of rediscovering Caldwell and describes this story, which, he feels, "belongs with the best of American fiction." Renek, "Rediscovering Erskine Caldwell," *Nation*, Vol. 219 (June 21, 1975), p. 758.

The Strawberry Season. *Pagany*, Vol. 1 (Winter), pp. 34–36.

On O'Brien's Roll of Honor for 1930.

*A Swell-Looking Girl. *Pagany*, Vol. 1 (Spring), pp. 43–46.

A Very Late Spring. *Scribner's*, Vol. 87 (June), pp. 636–639.

See the annotation for "The Mating of Marjorie" (1930).

1931

Stories:

American Earth. New York: Scribner's.

Caldwell's first collection includes twelve stories not previously published:

> The Dream
> Evelyn and the Rest of Us
> It Happened Like This
> The Lonely Day
> Memorandum
> *Molly Cotton-Tail
> Priming the Well
> The Rumor
> *Savannah River Payday
> *Ten Thousand Blueberry Crates
> The Visitor
> *Where the Girls Were Different

American Earth also includes the eleven stories published in 1929 and 1930, and four stories published in periodicals during 1931: "An Autumn Courtship," "The Corduroy Pants," "Dorothy," and "Hours Before Eternity." The collection is divided into three sections which distinguish the different geographic locations of the action of the stories. "Part I: Far South" is made up of "Dorothy," "Evelyn and the Rest of Us," "It Happened Like This," "Joe Craddock's Old Woman," "Memorandum," "Molly Cotton-Tail," "Saturday Afternoon," "Savannah River Payday," "The Strawberry Season," "A Swell-Looking Girl," and "The Visitor." "Part II: Farthest East," includes all the rest of the stories except for "Tracing Life with a Finger," "Inspiration for Greatness," and "Hours Before Eternity." These were combined to become *The Sacrilege of Alan Kent*, which in *American Earth* is "Part III: In the Native Land."

Subsequent editions of *American Earth* eliminate the three-part division and *The Sacrilege of Alan Kent*, which was published separately in 1936. The Uniform Edition of the collection (New York: Duell, Sloan and Pearce, 1950) has a brief introduction by Caldwell on pp. 7–8. In October, 1950 New American Library published the collection with the title *A Swell-Looking Girl*. Subsequent American paperback editions have continued to use the new title.

*An Autumn Courtship. *This Quarter*, Vol. 3 (Jan., Feb., March), pp. 466–472.

The Corduroy Pants. *Scribner's*, Vol. 89 (May), pp. 563–566.
  On O'Brien's Roll of Honor for 1932.

*Dorothy. *Scribner's*, Vol. 89 (April), pp. 396–400.
  In O'Brien's *The Best Short Stories of 1931* (New York: Dodd, Mead, 1931).

*The Empty Room. *Pagany*, Vol. 2 (Autumn), pp. 81–84.
  On O'Brien's Roll of Honor for 1932.

*Hours Before Eternity. *Pagany*, Vol. 2 (Winter), pp. 1–8.
  "Hours Before Eternity" was later published as the third part of *The Sacrilege of Alan Kent*. See listing for *American Earth* (1931) and for *The Sacrilege of Alan Kent* (1936).

*Rachel. *Clay*, No. 1 (Autumn), pp. 9–16.
  On O'Brien's Roll of Honor for 1932.

*We Are Looking at You, Agnes. *Clay*, No. 2 (Winter), pp. 16–19.
  On O'Brien's Roll of Honor for 1932.

1932

Stories:

  After-Image. *Pagany*, Vol. 3 (Spring), pp. 73–81.

  *The First Autumn. *Pagany*, Vol. 3 (Summer), pp. 71–76.
    In O'Brien's *The Best Short Stories of 1933* (Boston: Houghton, Mifflin, 1933).

  *Indian Summer. *Story*, Vol. 1 (Jan.–Feb.), pp. 3–15.
    On O'Brien's Roll of Honor for 1932.

  *Mamma's Little Girl. Published twice in 1932: in *Contact*, Vol. 1 (Oct.), pp. 59–61; and as a pamphlet entitled *Mama's Little Girl; A Brief Story*. Seventy-five copies of the pamphlet were published by Caldwell and Alfred Morang, who illustrated the story with drawings, at The Bradford Press, Portland, Me. Caldwell lived in Mount Vernon, Me. at the time; as a result the pamphlet is sometimes listed as having been published there.

  *The Midwinter Guest. *Story*, Vol. 2 (Aug.), pp. 7–15.
    On O'Brien's Roll of Honor for 1933.

  *Over the Green Mountains. *Contact*, Vol. 1 (May), pp. 29–36.
    On O'Brien's Roll of Honor for 1936.

  The People's Choice. In B. A. Botkin, ed., *Folk-Say IV: The Land Is Ours* (Norman, Okla.: U. of Okla. Press), pp. 215–222.

  *Picking Cotton. *Contempo*, Vol. 2 (May 25), pp. 1, 8.
    On O'Brien's Roll of Honor for 1933.

  The Picture. *New English Weekly*, Vol. 1 (July 28), pp. 349–351.
    On O'Brien's Roll of Honor for 1933.

  Warm River. *Pagany*, Vol. 3 (Winter), pp. 23–29.
    For reasons this critic doesn't understand "Warm River" is one of the most frequently reprinted Caldwell stories. In O'Brien's *The Best Short Stories of 1932* (New York: Dodd, Mead, 1932).

1933

Stories:

  We Are the Living: Brief Stories by Erskine Caldwell. New York: Viking. The first edition was limited to 250 copies printed on all-rag paper, numbered and signed by the author.

We Are the Living includes twenty stories, four published for the first time:
  *The Medicine Man
  *Meddlesome Jack
  *The Grass Fire
  *A Woman in the House
The other sixteen stories were published before 1933 or in periodicals during 1933: "After-Image," "August Afternoon," "Country Full of Swedes," "Crown-Fire," "The Empty Room," "The First Autumn," "Indian Summer," "Mama's Little Girl," "Over the Green Mountains," "The People's Choice," "Picking Cotton," "The Picture," "Rachel," "Warm River," "We Are Looking at You, Agnes," and "Yellow Girl."
*August Afternoon. *Esquire*, Vol. 1 (Autumn), pp. 22, 89, 110.
    On O'Brien's Roll of Honor for 1934.
*Country Full of Swedes. *Yale Review*, Vol. 22 (Winter), pp. 319–336.
    Received the *Yale Review's* 1933 award for fiction; on O'Brien's Roll of Honor for 1934; in Harry Hansen, ed., *O. Henry Memorial Award Prize Stories of 1933* (Garden City. N. Y.: Doubleday, 1933).
Crown-Fire. *Lion and Crown*, Vol. 1, No. 2, pp. 1–6.
    On O'Brien's Roll of Honor for 1934.
*Daughter. *Anvil*, No. 2 (Nov.–Dec.), pp. 3–6.
    On O'Brien's Roll of Honor for 1934 and 1936.
*Horse Thief. *Vanity Fair*, Vol. 41 (Nov.), pp. 37, 60, 67.
    In O'Brien's *The Best Short Stories of 1934* (Boston: Houghton, Mifflin, 1934).
The Man Who Looked Like Himself. *American Mercury*, Vol. 29 (May), pp. 59–62.
    The division of this story into three numbered sections is eliminated in subsequent publication.
*Masses of Men. *Story*, Vol. 2 (April), pp. 67–76.
    On O'Brien's Roll of Honor for 1934.
A Message for Genevieve. Published as a pamphlet entitled *A Message for Genevieve: A Brief Story* by Caldwell and Alfred Morang, who illustrated the story with a frontispiece, at the Old Colony Press, Portland, Me. One hundred copies, signed by Caldwell and Morang, were printed. Caldwell lived at Mount Vernon, Me. at the time; as a result, the story is sometimes listed as having been published there.
Slow Death. *New Masses*, Vol. 8 (Jan.), pp. 28–29.
Summer Accident. *Contempo*, Vol. 3 (June 25), pp. 1, 4–5.
*Yellow Girl. *Story*, Vol. 2 (Feb.), pp. 26–36.
    On O'Brien's Roll of Honor for 1934.

1934

Stories:
  *Back on the Road. *Metropolis*, Vol. 1 (Dec. 29), pp. 14–18.
  *The Cold Winter. *Story*, Vol. 5 (Dec.), pp. 41–45.
      In O'Brien's *The Best Short Stories of 1935* (Boston: Houghton, Mifflin, 1935).
  *Death of a Hero. In Carl Van Doren, ed., *Modern American Prose* (New York: Literary Guild), pp. 867–872.
      This is an excerpt from Chapter 17 of *God's Little Acre* (New York: Viking, 1933). It begins on p. 241 of the novel and continues to p. 252. The text of the novel is unchanged. A shortened version of the same excerpt was published in 1944 with the title "Carolina Cotton Mill."
  *Maud Island. "The Sunday Review" of the *Brooklyn Daily Eagle* (April 15), pp. 10–12.
      In Harry Hansen, ed., *O. Henry Memorial Award Prize Stories of 1934* (Garden City, N. Y.: Doubleday, 1934).
  The Sick Horse. *Esquire*, Vol. 1 (March), pp. 32, 138.
      On O'Brien's Roll of Honor for 1935.

1935

Stories:

Kneel to the Rising Sun and Other Stories. New York: Viking. The first edition was signed and limited to 300 copies.

The seventeen stories in this collection, all of which were published previous to 1935 or in periodicals during 1935, are "Blue Boy," "Candy-Man Beechum," "The Cold Winter," "Daughter," "A Day's Wooing," "The Girl Ellen," "The Growing Season," "Honeymoon," "Horse Thief," "Kneel to the Rising Sun," "The Man Who Looked Like Himself," "Martha Jean," "Masses of Men," "Maud Island," "The Shooting," "Slow Death," and "The Walnut Hunt."

The Uniform Edition of the collection (New York: Duell, Sloan and Pearce, 1951) includes a brief introduction by Caldwell on pp. v–vi.

*Blue Boy. *Anvil,* No. 10 (March–April), pp. 5–6, 18.

*Candy-Man Beechum. *Esquire,* Vol. 3 (Feb.), pp. 39, 146.

*A Day's Wooing. *Redbook,* Vol. 64 (March), pp. 50–51, 92–93.

On O'Brien's Roll of Honor for 1936.

The Girl Ellen. *Vanity Fair,* Vol. 43 (April), pp. 25 ff.

On O'Brien's Roll of Honor for 1936.

*The Growing Season. *Literary America,* Vol. 2 (April), pp. 293 ff.

In a review of *Kneel to the Rising Sun* Randall Jarrell says that "The Growing Season" is "one of the most extraordinarily ingenious stories" he has ever seen. Jarrell, "Ten Books," *Southern Review,* Vol. 1 (1935–36), p. 404. On O'Brien's Roll of Honor for 1936.

Honeymoon. *Direction,* Vol. 1 (Jan.–March), pp. 69–73.

On O'Brien's Roll of Honor for 1936.

*Kneel to the Rising Sun. *Scribner's,* Vol. 97 (Feb.), pp. 71–80.

Understandably, this is one of Caldwell's most frequently reprinted stories. On O'Brien's Roll of Honor for 1936.

*Martha Jean. *Esquire,* Vol. 3 (Jan.), pp. 50, 140.

*The Negro in the Well. *Atlantic Monthly,* Vol. 156 (Oct.), pp. 404–407.

*Return to Lavinia. *Esquire,* Vol. 4 (Dec.), pp. 50, 185–186.

The Shooting. *Scribner's,* Vol. 97 (June), pp. 349–350.

On O'Brien's Roll of Honor for 1936.

*The Walnut Hunt. *Literary America,* Vol. 2 (May), pp. 355–359.

On O'Brien's Roll of Honor for 1936.

Other:

Some American People. New York: McBride.

Though this book is usually listed as nonfiction, it does not entirely conform to that category. The second section of *Some American People,* "Cross Country," is a series of twenty-four prose pieces. Some are essays; some are short stories; most lie somewhere in between. A substantial number of the pieces can fruitfully be approached as fiction. The most interesting of these are:

On the Range
The Barber of the Northwest
After Eighty Years
Picking the Omaha Dump
Grandpa in the Bathtub
One More Day in Chillicothe
A Country That Moves
Joe Jendro
While a City Sleeps
Welcome Home

Four of these—"After Eighty Years," "The Barber of the Northwest," "A Country That Moves," and "Grandpa in the Bathtub"—appear in revised form in *When You Think of Me.* See listing for 1959.

1936

Stories:

**The Sacrilege of Alan Kent.* Portland, Me.: Falmouth Book House.

All three sections of this unusual and fascinating experiment with a series of brief, powerful narrative glimpses were published before the story as a whole was released in book form. "I. Tracing Life with a Finger" appeared in 1929, "II. Inspiration for Greatness" in 1930, and "III. Hours Before Eternity" in 1931. See the listings for these years. The entire story appeared as the final section of the original edition of *American Earth* in 1931, though it was eliminated from subsequent editions of that collection.

More recently, *The Sacrilege of Alan Kent* appeared with the early novels *Poor Fool* and *The Bastard* in paperback editions called *The Sacrilege of Alan Kent* (New York: New American Library, 1958 and New York: Macfadden-Bartell, 1966).

*Carnival. *Mid-Week Pictorial*, Vol. 44 (Oct. 24), p. 14.

*The Fly in the Coffin. *Mid-Week Pictorial*, Vol. 44 (Nov. 4), p. 12.

The Man Under the Mountain. *Mid-Week Pictorial*, Vol. 44 (Oct. 10), p. 16.

New Cabin. *College Humor*, Vol. 2 (July), pp. 6–9, 65.

*A Short Sleep in Louisiana. *Mid-Week Pictorial*, Vol. 44 (Nov. 11), p. 14.

*A Small Day. *New Yorker*, Vol. 12 (Aug 22), pp. 22–25.

On O'Brien's Roll of Honor for 1937.

*The Sunfield. *Parade*, (Spring), p. 5.

1937

Stories:

*Hamrick's Polar Bear. *Redbook*, (July), p. 54.

Here and Today. *Harper's Bazaar*, No 2692 (Feb.), pp. 56, 112, 122.

*Man and Woman. *New Yorker*, Vol. 13 (July 10), pp. 12–13.

In Harry Hansen, ed., *O. Henry Memorial Award Prize Stories of 1939* (Garden City, New York: Doubleday, 1939).

*The Night My Old Man Came Home. *New Yorker*, Vol. 13 (Dec. 11), pp. 24–26.

*Nine Dollars Worth of Mumble. *Harper's Bazaar*, No. 2693 (March), pp. 127, 148, 158.

The Only Love. *Signatures*, Vol. 1 (Dec. 6), pp. 297–301.

Snacker. *Cosmopolitan*, Vol. 103 (Dec.), pp. 101–102.

Other:

Caldwell and Margaret Bourke-White. *You Have Seen Their Faces.* New York: Viking.

This first Caldwell-Bourke-White collaboration includes ten first-person monologues. They are based presumably on Caldwell's observations but can be approached fruitfully as fiction.

1938

Stories:

Southways. New York: Viking.

Of the sixteen stories in this collection two were published for the first time:
Runaway
Wild Flowers

The other fourteen stories were published before 1938 or in periodicals during 1938: "Carnival," "The Fly in the Coffin," "Hamrick's Polar Bear," "A Knife to Cut the Corn Bread With," "Man and Woman," "The Negro in the Well," "New Cabin," "The Night My Old Man Came Home," "Nine Dollars Worth of Mumble," "Return to Lavinia," "A Small Day," "Snacker," "The Sunfield," and "Uncle Henry's Love Nest."

*A Knife to Cut the Corn Bread With. *Direction*, Vol. 1 (Jan.), pp. 7–9.

Uncle Henry's Love Nest. Originally published as "Uncle Mose's Love Nest." *Sunday Worker*, Vol. 3 (Jan. 23), Section 2 ("Sunday Worker Magazine"), pp. 2, 9.

1939

Stories:
*Balm of Gilead. *Story*, Vol. 14 (March–April), pp. 18–21.
*Big Buck. *College Humor*, Vol. 10 (Sept.), pp. 6–8, 46–47.
The People vs. Abe Lathan, Colored. *Esquire*, Vol. 12 (Aug.), pp. 26–27, 145.

    In O'Brien's *The Best Short Stories of 1940* (Boston: Houghton, Mifflin, 1940) and in Harry Hansen, ed., *O. Henry Memorial Award Prize Stories of 1939* (Garden City, N. Y.: Doubleday, 1939).

Other:
Caldwell and Margaret Bourke-White. *North of the Danube*. New York: Viking.

    This collaboration is one of Caldwell's finest books. It includes eight excellent sketches, all of which can be approached fruitfully as short fiction:

The Roads of Uzhorod
Bread in Uzok
The Train Through the Tatras
Wine of Surany
Peace in Brno
The Peasants of Dreharovice
The Dogs of Cesky Budejovice
Agent in Praha

Taken together, the sketches form a loose nonfiction novel about the coming of the Nazis to Czechoslovakia. Each of the sketches can stand alone, however, as is clear from the separate publication of five of them in 1939: "Bread in Uzok" appeared in *Town and Country*, Vol. 94 (Feb.), pp. 58–59, 75; "The Train Through the Tatras" appeared in *New Republic*, Vol. 98 (March 8), pp. 119–121; "The Peasants of Dreharovice" in *Vogue* (March 1), pp. 72–73, 131, with the omission of a few lines included in *North of the Danube*; "The Dogs of Cesky Budejovice" in *Direction*, Vol. 2 (March), pp. 4–6, with the ommission of a few paragraphs included in *North of the Danube*; "Agent in Praha" was published as "A Nazi Agent at Work" in *New Masses*, Vol. 30 (Feb. 28), pp. 5–7.

    "Bread in Uzok," "The Dogs of Cesky Budejovice," and "Wine of Surany" appear in *When You Think of Me*. See listing for 1959.

1940

Stories:
Jackpot: The Short Stories of Erskine Caldwell. New York: Duell, Sloan and Pearce.
    Of the seventy-five stories in *Jackpot* only one was published for the first time:
Uncle Jeff
The seventy-four previously published stories include all the stories from *American Earth* (1931) except "Molly Cotton-Tail," "Memorandum," "Joe Craddock's Old

Woman," and *The Sacrilege of Alan Kent;* all the stories from *We Are the Living* (1933) except "The Empty Room," "Picking Cotton," and "A Woman in the House"; all the stories from *Kneel to the Rising Sun and Other Stories* (1935) except "The Cold Winter"; and all the stories from *Southways* (1938) except "Uncle Henry's Love Nest" and "The Sunfield." *Jackpot* also includes six stories not previously collected: "Balm of Gilead," "Big Buck," "The End of Christy Tucker," "Handy," "The Midwinter Guest," and "The People vs. Abe Lathan, Colored." Two stories published in periodicals during 1941—"Handsome Brown and the Aggravating Goats" and "My Old Man Hasn't Been the Same Since"—are included with "The Night My Old Man Came Home" under the title "My Old Man." Before each of the stories in *Jackpot* Caldwell includes a brief comment, either about the specific story or about writing in general. These blurbs are generally amusing and illuminating.

The seventy-five stories in *Jackpot* were, in Caldwell's eyes, the best he had written. When he made the selection, he says he had exactly one hundred stories to choose from, "that being the number of published stories which I had set in 1930 as a goal. . . ." By the end of 1940 there were actually ninety-eight published stories, if one counts *The Sacrilege of Alan Kent* as a single story, 101 if the three parts of *The Sacrilege* are counted separately. See *Call it Experience,* p. 190, for Caldwell's comments about *Jackpot.*

The Day the Presidential Candidate Came to Ciudad Tamaulipas. Originally published as "A Mexican Presidential Candidate Comes to Ciudad Tamaulipas." *Town and Country,* Vol. 95 (Sept.), pp. 53, 72.

*The End of Christy Tucker. *Nation,* Vol. 150 (June 1), pp. 673–675.

An Evening in Nuevo Leon. *Harper's* (Nov.), pp. 605–607.

Handsome Brown and the Aggravating Goats. Originally published as "The Aggravating Goats." *New Republic,* Vol. 103 (Aug. 19), pp. 241–243.

*Handy. *New Republic,* Vol. 103 (Sept. 23), pp. 413–415.

In O'Brien's *The Best Short Stories of 1941* (Boston: Houghton, Mifflin, 1941).

*My Old Man Hasn't Been the Same Since. *Friday.*

The Thunderstorm. *College Humor,* Vol. 11 (July), pp. 6–8, 46.

1941

Stories:

*The Courting of Susie Brown. *Coronet,* Vol. 10 (June), pp. 113–118.

The Light. In Rae Beamish, ed., *American Signatures* (Rochester, N. Y. and Prairie City, Ill.: Black Faun Press), pp. 8–14.

My Old Man and the Grass Widow. *Coronet,* Vol. 9 (Feb.), pp. 91–96.

Squire Dinwiddy. *Esquire,* Vol. 15 (Jan.), pp. 33, 131.

Other:

Caldwell and Margaret Bourke-White. *Say, Is This the U.S.A.* New York: Duell, Sloan and Pearce.

This collaboration involves a variety of kinds of writing on Caldwell's part. Like *Some American People* it includes essays, stories, and hybrids of both. A substantial number of the individual sections can be approached fruitfully as fiction. The most interesting of these are:

The Boy in the Blizzard

The First Wild Woman to Set Foot in American Fork

B-Girl

The Box Maker

It seems possible that "The Box Maker" influenced Richard Wright's *The Man Who Lived Underground.*

1942

Stories:

Handsome Brown and the Shirt-Tail Woodpeckers. *Stag*, (Feb.).

*Handsome Brown's Day Off. Originally published as "Day Off." *Colliers*, Vol. 109 (May 30), pp. 16–17, 45.

A Soldier Is Born. *New York Herald-Tribune* (Jan. 11), "This Week Magazine," p. 2.
    This is a brief piece fictionalized from experiences Caldwell had in Russia in 1941. See the Sept. 27 entry in Caldwell's *Moscow Under Fire* (London: Hutchinson, 1942), pp. 102–103, for the probable source of this story.

The Windfall. *Story*, Vol. 20 (Jan.–Feb.), pp. 56–65.

1943

Stories:

Georgia Boy. New York: Duell, Sloan and Pearce.

Of the fourteen stories in this collection eight were published for the first time:

The Day We Rang the Bell for Preacher Hawshaw

My Old Man and Pretty Sooky

My Old Man and the Gypsy Queen

*My Old Man's Baling Machine

My Old Man's Political Appointment

The Time Ma Spent the Day at Aunt Bessie's

The Time Handsome Brown Ran Away

Uncle Ned's Short Stay.

The other six were first published before 1943: "Handsome Brown and the Aggravating Goats," "Handsome Brown and the Shirt-Tail Woodpeckers," "Handsome Brown's Day Off," "My Old Man and the Grass Widow," "My Old Man Hasn't Been the Same Since," and "The Night My Old Man Came Home."

The Uniform Edition of the collection (New York: Duell, Sloan and Pearce, 1950) contains a brief introduction by Caldwell on pp. iii–iv. The 1961 New American Library edition contains an "Afterward" by Robert Cantwell, which has been included in subsequent paperback editions. The original New American Library edition of 1950 includes the line drawings by Birger Lundquist which were originally published in the Swedish edition. Subsequent paperback editions include these drawings.

1944

Stories:

Stories by Erskine Caldwell. Selected and Introduced by Henry Seidel Canby. New York: Duell, Sloan and Pearce.

This is a collection of twenty-four previously published stories: "Part One" includes "August Afternoon," "A Day's Wooing," "Horse Thief," "Man and Woman," "Martha Jean," "Maud Island," "The Negro in the Well," and "New Cabin"; "Part Two" includes "Handsome Brown and the Aggravating Goats," "Handsome Brown's Day Off," "My Old Man's Baling Machine," and "The Night My Old Man Came Home"; "Part Three" includes "The Automobile That Wouldn't Run," "Country Full of Swedes," "The Grass Fire," and "The Midwinter Guest," and "Part Four" includes "Big Buck," "Candy-Man Beechum," "Daughter," "The End of Christy Tucker," "Kneel to the Rising Sun," "Nine Dollars Worth of Mumble," "The People vs. Abe Lathan, Colored," and "Saturday Afternoon."

This same collection was also published in 1944 by Grosset and Dunlap as *A Day's Wooing and Other Stories*. The only change was the placement of the title story first in the collection.

Carolina Cotton Mill. In Tremaine McDowell, ed., *America in Literature* (New York: Crofts), pp. 53–55.

Like "Death of a Hero" (see listing for 1934) this is an excerpt from Chapter 17 of *God's Little Acre* (New York: Viking, 1933), in this case from the beginning of the chapter to p. 248.

Sylvia. *Maryland Quarterly (Briarcliff Quarterly)*, Vol. 1 (Spring), pp. 36–39.

This story appears in revised form in *When You Think of Me*. See listing for 1959.

1945

Stories:

The Crack. In Harry Allen Smith, ed., *Desert Island Decameron* (Garden City, N. Y.: Doubleday), pp. 158–164.

This is an almost verbatim excerpt from Chapter 14 of the novel *Journeyman* (New York: Viking, 1935), pp. 139–147 of the first edition.

1946

Stories:

The Caldwell Caravan. Cleveland and New York: World.

This collection of previously published work includes *Tobacco Road*, *God's Little Acre*, and twenty stories: "August Afternoon," "An Autumn Courtship," "Balm of Gilead," "Candy-Man Beechum," "Country Full of Swedes," "A Day's Wooing," "The End of Christy Tucker," "Honeymoon," "Horse Thief," "Kneel to the Rising Sun," "The Mating of Marjorie," "My Old Man" (includes "The Night My Old Man Came Home," "Handsome Brown and the Aggravating Goats," and "My Old Man Hasn't Been the Same Since"), "The Negro in the Well," "Nine Dollars Worth of Mumble," "Priming the Well," "Savannah River Payday," "A Swell-Looking Girl," "Ten Thousand Blueberry Crates," "We are Looking at You, Agnes," and "Where the Girls Were Different." There is a brief introduction by Caldwell on p. 7.

Georgia Boy, and Other Stories. New York: Avon Modern Short Story Monthly, No. 30.

This collection of previously published work includes all fourteen stories from *Georgia Boy* (see listing for 1943) and six others: "Carnival," "Dorothy," "Hamrick's Polar Bear," "Handy," "Maud Island," and "The Rumor."

1947

Stories:

The Pocket Book of Erskine Caldwell Stories. Selected and Introduced by Henry Seidel Canby. New York: Pocket Books.

This collection of thirty-one previously published stories is basically the same as *Stories by Erskine Caldwell*, put together by Canby in 1944. One story in the earlier collection, "August Afternoon," was eliminated from "Part One"; and eight other stories were added: "The Medicine Man" and "Yellow Girl" to "Part One"; "My Old Man's Political Appointment" to "Part Two"; "The Rumor," "The Corduroy Pants," and "Over the Green Mountains" to "Part Three"; and "The People's Choice" and "Hamrick's Polar Bear," to "Part Four."

1948

Stories:
Midsummer Passion, and Other Stories. New York: Avon.

This paperback edition of fifteen previously published stories includes "The Automobile That Wouldn't Run," "The Dream," "Evelyn and the Rest of Us," "The Growing Season," "It Happened Like This," "The Lonely Day," "Midsummer Passion," "Molly Cotton-Tail," "Priming the Well," "Saturday Afternoon," "The Strawberry Season," "A Swell-Looking Girl," "Ten Thousand Blueberry Crates," "A Very Late Spring," and "The Visitor."

Where the Girls Were Different, and Other Stories. New York: Avon.

This paperback edition of fourteen previously published stories includes "An Autumn Courtship," "A Day's Wooing," "The Girl Ellen," "A Knife to Cut the Corn Bread With," "The Mating of Marjorie," "Meddlesome Jack," "The Medicine Man," "The People vs. Abe Lathan, Colored," "Rachel," "Savannah River Payday," "Snacker," "The Visitor," "Where the Girls Were Different," and "Yellow Girl."

1949

Stories:
A Woman in the House. New York: New American Library.

This paperback collection of nineteen previously published stories includes "After-Image," "August Afternoon," "Carnival," "Crown-Fire," "The First Autumn," "The Fly in the Coffin," "Handy," "Honeymoon," "Indian Summer," "Mama's Little Girl," "Return to Lavinia," "Runaway," "Slow Death," "A Small Day," "Uncle Jeff," "The Walnut Hunt," "We Are Looking at You, Agnes," "Wild Flowers," and "A Woman in the House."

1950

Stories:
A Swell-Looking Girl. New York: New American Library.

This collection is a retitling of the 1931 collection *American Earth*. All the stories published in *American Earth*, with the exception of *The Sacrilege of Alan Kent*, are included. The stories are not divided into sections according to the geographic location of the action, as they were in the first edition of *American Earth*. See the listing for 1931 for the specific stories and additional information.

1951

Stories:
The Humorous Side of Erskine Caldwell. Edited and Introduced by Robert Cantwell. New York: Duell, Sloan and Pearce.

This is a collection of short stories, all previously published, and excerpts from novels. The ten stories are "An Autumn Courtship," "Balm of Gilead," "Big Buck," "Country Full of Swedes," "A Day's Wooing," "Honeymoon," "John the Indian and George Hopkins," "My Old Man" (only two of the parts—"Handsome Brown and the Aggravating Goats" and "My Old Man Hasn't Been the Same Since"—of the three-part "My Old Man" published in *Jackpot* are included), "Ten Thousand Blueberry Crates," and "Where the Girls Were Different." The ten excerpts include "A Sack of Turnips," which is a condensation of the first four chapters of *Tobacco Road*; "Gold

Fever," a condensation of the first two chapters of *God's Little Acre*; "The Albino and Darling Jill," a condensation of Chapters 8 and 9 of *God's Little Acre*; "Spence Cooperates," a condensation of Chapter 10 of *Tragic Ground*; "The Doggone Douthits," a combination of the second half of Chapter 13 and Chapter 14 of *Tragic Ground*; "All Kind of Pep," a brief section of Chapter 12 of *The Sure Hand of God*; "A Big Mistake," which is Chapter 12 of *This Very Earth*; "Kathyanne and the Piggy Bank," a nine-page section of Chapter 2 of *Place Called Estherville*; "Romantically Inclined," a condensation of Chapter 2 of *Episode in Palmetto*; and "A Big Crop of Millet," the first four pages of the third section of Chapter 7 of *Episode in Palmetto*.

During 1951 this book was also published in paperback under the title *Where the Girls Were Different and Other Stories* by New American Library. This title is used in subsequent paperback editions.

1952

Stories:

The Courting of Susie Brown. Boston: Little, Brown.

This collection of seventeen previously published stories includes seven of the nine stories collected for the first time in *Jackpot*: "Balm of Gilead," "Big Buck," "The End of Christy Tucker," "Handy," "The Midwinter Guest," "The People vs. Abe Lathan, Colored," and "Uncle Jeff"; and ten stories not previously collected: "Back on the Road," "The Courting of Susie Brown," "The Day the Presidential Candidate Came to Ciudad Tamaulipas," "An Evening in Nuevo Leon," "Here and Today," "The Sick Horse," "Squire Dinwiddy," "Summer Accident," "Thunderstorm," and "The Windfall." A brief note by Caldwell precedes the text.

1953

Stories:

The Complete Stories. Boston: Little, Brown.

This is the most extensive collection of Caldwell's stories to date. It includes ninety-three stories, all previously published: all the stories collected in the original edition of *American Earth* (1931) except *The Sacrilege of Alan Kent*; all the stories in *We Are the Living* (1933) and *Kneel to the Rising Sun and Other Stories* (1935); all the stories in *Southways* (1938) except "The Night My Old Man Came Home"; and all the stories in *The Courting of Susie Brown* (1952).

The title of the collection is misleading, since there are a number of stories published before 1953 which are not included: the fourteen stories collected in *Georgia Boy* (1943), "The Light," "The Man Under the Mountain," "The Only Love," *The Sacrilege of Alan Kent*, "A Short Sleep in Louisiana," "A Soldier Is Born," "Sylvia," and the excerpts from Caldwell's novels published separately: "Carolina Cotton Mill," "The Crack," "Death of a Hero," and those in *The Humorous Side of Erskine Caldwell* (1951). Also, the four stories published in periodicals during 1953 are not in the collection.

A Gift for Sue. Originally published with the title changed to "Just a Quick One" without Caldwell's permission. *Cavalier*, Vol. 1 (Oct.), pp. 8, 68–69.

Girl with Figurines. Originally published with the title changed to "Figurines of Love" without Caldwell's permission. *Esquire*, Vol. 39 (May), pp. 56, 108–109.

Kathy. Originally published with the title changed to "The Motive" without Caldwell's permission. *Manhunt*, Vol. 1 (Sept.), pp. 85–91.

To the Chaparral. *Esquire*, Vol. 40 (Dec.), pp. 151, 236–237.

1954

Stories:
   *Soquots. Originally published with the title changed to "Second Cousin" without
   Caldwell's permission. *Manhunt*, Vol. 2 (Oct.), pp. 44–49.

1955

Stories:
   Her Name Was Amelie. Originally published with the title changed to "Epitaph"
   without Caldwell's permission. *Manhunt*, Vol. 3 (Jan.), pp. 83–88.
   In Memory of Judith Courtright. *Manhunt*, Vol. 3 (Oct.), pp. 28–36.
   Memento. *Manhunt*, Vol. 3 (March), pp. 133–138.

1956

Stories:
   Gulf Coast Stories. Boston: Little, Brown.
         This collection of twenty-one stories is the first book of short fiction since *Georgia
   Boy* (1943) to contain a substantial amount of new work. Six stories were published for
   the first time in *Gulf Coast Stories*:
         Girl on the Road
         The Last Anniversary
         Letters in the Mail
         A Little Candy for Tessie
         Miss Paddleford
         Vick Shore and the Good of the Game
   Of the other fifteen, eight were published before 1956: "A Gift for Sue," "Girl with
   Figurines," "Her Name Was Amelie," "In Memory of Judith Courtright," "Kathy,"
   "Memento," "Soquots," and "To the Chaparral." Seven were published in periodicals
   during 1956; see listing below.
   Advice About Women. *Playboy*, Vol. 3 (Jan.), pp. 10–11, 14, 65.
   Bud Perry's First Wife. *Dude*, Vol. 1 (Aug.), pp. 44–46, 68.
   Clyde Bickle and Dora. *Magasinet* (Denmark), No. 10 (March 10), pp. 1–2, 11–12.
   The Fifteenth Summer. *Swank*, Vol. 3 (Feb.), pp. 36–39, 97.
   Hat on the Bedpost. *Cavalier*, Vol. 4 (March), pp. 12–13, 90–91.
   The Pride of Miss Stella Sibley. *Gent*, Vol. 1 (Sept.), pp. 5–8.
   The Shooting of Judge Price. *Playboy*, Vol. 3 (May), pp. 23, 32, 71–72.

1957

Stories:
   Certain Women. Boston: Little, Brown.
         This is a collection of seven stories, all published for the first time:
         Anneve
         Clementine
         Hilda
         Louellen
         Nanette
         Selma
         Vicki

All stories are substantially longer and far, far weaker than Caldwell's earlier short fiction.

1958

Stories:

Molly Cottontail. Boston: Little, Brown.

This children's book is a revision of "Molly Cotton-Tail," which first appeared in *American Earth* in 1931. A major difference is the change from the original first-person to a third-person narrative.

Molly Cottontail is illustrated by William Sharp.

1959

Stories:

When You Think of Me. Boston: Little, Brown.

While this is a collection primarily of previously published material, it includes three stories which were published for the first time:

A Visit to Mingus County
The Story of Mahon
When You Think of Me

The collection is divided into four parts: the first, entitled "The Stories," includes "The Light," "A Message for Genevieve," "The Story of Mahon," "Sylvia," and "A Visit to Mingus County"; the second part, entitled "American Sketches," includes revised versions of "After Eighty Years," "The Barber of the Northwest," "A Country That Moves," and "Grandpa in the Bathtub," from *Some American People* plus "The Man Under the Mountain" and "A Short Sleep in Louisiana"; the third part, entitled "Czechoslovakian Sketches," includes three of the sketches originally collected in *North of the Danube*: "Bread in Uzok," "The Dogs of Ceske Budejovice," and "Wine of Surany." The fourth section is the long, maudlin story "When You Think of Me."

The difference between "stories" and "sketches" in this collection is very unclear.

1960

Nothing

1961

Stories:

Erskine Caldwell's Men and Women. Selected and Introduced by Carvel Collins. Boston: Little, Brown.

The twenty-two stories in this collections, all previously published, are in an order which, Collins explains in his introduction, loosely follows the subject matter from youth to old age: "Maud Island," "Indian Summer," "Where the Girls Were Different," "Horse Thief," "Candy-Man Beechum," "A Day's Wooing," "A Woman in the House," "Soquots," "Yellow Girl," "Meddlesome Jack," "The Medicine Man," "Clyde Bickle and Dora," "Midsummer Passion," "Handsome Brown's Day Off," "A Small Day," "The Growing Season," "Kneel to the Rising Sun," "Country Full of Swedes," "The Negro in the Well," "The Corduroy Pants," "The Fly in the Coffin," and "A Short Sleep in Louisiana."

The New American Library edition of *Erskine Caldwell's Men and Women* is the best paperback collection of Caldwell's stories presently available.

1962

Nothing

1963

Nothing

1964

Stories: Nothing
Other:
> *Around About America.* New York: Farrar, Straus.
>> Like most of Caldwell's nonfiction this book includes prose pieces which can be approached as fiction. While the material in *Around About America* is generally less interesting than that in earlier nonfiction books such as *Some American People*, *North of the Danube*, and *Say, Is This the U.S.A.*, there are sketches of interest:
>> Interim Two
>> Interim Four
>> Interim Fourteen
>> Burns, Oregon
> *Around About America* is illustrated by Virginia M. Caldwell.
>> "Interim Four" was later published with the title "I Don't Want to Get Fired" in G. R. Eriksson and Ivar Lindquist, ed., *Round the World* (Stockholm, 1970), pp. 10–12.

1965

Stories: Nothing
Other:
> *In Search of Bisco*, New York: Farrar, Straus and Giroux.
>> Like *You Have Seen Their Faces* this nonfictional examination of the race issue uses a series of first-person monologues which can be approached as fiction.

1966

Stories:
> *The Deer at Our House.* New York: Collier.
>> This is a children's book, an original story about a family's being bothered by shrub-eating deer.
> *The Deer at Our House* is illustrated by Ben Wohlberg.

1967

Nothing

1968

Stories: Nothing
Other:
> *Deep South.* New York: Weybright and Talley.

> The long first section of *Deep South* was originally published in England with the title *In the Shadow of the Steeple* (London: Heinemann, 1966). The second section, "At the Other End of Town," is new.

> This is Caldwell's best book of recent years. It contains reminiscences about his travels with his minister father, expository comments about aspects of religion in the South, and a number of effective first-person monologues in italics which can be approached as fiction.

1969–1975

Nothing

Notes

1. For years O'Brien published a combined work, *The Best Short Stories of [year] and the Yearbook of the American Short Story.* The first part of each annual volume included the prize-winning stories of the year. The second part, the *Yearbook*, presented extended listings of important stories and collections of stories which had appeared during the previous year. Individual stories were ranked by O'Brien as to quality by the use of one, two, and three asterisks, three designating stories of unusually high quality. A story receiving three asterisks was placed on the "Roll of Honor" for the year. In a different section of the *Yearbook* O'Brien listed the most significant collections of stories. When O'Brien died in 1941, the useful *Yearbook* died with him, for all practical purposes.

2. Otis Ferguson, "Story-Teller's Workshop," *Accent*, 1 (Spring 1941), 172–173.

3. There has been almost no criticism of Caldwell's stories outside of the generally favorable reviews which appeared around the country when the various collections were first published. The only article which discusses specific stories in detail is my "Repetition as Technique in the Short Stories of Erskine Caldwell," *Studies in American Fiction*, 5 (Autumn 1977), 213–225. This essay describes the various effects Caldwell has been able to create by using different types of repetition in such stories as "The Medicine Man," "Where the Girls Were Different," "August Afternoon," "Daughter," "Country Full of Swedes," "Candy-Man Beechum," and "The Fly in the Coffin." The introductions by Henry Seidel Canby and Carvel Collins for *Stories by Erskine Caldwell* (New York: Duell, Sloan and Pearce, 1944) and *Erskine Caldwell's Men and Women* (Boston: Little, Brown, 1961), respectively, make some interesting general comments. Canby, who considers Caldwell "primarily and essentially a short story writer," suggests that of the great American short story writers Caldwell is "the first who has consciously viewed the rich materials of his native experience as sociology, and then turned them into successful art" (Canby, p. ix). Canby praises Caldwell's love of vitality, his ability with tall tales, his humor, and his recognition of brutal social realities. He finds Caldwell extremely difficult to categorize, though he does see some interesting similarities between Caldwell's work and Goya's. Like Canby, Collins admires Caldwell's humor and the power of his social protest. Collins also comments on the dreamlike quality of some of the stories. Other critics who discuss Caldwell concentrate on the novels, mentioning the stories only in passing. This is the case even with James Korges, whose pamphlet is the most extensive critical work on Caldwell's career. Korges calls Caldwell "one of the American

masters of the short story," but spends only one paragraph in almost fifty pages on the stories. See Korges, *Erskine Caldwell* (Minneapolis: University of Minn. Press, 1969), pp. 45–46.

4. Letter from Erskine Caldwell to Scott MacDonald, Dec. 24, 1975.

5. A few brief listings of good Caldwell stories have been compiled by critics. These are so limited, however, as to be seriously misleading about the extent of Caldwell's accomplishment. Even Korges' list of twenty-two stories, the most extensive to date, only scratches the surface. Korges includes "Country Full of Swedes," "Kneel to the Rising Sun," "Candy-Man Beechum," "The Growing Season," "We Are Looking at You, Agnes," "An Autumn Courtship," "Meddlesome Jack," "The Negro in the Well," "Daughter," "Hamrick's Polar Bear," "Horse Thief," "Man and Woman," "Maud Island," "A Swell-Looking Girl," "Return to Lavinia," "A Woman in the House," "Yellow Girl," "The People vs. Abe Lathan, Colored," "After-Image," "An Evening in Nuevo Leon," "The Day the Presidential Candidate Came to Ciudad Tamaulipas," and "Wild Flowers." See Korges, pp. 45–46. I disagree with his inclusion of the final five stories.

6. In a very few instances I have not yet been able to locate complete bibliographical information. Because there are so few of these instances I felt it sensible and practical to publish the information I do have, rather than to wait any longer.

"Erskine Caldwell and the Literary Left Wing"

Sylvia Jenkins Cook*

> A new writer has been appearing; a wild youth of about twenty-two, the son of working class parents, who himself works in the lumber camps, coal mines, and steel mills, harvest fields and mountain camps of America . . . He is violent and sentimental by turns. He lacks self confidence but writes because he must—and because he has a real talent.
>
> He is a Red but has few theories. It is all instinct with him. His writing is no conscious straining after proletarian art, but the natural flower of his environment.
>
> New Masses *editorial, 1929*

In 1929, when Michael Gold issued his famous call to literary arms, "Go Left, Young Writers!" Erskine Caldwell was still struggling to publish his first novel and to achieve his characteristic personal style. He was not a "Red" though his instincts would soon lead him into that orbit as well as into the recognition that the Southern environment which produced him would also nurture his best fiction. He was in his mid-twenties, already well schooled in the poverty and violence of working-class America, having by his own (perhaps exaggerated) account worked as a stonemason's helper, plowed with a mule team on a Tennessee farm, shoveled cotton seed in a Georgia mill, operated a milk-delivery route, been a stock clerk in a variety store basement, ridden freight trains across the country and spent three days in jail as a suspected I.W.W. agitator.[1] His parents, though not exactly "working-class" had lived austerely, and, as the son of a rural Southern minister, Caldwell had witnessed early the consequences of extreme physical deprivation among the tenant farmers.

In many ways, including his obsessive need to write, Caldwell was a nearly ideal prototype of the young writer whom Michael Gold was trying to lure from "the temperamental, Bohemian left, the stale old Paris posing" and into the proletarian literary camp. The fact that Caldwell did produce so much of his best work during the 1930s, when he was most closely associated with the political radicalism of the Communist Party

*Reprinted from *Pembroke*, 11 (1979), pp. 132–39

and its wide variety of fellow-traveling intellectuals, raises the question of the artistic advantages for Caldwell of having an ideological framework in which to explore his themes. In his autobiographical writings, he has consistently portrayed himself as a writer consciously isolated from the literary and intellectual currents of his society, and especially from the critical, as opposed to the public, acceptance of his work. Yet in the most remarkable period of Caldwell's career there does seem to have been greater interaction between the writer and the liberal and leftist critics than he usually concedes. The history of this relationship reveals both the usefulness for Caldwell of a formal response to his work in the context of its ideas, and also the reason for his extreme wariness of critics, who, in this case, often ignored the unique nature of Caldwell's promise as a radical writer in their efforts to encourage him into a more colorless orthodoxy.

Some external evidence of Caldwell's political engagement in the 1930s may be briefly summarized: in September of 1932 he supported, along with fifty-two other artists and intellectuals, the candidacy of Foster and Ford, the Communist Party nominees, for the Presidency.[2] That same year he published in the *New Masses* under the title, "Ripe for Revolution," a review of Edward Dahlberg's *From Flushing to Calvary* in which Caldwell makes explicit his own adherence to revolutionary and Communist ideals.[3] In 1934, Caldwell became a correspondent for the *New Masses*, reporting on the terrorizing and lynching of Southern blacks; he also participated in that magazine's "Authors' Field Day"—a symposium on Marxist criticism; and in 1935 he contributed to Joseph Freeman's anthology *Proletarian Literature in the United States*. In 1937 and 1939 he signed the two proclamations of the League of American Writers, calling for their second and third congresses.[4] During this period Caldwell published three novels, including the two generally considered his best, *Tobacco Road* and *God's Little Acre*, two collections of short stories, his most stirring piece of non-fiction reportage, *Some American People*, and the picture text with Margaret Bourke-White, *You Have Seen Their Faces*. All of these works exhibit his concern for the poor and oppressed and were seriously reviewed in the social context of the Depression by liberal and left wing journals such as the *Nation*, the *New Republic*, and the *New Masses*.

Caldwell himself has tended to treat the books that he published before 1932, the year of his public commitment to revolutionary ideals, as rather amusing academic specimens of his literary apprenticeship, tentative, erratic, youthful rehearsals for the later career;[5] at one time he had desired them forgotten altogether.[6] These works, two novellas—*The Bastard*, 1929, and *Poor Fool*, 1930, the short story collection *American Earth*, 1930, and the prose-poem *The Sacrilege of Alan Kent*, published in parts from 1929–1931, display almost all the concerns of Caldwell's later fiction together with considerable uncertainty about matters of form, style and particularly of moral vision. *The Sacrilege of Alan Kent* has intrigued many critics with its strange and powerful imagist technique; the images—of violence and dismemberment, miscegenation, cruelty, lust, wandering, poverty and debasement—are those which will pervade his work, but the sensibility is different, more akin to that of the Greenwich Village Bohemianism that the later proletarian Caldwell would strongly abjure. There is a complete ideological revolution, for example, between this passage from Alan Kent: "Without the powerful hunger my body had always known, my soul would have died from lack of food,"[7] and the 1935 short story, "Masses of Men" in which lack of food for the body is shown to lead not to enrichment of the spirit, but to its utter depravity. The two early novellas each deal with a favorite Caldwell character, the naive young man who is alternately victim and victimizer of others and in each case equally unconscious of the forces that are acting on him. Gene Morgan of *The Bastard* and the boxer, Blondy, of *Poor Fool* are ingenuous murderers and rapists who are distanced from both sympathy and culpability by their own dulled sensibilities. This technique seems like a standard tool of literary naturalism whereby the individual's will is diminished by the oppressive forces of the environment but Caldwell already shows other tendencies that violate any easy response to his shocking material. Amidst all the squalor and suffering of *Poor Fool* the castrated rapist, Mr. Boxx, has a fantasy of descending under the earth to visit his dead wife and describes the sexual antics of the inhabitants of the grave with macabre relish. In a novel which emphasizes constantly the grim consequences of careless sexuality in Mrs. Boxx's appalling abortion clinic, this episode complicates any simple theory of determinism by inducing the reader's sympathetic laughter at human lust so powerful that it transcends even death. The distinctions made at the end of the work between "a poor fool" who is a hopeless product of circumstances and a "damn fool" who has more conscious control but ends up in an equally terrible state likewise blur the clear naturalistic thesis that proletarian critics came largely to prescribe. Kenneth Burke, noting this capacity in Caldwell for "muddling our judgments"[8] wondered if he would also be capable of stabilizing other judgments to give a positive perspective to his work.

The certainty of direction that Burke and other left wing critics hoped for in Caldwell began to appear in the collection of short stories, *American Earth*, which included, among its many tall tales of local life in the South and Maine and its many accounts of adolescent titillation, three stories, "Saturday Afternoon," "Savannah River Payday" and "Dorothy" which suggest a less ambiguous social vision than the early novellas. All three have a Southern setting; two of them concern racial persecution, the third the abuse and exploitation of women—and in all three the cruelty is unallayed by any compromising passages of whimsy. "Saturday Afternoon" is a lynching story which deals with the transference of guilt from white to black—the victim is a respectable, hardworking and successful black man who has always lived peacefully with his own wife. He is murdered by a group of lazy, dirty and salacious whites for having supposedly made a suggestive remark to a white woman. As in the other two tales, there is no formal authorial comment on the moral and economic standards of a society that permits and even encourages such atrocities, but the author's sympathies are clear in the understated ironic tone in which the repellent details are uncovered. This was the first of Caldwell's works to be seriously reviewed and the critics of both the *New Republic* and the *New Masses* were quick to spot a potential voice of the people—T.K. Whipple in the *New Republic* praised the folklore quality of these tales of "picaresque, proletarian, peasant America" and prayed that Caldwell might be "delivered from the highbrows";[9] Norman Macleod in the *New Masses* found him an idealist capable of good proletarian work who had yet to become aware of "the class struggle," "Russia," "the organized worker" and "The social scheme of things" and concluded his review, "We need writers like Caldwell. He should go left."[10]

When Caldwell followed the promise of *American Earth* in 1932 with *Tobacco Road*, he both pleased and confounded the critics who wanted a little more class-consciousness and a little less decadence for, in his first full length novel, he demonstrated that his mature style would be exactly a convergence of the two seemingly incompatible modes. While his own revolutionary political perspective is constantly reiterated in the novel's advocacy of co-operative and collective farming to replace the evils of the tenant and sharecropping system, the characters who voice this program are revealed not as sturdy future proletarians but as the hopelessly degenerate relics of the old corrupt system. The younger generation of Jeeter Lester's family is the most inept and decadent, the least likely to be the agents of change and their absurd antics force a paradoxical response from the reader: this situation is intolerably dehumanizing and must be changed—these dehumanized specimens are ludicrous and seem to merit no better than they have. The latter issue of merit, or the deservingness of the poor is a crucial one for American left wing writers of the 1930s and, of them all, only Caldwell dared to insist that the poor did not have to be depicted as stalwart, patient and vigorously noble in order for their poverty to be objectionable. It was a particularly sore point with the *New Masses* reviewer of *Tobacco Road* who commented of the Lester family, "They are all dying of pellagra and starvation, yet other organs beside their stomachs seem to plague them the most."[11] This prudish objection to the fact that the Lesters continue to seek sexual pleasure in the midst of their economic victimization and the further assertion that Caldwell "lacks social understanding" and is like a " 'bored and bilious God,' unmoved by his subjects' agonies," display a narrower comprehension both of literature and politics than Caldwell.

His simple style deceived his reviewers into believing that his conception of character was equally limited, yet *Tobacco Road* displays a more acute understanding than almost any other piece of left wing fiction of exactly those qualities in the dispossessed rural poor of America that separate them unfortunately from the heightened consciousness of their more revolutionary literary adherents. Thus, far from seeing religion as a distinctly reactionary force, Jeeter Lester attributes his worst suffering to the fact that " 'God is got it in good and heavy for the poor' "; after a full meal he smiles benignly on the rich and affirms with a sweep of his hat and a bow to a passing woman that such people " 'is just like us.' "[12] He clings in foolish loyalty to his devastated land rather than allying himself with the new urban proletarian in the mills and factories. Caldwell's refusal to make potential proletarians out of degraded peasants is given a further theoretical justification in his 1932 critical essay on Edward Dahlberg, in which he denies the possibility of a proletarian literature in America until a revolutionary change has taken place there: "We cannot expect to write or to read genuinely proletarian novels until we live in a proletarian world. At our present stage we find that we can only begin where our previous existence dumped us. We were dumped by a capitalist system on hard ground, and here we lie. Our first step is now being taken; we are scattered, broken, and bewildered; we are lifting our heads and looking ahead into the future."[13]

When Caldwell's next novel, *God's Little Acre*, 1933, was greeted with a pornography charge, it did not argue well for a shift toward greater proletarian orthodoxy, despite the fact that the book now dealt with the Southern urbanized factory worker as well as a less debilitated class of farmers than *Tobacco Road*. Caldwell in fact moves sexuality to the center of this novel by taking as his theme human hunger and the varied ways in which people need to satisfy it—searching fruitlessly for gold in the earth like Ty Ty Walden; begging sacks of flour and yeast from the State, like the striking mill workers; paying sexual homage to the voluptuous beauty of Darling Jill and Griselda, like Will Thompson; worshipping the godlike energy of factory machinery, like the girls who run back at night to press their bodies and lips against the mill walls. The novel takes the current correct position on the betrayal of workers by the AFL, on the need for solidarity between rural and urban poor and on the evils of the propertied classes, but it is about the vagaries of human nature whereby people act both foolishly and self-destructively while pursuing ideals that are sometimes noble, sometimes comic. The *New Masses* now felt that it was time to take Caldwell seriously to task on his ideological, and perhaps more significantly, his formal shortcomings. He was warned that his "over-emphasis" on sex would lead to latent (and unspecified) "decadent possibilities."[14] More interesting is the *New Masses* objection to the fantastic, legendary, almost mythical quality of Caldwell's writing in *God's Little Acre* which requires the use of grotesque characters and incidents that are distorted out of the realistic mold. The question of how far revolutionary criticism in the 1930s would support innovative, revolutionary fiction as opposed to fiction that merely advocated revolution is given a discouraging response in the case of Caldwell.

It is obviously impossible to know to what extent Caldwell responded consciously or unconsciously to the ideologues of the literary left although it may be assumed that he read them and noted their reprimands and advice since he still remained loyal in his public actions to the Communist-oriented League of American Writers. However, whether by personal choice or critical goading, Caldwell published in 1935 three books which show, for the first time in his career, a fracturing of the revolutionary—comic sensibility which seemed to pose such problems to the narrowly doctrinaire. The works comprise a novel, *Journeyman*, a collection of short stories, *Kneel to the Rising Sun*, and a book of documentary journalism, *Some American People*. The novel deals with a lewd, extravagant itinerant preacher, Semon Dye, who plays comic and outrageous confidence tricks on a gullible Southern community but it has few of the compassionate social insights which accompany this kind of humor in *Tobacco Road* and *God's Little Acre*. It is both sensational and trivial, since the grotesque comedy is no longer allied to a larger vision of humanity. The difference between this novel and *Tobacco Road* might be briefly illustrated by comparing the handling of a favorite symbol of Caldwell's that is common to both—a disintegrating automobile. Semon Dye arrives in the novel amid "a dense cloud of nauseating black smoke," "an ear-splitting backfire" and "a grinding vibration" that shakes his car from fender to fender.[15] It is both comic and violent, and certainly an appropriate medium for the devil himself—but it is also self-contained, echoing the myth it refers to without expanding on it. In *Tobacco Road*, the new automobile which is gradually dismembered by the reckless driving of Dude also has its source in folklore—this time in the many Southern tales of the violent dissection of people and animals—but in this novel the destructive havoc wreaked by and on the car is placed in a significant social context. It occurs while the Lester family comes to the absolute end of its food supply and provides a comment not only on the idiocy and profligacy of Dude, but more generally on the warped priorities of poor people in a voraciously consuming society. *Journeyman* is not wholly without serious undertones—it explores the Southern myth of the wandering, lecherous preacher and examines the psychology of religious conversion and "coming through" as consequences of deprivation and boredom, but it also shows, in a final comic twist, that the confidence trickster is himself drawn into his own frenzy, sees the light of God, and forgets to collect any money from his supposedly duped congregation. Nevertheless, the novel is less tied to the specific and contemporary social setting than any of the others.

By contrast, *Kneel to the Rising Sun*, containing some of the best proletarian short stories of the Depression, is a serious and horrifying expose of various facets of injustice in the South which employs revulsion without any complicating humor. The title story of the collection deals with racial prejudice and the ways it serves as a buttress to the class system in the South, dividing black and white sharecroppers against each other instead of uniting them against a brutal landlord who exploits black and white impartially. The tale is filled with the familiar horrific details in which Caldwell specializes—the landlord, Arch Gunnard, amuses himself by slicing off dogs' tails with calculating cruelty; his white cropper Lonnie makes no objection when the agony is inflicted on his own dog, as he later refuses to come to the aid of his black fellow-worker and defender, Clem, when Arch tracks him down with a lynch mob. The symbolic action of the story progresses through agony to anger, from the devouring of Lonnie's father by Arch Gunnard's snapping hogs to Lonnie's recognition in the redress of the dawn after Clem's murder of the betrayal in which he has participated. The story is a powerful one in the starkness of its indictment—Arch is an unmitigated villain, Clem an outspoken and valiant hero, Lonnie a naive and acquiescent dupe who slowly awakens to "try to say things he had never thought to say before."[16] It won Caldwell for the first time the unqualified critical approval of the *New Masses*: "one of the finest short stories any American has written"; "one of those rare pieces in which everything is right,"[17] as did several of the other stories in the collection such as "Slow Death" where working-class comrades discover their solidarity against the power of corrupt authority. Even among those stories which are not evidently revolutionary in content, a pervasive theme is that of the loathsomeness of the observer, the by-stander, the story-teller who reports but does not act—the whole collection conveys a sense of outrage against inertia in a world where suffering might frequently be averted. However, such a triumph in the field of left wing literature came for Caldwell at the expense of some curbing of a vision of human nature that was both more sardonic and more mysterious than the clear-cut sociological analysis that emerges in these stories.

Caldwell's separation of his talents into different genres was further marked in 1935 by the appearance of his first full-length work of non-fiction, *Some American People*, which deals with the contemporary plight of the poor in the West, in the Detroit auto industry and on Southern tenant farms. Caldwell showed in this work how adept he was in the new documentary medium of the age, in his capacity to interview and catch quaint images around which to build a report, and in his capacity to supply plenty of historical and economic background to further his analyses of Depression America. *Some American People* reveals a vision of humanity that is deterministic and sombre; there is neither irony nor foolishness to counteract the grim suffering that is exposed; many passages read like a sociological study of the same people who in *Tobacco Road* were the subjects of the artist rather than the social scientist:

Back on the hillsides the tenant families fell prey to various forms of religious excitement which served to take the place of normal entertainment. Physically, they became abject specimens of humanity. They ate what they could get, usually cornmeal and molasses. As a change many of them began eating the earth, and now communities of clay-eaters exist almost wholly on meal, molasses and clay. Clay-eaters may be identified by the color and texture of their skin, which looks and feels like putty.

In many such Georgia communities syphilis is as common as dandruff. Incest is as prevalent as marriage in these tenant regions where normal access to the outside is shut off because of the inability to travel.[18]

This journalistic method, with its omission of the humor of degeneracy and its concentration on cause rather than effect enables Caldwell to propose solutions to the plight of the poor which, in the more complicated world of the novels, would seem less than adequate; he appeared to be strongly drawn to the documentary method and returned to it again in his later books of photo-journalism with Margaret Bourke-White, most notably in *You Have Seen Their Faces*, 1937, and *Say, Is This the U.S.A.*, 1941. The first of these books, written and photographed when Caldwell was still strongly allied to the literary left, is an interesting mixture of sociology and imagination. It has long analytical essays on the history, geography, climate, ecology and economics of the South which pursue the same revolutionary thesis as *Some American People*—that only in the abolition of landlords and capitalism and the collectivization of farmland can the Southern farmer hope for a successful livelihood. However, the photographs are labelled not with factual details of their subjects but with invented remarks that Caldwell feels might be appropriate to them. In this slight step away from the naturalistic and into the imaginary world, Caldwell's penchant for the comic, the lazy, the repulsive and the idiotic in human nature surfaces again to qualify the certainty of the sociologist.

By 1939, when Caldwell signed the third call for a congress of the League of American Writers, the massive severing of allegiance with this organization by anti-Stalinists was well under way. Many of those who, like Caldwell, supported the League in the later days found their loyalty and energy diverted from it by the coming war. Caldwell's work for the next several years tended to be dominated by war-oriented journalism and when he returned later to fiction of the South it never again displayed the tension and the intellectual substance of the work done in the 1930s when there was the constant excitement of developing a fruitful dialectic between his artistic consciousness and his political sense of justice. It was then that he might have benefitted most from responsible and good-willed criticism. That the critics of the literary left wing and especially of the *New Masses* were grudging in their encouragement and unstinting in their criticism does not argue well for their ability to spot just the kind of young writer Michael Gold had publicly sought in his famous manifesto: one who was original, adventurous and sympathetic to the revolutionary cause, and who had, moreover, the capacity to draw a large following not perhaps from Party ideologues and academics, but from the masses themselves.

Notes

1. Erskine Caldwell, *Call It Experience* (New York: Duell, Sloan & Pearce, 1951), pp. 28, 14, 35, 27, 30.

2. Daniel Aaron, *Writers on the Left: Episodes in American Literary Communism* (New York: Octagon-Farrar, 1974), pp. 196, 423.

3. Erskine Caldwell, "Ripe for Revolution," *New Masses*, 8 (Dec. 1932), 26–27.

4. Eugene Lyons, *The Red Decade* (New Rochelle: Arlington, 1970), pp. 318, 320.

5. Erskine Caldwell, Introduction to *The Sacrilege of Alan Kent* (New York: New American Library, 1958).

6. Oscar Cargill, *Intellectual America* (New York: Cooper, 1968), p. 387.

7. Caldwell, *Sacrilege*, p. 26.

8. Kenneth Burke, "Caldwell: Maker of Grotesques," in *The Philosophy of Literary Form*, 2nd ed. (Baton Rouge: L.S.U. Pr., 1967), p. 353.

9. T.K. Whipple, in "Two Judgments of 'American Earth,' " *New Republic*, 67 (June 17, 1931), 130–31.

10. Norman Macleod, "A Hardboiled Idealist," *New Masses*, 7 (July 1931), 18.

11. Jack Conroy, "Passion and Pellagra," *New Masses*, 7 (April 1932), 24–25.

12. Erskine Caldwell, *Tobacco Road* (New York: Scribners, 1932), pp. 13, 186.

13. Caldwell, "Ripe for Revolution," p. 27.

14. Edwin Rolfe, "God's Little Acre," *New Masses*, 8 (Feb. 1933), p. 26.

15. Erskine Caldwell, *Journeyman* (New York: Duell, Sloan & Pearce, 1950), p. 12.

16. Erskine Caldwell, *Kneel to the Rising Sun* (New York: Duell, Sloan & Pearce, 1951), p. 244.

17. Hamilton Basso, "Sunny South," *New Masses*, 15 (June 11, 1935), 25.

18. Erskine Caldwell, *Some American People* (New York: McBride, 1935), pp. 261–62.

"Is That You in the Mirror, Jeeter?: The Reader and *Tobacco Road*"

Robert H. Brinkmeyer, Jr.*

Erskine Caldwell has written that the only purpose he had in mind when he wrote *Tobacco Road* was to describe as realistically as possible the lives of Southern poor whites. "I wanted," Caldwell writes in *Call It Experience*, "to tell the story of the people I knew in the manner in which they actually lived their lives from day to day and year to year without regard for fashions in writing and traditional plots." But one need not read far into the novel to realize that *Tobacco Road* is something quite other than a documentary. If indeed this is a mirror held up to the Georgia countryside, then it is one of those trick mirrors one sees at amusement parks which distorts everything into grotesque sizes and shapes. The world of *Tobacco Road* is, as just about every critic who has written on this novel has asserted, a realm of grotesque exaggeration, where everything—characters, settings, and situations—is twisted into bizarre and horrible shapes.

Caldwell's use of exaggeration has caused a good deal of consternation amongst critics who have tried to explain what he was really up to in this novel. Everyone accepts that Caldwell wrote the novel with a social purpose in mind, namely to draw attention to the plight of the tenant farmers and to make some suggestions on how to improve their condition. But why, then, the critic must ask, did he distort things to such an extreme, thereby making them comically absurd? And why did he apparently write the novel in the tradition of the Southwest humorists, a form whose history and very nature embody aristocratic disdain for backwoods people? Social realism and comedy, two separate and apparently incompatible purposes, seem to be at work in the novel; and the prevailing critical trend finds the novel flawed as a result of this mix: too comical for social indictment, and too socially zealous for pure humor.

But what I want to suggest here is that Caldwell's use of the bizarre and grotesque does not work against his sociological purpose, but actually is a part of a coherent narrative strategy designed to electrify the

*Reprinted from *Pembroke*, 11 (1979), pp. 47–50.

sensibilities of his readers and to arouse sympathy in them for the oppressed tenant farmer. Using comic exaggeration to arouse compassion
rather than contempt is a difficult line to walk, and many readers, not
surprisingly, have regarded Caldwell's comic exaggeration *merely* as
comic exaggeration. But this is not what Caldwell intended, and he con-
structs signposts along the way to guide the sensitive reader from this
interpretation.

Essentially what Caldwell tries to do with *Tobacco Road*, I believe,
is to lure the reader into believing he is reading a novel that is primarily
comic, written in the vein of the Southwest humorists, only to pull the rug
out from under him later in order to teach him a lesson. Caldwell's
strategy is to establish first in the reader a stance of detachment from the
material of the novel. He wants the reader—like the traditional audience
of the Southwest humorists—to look at the characters with curiosity and
detachment, and, most importantly, with condescension. "These are
mighty strange people," the reader is supposed to think for a while,
"thank God they have nothing to do with me!" This is all very comforting
for the reader since he implicitly affirms his own self-esteem by distancing
himself from the bizarre folks in the book.

The novel's opening scene works effectively to establish this posture
with the reader. The seduction of Lov (rape is a better word), the fight for
the turnips, the description of the wasted house, car, and countryside all
point to a world far removed from and irrelevant to most modern
Americans. Human actions are reduced to drives for animal
necessities—sex and food—and the emotions of love, respect, and sympathy are nonexistent. The old grandmother, we learn, survives only by
eating whatever grass and nuts she can scavenge from the woods, and is
scorned by the others because she sometimes pilfers food scraps. The
reader, working through this first scene, easily slides into the role of the
enlightened being looking down on his inferiors.

The rest of the novel progresses with scenes as grotesque as this first
one, continuously re-enforcing the reader's stance. But, at the same time,
and this is what makes *Tobacco Road* so bold and innovative, Caldwell
introduces information and situations which reveal the shortcomings of
assuming such a position. He suggests with this strategy not only the snobbery and ugly emotions which form the base of such an attitude, but also
the essential falsity of the stance itself: these folks whom you see only as
grotesques, having nothing to do with you, he implicitly suggests to the
reader, really have everything to do with you and your way of life.

One way Caldwell suggests this crosscurrent of meaning is through
his characterization of Jeeter Lester. At first glance Jeeter appears to be
totally lacking in any redeeming values: he is crude, selfish, violent, and
his wretchedness seems to strike no corresponding chords in the reader.
Rather than an instantaneous bond of identification, the basic impulse the
reader feels is rejection. But as Caldwell suggests time and again in the

novel, there is a lot in Jeeter which speaks directly to the reader. At the core of this superficially repulsive man lies a vital life-force which keeps him going against overwhelming odds. As Malcolm Cowley has pointed out in a review in *New Republic*,[1] Jeeter is not so much a figure of decay as "a sort of earth spirit, dirty, goatish, morally irresponsible." Jeeter emerges, on one level, as an embodiment of that typically American wish for backwoods freedom. "There have been hundreds of poems and stories," Cowley writes, "written in the vain attempt to introduce the god Pan into American folklore. Our woods are still unpeopled with fauns, nymphs or satyrs, but we do have Huckleberry Finn, who is sort of a river spirit, and we also have Jeeter Lester, who might be Huck in his old age." Jeeter is part of our collective consciousness.

Jeeter's plight as a farmer also speaks tellingly to the reader, for it represents the destruction of a central figure in American ideology and mythology, the independent husbandman. Besides possessing an unquenchable life-force, Jeeter also has a profound love of the land. Each spring, when the smells of burning sedge and newly plowed earth fill the air, his blood quickens and he yearns to be working the dirt. In another time and place, in an environment where he had the opportunity to work and to be rewarded fairly for his efforts, Jeeter might represent the classic American husbandman, the ideal farmer who Jefferson saw as the backbone of American democracy. In the twentieth century of this novel, however, Jeeter represents the figure of the small farmer gone bad, not so much through his own faults, but rather through the oppressive mechanisms of a social system which places no value on the individual. The actions of Captain John, Jeeter's farmer boss, who gave up the land, leaving his sharecroppers without farm supplies or credit backing, epitomize the cruelty of the present-day system:

> Rather than attempt to show his tenants how to conform to the newer and more economical methods of modern agriculture, which he thought would have been an impossible task from the start, he sold the stock and implements and moved away. An intelligent employment of his land, stocks, and implements would have enabled Jeeter, and scores of others who had become dependent on Captain John, to raise crops for food and crops to be sold at a profit. Co-operative and corporate farming would have saved them all (*TR*, 82–83).

Jeeter's ill treatment at the hands of Captain John represents more than just bad luck; it calls into question the entire economic system which destroyed him, and of which the reader is a part. Indeed, his fall illustrates the destruction of a traditional lifestyle and values in the name of "progress," and it calls upon the reader to open his eyes and ask himself whether this sort of heartless technological and economic development is really the true fruition of the American dream.

But Jeeter's fall has an even more significant message for the reader. Jeeter's family, as Caldwell tells us, was once well-to-do, and has for several generations experienced a devastating decline. Taxes, soil depletion, and low agriculture prices have slowly stripped the Lesters of a thriving family farm. The nadir of the decline is Jeeter's present plight—no land and no credit to buy the supplies needed to plant. Lively prosperity, by the time Jeeter comes along, has been reduced to stasis and starvation. The significant point here is that the Lester family was once a part of the system, but has been destroyed by it. The family which we see is surely grotesque and dehumanized, not because of their inherent nature but because they were twisted into these shapes by poverty and oppression. And the implicit message, devastating in scope, is that what happened to the Lester's could happen, under the present economic system, to anybody—the reader included! The Jeeters are at the mercy of an uncaring system; and anybody who falls victim to the debt collector may end up in the same boat with Jeeter.

While the Lesters no longer have any hold on the American scheme of things—the system has spit them out and passed them by—Caldwell makes it clear that they still hanker for the same material successes that the typical American does. As they grovel for food and money, Jeeter and his family become grotesque parodies of the American drive for wealth and power. And even more American is their lust for Bessie's new car, the central prestige symbol of American culture. Distorted as the images are, Jeeter's and his family's actions mirror those of American society.

All of these qualities of Jeeter and his family indicate the relevance of their story to the reader, and demonstrate the mistake that one commits if he reads these characters as merely comic grotesques that have nothing to do with the real world. Caldwell's message is a disturbing conclusion for the reader to come to, for Caldwell has set him up early to see the Lesters merely as comic misfits. The reader first watches the Lesters with disdain, only to come to the shocking realization that the Lesters are disconcertingly recognizable images of "normal" Americans. Caldwell's strategy accomplishes several things. First, it educates the reader by making him more aware of himself and his role in American society. Second, by showing the essential similarities between the characters of *Tobacco Road* and all Americans, the strategy creates a bond of sympathy and identification between the reader and the Lesters.

To realize a bond of sympathy and identification with the Lesters is not a flattering experience for anyone. The typical reader will go to any length to resist such a move by holding fast to his detached and condescending stance. So Caldwell with another narrative technique reveals to the reader the ugliness of those who maintain such a posture. Throughout the novel the Lesters and their clan come into contact with the "civilized" people of the modern city, in this case Augusta, Georgia. Time and again—the encounters with the loan company representatives (seen in a flashback), with the car salesmen, and with the proprietors of the hotel-whorehouse, to name several important instances—these city dwellers scorn helpless country people and take from them whatever they can get. Their laughter at and abuse of the Lesters and Bessie is a grotesque manifestation of the attitudes of the unsympathetic reader who also laughs at the Lesters. The heartless city people, Caldwell suggests, are no different from the genteel reader who refuses to recognize himself in the Lesters.

All of these narrative strategies used by Caldwell ultimately lead back to the social purpose of the novel—to call attention to the plight of the Southern poor white farmer and to enlist the reader's aid in helping to change things. By educating the reader both in the injustices of the economic order and the essential falseness of looking down on people like the Lesters, Caldwell hopes the reader will better sympathize with the cause which undoubtedly was a major motivating force behind the work—the destruction of the system of tenant farming.

That so many people read *Tobacco Road* as humor—and experienced the stage version (not written by Caldwell) in that way too—is, I think, not so much an indictment of Caldwell's art, but one of the American reading public. A comic interpretation is the easy way out, a way to disregard not only the plight of a segment of our population but also the injustices of the whole economic system, and the darker sides of ourselves which are mirrored in the people of *Tobacco Road*. Granted, Caldwell asks a lot of the reader. It's a bold challenge and not a glamorous one to take up. But Caldwell does his best to get us to rise to the occasion, and his effort is a poweful one. Alas, however, is it any wonder that the American public reduced this social commentary into local-yokel comedy?

Notes

1. Malcolm Cowley, "The Two Erskine Caldwells," *New Republic*, 111 (Nov. 6, 1944), 599–600.

"Erskine Caldwell's Nonfiction"

Sylvia Jenkins Cook

Like so many other writers in America, Erskine Caldwell began his literary career in journalism. From a high school summer job turning the handpress of the *Jefferson Reporter* he progressed to writing baseball columns for the *Augusta Chronicle*, obituaries and local news items for the *Atlanta Journal* and book reviews for the *Charlotte Observer*.[1] He dropped out of the University of Virginia in favor of further newspaper training and while there he was most drawn to sociology and English courses, disciplines which emphasized the same concerns as his journalistic interests—concerns with the shaping effect of the environment on people's lives and with an appropriate literary technique in which to embody them. It was a fruitful apprenticeship for a writer like Caldwell whose imagination has always sought out and tried to understand the whimsical and the fantastic among the mundane elements of human experience. Although journalism was a consciously abandoned stepping-stone to a career in fiction, Caldwell has, by his own account, felt the urge to return frequently to nonfiction writing throughout his life, both to vindicate his remembered sense of reality and to renew his spirits.[2] The books that have resulted from these excursions into the medium of reportage are *Some American People*, 1935; *You Have Seen Their Faces*, 1937; *North of the Danube*, 1939; *Say, Is This the U.S.A.*, 1941; *Russia at War*, 1941; *All-Out on the Road to Smolensk*, 1942; *Moscow Under Fire*, 1942; *Around About America*, 1964; *In Search of Bisco*, 1965; *Deep South*, 1968; and *Afternoons in Mid-America*, 1976. The quality of these books varies markedly, the best tending to coincide with the best of Caldwell's fiction in the 1930s and early 1940s when he was most ideologically, as well as aesthetically, engaged with his material. However, almost all of them not only give valuable insights into the vision of human nature that informs the fiction, but also display a style of documentary reporting that is as unique and individual as that of the novels, though in several ways quite distinct from it.

Caldwell's first nonfiction work, *Some American People*, was published in the heart of the Depression, in a decade that would later produce the great flowering of the documentary genre. An account of a personal journey through the agricultural and industrial states of mid-America, with a long excursion into Caldwell's native South, it appeared in the same year as Sherwood Anderson's journalistic picaresque book, *Puzzled America*, with which it has many affinities, not least of which is the sense that the South epitomized the most startling and extreme section of a devastated nation. Caldwell's book antedated similar American journeys of discovery by novelists James Rorty, Nathan Asch and Louis Adamic as well as the muckraking reporting of Hemingway and Steinbeck on the fate of World War I veterans and California migrant workers. Such a large-scale movement in the thirties from the more studied art of fiction to the immediacy of journalism has been variously explained by scholars as a rejection of the seeming frivolity of the imagined world in the light of the horrors of the real one; as a consequence of the failure of the traditional communications media to provide adequate information about the crisis, and a substitute for them; and as a turn to propaganda, illustrating the leftward swing in the political sympathies of so many artists and intellectuals seeking certainty in a time of bewilderment.[3] In Caldwell's case there is a measure of truth in all these explanations. By 1935 he had already achieved remarkable success with *Tobacco Road* and *God's Little Acre* but the novels had received a good deal of adverse criticism for their grotesque and exaggerated parodies of humanity under stress and for the unsatisfactory intrusion of sociological analysis and plans for improvement into the fictional text. The novels were accused of being both false and didactic in their fascination with human eccentricity, their horror of the dehumanizing effects of poverty and their effort to probe the historical and political significance of abandoned lives. *Some American People* became an effective nonfiction vehicle for achieving all these ends. The subject matter of the book—reporting on travels through midwestern farm districts, the Ford assembly lines in Detroit and the lives of Southern tenant farmers—took Caldwell back into contact with the deepest sources of his imagination and sympathy, with the South and victims of industrialism in particular and with the foibles of people in all circumstances. It permitted Caldwell to verify for himself and a sceptical public the extremities of degradation that might be uncovered anywhere in Depression America and to make constructive suggestions about improving conditions without being accused of tendentiousness and disguised propaganda. The technique Caldwell develops in *Some American People*, though different from that of his fiction, derives directly from what he says in *Writing in America* has been the main interest of his literary life—pondering the behavior of people and recording their "antics and motivations."[4] The language of the remark is important since it echoes the paradox that the fiction itself displays: "antics" suggests behavior that is both comic and irrational, "motivations" a naturalistic or rational explanation for that behavior. In the fiction this paradox is not resolved; in *Some American People* the humor and the sociology are large-ly separated and taken out of conflict. On the cross-country journey, Caldwell meets a wide variety of people who are recorded in amusing per-sonal anecdotes; although most are victims of the Depression and the Dust Bowl storms, they are not the scientifically determined products of them. By contrast, in the sections on the Detroit factories and Southern farms, there is neither comedy nor individuality but a sombre and angry exposé of conditions that virtually deprive people of their humanity. The greater the poverty and exploitation, the farther Caldwell moves from his comic vision—a situation directly contrary to the novels, where his imagination is capable of yoking and fusing the two. *Some American People* thus avoids the paradoxical complexity of the novels but makes a clearer ideological point by insisting that what is most appealing and worthy of literary note in human nature is also what is most threatened by material deprivation.

The most innovative reportorial techniques occur in the "Cross-Country" section of *Some American People*; and one sketch, "The Barber of the Northwest" may be taken as typical of much of Caldwell's early and best documentary writing. The narrator is in Bismarck, North Dakota, watching a baseball game between the local team and some visiting, bearded, House of David players when a Northern Pacific freight train disgorges a group of tramps onto the embankment above the ball park. One of them, after registering the score and the bewhiskered players, begins to unpack a rather elaborate set of shaving equipment. He is a freight train barber who recounts his story against the chorus of advanc-ing scores from the ball game. For a nickel or a dime, any tramp between the Great Lakes and the Rockies can have an in-transit shave or haircut by a graduate of the Kansas City Barber College who has abandoned wife and children in favor of a traveling life. The sketch combines many of Caldwell's most effective features: the laconic humor of the narrator; the absurdity of a tramp laying out an orderly collection of pearl-handled razors and whetstones on a railway embankment; the choral effect of the baseball game echoing in the background as the lather is mixed and the instruments sharpened; the repeated emphasis on the bearded House of David players; the mixture of whimsy and cruelty in Flynn, the barber, that leads him to speak so flippantly of the family he has abandoned and, underlying all, the evidence of the Depression that has driven him from his usual business into the ever-burgeoning migrant world. Flynn has a trick of concluding each of his remarks with a challenging "O.K.?" and the tale ends on the same word, dangling ironically at the end of a sketch of the less than satisfactory in contemporary America.

If there is a thesis in the first part of *Some American People*, it is clouded and modified by the variety of topics, characters and approaches in Caldwell's repertory. He ranges from extravagant tall tales of delusion in the Badlands to tragicomic accounts of paupers picking the Omaha dump and complacent Iowa farmers who subscribe to the *New Yorker* and educate their children at Harvard. The narrative voice shows comparable range. At times Caldwell is the impersonal researcher who is master of facts and figures: "Ranchers who had been buying hay at eighteen dollars a ton had reached the end of their rope; banks had long since stopped lending money to feed stock on a declining market; and the Federal Government had laid down a policy of not making feed loans on anything except breeding stock;"[5] at times he depicts himself in the third person as "the visitor"; at times in the first person, as "I" and "we" and at times in the second person of the colloquial "he says—you say" exchange. Underlying this diversity, however, certain constant elements emerge that reveal both Caldwell's understanding of personality and his ideological and political preoccupations in the thirties. Individual perverseness is pervasive; it is most aptly illustrated in the mystery of the derelict old panhandler in Fargo who stubbornly continues to beg for an insulting and loathsome subsistence when he might have both food and accommodation from the Transient Relief Agency. Habit and inertia prolong his degradation as much as any external circumstances and are unlikely to yield easily to optimistic public welfare schemes. Indeed, for all Caldwell's distress at the suffering he observes in the midst of the Depression, he seems even more concerned at the damage that may be done in trying to alleviate it. Even at the height of Caldwell's public commitment to a radical left-wing ideology, there is a conservative counter-current in his writing that fears the takeover of individuals by the government just as strongly as it promotes the ideals of union, power and fraternity. In considerable measure this conservatism is a nostalgia, frequently echoed at this time in the works of Steinbeck and Faulkner as well, for a rural American epoch that has died, partly because of the seeming treachery of nature herself against the farmers who believed the bounty was endless, partly because of the greedy, foolish and exploitative nature of the farming that developed. This double emphasis, on human quirkiness and intransigence and on the failure of Americans to conserve the land that brought them prosperity, runs throughout the first section of *Some American People*, but the mode is sardonic and frequently folksy so that it never seems unduly didactic. By contrast, the two remaining sections of the book display a rage and anguish that is unmitigated by any frivolity.

In the "Detroit" section the vein is still ironic but now it is savage satire of Henry Ford's insulated industrial kingdom where flower gardens cover the place where Ford's police gunned down his workers and employees mutilated by unsafe machinery are turned out onto the streets to scavenge for what they can get: "Once you become eight-fingered, you are a marked man in Detroit. Hotels will not hire negro porters if so much as one finger is missing. Transportation companies inspect the hands of applicants even before handing out application blanks. Store owners shake their heads at job seekers whose fingers are not all there.

Work for the eight-fingered narrows down to filling-station jobs and dish washing, and already there is a growing tendency to close these jobs to them. Eighteen or forty, it does not matter what the age may be; if you are eight-fingered, you are done for in Detroit" (172). This passage exemplified a familiar technique from Caldwell's fiction—a great intensity of meaning is coalesced into one grisly image, here the eight fingers with their immediate freakish suggestions; then the phrase is used repeatedly, cumulatively and finally obsessively.[6] However, unlike the fiction, its purpose here is directly propagandistic—the reader is shocked and frustrated but confronted at once with the correct response to this atrocity: "The mangling of hands and the crushing of life will only stop when workers succeed in forming their own rank and file union. There are no other means of forcing automobile manufacturers to reduce the speed-up and to install, and operate, safety devices that cannot be disconnected by the foreman" (172–3).

The final section of *Some American People* takes Caldwell to his Southern homeland and the familiar fictional territory of poor white tenants and sharecroppers. Like the people in *Tobacco Road* they are physically malformed and given to strange habits like dung and clay-eating; unlike them they are neither mysterious nor amusing. They are victims of a corrupt and wasteful agricultural system who must put their babies to suck at the teats of a dog because they have no other resources to offer. Again the horrific image is explored and reiterated; again it is a peculiarly appropriate horror in its unnaturalness, like Steinbeck's more famous use of a similar perversion of the act of nursing at the conclusion of *The Grapes of Wrath*. Again Caldwell advocates a union of sharecroppers as the first step towards a solution for these people. However, in contrast to the assurance of *Tobacco Road* that "Co-operative and corporate farming would have saved them all,"[7] Caldwell now finds the discovery of a new system of agricultural labor "problematical" (265) and hesitates between collective farming and a more Jeffersonian model of agrarian independence. *Some American People* thus proves finally more complex and less desperate in its political ideology than the fiction that preceded it, while it benefits immensely from the proven imagistic and repetitive techniques as well as the inventive skill of the story-teller. *Some American People* was well received by reviewers although one of them objected to Caldwell's frequent "lapses into fiction"[8] in a purportedly documentary book; however, these can scarcely be considered lapses so much as a conscious use of imaginative methods for an end quite distinct from the novels.

Between 1935 and 1937, the year of the publication of Caldwell's second nonfiction book, *You Have Seen Their Faces*, the desire of American artists to witness and record the lives of ordinary Americans during the Depression years was blossoming into the relatively new genre of the documentary, realized in the medium of Pare Lorentz's films, the oral history programs of the Federal Writers Project, and the photography project of the Farm Security Administration created by Roy Stryker. The mixing of these latter media of word and picture had also begun: Muriel Sheppard and Bayard Wootten had produced *Cabins in the Laurel* in 1935 and in the following year James Agee and Walker Evans had collected the materials of the three Alabama tenant families that would become *Let Us Now Praise Famous Men*. Thus, when the photo-text collaboration of Caldwell and Margaret Bourke-White appeared in 1937 it was not a wholly original experiment, but, like *Some American People*, it was innovative in Caldwell's insistence on mixing obviously imaginative material with more objective observation.

You Have Seen Their Faces is an exploration of the lives of rural poor people in the South, with blacks and whites sharing approximately equal attention. Caldwell has said that his purpose in writing it was "to show that the fiction I was writing was authentically based on contemporary life in the South," and that the decision to document it with photographs was also his.[9] He and Margaret Bourke-White spent the summer of 1936 touring the South and collecting their material, although the writing of the text was not done until later in the fall of that year. The form of the book is, on first appearances, a fairly simple alternation between sets of photographs, often with some thematic link, and sociological essays discussing the origins, development and decay of agricultural life and society in the region. However, although each photograph is given a quoted caption in the dialect and accent of its subject, Caldwell is careful to point out at the beginning that these are imagined, as are the monologues at the opening and closing of many of the essays, which speak again in the tones and language of the people themselves. Such documentary clearly makes no pretenses to scientific objectivity while contending all the while for the essential truthfulness of the material; it is an interesting and typical piece of ingenuousness on Caldwell's part that he can simultaneously insist that "no person, place or episode in this book is fictitious," while admitting that the quoted passages "do not pretend to reproduce the actual sentiments of these persons."[10] This distinction between the actuality and the authenticity of the sentiments recorded is crucial to any consideration of the documentary medium, especially as expressed in the 1930s. When James Agee and Walker Evans first tried to capture the "unimagined existence" of the Alabama tenant families, they wished to avoid not only the shaping imagination but, ideally, words themselves, because of their distorting intervention between the fact and the record of it. Caldwell, equally sceptical of reproducing pure documentary evidence, turns frankly to his own personal responses and recreates the reality he has witnessed.

The result of this mixture of subjective and objective methods and of the concentration on Caldwell's home region is a complicated and profoundly Southern work in which love struggles with hate, anger with understanding and hope with despair. Two consecutive paragraphs from the text will illustrate the conflict. Speaking of the South, Caldwell writes:

> This is the place where anybody may come without an invitation and, before the day is over, be made to feel like one of the home-folks. Scientists with microscopes and theologians with Bibles come to the South to tell it what is wrong with it, and stay to buy a home and raise a family. Gaping tourists come to pick its flesh to pieces, and remain to eat fried chicken and watermelon for the rest of their lives.
>
> Mark against the South its failure to preserve its own culture and its refusal to accept the culture of the East and West. Mark against it the refusal to assimilate the blood of an alien race of another color or to tolerate its presence. Mark against it most of, if not all, the ills of a retarded and thwarted civilization. (26)

Once again Caldwell focuses strongly on the destructive effects of neglect of the land through ignorance and inertia; the people can neither conserve nor adapt, the land suffers and because it does, the people suffer, becoming "god-forsaken, man-forsaken." The essays in *You Have Seen Their Faces* continue the use of Caldwell's repetitive techniques to recreate the vicious cycle of despair that every generation of Southern agricultural workers is trapped in. Their degradation is so extreme from a "back-breaking, spirit-crushing" existence that Caldwell feels obliged to assure us that "they are still people, they are human beings. They have life" (168). This statement reiterates the essence of Caldwell's fiction but whereas in the fiction having life and being human is most frequently exemplified by freakish behavior and preposterous attitudes, in the nonfiction such basic humanity insists on a practical solution for its predicament rather than a pessimistic shudder. At the end of *Tobacco Road* there is a marked dichotomy between Caldwell's rather desperate proposals for a revolutionary turn to collective farming and the actual world he depicts, where each generation is achieving new depths of incompetence and degeneracy and there is no person or agency to further the change. At the end of *You Have Seen Their Faces* Caldwell has resolved the conflict of *Tobacco Road* and the uncertainty of *Some American People* into a vaguer determination that the young people of the South, "With hope and a dream before them, . . . can change a hell into a living paradise" (169). By a sheer act of will, Caldwell reverses the tendency of the generations that he had noted in *Tobacco Road* and insists on action: "The older ones can be helped by charity and relief, and the remaining days they live can be made easier for them . . . The young people still have strong bodies and the will to succeed. They can change the agricultural system that broke the bodies and wills of their parents. They can stand up without fear and demand that they be paid adequately for their labor" (168). There is no mention now of precise plans for change although Caldwell's support of unions remains strong. One does not doubt for a moment the strength of the desire for improvement that lies behind this statement of Caldwell's convictions—yet at the point of their most forceful assertion, his imagination enters to undermine the moral simplicity of the essays. The legends invented by Caldwell to match the last series of photographs in the book depict an old woman saying, " 'I've done the best I knew how all my life, but it didn't amount to much in the end' " (183), while a young man admits, " 'It ain't hardly worth the trouble to go on living' " (185). This occurs in immediate juxtaposition to the last sentence of the "unimagined" text: "When fear has been banished, and self-respect restored, America will wake up to find that it has a new region to take pride in" (169). Such obstinate optimism from the author, allied to the fictional despair of his subjects, effectively points out the complex documentary medium that Caldwell creates in this book.

Margaret Bourke-White's photographs play an essential and equal role in *You Have Seen Their Faces*: of the three books she did with Caldwell, it is in this one that image and word seem most perfectly integrated. An early photograph in the volume shows a man with a two-horse plow moving across a sloping hillside, silhouetted against an overcast sky. The image suggests a primal, almost mythical relationship between the farmer and his land, and Caldwell's legend captures this sense of harmony in the simple terms of the farmer: " 'There's lots of things easier to do, and pay more money, but plowing the land and harvesting the crops give a man something that satisfies him as long as he lives' " (59). In the final section of the book a photograph of ravaged land undulating in gullies of dust is captioned, " 'It looks like God can't trust the people to take care of the earth any more' " (175). The photographs show the strength and beauty of poor people in the South as well as the many ways they may be distorted; they illustrate Caldwell's central thematic concerns in the essays with race, religion and land; their tone is both elegaic and angry, like the text. However, it must be admitted that some elements of caprice enter into Caldwell's imagined monologues for the photographic subjects: a black woman looking mournfully from behind prison bars says, "I've only been misbehaving," while a white man living in a delapidated, three-sided shack insists lazily that he likes his open-ended house better than when it had four walls. Some of the people express satisfaction, some humor, some mischief; the abstract truth of their victimization as a group is dispelled a little by the presence of their individual personalities. The captioned photographs replace the anecdotes in *Some American People* but fulfill a similar purpose by appearing to modify a didactic thesis while at the same time justifying the humane ends of such propaganda.

That most of Caldwell's nonfiction in the thirties was propaganda seems beyond dispute—the genre is almost inseparably yoked to it, but it is propaganda of high aesthetic rank, with subtlety, humanity and complexity. One of Caldwell's otherwise rather antagonistic critics says of his reportage that the best thing in it is, "the struggle of his fellow feeling against his ideology." This is said in response to Caldwell's capacity to like individuals and find them intriguing even when they do not share his political and economic attitudes or are themselves the embodiment of his opposition. Even beyond the question of "fellow feeling," there is, tempering Caldwell's rage against the human condition, a relish for discovering and appreciating how people live their lives, regardless of whether change is called for. One manifestation of this curiosity was Caldwell's enthusiasm, in 1938, to assume the editorship of a series of regional books, *American Folkways*, to be written by skilled writers from various parts of the country, and to describe, in his words, "the cultural influences implanted by the original settlers and their descendants and . . . explain the manner in which life in one region of the country differed from the way of life in another region."[12] The series, under Caldwell's direction, eventually comprised 23 volumes, generally very highly regarded. The emphasis in his plans for it is once again on the "antics and motivations" of people, but in desiring to represent the "indigenous quality of life in America" and to "reveal the ingrained character of America" Caldwell shows a native emphasis that is now as much ethnic, historical and cultural as it was economic and sociological in the earlier Depression years. Such an interest may have been spurred by Caldwell's and Bourke-White's trip to Czechoslovakia in the summer months of 1938 and the broadened perspective in Caldwell's thinking that is revealed in the book that resulted, *North of the Danube*, 1939.

The book is again a photo-text, structured similarly to *You Have Seen Their Faces*: eight essays, each set in a different region of Czechoslovakia is followed by a set of six to eight plates illustrating and complementing it. However, the photographs are factually, rather than imaginatively captioned, a small symbol of a major difference between the two books, for in *North of the Danube* Caldwell was working for the first time in a completely alien environment. He knew little of the customs and longer history of the country and he spoke neither of its major languages, getting by with German and English in the cities and Western regions, having immense difficulties in Eastern areas. Relatively few interviews were conducted with the subjects of the book and Caldwell's distance from its people may be measured in the relative dearth of humor in it, for if the comic/grotesque mode that dominates so much of Caldwell's writing is not to appear brutal, it depends on considerable intimacy with the lives of his people. In *North of the Danube* Caldwell wisely restricts the humor to situations where he himself, as the ignorant outsider, or the more prosperous and successful people, rather than the poor, bear the brunt of it. The peasants in the photographs do not speak directly—like their Southern counterparts, very few look straight at the camera—and the details that echo throughout the visual images are as foreign as the language and customs with which the writer has to deal. The people's lives are not invaded, either by Bourke-White's camera or by Caldwell's reporting—a reticence that is only partly due to their distance from the culture. There seems also to be a philosophical motive behind it, since invasion is the main political fact of the book. Czechoslovakia is seen as a fragile democratic union of national and ethnic groups that is being violated and dismembered to aggrandize the power-hungry surrounding countries. A culture sprung from diversity is being dismantled in favor of varieties of totalitarianism and greed.

However, *North of the Danube* is much more than a requiem for Czechoslovakia. It is both a celebration of human variety and cultural pluralism and a grim reminder of the exploitation and persecution that people are prone to in societies where such differences exist. In the early morning markets of the town of Uzhorod Caldwell notes with some pleasure that, "The wives of Czech railway workers and the wives of German bankers stood side by side with the wives of Jewish merchants and the wives of Gypsy traders. German and Jew, Czech and Gypsy, each in her own language, talked excitedly to the Ruthenian peasants, who understood nothing except the desire to sell their food and flowers."[13] When the day's business is ended, the Ruthenians, Czechs and Germans leave on bicycles, the Jews and Gypsies walk. On the land, a Czech vineyard owner notes the pattern of "Slovak workers, Hungarian overseers, and Czech landlords." Then he adds more grimly, "And over us all, the German God Almighty" (62). The ominous signs of impending war are everywhere in the book, from an ugly train incident in which a compartment of Czechs, Slovaks, Ruthenians and Hungarians stand passively by while a Jewish woman is attacked by a German, to a more explicit encounter in Prague with German propaganda agents who are determined to eradicate all that does not conform to their own monolithic dictates.

Lest one have any doubt of Caldwell's implicit political sympathies, he attaches to the end of each chapter quotations from politicians, historians and artists to make explicit his own more subtle emphasis: the chairman of a refugee commission says that these people have "found a haven in democratic Czechoslovakia" (79), while Hitler describes the country as "a tumor which is poisoning the whole European organism" (112). As with *You Have Seen Their Faces*, *North of the Danube* is undisguisedly partisan in its responses to prejudice and poverty, but it is also a travelogue in a new world for Caldwell and he responds to much of that novelty in the same way as to the eccentricity and whimsy of the people he encountered in *Some American People*, although in Czechoslovakia it is more to custom and incident than to individual personality. Two chapters, "Bread in Uzok" and "The Dogs of Ceske Budejovice," illustrate again the laconic narrative technique that finds an image around which to crystalize an experience and then develops and reiterates the image to the edge of absurdity. The motif in Uzok is the frenzy of people who have not so much as seen bread in six or eight years; when Caldwell and Bourke-White are chauffeured to visit them, they fill their trunk with loaves of bread and then discover they must fight off the peasants with knives and sticks in order to distribute it. The chapter is a fairly polemical statement on the shame of such hunger, illustrated through the most literal application of its common metaphor, bread. Caldwell is both appalled and intrigued by the familiar sight of poverty and its unfamiliar manifestations, such as the urban dog owners who sit hopefully all day on their doorsteps awaiting a summons to use their dogs and carts to transport small loads around the town. He discovers there are codes of conduct and rituals to be observed and conveys nicely the sense that what is exotic to him is merely part of a daily monotony of endurance for the people he describes. While a Czech farmer feasts Caldwell on wine and asparagus, he notes the farmer's overseer beating a stick on the knuckles of a Slovak peasant woman who has fallen behind in her hoeing. Ever alert to the signs of peonage, Caldwell is conscious in *North of the Danube* of a more comprehensive and complicated context for them than in preceding documentaries; for the first time he has neither solutions nor suggestions to offer—that would only be to abrogate the arrogance of the outsiders who are in the process of destroying Czech culture. Instead he concentrates on creating highly individual images of a rather bewildering society, which are richly supplemented by Margaret Bourke-White's photographs. She provides pictures of architecture, industry and urban life that modify Caldwell's rather agrarian and personal bias. The book is in some ways the most interesting of their three collaborations, since the camera provides what Agee called in *Let Us Now Praise Famous Men* a coequal study to the text, not merely an illustration of it, as in *You Have Seen Their Faces* or a tangent to it, as in their last work together, *Say, Is This the U.S.A.*

Published in 1941, *Say, Is This the U.S.A.* seems to suggest, for a variety of reasons, the temporary exhaustion of the photo-text medium. The book shows some of the ennui of the Missouri filling-station attendant whom Caldwell attempts to interview early in its pages:

> With a business-like gesture the attendant handed me a neatly printed card. It read as follows:
> "I am 36 years old. I smoke about a pack of cigarettes a day, sometimes more and sometimes less, but it evens up. I take an occasional drink of beer. I am a Baptist, an Elk, and a Rotarian. I live with my own wife, send my children to school, and visit my in-laws once a year on Christmas Day. I wear No. 9½ shoes, No. 15½ collar, and No. 7¼ hat. I shoot a 12-gauge shotgun and have a 27-inch crotch. I like rice, sweet potatoes, and pork sausage. I vote for F.D.R., pull for Joe Louis, and boo Diz Dean. I wouldn't have anything against Hitler if he

stayed in his own backyard. I don't know any Japs, but I've made up my mind to argue with the next one I see about leaving the Chinese alone. I'm in favor of the AAA, the CCC, the IOU, and the USA. If I have left anything out, it's an oversight. If you want your tank filled, just nod your head. If you don't want anything, please move along and give the next fellow a chance. I thank you. Hurry back."[14]

One critic has called this the epitaph for the "I've seen America" book of the thirties;[15] whether Caldwell's anecdote is real or imaginary, it effectively conveys a sense of the embarrassing surfeit of this approach to documentary.

For other reasons, too, Caldwell and Bourke-White's last joint enterprise is less successful than their earlier ones; for the first time there is an incompatibility between the photographs and the text—they are not quite parallel and not exactly complementary. Perhaps the problem lay in the breadth of the endeavor itself: Margaret Bourke-White wrote of it, "Our object was to give the impression and feel of America" (176). Such a task seems ironically more feasible when the society was an alien one to both artists, as was Czechoslovakia. Presumably they could then discuss and synthesize their attitude because they were fresh impressions: in the case of *You Have Seen Their Faces* Bourke-White was more obviously vindicating Caldwell's vision of agricultural poverty in the South, a narrowly defined topic on which he had considerable expertise. When the two came to create a mutual vision of America on the edge of war, they seemed to start from premises about American society that are distinctly at variance. Bourke-White's photographs in this volume are most clearly celebratory; a large proportion of them are angled from below the subjects, silhouetting them against landscape and sky, clearly anticipating the final heroic shot of the Statue of Liberty; her topics shift between farm and industry, work and play and the variety of ethnic groups that constitutes America, suggesting the diversity and democratic range of American life. The visual images of the book are thus consistent with a central theory of the progression of documentary ideology in the thirties: that it began in criticism of America's failures and ended by celebrating its successes.[16] However, Caldwell appears to have been less attuned to the affirmative note than Bourke-White. Where she sees ethnic variety, Caldwell still calls attention to racism; where she depicts industrial progress, he points to exploitation; her photographs show a rich and fertile land, his text turns once again to the decline of the old agrarian ideals. It is necessary to add that Caldwell's text is also frequently intensely nationalistic and patriotic; he has certainly never shown himself averse to the partisan uses of documentary and this book is not an exception. Nevertheless, *Say, Is This the U.S.A.* was clearly not conceived to serve Caldwell's personal ideological concerns and the book is not helped by this dividing of loyalties. It is not a dichotomy that Caldwell seems fully in control of, as he is with the inconsistencies and incongruities of his earlier work. Opposite Bourke-White's titanic image of the State of Liberty Caldwell's caption reads: "Car hops and bobbin boys, auto courts and night shifts, hitch hikers and hotel greeters, beauty queens and bank nights, prayer services and union meetings, personal appearances and gossip columns, all-night movies and bunion derbies" (174). This is certainly an amused and appreciative and gently ironic description of the diverse life of New York City but it seems in somewhat embarrassing contrast to the heroic overtones of the photograph: almost as though Caldwell were developing a kind of unconsciously dialectical argument with Bourke-White's imagery. Earlier in the book, in response to a photograph of school children seated around a piano, an American flag in the background and a pretty teacher playing to them, Caldwell writes as the legend: "They like to tell their teacher when their fathers have jobs and are working, but they do not like to talk about it when their fathers cannot find any work to do" (102); opposite a picture of the bountiful wheat fields of Kansas, the caption tells us, "In Kansas City a man is arrested on a charge of vagrancy because he begged for something to eat" (12).

Not all of Caldwell's captions are of this rather contentious nature. Many of them are somewhat Whitmanesque catalogues of local activities or produce associated with the photo images; they show a fascination with language and a mastery of colloquialism and slang that is much less in evidence in Caldwell's fiction where the vocabulary seems pruned to the barest minimum. For perhaps the first time in Caldwell's writings one sees the author's sheer delight in the resources of language rather than its wilful limitations, a freight train entering Dodge City is captioned, "Skippers, rail benders, rear stacks, hog heads, tallow pots, smoke artists, snakes, bull snakes, goats, pig snouts, and Mae Wests" (20); a Texarkana stock market picture bears the description, "Foals, colts, yearlings, fillies, mares, dams, geldings, stallions, mustangs, pintos, palominos, bronchos, cayuses, plugs, jackasses" (128).

In the text itself, Caldwell continues his method of relating personal anecdotes built around a kind of choral image, like that of the B-girl who is sick of drinking champagne for a living or the New York cab-driver who is too engrossed in his income tax to take any customers; though the Depression is over for these two, their newfound prosperity is still distasteful. Occasionally, as he had done with the anecdote of "Bread in Uzok" in *North of the Danube*, Caldwell seems to stumble almost innocently on a symbol that taps a kind of primal mythology, even while he is presenting it in rather mundane circumstances. Such is certainly the story of the black coffinmaker whom Caldwell bumps into one dark night in a deserted city street. He is literally an underground man—three years on a Georgia chain gang have driven him out of this world to take up residence in a dark basement where the daylight never penetrates. There he plies his trade, making boxes for the burial of his fellow blacks.

Caldwell presents the encounter with restraint but the image of America implicit in it has no parallel in the photographs. Indeed it is difficult to imagine that any medium other than words could convey the subterranean gloom of its suggestions.

Caldwell and Bourke-White attempted one more collaboration after *Say, Is This the U.S.A.*; originally intended as a more contemplative text on the Soviet Union, the pressure of events there in 1941 turned it into a more immediate piece of journalism, *Russia at War*, compiled from Caldwell's newspaper articles on the war with photographs selected by Bourke-White from her collection. In 1942 Caldwell and Bourke-White's divorce culminated the professional split that seems imminent already in *Say, Is This the U.S.A.* Apart from two books, *All-Out on the Road to Smolensk* and *Moscow Under Fire*, published in 1942 and hastily concocted from wartime correspondence diaries and broadcast notes, this was to be Caldwell's last major engagement with nonfiction writing for a very long time—in fact until another crisis in public life that engaged his sympathies in the same way as the Depression: this was the growing Civil Rights movement of the 1960s. Caldwell's nonfiction, like his best fiction, seems to have flourished best when his ideological commitment was strong, and his two main works of reportage in the sixties, *In Search of Bisco*, 1965, and *Deep South*, 1968, take him back once again to the concerns of poverty and racial injustice on his native grounds. Both books have a more directly autobiographical format than any of the earlier ones, although they seem, like so much of Caldwell's nonfiction, to dwell in a world somewhere between the real and the imaginary. *In Search of Bisco* was clearly spurred by the Civil Rights movement and Caldwell's strong support for it, although its method is not so fully adjusted to the modern issues with which the movement sought to deal; Caldwell is clearly still more at home aesthetically with accounts of chain gangs, lynchings and miscegenation than desegregating schools and lunch counters. The narrative motif is based on his search throughout the South for Bisco, a black childhood companion, with whom he had lost touch. Through Bisco, and his own mother's refusal to let him sleep and eat with the black child, Caldwell discovered racism at an early age. His adult search for Bisco is a device to explore Southern attitudes, black and white, to race; the inevitable discovery that he makes is that every black may be Bisco, his lost and betrayed friend. The book cannot be said to add any profound insight into the origins of the Civil Rights movement, but it does suggest the human consequences of segregation and exploitation in the South and explore candidly the normally unarticulated prejudices of the whites. Caldwell's talent for uncovering the incongruous situation and the absurd character is focused here exclusively on the mechanism of bigotry: " 'What they don't understand up North is that niggers—or Negroes, as they say it—haven't gone through evolution as far as white people. They're still primitive—just like wild Indians used to be. They just don't have the intelligence we've got and it's going to take time for their brains to grow bigger so they can go through their cycle of evolution like we've already done.' "[17] One reviewer felt that, because of characters like this, the book rang "disturbingly of fiction" although the major impact was its tone of "piercing reality and immediacy."[18] In fact, Caldwell had made fiction a tool of nonfiction as a partial method in his early works of reportage but increasingly so in the two 1960s books until the barrier between fact and fancy virtually disappears.

Deep South, another autobiographical work, is built around Caldwell's memories of his clergyman father, Ira Sylvester Caldwell, and is an obvious vehicle for exploring the varied manifestations of religious feeling in the South, from stiff, upperclass society churches to all the fanatical extremes of fundamentalism: snake handling, coming through, head-banging, and glossolalia. One of Caldwell's main interests here is the way the South's poor whites have evolved a religion away from ethics into violence and hysteria, and the consequent appeal of such movements as the Ku Klux Klan. In the treatment of the wealthier churches, Caldwell's radical political perspective is again evident; he detests privilege and spends a good deal of time satirizing the alliance of such churches to money, business and the stock exchange. Underlying the treatment of both poor and wealthy white churches is the ethical issue of racism. In the second part of the book, Caldwell turns to the black churches, exploring their history and customs and moving now beyond the religious context to discuss further the topic of *Bisco*, the intolerable position of blacks in the South.

The book is unified by the device of exploring Caldwell's father's job, as a kind of trouble-shooter in the congregations of the Associated Reformed Presbyterian Church. This gives Caldwell a good opportunity to return to the methods of documentary that had succeeded so well for him in the thirties—a mixture of personal histories and generalized commentary, with a balance between humor and fairly partisan speculation. Once again we meet varieties of people in outlandish situations; the Rev. I. S. Caldwell officiates at literal shotgun marriages and tries to arbitrate between the factions of a congregation that has split over the issue of whether or not to carpet the church floor: "As a result of the controversy, the bare-floor and the carpet-floor advocates had stopped speaking to one another, two divorces had occurred in intermarried families, and there had been a shooting affray in which one member was killed and another paralysed for life."[19] This is clearly the material of fiction, and a fairly tall tale at that, yet it captures the combination of pettiness and fanaticism that Caldwell finds everywhere in the churches. In analysing this, Caldwell comes closer to making explicit the implicit assumptions of his fiction than anywhere else in his writing: in addition to the physical and spiritual deprivations of poverty, he argues, the Southerner is the heir to a rabid anti-intellectualism nourished by a powerful church that permits no speculative thinking. Thus the poor are institutionally aided in becoming superstitious, bigoted, reactionary, foolish and unethical: "As is to be expected among people dedicated to fundamentalistic Protestantism, their extreme conservatism is in keeping with the traditional sharecropper-plantation system, the segregated racial pattern, states rights, and one-party political domination. In both city and country, where such principles have prevailed for generations, the glorification of ruralism and anti-intellectualism is the predominating social, economic, and political influence" (55). This does not perhaps offer a complete explanation for the antics of Jeeter Lester, Ty Ty Walden and Semon Dye, but it does show the extent to which Caldwell's seemingly naive material and technique is the result of a conscious and rather more sophisticated perspective.

In 1976, when Caldwell was in his seventies, he produced his latest work of nonfiction, *Afternoons in Mid-America*. The tendency in Caldwell's later nonfiction to drop the guise of simplicity and permit himself a broader range of omniscient speculation is furthered here where Caldwell's perspective on Middle America is that of the urbane world traveler who has visited spas in Czechoslovakia, dined with Picasso and met European monarchs; his vocabulary is also markedly different in range from the novels—in fact it is only by reading Caldwell's nonfiction that one becomes aware of the extent to which the fictional voice and tone is consciously, rather than genuinely, naive. However, the middle-Western states in the seventies do not provide Caldwell with the kind of stimulus necessary for his best work; although he returns again to some of his enduring concerns, such as the preservation of the land and the relations between races and ethnic groups, what he sees provokes neither outraged laughter nor concerned pity. Farmers are now aware of the need for conservation: " 'the good rich soil we're blessed with here in the valley is a precious thing, and every inch of it ought to be protected against erosion and abuse;' "[20] and although racial divisions are still keen, Caldwell protests in this book not against lynching and chain gangs but against "sick jokes and ethnic anecdotes" (121). Caldwell is still moved by poverty and injustice but his perceptions of them are less harsh, and a mellow Erskine Caldwell is not much Caldwell at all. Almost without exception, the liveliest parts of *Afternoons in Mid-America* are reminiscences of Caldwell's childhood and his Southern background which evoke the familiar blend of cruelty, titillation and compassion, although such stories can scarcely be justified as relevant to the main material of the book. Caldwell's imagination and his conscience, the two key elements of his nonfiction, have always functioned best in an extreme environment; with neither crisis nor chronic perversion of normality to encourage him, he resorts to the memory of these in the Depression and the South in order to recapture his personal tone.

Any final assessment of Caldwell's contribution to the documentary genre in America must rest on the work he did in the 1930s, when he developed the techniques that have served him throughout his literary career. He recognized from the outset that documentary truth has more kinship with the authenticity of fiction than with scientific poll-taking and therefore never assumed a factitious air of disinterestedness about the material he recorded. Documentary and nonfiction writing has always been for Caldwell partisan, personal and highly selective; his imagination has played as vital a part in it as his conscience and observation. Yet there are clear stylistic and ideological distinctions between Caldwell's fiction and nonfiction. Despite the obvious inventive quality of much of his reporting which has led several of his critics to label it fiction, Caldwell maintains a separate persona, vocabulary, technique and even point of view in his nonfiction. While the fiction is almost consistently notable for the author's disengaged stance from the "antics and motivations" of the characters, the nonfiction permits an intrusive author, calling attention to his presence, his awkwardness, his anger and his sympathy. The more sophisticated vocabulary of the nonfiction reveals to what extent the ingenuous style of the fiction is a consciously contrived technique, while the tendency to separate comedy from degradation in the nonfiction suggests a different ideological purpose—reform rather than despair for the victims of economic and racial exploitation. While the underlying vision of human nature and society, especially as symbolically manifested in the South, is consistent in all his work, it is in the nonfiction that the intensity of Caldwell's moral purpose is most evident; by developing a carefully wrought, inventive literary method for his documentary reporting, he has succeeded in his best works, in negating the conventional distinction between effective propaganda and genuine aesthetic merit.

Notes

1. Erskine Caldwell, *Call It Experience: The Years of Learning to Write* (New York: Duell, Sloan and Pearce, 1951), pp. 16, 19, 36–37, 42.

2. Caldwell, *Call It Experience*, pp. 161–62.

3. Daniel Aaron, *Writers on the Left: Episodes in American Literary Communism* (New York: Harcourt, Brace & World, Inc., 1961), p. 393; William Stott, *Documentary Expression and Thirties America* (New York: Oxford University Press, 1973), pp. 67–73; Richard H. Pells, *Radical Visions and American Dreams: Culture and Social Thought in the Depression Years* (New York: Harper Torchbooks, 1973), p. 195.

4. Erskine Caldwell, *Writing in America* (New York: Phaedra Publishers, 1967), introduction, unpaged.

5. Erskine Caldwell, *Some American People* (New York: Robert M. McBride & Company, 1935), pp. 32–33. Subsequent references to this edition will be made in the text.

6. See Scott MacDonald, "Repetition as Technique in the Short Stories of Erskine Caldwell," *Studies in American Fiction*, 5 (1977), 213–25.

7. Erskine Caldwell, *Tobacco Road* (New York: Duell, Sloan and Pearce, 1932), p. 83.

8. Robert Van Gelder, *New York Times* (15 December, 1935), 9.

9. Caldwell, *Call It Experience*, p. 163.

10. Erskine Caldwell and Margaret Bourke-White, *You Have Seen Their Faces* (New York: Arno Press, 1975), p. 4. Subsequent references to this edition will be made in the text.

11. Stott, *Documentary Expression*, p. 243.

12. Caldwell, *Call It Experience*, p. 183.

13. Erskine Caldwell and Margaret Bourke-White, *North of the Danube* (New York: Viking Press, 1939), p. 11. Subsequent references to this edition will be made in the text.

14. Erskine Caldwell and Margaret Bourke-White, *Say, Is This the U.S.A.* (New York: Duell, Sloan and Pearce, 1941), pp. 10, 12.

15. Stott, *Documentary Expression*, p. 256.

16. Stott, *Documentary Expression*, p. 237.

17. Erskine Caldwell, *In Search of Bisco* (New York: Farrar, Straus and Giroux, 1965), pp. 86–87. Subsequent references to this edition will be made in the text.

18. C. L. Cooper, *Saturday Review*, 48 (1 May, 1965), 39.

19. Erskine Caldwell, *Deep South: Memory and Observation* (New York: Weybright and Talley, 1968), p. 18. Subsequent references to this edition will be made in the text.

20. Erskine Caldwell, *Afternoons in Mid-America: Observations and Impressions* (New York: Dodd, Mead & Company, 1976), p. 142. Subsequent references to this edition will be made in the text.

INDEX

Adamic, Louis 376
Adams, Franklin P. 28
Adams, J. Donald 29
Ade, George 258
Adlow, Judge Elijah 251
Adventures of Huckleberry Finn, The
    301–302 372
Agamemnon 36
Agee, James 380, 385
Agrarians 58
"Alibi Ike" 68
Allen, Walter xiii
The Ambassadors xxviii
Amber Satyr 75
Anderson, Sherwood xxi, xxix, 4, 8,
    74, 80, 239, 241, 266, 290,
    319, 376
Ansermoz-Dubois, Félix 257
Arban, Dominique 242–243, 259
Aristophanes 30, 252
Armstrong, Louis 296
Arnavon, Cyrille 260
Asch, Nathan 376
As I Lay Dying xxi, 237, 289, 294
Avret, J. T. 133

Balzac, Honore de 183, 249, 317
Barbezat, Marc 240, 260
Barlow, James Jr. 111
Basso, Hamilton 38–39
Baudelaire, Charles 255, 257
Beach, Joseph Warren xi–xii, xxxii,
    180–197, 317
The Bear 326
Bellow, Saul xxvii
Benchley, Robert 258
Benedict, Stewart H. xxxii, 255–261
Bergson, Henri xii, 170, 185–186
Bessie, Alvah 43
Bierce, Ambrose 36
Birthright 75
Blanzat, Jean 241–242, 244, 260
Boccaccio, Giovanni 30, 160
Bode, Carl xiii, 246–248, 260
Bok, Judge Curtis 252–253
Böll, Heinrich 261
Borovoy, Leonid 264, 265

Bosch, Hieronymus xxvi
Bourke-White, Margaret xxvi, 53, 55–
    56, 58, 59–62, 71–72, 181, 296,
    297, 317, 326, 368, 380, 382,
    383–388
Bradbury, John M. xiii
Brecht, Bertolt xv, 309
Brinkmeyer, Robert H. Jr. xv–xvi,
    370–374
Brodin, Pierre 238, 242, 260
Brooks, Cleanth xii
Broun, Heywood 249
Brown, John 259
Brown, John Mason 29
Browning, Tod 325
Burke, Kenneth xi, 167–173, 261, 329,
    363
Burnett, Whit 43

Cabins in the Laurel 380
Cain, James M. 243
Caldwell, Caroline Preston Bell 318
Caldwell, Erskine
    biography 215, 315–329
    definition of fiction xviii–xix
    as humorist ix–xvi, xxiv–xxv, 19,
        25, 67, 78–79, 156, 185–186,
        198–213, 217–218, 258,
        281–282, 299–314
    as maker of grotesques xxiii–xxiv,
        167–173, 210, 298–299
    marriages 316–317, 318, 388
    method of composition xvii–xxi,
        282–286, 290–291
    parents. *See* Caldwell, Caroline
        Preston Bell and Caldwell, I. S.
    "plain style" xx, xxi, xxvi, 195, 264
    as social critic ix–xvi, xxiv–xxv, 15,
        24, 56–67, 97–152, 175–179,
        198–200, 201, 213
    works (novels, nonfiction books,
        pamphlets, collections)
        Afternoons in Mid-America 390
        All Night Long xii
        All-Out on the Road to Smolensk
            388
        American Earth 3–11, 13, 25,

172, 196, 221–222, 237,
    255–256, 315, 345–346, 354,
    363–364
American Folkways Series xxxiv,
    211, 383
Around About America 264, 358
The Bastard xiv, 4, 10, 80, 186–
    187, 325, 362–363
Caldwell Caravan, The 353
Call It Experience xiv, xx, 245,
    264, 320–324, 370
Certain Women 273, 277, 356–
    357
Claudelle Inglish 273
Close to Home xiv, 263, 275, 282
Complete Stories of Erskine
    Caldwell, The 247, 355
Courting of Susie Brown, The 355
Day's Wooing and Other Stories.
    A 353
Deep South xxvi, 268–269, 274–
    275, 277, 328, 359, 389–390
Deer at Our House, The 358
Episode in Palmetto 269–270
Erskine Caldwell's Men and
    Women 357–358
Georgia Boy xiii, 201–203, 217,
    218, 245, 263, 264, 304, 352
Georgia Boy, and Other Stories
    353
God's Little Acre xii, xiii, xvi,
    xxii, 23–33, 40, 41, 70, 81,
    84–85, 91–93, 156–166, 168,
    169, 170–172, 178, 191–194,
    199, 208, 210, 212, 225–226,
    237–240, 244, 246–247,
    249–252, 254, 255–257, 265,
    271–272, 275–276, 295, 296,
    304–313, 316, 317, 327–328,
    329, 340, 365–366, 376
Gulf Coast Stories 356
House in the Uplands, A xii, 82–
    84, 87, 209, 233–234, 244, 275,
    312
Humorous Side of Erskine Cald-
    well, The xiii, 354–355
In Search of Bisco xiv, 264, 274,
    328, 358, 388–389
Jackpot 200, 214, 219, 350–351
Jenny By Nature 263, 273
Journeyman xvi, xxii, 38, 39–41,
    168, 169, 170, 172–173,
    188–190, 202, 209–210,
    229–230, 245, 255, 265, 270,

271, 274, 366
Kneel to the Rising Sun xiii, 33–
    39, 181, 227–228, 239, 256,
    342, 348, 366–367
Lamp for Nightfall, A xiii–xiv,
    xxxiii, 245, 257, 264
Last Night of Summer, The 291
Love and Money 257
Mama's Little Girl 346
Message for Genevieve, A 347
Midsummer Passion, and Other
    Stories 354
Miss Mamma Aimee xiv, 273
Molly Cottontail 357
Moscow Under Fire 388
North of the Danube xiv, xxvii,
    71–72, 350, 383–385
Place Called Estherville xii, 89–
    90, 245, 256, 274, 275
Pocket Book of Erskine Cald-
    well Stories, A 353
Poor Fool xiv, 80–82, 186–187,
    241–242, 325, 362–363
Russia at War 388
Sacrilege of Alan Kent, The 4, 5–
    6, 8, 9, 26, 167, 172, 239, 315,
    320, 329, 344, 345, 346, 349,
    354, 362–363
Say, Is This the U.S.A. xiv, xxvi,
    344, 351, 368, 385–388
Some American People xiv, xxv,
    xxvi, 41–44, 181, 270, 344,
    348–349, 367–368, 375–379,
    382, 384
Southways 67–70, 245, 256, 342,
    349–350
Stories by Erskine Caldwell 352–
    353
Summertime Island 291
Sure Hand of God, The xii, 87,
    245, 255, 272–273, 276
Swell-Looking Girl, A 346, 354
Tenant Farmer xxv, 39
This Very Earth xii, 86–88, 233,
    235–236, 245
    236, 245
Tobacco Road xii, xv, xvi, xxii,
    xxv, 10–19, 23, 25, 31, 32–33,
    38, 41, 81, 107, 156–157, 168,
    170–173, 174–179, 181,
    184–188, 194, 198–199, 202,
    208, 209, 210, 217, 223–224,
    237–240, 244, 255–257, 262,
    265, 276–277, 283, 295–297,

299–300, 304–313, 316, 329,
364–366, 370–374, 376, 381
Tobacco Road (dramatic version)
32–33, 44–53, 107, 136, 215,
243, 251, 316, 317
Tragic Ground xii, xvi, xxii, 78–
79, 84–85, 199–200, 205–208,
210, 231–232, 240–241, 243,
244, 251, 256, 276, 304
Trouble in July xvi, xx, xxiii, 72–
78, 190–191, 199, 203–205,
208, 210, 213, 233, 243–244,
255, 262, 265, 275
We Are the Living 81, 156–157,
172, 237, 239, 244, 255–256,
346–347
Weather Shelter, The 291, 328
When You Think of Me 357
*Where the Girls Were Different,
and Other Stories* 354, 355
Woman in the House, A 354
Writing in America 376
You Have Seen Their Faces xiv,
xxv, xxvi, 53–67, 181, 270, 314,
317, 349, 368, 379–382, 384,
386
works (individual short stories,
sketches, essays)
"After Eighty Years" xxvi
"After-Image" 360
"August Afternoon" 331, 333–334
"Automobile That Wouldn't Run,
The" 331
"Autumn Courtship, An" 360
"Barber of the Northwest, The"
xxvi, 377
"Big Buck" 216, 217, 340
"Blue Boy" 38, 341
"Box Maker, The" 351, 387–388
"Bread in Uzok" 384–385
"Caldwell Declares AAA Ruins
Thousands in South" 140–142
"Candy-Man Beechum" 216, 217–
218, 248, 325, 337–339, 360
"Cold Winter, The" 37, 264
"Corduroy Pants, The" 25
"Country Full of Swedes" xxii,
173, 200, 216, 262, 334–336,
360
"Crown-Fire" 172
"Daughter" 195, 200, 265–266,
336–337, 360
"Day the Presidential Candidate
Came to Ciudad Tamaulipas,

The" 351, 360
"Day's Wooing, A" xxii, 195
"Day We Rang the Bell for
Preacher Hawshaw, The" 314
"Dogs of Ceske Budejovice, The"
384–385
"Dorothy" 10, 243, 341, 363–364
"End of Christy Tucker, The" 218
"Evelyn and the Rest of Us" 248
"Evening in Nuevo Leon, An"
341, 360
"First Autumn, The" 341
first publication of 344–359
"Fly in the Coffin, The" xxii,
337–339
"Georgia Land Barons Oust
Dying Girl and Her Father"
102–105
"Georgia Poverty-Swept, Says
Caldwell" 97–100
"Georgia Tenants, Ousted by
Landlords, Eat Dirt as Change
from Bread and 'Lasses"
149–152
"Gift for Sue, A" 355
"Girl with Figurines" 355
"Grandpa in the Bathtub" xxvi
"Grass Fire, The" 70, 217
"Growing Season, The" xxii, 37,
195, 341, 360
"Hamrick's Polar Bear" 360
"Handsome Brown's Day Off"
314
"Here and Today" 248
"Her Name Was Amelie" 356
"Honeymoon" 195
"Horse Thief" 200, 341, 360
"Indian Summer" 341
"Introduction" (to *American
Earth*) 221–222
"Introduction" (to *God's Little
Acre*) 225–226
"Introduction" (to *A House in
the Uplands*) 233–234
"Introduction" (to *Journeyman*)
229–230
"Introduction" (to *Kneel to the
Rising Sun*) 227–228
"Introduction" (to *This Very
Earth*) 235–236
"Introduction" (to *Tobacco Road*)
223–224
"Introduction" (to *Tragic
Ground*) 231–232

"Joe Craddock's Old Woman" 266
"John the Indian and George Hopkins" 10
"Kathy" 355
"Kneel to the Rising Sun" xxii, 34, 37, 38, 168, 217, 218, 248, 317, 341, 348, 360, 367
"Knife to Cut the Corn Bread With, A" xxii, 70, 275
"Landlords Chiseling South's Poor on FERA" 143–145
"Lonely Day, The" 25, 247
"Mama's Little Girl" 341, 346
"Man and Woman" 218, 360
"Martha Jean" 216, 218
"Masses of Men" 34, 40, 263, 340, 363
"Mating of Marjorie, The" 9, 341, 345
"Maud Island" 200, 218, 360
"Meddlesome Jack" 156, 157, 325, 341, 360
"Medicine Man, The" 156, 248, 331–332, 340
"Memorandum" 341
"Message for Genevieve, A" 347
"Midsummer Passion" xxi–xxii, 25, 222, 344
"Midwinter Guest, The" 217
"Mr. Caldwell Protests" 32–33
"Molly Cotton-Tail" 196, 357
"My Old Man" 217, 219
"My Old Man and the Gypsy Queen" 314
"My Twenty-five Years of Censorship" 249–254
"Negro in the Well, The" xxii, 200, 341, 360
"Negroes Who Ask Pay Beaten in Alabama" 145–148
"New Cabin, The" 264
"Night My Old Man Came Home, The" 70, 200
"Nine Dollars' Worth of Mumble" 340–341
"Over the Green Mountains" 157, 341
"People vs. Abe Lathan, Colored, The" 200, 360
"Picking Cotton" 341
prizes and awards 342, 344–359
"Rachel" 40
"Return to Lavinia" 70, 360

"Ripe for Revolution" 20–23, 362, 365
"Rumor, The" 25
"Saturday Afternoon" 7, 25, 216, 217, 325, 331, 345, 363–364
"Savannah River Payday" xxii, 363–364
"Short Sleep in Louisiana, A" xxii
"Slow Death" 275, 341, 367
"Small Day, A" 68–69, 194
"Soldier Is Born, A" 352
"Soquots" 356
"Starving Babies Suckled by Dog in Georgia Cabin" 105–107
"Swell-Looking Girl, A" xxii, 331, 360
"Sylvia" 353
"Tobacco Roads in the South" 50–53
"Uncle Henry's Love Nest" 70, 350
"U.S. Aid Forces Out Georgia Share Croppers" 100–102
"Very Late Spring, A" 345
"Warm River" 346
"We Are Looking at You, Agnes" 263, 336, 360
"Where the Girls Were Different" 331, 332–333
"Wild Flowers" 70, 360
"Woman in the House, A" xxii, 341, 360
"Yellow Girl" 341, 360
Caldwell, I.S. 12, 107, 113, 116, 118, 119, 130, 131–132, 140, 269–270, 274, 317–318, 328, 389
Calvinism 276
Canby, Henry Seidel xxxii, xxxiv, 29, 200, 214–220, 249, 352, 353, 359
Candide 207
Cantwell, Robert xiii, xxxiii, 271, 352, 354
Casanova, Giacomo 160
Cather, Willa 80
Caucasian Chalk Circle, The 309
Céline, Louis-Ferdinand 204, 212
Cellini, Benvenuto 160
censorship 15–16, 27–33, 44–48, 84–85, 91–93, 249–254
Cervantes, Miguel de 253

Chalk Face 75
"Champ, The" 68
Chaplin, Charles 258, 259
Chaucer, Geoffrey 30, 183, 317
Chekhov, Anton 219, 266–267
Cocteau, Jean 261
Cohen, Octavus Roy 288
Coindreau, Maurice Edgar 80–82,
    237, 238, 239, 241, 242, 259,
    260, 317
Collapse of Cotton Tenancy, The 178
Connelly, Marc 29, 249
Conrad, Joseph 288, 324, 326
Conroy, Jack 17–18
Collins, Carvel xxxiv, 357, 359
Cook, Sylvia Jenkins xvi, xxxiii, xxxv,
    361–369, 375–392
Couch, W. T. 56–59
Country Wife, The 75
Cowley, Malcolm xii, xiv, xvi, 4–6,
    29, 54–56, 198–200, 249, 261,
    294–295, 315–329, 372
Crime and Punishment 240
Cummings, E. E. 17
cyclorama 233, 291, 326, 328
Cyrano de Bergerac 44

dadaism xi, 171
Dahlberg, Edward 16–17, 20–23, 362,
    365
Dalí, Salvador xxvi
Daniels, Jonathan 28, 67–68, 78–79,
    89, 90, 261
Davidson, Donald x, 59–67
Deen, Rep. Braswell 48–50, 50–51,
    251
Defoe, Daniel 249, 253
Delpech, Jeanine 238–239, 259
d'Houville, Gérard 244
Dickens, Charles 175, 176, 183, 317
Dickey, James 330
Divided We Stand 65
Don Quixote 253
Dos Passos, John 327
Dostoevski, Fyodor 240, 326
Dreiser, Theodore xxi, xxxiv, 48, 80,
    219, 241, 255, 290
Droll Stories 249
"Dry September" 325
Duhamel, Georges 261

Eastman, Max 249
Eisner, Mark 29, 249
Elliot, George xxvii

Ellis, Havelock 258
Enormous Room, The 17
Ernst, Morris 253
Erskine College 318, 319
Evans, Walker 380

Fadiman, Clifton 249
Fairhurst, Judge 252
Farrell, James T. 25–27, 28, 39–41,
    246, 252
Faulkner, William xx, xxi, xxvi, xxvii,
    xxviii, xxix, 16, 84, 204, 205,
    210, 213, 215, 237, 238, 239,
    241–242, 248, 252, 255, 266,
    289, 294–295, 299, 302, 319,
    324–326, 327, 339, 342
Ferguson, Otis 69–70, 342
Fiedler, Leslie A. 260
Fielding, Henry 12
Fields, W. C. 258
*Fifth Column and the First Forty-
    Nine Stories, The* 342
Finkelstein, Sidney xiii–xiv
Finnegans Wake xxviii
Fitzgerald, F. Scott xxix, 342
Flannagan, Roy 75
Flaubert, Gustave 255, 257
Flowering Judas 342
Forster, E. M. 75, 312
France, Anatole 253
Frank, Waldo 75
Frohock, W. M. xii, 201–213
From Flushing to Calvary 20–23, 362

Gamblers, The 265
Gang Rule in New York 78
Gannett, Lewis 29
Georgia Scenes 300–301
Gide, André 260
Gingrich, Arnold 44
Glasgow, Ellen 300, 312
Go Down, Moses 307
Gogol, Nikolai 265
Gold, Michael 361
Gone With the Wind 257
Gorky, Maxim 183, 317
Gossett, Louise Y. xiii
Goya, Francisco de 36, 219
Graham, Billy 280
Grapes of Wrath, The 205, 379
Gray, James x, 13–15
Gray, R. J. xv, 298–314
Great Gatsby, The 305
Greenspan, City Magistrate Benjamin

E. 27–31, 249–250
Gregory, Horace 28, 168
Gruenberg, Sidonie M. 29
Gulliver's Travels 253
Gurko, Leo 260
Guyot, Charly 244, 260

Halper, Albert 41–44
Hamlet 211
Hardy, Thomas xxvii, 288
Harris, George Washington xv, 302–308, 311, 312
Harte, Bret 12, 19, 216
Hatcher, Harlan 261
Hawthorne, Nathaniel 215, 253, 255
Hazel, Robert 314
Hemingway, Ernest xxi, xxvi, xxvii, xxviii, xxix, xxx, 7, 8, 19, 80, 168, 204, 213, 217, 255, 259, 289, 319, 324, 327, 339, 342, 376
Hicks, Granville 261
Hindus, Maurice 71–72
Hitler, Adolf 71, 384
Holley, Judge W. H. 44
Hollywood 155, 292, 325, 326
Holman, C. Hugh xxxiii, 340
Holmes, L. E. 134
Howard, Leon 261
How the Other Half Lives 179
Hugo, Victor 175, 205

Ibsen, Henrik 47
In Dubious Battle 205
Irving, Washington 215
I Was a Share-Cropper 58–59

Jackson, Joseph Henry 28
James, Henry xxviii, xxix, 255, 324
Jarrell, Randall x, 35–37, 284
Jewett, Sarah Orne 215
Johnson, Gerald 64
Jones, Howard Mumford 211
Joyce, James xxviii, 250, 324, 326
Juvenal 252

Kallen, Horace M. 29
Kashkeen, Ivan 262, 263, 264–265
Kazin, Alfred 261
Kelly, Mayor Edward J. 44–45, 51, 251
"Killers, The" 217
King Lear 36
Kinsey report 253

Kirkland, Jack 32, 49, 215, 251, 316, 317
Klevar, Harvey xxxiv
Korges, James xiv, xvi, 340, 359–360
Kreymborg, Alfred 318
Kroll, Harry Harrison 58–59
Kronenberger, Louis 28
Kubie, Lawrence S. 81, 159–166, 171, 196–197
Ku Klux Klan 77, 389

Lalou, Rene 260, 261
Landor, Mikhail xxxiii, 262–267
Lannigan, Helen 318
Lardner, Ring 68
Las Vergnas, Raymond 245
Lawrence, D. H. 24, 168, 238, 239, 255
Let Us Now Praise Famous Men 380, 385
Lewis, John R. 109, 110, 112, 113–115, 125–126
Lewis, Sinclair 29, 80, 241, 249
Lindey, Alexander 253
Lindsay, Vachel 214

Long, Huey 97, 104
Longstreet, Augustus Baldwin 300–301, 308
Long Valley, The 342
Lorentz, Pare 379
Lowenstein, Solomon 29
Lucet, Charles 240
lynching 72–78, 190
Lynn, Kenneth 313

Macaulay, Thomas B. 252
McCullers, Carson xxi, 294
MacDonald, Scott ix–xxxv, 330–360
Macleod, Norman ix–x, 6–7, 364
Magny, Claude-Edmonde 244, 260
Magritte, René xxvi
Main Street 179
Malcolmson, Charles 148–149
Malraux, André 204
March, Joseph Moncure 80
Marion, J. H. Jr. x, 174–179
Marx, Harpo 258
Maulnier, Thierry 260
Maupassant, Guy de 239, 255, 259
Maurois, André 237–238, 240–241, 261, 317
Maxwell, Gilbert 175
Melville, Herman 255

Mencken, H. L. 64, 2´9
Merle, Robert 245
Michel-Tyl, Ed 239
Miller, Judge Guy A. 46, 47–48
Miller, Henry 243
Miner, Ward L. xxxii, 237–245
Mission to Moscow 326
Moll Flanders 249
Moravia, Alberto 261
Mother Courage 309
Muller, Herbert J. 260
Mumford, Lewis 249

Nausée, La 212
Nichol, Anne 45

O'Brien, Edward J. 43, 342, 359
O'Connor, Flannery xxi, 294
Of Mice and Men 74
Ottinger, Nathan 29
"Outcasts of Poker Flat, The" 216

Page, Thomas Nelson 177
Pamela 253
"Pantaloon in Black" 325
paperback books 85, 327–328
Paradise Lost xxix
Parker, Dorothy 249
Passage to India, A 75
Pembroke Magazine (Caldwell issue)
    xv
Perelman, S. J. 258
Perkins, Maxwell xxxiii, 283–284,
    321–322
Petrov, Evgeni 262–263
Phelps, William Lyon 32
Phillips, John R. Sr. 111–112
Pilcher, J. J. 122–125
Pierce, Warren H. 115–116
Poe, Edgar Allan 215, 255
pornography 290
Porter, Katherine Anne 342
Powys, John Cowper 29
Pratolini, Vasco 261
Preface to Peasantry 178
Proust, Marcel 324
Puzzled America 376

Rabelais, Francois 12, 160, 238, 239,
    255, 257, 259
Rahv, Philip 294
Raper, Arther 178
Rascoe, Burton 74–78, 249
Raymond, Allen 78

Raymond, Louis-Marcel 260
regional writing xix, 292–293
Renek, Morris 345
repetition xvi, 173, 330–341
Rice, Elmer 29, 249
Richardson, Samuel 253
Riis, Jacob 179
Roberts, Elizabeth Madox 16, 300,
    312
Roberts, Oral 280
Robinson Crusoe 253
Rolfe, Edwin 23–25
Romains, Jules 261
roman noir 212
Rorty, James 376
Ruhl, Arthur x, 33–35
Runyon, Damon 292

Sale, Richard B. xix, 279–293
Sanctuary 237, 252, 325, 326
Saroyan, William 43, 292
Sartre, Jean-Paul 204, 212
Scarlet Letter, The 253
School for Wives 207
Scott, Les 248
Scott, Sir Walter 176, 253
Scribner, Charles Jr. 284
Seldes, Gilbert 28, 249
Shakespeare, William 205, 326
Sheppard, Muriel 380
Simms, William Gilmore 177
Simon, Jean 245, 259, 260
Smith, Sen. Ellison D. 148–149
Smith, Harrison 82–84, 89–90, 261
Smith, Lillian 217
Smith, Thelma M. xxxii, 237–245
Snell, George xxxiii, 261
"Some Like Them Cold" 68
"Song of Myself" 320, 321
Soskin, William 28
Sound and the Fury, The xxviii, 294
Soupault, Philippe 237
southwestern humorists xv, 157, 298–
    314, 329, 370
Spalding, Justice 91–93
"Spotted Horses" 325
Startsev, Abel 266
Stein, Gertrude xx, xxvii, 330, 339
Steinbeck, John xxi, xxvii, xxix, 74,
    204–205, 213, 241–242, 289,
    327, 342, 376, 379
Stowe, Harriet Beecher 136, 176
Strange Fruit 217
Strauss, Harold xxxii

Stribling, T. S. 75
Studs Lonigan 252
Sumner, John S. 27–31, 249
surrealism xi, 171
Sut Lovingood's Yarns 302–308
Sutton, William A. 318–319, 321
Swift, Jonathan 253, 255
Swope, Herbert Bayard 29
Sykes, Gerald 7–8

Talmadge, Gov. Eugene 51, 97, 101,
    104, 111, 139
Tanner, Tony 313
Taps at Reveille 342
Teeftallow 75
Tharpe, Jac Lyndon xviii, xxxiv
"That Evening Sun" 326
Thiébaut, Marcel 238, 260
Thompson, Craig 78
Thompson, James J. Jr. xxxiii–xxxiv,
    268–278
Thompson, Ralph 56
Thorp, Willard 260
Thurber, James 294
Tinkle, Lon 87–88
"tobacco-road" 213
To Have and Have Not 55
Tom Sawyer 253
Turgenev, Ivan 43
Twain, Mark xxi, 12, 19, 157, 202,
    217, 239, 253, 255, 301, 313

Ulysses xxviii, 31, 250
"Uncle Remus" 177
Uncle Tom's Cabin 59, 82, 83, 136,
    176, 179
Uncle Tom's Children 342
University of Virginia 318, 319, 375
Unvanquished, The 342

Valéry, Paul 36
Vallette, Jacques 242
Van Doren, Carl xi, 29, 74, 155–158,
    179, 313

Van Doren, Dorothy 68–69
Van Gelder, Robert 53–54
Van Loon, H. W. 249

Wade, John Donald x
Wagenknecht, Edward 260, 261
Waiting for Lefty 46
Wall, Vincent 8–9
Watkins, J. Raiford 11–13
Weaver, Raymond 29
Webb, Walter Prescott 65
Warren, Robert Penn 294
Welty, Eudora 294
Wessberge, E. H. 239, 260
West, Mae 258
West, Nathanael 319
West, Ray B. xiii
Wharton, Edith 80
Whipple, T. K. 3–4
White, Kenneth 18–19
Whitman, Walt 319, 320, 321
Willingham, Calder 294–297
Winesburg, Ohio 324
Wings of the Dove, The xxviii
Winter, William 47
Wolfe, Thomas xxix, 258, 294, 327,
    330
Woolsey, Judge John 250
Woollcott, Alexander 249
Wootten, Bayard 380
Work, Monroe W. 76
Wright, Richard 72–73, 244, 342,
    351
Wycherly, William 75

Yatsenko, Vadim 265–266
*Yearbook of the American Short Story,
    The* 342
You Know Me, Al 68

Zola, Emile xxxiv, 175, 179, 219, 240,
    253